Fifth Edition

PRACTICAL RESEARCH
Planning and Design

PAUL D. LEEDY
The American University

MACMILLAN PUBLISHING COMPANY
New York

MAXWELL MACMILLAN CANADA
Toronto

MAXWELL MACMILLAN INTERNATIONAL
New York Oxford Singapore Sydney

Cover Art: David Cutler
Editor: Robert B. Miller
Production Editor: Sheryl Glicker Langner
Art Coordinator: Lorraine Woost
Text Designer: Susan E. Frankenberry
Cover Designer: Cathleen Norz
Production Buyer: Pamela D. Bennett

This book was set in Baskerville by V & M Graphics and was printed and bound by Semline, Inc., a Quebecor America Book Group Company. The cover was printed by Phoenix Color Corp.

Printed in the United States of America

Macmillan Publishing Company
113 Sylvan Avenue, Englewood Cliffs, NJ 07632

Library of Congress Cataloging-in-Publication Data
Leedy, Paul D.
Practical research : planning and design / Paul D. Leedy.—5th ed.
p. cm.
Includes bibliographical references and index.
ISBN 0-02-369242-1
1. Research—Methodology. I. Title.
Q180.55.M4L43 1992
001.4—dc20 92-18313
CIP

Printing: 4 5 6 7 8 9 Year: 5 6 7

With special appreciation
to
Two Girls
and
One Boy:
Renie,
Kathy,
and
Tom

Acknowledgment and Appreciation

No man is an Iland, intire of it selfe; every man
is a peece of the Continent, a part of the maine. . . . .

So wrote the great Dean of St. Paul's Cathedral in the seventeenth century. And, so write I now.

Those who have had a part in the making of this book, known and unknown, friends and colleagues, gentle critics and able editors—all—are far too many to salute individually. Those of you who have written in journals and textbooks have added insight to my own thoughts, the generations of graduates and undergraduates who have taught me more than my academic mentors, the kindly letters that so many of you have voluntarily written to tell me how this little book has helped you in your own research endeavors—a noble company: to all of you, I owe acknowledgment and appreciation wherever you may be.

You have had a greater part in bringing this book through its four previous editions than you will ever know. And now we have produced edition number five. To this edition especially, four of my colleagues have richly endowed it with their constructive and insightful critiques. I acknowledge their assistance with gratitude: Professor Jane Whitney Gibson, Nova University; Professor John N. Olsgaard, University of South Carolina—Columbia; Professor Thomas A. Romberg, University of Wisconsin—Madison; and Professor Paul Westmeyer, University of Texas—San Antonio.

No author is an island, entire of itself. Every author has had many hands guide his pen and many minds illuminate his thoughts. All of you have been helpful; all of you have been "a piece of the continent, a part of the main." I am deeply indebted indeed to each of you. And to all of you, the best that I can give: my humble and hearty thanks.

Paul D. Leedy

Contents

PART 3

PART I

THE FUNDAMENTALS

Introduction

The Purpose of This Book

Practical Research: Planning and Design is a broad-spectrum book suitable for all courses in basic research methodology. Unlike many texts, *Practical Research* was not written for any specific course or discipline. The methodology of research transcends the limitations of academic area as a general approach for conducting any basic research project. For most academic disciplines it is accepted under the rubric of experimental research or, as it is sometimes called, the *scientific method.*[1] It is important, however, to distinguish between the procedure employed in executing a research project and the method employed in gathering the data necessary to the project. The means by which the information is secured may vary; the actual procedures of executing the research remain the same.

For example, the neurosurgeon seeking to determine the difference in neurotransmitters in the brains of normal patients and those afflicted with Alzheimer's disease and the sociologist seeking the cause of hostility between two social groups have precisely the same goal: to find the answer to an unsolved problem. And in pursuing that goal each will, perhaps, follow the same or very similar procedures. That is, each will employ the same methodology. But each will need specific factual information to reach their respective goals, and in securing that information each will employ a different approach.

One Process for All

The biologist gathers data by way of the microscope, the sociologist by using a questionnaire or by surveying a population, and the psychologist, by tests and observations of behavior. From there on, the basic procedure of each is identical. Each processes the information, interprets it, and reaches a conclusion that the facts seem to warrant. Students in education, nursing, sociology, the natural sciences, business administration, geography, landscape architecture, and allied academic disciplines have used this text as a guide to the successful completion of their research projects.

Practical Research guides the student from problem selection to completed research report with practical suggestions based on a solid theoretical framework and an educationally sound learning procedure. The student comes to understand not only that research needs planning and design but also—and, perhaps, more importantly—*how* one's own research project may be executed in a professional and acceptable manner. Essentially, this is a do-it-yourself, understand-it-yourself manual. From that standpoint, it is a guide for students who are left largely to their own resources in executing their research projects. The book, supplemented by occasional counseling by one's academic advisor, will guide the student to the completion of a successful research project.

Learning Pure Research Cannot Begin Too Early

Many undergraduates have found that *Practical Research* has helped them both to understand the nature of the research process and to complete their research projects. Its simplification of research concepts and its reading ease commend it to those undergraduate situations where

[1]The scientific method is described in chapter 5.

students should be introduced, perhaps for the first time, to genuine research methodology. All too often such students labor under the deception that merely transferring facts from one place to another and incorporating them into an extended footnoted paper is a genuine research endeavor. Nothing could be further from the truth.[2]

Unfortunately, this misconception has been witnessed by all too many graduate professors, whose students come to the threshold of their doctoral dissertation only to realize that they are required to do, at that point, what is entirely foreign to anything that they have been led to believe about the nature of research during their long years of previous schooling. Something has gone tragically wrong with the education of students who have been permitted to practice such a misconception of research from grade school to graduate school.

Countless students have labored to the point of frustration to try to present an acceptable research proposal only to be told by their professors, "This is really not an acceptable proposal," or more bluntly, "This is just not research." And, without an understanding mentor or a helpful text, such students face a blank wall of frustration and discouragement.

One has only to sit on a panel for the review of proposals for governmental grants, as I have done on many occasions, to realize how many of these are rejected for one reason only: the lack of a clear understanding of the nature of basic research.

Research has one end: the ultimate discovery of truth. Its purpose is to learn what has never been known before; to ask a significant question for which no conclusive answer has been found and, through the medium of relevant facts and their interpretation, to attempt to find the answer to that question.

Students Work on Practical Research Project

Practical Research is dedicated to one end: to teach students basic research methodology and the scientific method. The approach of the text is broad. It cannot be appropriated solely by any one academic discipline. The research principles set forth in this text are equally applicable to all disciplines where the tenets of the scientific method are valid for the solution of problems and the ultimate pursuit of truth.

At no point in this text are students left open-ended. The chapters do not end in a section that merely asks questions and provides little or no leadership in answering them. The chapters do not end in sections entitled "exercises" or "review questions." With but one or two exceptions, the chapters end with a section entitled "Practical Application." This is a specifically designed feature of *Practical Research.* It compels students to *apply* the principles presented in the chapter rather than merely answer questions about what they have read. Sometimes, I do not delay this practicum in learning until the end of the chapter, but insert it at any point where the principles that have been discussed need reinforcement by a practical application in a simulated research setting.

The "practical application" feature of this text is unique. It aims to do two things: (1) to instruct students in the principles of basic research methodology, and (2) to have students do precisely what the subtitle of the text suggests: to "plan" and "design" a research project. Every "practical application" unit guides the students toward this goal. In other words, as they progress through the text, they are concurrently planning and designing a "practical research" project so that, when they have completed reading the text, students will also have planned and designed a viable research proposal. "We learn to do by doing" is still a valid aphorism in education. The logo of a quill pen and an inkstand will alert you to each of these practical application sections.

I am not a wistful dreamer. I have seen the behavior of too many students to be deceived with happy expectations that they will obediently follow all the directions in this textbook. Students, for example, are not prone to flip over hundreds of pages to find a practical application unit in some unobtrusive appendix or to study a proposal that is hidden in the hind parts of the text.

[2]For an amplification of this statement, see p. 10.

For that reason, the practical application units of the material that has just been discussed in the text and corresponding significant parts of a student's actual research proposal have been relocated in this edition in juxtaposition to the chapter material that is relevant to their purpose. In this position, what was remote is now immediate, and the application of the principles of research discussed in each chapter will also be immediately applied to students' own research proposals or projects.

For those seeking to prepare a proposal either for approval for an academic degree or as part of the process of applying for a research grant, a fully annotated proposal is presented in installments to illustrate the discussion in certain chapters. The first of these appears in chapter 3, and other sections in chapters 4 and 7. Thus, the major portions of an entire proposal are offered as a model for those who wish to write a similar document. Former generations of students who have used this text found the proposal to be a significant guide and many of them have strongly recommended that it be included in this edition.

Research Methodology Is More Than An Academic Requirement

In revising this text for the fifth edition I attempted to determine some of the problems associated with previous editions. To this end, I actively sought the reactions of both the students who used the text and the instructors who taught it. I sent questionnaires to instructors who used the previous edition of this text and their recommendations were adopted for the changes that have been made in this edition.

From these inquiries and long professional observation of the many generations of students who have taken my course in research methodology, certain facts and student attitudes have become clear. The most sobering of these was that students all too frequently think of a course in research methodology as merely an academic requirement. Students get academic myopia easily. It arises here from considering research as merely an unimaginative banality for fulfilling a requirement to write a thesis, final document, or a "research report." Many students think of it as just one more hurdle to cross before receiving one's degree. This provincial and shortsighted thinking is, sadly, all too common. The process of thinking that one develops by applying the scientific method to the solution of problems; namely, to see the problem, get the facts, interpret the meaning of those facts and, on the basis of them, make a decision, is a valuable asset for attacking many problems in everyday living. A satisfying research course can help students appreciate these assets.

We need to see the study of research methodology in a broader perspective. It has more important implications than that of merely satisfying a parochial "course requirement." Research methodology and its application to the solution of problem situations is an acquisition that will serve you for the rest of your life. Rightly considered, it should give you an opportunity to look beyond the academic campus to the realistic world of research activity on the other side. And what you will see is unbelievably exciting.

The real world is alive with problems and, consequently, concomitant research activity! It is everywhere. The media is replete with fascinating reports of life-saving discoveries, of wonders on the earth and discoveries in the vastness of the universe, all the results of research. Research is not an academic banality; it is a vital and dynamic force that is indispensable to modern progress. Ultimately, perhaps, research may be the last hope of the human race and the key to the very existence of the human species on this planet.

More immediate, however, is the need to apply research methodology to those lesser daily problems that nonetheless demand a thoughtful resolution. Those who have learned how to analyze problems dispassionately and who have been disciplined by the scientific method will live with more self-assurance and less panic than those who have shortsightedly dismissed the discipline of research as merely a necessary impediment on the way to a degree. Compared with the advantages that the research viewpoint produces, considering an academic research requirement as annoying and irrelevant is untenable.

What's New?

In this edition of *Practical Research,* at the end of each chapter, a section is signaled by a logo vignette of a microscope and entitled, "Significant and Influential Research." The fourth edition examined one significant research project per chapter. This edition will provide you with a directory and reading list of contemporary research efforts over a wide academic spectrum. At the end of the first chapter is a list of journals to be found in most academic libraries. In these periodicals, legions of men and women report their ongoing research and reveal their findings. From chapter 2 onward, each chapter also concludes with a reading list of significant research published over a broad range of academic interest. The idea is to make the study of research methodology a means by which the student may understand how problems are solved in the real world through the medium of research and how insights into new knowledge are obtained.

These references will suggest that the application of research methodology is a dynamic and indispensable force in modern life. Also, they may suggest that research as an empirical learning experience in college and research as an indispensable element in shaping modern life are complementary. The "Significant and Influential Research" section in each chapter of *Practical Research* is an attempt to reinforce that interrelationship.

The Computer and the Researcher

Elemental computer literacy is an absolute "must" for the present-day researcher. For that reason a series of presentations relating to computerization will be found in this edition. You will be alerted to these sections by the logo of a computer monitor in the margin of the text at the beginning of each discussion. Like statistics, an extended discussion of the computer as a tool of research is beyond the limits of this text. These installments contain suggestions for ways to computerize research and do not presume to go beyond a surface presentation. For those who wish to pursue the discussion topic further, an extensive bibliography and list of leading vendors of software, database services, and other aspects of computer-assisted research complete certain discussions.

And So . . . *Bon Voyage!*

Now you have seen the structure, the rationale, and the philosophy of this text. In this introduction, I have shared with you some of my reasons for writing the text and some reasons why research methodology is not a transient curricular bubble but an unparalleled opportunity for you to learn how to handle any problem better for which you do not have a ready solution. In a score of years you will look back upon your course in research methodology as one of the most rewarding and practical courses in your entire educational experience. I have found it so in my own experience; scores of my students have confessed to me that they likewise have had the same experience.[3]

[3]An article by George Kress, appearing in *Marketing News,* July 17, 1989, pages 10–11,17,24, entitled "More grads than deans urge MBA students to study research," indicates the importance of a research course in their degree program. "Almost 95% of the MBA grads indicated that MBA students should take a research course," and, furthermore, "almost 65% of the MBA grads felt that students should perform a major research project in their [degree] programs."
See also *Marketing News,* January 2, 1989, page 36, Gilberto de los Santos and Vern Vincent, "Student research projects are gaining in popularity."

CHAPTER 1

The Dimensions of Research

Everywhere our knowledge is incomplete and problems are waiting to be solved. We address the void in our knowledge, and those unresolved problems, by asking relevant questions and seeking answers to them. The role of research is to provide a method for obtaining those answers by inquiringly studying the facts, within the parameters of the scientific method.

Dimension One: Why Research?

Research powers the world. Not the planet itself, of course, but the more intimate and intricate world of human activity. That world is in ferment. It is changing constantly because of the discovery of new information and the resolving of old problems. In the vanguard of this change is a relatively small cadre of dedicated men and women who make it happen. They are the movers and shakers of our age. They attempt to know the unknown and to do the undoable. These are those who do research.

Hidden away in laboratories, offices, libraries, and archives, and mingling on city streets with the surging tides of everyday life, unrecognized observers of the rest of us, these individuals are at work discovering the facts that will make the world of tomorrow as different from the world of today as the last century was from this one.

A century ago, we tapped out messages in Morse code and sent them along copper wires that for the most part paralleled the railroad tracks. Today we fax our messages and transmit them at the speed of light. In the Civil War, men died of their wounds because of raging infection. Today, we have the miracle of antibiotics. At the turn of the century, we cranked the telephone on the wall to talk to a neighbor over a strand of wire that served the communication needs of multiple subscribers. Now, on a fiber of glass thinner than a human hair, our words are carried across a continent or beneath the sea on a wavelength of light. Far above, at the edge of space, we survey the activities of other nations, check global weather patterns, and explore the outer reaches of the universe. Television permits us to see the history of tomorrow as it happens today. The kitchen stove has been replaced by the microwave oven, and instead of laboriously writing out this edition of *Practical Research* in longhand, it was typed, juggled, and edited on a personal computer using convenient word processing software. These are but a few examples of the power of research to revolutionize our way of life. But despite all this, the present is merely prelude. An unconquered universe lies out there, and we are surprisingly ignorant of either its dimensions or its nature.

Let us go from the infinite to the infinitesimal. The atom, for all we have discovered about it, is still largely a mystery. We have just begun to understand the complexity of its dynamics. Our theories of both universal and of subatomic structure change almost daily. The few examples that we have suggested merely skirt the universe of the Great Unknown. There is an awesome black hole of ignorance out there that baffles and confounds the most insightful minds of our day.

Look in the mirror and you will see a creature that to modern medicine in many ways remains an eternal enigma. After all of the sophisticated advances that we have made, AIDS, Alzheimers, and arthritis still mock the skill of the wisest physicians and remind us of how much there is yet to know.

Near the end of his life, Alexander the Great expressed disappointment that he had "no more worlds left to conquer." Alexander the Great was dead wrong! Legions of worlds are still waiting to be conquered, containing a plethora of problems that challenge the resourcefulness of modern research.

Every industry thrives because of specialized research. So much so, that the phrase "research and development" has become a commonplace that we merely identify with the cryptic letters R & D. Without the "R," however, there could be no "D." Research indeed powers the modern world. After this evidence, we hardly need ask: Why research?

Dimension Two: A Temporal View of Research

Research has one prime goal: *discovery*. But that goal is as old as the human race. Discovery was essential for primal existence: how to make fire; how to cover distances more efficiently, more quickly, and without the fatigue of walking; how to cook food and make it more nutritious and palatable. These and other problems faced primeval humans, who needed to find practical ways to solve them.

Let's look for a moment at the first of the problems suggested above. Our ancestors needed to discover how to kindle a fire. The first fire they experienced was probably a gift from the heavens. A storm approached. Lightning struck. Thunder crashed, and—Behold! there was fire. But how does one kindle a fire without the pyrotechnics of a storm? Our early ancestors needed fire on demand: for comfort, for cooking, for protection. They could not always wait for lightning to start a blaze. How, then, could fire be created? This was, perhaps, one of the earliest problems for research that the human race encountered and, after some experimentation, finally resolved.

Some early experimenter discovered that if two sticks were vigorously rubbed together, they became warm. Aha! A brilliant idea exploded within that skull: Fire was in the stick. This was probably the first research hypothesis! Rub the sticks long enough and vigorously enough and the sticks would smoke. Ultimately, the smoke would ignite, solving one of humanity's earliest problems. And it was resolved by research methodology, although certainly unwittingly and unplanned.

The method was empirical. It was elemental. It was simple. But it *was* the first research method. The term *research methodology* merely means *the way in which we proceed to solve problems,* and that is what this text will explain.

At first glance it may seem superfluous, and hardly worth devoting an entire text or a college course to such an apparently simple end. But, on closer examination, we see that gathering data, managing those data, solving problems, and formulating valid conclusions as an outcome of an investigation may not be as simple as it appears.

The Essence of Research Methodology

We have started with a simple example to illustrate two basic facts:

1. the methodology of research is a basic procedure, and
2. the steps in solving an unsolved problem are practically the same for the modern researcher as they were for our first ancestors.

Let's review those steps briefly:

1. In the beginning was a *problem*: How can humans kindle a fire?
2. Then came the recognition that there were[1] *data relating to the problem*: sticks rubbed together became warm. That was *fact.*
3. Next, came a rationalization and a guess: a *hypothesis,* we call it. Logical reasoning entered the process: The sticks are warm. Fire is warm. Therefore, fire is in the stick. Further data were amassed to see whether the hypothesis should be supported or rejected.
4. The sticks were rubbed against each other with increasing force and vigor. They began to smoke. There was another *fact.*
5. These additional data seemingly *confirmed the hypothesis* and was leading apparently to solving the problem: further rubbing caused the temperature to rise to the kindling point—the smoke ignited. Fire!
6. *The problem was resolved,* and our ancestor's guess (hypothesis) proved to be correct.

We have just detailed the modern research procedure:

1. It originates with a *problem;*
2. It ends with a *conclusion.*
3. The entire process is based upon observable *facts,* called *data.*
4. It is *logical.*
5. It is *orderly.*
6. It is *guided by a reasonable guess.*
7. It *confirms* or *rejects* the reasonable guess (the hypothesis) on the basis of fact alone.
8. It arrives at a conclusion on the basis of what *the data,* and *only* the data, dictate.
9. The conclusion resolves the problem.

The process of research, then, is largely circular in configuration: It begins with a problem; it ends with that problem resolved. Between crude prehistoric attempts to resolve problems and the refinements of modern research methodology the road has not always been smooth, nor has the researcher's zeal remained unimpeded.

The "Black Hole" in the History of Research

In the blackout of inquiry and the right to question the established dogmas and doctrines during the Middle Ages, research had a perilous time. Doctrine and dogma were substituted for observation and fact, and logic was shaped to support a preconceived belief. The Church stood firmly astride the practice of empirical investigation. Not until the Renaissance did those pioneers of modern research, whose primary interests were a search for the truth and an investigation of the accepted status quo, muster enough courage to withstand the forces of dogmatism and ecclesiastical tyranny.

Galileo Galilei dared to question the immobility of the earth, and Copernicus doubted the centrality of the earth and the architectural structure of the heavens. Leonardo, Durer, Michelangelo, and Raphael all studied the human body and rendered it truthfully upon their canvases. Vesalius was distinguished for his studies in anatomy and for his refutation of the earlier teachings of Galen. These were the pioneers of modern research. They signalled the beginnings of the decline of relying solely upon superstition, tradition, authoritarianism, and rationalistic dogmatism.

The new procedure, ushered in by the Renaissance, had an entirely new and naive approach. It simply *looked at facts as they really were.* No longer was the earth flat and "stretched out beneath the heavens." It was a fact, as anyone could see by simply standing on the seashore

[1]Note the plural. *Data* is the plural form of *datum,* and so always is used with the plural form of the verb.

and looking at the horizon, that the line between "heaven" and earth was not a straight, flat, horizontal line—as it would had to have been, had the earth been flat—but that the horizon *curved.* It was merely an arc of a much greater circle. The earth was not flat. It was round like a ball! Any seaman could see that, had he really looked—and thought.

We could go on, example after example; the history of the Renaissance is replete with them. This process of merely looking at life and the world in the cold, factual light of observation and drawing conclusions from the facts—and *only from the facts*—was called "the scientific method."[2] And, within that general rubric, we now think of it as the basis for research methodology.

Erroneous Contemporary Concepts of Research

Research. It is probably one of the most misused words in the English language. No word in everyday speech has been used with more meanings and given rise to more erroneous concepts than the word *research.* Students have been misled through incorrect teaching and false usage of the word by their instructors. The uninformed insert it into their speech to add a touch of counterfeit prestige and distinction, while others capitalize on the aura of mystique that the word evokes. Merchandisers profit from the ignorance of "those who know not, and know not that they know not" and offer them a myriad of articles, touting them as being "the result of years of research," the magic phrase that stimulates business and which the gullible readily accept.

Let's clear up some of the false concepts stemming from erroneous use of the word research.

Research Is the Act of Finding and Transferring Information. From elementary school to graduate school, teachers, instructors, and professors send students to the library "to *research* a particular subject" or to "write a *research* report" on an assigned topic.

And so, what does the student do? In all likelihood, the student goes to the library, looks up a given topic, scratches down some notes or photocopies an assortment of articles, and assembles this potpourri of data into a written account that the student then presents to the instructor as a purported "*research report.*"

To mislead a student into thinking that fact transferral is research is sheer academic deception. Why not call a procedure of this kind precisely what it is—a learning experience for the student? Call it an exercise in information gathering, fact transferral, or self-enlightenment, but don't call it *research.* In its skeletal form, it is nothing more or less than factual data that has travelled from the book in the library to the student's paper. To delude the student into thinking that this is research when it in fact meets none of the criteria for genuine research (described in the next section of this chapter), casts umbrage upon the ethics of the whole instructional process.

And the report, despite what the teacher or the instructor may have called it, is *not* research. But the student has footnoted the paper. That is commendable. It is simple honesty on the part of the student. It merely acknowledges who "owns" the information. Unfortunately, however, footnoting the origin of a fact does not make the student's effort a research project.

Rummaging through books and magazines and journals for tidbits of information and acknowledging where you found these scraps of knowledge must not be confused with the *interpretation of the data and the discovery of their meaning.* They are simply not the same.

Garnering facts is certainly not to be demeaned. It is a *part* of the research process—but it is only a part. Research happens inside the head of the researcher. When you, the researcher, gather fact after fact until you have accumulated a mountain of data, and then out of all of these facts have a sudden insight—a realization, a flash of *discovery*—of a significance of these facts that you never saw before (and that perhaps no one else has): *That is research!*

[2]For a fuller explanation of the scientific method, see chapter 5.

Research Is Merely a Word That Is Used to Impress Others. Some words have an esoteric mysticism about them, and research is one of these. It is a word that conveys an erudite ambiance. Relatively few people know precisely what research is. Hence, we use it, frequently glibly and meaninglessly, because it sounds important and invests us with a counterfeit prestige.

An example will make the point. The house across the street is for sale. It is a desirable property and I would buy it, if I knew the sales value of my own property. I call my real estate broker and ask him to determine the market value of my property. He tells me that he "will *research* the matter" and advise me. What he intends to do is to make a comparison: to see what properties similar to mine sold for in the past few weeks, and from that, give me an estimate as to the probable sales figure for my property.

Nothing that he will do is research; it is merely looking for similarities and venturing a guess. But his willingness to "research the matter" sounds very impressive indeed. But to review the sales figures of similar properties is not research.

Research Is a Catchword That Exudes Pomposity and Snares the Gullible. The morning's mail brings me a letter. I open it, and see in boldface type:

Years of research have produced a miracle car wash! Banish that dull, lifeless look on that set of wheels you are now driving. Get S*P*A*R*K*L*E C*A*R today!

I look out the window at my pitiable five-year-old sedan. I think, "this 'miracle of research' is for me." I send for a six-ounce trial size of "Sparkle Car" for $12.00. A little expensive, I think, but look at the "years of research" that have gone into the development of this product. Two weeks pass, and my sample arrives. And what do I get? A six-ounce bottle of dishwashing detergent. The content description announces that it contains "anionic and nonionic surfactants"—the identical wording that is on an eighty-nine cent bottle of soap I can purchase at the supermarket. The "years of research" catchphrase lured my dollars. The gullible are the victims of the catchphrase artist!

Dimension Three: What Is Research?

I have already indicated the nature of research. We looked at the aborigine attempting to produce fire and suggested that this might have constituted a primitive type of research. Now we shall spell out precisely what research is and what makes it a unique procedure, separate from all the pseudoresearch situations that we have discussed above.

We begin with a basic definition. It is perhaps the most comprehensive and poignant definition that I have ever seen, and it comes from one of our most accessible sources: *Webster's Dictionary of the English Language*:[3]

> *Research.* A studious inquiry or examination, especially a critical and exhaustive investigation or experimentation having for its aim the *discovery* of new facts and their correct *interpretation*, the revision of accepted conclusions, theories, or laws in the light of newly *discovered* facts or the *practical* application of such conclusions, theories, or laws.

Now, let us look at that definition more intensively. Notice the italicized words. They are important in comprehending the nature of basic or academic research.

We begin with an axiom: *If there is no discovery, there is no research.* Consider the student's information quest that we cited above. The student had an accumulation of facts. That's all. The student did not *interpret* any of that body of information. There was no focal point where

[3]*Webster's Third New International Dictionary of the English Language* (Springfield, MA, 1971), 1930.

all the facts came together and, analyzing them, a burst of discovery exploded within that student's brain and the student exclaimed, "Look! All of this factual data means . . . *this!*" That's what we mean by the phrase, *the interpretation of the data.* It is *a sudden, enlightening awareness of what the facts mean.* And, unless there is a discovery of the meaning of the data, there is no research.

Research Follows a Basic Procedure

Research is not a haphazard activity. It follows a standard procedure in a logical sequence of steps that form its methodology. And that methodology has eight distinct characteristics:

1. *Research begins in the mind of the researcher.* Research originates in a curious, observant, inquisitive attitude that recognizes that problem situations exist that need further investigation.
2. *Research demands that the researcher articulate a specific goal for the investigative process.* This is known as *the statement of the problem for research.*
3. *Research demands a specific plan of procedure.* This is also called *the research method.*
4. *Research generally recognizes that a frontal attack on the entire problem is too much to attempt at one time.* Every problem can be divided into *subproblems.* By subdividing the problem, it becomes more manageable. You solve a part at a time.
5. *Research is generally guided by constructs called hypotheses.* We mentioned and partly defined hypotheses earlier.[4] We will have more to say about them in the paragraphs ahead.
6. *Research accepts certain critical assumptions* that are axiomatic and essential for the research process to proceed.
7. *Research countenances only specific, measurable data* as admissible in resolving the problem.
8. *Research is, by nature, a circular* or more exactly, *a helical process.*

Characteristics of Basic or Pure Research

Now, we shall discuss each of the characteristics of research at greater length.

1. The first characteristic is subjective. It is the ability to observe: the ability to look at a situation and to see in it unresolved questions. Everywhere we look we observe facts that cause us to wonder, to speculate, to form questions. And, by forming these questions in our own minds we strike the first spark that culminates in the research process. *An inquisitive mind is the beginning of research.* There is so much that we do not know, that we do not understand! The hope of lessening our ignorance lies in the questions we ask and the facts that we summon. It is in the *collective* meaning of those facts that ultimately we hope to find insight.

Look around you. Consider the unresolved situations that evoke the questions: Why? What is the cause of that? What does it all mean? These are everyday questions; they are also the sparks that ignite research. If you have trouble in finding a research problem, don't ask your advisor to suggest one; don't scramble through the pages of books—think! From the very outset your ability to think will determine the quality of your research endeavor.

2. *Research requires the skill of articulation.* You must be able to put into words clearly and unambiguously precisely what the problem is that you intend to research. No place for fuzzy heads and foggy thinking here. You must state your research goal with crystal clarity.

"But," you say, "I don't know precisely what it is that I intend to research."

Stop! Go no further until you *do* know and are able to express your research intent precisely and succinctly. There is no purpose in attempting to go somewhere, if you don't know where you're going!

[4]See Introduction.

I have seen students repeatedly attempting to do research with a half-articulated problem. Such a procedure is merely a failure waiting to happen. I have found that perhaps ninety-nine percent of research project crashes have been because the student either had not been specific enough in thinking about the project or had not planned carefully enough the research procedure.

3. *Planning means just that: having in mind some practical and specific ideas how your research might be accomplished.*

For example, from what we have said thus far in the chapter, you should be prepared to face head-on the following questions and to attempt to answer them honestly, without any excuses or mental reservations.

1. Do you have *clearly* in mind precisely what your research effort will seek to accomplish?
2. If you have decided upon the goal of your research, can you state that goal in clear, unambiguous language?
3. Have you made that statement? If not, do it now.

Procrastination has no place on the agenda of the researcher. Those who intend to do research cannot afford the luxury of the Scarlett O'Hara syndrome: "I'll think of that tomorrow."

Research is not an excursion into happy expectations, of fondly hoping that all will turn out well. It is no luxury safari in which you can bask in a fog of indecision and procrastination. Research demands hard, strenuous thought, precise articulation, and the laborious accumulation of a body of specific facts. It is a carefully planned attack upon a sometimes intransigent problem, the solution of which seems elusive and difficult. It is a search-and-discover mission *explicitly designed in advance.* Consider the title of this text: *Practical Research: Planning and Design.* The words following the colon are the important ones.

The second aspect of research methodology considered the goal. That was *what* you intend to do. Now, you state the plan and the design; you are concerned with *how* you will reach that goal.

You must not wait until you are chin-deep in the project to begin to plan and design your strategy. The moment that you select a problem for your research, you must look at the statement of that problem critically:

1. Is it feasible? Can *you* do it?
2. If so, where will you find the data?
3. Even if the data exist, can you get access to them?
4. Presuming that you have access to the data, what will you do with them after they are in your possession?

We might go on and on. These questions merely indicate what you must initially consider concerning your problem. Obviously, you cannot answer some of these questions in this early stage of your research experience. They are presented here with only one purpose: to answer the question posed in the title of this section, "What Is Research?" One answer is that research is a process that demands precision, clarity of thinking, foresight, specificity, planning, and the ability to wrestle with difficult questions and find answers to them. Research is *not* happy little excursions to the library and writing "documented" papers from the factual gleanings you have amassed.

4. *Researchers soon realize that the total research problem is usually too large an investigative area to be managed as a whole.* To make the research problem more manageable, researchers usually divide the problem into *subproblems.* The whole is composed of the sum of its parts. That is a universal law. It is also a valuable guideline to observe when thinking about one's goal for research.

We operate through subproblems much more frequently than many of us realize. For example, I want to get from Researchville, where I live, to Goalsburg, a village 75 miles away. There is my main problem: to get from one location to another. Look how it easily breaks down into subproblems:

Main problem:
How do I get from Researchville to Goalsburg?

Subproblems:

1. What is the most direct route? (The highway.)
2. How far do I travel on the highway?
3. Where do I exit from the highway?
4. Are there any signs, or landmarks, to direct me?
5. After I exit from the highway, what do I do then?

The main problem—how I get from one town to another—seems simple enough. But zoom in on it and its simplicity begins to evaporate. Other questions arise that must be answered before I can resolve the main question. Only when I begin thinking analytically do I begin to realize that the five corollary questions are all integral parts of a simple request for direction.

Research problems break down in the same way, but it takes analytical thinking to isolate the subproblems. Inspect the main problem for research, and you will soon find subordinate, logical additional problems beginning to surface. These invariably are more detailed than the main problem. And resolving the subproblems will ultimately resolve the main problem.

5. *Research seeks direction through appropriate hypotheses.* Having stated the problem and its attendant subproblems, the researcher then develops a construct called a *hypothesis.* What is a hypothesis? It is an intuitive feeling, a hunch, a supposition, or an educated guess with respect to the outcome of the problem.

Hypotheses are tentative. The facts carry the ball. And the facts that you discover concerning the problem or subproblem determine whether the hypothesis that you posed is valid or not. In research we use the word *supported* with hypotheses: the facts either support the hypothesis, or the facts do not support it. There is no middle ground.

But whether hypotheses are supported or not is relatively unimportant. If the facts support the hypothesis, it merely means that your initial guess was correct; if the facts do not support the hypothesis, that merely means you were incorrect. But they do fulfill one important function: they help to give you a sense of orientation, a direction in which to look for facts. Supporting the hypothesis does not solve the problem.

We should clarify here that we are discussing a *research hypothesis.* The *null hypothesis,* which is discussed in chapter 3, is an entirely different kind of hypothesis. These two distinct types of hypotheses should not be confused with each other.

Hypotheses are nothing new. They are common, recurring features of everyday life. For example, you come home after dark, having driven en route through a severe thunderstorm. You open the door of your home, reach to switch on a lamp and . . . no light! At this point the main problem races through your mind: Why no light? Then you begin to hypothesize; you construct a series of reasonable guesses that will help you to look for the cause of the lamp failure:

1. The bulb has burned out.
2. The lamp is not plugged into the wall socket.
3. Lightning from the thunderstorm has interrupted the electrical service.
4. The wire from the lamp to the wall is defective.

Each of these hypotheses provides a channel for gathering facts and verifying whether the facts support the conjecture. Note that you are not trying to prove the hypothesis. Hypotheses are never proved. They are merely *temporary constructs* that the facts will either verify (support) or discover to be false (reject).

Now you go on a search to "test" the acceptability of your hypotheses.

1. You install a new bulb in the lamp. The lamp fails to light. (Hypothesis one is rejected.)
2. A glance at the wall outlet verifies that the lamp is plugged into the outlet. (Hypothesis two is rejected.)
3. You look at your neighbors' homes. Everyone has electrical power. The walks and driveway of your home are dry. Your community was not touched by the storm. (Hypothesis three is rejected.)
4. You touch the wire to your lamp. The lamp lights and then goes out. You touch the cord a second time. The lamp lights and goes out. The connecting wire is defective. (Hypothesis four is supported.)

6. *Assumptions provide the foundation upon which the entire research structure rests.* In research, they are equivalent to axioms in geometry: self-evident truths, the *sine qua non* of research. The assumption must be valid or the research cannot proceed. For this reason, careful researchers—certainly in academic research—set forth a statement of the assumptions as the bedrock upon which the study must rest. In your research, therefore, it is important that others know what you assume with respect to your project. For, if one is to judge the quality of your study, then the knowledge of what you assume as basic to the very existence of your study is vitally important.

An example will clarify the point. Your problem is to investigate whether students acquire greater facility in grasping the ambience of a language more quickly by learning only one foreign language at a time or attempting to learn two foreign languages concurrently. By *ambience* we mean the native accent, a comprehension of the expressive characteristics of grammatical, idiomatic, accentual, and similar unique aspects of the language.

Now, what assumptions would underlie such a problem?

1. It would be assumed that the teacher would be competent to teach the language or languages and would have mastered the linguistic ambience.
2. It would be assumed that those students taking part in the research are readily capable of hearing the subtleties of accent and alert to other unique characteristics of the language.
3. It would be assumed that the languages selected would have distinguishable ambience characteristics that could be recognized and learned and practiced by the students selected for the study.

And we could go on, if necessary, to other assumptions that without which the study would not be feasible or, if done, would be faulty in basic design.

7. *The data for research must be specific and measurable.* Research can arrive at valid conclusions only on the basis of specific, hard, verifiable, and measurable fact. Remember one of the great statements in education: "If it exists, it can be measured." We shall discuss fully the process of measurement in chapter 2, "Tools of Research."

The data used in research also must *be interpreted.* What do we mean by interpreted? *Interpretation* simply means that after the data have been accumulated and processed—arranged into categories, converted to graphical presentation, analyzed statistically, or by any other means of manipulating them—there must be finally a *discovery* of the meaning of those data, as discussed at the beginning of this subsection. They cannot remain in their raw state. All research ends in a conclusion or series of conclusions, and these are reached by searching the data to determine what, collectively, these data connote.

Perhaps you will see now why we indicated that going to a library, gathering an accumulation of facts on a particular topic, and presenting these facts in a written paper is not research.

One of the virtues of research is that it teaches a researcher to be scrupulously honest. A pile of facts is merely a pile of facts—nothing more. That you level out the pile by scattering these through a written document, with or without benefit of footnotes, does not change the nature of the material. All you have are dispersed data.

8. *By its nature, the research process is circular.* The research process is cyclical and begins simply: with a curious inquiry within a human brain. It follows logical developmental steps:

1. A questioning mind observes a particular situation. (This is the subjective origin of research.)
2. Being curious, the mind asks, "Why?" "What caused that?" "How come?"
3. The answer to those questions becomes formally stated as a problem. (This is the overt beginning of research.)
4. Facts are discovered that seem to bear on the problem.
5. The facts seem to point to a tentative solution of the problem. A guess is made; a hypothesis is formed.
6. The quest for more facts continues.
7. The body of fact is processed and interpreted.
8. A discovery is made; a conclusion is reached.
9. The tentative hypothesis is either supported by the facts or it is not supported.
10. The cycle is complete.[5]

But, what seems like a neatly *closed* circle is deceptive. Research never dead-ends into finality. The"circle of research" might be described more accurately as a *helix* or *spiral* of research. We have mentioned the inquisitive mind of the researcher. To the curious and inquisitive mind, additional problems invariably arise that need resolving. Research begets research. The pursuit of undiscovered knowledge is endless.

To view research in this way is to see research as dynamic. That is its true nature. This is a far cry from the conventional view that regards research as a one-time act: static and self-contained. The student who produces the erroneously called "research" paper finds no other worlds to conquer.

Quite to the contrary, genuine research expands the researcher's horizon until it extends to infinity. Like a will-o'-the-wisp, the quest for the discovery of Truth is ever elusive, but in the pursuit of it, you will be continually lured by divergent avenues that lead to unexplored and irresistibly enticing problems. These problems may prove unrelated to your inquiry, and may thus be either diversions or hindrances. Then again, they may be too important to ignore and, unless pursued, may bar you from ever again glimpsing the broad throughway to the ultimate end of your present quest.

We have mentioned two concepts of the research process. The first of these is the circular concept, shown in Figure 1.1.

A far more dynamic and challenging concept of the research process is represented by the *helical concept.* We have described it briefly above. It takes the researcher out to the open road. Here one can see beyond the immediate concerns of one's own problem area.

When you can see your immediate problem against the long vista of related problems, it gives perspective to your own research. It is both humbling and exhilarating. It teaches the researcher that one's problem is not all important, but merely a link in a long chain of associated problems: that your endeavor is but a molecule in a helix that winds upward toward the ultimate discovery of Truth. You might conceive of it as shown in Figure 1.2.

[5]Compare the above procedure with that of the aborigine at the beginning of the chapter.

Figure 1.1 The Research Cycle

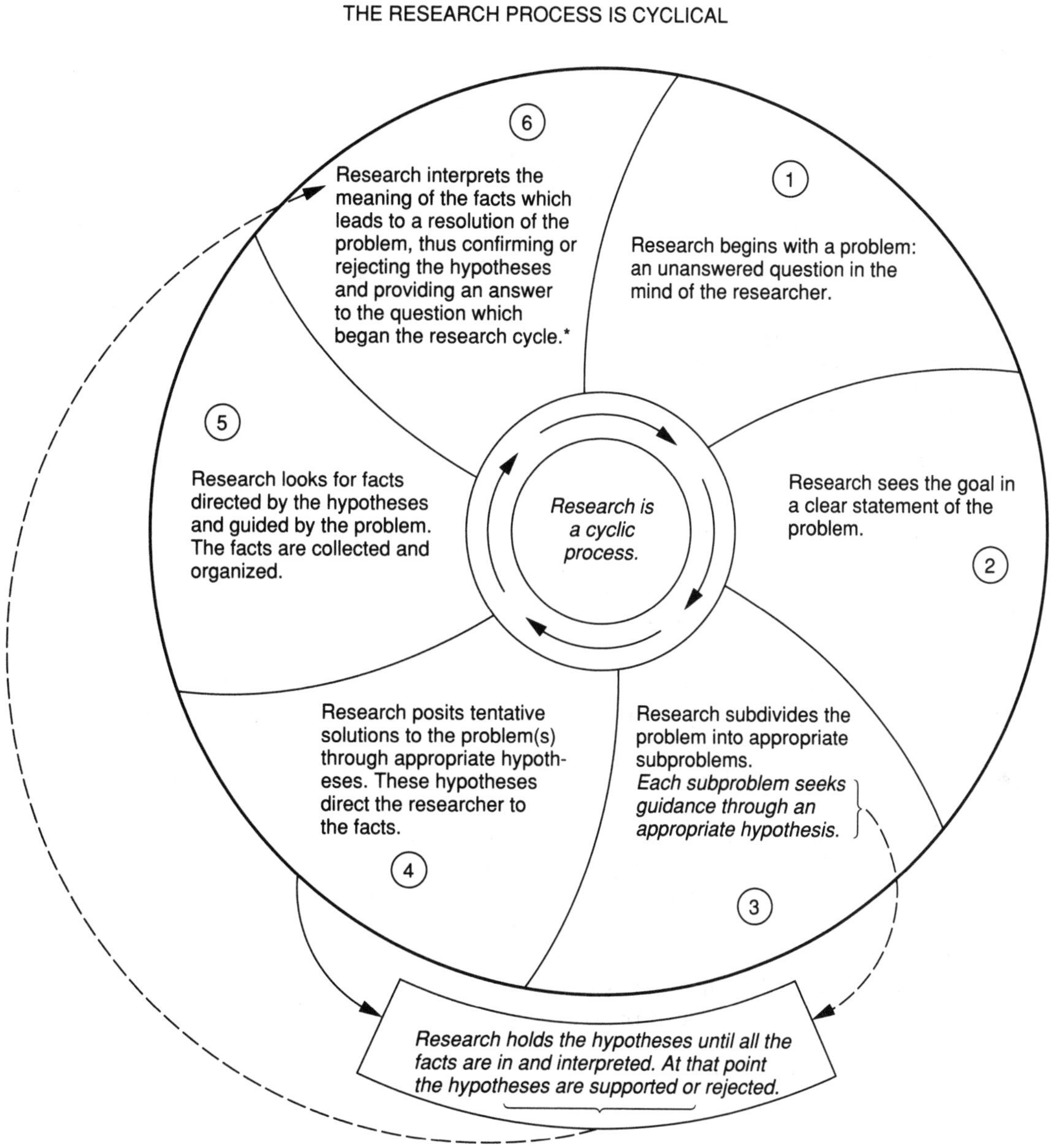
THE RESEARCH PROCESS IS CYCLICAL
6
Research interprets the meaning of the facts which leads to a resolution of the problem, thus confirming or rejecting the hypotheses and providing an answer to the question which began the research cycle.*
1
Research begins with a problem: an unanswered question in the mind of the researcher.
5
Research looks for facts directed by the hypotheses and guided by the problem. The facts are collected and organized.
Research is a cyclic process.
Research sees the goal in a clear statement of the problem.
2
Research posits tentative solutions to the problem(s) through appropriate hypotheses. These hypotheses direct the researcher to the facts.
4
Research subdivides the problem into appropriate subproblems.
Each subproblem seeks guidance through an appropriate hypothesis.
3
Research holds the hypotheses until all the facts are in and interpreted. At that point the hypotheses are supported or rejected.

Dimension Four: Where Do We Find Research?

This chapter opened with a dynamic statement: *Research powers the world!* At the time, those words perhaps failed to deliver their full shock to your awareness. And this chapter, despite its effort to bring research down to earth, may still have left it hovering just beyond your grip.

Now it is essential that we see the implication of those words in all its reality. No more hypothetical examples. No more abstract discussions *about* research. No assignments in academic busywork that do not come shoulder to shoulder with the research that *does* power the world.

We mentioned that "relatively small cadre of dedicated men and women [who] attempt to know the unknown and do the undoable." But who are these esoteric creatures? Where do

Figure 1.2 A Helical Concept of the Research Process Is Probably a More Realistic Representation

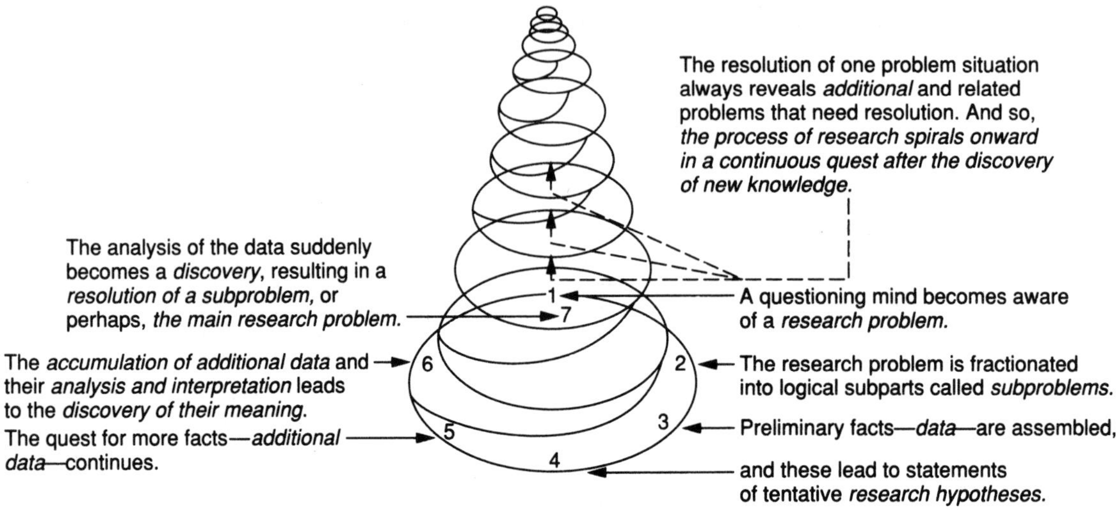
The resolution of one problem situation always reveals *additional* and related problems that need resolution. And so, *the process of research spirals onward in a continuous quest after the discovery of new knowledge.*
The analysis of the data suddenly becomes a *discovery*, resulting in a *resolution of a subproblem*, or perhaps, *the main research problem.*
1
7
A questioning mind becomes aware of a *research problem.*
The *accumulation of additional data* and their *analysis and interpretation* leads to the *discovery of their meaning.*
6
2
The research problem is fractionated into logical subparts called *subproblems.*
The quest for more facts—*additional data*—continues.
5
3
Preliminary facts—*data*—are assembled,
4
and these lead to statements of tentative *research hypotheses.*

they emerge from their clandestine existence and give evidence of their existence and present the fruits of their labors?

In case you are not aware, or intimately acquainted, with the stage upon which all of this happens, we shall indicate where you may learn of the tremendous research activity that has been reported during the last year. The total of it staggers the imagination.

You will find this information in the major indexes and reviews in some well-known volumes in the library, or computerized and available to you on the library system. Perhaps to begin, it may be more rewarding to go to the reference section of your library and get the printed copies of the volumes below that report the recent research in your particular area of interest.

Browse in these volumes, just to get acquainted with them. You may be amazed at what you discover. A broad spectrum of academic disciplines is represented in the following list. Go first to those that tweak your interest. Then, get acquainted with as many of them as possible. Competent researchers should have general knowledge of the sources available to their field.

Obviously, listing all such indexes or reviews would require a separate volume. We present here merely the principal and representative ones.

1. *Behavior Research Methods*
2. *Biological Abstracts*
3. *Chemical Abstracts*
4. *Child Development Abstracts*
5. *Communications Research*
6. *Current Psychological Research and Reviews*
7. *Dissertations Abstracts International*
8. *Editorial Research Reports*
9. *Environmental Research*
10. *Journal of Business Research*
11. *Journal of Labor Research*
12. *Journal of Psycholinguistics Research*
13. *Journal of Research on Crime and Delinquency*
14. *Journal of Research of the National Bureau of Standards*
15. *Journal of Speech and Hearing Research*

16. *Nursing Research*
17. *Psychological Abstracts*
18. *Research in Communication Science*
19. *Research in Nursing and Health*
20. *Research in Physical Education*
21. *Research on Aging*
22. *Research Quarterly in Exercise and Sports*
23. *Research Reports* (Economics)
24. *Review of Educational Research*
25. *Sociological Methods and Research*
26. *Sociology and Social Research*
27. *Year's Studies in English*

Obviously, a student doing research in any one academic discipline would want to examine a number of journals from the above list which may contain research appropriate to that particular area of study. A researcher in education, for example, may find, aside from the *Review of Educational Research* (No. 24 in the above list) important studies in the journals numbered 1, 4, 6, 7, 12, 17, 20, 24, and 26 above. Other disciplines will find an equal constellation of appropriate journals. Inspect the list to consider *all* the applicable possibilities it contains.

Significant and Influential Research

We mentioned earlier in this chapter the apparent remoteness in popular thinking of the role and relevance of research and the researcher from everyday living. Even graduate students, working on a thesis or a dissertation, may feel a sense of isolation and consider their task mere academic busywork that has no intimate relation to the world outside the campus precincts. This is simply not true. The research demanded in the production of an acceptable thesis or dissertation is one of the most valuable educational experiences an individual can have. It has an immediate connection with the profound research activity in the practical world, which advances the welfare and comfort of all of us. Great discoveries that push back the frontiers of knowledge and enhance our well-being are commonplace announcements in the contemporary media. To make the whole research process more intimate, it may help if you could see its benefits and realize that what you are doing is but a link in that ongoing endeavor. The purpose of this section, at the close of each chapter in this text, is to give you an opportunity to see *your* research against the backdrop of some of the important and significant research of the past and present. To go to the library to read some actual research reports by notable researchers (to which you will be given specific bibliographical references), that have been influential in changing our lives and our thinking, is to bring significant research home to you in an intimate way that students normally do not experience during *their* academic research. Going to the source of some significant research, therefore, may make the whole discipline of research more intimate and more interesting.

Generally, we shall be concerned with primary sources, but occasionally, when a survey of significant research is in book form, we will suggest the title. One of these is a small volume edited by Eugene H. Kone and Helen J. Jordan, *The Greatest Adventure: Basic Research That Shapes Our Lives* (New York: The Rockefeller Press, 1974). *The Greatest Adventure,* according to its Preface, "is problem oriented and focuses on vital research in various scientific disciplines . . . that has special pertinence today."

The Computer as a Tool of Research

Introductory Statement

We are in the age of computerization. In research the computer can be a particularly valuable tool. We discuss this topic as a tool of research in chapter 2; but most books just discuss it, and leave it there. This text is different. It is devoted to the proposition that if computerization has any relevance to the research process, then throughout the book, at the end of each chapter, specific suggestions should be given as to *how* computers can be of assistance to the researcher. Some of you may have personal computers (microcomputers), some may not; but all of you at one time or another will need to use a computer to obtain information.

A word of caution: The art of computerization is advancing at supersonic speed. Some of the information that may be appropriate at the time of revising this text may be superseded by the time it appears in bound copy. In any event, we shall try to keep this section as up to date as possible. We will introduce you to some general informational readings and to some standard journals that are particularly concerned with computer applications to specific research areas and needs. Special attention will be given to the use of the microcomputer.

Practical Application

This text is more than a theoretical discussion of research methodology. You become a researcher by putting into practice the principles that form the basis of the discussion in the chapter. Following each major discussion area, you will be asked to pause and engage in a Practical Application of the principles that have been covered up to that point. In long chapters, delaying the application of the principles discussed may not be optimal, so the Practical Application section may occur at a feasible point within the chapter.

As we get further into the text, the Practical Application sections will be structured so that each one successively helps you to construct an actual research proposal for your chosen problem.

Project 1

Early in this chapter we discussed the way that factual observation gradually replaced superstition and dogma as the primary source of information about the world. List at least five superstitious beliefs that still prevail without any factual confirmation. Indicate which of these may be amenable to research confirmation and suggest the procedure that one might follow to confirm or invalidate these superstitions.

Project 2

Within a given period of time (a week or month), jot down examples—in conversation, in the media (TV commercials, newspapers, etc.)—where you have noted the word "research" used incorrectly, as discussed in the chapter.

Project 3

Here is a chance for you to evaluate your qualifications as a researcher. You will make a self-evaluation by noting those personal areas of strength and those that need improvement. Many students are handicapped by having undesirable qualities that they do not recognize and which hinder their ability to become a skilled researcher. Here is an opportunity to measure your own research aptitude.

Personal Research Aptitude Test

Directions: Check the "Yes" or "No" column honestly as the question applies to you. You will gain nothing by giving the response that *you* may *think* is desirable. Just answer *honestly* what you do.

Personal Quality	YES	NO
1. Do you refuse to procrastinate, coming to grips immediately with situations that need resolving?	_____	_____
2. Have you an inquisitive mind? Are you curious in your thinking?	_____	_____
3. Do you always look for facts before making up your mind about a situation?	_____	_____
4. Can you keep the central issue—the problem—foremost in your thinking in a discussion or an argument?	_____	_____
5. Do you analyze problems, thinking of the problem in terms of subproblems, rather than looking at the problem as a whole?	_____	_____
6. Do you look for causes, forming hypotheses for a situation?	_____	_____
7. Are you a planner? Do you consider how you will accomplish a certain task before you begin it?	_____	_____
8. Do you wait to hear all sides of an issue before making up your mind?	_____	_____
9. Do you find it easy to accept the facts of a situation even though these may run counter to what you would like to think?	_____	_____
10. Are you articulate? Is it easy for you to put your thoughts in words?	_____	_____

What is your score? Multiply the total YES responses by 10. Enter here _____. This is the percentage of your desirable qualities as a researcher.

Multiply the number of check marks in the NO column here _____. This is the percentage of qualities that need improving.

Project 4

This chapter has outlined the eight qualities to be found in valid research. You have just been given a list of journals that report research (See "Significant and Influential Research"). Go to any of the journals in that list. Read five studies that purport to be research. Evaluate each of these studies according to the following checklist.

Checklist for Evaluating Research*

Author of Research Report ______________________________
Last Name First Name Initial

Title ______________________________
Title of research report/ thesis/ dissertation

Appearing in ______________________________
Journal (title) Volume Month Year Pages

Directions: Check the appropriate column after carefully reading the research report to determine if it contains the item designated.

Factor	Yes	No
1. A clear statement of the research problem.		
2. Are any subproblems stated?		
3. Is ( )a hypothesis ( )hypotheses [check which] stated?		
4. Is the report organized under appropriate headings?		
5. Are the data analyzed and interpreted?		
6. Is any indication given whether the hypothesis(-es) is either supported or rejected?		
7. Does the article refer to any related literature or supporting studies?		
8. Are the conclusions clearly stated?		
9. Are any further studies or needed research suggested?		
10. Did you understand the research and comprehend what the researcher was attempting to do?		

Number of check marks in each column (Enter these here) _____
Multiply each check mark in the YES column by 10 _____
Place a 0 in the NO column _____
THE TOTAL SCORE for all your articles is found by adding all of the individual scores in the YES column and dividing by the number of articles you have read _____
Total Score

Conclusions with reference to the above survey

You have briefly sampled some research studies. Now, look over your findings. What conclusions can you state in terms of what you have discovered?

*Permission is granted by the author and by Macmillan Publishing Co. for the student to make as many photocopies of the "Checklist for Evaluation of Research" as necessary to complete the project in evaluation. Photocopying any other parts of the text (except where express permission is granted) is strictly forbidden. See statement on reverse side of title page.

For Further Reading

Barzun, Jacques, and Henry Graff. *The Modern Researcher.* 4th ed. New York: Harcourt, Brace, Jovanovich, 1985.

Beveredge, I. B. *Seeds of Discovery: A Sequel to the Art of Scientific Investigation.* New York: W. W. Norton, 1980.

Bloom, Martin. *The Experience of Research.* New York: Macmillan, 1986.

Calnan, J. *One Way to Do Research: The A–Z for Those Who Must.* New York: W. S. Heinman, 1976.

Campbell, H. M. "Some Common Sense Suggestions for Nurses New at the Research Game." *Canadian Nurse* 77 (November 1981): 32–33.

Davitz, Joel R., and Lois Jean Davitz. *A Guide for Evaluating Research Plans in Psychology and Education.* New York: Teachers College Press, Columbia University Teachers College, 1967.

Ford, Lee E. *Women of the Eighties: The Woman in Research.* Vol. 3. Auburn, IN: Ford Associates, 1981.

Franklin, Billy J., and Harold W. Osborne. *Research Methods: Issues and Insights.* Belmont, CA: Wadsworth, 1971.

Freed, Melvyn, N., Robert K. Hess, and Joseph M. Ryan, *The Educator's Desk Reference,* New York: American Council on Education and Macmillan, 1989.

Gibbons, Robert J., ed. *Research Philosophy and Techniques: Selected Readings.* Malvern, PA: Insurance Institute of America, 1983.

Hawkins, C., and M. Sorgi, eds. *Research.* New York: Springer-Verlag, 1985.

Heidgerken, Lovetta. "The Research Process." *Canadian Nurse* 67 (May 1971): 40–43.

Helmstadter, G. C. *Research Concepts in Human Behavior.* New York: Appleton-Century-Crofts, 1970.

Husen, Torsten and T. Neville Poslethwaite, *The International Encyclopedia of Education: Research and Studies.* 10 vols. Elmsford, NY, 1985.

Kane, Eileen. *Doing Your Own Research.* New York: Charles Scribner's, 1985.

Kerlinger, Fred N. *Foundations of Behavioral Research.* 2nd ed. New York: Holt, Rinehart & Winston, 1973.

Kovacs, Alberta. *The Research Process: Essentials of Skill Development.* Philadelphia: F. A. Davis, 1983.

Leedy, Paul D. *How to Read Research and Understand It.* New York: Macmillan, 1981.

Lewin, Miriam. *Understanding Psychological Research: The Student Researcher's Handbook.* New York: John Wiley, 1979.

Luczun-Friedman, M. E. "Introduction to Research: A Basic Guide to Scientific Inquiry." *Journal of Post Anaesthetic Nursing* 1 (February 1, 1986): 64–75.

McElroy, M. J. "Starting Your Own Research." *Ohio Nurses Review* 61 (August 6, 1986): 11–12.

Mitzel, Harold E. *Encyclopedia of Educational Research.* 5th ed. 4 vols. New York: Macmillan and The Free Press, 1982. [Revised and updated approximately every ten years.]

Neale, John M., and Robert M. Liebert. *Science and Behavior: An Introduction to Methods of Research.* 2nd ed. Englewood Cliffs, NJ: Prentice-Hall, 1980.

Reed, Robert D. *How and Where to Research Your Ethnic-American Cultural Heritage.* Saratoga, CA: R. D. Reed. n.d.

Saslow, Carol A. *Basic Research Methods.* New York: Random House, 1982.

Sheehan, J. "Research Series: I. "Starting the Study." *Nursing Mirror* 160 (May 1985): 17–18.

Shropshire, Walter, Jr., ed. *The Joys of Research.* Washington, DC: The Smithsonian Institution, 1982.

Stacks, D. W., and J. J. Ghalfa, Jr. "Undergraduate Research Team: An Applied Approach to Communication Education." *Communication Education* 30 (April 1981): 180–183.

Valiga, T. M. et al. "Formulating a Researchable Question." *Topics in Clinical Nursing* 7 (July 1985): 1–14.

Wandelt, M. A. *Guide for the Beginning Researcher.* New York: Appleton-Century-Crofts, 1970.

Webster, E. et al. "Beginning Research." *American Association of Registered Nurses Newsletter* (June 4, 1986): 14.

CHAPTER 2

Tools of Research

Every worker needs tools. The carpenter needs a hammer and saw;
The surgeon, a scalpel; the dentist, a drill; And the researcher needs an array of means by which data may be discovered and manipulated, and facts made meaningful. The tools of research are merely ancillary to the ultimate goal of research itself: to derive conclusions from a body of disparate fact and discover that which was hitherto unknown.

What Are Tools of Research?

Let us simplify the phrase, "tools of research." We all need tools to work efficiently. Without tools, no house would be built, no life saved, no tooth filled. Tools are indigenous to the task. Every trade, every profession, every academic discipline has its own precise tools. Researchers, likewise, have their own kit of tools to help them achieve their goals and carry out their plans. In some instances, these may not be as tangible as a hammer and saw. Nevertheless, they serve to assist the researcher to reach the final target of all research—the resolution of a problem and the discovery of new knowledge.

Tools vary according to the job to be done. The tools some researchers use to achieve their goals are distinctly different from those of their investigator colleagues. The microbiologist needs a microscope; the attorney, a library of legal decisions and statute law. But these are *specialized* tools, intrinsic and necessary for the solution of research problems within a specialized area. Every academic discipline has its own unique tools of research, and without them, the research of that discipline would be immobilized. Can you imagine attempting to do research in microbiology without a microscope?

In this text, however, our concern will be with the more *general* tools of research that all researchers, regardless of discipline or situation, are likely to need to derive meaningful and insightful conclusions from their unique data.

The General Tools of Research

For most researchers, there are five general tools of research:

1. The library and its resources
2. Techniques of measurement
3. Statistics

4. The computer and its software
5. Facility with language: both English and required foreign languages

Volumes have been written on each of these. In this text, we will simply introduce each general tool so that those unfamiliar with its use or its recent developments may begin employing it effectively.

A cautionary word, however. With research especially, we should be careful not to equate the *tools* of research with the *genre* or *methodology* of research. The tool is ancillary; the methodology is indigenous. Let's say it another way. The tool is what the researcher employs to amass data or manipulate them to extract meaning from them. The methodology of research is the particular characteristics that the whole research project assumes because of its procedures or the character of its data.

Confusing the Tool with the Method

Confusing the tool with the research method is immediately recognizable. Such phrases as "library research" or "statistical research" are telltale signs, and largely meaningless. They suggest immediately that those who use such phrases fail to understand the nature of pure or basic research. They demonstrate, more seriously, a confusion in thinking. They reveal the failure to differentiate between tool and method.

The library is merely a place for locating or discovering certain data that will then be analyzed and interpreted later in the research process. Likewise, statistics is merely a way to represent data numerically. By so doing we are able to manipulate those data: to view them in a new environment so that we may see more clearly their nature and significance. The more angles from which we view data, the more meaningful those data become.

Statistics can tell us where the center of an accumulation of data lies, how broadly they are spread, the degree of relationship that exists between one set of data and another, how nearly they conform to an ideal distribution, and other surface characteristics of the data. But statistics cannot *interpret those data and arrive at a logical conclusion as to their meaning.* Only the mind of the researcher can do that. The human brain is the most magnificent research tool of all! Its functioning dwarfs all other gadgetry. Nothing equals its power of comprehension, of insight, and of integrative reasoning.

For those who are avidly dedicated to the dogma that unless research is basically statistical, then it is not valid research, a gigantic fact looms across their path, demanding reconciliation with such an intractable viewpoint:

A great body of genuine and carefully designed research is extant in which not one statistical process was employed and, for the consummation of which, not one library was presumably entered. To deny, therefore, validity and the status of true research to such studies is to pontificate a narrow and indefensibly parochial concept of research. Those who maintain such a stance would claim that many studies in philosophy, archaeology, history, religion, musicology, language, and literature are not research.

We cannot support a provincialism that would vilify respectable research colleagues whose only "transgression" is that they dared to pursue knowledge by following a different route from that dictated by an elite and self-ordained academic guard. Their only fault lies in the fact that they have deigned to use different tools and a divergent methodology.

Besag has put it succinctly:

> Researchers should remember that the task before us is to answer the research question, not to revalidate our methodology. We should be open to all types of knowledge and methodologies, including probability, insight, common sense, and anything else that can help us answer the question. The question should determine the methodology. The methodology should not determine the question.[1]

[1]Frank Besag, "Reality and Research," *American Behavioral Scientist* 30 (September-October 1986): 13. Reprinted by permission of Sage Publications, Inc. See also Peter S. Graham, "Research Patterns and Research Libraries: What Should Change?" *College & Research Libraries* 50 (July 1989): 433–40.

Let us now consider each of the general tools of research separately.

The Library and Its Resources

For thousands of years, the library had one basic function. It was a repository of writings, books and manuscripts: the thought and knowledge of great and lesser minds. From the great libraries of antiquity—the clay tablet collections of Babylonia, the temple libraries of Egypt, the renowned library of Ashurbanipal at Nineveh, and the famous collections at Alexandria and Pergamum—to those of the present day, their sole *raison d'être* has been preserving the sources and expressions of human wisdom.

Traditionally, the library has been a kind of literary mausoleum: a place where manuscripts and books were kept and added to as the slow advance in literature or factual enlightenment became available. It was, for the most part, a static or slowly expanding universe of knowledge, one that could be comfortably contained within masonry walls.

In the twentieth century—and especially in the latter half of the century—the role of the library changed. We had an explosion of information, of knowledge. Research altered old ideas in practically every domain of human interest. Never have the words of Abraham Lincoln been more appropriate: "The dogmas of the quiet past are inadequate for the stormy present. We must think anew, and act anew. We must disenthrall ourselves."

Words that were appropriate for a national crisis in the nineteenth century have become a manifesto for the informational crisis in the closing years of the twentieth. And this is especially true for the library.

The avalanche of new knowledge has caught many libraries unprepared. Most are struggling to revamp their original purpose of providing a repository of written thought and factual information. Today, journals carrying announcements of new discoveries have proliferated in every segment of human endeavor. Books are out of date before they can be put on shelves. One rocket fired into space revises our knowledge and invalidates many of our previous concepts of the universe and our planet. In previous editions of this text, this section gave directions for acquainting the student with the traditional library. Much of that information is now passé. A modicum of it is given here, in the final pages of this section, merely because some students still need it. Knowledge does not march forward any more; it arrives with the speed of light.

The Library of the Quiet Past . . .

When some doctoral student in the twenty-first century writes a dissertation on the epistemological revolution of the twentieth, the most interesting chapter will probably be on the speed with which that revolution occurred. The shock waves associated with it have reached every segment of contemporary society. Directly above its epicenter, the college and university library has perhaps felt its most severe and uncompromising jolts.

Let's witness a contrast in a student's acquisition of knowledge, then and now. Imagine, if you will, that you are a student of yesteryear. When you went to the library to gather information, you most probably headed straight to the card catalog—a series of drawers containing three 3×5 inch cards for each book in the library—and sorted through, card by card, the titles and content descriptions of the books in each category in which you were interested. You noted down information to help you locate the titles most likely to contain the information you desired. Next, you went to the stacks to inspect those titles.

If you wanted further information, the periodical indexes were your next line of assault. Ponderous volumes arranged in long rows on the reference shelves, they contained cross-indexed references to current literature, and had such titles as *Readers' Guide to Periodical Literature, Education Index, New York Times Index, Business Periodicals Index,* and so on seemingly ad infinitum. You worked your way through each sizable volume until you found material on your area of interest, and then you made notes of the article: author, title, periodical, volume, pages, and date.

Then you began a second search seeking out each likely title, roaming long corridors. Finally, you found a nugget or two of information and carefully jotted them down on a note pad or on three-by-five inch cards. Such was the acquisition of knowledge in the library of the quiet past. It was a laborious, time and energy consuming and inefficient process that simply could not work under the sudden torrential onrush of the information revolution.

. . . And the Library of the Stormy Present

Even the most unobservant adult who grew up in the era of the library of the past must be struck by the entirely different ambience in the college library of the stormy present. Instead of a card catalog, which may still be stowed away in some out-of-the-way corner of the building, there are batteries of computer terminals and keyboards. These are standard equipment for most college libraries. This is no great innovation for the contemporary college student. Beginning in the elementary school, we have been rearing a generation of computer literates. The computer keyboard is a familiar adjunct for acquiring information, and most students are adept at using it.

Strangely enough, what is fermenting change within the modern library is powered by the needs and patterns of contemporary research. On March 30, 1987, Francis L. Miksa addressed the Fifth Annual Conference of Directors of Research Libraries.[2] He observed that research is now much more analytic and highly structured, and that quantitative methods are more generally employed. For such a research structure, the computer is ideally appropriate. With it the researcher can access vast universes of information, search countless online databases, and manipulate factual information with a facility that saves time, increases accuracy, and boggles the mind at its efficiency.

Not only has the college library hardware changed but the conventional view of knowledge has changed.[3] To look at the average college catalog, you would infer that human knowledge was an accumulation of separate disciplinary studies, each neatly boxed and bearing labels such as anthropology, biology, chemistry, economics, and so on. In the typical college or university, these little boxes of knowledge (whose partitions are largely nonosmotic) are called "departments." They are inimical to the concept of a universe of knowledge. Like the physical universe, the quest for truth knows no boundaries or artificial departmentalization. Modern research cannot tolerate the concept that the academic "right hand knoweth not what the [academic] left hand doeth." There are no dichotomies, no divisions, no cellular capsules of knowledge; there is instead a streaming off toward omniscience and omnipresence. With reference to knowledge and its character, Miksa comments that "the very core of a universe-of-knowledge . . . is the assumption that all knowledge, whether old or new, is by its very nature a single, cohesive, interwoven whole."[4]

Research has become less disciplinary and more global in both its problems and methodology. This has created demands that libraries have never faced before. What are some changes in information management that research has imposed on the library? To answer that question requires appreciating the need to access the whole realm of global knowledge quickly and comprehensively.

Some authorities in library science have even questioned the stability of the library as primarily a center for the printed page. Lancaster envisions a library in which the communica-

[2]Francis L. Miksa, *Research Patterns and Research Libraries* (Dublin, OH: OCLC, c. 1987). Text of an address given at the Fifth Conference of Directors of Research Libraries. For a discussion of Miksa's views, see Graham, "Research Patterns and Research Libraries."

[3]See David W. Lewis, "Inventing the Electronic University," *College & Research Libraries* 49 (July 1988): 291–304.

[4]Miksa, *Research Patterns*, p. 8.

tion channels will be largely paperless (electronic).[5] He presents a scenario for a paperless communication system, and his article urges library professionals to give immediate and serious consideration to the role of the library in an electronic society.

How to Access Global Knowledge Quickly and Efficiently

Most college libraries have replaced the card catalog with an electronic database containing the total resources of the library. You sit before a keyboard and type in the area of knowledge or the title of the book. With a flick of the finger the information about the book formerly on the catalog file card is instantaneously displayed on the monitor screen. No more pawing through long trays of individual cards in a catalog file. And no more searching through heavy index volumes for a periodical article that may turn out to be irrelevant to your needs.

The principal publishers of indexes, those listed at the end of this chapter and others, are encoding their information electronically. Sit down at any monitor retrieval location and type "Research: Information Technology." Immediately, a complete bibliography of all the recent articles dealing with information technology and research will flash on the terminal screen.

College Consortium Databases

Many colleges within a convenient geographical area have pooled their resources electronically, creating a regional database of library holdings. Messiah College is an excellent example. A small liberal arts institution located in the broad Cumberland Valley of Pennsylvania, Messiah College is one of a cluster of similar institutions in the region whose acquisitions are readily available to each other through interlibrary loan. To locate any book or periodical owned by any one of these institutions you would have only to go to the Messiah College Murray Learning Resources Center—a more appropriate name for a college library today—to query the regional college consortium library database and, if any of the libraries within the consortium has your desired publication, its location and the information pertaining to it is instantly on the monitor screen. Here is a sample response to a query: On one occasion, I was interested to know whether a copy of the first edition of this text (published in 1974) was owned by any of the consortium libraries. I entered my last name and the title of the book. I touched the "print" key, and the information was printed out as follows:

Title:	Practical research: planning and design [by] Paul D. Leedy	
Publisher:	New York, Macmillan [1974]	
Collation:	x, 246 p. illus. 28cm.	
Location:	F&M ....:	Stacks Q180.A1 L43
	KUTZTOWN ....:	001.43 L517p
	MESSIAH ....:	Q180.A1 L43
	MILLERSVILLE .....:	Regular Collection 001.43 L517
	SHIPPENSBURG....:	General Collection A180.A1 L43

But say you are new to the area, and the location of the consortium institutions is unfamiliar to you. Touch a function key and a map of the consortium area appears (Figure 2.1), that gives you the precise location of all of the member libraries with the major highway routes leading to each. Acquisition of knowledge was never like this in the "library of the quiet past"!

[5]See F. Wilfred Lancaster, "Whither Libraries? or, Wither Libraries," *College & Research Libraries* 50 (July 1989): 406–419. An equally insightful article is by Susan K. Martin, *College & Research Libraries* 50 (July 1989): 397–405.

Figure 2.1

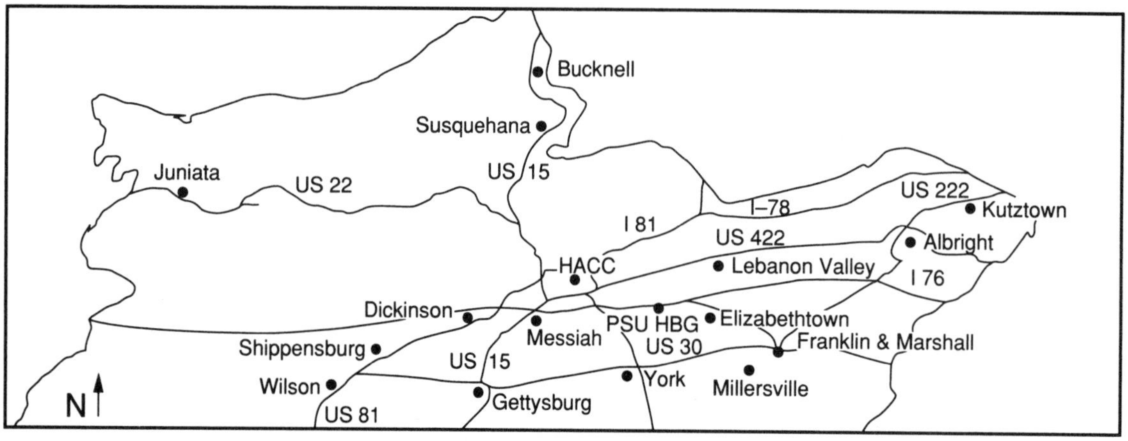

The Power of CD-ROM

College libraries are gradually acquiring another means of accessing vast amounts of information in an incredibly compressed space. This is an electronic storage system known as CD-ROM. *CD* stands for *compact disk*—a disk of the same size and appearance that has become commonplace in music reproduction. *ROM* is the acronym for *read only memory*. These disks may be read for the information they contain but cannot be recorded with additional material. They are constantly updated by the agency that prepares and issues them.

The amount of information that can be encoded on a single disk simply staggers one's comprehension. On a single CD-ROM disk, 5 inches in diameter, it is possible to encode the equivalent of 275,000 pages of text, the capacity of 1,800 double-density floppy disks. A single ROM disk may also contain thousands of images, many of which may be in brilliant color. One disk contains the total text of the 21 volumes, with illustrations, of *The New Grolier Encyclopedia.*[6] Another single disk holds the complete text of a shelf of reference works, including *The New York Public Library Desk Reference, Webster's New World Dictionary,* Third College Edition, *Webster's New World Thesaurus, Guide to Concise Writing, Dictionary of 20th Century History, J. K. Lasser's Legal and Corporation Forms for the Smaller Business, Dictionary of Quotable Definitions,* and *The National Directory of Addresses and Telephone Numbers.*[7]

L. R. Shannon, in the "Peripherals" column of *The New York Times,* quotes John Metcalfe, marketing manager of Nimbus Info Systems. "A CD-ROM disk is made in the same way as an audio disk . . . except that you've got a total of 666,000,000 characters on one disk. That's equivalent to a quarter of a million pages of text, which would be a 35-foot-high pile of 60 gram paper, printed on both sides—or, to the ecologists, and we feel very proud of this, it's the equivalent of eight trees on one disk."[8]

Many college libraries are acquiring CD-ROM equipment and data, especially index information that previously was accessible only in a ponderous reference volume on a library shelf. CD-ROM makes any information in such an index immediately available by merely typing a key word and viewing a monitor.

Because using this computerized data is unfamiliar to some students, instructions are usually posted near the system, or library personnel will assist students in learning how to use it.

[6] "CD-ROM Power: Knowledge in Hand," *PC Computing* 3 (February 1990): 64–75.
[7] Issued by The Software Toolworks, 40 Leveroni Court, Novato, CA 94949.
[8] *The New York Times,* Section C, June 18, 1991.

But things move fast in any new developmental and innovative field. Already there are rumors that Sony Corporation will soon have a 2.5-inch disk upon which one can record and read even a greater amount of data. And "a chemistry professor and researcher at the University of California at Irvine has invented a laser-based device that can store 6.5 trillion bits of information—the equivalent of one million novels—in a computer memory unit the size of a sugar cube."[9]

As rapidly as research in the storage and retrieval of information is progressing, perhaps no part of this book will be outdated more quickly than this discussion, and no developments in computer science will be more amazing than those in this area.

Stacks Are Probably Here to Stay

Library stacks and book collections will probably still remain, however, to be the solid core of information and thought housed in the library. We cannot close this section without discussing how to use this body of information.

Books are arranged on the library shelves in accordance with two principal systems for the classification of all knowledge: the Dewey Decimal classification system and the Library of Congress system. Most libraries are organized according to one of these systems; a few classify their collections according to both.

For students who wish to browse, or to locate books in a particular category of knowledge, a guide to each system of classification may be helpful. Table 2.1 shows a parallel equivalency chart of the two systems.[10]

Read down the "Subject" column to locate the area of knowledge in which the book may be located. The column of numbers to the left gives you the Dewey Decimal classification. The letters in the column to the right indicate the corresponding Library of Congress system classification symbols.

Does Your Library Still Have the Card Catalog? For those who are still using the card catalog file to locate titles, four simple rules govern the placing of individual cards in the file drawer:

1. Books *by* a person precede books *about* the person.
2. Collected works usually precede individual works.
3. When the same word is common for (a) a person, (b) a place, or (c) a thing, the cards in the catalog will be arranged in that order. For example, (a) cards pertaining to Lincoln, Abraham, precede (b) cards pertaining to Lincoln, Nebraska; these precede (c) cards pertaining to the Lincoln Warehouse Corporation.
4. Saints, popes, kings, and others are arranged in that order of hierarchical precedence.

And so, we come to the last word on the best way to learn the research tool that is the library: Use it! Go in, explore, take stock of its resources; try electronic searching; browse in the reference room; go into the stacks, browse some more. You may be surprised what a magnificent tool of research the library really is.

Measurement as a Tool of Research

An old adage says, "If it exists, it is measurable." In research, we go one step further: If it exists, then it *must* be measurable.

[9] *The New York Times*, Campus Life section, September 1, 1991, p. 43.

[10] This arrangement of the dual classification systems was conceived by Mr. Roger Miller, former director of the Murray Resources Learning Center, Messiah College, Grantham, PA. Reprinted by permission from Mr. Miller and Messiah College.

Table 2.1 A Conversion Chart: Dewey Decimal Classification vs. Library of Congress System

DC	Subject	LC	DC	Subject	LC
630	Agriculture	S	400	Language	P
570	Anthropology	GN	340	Law	K
913	Archeology	CC	020	Library Science	Z
700	Art	N	800	Literature	P
220	Bible	BS	810	Literature, Amer.	PS
010–020	Bibliography	Z	820	Literature, English	PR
920,92	Biography	CT	840–860	Literature, Romance	PQ
560	Biology	QH	658	Management	HD
580	Botany	QK	510	Mathematics	QA
650	Business	HF	610	Medicine	R
540	Chemistry	QD	355–358	Military Science	U
155.4	Child Development	BF	780	Music	M
260–270	Church History	BR	560	Natural Science	QH
330	Economics	HB–HJ	359	Naval Science	V
370	Education	L	610	Nursing	RT
378	Education, Higher	LD	750	Painting	ND
030	Encyclopedias	AE	615	Pharmacy	RS
400	English	PE	100	Philosophy	B
600	Engineering	T	770	Photography	TR
700	Fine Arts	N	530	Physics	QC
440	French Language	PC	320	Political Science	J
000	General	A	150	Psychology	BF
910	Geography	G	200	Religions	B
550	Geology	QE	500	Science	Q
430	German Language	PF	730	Sculpture	NB
740	Graphic Arts	NC	300	Social Science	H
480	Greek Language	PA	301–309	Sociology	HM–HX
930–960	History, (except American)	D	460	Spanish Language	PC
			790	Sports	GV
970–980	History, American (General)	E	310	Statistics	HA
			230	Theology, Doctrinal	BT
970–980	History, US (Local)	F	250	Theology, Practical	BV
640	Home Economics	TX	590	Zoology	QL
070	Journalism	PN			

But what is measurement? Most of us think of measurement in terms of rulers and yardsticks, scales and dials, and values of squared surfaces or cubic units of volumetric objects. In research, measurement takes on an entirely new meaning. The following definition is probably an entirely new concept of measurement, different from any you have held previously:

Measurement is limiting the data of any phenomenon—substantial or insubstantial—so that those data may be examined mathematically, and, ultimately, according to an acceptable qualitative or quantitative standard.

Definitions frequently contain more fog than clarity. Their verbal compression often produces such density that discerning the concepts and meanings is almost impossible. Because of its etymological overtones, this may be one such, and so let's try to clear the fog and let some light filter through these twenty-nine words. As researchers, we need to understand *precisely* what measurement *really* is.

Measurement is limiting the data . . . Measurement is conceived as being done with yardsticks, scales, pressure gauges, numerical values, or similar interpretive devices. But in the first five words of our definition nothing even remotely suggests any of these tools.

Let's look at history: The word *measure* came into the English language in the early thirteenth century, and originally meant "to restrain or limit in quantity." This is the basic concept that runs through all ideas of measurement: to "set a limit," to "restrain" the data. It suggests erecting a barrier beyond which those data cannot go. We still use this concept. What is a foot, a mile, a pound? Each is a unit of *measure* governed by a numerical *restraint.* Twelve inches restrain a foot; five thousand two hundred and eighty feet, a mile; and sixteen ounces avoirdupois, a pound.

Now let's look at the next six words: . . . *of any phenomenon—substantial or insubstantial—* . . . That is all-inclusive. Nothing exists that the researcher cannot measure.

Measurements may be of *things,* i.e., objects. These are *substantial* measurements. An engineer measures the span of a bridge; a chemist the weight of a compound both before and after removing the water vapor or gas from it. A Greek scholar, Erastosthenes, attempted to measure the circumference of the earth by comparing two shadows of a gnomon (the rod of a sundial) in different cities. These are attempts to measure *substantial* phenomena.

We may also measure those things—if "things" they be—that are *insubstantial;* that exist only as concepts, ideas, opinions, feelings: the status of business, the quality of an individual's mental ability. We seek to measure these intangibles, not with lineal tape, weights and balances, and shadows of disparate lengths; but by questionnaires, by Gallup opinion surveys, by the Dow-Jones index, and by IQ tests. These are efforts to measure life's intangibles, those airy nothings and elusive incorporalities that we cannot see, hear, touch, or perceive in any substantial form and yet which exist as truly as do a bridge span, a chemical compound, or the circumference of the earth.

For certain researchers—such as those in the social sciences, the humanities, psychology, education, and economics—measuring intangibles is a primary stock-in-trade. We shall discuss the art of measuring the vacuity of nothingness with a typical example.

Measuring Airy Nothings

Let's see this matter of measuring intangibles at closer range. Nothing is perhaps more wispy and elusive than the interpersonal dynamics within a group of individuals. A group of nine people is shown below. They have interpersonal relations within the offices of a large corporation. They are arriving for a recognition dinner at an exclusive hotel.

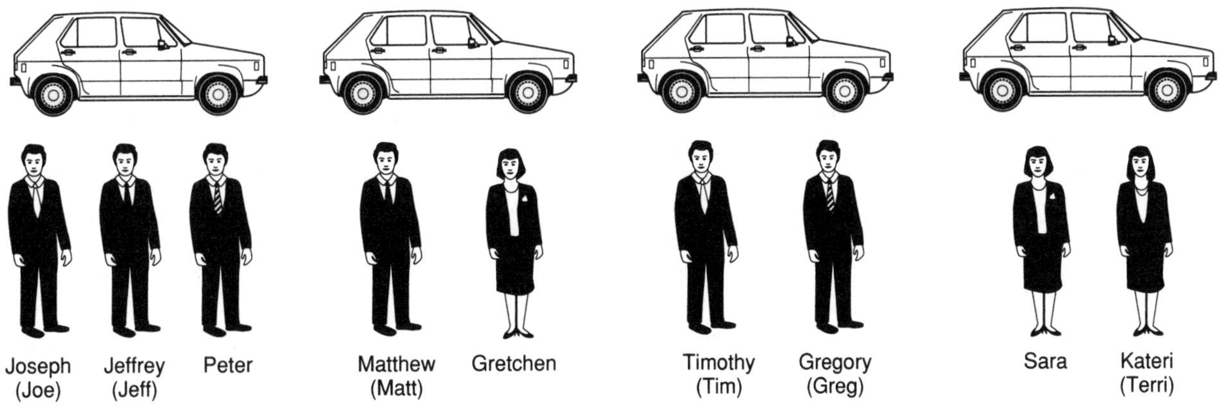

They have arrived in four cars. They enter the hotel in the following order: Timothy, Gregory, Kateri, Gretchen, Sara, Peter, Jeffrey, Matthew, and Joseph. They greet each other by their nicknames, which we too will use. They have time for a brief conversation before dinner. They position themselves in the conversation groups shown here.

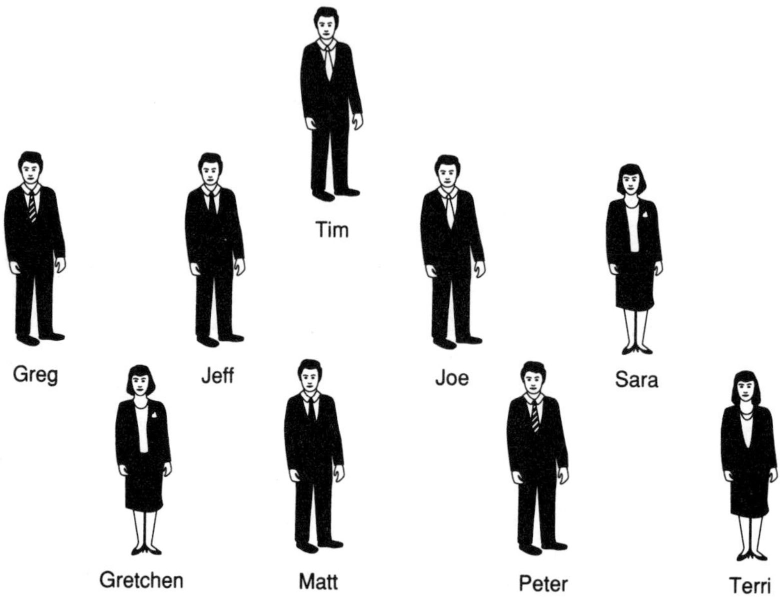

To the perceptive observer, the normal interpersonal dynamics of attraction and exclusion will soon become apparent. Who greets whom with enthusiasm or with bland indifference? Who joins in conversation with whom and helps to form an intragroup clique? Who comprises a subgroup to the principal clique? Who is excluded from either group? If, among the guests, there were "personal magnetic fields," we might easily detect the strength of these with proper instrumentation. But there are no such objective sensors of personal attraction, indifference, and rejection. And, since we have no objective way to compare these enthusiasms and indifferences, we may observe but not measure them. *To merely observe the behavior of individuals in a particular situation is not to measure it.*

One measurement method that is sometimes productive is to get each of the individuals in a group to talk about the others. It takes a skilled interviewer to do this type of inquiry. Discuss the group in terms of "best liked," "least liked," and neutrality. Conversation reveals much. Note the responses when a member of the group is mentioned. It takes keenness of perception and great tact to gather data in this way. But remember the basic axiom: If anything (interpersonal dynamics included) exists, then it *must* be measurable.

Another method is to give each individual in the group a slip on which to record three choices: (1) the individual in the group the person likes most, (2) the person liked the least, and (3) the person for whom the recorder has no strong feeling one way or another. When using this method, you must guarantee that every response will be kept confidential and, if possible, poll each person in the group individually.

We might then draw a chart, called a *sociogram,* of these intensities of personal reaction, that might look something like Figure 2.2.

We might also "weight" the data into three numerical categories: +1 for a positive choice, 0 for bland indifference, and −1 for a negative reaction. Categorizing the data in this way, we may then construct a *sociometric matrix.*

To create a matrix, we arrange the names of each person twice: horizontally across the top of a grid, and in the same order vertically. The result is shown in Table 2.2.

Certain relationships begin to emerge. As we represent group dynamics in multiple forms, certain constellations of facts suggest the following conclusions:

1. Jeff is the informal or popular leader (sometimes called the "star") of the group. He received five choices and only one rejection. The sociogram confirms the matrix total.

2. Probably some schism and tension is present in this group. Note that Peter, Sara, and Terri form a subclique, or "island," that is separated from the larger clique that Jeff leads. The liaison between these two groups is Joe, who has mutual choices with both Jeff and Peter.
3. There are friendship pairs that may lend cohesion to the group. Note the mutual choices: Matt and Gretchen, Peter and Joe, Jeff and Joe, Sara and Terri, Gretchen and Jeff. Only the sociogram reveals these alliances dramatically.
4. Tim apparently is the isolate of the group. He received no choices; he is neither liked nor disliked. In such a position, he is probably the least influential member of the group.

We have presented this sociometric data in its various forms to show how intangible data can be measured. Many other ways *can* be devised to measure airy nothings. In fact, there are other methods of drawing sociograms aside from the illustration above, such as the alternative suggested by B. B. Chaatterjee and A. K. Srivastava.[11] Their method is useful for larger popu-

Figure 2.2 Sociogram of Interpersonal Dynamics

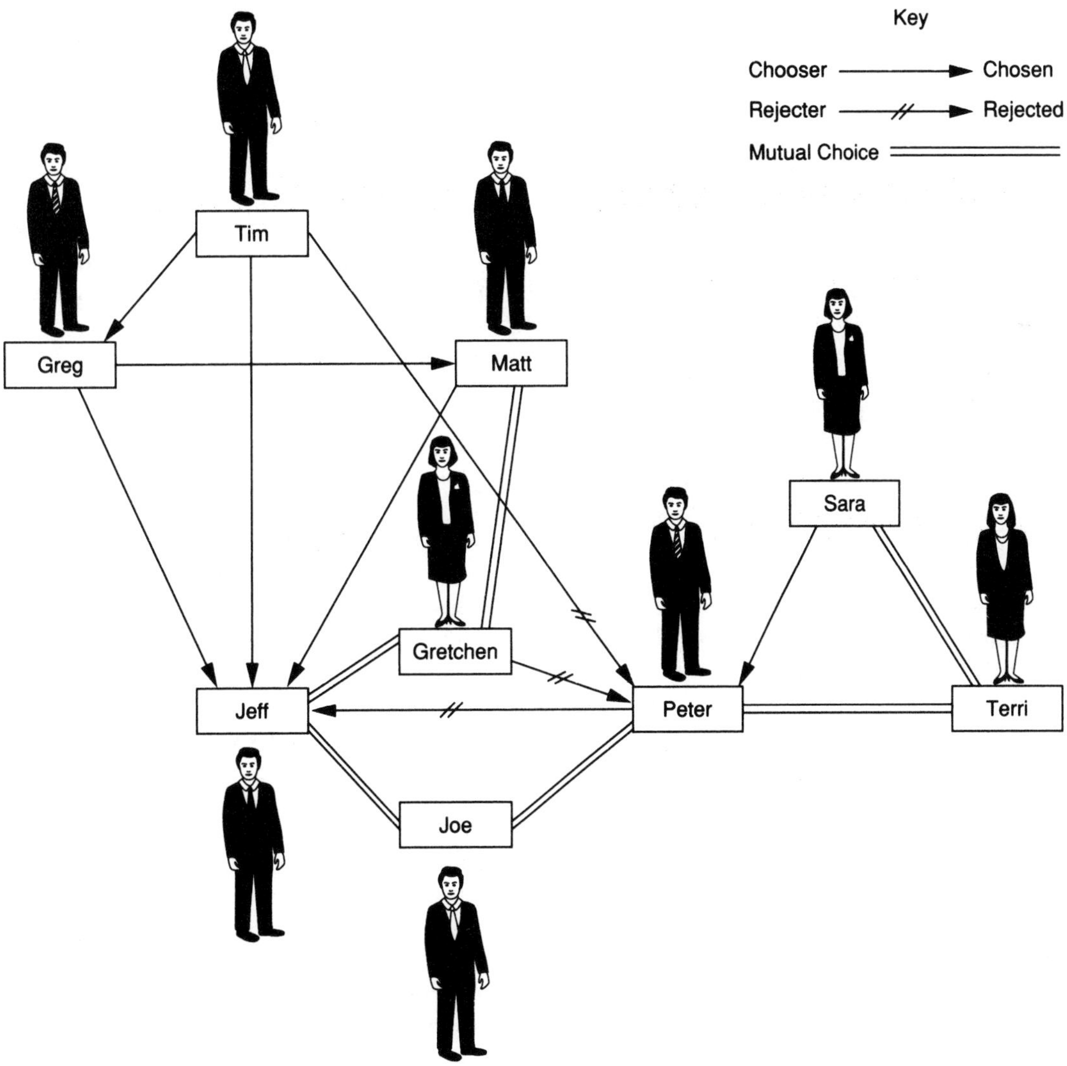

[11]B. B. Chaatterjee and A. K. Srivastava, "A Systematic Method for Drawing Sociograms," *Perspectives in Psychological Researches* 5 (April 1982): 1–6.

Table 2.2 Data from Figure 2.2 Presented as a Sociometric Matrix

	Gretchen	Joe	Greg	Sara	Peter	Jeff	Tim	Matt	Terri
Gretchen	—	0	0	0	−1	+1	0	+1	0
Joe	0	—	0	0	+1	+1	0	0	0
Greg	0	0	—	0	0	+1	0	+1	0
Sara	0	0	0	—	+1	0	0	0	+1
Peter	0	+1	0	0	—	−1	0	0	+1
Jeff	+1	+1	0	0	0	—	0	0	0
Tim	0	0	+1	0	−1	+1	—	0	0
Matt	+1	0	0	0	0	+1	0	—	0
Terri	0	0	0	+1	+1	0	0	0	—
Totals	2	2	1	1	1	4	0	2	2

lations and should be studied by those interested in studying social forces within extended groups.

The above analyses give us a mathematical insight into the social dynamics within a typical group. But *mathematics* is an easily misunderstood word, especially if we are thinking of it in the narrow sense only—that is, as the science of mathematics. We must divorce ourselves from this connotation.

Mathematical Examination of the Data

The ultimate criterion of any type of measurement is contained in the next eight words of our definition: . . . *so that those data may be regarded mathematically*. . . . We are now on very slippery terrain. Unless we read insightfully, we will miss the essential idea conveyed by the word *mathematical*, perhaps because the term inevitably conjures up another word, *numerical*. There's the danger. You are likely to jump to an unwarranted connotation. We must carefully distinguish between the basic meanings of these two terms. They are not synonymous, and have entirely different origins.

Mathematical comes from the Greek word *mathema*, meaning "science" or "knowledge," which is derived from the Greek verb meaning "to learn." Mathematical measurement, therefore, is a tool of research that provides increased insight into the data. The result is a fuller *knowledge*, or awareness, of what those data mean. This comes very close to what we shall later refer to as "the interpretation of the data."

On the other hand, a *numerical* view (from the Latin *numerus*, number) merely identifies data by having numbers assigned to them. To the genuine researcher, numbers are largely superficial. They become merely an exercise in arithmetic, very different from true mathematical insight. The latter is a revelation and a glimpse into a factual world that has never been seen before. It is a journey into discovery.[12] It's what Keats expressed in those two lines in "On First Looking into Chapman's Homer":

> Then felt I like some watcher of the skies
> When a new planet swims into his ken.

That's the thrill, the sheer excitement, that those who do research feel when they have a sudden mathematical insight of the disparate data with which they have been working. They experience an explosion of meaning! The data have been *interpreted: they have been transformed into facts, into units of discovery, of revelation, of enlightenment, of insight that the researcher has never seen before.* That's *true* research. That's what "regarding the data mathematically" means in our definition of measurement.

[12]Note the definition and the discussion in chapter 1 of discovery as a prime element of research.

We have demonstrated what it means to regard data mathematically by glimpsing the ebb and flow of emotional forces lying deep within nine individuals, presumably amicably assembled for a dinner occasion. There we have looked below the surface to discover hidden social dynamics in their reactions to one another.

Now, we finish the definition: ". . . *and, ultimately, according to an acceptable qualitative or quantitative standard.*" There must be a goalpost, a true north, a point of orientation. In research, we call these standards *norms, averages, conformity to expected statistical distributions, goodness of fit* and the like.

Measurement is ultimately a comparison: a thing or concept measured against a point of limitation. We compare the length of an object with the scale of a ruler or a measuring tape. We "measure" an ideology against the meaning of it as articulated or suggested by the originator of the ideology. The meaning of freedom and democratic idealism is best articulated in the Declaration of Independence and The Constitution of the United States; the essence of a religious belief resides in its sacred writings, in the precepts of its great teachers, and in its creed; the essence of a philosophy arises from the writings and teaching of its founder: Platonism from Plato, Marxism from Karl Marx, and romanticism perhaps basically from Jean Jacques Rousseau. Against these original sources it is possible to measure the thoughts and ideas of others and approximate their similarity or deviance from them.

Data that are examined statistically are constantly being interpreted in comparison to statistical norms: the Gaussian curve, point of central tendency, degree of dispersion, and other accepted statistical standards.

We see, therefore, that our definition implies much more than a surface reading might suggest. Measurement is indeed a tool by which data may be inspected, analyzed, and interpreted so that the researcher may probe meaning, which lies below superficial fact.

The Classical Measurements of Research

In 1946, S. S. Stevens suggested a hierarchy of levels for the measurement of data that has become a classic of categorization for statisticians and researchers.[13] Stevens suggested four levels, or types, of measurement, which he called (1) *nominal*, (2) *ordinal*, (3) *interval*, and (4) *ratio.* Basic to all measurement, however, is the *nature of the data.* The nature of the data will dictate the statistical procedure that you can use in processing the data, and will prescribe the appropriate type of measurement. To appreciate this fact, we shall consider each level of measurement and its characteristics.

Nominal Level of Measurement. The word *nominal* comes from the Latin *nomen,* meaning "a name." Hence we can measure data by assigning names to them. Remember the earlier discussion of *measure,* where we suggested that its basic meaning was to restrict, to limit. That's what nominal measurement does—and just about all that it does. Assign a specific name to anything and you have restricted that thing to the meaning of its name. For example, we can measure a group of children by dividing it into two groups: girls and boys. Each subgroup is thereby measured—"restricted"—by virtue of gender to a particular category. By assigning a *name,* we create a measurement.

There are an infinite number of ways of measuring nominally. We can measure the groups above according to the home site of each child. In the town in which they live, Main Street, extending east and west, cuts the town in half: those who live north of Main Street are "the Northerners," and those who live south of it are "the Southerners." In one period of our history we measured the population of the entire nation in just such a manner.

Nominal measurement is elemental and unrefined, but it does divide data into discrete categories that can then be compared with each other. Let's look at nominal measurement a little further. We have six individuals: Irene, Paul, Kathy, Tom, Ginger, and Nicky. They can be

[13]S. S. Stevens, "On the Theory of Scales of Measurement," *Science* 103 (7 June 1946): 677–80.

measured into six units of one each; they can also form two groups: Irene, Kathy, and Ginger in one; Paul, Tom, and Nicky in the other. Let us think of them as a class that meets in room 12 at Thompson's Corner School. By assigning a room number, we have provided it with a name, even though that "name" may be a number. However, that number has no quantitative meaning: room 12 is not necessarily bigger or better than room 11, or inferior to room 13.

Nominal measurement is, nevertheless not merely a measuring convention. It can be processed statistically, for example by locating the mode: the most individuals by the name of Paul or Tom, or Irene, or Kathy in a family, a school, or a town. By means of statistics, we can also find the percentage of one subgroup to another subgroup or to the total group, or gain some insight to the normalcy of the group or groups by comparing them using the chi square test. We will discuss statistics more fully in the next section of this chapter.

Ordinal Level of Measurement. In the ordinal scale of measurement we think in terms of the symbols > (greater than) or < (less than). The ordinal scale implies that the entity being measured is quantified in terms of being of a higher or lower, a greater or lesser *order* (from which we get the name of the scale, *ordinal*) than a comparative entity.

In measuring on the ordinal scale, there is always an asymmetrical relationship. Something is always greater than, less than, older than or younger than, more intelligent than, more desirable than, more tactful than—we could go on and on.

We measure level of education grossly on the ordinal scale by classifying people as unschooled, or as having an elementary, high school, college, graduate school, or professional school education. Likewise, we measure members of the work force by grades of proficiency: unskilled, semiskilled, or skilled.

The ordinal scale expands the range of statistical techniques that can be applied to the data. Using the ordinal scale we can find the mode and the median, determine the percentage or the percentile rank, and test by the chi square.

By means of rank correlation, we can also indicate relationships within the data.

Interval Level of Measurement. The interval scale is characterized by two features: (1) it has equal units of measurement, and (2) its zero point has been established arbitrarily.[14] Thermometric scales are probably the most familiar interval scales. In both the Fahrenheit and the Celsius scales, each degree is equal to the others and the zero point has been established arbitrarily. Perhaps the Fahrenheit scale shows the arbitrariness of the setting of the zero point most clearly. Gabriel Fahrenheit first took as his zero point the coldest temperature observed in Iceland. Later, he made it the lowest temperature obtainable with a mixture of salt and ice. This was purely an *arbitrary* decision. It placed the freezing point of water at 32 degrees, and the boiling point at 212 degrees, above zero.

We have alluded to the common standard measurements utilizing interval units. A common use of interval measurement is in the *rating scales* employed by many businesses, survey groups, and professional organizations. One college uses the following ten-point measurement of its faculty's teaching effectiveness. Students are asked to rate their teachers on specific qualities of effectiveness. One segment of the scale looks like this:

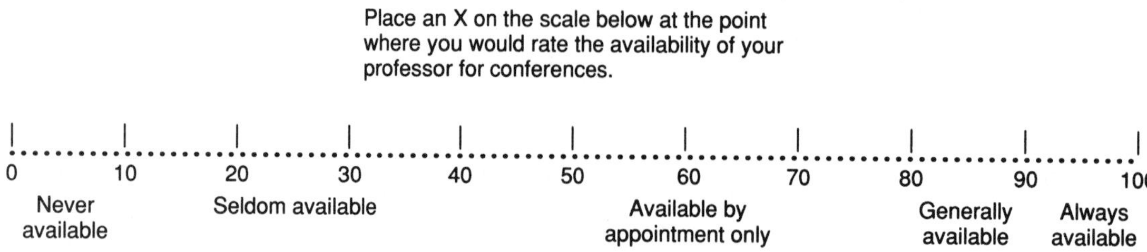

[14]David Sills, ed., *The International Encyclopedia of the Social Sciences*, Vol. 13 (New York: Macmillan and the Free Press, 1968), 97.

Note that the scale above has ten *equidistant* points. The equidistance creates a standard scalar unit and is thus comparable to the second, minute, or hour intervals of time.

Look at the above rating scale a little more closely. On it are ten reference points and five judgment categories. The fineness of gradation of the scale might be improved by adding five intermediate points between each of the locations on the ten-point scale. This will create a scale of 50 points for a five-category placement. If, on the other hand, ten points are inserted between each of the above locations, we then have a 100-point scale upon which to make judgments. For indicating the availability of a professor, such finesse of discrimination may not be either possible or desirable, but one may conceive situations in which such a degree of discrimination may be required.

Ratio Level of Measurement. Two measurement instruments may help you understand the difference between the interval and ratio scales: one is for measuring temperature (a thermometer), and one is for measuring space (a yardstick). For example, we cannot say that 80 degrees Fahrenheit is twice as warm as 40 degrees Fahrenheit. Why? Because, as we discussed above, the Fahrenheit (as well as the Celsius) scale does not originate from a point of absolute zero. There is no solid foundation upon which the scale rests. If the scale arose from absolute zero, there would be nothing to measure, in terms of temperature *below* the zero point. But as all of us know, on a cold winter day it is not unusual for the temperature to register considerably below zero. With the yardstick, however, the beginning of linear measurement is absolutely the beginning. If I measure my desk from the left edge to the right edge, that's it. There is no more desk beyond those limits. Fox puts it succinctly: He defines *true zero* as "the total absence of the quantity being measured."[15] You cannot measure a minus distance. Also, the units of measurement on a yardstick are all equal: The distance between the first and second inch is the same as that between the thirty-fifth and the thirty-sixth inch.

Remember the scale given above that measures the availability of the professor? That scale could never be considered a ratio scale. Why? Because there is only one condition in which the professor would be *absolutely* unavailable: if the professor were *dead*! Under that condition, all the rest of the degrees of availability would evaporate, and the scale would vanish.

A characteristic difference between the ratio scale and all the other scales is that *the ratio scale can express values in terms of multiples and fractional parts*, and the ratios are *true* ratios. A yardstick can do that: a yard is a *multiple* (by 12) of a 3-inch distance; 3 inches is one-fourth (a *fractional part*) of a foot. The ratios are 3:36, or 1:12, and 3:12, or 1:4.

In summary, perhaps Senders has encapsulated this discussion in the following simple test for various kinds of data measurement.[16]

If you can say that:

one object is different from another, you have a *nominal scale*;
one object is bigger or better or more of anything than another, you have an *ordinal scale*;
one object is so many units (degrees, inches) more than another, you have an *interval scale*;
one object is so many times as big, or bright, or tall, or heavy as another, you have a *ratio scale*.

We have perhaps belabored these types of data measurement enough. But it is very important for you to have a clear concept of each of the four scales and for you to understand the relationship between measuring and the statistical treatment of data. The type of statistical analysis to which data are subjected depends many times upon the type of measurement applied to the data.

[15]David J. Fox, *Fundamentals of Research in Nursing* (New York: Appleton-Century, 1976), 73.
[16]Virginia L. Senders, *Measurement and Statistics: A Basic Text Emphasizing Behavioral Science* (New York: Oxford University Press, 1958), 51.

The following Summary of Measurement Scales (Figure 2.3) will provide a quick reference table of the various types of scales, their distinguishing characteristics, and the statistical possibilities of each scale. Later, when we consider the statistical interpretation of data, you may wish to refer to this table to determine whether the type of data measurement you have employed will support the statistical operation that you may be contemplating.

Validity and Reliability

With any type of measurement, two considerations are very important. One of these is *validity*; the other is *reliability*. *Validity* is concerned with the soundness, the effectiveness of the measuring instrument. Take a standardized test, for instance. Validity would raise such questions as: What does the test measure? Does it, in fact, measure what it is supposed to measure? How well, how comprehensively, how accurately does it measure it?

Refer back to the scale that measures a professor's availability. Let's look at it with respect to the validity of its measurement. Note how fuzzy some of the category words are. The professor is "always available." What does "always" mean? Twenty-four hours a day? Could you call the professor at 3 A.M. any day of the week? Whenever the professor is on campus? If so, could you call your professor out of a faculty meeting or out of a conference with the president of the college?

All right, you say, let's eliminate the "always" category. Now, what happens? This leaves only four categories, upping the value of each to 25 percent. This does not solve your basic problem. It leaves you with the next category descriptor, "generally." What does "generally" mean? How general is *generally*? The same goes for "seldom" available. And is "never" available possible, short of the death of the professor?

What seems at first glance to be a scale anyone could understand is on careful inspection open to very serious question as to its validity and, in fact, its practical usefulness *as a measuring instrument* for research purposes.

Figure 2.3 A Summary of Measurement Scales, Their Characteristics, and Their Statistical Implications

Measurement Scale		Characteristics of the Scale	Statistical Possibilities of the Scale
Non-interval Scales	Nominal scale	A scale that "measures" in terms of names or designations of discrete units or categories.	Can be used for determining the mode, the percentage values, or the chi square.
	Ordinal scale	A scale that "measures" in terms of such values as "more" or "less," "larger" or "smaller," but without specifying the size of the intervals.	Can be used for determining the mode, percentage, chi square, median, percentile rank, or rank correlation.
Interval Scales	Interval scale	A scale that measures in terms of equal intervals or degrees of difference but whose zero point, or point of beginning, is arbitrarily established.	Can be used for determining the mode, the mean, the standard deviation, the *t*-test, the *F*-test, and the product moment correlation.
	Ratio scale	A scale that measures in terms of equal intervals and an absolute zero point of origin.	Can be used for determining the geometric mean, the harmonic mean, the percent variation, and all other statistical determinations.

There are several types of validity. The more common types of validity, with a brief description of each, are listed below.

A Summary of the More Common Types of Validity

1. **Face validity:** This type of validity relies basically upon the subjective judgment of the researcher. It asks two questions, which the researcher must finally answer in accordance with his or her best judgment: (1) Is the instrument measuring what it is supposed to measure? (2) Is the sample being measured adequate to be representative of the behavior or trait being measured?
2. **Criterion validity.** Criterion validity usually employs two measures of validity; the second, as a *criterion,* checks against the accuracy of the first measure. The essential component in criterion validity is a reliable and valid criterion—a standard against which to measure the results of the instrument that is doing the measuring. The data of the measuring instrument should correlate highly with equivalent data of the criterion.
3. **Content validity.** This type of validity is sometimes equated with *face validity.* Content validity is the accuracy with which an instrument measures the factors or situations under study; i.e. the "content" being studied. If, for example, we are interested in the content validity of questions being asked to elicit familiarity with a certain area of knowledge, content validity would be concerned with how accurately the questions asked tend to elicit the information sought.
4. **Construct validity.** A *construct* is any concept, such as *honesty,* that cannot be directly observed or isolated.[17] Construct validation is interested in the degree to which the construct itself is actually measured. To this end a significant procedure has been developed by Campbell and Fiske known as the Multitrait-Multimethod Matrix.[18] It makes use of the traits of *convergence* and *discriminability. Convergence* looks to the focal effect of various methods of measuring a construct. Different methods of measuring the same construct should "converge" or "focus" in their results. *Discriminability* means that the measuring instrument should be able to discriminate, or differentiate, the construct being studied from other similar constructs.
5. **Internal validity.** This term, and the one following, should not be confused with internal and external criticism, which are tests of validity in historical research and are discussed later in this text. *Internal validity* is the freedom from bias in forming conclusions in view of the data. It seeks to ascertain that the changes in the dependent variable are the result of the influence of the independent variable rather than the manner in which the research was designed.
6. **External validity.** This type of validity is concerned with the generalizability of the conclusions reached through observation of a sample to the universe; or, more simply stated, can the conclusions drawn from a sample be generalized to other cases?

Validity looks to the end results of measurement. The principal question that validity asks is: Are we really measuring what we think we are measuring?

The naive assume that because a test is designed to measure a certain factor or attribute, it does precisely that. Take, for instance, a paper-and-pencil test of personality factors. By a series of check marks the individual indicates his or her most representative traits or actions in given situations—these traits and behaviors are presumed to reveal the characteristics of personality. The question that validity asks is: Does such a test *in fact* measure the individual's *personality*

[17]Mary G. Kweit and Robert W. Kweit, *Concepts and Methods for Political Analysis* (Englewood Cliffs, NJ: Prentice-Hall, 1981), 21, 350.

[18]D. T. Campbell and D. W. Fiske, "Convergent and Discriminant Validation by the Multitrait-Multimethod Matrix," *Psychological Bulletin* 56 (1959): 81–105.

factors, or does it measure something else, quite removed from pure personality traits? No doubt the questions are directed toward one's behavioral traits and actions, but the check marks may represent only those by which the student wishes to be represented. Hence, this is not a *valid* evaluation of the student's *real* personality but rather an idealized portrait of the way in which the student hopes that others may regard him or her.

We have now come very close to the second consideration in measurement, and that is reliability.

Reliability. Reliability deals with accuracy. It asks such questions as, How accurate is the instrument that is used in making the measurement? Take the measurement of time, for example. A sundial may measure time, and within certain broad parameters it may be useful in our knowing whether it is morning, noon, or afternoon. But as a measure of time, a sundial is not too *reliable.* A person would not use one for catching planes or keeping appointments.

Mechanical timepieces are much more reliable. But even these run fast or slow, depending on their quality and their maintenance. They are *fairly reliable* for everyday needs. If, however, we are transiting stars, tracking satellites, and doing other ultraprecise research, we need the reliability of the cesium atomic clock of the Naval Observatory or the National Institute of Standards and Technology. Reliability asks one question above all others: With what *accuracy* does the measure (test, instrument, inventory, questionnaire) measure what it is intended to measure?

No research can proceed without data. But merely collecting data in their raw, undisciplined state serves little purpose. We must find some way of corralling data by submitting them to the process of measurement. This consists in seeing facts in orderly fashion. The common procedure is to measure them by one of the four scales we have already discussed. Measurement, then, is merely the process of taking data in their raw state and arranging them along some scale of comprehensible values. It provides a means of "seeing" the data in terms of some specific, manageable unit.

But, having done this, we have done little more than create order from the chaos of unrelated and undisciplined fact. Before the data can be really useful to the researcher, more remains to be done. In many instances, another tool of research must be used to process the data further, so that by such processing we may still further discern their meaning. This tool is statistics.

Statistics

Statistics is merely a *tool* of research, nothing more. It provides a means by which the researcher may more comprehensively view data. And viewing data properly is one of the major secrets of successful research. Data should *always be viewed from as many angles as possible:* statistically, logically, inquisitively, comparatively, and so forth. Because of the undue emphasis that has been placed upon statistics both in textbook and classroom, students frequently consider this as the only way data may be significantly comprehended. Despite that, statistics is a most insightful tool and its importance should not be undervalued in the role it plays in comprehending the meaning of the data.

Whether they be the contents of the metal chest of the mechanic or the delicate instruments of the scientist, tools should be appreciated in terms of their potential. What value have they? For what *specific* task were they designed? What *single* purpose does the use of the tool fulfill? Whether the tool is a screwdriver or a coefficient of correlation, these questions are relevant.

A screwdriver has one functional purpose: to insert or remove screws. I had a friend, however, that used a screwdriver for any exigency that arose: to pry off lids, punch holes, as a leverage device, to scratch off unwanted accretions of foreign matter, and so on. I do not deny that the end was not accomplished by so using the tool—or rather, *misusing* it—but the purpose for which the tool was designed was totally invalidated.

So with statistics. It is a powerful tool when used correctly. But we must consider its limitations. Statistical values are never the consummation of the research endeavor. They are not the final answer to the research problem. Behind statistics lie the facts, to which the statistics refer. The final question in research is: *What do the facts indicate?* Not what is their numerical configuration; where they cluster, how broadly they spread, or how closely they are related. Statistics gives us *information* about the facts, but a careful researcher is not satisfied until the *meaning* of the facts is revealed.

A statistical conclusion usually implies a deeper significance hidden within the data. After the statistical result, the significant questions then begin to float to the surface. These are the questions of How? Why? and What does it all mean? Even the simple arithmetic mean may tell us nothing until we look at the data curve. What is its configuration? Is it skewed? If so, how? How is this skew reflected in the population? Is it bimodal? What does the skew and the bimodality tell you that the arithmetic mean does not? Much lies below a simple point such as central tendency that the researcher who draws conclusions from statistical sources only misses entirely.

The acid test of research is: Does the conclusion arise solely from the *interpretation of the data*? Does the conclusion answer the questions raised by the research problem? The instant the researcher concludes that the problem or subproblem has been resolved that researcher should reread that problem or subproblem to determine whether what *purports* to answer the research question *really is an answer supported by the data.*

There is no substitute for the task the researcher ultimately faces: to discover the significance of the data and the relevance of that significance to the research problem. Any statistical process that you may employ is merely ancillary to this larger quest.

The Seductiveness of Statistics

Statistics can be the voice of a bevy of sirens to the neophyte researcher. For those who have forgotten their Homer (or, sadly, have never read him), the *Odyssey* describes the perilous straits between Scylla and Charybdis. On these treacherous rocks sat an assembly of Sirens—svelte maidens who, with enticing songs, attempted to lure sailors and, by so doing, caused ships to drift and founder upon the jagged shores.

For many students, statistics holds a similar lure. They forget that statistics is merely a *tool* of research. Treating data by subjecting them to elegant statistical routines may lure students into thinking they have made a substantial discovery, one that in fact may be little more than a numerical value indicating a deeper and more significant revelation. Students become fascinated in playing with the tool. They forget that behind every statistic lies the as-yet-undiscovered, substantial body of *fact* that will resolve the research problem. The uncompromising, real, observable world, of which the statistic is only an indication, is the arena in which the mind of the researcher must wrestle with the facts. It is this world of facts, and not that of statistics, that will ultimately yield the evidence that will solve the problem.

Elegant Statistics Entice. The lead editorial in the 1987 issue of *Research in Nursing and Health* puts the role of statistics poignantly and reasonably:

> Occasionally, we see manuscripts in which descriptive data are omitted but detailed results of several multivariate analyses are reported. One can only surmise, in those instances, that the investigator was indeed seduced by the elegant manipulations made possible by the computer and by statistical programs. The cavalier treatment of descriptive data also may be accompanied by cavalier treatment of the assumptions upon which the statistical procedures are based. Those who "do their own statistics" may not be as thoroughly conversant with the nuances of the procedures employed as would be desirable. . . .

> The use of elegant statistics can never compensate for inelegant conceptual bases. The new evaluative procedures are exciting because they enable examination of data in ways previously not possible. The bottom line remains the same, however. One cannot draw large savings out of an account into which little has been deposited. Neither can one draw useful meanings from studies into which less-than-important notions have been entered.[19]

The Primary Functions of Statistics

Statistics has two principal functions: descriptive and inferential. Statistics can aid the research process in only two ways: (1) By describing the contour of data and, in the case of two or more groups of data, their proximity or remoteness of relationship. This is *descriptive* statistics. (2) By suggesting certain inferences as to the nature of the data. This is *inferential* statistics. Inferential statistics attempts to do with data what a tailor does when creating a suit. The tailor attempts to make the suit conform as nearly as possible to the contour of the individual being fitted. Inferential statistics seeks to fit data to the ideal form of a statistical model. Neither branch of statistics has ever solved a research problem. As stated, only a thorough examination of the collected data can do that. Statistics can illuminate contour, but the researcher's principal interest is not to see the contour but to account for its configuration in terms of the research problem. The task is identical to that of the geologist in seeing the configuration of an area of land. Both researcher and geologist are looking for the *cause* for the configuration, neither is content with merely observing it.

I do not at all mean to disparage statistics as a tool of research. It is a powerful tool, and it plays an important role in manipulating data and comprehending the entire research process. Indeed, a major service—perhaps the primary one—that statistics exerts is to help the human mind comprehend disparate data as an organized whole.

Assume that we have accumulated a body of data from a selected population. The statistical questions now arise: How typical is this population? How divergent are certain characteristics of it? What is the point where the group is most homogeneous? What is the goodness of fit of the collected data to the graceful curve of the idealistic model? What is the probability that a certain event will happen? The answers to these questions will not in any way resolve the central problem of the research. Each question is nothing more than a signpost pointing toward that inevitable and final encounter with the original research question, whose answer can be extracted only from the raw data that initiated the statistical quest.

While no statistical question is terminal, all have their place in advancing the research process. They give us added insight into the nature of the data and its characteristics and can be very helpful. But we must keep them in perspective. We cannot allow them to lure us off our main course: to pursue our solution unerringly. Statistics is a powerful and necessary tool, but is not a consummation devoutly to be wished. It cannot provide the final answer to a major research problem, but it can indicate important characteristics of the data amassed for the solution of that problem that would otherwise not be revealed.

Statistics Often Create That Which Has No Counterpart in Reality

Generally, we accept the arithmetic mean—commonly called the "average"—without question or reservation. But take a simple example: Four students have parttime jobs on campus. One works 24 hours a week in the library, the second works 22 hours a week in the campus book store, the third works 12 hours a week in the parking lot, the fourth 16 hours a week in the cafeteria.

Now data presented in this form is unorganized and random. All facts, as they come to us from the real world are unorganized, separate bits of undisciplined information. They have no focus; they need to be managed. How do we do this?

[19]"Use of Elegant Statistics," *Research in Nursing and Health* 10 (1987): iii.

Let us enlist the aid of statistics. We need to get some organization out of the random hours that four students are extracurricularly employed. So what can we do? We can find the arithmetic mean. This reveals that these students work "on the average" 18.5 hours a week. Now the four unrelated working periods are beginning to become meaningful. We begin to feel much more comfortable. We have "learned" something about these four students and their working hours—even though what we have "learned" is mythical: no student has worked 18.5 hours a week. That figure represents absolutely no fact in the real world.

Apparently we have solved one problem only to create another. We have created a dilemma. If statistics offer us only an unreality, then why statistics? Why create myth out of hard, demonstrable fact?

The answer lies in the nature of the human brain. It is difficult for the human mind to comprehend any concept other than unity arising from a dispersion of uncoordinated data. Present to the brain a disunity, a confusion, and the brain cannot cope; it abhors confusion. And so, to accommodate the psychological need for a unified concept, we have devised a system that will satisfy our mental requirements, despite the fact that in so doing we will create unreality.

Nevertheless, statistics *does* take unconnected facts and tie them together meaningfully. It provides a hypothetical platform from which we may view even great masses of data. To acquire this view, we convert each individual datum into a hypothetical coagulate from which, with the aid of statistical processing, the mind of the researcher can extract a substantial, though frequently entirely nonexistent, concept. Think about the average, the standard deviation, a correlation of one variable to another variable, and so on. Each is insubstantial. Averages and all other statistical concepts are figments, for mental convenience only. Statistics, then, may be defined as that numerical system that aims to make diverse and complex data garnered out of the real world unified and comprehensible to the human mind.

So much, therefore, for a discussion whose sole purpose was to present the nature, rationale, and potential of statistics as a general tool of research. It is a valuable tool, and we must not underestimate its capacity to give us insight into the depths of factual significance, beyond which lies the realm of Ultimate Truth.

Using the Computer for Research

The computer is perhaps the workhorse of the generalized tools of research. The variety of things it can do is incredible. The speed with which it works is incomprehensible. But, like any tool, no matter how powerful, it has its limitations. It is a truism that a computer cannot do anything that you cannot do with pencil and paper, although it can do it in much shorter time. But you can do what no computer can ever do: dream, imagine, plan, and create. No computer on earth has this ability.

As tools of research, computers are becoming increasingly commonplace. But to the uninitiated, they still have an aura of mystery. They are sometimes considered a panacea for any problem that the researcher faces. "Let the computer do it" is the contemporary equivalent for the older shibboleth "Let George do it." We often seem to think that whenever the task becomes difficult or the thinking begins to pain, a computer will solve all our problems. Nothing could be further from the truth.

Computers are not human brains. Yes, a computer can certainly calculate, compare, search, retrieve, sort, and organize data more efficiently and more accurately than you can. But compared to the magnificence of the human brain, computers are pitifully limited machines that, in their present stage of development, depend totally upon a person at the keyboard to tell them what to do. When it comes to initiative, computers have none!

For those who are awed by the computer's amazing memory and performance, let them be told that the IQ of the computer is so awe-inspiring that its total "brain power" can handle only two things: the awareness of an electrical impulse or of the absence of an electrical impulse—whether a circuit is on or off. It cannot do more.

With such a limited "brain," how then does a computer work? Like this: everything that goes into it is put there directly or indirectly by humans. Each letter, number, punctuation mark, symbol that you strike—even spacing—is coded into an electronic impulse that the computer then manipulates according to instructions written by a computer programmer. A computer program is nothing but a set of written instructions that tell the computer how to manipulate the data that is put into it, how to process it and display it on the monitor screen.

This is, of course, a very sketchy explanation of how the computer works. We need go no further to give you an appreciation of the amazing electronic complexity of what happens behind the monitor screen, and all at nearly the speed of light!

But our main purpose here is to consider the computer as a tool of research. It has a multitude of applications. Unfortunately, many people have a general impression that the principal function of a computer is to "compute"—merely to perform mathematical and statistical operations. And perhaps this *was* its primary function when it was first developed. But no more. Word processing has assumed a major role in computer use and has greatly enhanced the computer's value as a research tool. Through word processing we are able to create documents, edit them, emphasize certain ideas within them with boldface or italics, move sections of text or transpose paragraphs, create footnotes and running heads, automatically number pages, check spelling, call upon a thesaurus to supply a synonym, or adjust our writing style.

To understand computers, two key words are of consummate importance: *hardware* and *software. Hardware* consists of all those tangible parts of the computer system: the computer itself—the box containing the electronic components and circuitry; the keyboard, which sends messages to the computer; the monitor, or cathode tube, on the face of which the words and symbols appear; the disk or tape drives that store computer data for later retrieval, and the printer, which produces the *hard copy* of the material that has appeared on the monitor screen and is stored in the memory of the computer. The *software,* on the other hand, consists of the programs that tell the computer what to do, that issue the battery of commands that instruct the computer how to perform certain specific tasks.

In the bibliography section at the conclusion of this chapter, we will list some of the principal directories to computer software. It is difficult to be up-to-date in bibliographical citations, because the computer industry is developing so fast that changes occur almost daily.

For the serious researcher, one further use of the computer as a research tool should be mentioned: online databank resources. These can be accessed by telephone from a personal computer. Usually, there is a one-time hookup or access fee, and then a variable hourly rental fee. Data from a databank can be recorded upon reception directly into the computer memory or hard disk, on diskette (floppy disk), or saved as printed hard copy.

The databank is an information retrieval reservoir. Some databanks store an awe-inspiring amount of information. Akin to the databank is another source of information, CD-ROM, mentioned earlier in this chapter. CD-ROM, a recent development in information storage and retrieval, is fast becoming a popular data source for personal computer users as well as for libraries and businesses.

Like most data that is stored in disk files, databanks, or on diskettes, the information on CD-ROM can be printed out if hard copy is needed.

All of us are familiar with computer printouts. Every time we go to the supermarket and the checkout clerk hands us an itemization of our purchases, we have received a *computer printout.* This is *hard copy* text made by a computer printer. The data need not be recorded in this form. Data can be stored in the memory of the computer until we are ready to use it. Such storage is, however, a case of all's well that ends well. Should the current be interrupted while the computer is operating, should someone accidentally pull the plug to the power source, or should the voltage surge when your computer isn't protected against such current spikes, you could lose all the data stored in the memory. You should, of course, have a reliable protective device to control voltage surges. Such surges can seriously damage the computer itself, as well as obliterate the stored data.

It is always a good idea to have backup sources of your data. Prudent researchers store their data regularly on diskette or tape (by which it can be reinstalled into the computer, if need be) or directly on *hard copy*. In using a computer, preserving data is a very important consideration.

This has been a brief and superficial discussion of the computer as a tool of research—what a computer can and cannot do. We exit with the same advice with which we started: *The computer is not a miracle worker. It cannot do your thinking for you.* It can, however, be a very fast and faithful servant. It must be told exactly what to do, and it must be given instructions for precisely how to do it. Understood in this manner, the computer is one of the researcher's best friends.

Language and the Ability to Use It

All research, to be generally useful, must ultimately be issued as a written document. To be able to produce such a document, the researcher must possess the ability to use language to communicate with a degree of skill and accuracy that will clearly delineate all aspects of the research process. We usually refer to the written document as the *research report*. The basic requirement for writing such a report is the ability to use the English language—to write clear, coherent exposition—so that your document will leave no doubt in the reader's mind precisely what the research problem is and what steps and considerations resulted in its solution.

The problem of research must be set forth with such clarity that it will be impossible not to comprehend precisely what is being investigated. It requires you to have a vocabulary that is adequate for the common exigencies of exposition. But this is a surface manifestation of certain elements of expression that lie much deeper.

No one speaks—or writes—clearly who does not first *think* clearly. Clear thinking is based on the ability to think logically, sequentially, and concretely. There is no place in research reporting for using "you-know-what-I-mean," a phrase we often use to cover our ignorance or our intellectual laziness. It indicates either that we do not know something or that we do not have the ability to express a thought in communicable form. Do not be duped into thinking that such a lack of mental energy will suffice in doing research. Those who operate on that premise are doomed to disaster.

We write the way we do because we think the way we do. Good writing is merely precise, sensitive thinking mirrored in carefully chosen, logically presented words. Sentences lumber across the page because those who wrote them have lumbering minds—minds that have little facility in clothing thoughts with words. Those minds have never been taught to think with verbal precision.

But there is another aspect to language used as a tool of research. We cannot assume that all significant research is reported in English. Most doctoral programs have language requirements, which usually require students to demonstrate a reading competency in two foreign languages in addition to proficiency in writing English. The choice of those languages is usually linked to the area of proposed research.

In the *Guide to American Graduate Schools,* Harold Doughty and Herbert Livesey have this to say about the language requirement:

> Perhaps one-third of the nation's graduate schools require some sort of ability in at least one foreign language for the master's degree. Nearly all schools, however, demand knowledge of at least one language, and often two, for the doctorate. The language requirement has evolved from the traditional French and/or German of the early years of graduate study in the United States to a variety of present forms.

For the master's degree, the language requirement is generally stated as a "reading knowledge of 1 modern foreign language, usually French, German, or Russian." The requirement is usually school-wide, but many departments stipulate this reading knowledge when their schools do not. On the doctoral level, two of the above-named languages may be specified. Several variations of this customary requirement for the doctorate have cropped up in recent years, however. These include: (1) a reading, speaking, and writing knowledge of one foreign language, *or* reading knowledge only of two languages; (2) a reading knowledge of one language plus proven ability to use another appropriate research tool such as statistical methods; (3) reading knowledge of only one language.

Although some graduate schools adhere to the traditional French and German requirement for the doctorate, most now permit substitution of another language deemed appropriate for a particular area of specialization for at least one of the two languages.[20]

The language requirement is a reasonable one. Human enlightenment has spread across the world at an astounding rate because of research and discovery. The Soviet Union, for example, during its existence made gigantic strides in science, especially in the areas of physics and space science. The Japanese have pushed back the frontiers in electronics and robotics. Many such new discoveries are reported in the native language of the researcher.

A researcher doing a doctoral dissertation that demands knowledge of research in other languages must be able to gain access to it through at least a reading competency in the languages in which the research is reported. When I began my doctoral research, I fully anticipated that the material relevant to my investigation would all be in English. Midway into the research, I found to my utter surprise that I needed a reading knowledge of Latin, French, and German to complete my study successfully. Anyone who has ever done research realizes that the quest for data leads one through unexpected turns and into unimagined areas.

Open a volume of the *Index Medicus.* Note how much medical research is reported in languages other than English. The same is true in other fields. To open the door to knowledge of this research, the researcher needs a tool to force open the lock. That tool is a facility with the language in which the research is reported.

For a case in point, let's take an article that appeared in the *Journal of African History* in which the author was studying "the significance of the Atlantic slave trade for African history [, which] has been the subject of considerable discussion among historians and merits attempts from time to time to review the literature."[21]

Two paragraphs from this article, with text citations (but not the notes themselves) are reproduced below. [22] The author acknowledges that new material on the controversial position that the slave trade had a devastating effect on African societies have not welcomed a hard look at facts and statistical probability.

Any assessment of the impact of the slave trade on Africa has to estimate the scale of exports over time and for specific exporting regions, and hence has to deal with the projections based on existing knowledge, always allowing for gaps in the data. Many studies of this type have been completed, and more are likely to be done.[16] Analysis depends upon a continuing reassessment of the volume and direction of the export trade as new material becomes available.

The most important new material pertains to the French trade, assembled in Jean Mettas, *Répertoire des expéditions négrières françaises au XVIII siècle.*[17] Mettas's data are analyzed by Charles Becker and David Richardson.[18] Richardson has also compiled new material on the British trade in the eighteenth century and has reinterpreted the available data on the North American trade.[19] Finally, José Curto has uncovered new material on the Portuguese trade.[20]

[20]Harold R. Doughty and Herbert B. Livesey, *Guide to American Graduate Schools,* 4th ed. (Baltimore, MD: Penguin, 1982), 19.
[21]Paul E. Lovejoy, "The Impact of the Atlantic Slave Trade on Africa: A Review of the Literature," *Journal of African History* 30 (1989): 365–394.
[22]Lovejoy, "Impact," 368.

"Analysis [of this problem] depends upon a continuing reassessment of the volume and direction of export trade as new material becomes available." Now, notice how Lovejoy would be stopped were he not conversant in reading French. He readily admits that "the most important new material pertains to the French trade, assembled in Jean Mattas, *Répertoire des expéditions négrières Françaises au XVIII siècle.*" Notice also the extent to which he notes that other researchers have used other French documentary sources, the checking of which would be obligatory if one were only to review the literature, let alone do research in this field.

Significant and Influential Research

The time: February 13, 1929. The place: St. Mary's Hospital, London. The occasion: the reading of a paper before The Medical Research Club. The speaker: a member of the hospital staff in the Department of Microbiology. That was the setting for the presentation of one of the most significant research reports of the early twentieth century. It was the report of a discovery that has transformed the practice of medicine. Dr. Alexander Fleming presented to his colleagues his research on penicillin. The group was apathetic. No one showed any enthusiasm for Dr. Fleming's paper. Great research has frequently been presented to those who are imaginatively both blind and deaf.

Dr. Fleming, however, knew the value of what he had done. The first public announcement of the discovery of penicillin appeared in the *British Journal of Experimental Pathology*.[23] It is a readable report—one that André Maurois calls "a triumph of clarity, sobriety, and precision." Get it; read it. You will be reliving one of the great moments in twentieth-century medical research.

Soon two other names became associated with the development of penicillin: Ernst B. Chain and Howard W. Florey.[24] Together they developed a pure strain of penicillin. Florey was particularly instrumental in initiating its mass production and its use as an antibiotic for wounded soldiers in Word War II.[25] Reading these reports takes you back to the days when the medical urgency of dying people called for a massive research effort to find ways to make a newly discovered antibiotic available for immediate use.

October 25, 1945: The Nobel Prize in medicine was awarded to Fleming, Chain, and Florey.

For those of you who wish to know more about the discovery of penicillin, read André Maurois's *The Life of Sir Alexander Fleming*, the definitive biography done at the behest of Dr. Fleming's widow.[26] It is a document that will give you an insight into the way great research comes into being.

The procedures of great research are identical to those every student follows in doing a dissertation, a thesis, or a research report. All research begins with a problem, an observation, a question. Curiosity is the germinal seed. Hypotheses are formulated. Data are gathered. Conclusions are reached. What *you* are doing in research methodology is the same as what has been done by those who have pushed back the barriers of ignorance and made discoveries that have benefited the human race.

This has been the first of a series of silhouettes of influential research that will appear in this section in each chapter. In succeeding chapters we will cover significant research

[23]Alexander Fleming, "On the Antibacterial Action of Cultures of a Penicillium with Special Reference to Their Use in the Isolation of *B. influenzae*," *British Journal of Experimental Pathology* 10 (1929): 226–36.
[24]E. Chain, H. W. Florey, A. D. Gardner, N. G. Heatley, M. A. Jennings, J. Orr-Ewing, and A. G. Sanders, "Penicillin as a Chemotherapeutic Agent," *Lancet* 2 (1940): 226. See also H. W. Florey, E. Chain, et al., "Further Observations on Penicillin," *Lancet* 2 (1940): 177–88.
[25]Robert D. Coghill, "Penicillin—Science's Cinderella. The Background of Penicillin Production," *Chemical and Engineering News* 22 (1944): 588–93. See also R. D. Coghill and Roy S. Koch, "Penicillin—a Wartime Accomplishment," *Chemical and Engineering News* 23 (1945): 2310.
[26]André Maurois, *The Life of Alexander Fleming: Discoverer of Penicillin* (New York, E. P. Dutton, 1959).

in a broad range of academic disciplines. The research reported will revolutionize some of the concepts that we have accepted as "facts." It will change some teachings in traditional texts.

For each chapter installment, go back to the research reports or the documentation cited. Reading the research reports that announced a new discovery, a new departure in human knowledge will take you to the front line of research activity.

The Computer as a Tool of Research

Software

In a chapter in which we have been discussing the subject of tools of research, perhaps it might be well to discuss also the tools that the computer needs so that it can be a tool of research. Listen to Robert A. Froehlich: "The computer is a dumb tool. When a computer user needs useful work from his or her computer, software is needed to drive the machine to perform. Personal computers can accomplish a great variety of tasks, but the computer's ability to accomplish a function depends on the software used. Software, then, is the driving force, the necessary ingredient to get your computer to do useful things."[27]

In thinking of software, one word is supremely important: *compatibility.* Compatibility means that the software must be able to be used with a particular make of computer. Nothing is more unsettling than to purchase software that will not work with the computer that you are using. Be sure, therefore, that the software that you are anticipating using is compatible with the computer you expect to use. Any dealer in computers and software can advise you on compatibility.

For a brief introduction to locating software, the following articles may be of assistance:

Periodicals

Barden, William. "How to Buy Software." *Popular Computing* 2 (January 1983): 54–57.

Kelley, Mahlon G. "Buying Software." *Popular Computing* 1 (April 1982): 29–30.

Levin, Dan. "These Experts Can Wake You from the Software Nightmare." *The Executive Educator* 4 (March 1982): 26–28.

P.C. World: The Comprehensive Guide to IBM Personal Computers and Compatibles. Annual Software Review. Special edition on software each Winter quarter of the periodical.

Price, Robert. "Free and Inexpensive Software Review." *Educational Computer Magazine* 3 (February 1983): 54–55.

Price, Robert V. "Selecting Free and Inexpensive Computer Software." *Educational Computer Magazine* 2 (May–June 1982): 24–26.

"Quality Software: How to Know When You've Found It." *Electronic Learning* 1 (November–December 1981): 33–36.

"'Shareware' . . . Make It Your First Software Purchase." *Online* 9 (May 1985):44–50.

Software, a bimonthly journal published by Fast Access, 2801-B, Ocean Park Boulevard, Santa Monica, CA 90405.

Software Canada, 11 issues yearly by Maclean-Hunter Ltd., Business Publications Division, M-H Building, 777 Bay Street, Toronto, Ontario M5W 1AT Canada.

"The Software Dilemma." *School Business Affairs* 51 (May 1985): 28–29.

Software Catalog: Microcomputers. A quarterly journal. New York: Elsevier Science Publishing Company, Inc., 52 Vanderbilt Avenue, New York, NY 10017.

Software Critic. A bimonthly publication. Timothy J. Pettibone, Editor-Publisher, 1431 Cherokee Trail #101, Knoxville, TN 37920.

[27]Robert A. Froelich, *The Free Software Catalog and Directory* (New York: Crown, 1984): 3.

Software Digest Ratings Newsletter. Published by Software Digest, Inc., 1 Winding Drive, Philadelphia, PA 19131.
"Software, Libraries, and the Copyright Law." *Library Journal* 110 (July 1985): 33–39.
Software News. Sentry Publishing Company, 1900 West Park Drive, Westborough, MA 01581.
Software Times. Connie Zane, Editor, Software Marketing Division, 11050 White Rock Road, Ste. 100, Rancho Cordova, CA 95670.
Systems Software Reports (Formerly *Auerbach Software Reports*), Faulkner Publishers, Inc., 6560 North Park Drive, Pennsauken, NJ 08109.
"What's New in Software?" *Journal of Reading, Writing, and Learning Disabilities International* 1 (1985): 105–11.
Whole Earth Software Catalog. New York: Quantum Press-Doubleday. (Four issues annually.)

Conclusion

This chapter has had but one purpose: to provide an introductory orientation to some of the tools of research. In none of the sections of the chapter has any attempt been made to present comprehensive coverage. To do so would be far beyond the province of this book. There are excellent volumes on library research and resources, on measurement and evaluation, on statistics, and on computers and computerization. Should you need additional information in any of these areas, the search terminals or card catalog of the library, or a periodical index, will probably point you in the right direction.

Should you desire to read further in the principal areas presented in this chapter, the following list of references may be helpful. The references merely begin exploration of the several areas. For a more in-depth investigation, consult the resources of your library.

For Further Reading

Further Reading in Using the Library

Ashworth, Wilfred. "The Information Explosion." *Library Association Record* 76 (April 1974): 63–68.

Becker, Joseph, and R. M. Hayes. *Information Storage and Retrieval: Tools, Elements, Theories.* New York: Wiley, 1963.

Berry, Dorothea M. *A Bibliographic Guide to Educational Research.* 2d ed. Metuchen, NJ: Scarecrow, 1980.

Comprehensive Dissertation Index, Ann Arbor, Michigan: University Microfilms International, Annual supplements. [Endeavors to index every doctoral dissertation accepted by North American universities since 1861.]

Cook, Margaret G. *The New Library Key.* 3d ed. New York: H. W. Wilson, 1975.

Courtney, Winifred F. *The Reader's Adviser.* 2 vols. 11th ed. New York: R. R. Bowker, 1969.

Diebold, John. *Making the Future Work: Unleashing Our Powers of Innovation for the Decade Ahead.* New York: Simon & Schuster, 1984.

Gates, Jean K. *Guide to the Use of Books and Libraries.* 4th ed. New York: McGraw-Hill, 1979.

Goodrum, Charles A. *The Library of Congress.* New York: Praeger, 1974.

Gore, Daniel, ed. *Farewell to Alexandria: Solutions to Space, Growth, and Performance Problems of Libraries.* Westport, CT: Greenwood, 1976.

Jacob, Herbert. *Using Published Data: Errors and Remedies.* Newbury Park, CA: Sage, 1984.

Kane, Eileen. *Doing Your Own Research.* New York: Marion Boyars, 1985.

Katz, William A. *Introduction to Reference Work.* 2d ed. New York: McGraw-Hill, 1974.

Martin, Susan K. "Information and Libraries: Toward the Year 2000." *College and Research Libraries* 50 (July 1989): 397–405.

More, Grant W. *The Concise Guide to Library Research.* New York: Washington Square, 1966.

Sheehy, Eugene P. *Guide to Reference Books.* 9th ed. Chicago: American Library Association, 1976.

"Visions of Tomorrow," *Life* 12 (February 1989): 77.

Further Reading in Understanding Measurement

Bonjean, Charles M., Richard J. Hill, and S. Dale McLemore. *Sociological Measurements: An Inventory of Scales and Indices.* San Francisco, CA: Chandler, 1967.

Cronbach, Lee J., and Lita Furby. "How We Should Measure 'Change'—or Should We?" *Psychological Bulletin* 74 (July 1970): 68–80.

Cutright, P. "National Poetical Development: Measurement and Analysis." *American Sociological Review* 27 (1963): 229–45.

Dellow, E. L. *Methods of Science: An Introduction to Measuring and Testing for Laymen and Students.* New York: Universe, 1970.

Froelicher, E. S. S., "Understanding and Reducing Measurement Errors," *Cardiovascular Nursing* 24 (November–December, 1988): 48.

Gold, R. S. et. al., "Measurement Issues in Research Design." *Health Education Research* 3 (June 1988): 127–29.

Guttman, Louis. "A Basis for Scaling Qualitative Data." *American Sociological Review* 9 (1944): 139–50.

Likert, R. "A Technique for the Measurement of Attitudes." *Archives of Psychology* 21, No. 140.

Lord, Frederic M. "The Measurement of Growth." *Educational and Psychological Measurement* 16 (Winter 1956): 421–27.

Lynch, M. D., H. M. Nettleship, and R. C. Carlson. "The Measurement of Human Interest." *Journalism Quarterly* 45 (1968): 226–34.

Miller, Delbert C. *Handbook of Research Design and Social Measurements.* 3d ed. New York: David McKay, 1977.

Oppenheim, A. N. *Questionnaire Design and Attitude Measurement.* New York: Basic Book, 1966.

Osgood, C. E., C. J. Suci, and P. H. Tannenbaum. *The Measurement of Meaning.* Urbana IL: University of Illinois Press, 1957.

Payne, David A., and Robert F. McMorris. *Educational and Psychological Measurements* 2d ed. Morristown, NJ: General Learning, 1975.

Payne, James. *Principles of Social Science Measurement.* College Station, TX: Lytton, 1975.

Rice, V. H. "Issues in Outcome Measurement: Evaluating Quality of Measuring Tools." *Cardiovascular Nursing* 24 (November–December 1988): 47–48.

Rivers, W. *Finding Facts: Interviewing, Observing, Using Reference Sources.* Englewood Cliffs, NJ: Prentice-Hall, 1975.

Robinson, J.P., and P. R. Shaver. *Measures of Social Psychological Attitudes.* Ann Arbor, MI: Institute for Social Research, University of Michigan, 1969.

Shaw, M.E., and J. M. Wright. *Scales for the Measurement of Attitudes.* New York: McGraw-Hill, 1967.

Sheehan, J. "Starting the Study (Research Series)." *Nursing Mirror* 1 (May 1, 1985): 17–18.

Stanley, Julian C., and Kenneth D. Hopkins. *Educational and Psychological Measurements and Evaluation.* Englewood Cliffs, NJ: Prentice-Hall, 1972.

Thorndike, Robert L., and Elizabeth Hagen. *Measurement and Evaluation in Psychology and Education.* 3d ed. New York: Wiley, 1969.

Tull, Donald S. *Marketing Research: Meaning, Measurement, and Method.* New York: Macmillan, 1976.

Weinert, C. et. al., "Measures of Social Support: Assessment of Validity." *Nursing Research* 39 (July–August 1990) 212–16.

Further Reading in Understanding Statistics

Anderson, Theodore R., and Morris Zelditch, Jr. *Basic Course in Statistics with Sociological Applications.* 2d ed. New York: Holt, Rinehart & Winston, 1968.

Arkin, Herbert, and R. Colton. *Statistical Methods.* 5th ed. Barnes and Noble Outline Series, New York: Barnes & Noble, 1970.

Blalock, Hubert M., Jr. *Social Statistics.* 2d ed. New York: McGraw Hill, 1972.

Ferguson, G. A. *Statistical Analysis in Education and Psychology.* 4th ed. New York: McGraw-Hill, 1976.

Hardyck, Curtis D., and Lewis F. Petrinovich. *Statistics for the Behavioral Sciences.* Philadelphia: W. B. Saunders, 1969.

Hinkle, D. E., W. Wiersma, and S. G. Jurs. *Applied Statistics for the Behavioral Sciences.* Boston, MA: Houghton Mifflin, 1979.

Keppel, Geoffrey. *Design and Analysis: A Researcher's Handbook.* Englewood Cliffs, NJ: Prentice-Hall, 1973.

Key, V. O., Jr. *A Primer of Statistics for Political Scientists.* New York: Thomas Y. Crowell, 1954.

McCall, Robert B. *Fundamental Statistics for Psychology.* 2d ed. New York: Harcourt Brace Jovanovich, 1975.

Minium, Edward W. *Statistical Reasoning in Psychology and Education.* 2d ed. New York: Wiley, 1978.

Neyman, J. "Statistics—Servant of All Sciences." *Science* 122 (September 2, 1955): 401.

Novick, Melvin R. *Statistical Methods for Educational and Psychological Research.* New York: McGraw-Hill, 1974.

SAS Institute, Inc. *SAS User's Guide: Statistics, Version 5 Edition.* Cary, NC: SAS Institute, 1982.

Weiss, R. S. *Statistics in Social Research: An Introduction.* New York: Wiley, 1968.

Further Reading in Understanding Computers and Computerization

Aker, Sharon Z. *The Macintosh Companion.* Reading, MA: Addison-Wesley, 1991.

Armor, David J., and Arthur S. Couch. *Data Text Primer: An Introduction to Computerized Social Data Analysis.* New York: The Free Press, 1972.

Athey, Thomas H., and Zmud, Robert W. *Introduction to Computers and Information Systems.* Glenview, IL: Scott Foresman, 1986.

Baker, W. O., W. S. Brown, M. V. Matthews, S. P. Morgan, H. O. Pollak, R. C. Prim, and S. Sternberg. "Computers and Research." *Science* 195 (March 18, 1977): 1134–39.

Behling, Robert. *Computers and Information Processing: An Introduction.* Kent, OH: Kent State University Press, 1986.

Bender, T. K. "Innovations in the Format of Literary Concordances and Indexes." *Linguistics* 194 (July 23, 1977): 53–63.

Blotnick, S. *Computers Made (Ridiculously) Easy.* New York: McGraw-Hill, 1984.

Borko, Harold, ed. *Computer Applications in the Behavioral Sciences.* Englewood Cliffs, NJ: Prentice-Hall, 1962.

Deitel, Harvey M., and Barbara Dietel. *Introduction to Computers and Data Processing.* San Diego, CA: Academic Press, 1986.

Gersting, Judith, and Michael Gemignani. *The Computer.* New York: Macmillan, 1986.

Gille, Frank H., ed. *Computer Yearbook and Directory of Information on University Computer Systems.* 2d ed. Detroit: American Data Processing, 1968.

Goodman, D. *Danny Goodman's Macintosh Handbook: Featuring System 7.* New York: Bantam, 1992.

Hellwig, Jessica. *Introduction to Computers and Programming.* New York: Columbia University Press, 1969.

Hockey, Susan. *A Guide to Computer Applications in the Humanities.* Baltimore: Johns Hopkins University Press, 1980.

Hy, Ronn J. *Using the Computer in the Social Sciences: A Nontechnical Approach.* New York: Elsevier Science, 1977.

Janda, Kenneth. *Data Processing: Applications to Political Research.* Evanston, IL: Northwestern University Press, 1965.

Johnston, J. M. *Computers, Beeps, Whirs, and Blinking Lights.* New York: Dell: 1983.

Lewis, David W. "Inventing the Electronic University." *College and Research Libraries* 49 (July 1988): 291–303.

Loehrmann, Arthur. *Introduction to Computer Applications.* New York: McGraw-Hill, 1985.

McWilliams, Peter. *The Personal Computer Book.* Los Angeles: Prelude, 1990.

Rossman, Parker. *Computers: Bridges to the Future.* Valley Forge, PA: Judson, 1985.

Savage, John E. et al. *The Mystical Machine: Issues and Ideas in Computing.* Reading, MA: Addison-Wesley, 1986.

Volpe, Joseph B. *Basic Keyboard Skills.* Englewood Cliffs, NJ: Prentice-Hall, 1983.

Williams, Martha E. *Computer-Readable Data Bases: A Directory and Data Sourcebook.* White Plains, NY: Knowledge Industry, 1979.

Wolfart, H. O., and F. Pardo. "Computer Aided Philology and Algorithmic Linguistics." *International Journal of American Linguistics* 45 (April 1979), 107–22.

Wortham, A. William. *I Hate Computers.* New York: Vantage, 1986.

Further Reading to Help You Find Software

For an exhaustive list of publications in software and relating to software, see the most recent edition of *Books in Print* (Subject Titles). A brief list is given here.

Aker, Sharon Z. et al. *The Macintosh Bible.* 3d ed. Berkeley, CA: Goldstein & Blair, 1987.

Bowker's Complete Sourcebook of Personal Computing. New York: R. R. Bowker, 1985.

Freed, Melvyn N., Robert K. Hess, and Joseph M. Ryan, *The Educator's Desk Reference,* New York: Macmillan, in collaboration with the American Council on Education, 1989. See especially section B, chapter 3, "Microcomputer Software Publishers in Education and Academic Subjects," pp. 175–210.

Froelich, Robert A. *The Free Software Catalog and Directory.* New York: Crown, 1984.

Jussawalla, Meheroo. *The Economics of Intellectual Property in a World Without Frontiers: A Study of Computer Software.* Westport, CT: Greenwood, 1992.

Morrow, Blaine V. *CD-ROM Retrieval Software: An Overview.* Westport, CT: Meckler, 1992.
Nagel, Stuart S., ed. *Applications of Decision-Aiding Software.* New York: St. Martin's Press, 1992.
Parker, Steven W. *Corporate Technology Directory.* 4 vols. Technology Information Services, 1992.
Professional Industries Software: For IBM and Compatible DOS Computers. Indianapolis: ICP, 1990.

Selected Magazines Devoted Especially to Computers

Byte (Monthly). P. O. Box 590, Martinsville, NJ 08836.
The Computer Journal. British Computer Society, Spectrum House, London NW4 JQ UK.
Computer Education. Polytechnic Computer Center, Blackheath Lane, Staffordshire, UK.
Computers and the Humanities. Pergamon Press, Inc. Elmsford, NY 10523.
MacUser (Monthly). P. O. Box 56986, Boulder, CO 80321.
MacWorld (Monthly). P.O. Box 54529, Boulder, CO 80323.
Infoworld (newsweekly). 375 Cochituate Road, P. O. Box 880, Framingham, MA 01701.
Personal Computing. (Monthly) P. O. Box 2941, Boulder, CO 80321.
Popular Computing. (Monthly) P. O. Box 307, Martinsville, NJ 08836.

PART **II**

RESEARCH PLANNING AND DESIGN

CHAPTER 3

The Problem: The Heart of the Research Project

The problem is the axial center around which the whole research effort turns. The statement of the problem must be expressed with the utmost verbal precision. The problem is then fractionated into more manageable subproblems. So stated, we can then see clearly the goal and the direction of the entire research effort.

At the very heart of every research project is the problem. It is paramount in importance to the success of the research effort, and it should be so considered by every researcher. The situation is quite simple: no problem, no research. To see the problem with unwavering clarity and to be able to state it in precise and unmistakable terms is the first requirement in the research process.

Where Are Research Problems Found?

Problems for research are everywhere. Take a good look at the world around you. It teems with researchable problems. Whatever arouses your interest, tweaks your curiosity, and raises questions for which as yet there are no answers or where answers exist but where dispute arises as to their validity—there is fertile ground for the discovery of a *researchable* problem.

At the outset, it is extremely important that you distinguish between two basic types of problems: *personal* problems and *researchable* problems. When some students think of problems, they lump together all of the perplexities they are faced with and fail to distinguish between their essential characteristics. *You* may have a problem: how to get along with your mother-in-law, how to ask the boss for a raise, how to make a success of your life. And these problems are real, but they are not *researchable.* Researchable problems fit the requirements of the scientific method, which we will discuss more fully in chapter 5. And there is no scarcity of them.

The human race does not have the final word on most of the problems that are important to it. Inspect any segment of life, any phenomena happening at this moment, any of the events that swim before your eyes. In all of these situations lie innumerable problems to claim the attention of the researcher.

Where does your interest lie? Is it in agriculture, chemistry, economics, education, electronics, engineering, health sciences, languages and literature, medicine, music, political science, physics, sociology, zoology, or perhaps in any one of dozens of other categories? Go to the library; inspect any volume of *Dissertation Abstracts International* under the general heading of your interest and you will suddenly be aware how intimately the world of research and the world of everyday life have become intertwined. You will see research intimately related to the ever-expanding and exploding universe of knowledge. You may also realize after such an experience that all you need is to see your own area of interest in sharp, clear focus and then enunciate the problems indigenous to it in precise lucid terms, and you will have a problem for your own research efforts. But it is with an unmistakably clear statement of the problem that research begins.

Problems for research are usually found at two theoretical levels: (1) the problems whose aim it is to increase our knowledge, and (2) the problems whose prime purpose it is to make life better. There is usually a link between the two. We find a researcher interested in the effect of a stimulus on rats and, frequently, we say to ourselves, "Of what use is the expenditure of this time and money?" But the regimen keeps the rats active and busy into their old age. At the death of each rat, its brain cells are closely examined. A startling difference appears between the brain cells of the active, stimulated rats and those who have lived out their days in an impoverished and restricted environment.

Other researchers attack the problem from different angles, calling upon other means of stimuli. They come to similar conclusions. We are now coming very close to knowledge that, transferred from rat to human, may say much in the matter of aging. The wise choice of a researchable problem can lead the researcher into a truly unexpected and fascinating domain.

Problem begets problem and the helical process, which we discussed in chapter 1, begins. By its very nature, research always suggests more problems than it resolves. Both danger and challenge reside in this phenomena. The danger is that, for the mind that cannot lock on a single problem and pursue it purposefully, the research effort may be more of a scatteration than a concentration. The challenge lies in the magnificent unexplored vistas that are a fertile domain for future investigation.

Keeping the Research Process in Focus

Research, as a process utilizing the scientific method, is a new concept to many students. This becomes obvious when they attempt to formulate a researchable problem. In chapter 1, we discussed briefly some types of pseudoresearch and false concepts of the research process that have become a part of many students' earlier education. In learning a new orientation to research, confusion arises easily.

At the very beginning of the research process, students are confronted with stating a *problem* for research. Many students find it difficult to formulate an acceptable *research problem.* The heart of their trouble usually lies in their inability to appreciate the struggle between thinking and doing. One of the first things that any researcher must learn is to distinguish between what it is to *think* with respect to the data and what it is to *do* with respect to the data.

In research, it is very easy to become entranced with action, with merely doing—making notes, sleuthing facts, comparing, collating, correlating. Just so long as you are doing something, you can convince yourself that you are making progress in "*doing* research." Perhaps that phrase itself suggests to the researcher action rather than thought. There is also a certain euphoria that accompanies the discovery of a fact. Research has a way of becoming an inspired dedication to the researcher. This dedication can become a vicious cycle of finding more facts, making more notes, applying statistical tests and measurements to the data already in hand, digging further and deeper—always doing, doing, doing!

If you become aware that you are developing such a frame of mind, and if the elation of fact finding becomes a driving force in your enthusiasm to do research, slow down and look at the situation with detachment and objectivity. Remember, the heart of the entire research project is the problem. The first responsibility of the researcher, therefore, is to articulate an acceptable problem. Whatever you do should have but one purpose: *to formulate a problem that is carefully phrased and represents the single goal of the total research effort.*

For this reason, successful researchers, at every step in the process, ask themselves constantly, "What am I doing, and for what purpose am I doing it?" These questions discipline your thinking concerning the ultimate purpose for garnering the facts: to resolve the problem.

There is nothing wrong with frenzied data acquisition, except that you need to monitor the data constantly and keep your purpose in mind. The euphoria, the inspiration in doing research, can in fact be a very salutary force in the overall research effort.

A colleague of mine once said,

> There *is* an inspiration in doing research that few other academic activities afford. But that inspiration is quite different from the common understanding of the term. The inspiration of research is not an ethereal afflatus that transports the spirit aloft and leaves the brain behind: that sends the researcher into tailspins of uncontrolled activity. It is, rather, the excitement of the mind that, in contemplating a galaxy of data, discerns the unexpected flare of a factual nova in the area of the research problem—a glimpse of new meaning—where previously there was nothing but a black hole of inchoate fact. That is the excitement—the inspiration—that accompanies the research process.[1]

The Wording of the Problem

The statement of the research problem *must* imply that, for the resolution of that problem, *thinking on the part of the researcher* will be required. Such analytical thinking, which squeezes meaning out of the mere accumulation of fact, is what we call *the interpretation of the data.* Those who read the statement of the research problem must explicitly understand that at the summit of the research you will dispassionately analyze the accumulated facts to discern what those facts say in terms of the resolution of the problem.

Consider the difference between an accumulation of data in a research project and a mass of data as you find it in, for instance, *The World Almanac.* The *Almanac* is a treasury of fact, but there it ends. The facts in *The World Almanac* are certainly full of meaning, yet they remain sterile—static and frozen upon the page. Let the thoughtful mind of the researcher contemplate any galaxy of facts and meanings will begin to emerge. Yet, how many students attempt to produce a research document in the tradition of *The World Almanac?* They are completely comfortable in their delight at merely having "found the facts," hypnotized by the discovery and accumulation of facts. There is no research whatever in what they have done.

What Is Not a Research Problem

The above discussion suggests that certain problems may not be suitable for research. This is primarily because they lack the "interpretation of data" requirement, they lack the "mental struggle on the part of the researcher to force the facts to reveal their meaning." Here are a few situations to avoid in considering a problem for research purposes:

- *Don't use a problem in research as a ruse for achieving self-enlightenment.* All of us have great gaps in our educations, and diminishing them is the joy of learning. But *it is not the purpose of research to educate you.* Your lack of information may be a *personal* problem, and you may want to know more about a certain area of knowledge. That is laudable. You may find gathering facts and dissipating your own informational deficiency gratifying. That is good. But do not confuse gathering data with a similar activity that is characteristic of the research process. From the standpoint of the purpose for which they are initiated, the two are entirely different.

[1] See the discussion relative to this same point in chapter 2.

A student submitted this as the statement of a research problem:

> The problem of this research is to learn more about the way in which the Panama Canal was built.

We stated above that for a research problem to be valid, the statement of the problem must indicate that at the summit of the research effort there will be dispassionate looking at the galaxy of facts to discern what whose facts say in terms of the solution of the problem. For this student, the summit of the fact-finding effort will provide only the satisfaction of having gained more information about a particular topic. Personal satisfaction and self-enlightenment are not the goals of research.

- *Problems whose sole purpose is merely to compare two sets of data are not suitable research problems.* The statement of the problem must be taken at its face value. We assume you intend to do precisely what the wording of the problem statement says you will do.

Take this proposed problem for research:

> This research project will compare the increase in the number of women employed over 100 years—from 1870 to 1970—with the employment of men over the same time span.

Fine! We can do that without any effort. And we can complete this "research effort" in two lines:[2]

	1870	**1970**
Women employed	13,970,000	72,744,000
Men employed	12,506,000	85,903,000

- *Finding a coefficient of correlation between two sets of data merely to show a relationship between those data sets is not acceptable as a problem for research.* Why? Because the basic requirement for research is ignored. Nowhere can we see a human mind struggling with facts. What we do see, however, is a proposal to perform a statistical operation that a computer can do infinitely faster and more accurately than a person can. A coefficient of correlation is merely a decimal fraction to express within a range of 100 degrees how closely two sets of data are related to each other. Aside from being a decimal fraction, a coefficient of correlation is merely a signpost. It points in the direction of a meaningful relevancy.

Under every coefficient of correlation lies an ulterior cause. Statistics look for the decimal indication of the proximity of the variables in the relationship; research, on the other hand, derives a correlation coefficient as a signpost to look deeper into the *cause* for that relationship.

We feel most pompous at times when we collect data and by means of a statistical procedure determine that two variables are closely related (the intelligence quotients of parents and their offspring, for example). We go off trumpeting to the world that "research has shown that the correlation between the intelligence of the parents and that of their children is point—." We are blindly mistaken. *Research* hasn't shown that; *a tool of research* has given us this tantalizing fact. It has suggested a problem *for* research. The problem for research is: Wherein lies the cause of that intellectual relationship? Is it genetic? Is it social? Is it environmental? Is it a combination of certain or all of these?

To find the answer to these questions and to isolate the causal basis for the relationship—*that* is research; *that* takes *thinking* on the part of the researcher; and when we have discovered what underlies the correlation, *that* is the supernova that illuminates our ignorance. But to

[2] Source: *Historical Statistics of the United States: Colonial Times to 1970.* Part I. Bicentennial Edition. Washington, DC: United States Department of Commerce, 1975.

plug data into a mathematical formula and get a decimal value—that is merely to demonstrate one's ability to work an equation. It is no more than stopping by the wayside to discover a signpost that points to truly adventurous country beyond.

- *Problems that result in a yes or no answer are not suitable problems for research.* Why? For the same reason that merely finding a correlation coefficient is not satisfactory. Both situations look at the froth on the top of the mug and mistake it for the substantive drink below!

"Is homework beneficial to children?" That is no problem for research, certainly not in the form in which it is stated. It simply misses the point. If homework produces better students, then it is beneficial; if it does not, then it is not beneficial. But like an ignis fatuus, the question as originally asked hovers over the *real* research issue as elusively and insubstantially as marsh gas. A question as flimsy as that need not involve the power and complexity of the scientific method for its resolution. Action research can answer that question in a hurry. If all you want is a simple yes or no, give the students homework to see what happens.

The researchable issue is not *whether* homework is beneficial, but wherein the benefit of homework, if there is one, lies. What factual components of homework are beneficial in the process? Which ones are self-defeating? If we knew the answers to those questions, then our wisdom would be enlarged, and we could structure the homework assignment with more purpose and greater intelligence than we can now. We could also educate our children much more efficiently. Finding the answers to these problems demands the full power of the scientific method and perhaps the ancillary help of statistics, computerization, discriminative and analytical thinking, creative research methodology, a critical consideration of factors that have a tendency to pollute the data (bias, attitude, emotional reaction, etc.), and a very careful use of language so that the research findings might be expressed in the most accurate manner possible. There is quite a difference between this view of the benefit of homework and the superficial question, "Is homework beneficial to students?"

The Statement of the Research Problem

There are bad habits in research just as there are bad habits in other areas of human behavior. One of the worst is the habit of mumbling fragmentary nothings begotten of fuzzy thinking and mental lassitude.

Some students try to state a research problem by jotting down meaningless groups of words—verbal fragments—in lieu of a well thought-out and fully articulated statement. Such wisps of verbal fog are no help in seeing the problem clearly. There is a basic directive for the statement of the problem: *Always state the problem in a complete grammatical sentence in as few words as possible.*

Your problem should be so clearly stated that anyone anywhere in the world (who reads English) may read it, understand it, and react to it without help. If the problem is *not* stated with such clarity and precision, then you are merely deceiving yourself that you know what the problem is. Such self-deception will merely cause you trouble later on.

Here, for example, are some meaningless half-statements, mere verbal blobs that only hint at the problem. Students submitted these at the beginning of their course in research methodology:

A student in sociology submitted this:
Welfare on children's attitudes.
A student in music, this:
Palestrina and the motet.
A student in economics proposed this:
Busing of schoolchildren.

Finally, this from a student in a school of social work:

Retirement plans of adults.

All four students uttered uncommunicative nothings. Generally, fragments such as these demonstrate that the researcher either cannot or will not think in terms of specifics. Although it may be irksome to express your thought accurately and completely—if you are one of those who think in terms of scraps and pieces—you had better begin to think in terms of specific researchable goals expressed in complete communicative statements.

We shall take the preceding half-utterances and develop each of them into a complete statement that expresses a fully researchable problem.

Welfare on children's attitudes becomes:

What effect does welfare assistance to parents have on the attitudes of their teenage children toward work?

Palestrina and the motet becomes:

This study will analyze the motets of Giovanni Pierluigi da Palestrina (1525?-1594) written between 1575 and 1580 to discover their distinctive contrapuntal characteristics and will contrast them with the motets of his contemporary William Byrd (1542?-1623), written between 1592 and 1597. During the periods studied, each composer was between 50 and 55 years of age.

Busing of schoolchildren becomes:

What factors must be evaluated and what are the relative weights of those several factors in constructing a formula for estimating the cost of busing children in a midwestern metropolitan school system?

Retirement plans for adults becomes:

How do retirement plans for adults compare with the actual realization in retirement of those plans in terms of self-satisfaction and self-adjustment, and what does an analysis of the difference between anticipation and realization reveal for a more intelligent approach to planning?

Note that in the full statement of each of these problems the areas studied are carefully limited so that the study is of manageable size. The author of the Palestrina-Byrd study carefully limited the motets that would be studied to those written when each composer was between 50 and 55 years of age. A glance at the listing of Palestrina's works in *Grove's Dictionary of Music and Musicians* will demonstrate how impractical it would be for a student to undertake a study of *all* the Palestrina motets. He wrote some 392 of them!

Think, Consider, and Estimate

Students sometimes rush into a problem without thinking through its implications. Take the student who proposed the following:

This study proposes to study the science programs in the secondary schools in the United States for the purpose of . . .

Let's think about that. There are 22,383 public secondary schools in the United States and 2,237 private secondary schools, for a total of 24,620 "secondary schools in the United States"—in the words of the student's proposal. These schools, north to south, extend from Alaska to the tip of Florida; east to west, from Maine to Hawaii.

Certain practical questions immediately surface: How do you intend to contact each of these 24,620 schools? By personal visit? Being very optimistic, you might be able to visit two schools per day—one in the morning, one in the afternoon. That will amount to 12,310 visitation days. Counting the number of school days in the average school year (180), it will take you more than 68 years to gather the data. Now add in 11.8 years of "dead time" during which schools will not be in session because of holidays or summer vacation. Assuming that you are ready to do your graduate thesis or dissertation by the age of 25 (and very few people are!), you will be older than 105 by the time you have collected the data. And you have just begun your study!

Another important question is, have you estimated what the financial outlay for this project will be? Being very conservative, a reasonable estimate is that you will not be able to live for less than $75 per day (including on-the-road lodging). The traveling expense *alone* will amount to almost a million dollars—$923,265 to be exact. During the 11.8 years when you will be immobilized because of vacation days and summer recess, your daily living expense (rent, food, clothing, incidentals) is only half of your traveling expense. This will still add another $161,512 to your total. Now you are looking at a total of $1,004,777—over a million dollars! And this is the cost of just collecting the data.

But, you explain, I plan to gather the data by mail, with a questionnaire. Fine! Each letter to the 24,620 schools, with an enclosed questionnaire and a return postage-paid envelope, will cost 58 cents. The total cost for letters to all the schools is $14,279.60. But you have overlooked the fact that you will need a second, and perhaps a third, mailing. A 50 percent return on the first mailing would be considered a good return. But for the nonreturnees you will need another mailing at a cost of $7,139.80. Now the mailing bill stands at $21,419.40.

In addition to this figure you will have the cost of envelopes, stationery, questionnaire duplication, and miscellaneous items for a total of 37,000 questionnaires and an additional 37,000 cover letters explaining your reason for sending the questionnaire. Add to this the processing of some 18,500 questionnaires, programming the data, computer time, and the compilation and typing of a research report, and you will realize that the project you have proposed is not an inconsequential undertaking. $40,000 to $60,000 would not be an unrealistic estimate!

But, you protest, I had no idea of surveying *all* of the secondary schools in the United States. No? This, then, brings up a matter of utmost importance.

Say Precisely What You Mean

If you did not mean what you said in the statement of your problem, you should have corrected the error right up front—in the statement of the problem itself. There is no place for evasion, equivocation, or mental reservation in research. You must mean what you say and assume total responsibility for the message your words convey. You cannot assume that others will know what is in your mind. In the statement of the research problem, there is no room for the words, "Well, what I mean is—." Others will always take your words at their face value: You *mean* what you *say*. That's it.

Your failure to be careful with your words can have grave results on your standing as a scholar and a researcher. In the academic community, a basic rule prevails:

Absolute honesty and integrity is assumed in every statement that a scholar makes.

You should say *precisely* what you mean. We assume that you mean to fulfill precisely what you have stated. No double talk, no pleading thoughtlessness, no avoiding the obligation to perform strictly what you have committed yourself to do. Had you intended *not* to survey "the science programs in the secondary schools in the United States," then you should have said so plainly: "This study proposes to survey the science programs in *selected secondary schools throughout the United States.*" Or perhaps you should have limited your study to a specific geographical area or to a student population within certain designated limits. That would give the problem a limitation that the original statement lacks and would honestly communicate to others what you intend to do. Furthermore, and vastly more important, it would have preserved your reputation as a researcher of integrity and precision.

One further haunting thought lingers with respect to the statement of the problem. If a researcher cannot be completely responsible for the statement of the problem and its attendant parts, one might question seriously whether such a researcher is likely to be any more responsible in gathering and interpreting the data. And this, indeed, is very serious, for it reflects upon the basic responsibility of the whole effort. It can be a brutal blow to one's degree aspirations.

We have discussed two of the three most common difficulties in the statement of the problem: fragmentary and meaningless splutter, and irresponsible and extravagant wording. To these we now add a third: generalized discussion that ends in a foggy focus. Occasionally, a researcher will announce an intention to make a statement of the problem. From that point the discussion becomes foggier and foggier. Such a researcher talks *about* the problem instead of clearly stating it. Under the excuse that the problem needs an introduction or needs to be seen against a background, the researcher launches into a generalized discussion, continually obscuring the problem, never clearly articulating it.

Take, for example, what one student wrote under the heading of "Statement of the Problem":

> The upsurge of interest in reading and learning disabilities found among both children and adults has focused the attention of educators, psychologists, and linguists on the language syndrome. In order to understand how language is learned, it is necessary to understand what language is. Language acquisition is a normal developmental aspect of every individual, but it has not been studied in sufficient depth. To provide us with the necessary background information to understand the anomaly of language deficiency implies a knowledge of the developmental processes of language as these relate to the individual from infancy to maturity. Grammar, also an aspect of language learning, is acquired through pragmatic language usage. Phonology, syntax, and semantics are all intimately involved in the study of any language disability.

Is there a statement of problem here? If so, where is the problem explicitly stated? Several problems are suggested. None is articulated with sufficient clarity that we might put a finger on it and say, "There, that is the problem."

You need not write an orientation essay in order to state a problem. Earlier in this chapter, we invited you to go to *Dissertation Abstracts International* to see how the world of research and the real world of everyday living are intertwined. Now return to that same source, and note with what directness the problems are set forth. The problem is stated in the very first words of the abstract: "The purpose of this study is to. . . ." No mistaking that; no background buildup necessary—just a straightforward plunge into the depths of the business at hand. All research problems should be stated with the same clarity.

Edit Your Writing

The difficulties we have been discussing can be avoided by carefully editing your words. Editing is sharpening a thought to a gemlike point and eliminating useless verbiage. Choose your words precisely. To do so will clarify your writing.

The sentences in the previous paragraph began as a mishmash of foggy thought and jumbled verbiage. The original version of the paragraph contained 71 words. These were edited down to 38 words. That is a reduction of 46 percent, an improvement in readability of 100 percent. Figure 3.1 shows the original version and the manner in which it was edited.

Note the directness of the edited copy. We eliminated garrulous phrases—"relating to the statement of the problem," "a process whereby the writer attempts to bring what is said straight to the point"—replacing the verbosity with seven words: "sharpening a thought to a gemlike point." Clichés are trashed; inanities are junked. "By editing the words we have written. . ."—Well, who else do you think wrote them? Such language is inane. People who write

Figure 3.1

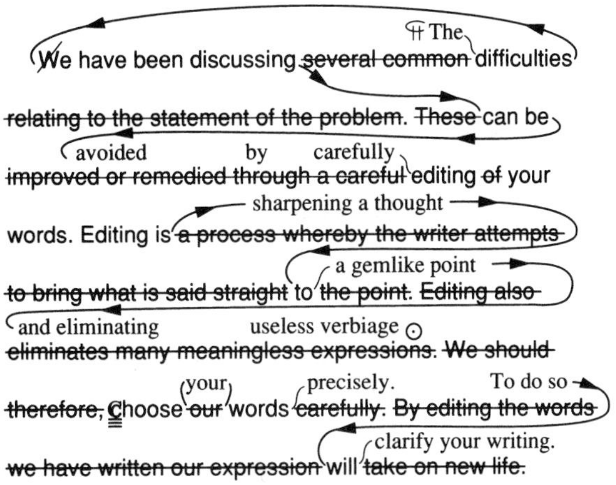

like this throw their heads out of gear before their pens get going! And remember, I myself wrote those silly phrases in the original version of that paragraph.

Editing almost invariably improves your thinking and your prose. Many students think that any words that approximately express a thought in their own minds are adequate to convey it to others. This is not so. Approximation is never precision.

You need to be rigorous with the words you write. Punctuation will help you. A colon will announce that what follows it explains the general statement that precedes it. Similarly, the semicolon, the dash, quotation marks, parentheses, brackets, and italics are all tools in clarifying your thought. Learn to use the comma correctly.

Any good dictionary will usually have a section dealing with punctuation usage. Most handbooks of English will help you to write clear, concise, and effective sentences and help you to combine those sentences into unified and coherent paragraphs.

Cliches, colloquialisms, slang, jargon, and the gibberish of any group or profession usually obscure thought. The irresponsible use of professional jargon is evidence of a lazy mind. Those who employ it do so usually because they feel that it is impressive or that it adds importance to what they are saying. They are almost always wrong.

The thought's the thing. It is clearest when it is clothed in simple words, concrete nouns, and active, expressive verbs. Every student would do well to study how the great writers and poets set their thoughts in words. They have much to say by way of illustration to those who have trouble putting their own thoughts on paper.

In general, however, some basic guidelines for clear writing may help you to express problems and subproblems effectively.

1. Express the thought fully with the least words possible.
2. Use a thesaurus: It will help you find the exact word.
3. Never use a long word where a short one will do. In straightforward discussion, use one- or two-syllable words rather than longer ones.
4. Keep your sentences short. Vary the length, of course, but break up those long, contorted sentences into shorter, more succinct ones.
5. Look critically at each thought as it stands on the paper. Do the words say exactly what you wish them to say? Read carefully phrase by phrase. See if one word will carry the burden of two or more. Throw out superfluous words.
6. Be alert to modification. Misplaced phrases and clauses can create havoc with the thought.

Here is an example of misplaced modification: "Piano for sale by a woman with beautifully carved mahogany legs that has arthritis and cannot play anymore." Place the modifier correctly and all's well that ends well: "FOR SALE: A piano with beautifully carved mahogany legs by a woman that has arthritis and cannot play anymore."

Practical Application

Up to this point we have been merely discussing the problem for research. Now, you will apply the principles governing the problem in a Practical Application. What you will be asked to do is not a mere exercise or a review assignment. It is the first step in preparing a final proposal for a research endeavor. You will be guided in framing a statement of a problem for research.

Future Practical Applications will build on the problem statement that you are now about to articulate. When you have completed all of the Applications in this text you will have a final proposal suitable for submission as an actual research endeavor.

Stating the Research Problem

1. Write a clear statement of a problem for research:

   A. Is your problem fully stated in the form of a complete, grammatical sentence?
   _____ Yes _____ No
   If yes, go on to subsection B; if no, do not continue until you have stated the problem clearly, and can answer this question "yes."

   B. Is the fact of interpretation of the data apparent in the statement of your problem?
   _____ Yes _____ No

   C. If yes, quote the section of the statement of the problem that implies interpretation of the data: ____
   ____

   D. If no, rephrase the problem, or revise it, or get a new problem that fulfills the demands of B and C above.

   E. Have you said precisely what you mean to do in your research endeavor?
   _____ Yes _____ No

2. Have you edited your problem? _____ Yes _____ No
   If yes, write the original statement of your problem; write it immediately below the edited version.

3. Evaluate your problem according to the following Checklist for Evaluating the Problem.

Checklist for Evaluating the Problem

The following checklist will assist you in evaluating your problem. It may indicate to you those aspects of your problem that need further refinement. In using the following checklist, *be realistic.* Read the problem as you have it written; read the checklist statement; then, to the best of your ability, try to decide whether the checklist item is applicable. There is no value at this point in wishful thinking. Either the item is applicable or it is not. Check the appropriate column.

Faults Resulting from Lack of Understanding of the Nature of Research

	Yes	No
1. Problems seem to be merely an exercise in gathering data on a particular subject. ("I don't know anything about the subject; I'd like to learn more by 'researching' it.")	____	____
2. Problem seems to be little more than a simple comparison.	____	____
3. Problem can be resolved finally with a yes or no answer.	____	____
4. Problem seems to indicate that all you will have ultimately is a list of items.	____	____
5. Problem seems to indicate that your study will be little more than an exercise in finding a correlation coefficient—the discovery that there is a relationship between various data.	____	____
6. Problem has no identifiable word within it that indicates the need for interpretation of the data.	____	____

Diagnosis of your difficulty: If you have checked any items in the yes column, you need to go back to the text. After you have reread the chapter, and restudied your problem in terns of items 1-6, check here. ________

Faults Relating to Pseudoproblems

	Yes	No
7. You do not have a problem *per se* but rather an expression of an opinion that you would like to defend or prove.	____	____
8. Your problem does not focus on *one* research aim or goal but rather diffuses into several problems.	____	____
9. The problem is too broad; it attempts to research too much—too large a geographical area, too great a population.	____	____
10. The problem seems to suggest that you wish to learn more about the particular area you propose to research and that you are using the project as a means of gathering such information.	____	____
11. The problem seems to be more in the area of *applied* research than in that of *basic* research: You wish to research the problem merely because it has a practical application—"it needs to be done"—rather than because it seeks to discover a basic truth underlying a practical application.	____	____

Diagnosis of your difficulty: If you have checked any items in the yes column in the preceding section, you need to go back to the text. After you have reread the chapter, and restudied your problem in terms of items 7-11, check here. ________

Faults Relating to the Language and Manner in Which You State the Problem

	Yes	No
12. Problem statement is a meaningless fragment: you have no sentence.	____	____
13. Read your problem *literally, phrase by phrase.* Are there any areas in the wording where the words do not say precisely what you *mean?* Is there any fogginess in the statement?	____	____
14. Problem is stated in clichés or in other inexact or involved language that does not communicate clearly.	____	____

15. You use reference words with no referents: pronouns without antecedents. ____ ____
16. You have additional discussion: a preamble, apology, statement why you have an interest in the problem area, or other discussion. You have written more than simply the statement of the problem. ____ ____

Diagnosis of your difficulty: If you have checked any items in the yes column in the preceding section, you have trouble in an area that is corollary to the domain of this book: you need to develop your skills with written English. Many people have difficulty in putting their thoughts in writing. Read the chapter material again and follow the suggestions given there.

After you have read the preceding pages (and whatever other sources were necessary) and have edited your work and are satisfied with it—and do not be too easily satisfied with your own efforts—check here. ________

Now rewrite the statement of your problem, if necessary, precisely as you wish it to stand after checking it out and editing it according to the preceding sixteen criteria.

The Subproblems

Most problems in their entirety are too large or too complex to be solved without subdividing them. The strategy, therefore, is to divide and conquer. Every problem can be broken down into smaller, discrete units. From a research standpoint, these units are easier to comprehend and resolve. From here on, the matter is one of the simple axiom of numbers: The sum of the parts equals the whole.

The subparts of the main problem are called *subproblems,* discussed briefly in chapter 1. By viewing the main problem through the subproblem, the researcher frequently gets a better global view of the entire research endeavor. Always think of a problem, therefore, in terms of its component parts.

Characteristics of Subproblems

Because some researchers may not be entirely familiar with the nature and the purpose of subproblems, we will discuss them briefly.

- *Each subproblem should be a completely researchable unit.* A subproblem should constitute a logical subarea of the larger research undertaking. Each subproblem might be researched as a separate subproject within the larger research goal. The solutions of the subproblems, taken together, combine to resolve the main problem of research. It is necessary, therefore, that each subproblem be stated clearly and succinctly. Often, a subproblem is stated in the form of a question. A question tends to focus the attention of the researcher more directly on the research target of the subproblem than does a mere declarative statement. After all, the interrogative attitude is the normal psychological condition of every true researcher's mind.
- *Pseudosubproblems are not researchable subproblems.* Each researcher must distinguish subproblems that are an integral part of the main problem from what look like problems but are nothing more than procedural indecisions. These latter we call *pseudosubproblems.* These pseudosubproblems arise quite logically from the ambience of the research situation. They are, in fact, merely decisions that the researcher must resolve before further progress toward the resolution of the research problem is possible. We need to think acutely. Pseudosubproblems are problems for the researcher, not subparts of the research problem. They are decisions that must be made outside of the principal research environment. Consider these:

What is the best way to choose a sample?

What instruments or methods should be used to gather the data?

What measurement instruments are available for measuring the strength of a person's convictions?

How large should a representative sample of a population be?

How do I find the subproblems within the main problem?

The last of these questions we will resolve for you later in this chapter. Note that these pseudosubproblems result from either a lack of knowledge or a demand for creativity on the part of the researcher. You cannot research any of these problems by gathering and interpreting data.

Deal with pseudosubproblems forthrightly by making a firm decision with respect to them, and then get on with the solution of the research problem. To deal with pseudosubproblems, two avenues are open to you. You must decide: 1)—and try this first—whether a little common sense and some creative thinking might not help to solve your "problem," or 2) whether this is a purely *factual deficiency* on your part: you simply lack knowledge; in this case you have three options:

1. Turn to the index *of this text* to see if the "problem" (pseudosubproblem) is discussed. Look under "Subproblems, how to find."
2. Peruse carefully the suggested sources in "For Further Reading" at the end of each chapter in this book to see if they contain any references that may help you. Be alert for standard research references, such as the *Encyclopedia of Educational Research* or the *International Encyclopedia of Educational Research and Studies.* Consult these and similar works.
3. Go to a library—preferably a college or university library—and consult the listings under the heading "Research Methodology." Consult the indexes of these texts, as you did with this text. Also check the leading periodical indexes under the heading "Research Methodology" to determine if you can locate any articles on the subject of your query. Determine whether the library has the periodical or periodicals that you need.

• *Within each subproblem, interpretation of the data must be apparent.* At some point in the statement of the subproblem—as, indeed, within the main problem—the fact that data will be interpreted must be clearly evident. This may be expressed as a part of each subproblem statement, or it may occupy an entire separate subproblem.

• *The subproblems must add up to the totality of the problem.* After you have stated the subproblems, check them against the statement of the main problem to see (1) that nothing in excess of the coverage of the main problem is included, and (2) that you have no omissions, so that all significant areas of the main problem are covered by the several subproblems.

• *Proliferation of subproblems is circumspect.* If the main problem is carefully stated and properly limited to a feasible researchable effort, the researcher will find that it usually contains in the vicinity of two to six subproblems. Sometimes the inexperienced researcher will come up with as many as ten, fifteen, or twenty problems. When this happens it generally means that a careful review of the problem and its attendant subproblems should be undertaken. The researcher should study each subproblem to see whether it is truly a subproblem of the main problem or whether it falls into one or more of the following categories:

1. *The researcher has confused his or her personal problems with problems for research.* Has the researcher stated as subproblems procedural decisions that need to be made before the research can proceed?
2. *The researcher has fragmented the true subproblems.* Can any of the subproblems be combined into larger researchable units lesser in magnitude than the main problem?

3. *There may be a mixture of the preceding errors.* If so, a careful study of each subproblem is necessary to separate procedural questions from purely researchable goals.

- *Beware of unrealistic goals.* Be cautious of committing yourself beyond what is possible to achieve. We have discussed this area with respect to the main problem. If it is there controlled, the researcher then will experience little difficulty with it in the subproblems. But be mindful of this tendency with respect to the subproblems also.

How to Locate the Subproblems

Students frequently have difficulty in locating the subproblems within the main problem. Here are some guidelines:

- *Begin with the problem itself.* If the problem is correctly written you will be able to detect within the problem the subproblem areas that may be isolated for further study. The old axiom that the sum of the parts equals the whole applies here. All of the subproblems must add up to the total problem.
- *Write the problem. Then box off the subproblem areas.* Take a clean sheet of paper. Then:

1. Copy the problem on it, leaving considerable space between the lines.
2. Read the problem critically to discover the areas that should receive in-depth treatment before the problem can be resolved. Box off these areas. Within each of the boxes lies a subproblem.
3. Every subproblem should contain a word that indicates the necessity to *interpret* the data within that particular subproblem. Underline this word.
4. Arrange the entire problem, which will now have the subproblems boxed off, into a skeletal plan that will show the research structure of the problem. You should now have a structure of the whole research design.

Let us take the problem of the motets of Palestrina. (This procedure for finding subproblems will work for *any* problem in *any* academic discipline. A problem in musicology is used here merely to illustrate the technique.) We will do exactly as we have suggested above. We will delete the factual matter, such as life–span dates and the fact that these men were contemporaries. These facts merely help to give a rationale for certain elements within the problem. Slimmed down to its essential parts, the motet problem reads as follows:

> The purpose of this study will be *to analyze* the motets of Palestrina written between 1575 and 1580 to discover their distinctive contrapuntal characteristics and *to analyze* the same characteristics in the motets of William Byrd [to determine what a *comparative study of these two analyses* may reveal].

Note that we have transposed the "and will contrast them with" phrase in the original statement of the problem to the wording in brackets to provide the logical third subproblem, which, incidentally, resolves the main problem.

Note also the words in italics. The research process demands the intervention of the mind of the researcher at the point where the researcher needs to analyze the two groups of compositions and determine what a comparative study of these analyses may reveal. This is where the data will be regarded analytically, the point where *the interpretation of the data* will take place.

Recall the statement made earlier in this chapter: "The statement of the research problem must indicate that, for the resolution of that problem, thinking on the part of the researcher will be required." Those were not idle words. You are probably beginning to see how this requirement is being implemented.

Figure 3.2 A Structural Representation of the Palestrina-Byrd Problem

The purpose of this study will be:

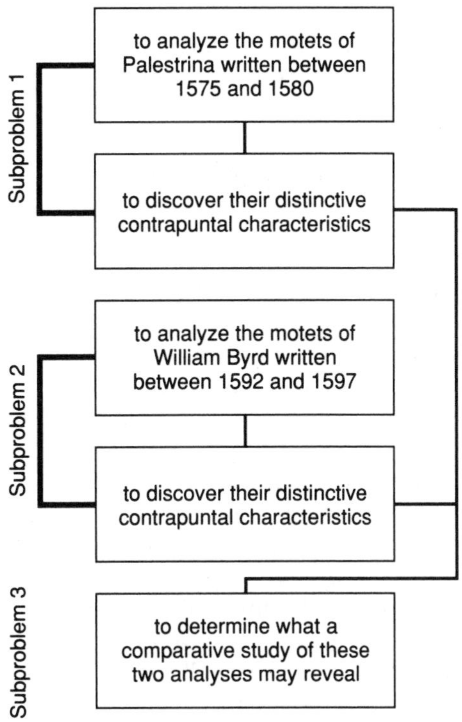

Let us now take that problem and arrange it so that we may see precisely what the design will be. Figure 3.2 is a structural chart of the problem. We have taken the problem and divided it into three subproblems. The first and second of these have the same general structural configuration. The analytical aspect of the subproblem is stated first, in the first of the two boxes, then the purpose of the analysis is stated in the accompanying box immediately beneath the first one. The third subproblem, in effect, analyzes the findings of the two preceding subproblems to determine what actually has been discovered.

Every Problem Needs Further Delineation

Up to this point we have been discussing only the problem and its subparts. The statement of the problem establishes the goal for the research effort. The subproblems suggest ways of approaching that goal in a more manageable way. But a goal alone is not enough.

Confusion can arise, and if we are to comprehend fully the meaning of the problem, we need to have information other than merely the statement of the research goal. The discipline of research is based upon a clear understanding of every detail in the process, both on the part of the researcher and on the part of those who read the research.

In every research endeavor, the researcher should eliminate any possibility of misunderstanding certain matters by:

1. *Delimiting the research:* giving a full disclosure of what he or she intends to do and, conversely, does *not* intend to do.
2. *Defining the terms:* giving the meaning of all terms used in the statement of the problem or subproblems that have any possibility of being misunderstood.

3. *Stating the assumptions:* offering a clear statement of all assumptions upon which the research will rest.
4. *Stating the hypotheses:* offering a complete statement of the hypotheses that are being tested.

All these matters are important for the researcher in facilitating the research and for the consumer in facilitating understanding of the research. Taken as a whole, they comprise *the setting of the problem.* We shall look at each of these components in more detail in the following paragraphs.

Components Comprising the Setting of the Problem

Delimiting the Research Problem. We need to know precisely what the researcher intends to do. We need to know with equal candor precisely what the researcher does *not* intend to do.

What the researcher intends to do is stated in the problem; what the researcher is not going to do is stated in the *delimitations.* The limits of the problem should be as carefully bounded for a research effort as a parcel of land is for a real estate transfer.

Problems arise out of a much more expansive area than is covered by the statement of the problem. The researcher can very easily be beguiled by discovering interesting facts that lie beyond the precincts of the problem under investigation. In the Palestrina-Byrd problem we have just discussed, it is possible, since the two men were contemporaries, that Byrd may have met Palestrina or at least have come in contact with some of his motets. Such contact may have been a determinative influence upon Byrd's compositions. We are not, however, concerned with *influences on,* but rather with *characteristics of,* the motets of the two composers. We are interested in analyzing musical style, musical individualism, the contrapuntal likenesses and differences in the motets of these two composers. To study the contrapuntal characteristics—that is what a researcher of this problem will do. What that researcher will *not* do is become involved in any facts extraneous to this one goal—no matter how enticing, interesting, or appealing such an exploratory safari may be. Only a researcher who thinks carefully about the problem and its focal center will distinguish between what is relevant and what is not relevant *to the problem.* All irrelevancies to the problem must be firmly ruled out in the statement of delimitation.

Figure 3.3 may make the matter of delimitations more understandable.

Defining the Terms. What precisely do the terms in the phrasing of the problem and the subproblems mean? For example, if we say that the purpose of the research is to analyze the harmonic characteristics of motets, what are we talking about? What are harmonic characteristics? Without knowing explicitly what a term means, we cannot evaluate the research or determine whether the researcher has carried out what, in the problem, was announced as the principal thrust of the research.

A term must be defined operatively; that is, the definition must interpret the term *as it is employed in relation to the researcher's project.* Sometimes students rely on dictionary definitions, which are seldom either adequate or helpful. In defining a term, the researcher makes that term mean whatever he or she wishes it to mean within the particular context of the problem or its subproblems. We must know how *the researcher* defines the term. We need not necessarily subscribe to such a definition, but so long as we know what the researcher means when employing a particular term we are able to understand the research and appraise it objectively.

Formal definitions contain three parts: (1) *the term* to be defined, (2) *the genera,* or the general class to which the concept being defined belongs, and (3) *the differentia,* the specific characteristics or traits that distinguish the concept being defined from all other members of the general classification. For example, *harmonic characteristics* (the term to be defined) shall mean *the manner* (the genera) in which tonal values are combined *to produce individualized polyphonic patterns associated with the works of a particular composer* (the differentia: telling what particular "manner" we mean).

Figure 3.3 Delimitation of a Problem

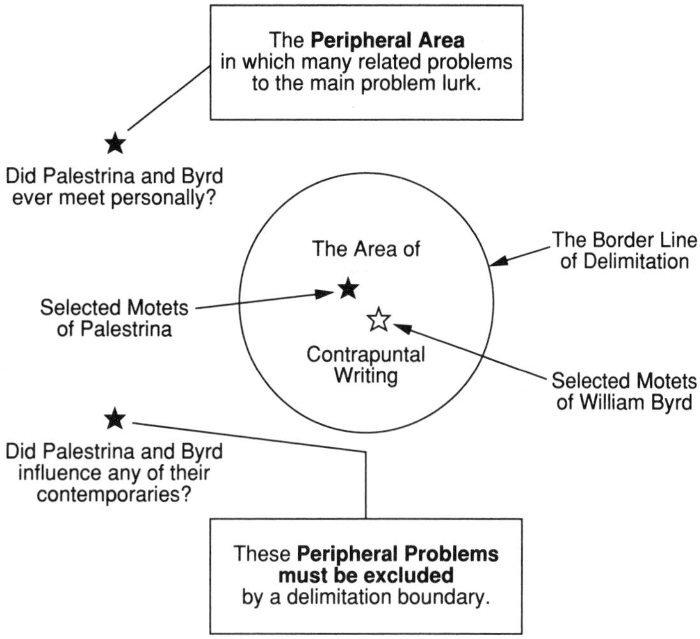

A spurious type of definition, commonly called a *circular definition,* or defining in a circle, is sometimes encountered. The most classic example is perhaps Gertrude Stein's, "a rose, is a rose, is a rose." Defined in a circle, *harmonic characteristics* would be "those *characteristics* that derive from the *harmonic* patterns found in the works of a particular composer." In circular definitions, the term to be defined is employed in defining that term, as above, where *characteristics* and *harmonic* are used to define *harmonic characteristics.*

Stating the Assumptions. We discussed the matter of the assumptions briefly in chapter 1. Here, however, the matter needs further discussion. Assumptions are so basic that without them the research problem itself could not exist. For example, we are attempting to determine by means of a pretest-posttest whether a particular method of teaching has produced the results hypothesized. A basic assumption in such a situation must be that the test measures what it is presumed to measure. We must assume also that the teacher can teach. Without these assumptions, we have no problem, no experiment.

Assumptions are what the researcher takes for granted. But taking things for granted may cause much misunderstanding. What I may tacitly assume, you may never have thought of. If I act upon my assumption, and in the final result such action makes a vast difference in the outcome, you may face a situation that you are totally unprepared to accept. For each of us to know, therefore, what is assumed is basic to an understanding of the research results. If we know the assumptions a researcher makes, we are then better prepared to evaluate the conclusions that result from such assumptions. To many students, the stating of assumptions may be tantamount to stating the obvious, but because in research we try to leave nothing to chance in the hope of preventing any misunderstanding, all assumptions that have a material bearing upon the problem should be openly and unreservedly set forth. To discover assumptions, ask, "What am I taking for granted with respect to the problem?" The answer to that question will bring your assumptions into clear view.

Stating the Hypotheses. We also discussed hypotheses in chapter 1. There we pointed out that hypotheses are *tentative, intelligent guesses posited for the purpose of directing one's thinking toward the solution of the problem.* Hypotheses are necessary because the researcher needs to have some point around which the research may be oriented in searching for relevant data and in establishing a *tentative* goal against which to project the facts.

We should keep in mind that hypotheses are neither proved nor disproved. They are *tentative propositions set forth as a possible explanation for an occurrence or a provisional conjecture to assist in guiding the investigation of a problem.* To set out deliberately to prove a hypothesis would defeat impartiality in research. The researcher would bias the procedure by looking only for those facts that would support the hypothetical position. Difficult as it may be at times, we must let the chips of fact fall where they may. Hypotheses have nothing to do with proof. Rather, their *acceptance* or *rejection* is dependent on what the facts—and the facts alone—ultimately reveal.

Hypotheses may originate in the subproblems. A one-to-one correspondence might well exist between the subproblems and their corresponding hypotheses. Generally, we have as many hypotheses as we have subproblems. Each hypothesis becomes, in a sense, a target against which the data of each subproblem may be projected. As a point of reference, a hypothesis is to a researcher what a point of triangulation is to a surveyor: It provides a position from which the researcher may begin to initiate an exploration of the problem or subproblem and also acts as a checkpoint against which to test the findings that the data seem to reveal.

If, however, the facts do not ultimately support the hypothesis, you should not let such an outcome disturb you. It merely means that your educated guess as to what the outcome of the investigation should have been was wrong. Frequently, unsupported hypotheses are a source of genuine and gratifying surprise for the researcher. When such an outcome occurs, you have truly made an unexpected discovery.

We must introduce one further type of hypothesis here: the *null hypothesis.* The null hypothesis is an indicator only. It reveals that some influence, force, or factor has either resulted in a significant statistical difference (one that cannot be accounted for by mere chance, that occurs within certain arbitrary statistical limits) or in no such difference. Much research stops at this point. This is comparable to getting off at the mezzanine instead of descending to the subbasement where the foundations of the building are located. If the null hypothesis shows the presence of dynamics that have caused a change, then the logical next questions are *What* are these dynamics? *What* is their nature? *How* can they be isolated and studied?

A social worker finds statistically that a particular social program is making a great difference in the attitudes of those exposed to it. The hypothesis stating that the program will make no difference has been rejected. Fine! That's encouraging news. But it's a mezzanine conclusion. What dynamics were at work below the surface that were merely registered on the statistical dial upstairs? What specifically was the factor or factors within the program that caused the null hypothesis to be rejected? These are fundamental questions, the answers to which will uncover facts that may lie very close to the discovery of new substantive knowledge. That is the purpose of all research.

The Importance of the Study. Within the dissertation or research report, the researcher frequently sets forth the reason for undertaking the study. In the proposal, this section may be very important. Some studies seem to go far out into the rarified atmosphere beyond contact with everyday reality and beyond any relationship to the practical world. Of such research efforts one inwardly, if not audibly, asks, "Of what *use* is it? What *practical value* does the study have?"

In the 1970s, contemplating the space exploration flights to the moon, the average citizen frequently asked, "What good is it? What's the use of it all? How will all this expenditure of money in space flights benefit anyone down here?" Perhaps those engaged in space research did not set forth clearly and succinctly enough the reasons why the missions were undertaken. Only now are we beginning to appreciate the *practical* value of those early missions.

The Rationale for the Order in Which the Topics in This Text Are Presented

This chapter inaugurates a rationale for the succeeding chapters of this text. You will find a one-to-one correspondence between the discussions in this text and the sequence of topics that appear in a research proposal or research report. In any document, the first order of business is to present the problem and its setting. Generally, the document opens with a statement of the problem for research. This is followed by the subproblems. The hypotheses concerning the subproblems are then stated. Some authors prefer to arrange the subproblems and then the corresponding hypotheses in parallel fashion. What is important is that no matter how you present these items, your order of presentation should be logically sequential.

Once the problem and its component parts have been articulated, the rest of the items comprising the setting of the problem are presented, generally beginning with a statement of the delimitations, followed by the definitions of terms, the assumptions, and a statement with reference to the importance of the study.

In a proposal or research report, these items usually comprise the first chapter. The report then generally continues with a discussion of the investigations that others have done, normally entitled "The Review of the Related Literature." This is the topic that we will discuss in the next chapter.

Practical Application

In the previous Practical Application for this chapter, you stated you main problem for research. This was the beginning step in creating a research proposal. Now you will add the rest of the "setting" of the problem: defining the subproblems and delimitations, defining the terms, and stating the assumptions and hypotheses. The main problem and the subproblems should each have one hypothesis.

To show you how your proposal should look, the first section of an actual proposal that was submitted to an academic research committee follows this Practical Application. The candidate was seeking approval of the proposal as a draft of the final document to be presented for an advanced degree. Note the comments and directives jotted in the margin.

Stating the Subproblems

On a separate sheet of paper, copy your research problem statement. Allow considerable space between the lines. Now do the following, after inspecting the problem carefully:

1. Box off within the problem those areas that must receive in-depth treatment if the problem is to be fully explored. Number each of the boxed-in areas consecutively.
2. Enclose within dotted lines those specified words within your statement of the problem that indicate your intention to interpret the data.
3. Below the problem, which has been thus treated, write in complete sentences the several subproblems for your study.

Completing the Problem Statement and its Setting

Now having stated the problem and the subproblems, you are ready to finish the entire first section of your proposal. Turn to the following sample proposal and study it carefully. Note especially the running comments in the right-hand column. These comments will guide you with respect to important points to be observed. Note carefully the use of the headings in presenting the material in a clear, logical format.

Now do the following:

- *Write the hypotheses.* Read again what has been said about hypotheses in this chapter. Study the way in which the author of the sample proposal posited his hypotheses. They are precisely parallel with his subproblems.
- *Write the delimitations.* Review again what was said in the text. Study the way in which the author has ruled out in the sample proposal those areas that, although contiguous to his research effort, his study will not consider.
- *Write the definitions of terms.* Before writing your definitions reread the section earlier in the chapter. It may help to number 1, 2, 3 the parts of the definition as we did in the text or to "box in" the several parts of your definition, labeling each as "term," "genera," or "differentia." Study the handling of the definitions section in the same proposal. (Take out the numerals in the final draft of the proposal.)
- *Write the assumptions.* Reread the text material and study the section of the sample proposal dealing with assumptions.
- *Write the section dealing with the importance of the study.* In a short, succinct statement, point out to the reader the importance of your study. Generally, you will not need more than two or three well-written paragraphs. Edit out all but essentials. Study the section that establishes the importance of the study in the sample proposal.

Using now the sample proposal as a format, type your proposal, using the style and format shown.

You now have the first section of your research proposal completed. After you have your proposal typed, compare the appearance of your page with that of the sample proposal. Do they resemble each other? They should.

A Sample Research Proposal

On the pages that follow is a reprint of part of the text for a research project submitted to the faculty of the School of Education of The American University, Washington, D.C. The proposal is presented here to give the student a clearer concept of precisely what a proposal is, the form it should take, and a suggested arrangement of its several parts. The proposal is shortened, since it is unnecessary and uneconomical to present the entire document. Other portions are presented in chapters 4 and 7.

Every proposal is essentially the same whether it is an outline for a thesis or dissertation or an application for a grant to underwrite an independent research endeavor. Notice the degree of fullness and the precise care with which the details are spelled out.

The greater the investment of time, money, and effort, the fuller and more specific the proposal should be. Certainly there are variations to the format presented here. No brief is made for the form of this proposal over any other equally logical presentation.

Underlying the sample proposal was a substratum of reasoning similar to this: Everyone desires to succeed. People are more likely to succeed if they are engaged in work they like to do. Therefore, a person's interest can in part be a key to the probability of vocational success. One must do what one is interested in doing. Interests are identified objectively by measuring the degree of like or dislike with which a person reacts to a vicarious activity.

Of the several general inventories, the *Strong Vocational Interest Blank* has been one of the most widely used and intensively studied. Interest scales have been developed on the Strong inventory for 54 occupational groups. No scale has ever been developed for cartographers, however, either on the Strong or on any other interest-measuring instrument.

Cartographers, and the nature of their professional activities as mapmakers, are little known to the general public. Furthermore, the annual production of cartographers is only one percent of the annual requirement.

If, therefore, some way could be found to match people who have interests kindred to those of cartographers with the vocational opportunities for which there is a 99 percent demand, we may have come to grips with a very practical problem: supplying a professional group with needed personnel and guiding individuals with the particular skills and aptitudes for cartography into a satisfying and rewarding profession. Here is the researcher's problem. Here is even a broader problem for an entire profession. It is to seek a possible solution to this problem through research that this proposal addresses itself.

One further word should be said about the form in which the proposal is presented here. As we have said earlier, the typescript is *a verbatim reprint of the proposal as it was presented by the student.* Its value to the user of this book will lie in both (1) seeing its original form, and (2) seeing how, excellent as it is, even this proposal might have been improved.

Two conventions have, therefore, been employed in this presentation: (1) the usual proofreading marks to indicate editorial changes, and (2) a running commentary in the right-hand margin, pointing out both the excellent features of the proposal and those areas in which improvement might have made the proposal even more effective.

The proposal is not meant to be slavishly emulated. It is presented in the hope that it will crystallize the material presented in the text in a specific document that *demonstrates* in concrete form the features of a practical and successful proposal dealing with a very pragmatic and substantial problem.

THE PROBLEM AND ITS SETTING

The Statement of the Problem

This research proposes to identify and evaluate the existing discrete interests among Federally employed male cartographers and to develop a scale for the revised Strong Vocational Interest Blank to aid recruitment of cartographers into Federal employment.

The Subproblems

1. The first subproblem. The first subproblem is to determine whether male cartographers employed by the Federal government have a discrete pattern of interests different from those of men in general as measured by the Strong Vocational Interest Blank.

COMMENTS ON ITEMS WITHIN THE PROPOSAL

Note the use of the headings to indicate the organization and outline of the proposal. (Refer to the discussion of this matter in Chapter 12.)

The phrase "existing discrete" is useless verbiage. If they are "discrete interests," they do "exist."

Note the underscoring, indicating italics, for published titles.

Note also that only the words are italicized. It is impossible to italicize spaces. Hence, the line is broken and not solid as so often written.

The numbering here is superfluous. The ¶ sidehead makes it clearly apparent that this is the first subproblem. No need, therefore, to number it 1.

This is the first of three parts of a research proposal submitted by Arthur L. Benton to the American University, Washington, D.C., in partial fulfillment of the requirements for the degree of Doctor of Philosophy. Reprinted (with alterations) with permission of Dr. A. L. Benton.

2. The second subproblem. The second subproblem is to construct a scoring key for the Strong Vocational Interest Blank to differen-
the interest of those of also from the interests of
tiate^cartographers from ^men in general and^other occupational groups.

Here the researcher is not thinking what he is saying. What he says is that he wants to differentiate cartographers. That is not so. He wants to differentiate the interests of cartographers. The edited additions bring the thought into correct perspective.

to
3. The third subproblem. The third subproblem is to analyze and^ interpret the treated data so as to evaluate the discovered interests in terms of their discreteness in recruiting cartographers.

Note the correction in syntax. A correlative connects two like constructions; thus the insertion of the to.

Note that the three subproblems add up to the totality of the problem.

The Hypotheses

Note the spacing between the freestanding sidehead and the first line of text. Such spacing causes the heading to stand out prominently for ease of reading. Crowding is the worst typing fault of most students.

The first hypothesis is that male cartographers employed by the Federal Government have a discrete pattern of interests different from those of men in general.

Note the position of the hypothesis section. It immediately follows the subproblems. It facilitates seeing the one-to-one correspondence between the subproblem and the hypothesis pertaining to that subproblem.

The second hypothesis is that the Strong Vocational Interest Blank can identify the existing discrete interests of cartographers differentially
those of those of
from^men in general and^other occupational groups.

"Edited-in" words express precisely what the writer of the proposal means.

The third hypothesis is that the development of an interest scale can aid the recruitment of cartographers into Federal employment.

This hypothesis goes beyond the limits of the problem. The researcher does not intend to investigate the actual recruitment of cartographers, yet, unless he does he cannot know whether his hypothesis will be supported or not.

The Delimitations

The study will not attempt to predict success of cartographers.

The study will not determine nor evaluate the preparation and training of cartographers.

Delimitations indicate the peripheral areas lying contiguous to the problem which the researcher expressly rules out of the area of his investigation.

The study will be limited to male cartographers who have attained, within the U.S. Civil Service classification system, full performance ratings of GS-09 or higher in Occupation Series 1370.

any cartographers who may be also
The study will not evaluate^uniformed military personnel.

Again, the researcher is not saying what he means precisely. The interpolation clarifies what he intends to say.

The Definitions of Terms

Note that the word to be defined is given in the ¶ sidehead. Then follows a complete definition comprising the three parts discussed in chapter 3. The small numbers over the first definition indicate: 1 = the term to be defined, 2 = the genera, 3 = the differentia.

1 2
Cartographer. A cartographer is a professional employee who
3
engages in the production of maps, including construction of projections, design, drafting (or scribing), and preparation through the negative stage for the reproduction of maps, charts, and related graphic materials.

Discrete interests. Discrete interests are those empirically derived qualities or traits common to an occupational population that serve to make them distinct from the general population or universe.

Again the definition is formal in that it begins with the term to be defined (discrete interests); it states the genera to which the term belongs (empirically derived qualities or traits); and then the differentia (e.g., common to an occupational population).

Abbreviations

SVIB is the abbreviation used for the Strong Vocational Interest Blank.

USATOPOCOM is an acronym for the U.S. Army Topographic Command.

CIMR is an abbreviation used for the Center for Interest Measurement Research.

SD is the abbreviation used for standard deviation.

This section was not discussed in the text, but it is perfectly appropriate. Whatever makes reading easier and aids in giving the problem an appropriate setting is worth including in this part of the proposal.

Assumptions

The first assumption. The first assumption is that the need for cartographers in Federal service will continue.

The second assumption. The second assumption is that the revised Strong Vocational Interest Blank will continue in use as a vocational guidance tool.

Note that the assumptions are set up with appropriate paragraph subheads. Perhaps this is one feature that might have enhanced the presentation of the hypotheses. Had they been set up, as, for example, The first hypothesis, each section would have been parallel in format.

The third assumption. The third assumption is that the recent revolutionary advances in the cartographic state of the art will not alter the interests of persons in the employment of the Federal Government as cartographers.

As we said earlier, clarity is most important in the writing and structuring of a proposal. The writer of this proposal has presented his material in a delightfully clear manner.

The fourth assumption. The fourth assumption is that the criterion group consisting of the population of cartographers employed by the USATOPOCOM at Washington, D.C.; Providence, Rhode Island; Louisville, Kentucky; Kansas City, Missouri; and San Antonio, Texas, is representative of the universe of Federally employed cartographers.

Note that the writer repeatedly gives evidence of working with care and precision. He does not try to cut corners. Here he spells out fully the name of the state, rather than employing abbreviations.

The Importance of the Study

Cartographers and the nature of their work is little known in American society. The total annual production of graduates, at the bachelor's level, with competence in the broader field of survey engineering within which cartography is subsumed, is currently less than one percent of the annual requirement. The addition of a cartographer scale to the occupations routinely reported for the Strong Vocational Interest Blank would potentially bring to the attention of everyone involved with the existing vocational guidance system the opportunities within the field of map-making and serve to attract serious and capable students into the appropriate preparatory college programs.

This section gives the reader of the proposal a practical rationale for undertaking the study. It shows a utilitarian connection between the problem for research and the exigencies of real life.

Here the researcher points out that chance produces less than one percent of graduates required for the demand of the cartographic profession. If he can identify potential candidates for the profession in terms of their discrete interests on the SVIB, it may attract serious and capable students into courses that might prepare and lead them toward cartography as a life's work.

Significant and Influential Research

"But worse than any loss of limb is the failing mind, which forgets the names of slaves, and cannot recognize the face of the old friend who dined with him last night, nor those of the children whom he has begotten and brought up."—Juvenal

Such, in varying degrees of severity, were the normal expectations of aging. In discussing the aging mind, psychology texts of a generation or two ago invariably focused on mental deterioration. This was probably the belief responsible for retirement-age policies. The deterioration of mental faculties—the "onset of senescence"—was as commonly and tacitly accepted as normal for the individual as were the needs for food, companionship, and shelter. Physical and mental deterioration were merely a fact of life and were not open to question.

Recent research has dealt a devastating blow to this belief. A recent study offers solid evidence that people lose their mental skills when they stop using them. Many older people who retire just "let down." The daily pressure of occupational demands is off, retirees grow lackadaisical, interest sags, and the "old age" syndrome sets in.

But the research of Professor K. Warner Schaie, of Pennsylvania State University, in collaboration with Professor Sherry Willis, which covered a 28-year period and involved 4,000 people, has produced data that suggest that skills that had been allowed to deteriorate could be reacquired.[3] Deficiencies differ from individual to individual. But many individuals show significant improvement after diagnosis and a series of tutorial sessions designed to rekindle interests, provide mental challenges, and make demands on the use of problem solving, numerical, and verbal skills. More dramatically, 40 percent of the group studied regained the level of skill proficiency they had nearly 15 years earlier.

An active life style, flexibility, and support of family and friends have been shown to contribute to regaining and maintaining mental sharpness. Up to the age of 60, most individuals are relatively safe. There is practically no decline in their mental abilities. But with many adults retiring at an earlier age and a rapidly growing senior citizen population, this research is certainly significant. Perhaps mental stimulation in the form of continuing education and social involvement is one of the best means of avoiding the "old age" syndrome. Research seems to indicate this is so.

[3] See K. Warner Schaie and Sherry Willis, "Can Decline in Adult Intellectual Functioning Be Reversed?" *Developmental Psychology* 22 (No. 2, 1986): 223-32.

The Computer as a Tool of Research

Online Informational Databases

Through a microcomputer, you can reach out worldwide and access information from thousands of sources on every conceivable subject. And you can use your telephone line to do it.

In the discussion of the computer as a tool of research in chapter 2, we mentioned briefly the databank and its accessibility through the use of the personal computer. One has only to look at a copy of *The North American Online Directory* to realize the vastness of the universe of information available to the owner of a microcomputer. The latest edition of the Cuadra Associates' *Directory of Online Data Bases* lists over 2,200 separate data-bases, produced by over 1,000 companies and marketed by more than 300 online services.

Do these figures overwhelm you? If so, they should also enlarge your vision. All this information is systematically available to any microcomputer owner who has the proper hardware and who can afford the fees and rental time associated with garnering the facts he or she seeks. Many universities subscribe to online databases and make these available to graduate students at no charge.

What do you need to dip into this well of facts and figures and to pipe the desired information through your computer and onto your monitor screen? Aside from your microcomputer and monitor, you need a modem and a telephone.

Your computer generates *digital* signals. The telephone line operates on *analog* signals. If your computer is to "talk" to another computer over a telephone line, it needs to convert its digital signals to analog signals that are compatible with telephonic transmission characteristics. The modem is the converter that does this. Conversely, when the distant computer replies to yours, it converts *its* digital signals to analog ones. For your computer to accept this information, however, it must be reconverted to digital data. The conversion from digital to analog is called *modulation,* and, conversely, the conversion from analog back to digital is called *demodulation.* Take the initial letters of each term and you have *mo* + *dem.* Figure 3.4 illustrates the entire process.

There are many different commercial software applications to help your computer transmit and receive data, and there are several distinct types of modems. It would be well for you to talk to a computer specialist before you go any further with modems and online information planning.

How do you locate available databases? Here is a partial list of database directories and their respective publishers:

Datapro Directory of On-Line Services. 2 volumes. Datapro, 1805 Underwood Boulevard, Delran, NJ 08075. Updated monthly.

Directory of Online Databases. Cuadra Associates, 2001 Wiltshire Boulevard, Suite 305, Santa Monica, CA 90403. Two complete issues and two supplements each year.

Directory of Online Information Resources: Semi-Annual. CSG Press, 11301 Rockville Pike, Kensington, MD 20895.

Figure 3.4

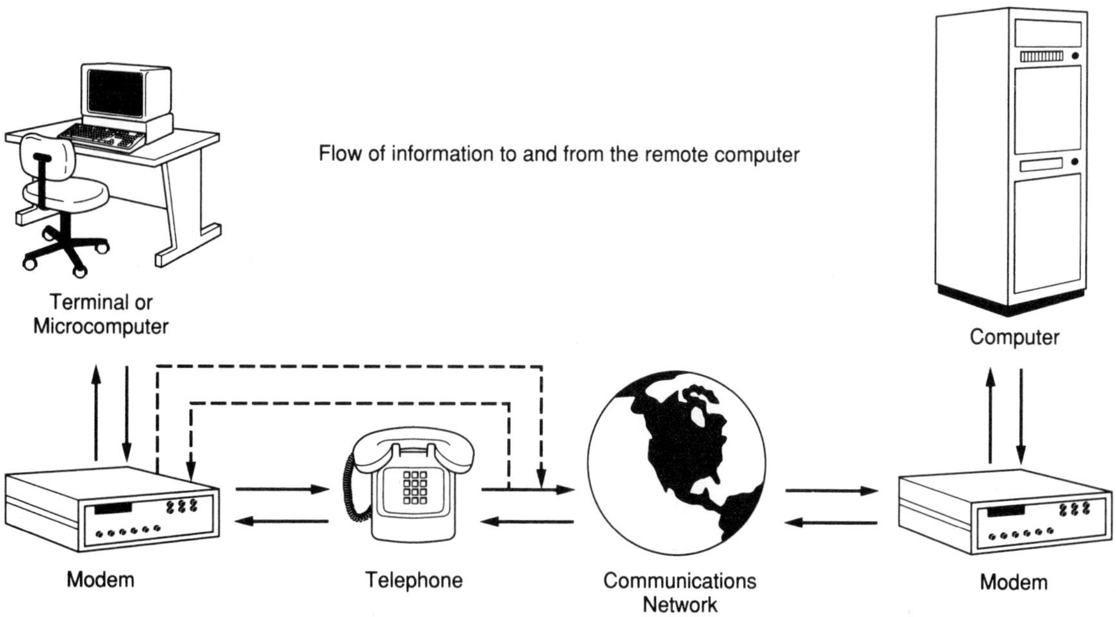

This drawing adapted from that appearing in Carol Hansen, *The Microcomputer User's Guide to Information Online,* Hasbrouck Heights, NJ: Hayden Book Co., n.d.

Encyclopedia of Information Systems and Services. 5th ed. (1982), Gale Research Company, Book Tower, Detroit, MI 48226.

Lesco, M. *The Complete Data and Data Base Source Book.* New York, Avon, 1984.

Motley, Lynne. *Modem U.S.A.: Low Cost & Free Online Sources for Information. Databases & Electronic Bulletin Boards Via Personal Computer and Modem in 50 States.* Allium Press, 1991.

Omni Online Database Directory. New York: Macmillan, 1983.

Online Bibliographic Databases. 3d ed. (1983), Gale Research, Book Tower, Detroit, MI 48226.

Online Business Information Sources: Your Guide to Profits Through Information (1983), News Net, Inc., 945 Haverford Road, Bryn Mawr, PA 19010.

Online Reference and Information Retrieval. 2d ed. Littleton, CO: Libraries Unlimited, 1987.

Rittner, Don. *Ecolinking: Everyone's Guide to Online Environmental Information.* Peachpit Press, 1992.

Rittner, Don. *Ecolinking: Online Resources for the Environmental Community.* Peachpit Press, 1992.

Periodicals

Computer Data Report. Quarterly. Information USA, 12400 Beall Mountain Road, Potomac, MD 20854.

Data Base Alert. Monthly. Knowledge Industries Publications, 701 Westchester Avenue, White Plains, NY 10604.

Database: The Magazine of Database Reference and Review. Quarterly. Online, 11 Tannery Lane, Weston, CT 06883.

Online. Bimonthly. Learned Information, 11 Tannery Lane, Weston, CT 06883.

General Reading about Online Databases

Aluri, Rao, and D.A. Kemp. *Subject Analysis in Online Catalogs.* Littleton, CO: Libraries Unlimited, 1991.

Auster, Ethel, ed. *The Online Searcher.* New York: Neal-Schuman, 1990.

Byerly, Greg. *Online Searching: A Dictionary and Bibliographic Guide.* Littleton, CO: Libraries Unlimited, 1983.

Date, C.J. *Database: A Primer,* Reading, MA: Addison-Wesley, 1990.

Fenichel, Carol H., and Thomas H. Hogan. *Online Searching: A Primer.* Medford, NJ: Learned Information, 1984.

Goldmann, Nahum. *Online Information Hunting.* Blue Ridge Summit, PA: TAB, 1992.

Goldman, Nahum. *Online Research and Retrieval with Microcomputers.* Blue Ridge Summit, PA: TAB Books, 1985.

Hansen, Carol. *The Microcomputer User's Guide to Information Online.* Hasbrouck Heights, NJ: Hayden, 1984.

Hildreth, Charles. *Online Public Access Catalog: The User Interface.* Dublin, OH: OCLC Online Computer Center, 1982.

Hiltz, S.R. *Online Communities.* Edited by Ben Schneiderman. Norwood, NJ: Ablex, 1984.

Newlin, Barbara. *Answers Online: Your Guide to Informational Data Bases.* Berkeley, CA: Osborne McGraw-Hill, 1985.

Palmer, Ian R. *Data Base Systems: A Practical Reference.* Wellesley MA: QED Information Sciences, 1975.

Tuman, Myron C., ed. *Literacy Online: The Promise (& Peril) of Reading & Writing with Computers.* Pittsburgh, PA: University of Pittsburgh Press, 1992.

For Further Reading

Beckingham, Ann C. "Identifying Problems for Nursing Research." *International Nursing Review* 21 (1974): 49–50.

Borg, Walter R., and Meredith D. Gall. *Educational Research: An Introduction.* 3d ed. New York: Longman, 1979. In chapter 2 is a discussion of "The Research Problem." *

Brink, Pamela J., and Marilyn J. Wood, *Basic Steps in Planning Nursing Research.* North Scituate, MA: Duxbury, 1978. See chapter 2, "From Question to Problem," and chapter 3, "The Full and Final Problem."

Charles, D.C. "Early Research in Educational Psychology." *Educational Psychologist* 23 (Summer 1988): 221–33.

DeBakey, Selma, and Lois DeBakey. "The Title: What's in a Name?" *International Journal of Cardiology 2* (1983): 401–6.

Diers, Donna. *Research in Nursing Practice.* Philadelphia: J.B. Lippincott, 1979. See chapter 1, "Research Problems," and chapter 2, "Statement of the Problem."

Gephart, William J., and Robert B. Ingle. *Educational Research: Selected Readings.* Columbus, OH: Merrill, 1969. See chapter 2, "Problem Identification, Hypothesis Development."

Good, Carter V. *Essentials of Educational Research Methodology.* 2d ed. New York: Appleton–Century–Crofts, 1972. See chapter 2, "The Problem and Hypothesis."

Horner, J., and D. Thirlwall, "Online Searching and the University Researcher." *Journal of Academic Librarianship 14* (September 1988): 225–30.

Kerlinger, Fred N. *Foundations of Behavioral Research.* New York: Holt, Rinehart and Winston, 1964. See chapter 2, "Problems and Hypotheses."

—. *Behavioral Research: A Conceptual Approach.* New York: Holt, Rinehart and Winston, 1979. See chapter 3, "Problems, Hypotheses, and Variables."

Lindeman, C.A. "The Research Question." *Journal of Nursing Administration 12* (January 1982): 6–10.

Manheim, Henry L., and Bradley A. Simon. *Sociological Research.* Homewood, IL: Dorsey, 1977. See chapter 6, "The Formulation of a Research Problem."

Mosenthal, P.B. "Research Views: Defining Problems in Reading Research." *Reading Teacher 42* (May 1989): 718–19.

Mouly, George J. *The Science of Educational Research.* New York: Van Nostrand Reinhold, 1970. See chapter 4, " The Research Problem."

Notter, Lucille E. *Essentials of Nursing Research.* 2d ed. New York: Springer, 1978. See chapter 3, "Selecting a Problem."

Polit, Denise, and Bernadette Hungler. *Nursing Research: Principles and Methods.* Philadelphia: J.B. Lippincott, 1978. See chapter 5, "Selecting and Defining a Nursing Research Problem."

Rajabally, M.H. "Research Problems: Objectivity." *Nursing Papers* 16 (Fall 1984): 9–11.

Resta, Paul E., and Robert L. Baker. *Formulating a Research Problem.* Inglewood, CA: Southwest Regional Laboratory for Educational Research and Development, 1967.

Sweeney, Mary Ann, and Peter Oliveri. *An Introduction to Nursing Research.* Philadelphia: J.B. Lippincott, 1981. See chapter 5, "Starting to Develop the Research Problem."

Travers, Robert M.W. *An Introduction to Educational Research.* New York: Macmillan, 1978. See Chapter 4, "Methods of Finding a Problem."

*In the periodical and separately published literature, a phenomenal void occurs in the discussion of the research problem. Most of such discussions are found in texts of research methodology. This will explain the predominance of such references in this bibliography.

Valiga, Theresa M., and Virginia M. Mermel. "Formulating the Research Question." *Topics in Clinical Nursing* 7 (July 1985): 1–13.

Verhonick, Phyllis J., and Catherine C. Seaman. *Research Methods for Undergraduate Students in Nursing.* New York: Appleton-Century-Crofts, 1978. See chapter 2, "The Research Problem."

Vockell, Edward L. *Educational Research.* New York: Macmillan, 1983. See chapter 18, 331–32.

Watson, P.G. "On Conducting Research: Definition of Terms." *Journal of Enterostomal Therapy* 11 (November-December 1984): 242–44.

Williamson, John B., David A. Karp, and John R. Dalphin. *The Research Craft: An Introduction to Social Science Methods.* Boston, MA: Little, Brown, 1977. See chapter 2, "Generating and Testing Ideas."

CHAPTER 4

The Review of the Related Literature

Those who do research belong to a community of scholars, each of whom has journeyed into the unknown to bring back a fact, a truth, a point of light. What they have recorded of their journey and their findings will make it easier for you to explore the unknown: To help you also to discover a fact, a truth, or bring back a point of light.

Understanding the Role of the Review

As a general rule, students do not understand the purpose of investigating the literature related to their research problem. Simply put, it is fundamental among researchers that the more you know about the peripheral investigations germane to your own study, the more knowledgeably you can approach your particular problems.

Such exploration and discussion occupies the section in the research proposal or in the completed research report known as the *review of the related literature.* The italicized words are emphasized intentionally to stress what needs stressing. They describe precisely what the related literature section does. Its function is to "look again" *(re+view)* at the *literature* (the reports of what others have done) in a *related* area: an area not necessarily identical with, but collateral to, your own area of study.

The Purpose of the Review

What, then, is the purpose of this review? It has several purposes. Primarily, it is to assist you in attacking your problem for research. In any research undertaking, *your own research problem* is always central. Everything that you do, you do because it helps you resolve your problem. When you know what others have done, you are better prepared to attack the problem you have chosen to investigate with deeper insight and more complete knowledge. But this is only the principal reason for investigating the literature. Such a review can provide you with many benefits:

1. It can reveal investigations similar to your own, and it can show you how the collateral researchers handled these situations.
2. It can illuminate a method of dealing with a problem situation that may suggest avenues of approach to similar difficulties you may be facing.
3. It can reveal to you sources of data that you may not have known existed.

4. It can introduce you to significant research personalities, of whose work and collateral writings you may have had no knowledge.
5. It can help you to see your own study in historical and associational perspective and in relation to earlier and more primitive attacks on the same problem.
6. It can provide you with new ideas and approaches that may not have occurred to you.
7. It can help you evaluate your own research efforts by comparing them with the similar efforts of others.

How to Begin a Search for Related Literature

Go to the Indexes and Abstracts. Refer back to chapter 2, "The Tools of Research." Read again the section dealing with the library. There we discussed the master keys to the library and gave you a list of general reference works.

As a rule, begin with the indexes and abstracts of the periodicals in your academic area: *Biological Abstracts, Chemical Abstracts, Child Development Abstracts, Dissertation Abstracts International, Psychological Abstracts, Education Index, Index Medicus, Index of Science and Technology, Science Citation Index.* These are simply the more common indexes and abstracts. You will doubtless discover others in your own library. They will provide you with principal current studies and related research projects.

For contemporary events, do not overlook *Facts on File* and *The New York Times Index.* For a guide to the periodical literature of the nineteenth century, such works as *Poole's Guide to Periodical Literature* and the *Nineteenth Century Readers' Guide* are indispensable.

Be sure to examine published bibliographies. Perhaps one of the best current sources is the *Bibliographic Index.* Besterman's *Bibliography of Bibliographies* and similar standard reference sources are helpful. For locating books, *Books in Print, Paperback Books in Print,* the *Cumulative Book Index, The Book Review Digest,* and the various catalogs of the Library of Congress, the British Museum, the Bibliothèque Nationale, and other great libraries of the world are found in multivolume form in many libraries.

Also, you should not be unmindful of the wealth of information on microfilm. The informational services, such as MEDLARS, ERIC, and University Microfilms, which reduce significant research to microfilm, microfiche, or microprint and make it available to the researcher at nominal cost, have centers located at strategic points throughout the nation. In chapter 2, we included in the list of master guides to basic reference literature the *Guide to Microforms in Print.*

Database Access to the Literature. In chapter 3, in the section devoted to the computer as a tool of research, we presented in some detail the matter of information stored in databanks and their accessibility with the aid of the personal computer. In considering the review of the literature, those who have microcomputers should not overlook the vast potential of this source of data. Perhaps you might want to refer to one or more of the following, which were not cited in the references in that discussion:

Donald T. Hawkins, *Online Information Retrieval Bibliography, 1987–1989* (Learned Information, Inc., 1990).

"Information Retrieval Systems for Microcomputers," *Library Hi-Tech* 3 (1985): 41–54.

"Data Networks Shrink Research Frontiers," *Informational Management* 38 (July 1984): 31–32.

"Fifty 'Best' Databases and File Management Packages for Academic Libraries," *Library Software Review* 4 (March–April 1985): 59–62.

Subject Guide to Books In Print, 1991–1992 (New York: R. R. Bowker, 1992).

"Microsearch: The Many Uses of a Downloaded Database," *Microcomputers for Information Management: An International Journal for Library and Information Management Services* 2 (March 1985): 25–32.

The Treasury of Government Publications. Another vast source of information should not be overlooked: the Depository Libraries of the United States Government. The United States Government Printing Office is the largest publisher of printed material in the world. The policy of distributing to the public the documents issued by the printing office began in a resolution passed by Congress December 27, 1813.

With changes over the years, the Depository Library Act of 1962 finally established the matter of depository libraries.[1] A message from the chairman of the congressional Joint Committee on Printing states that "the laws establishing the depository library system are among the oldest right to know statutes passed by the U.S. Congress. In nearly 1,400 congressionally designated libraries throughout the United States, the public has access to information about its government. The depository libraries in accepting this designation pledge themselves to provide free public access to all Government documents entrusted to them." The preceding statement is taken from *A Directory of U.S. Government Depository Libraries, March 1987.* This document is available for sale from the Superintendent of Documents, U.S. Government Printing Office, Washington, DC 20402, and lists each of the nearly 1,400 depository libraries by state, city, and congressional district. A few of the many publications available are *Statistical Abstract of the United States, Survey of Current Business, United States Government Manual, Public Papers of the Presidents, Monthly Labor Review,* and information about the federal government, nutrition, environment and weather, careers, science and technology, business opportunities, health care, energy, and education.

A comprehensive list of the government publications that may be found in all regional depository libraries and in the subregional depository libraries (listed in the document cited above) is found in a nearly 200-page publication of the Government Printing Office entitled *List of Classes of United States Government Publications Available for Selection by Depository Libraries,* which bears the classification number GP3.24:987/3. Not all depository libraries may carry the full contents of this list, but you should request it when you visit a depository library to appreciate the wide spectrum of material that is available through government sources.

A free catalog of books, hard- and softcover (in contradistinction to the above pamphlet and report materials found in the depository libraries), published by the government on a wide range of subjects is available by request from Free Catalog, P.O. Box 37000, Washington, DC 20013.

The Government Printing Office also issues the "GPO Sales Publications Reference File," or PRF, a 48X microfiche catalog of publications sold by the Superintendent of Documents. Out of the nearly 1,400 depository libraries, about 1,150 receive the PRF.

A letter addressed to the Superintendent of Documents, U.S. Government Printing Office, Washington, DC 20402 (telephone 202-275-2051) will bring you a packet of informational material.

A title that may be in the reference section of your college or university library is also a guide to government publications: *Information U.S.A.*, compiled by Matthew Lesco (New York: Viking, 1983). It bears the subtitle, "The ultimate guide to the largest source of information on earth: How to get information from the U.S. Government."

Go to the Library Armed with Data-gathering Tools. You'll need bibliography cards and a container to carry them in. This may be a filing box or an expandable envelope. Bibliography cards are valuable not only for gathering and recording the information but also for locating it again at a future date, should that be necessary, without continual return trips to the library. Have a standard form on which to record every bibliographic item that you inspect. Below we have given a suggested form for such a card. It contains the essential information concerning a bibliographical source. It may be well to duplicate as many of these cards as necessary and always to have a supply with you whenever you go to the library. Sometimes very valuable ref-

[1]See Yuri Nakata, *From Press to People: Collecting and Using U.S. Government Publications* (Chicago: American Library Association, 1979).

Figure 4.1 Bibliographic Reference Card

Serial No. ________________

Author(s) ________________

Title of article ________________

Journal title ________________

Vol. _____ *No.* _____ *Month* _____ *Year* _____ *Pages* ________________

Place of publication, publisher, date, edition (books only)

____

Library where info. is located __________ *Call No.* ________________

Source of bibliographic info. ________________

How item relates to research problem ________________

Use reverse side for additional comment. (if used, check here) ☐

erences are encountered unexpectedly, and you may not always be able to get a printout of the library's computerized listing. In addition, you will want to make notes on the document's relation to your project. In the interest of conserving space and aiding in duplication of the bibliographical item, 20-pound bond paper, cut to 3- × 5-inch size, is convenient for card making. It gives the necessary sturdiness for filing, yet it is thin enough to permit making multiple copies of the same note or bibliographic reference.

A sample card might look something like Figure 4.1.

Make as Many Copies of the Bibliographic Item as Necessary. You should make at least two copies of every bibliographical item and set up two files. One should have the cards arranged by author's last name, alphabetically; the other should have the cards arranged serially, by number. If you can't afford the copying fees, carbon paper slipped under the original when you make the original notation will make two or more copies at one writing.

In making notes, it is frequently convenient to have a single symbol for a complete source. In the upper right-hand corner of the sample card are the words *Serial No.* If, as you write each item of bibliography, you assign to that bibliographical source a number, you will save time and effort when making notes from that source by indicating the page and serial number of the bibliographical source from which the note was made. A colon may be used to separate the serial number of the source from the page notation. Suppose in a certain work whose bibliographical serial number is 63, we were to extract certain items of information from pages 24, 26, and 29. You would have probably three note cards, each with one item of information from each of the three pages. To identify the source of each reference, therefore, the cards would bear the symbols 63 (the bibliographical serial number): 24 (the page), 63:26, and 63:29, respectively.

It is important to have an *alphabetical* file of bibliography cards (by authors' last names, followed by first names and initial), as well as a *numerical* one. Take this, for instance: you are reading other studies, and a work is mentioned that you know you have inspected. You have been working at several libraries. By having the author's last name, you can readily find the information on the work mentioned and the library that owns it, if you consult the alphabetical file under the last name of the author.

Parallel card files thus serve distinctly different purposes; but for an extended research effort, in which you may be inspecting hundreds of items, each file in its own way may be indispensably important and save hours of futile search.

Computerize as Much as Possible. For those of you who have personal computers, open a file and computerize your data as much as possible. The "sort" feature of your database software will alphabetize the data or will arrange it according to date: from the most recent to the most remote or vice versa. You may also create and maintain in this fashion the parallel bibliographic files discussed above. (Be sure to enter the results of each day's data gathering at the end of the day. Few prospects are more frustrating than facing a mountain of backlogged data entry—more than one promising project has been shelved forever because the researcher just couldn't conquer the task!) The versatility of the computer makes editing simple. Moving data and merging items is a routine procedure. All this simplifies the management of your data and may save hours of time in filing, copying, and note taking.

Be as Fast and as Accurate as Possible. Photocopying is a common means of getting data both quickly and accurately. Copying great quantities of material, however, has its limitations. In college and university libraries, one frequently is frustrated by long lines of students waiting to copy equally great quantities of material on a limited number of copy machines.

A good camera and a copying lens attachment can add both speed and accuracy in copying data. In doing my own doctoral dissertation, I copied a vast store of material with a tripod, camera, and copying lens. I collected and amassed great quantities of material, taking it to a remote part of the library where I had set up my tripod and camera. I had previously scanned each selection for copying and marked it with a slip of paper. As fast as possible, I slipped one book or bound journal after another under the field of the camera, and with a snap of the lens copied an entire page or two. I then developed the film and printed the images. I carefully stored the developed film in canisters in a 4" × 6" filing drawer, making sure that each canister was appropriately labeled as to contents or numbered for identification. If, in your area there is an amateur photography club, or an individual or group of individuals interested in photography, you might be able to get them to do your developing and printing at substantially less than commercial rates, or you may provide the processing chemicals and enlargement paper and reimburse them for their time and effort. Use your imagination. There are ways to circumvent the queues at the copy machine.

Be Systematic and Thorough. "Make haste slowly" is a sound rule for the researcher. Too many students make careless, half-complete jottings that, when consulted later, after their having consulted scores of other sources in the meantime, are either entirely unintelligible or are so lacking in essential information that they are practically useless. Write legibly, or print clearly. Not being able to distinguish between undotted *i*'s and closed-up *e*'s, carelessly made *a*'s and *o*'s, will either send you scurrying back to sources to see exactly what is correct, or, without confirmation, will fill your document with error.

The original time spent seeking out the item can be totally wasted. It would be much better to take care and do the job right in the first place. Little is gained by rushing so that you fail to get adequate or accurate information the first time around and cannot read it accurately when referring to it later.

Relate Your Bibliography to Your Problem. Always keep your research *problem-oriented.* In gathering your bibliography, ask yourself, how does this item of literature relate to my problem? Discover links between the problem and the literature. This will be a safeguard against the temptation of merely building a haphazard bibliographic collection. Some students think that the more sources they are able to cite, the more impressive and thorough their literature search will seem. Irrelevant literature soon becomes apparent, and a little will ruin a lot of conscientious work.

To avoid being accused of irrelevancy, on each bibliographical source card indicate precisely how that particular item relates to your problem. The specimen card in Figure 4–1 includes a space for this information. The competent researcher never forgets that everything is done for only one purpose: to contribute to the solution of the problem.

How to Write the Section on the Related Literature

After they have amassed an impressive bibliography, many students do not know what to do with it. They have their cards arranged in order, but are at a loss to know how to present their findings. A few simple guidelines may help.

Get the Proper Psychological Orientation. You need to be clear in your own thinking. Know precisely what it is that you are attempting to do. The review of the related literature section is a *discussion* of the studies, research reports, scholarly or broad spectrum writings that bear directly upon your own effort. Consider the review of related literature section in your document as a discussion with a friend (the word *discussion* is italicized above to emphasize its essential nature) about what others have written in relation to what you plan to do. Viewing the literature section in this way will help you develop the proper psychological perspective and will help you see your own effort in relation to the efforts of other researchers.

Too many students consider the related literature section as an unnecessary appendage standing in the way of their real goal. They are eager to get on with the research. To the contrary, a conscientious and thorough review of the literature related to the problem can open up new possibilities and new ways of looking at the problem that may otherwise be totally missed.

Have a Plan. Too many discussions of related literature are unplanned and disorganized ramblings. The student lists whatever comes first to the attention. Design is lacking. The entire effort lacks structure, unity, and coherence.

Before beginning to write the review of the related literature, you should outline the discussion that will follow. Perhaps one of the best guides for such an outline is the problem itself. A careful consideration of the problem should suggest relevant areas for discussion and indicate the direction that the discussion of the related literature should take.

First, there are always the classic studies, the historically oriented writings that have prepared the way for your research effort as well as those of others. These studies are the efforts of the trailblazers of the discrete area within which your problem lies. They connect your special realm of interest to the broad historical horizon from which you can gain perspective for your own efforts. Those who developed the laser utilized the efforts and writings of those who explored relativistic quantum mechanics and the theories of matter and light in electromagnetic fields.

Begin your discussion of the related literature from a comprehensive perspective, like an inverted pyramid: broad end first. Then you can deal with more and more specific or more localized studies that focus more and more on your specific problem.

After the Practical Application that follows this discussion, you will find a section of our sample proposal dealing with "The Review of the Related Literature." Here the writer of the proposal is interested in searching the literature pertaining to his problem. Where does this discussion of related literature, therefore, begin? It begins with the writings of the basic educational theorists of the eighteenth century who have dealt with the role of human interest and its relation to learning. Note his opening sentence: "The role of interests within the behavioral sciences is not new." That sentence takes you immediately into the eighteenth century and to the beginning of the nineteenth century with a discussion of the writings of Jean-Jacques Rousseau (1712–1778) and Johann Friedrich Herbart (1776–1841).

Note the organizational outline that the author follows in presenting the related literature dealing with his problem. We have arranged these topics in the form of an inverted pyramid so that you will be able to see how the author of the sample proposal has done precisely what we have already discussed in terms of an overall plan.

Outline of the Review of the Related Literature

Historical Overview (indicating the studies that underlie the whole problem group)
Interest Measurements as a Vocational Guidance Technique
The Measurement of Interests of Cartographers
The Strong Vocational Interest Approach
The Validity of the Approach
The Construction of a
Scoring Key
Summary

Throughout your discussion of the related literature, the plan of its organization should be clear. Clarity will be enhanced if you use headings and subheadings to indicate the organization of the discussion. (Headings are discussed in detail in chapter 12.)

Emphasize Relatedness. Keep your reader constantly aware of the manner in which the literature you are discussing is related to your problem. Point out precisely what that relationship is. Remember that you are writing a review of the *related* literature.

Too many discussions of the literature are nothing but a chain of pointless, isolated summaries of the writings of others. Jones says . . .; Smith says . . .; Green says. . . . This is the format students generally use. This is also, perhaps, the worst form of a discussion of related literature. There is no discussion, no attempt to demonstrate the *relatedness* of the literature to the problem being researched.

Whenever you cite a study, make yourself account for that particular study in terms of the problem you are researching. Be sure that you specifically point out to the reader in your discussion precisely what the relationship is. Unless you can establish such accountability, you would do well to consider whether you should include the study at all. Use a simple structural device such as a skeleton outline to assist you in establishing the relationship of the literature to the problem.

Review the Literature; Don't Reproduce It! The literature review section of a proposal or a dissertation is perhaps one of the most challenging to write. It requires that you keep a clear focus on just what this section is intended to do. Many students seem to think that here they have the opportunity to quote long passages from the literature, to cite at length the words or ideas of others. More important is what *you say about the study* than what *the author says in the study.* A valued colleague gives this advice to his students:[2]

1. Present your own discussion.
2. Paraphrase (précis, résumé, give a synopsis, an epitome).
3. Use short, direct quotations if necessary.
4. Long quotations are a last resort. Use them only for a *very good reason.*

That is sound advice. Too often students consider the section devoted to the discussion of the related literature as merely conventional filler in the document—something that everyone does and, therefore, needs to be done. They fail to see how such a discussion shows the relatedness of the research project to the broad environment of similar research that has been

[2]Alvin J. Stuart, Department of Education, Indiana University of Pennsylvania, Indiana, PA.

done by others. This is the sole purpose of the literature discussion. In a very real sense, it forms the *raison d'être* for the problem the student is proposing to research.

Showing the Relatedness of the Literature to the Research Project

Since many discussions of the related literature never quite make the connection between the discussion of the literature others have produced and the research that one is doing, the following procedure is recommended to prevent such a hiatus:

1. Write your problem at the top of the page where you cannot lose sight of it. In this location, you will be constantly reminded of the central axis around which everything else revolves.
2. Dissect the problem by numbering its various subparts.
3. Divide the page into two columns by drawing a vertical line down the middle of the page, starting below the statement of the problem.
4. Cite each specific study in the left-hand column.
5. In the right-hand column, opposite each study, note the particular subdivision of the problem to which the study relates, and note also the rationale for including it in the review of the literature.
6. Gather together all the citations that refer to a particular aspect of the problem, so that you have as many groups as you have subdivisions of your main problem.
7. Study these groups in relation to each other, with the view of planning and organizing the discussion of the related literature.
8. Write the review. Head each section with headings whose wording contains *the identical words* found in the statement of the problem.

By following this procedure, you will avoid mere bibliographical prattle under the guise of reviewing the literature presumably related to your problem.

Summarize What You Have Said

Every discussion of literature and associated research relating to the problem under consideration should end with a brief section in the form of a summary in which the author gathers up all that has been said and sets forth its *significance* in terms of the research problem. Perhaps the most important question that any researcher can ask—and should ask continually throughout the whole progress of the research study—is, *Now, what does it all mean?* Too many studies end in a fuzzy blur of verbiage without coming to any focal point. At the end of each section of the discussion of the literature, at the end of the presentation and processing of data in the research report, in the final summary of the disparate subproblems, one question is *always* appropriate: "What does it all *mean*?" One heading is always in order: the heading entitled, "Summary," which epitomizes the discussion and shows its direct relationship to the problem under study.

Points of Departure

Perhaps one of your most perplexing moments in undertaking a search of the literature will come when you seek a point of departure that will lead you to the significant research studies in your field. Start by inspecting certain general works: abstracts, indexes, and accessible online databases. A brief list of some of the most important of these follows. You will discover many more as you proceed with your search. There has been no attempt at comprehensiveness in the list that follows.

Abstracts

An abstract is a summary of an article or a study. It gives the source of the original study, should a reader wish to refer to it. Here are some of the better-known periodicals' publishing abstracts.

African Abstracts
Abstracts of Hospital Management Studies
Abstracts of Reports and Studies in Nursing
Abstracts of Studies in Public Health Nursing
Biological Abstracts
Chemical Abstracts
Child Development Abstracts
Dissertation Abstracts International
Historical Abstracts 1775–1945: Bibliography of the World's Periodical Literature
International Political Science Abstracts
Nursing Abstracts
Pollution Abstracts
Psychological Abstracts
Public Administration Abstracts
Race Relations Abstracts
SAGE Public Administration Abstracts
SAGE Urban Studies Abstracts
Sociological Abstracts
Urban Affairs Abstracts
Women Studies Abstracts

The most comprehensive and relevant abstract *index* for the political scientist is that edited by Alfred de Grazia, *The Universal Reference System: Political Science, Government, and Public Policy Series* (Princeton, NJ: Princeton Publishing, 1967). It consists of ten volumes and is updated through annual supplements.

Indexes

Indexes are compilations listing articles, studies, and research reports in certain specified areas. In using an index, you may do well to look first under the heading of "Research." Indexes are arranged alphabetically. The principal indexes that will provide you with a good starting point are the following.

Agricultural Index
Applied Science and Technology Index
Bibliographic Index: A Cumulative Bibliography of Bibliographies
Biography Index
Book Review Index
British Humanities Index
Business Periodicals Index
Canadian Periodical Index
Comprehensive Dissertation Index: 1861–1972
Current Index to Journals in Education
Education Index
Index of Economic Journals

Index to Foreign Legal Periodicals
Index to Latin American Periodicals
Index to Legal Periodicals
Index Medicus
Index of Publications of Bureaus of Business and Economic Research
Index to Selected Periodicals
International Index: A Guide to Periodical Literature in the Social Sciences and Humanities
Michigan Index to Labor Union Periodicals
National Union Catalog of Manuscript Collections
New York Times Index
Nursing Literature and Allied Health Literature Index
Poole's Index to Periodical Literature, 1802–1889
Serial Bibliographies in the Humanities and Social Sciences
Social Sciences Citation Index
Social Sciences Index
Special Issues and Indexes of Periodicals
United Nations Documents Index
Wall Street Journal Index
Witness Index to United States Congressional Hearings, 1839–(to present)

Practical Application

In chapter 3, you began to construct your own research proposal by stating the problem and the subproblems. Now, you will plan the Review of Related Literature section of your developing proposal.

Defining the Scope and Indicating the Sources of the Related Literature

Step 1. The purpose of this project is to help you plan in a systematic and organized manner the search of the related literature with respect to your problem. The literature that you will review is related only to your problem and to nothing else. To help you keep that fact foremost in your mind, write your problem in the following space:

Step 2. Now read the problem analytically and insert 1, 2, 3, 4, and so on before each separate subarea of your problem, thus isolating the several subareas of your problem into topics under which you might look in indexes, abstracts, bibliographies, and similar reference works in order to find specific items related to your problem. List the key words or phrases that will guide you in your search in the following spaces:

Step 3. Begin your search of the related literature by consulting the following eight general reference works, noting in each instance the library where the book was consulted, the edition, the pages on which relevant material was found, and any comments that you may wish to make. Table 4.1 gives you a sample format for these notes.

Keys to the Treasury of Printed Knowledge

Eight keys will unlock for you the treasury of printed knowledge. These are master guides to the basic reference literature of the world, and are found in most libraries. All researchers, though they may not have a personal reference library, should have several of these books, among others, on their shelves. Go into your university library—in the 000–099 category of the Dewey decimal classification system or the Z classification of the Library of Congress system—to explore the eight titles below. You should be intimately acquainted with the format, the content, and the specific purpose of each.

Burke, Arvid J., and Mary A. Burke. *Documentation in Education.* New York: Teachers College Press, Columbia University, 1967.

Hillard, James M. *Where to Find What.* Metuchen, NJ: Scarecrow Press, 1975.

Murphey, Robert W. *How and Where to Look It Up.* New York: McGraw-Hill, 1958.

Prakken, Sarah L., F. J. Sypher, and Jack A. Clark, eds. *The Reader's Adviser: A Layman's Guide to Literature.* 3 vols. 12th ed. New York: R. R. Bowker, 1977.

Sheehy, Eugene, ed. *Guide to Reference Books.* 9th ed. Chicago, IL: American Library Association, 1976, and *Supplement,* 1980.

Table 4.1 Master Key to Reference Materials

Title	Library	Edition	Pages	Comments

Figure 4.2

BIBLIOGRAPHIC REFERENCE CARD
For Abstracts, Bibliographies, Indexes, etc.

Title ______________________

Volume ______ Date ______________

Categories consulted:

Type of Reference
Abstract (Check) [ ]
Bibliography [ ]
Index [ ]

Library ______________ Book call number ______________

See other side for additional notes

Walford, Albert J. *Guide to Reference Material.* 3 vols. 3d ed. London: The Library Association, 1981.

Walsh, John J., ed. *Guide to Microforms in Print.* Westport, CT: Microform Review, 1977.

Wynar, Bohdan S., ed. *American Reference Books Annual.* Littleton, CO: Libraries Limited. Issued annually.

Step 4. On the basis of the references suggested to you in the several master reference works, make up a bibliographic reference card similar to that shown in Figure 4.2 and duplicate it in sufficient quantities for your use. This is the first step in locating specific items: to go to the indexes, abstracts, bibliographies, and similar works to find the particular bibliographic item in the literature.

Step 5. Finally, using the suggested bibliography card given in the chapter, copy down the specific references in the literature as given in the abstract, bibliography, or index. Use one card for each item. Fill in the author's name, the title of the article, the title of the journal in which the article is to be found, together with the volume of the journal, the pages, and the month and year of publication, and finally the source of your infor-

Figure 4.3

Serial No. ______

Author(s) ______________________
(Last names first, first name, initial)

Title of article ______________________

Journal title ______________________

Volume ______ Pages ______ Month ______ Year ______

Place of Publication, Publisher, date (books only) ______________

______________________ Edition ______

Source of bibliographic information ______________________

Library where information is located ______________________

Call number of book ______________________

How item relates to problem: ______________________

____

Use reverse side for additional comment. (If used, check here ☐.)

mation (the bibliographic reference that you are using). You are now ready to go to the library to begin reading.

A reduced copy of the bibliography card is shown in Figure 4.3. Reread the section in the text entitled "How to Begin a Search for Related Literature" before you actually begin collecting the data for the related literature discussion.

Step 6. By this time you should be reading the literature related to your problem. Write as much as you can of "The Review of the Related Literature" section. Check your presentation against the criteria given in the chapter and in the following sample proposal. Submit your draft to your instructor for comments and suggestions.

A Sample Research Proposal

This is the second of three parts of an actual submitted academic research proposal. (The two other sections appear in chapters 3 and 7.) Study this example with its marginal comments. It will illustrate how the principles discussed in the chapter have guided the student in writing this part of his proposal.

THE REVIEW
OF THE RELATED LITERATURE

A Historical Overview

The role of interests within the behavioral sciences is not new. Rousseau (1712–1778) in the eighteenth century spoke to the matter of interests:

> . . . Education . . . is a development from within, not an accretion from without; it comes through the workings of natural instincts and interests and not in response to external force; it is an expansion of natural powers, not an acquisition of information; it is life itself, not a preparation for a future state remote in interests and characteristics from the life of childhood.[1]

Herbart (1776–1841) stressed virtue as the ultimate purpose of education but recognized the need for arousal of interest in order to secure the attention and appropriation of new ideas. [2]

Within the same context of educational and psychological thought, James (1842–1910) said:

[1] Paul Monroe (ed.), History of Education (New York: Macmillan, 1909), p. 566.
[2] Ibid., p. 752.

This section makes no attempt to present a complete discussion of the related literature with respect to this problem. It does, however, select a representative sampling of each section from the complete discussion so that the student may see how the discussion of related literature is presented.

Note the centered heading, all caps. This is the second main division of the proposal, a fact which the position and all-capitalization of the heading indicates (See chapter 12.)

The reader is introduced to the problem through the perspective of its historical background. Note that the discussion begins with the earliest reference to interests in the eighteenth century and progresses strictly chronologically from J.J. Rousseau (1712–1778) to Guilford (1965).

Extended quotations are single spaced, indented. Ellipsis is indicated by three periods alternating with single space distances (. . .). Ellipsis indicates that words, or perhaps even sentences, have been deleted from the original text. If an entire paragraph is omitted, such omission is marked by an entire line of double-spaced periods:

. . . .

Herbart is discussed as having been interested in the subject of interest.

Here the author should have gone to the original sources—to the writings of J.J. Rousseau (definitive edition) and cited the location of the quotation from the work in which it appears.

Note that here the author of the proposal does cite the prime source of the quotation (footnote 3). This is the way the Rousseau and Herbart quotations should have been cited.

Again the reader should be referred to the specific location in Herbart's writings where the idea discussed is found. In addition, the use of "Ibid." and "Op. Cit." is discouraged in favor of a shortened form of the title cited. See one of the major style manuals for examples of this form.

> Millions of items of the outward order are present to my senses which never properly enter into my experience. Why? Because they have no interest for me. My experience is what I agree to attend to. Only those items which I notice shape my mind--without selective interest, experience is utter chaos. Interest alone gives accent and emphasis, light and shade, background and foreground--intelligible perspective, in a word.[3]

Note again that an extended quotation is single spaced, and indented from both margins of the page.

Psychologists and educators alike have sought to define the desires, interests, and satisfactions that initiate behavior and have applied the term motivation to the concept. Ryan remarked that a postulated "X" which energizes and directs behavior is still the common core across widely different theories of behavior.[4]

Ryan and Guilford are cited and the footnotes refer the reader to the original sources.

Guilford perhaps ~~comes~~ came close to explaining motivation in terms of his informational psychology when he addressed the Nebraska Symposium on Motivation in 1965, saying ". . . there is goal information and this is in the form of the product of anticipation. Human goals are almost entirely developed by experience in the form of anticipated values, and anticipations are implications."[5]

Note the change in tense. Precision of expression is paramount in research writing and reporting. The broad rule for tense usage is generally that since a research report recounts what has been done, the tense employed should generally be the past tense. If present or future tenses are used they should represent facts that will be true at any time the document is read. Here comes is inaccurate. Guilford came close to explaining motivation in 1965 at the Nebraska Symposium. Other changes in tense will be made where necessary.

. . . .

A hiatus in the manuscript.

The area of guidance and vocational guidance which has devoted an entire volume to the Counseling Use of the Strong Vocational Interest Blank.[19]

In the previous section, we were discussing "Interest Measurement in Counseling and Guidance" generally. Now the subject narrows to the measurement of interests among a specific occupational group: cartographers.

Measurement of Interests Among Cartographers

The literature ~~contains~~ contained no references directly to the measurement of interest among cartographers nor to the skills subsumed therein, i.e. photogrammetrist, map-analyst, geographer, surveyor, geodesist, or compiler.

Note tense change. When the researcher searched the literature (in the past) the literature "contained."

Research done with the SVIB has resulted in some fragmenting of the broader vocational fields. The physician scale, for example, ~~is~~ was based upon a composite made up of nine specialties plus interns.[20] Similarly,

[3] William James, The Principles of Psychology (New York: Henry Holt, 1908), Vol. I, 402.

[4] T. A. Ryan, "Drives, Tasks, and the Initiation of Behavior," American Journal of Psychology LXXI (January 1958), 74–93.

[5] J. P. Guilford, "Motivation in an Informational Psychology," David Lewine (ed.), Nebraska Symposium on Motivation (Lincoln: University of Nebraska Press, 1965), pp. 313–333.

[19] W. L. Layton, Counseling Use of the Strong Vocational Interest Blank (Minneapolis, Minnesota: University of Minnesota Press, 1958).

Note the footnote form here for citations with reference to journals. Here for the volume the writer uses Roman numerals, the date in parentheses, and merely the numbers—without pp.—for the pages. There are several forms for footnote citation, which we shall discuss later in the text.

the engineer criterion group ~~includes~~ included mining, mechanical, civil, and electrical engineering.[21] In the latter case, Dunnette has compared the responses of several types of engineers to the SVIB and concluded that the SVIB potentially ~~can~~ could discriminate between the fields within the engineering disciplines.[22]

Note that the tense has again been changed to the past: could is the past tense of can. Also, would, should, and might for will, shall, and may.

In present practice, Campbell ~~reports~~ reported that counselors usually extrapolate from the available SVIB scales to occupations not listed on the profile.[23] This technique, although weak, might be appropriate to parcel out the geologist from potentially relevant engineer and chemist scales. However, to apply the technique when a larger number of existing scales appear applicable to the occupation would considerably weaken any resulting interpretation. The presently available scales ~~do~~ did not identify a single occupation even remotely related to cartography.

The Kuder Preferential Record, the Minnesota Vocational Interest Inventory, the Guilford-Sheidman-Zimmerman Interest Survey, the Occupational Interest Inventory, and the Vocational Interest Analysis ~~are~~ were not scored for cartography nor for any related occupation.

Again, the discussion narrows from the broad discussion of "measurement of interests among cartographers" to a particular method or means of measuring interests among cartographers; namely, "the Strong Vocational Interest approach."

The Strong Vocational Interest Approach

The research generated by the SVIB ~~is~~ was probably exceeded only by ^that of the Rorschach.[24] The SVIB is so well known as to need no description in detail. To repeat here all the information available on the construction of scoring keys for particular occupations does not seem at all pertinent. But the necessary information which is relevant to the

The research "generated by the SVIB" was superseded by the Rorschach in 1969, when Benton wrote his proposal.

Also note the insertion of "that of" expresses precisely the thought the author wished to express.

. . . .

Another hiatus in the manuscript.

The Validity and Reliability of the Strong Approach

Now the author discusses the matter of validity and reliability of the Strong approach to assessing interests.

The criteria for judging the value of a test have long constituted a controversial issue and are beyond the scope of this review. The American Psychological Association, attempting to aid both the test-maker and the test-user, has published a helpful document, "Technical Recommendations for Psychological Tests and Diagnostic Techniques."[32] Cronbach

Note the way in which the author has delimited the discussion by openly stating whatever he feels is beyond the province of his discussion.
Note the general discussion of test validity here.

[20]Campbell (1968), op. cit., p. 26.
[21]Campbell (1966), op. cit., p. 59.
[32]American Psychological Association, "Technical Recommendations for Psychological Tests and Diagnostic Techniques," Psychological Bulletin Supplement, LI (March, 1954), 1–34.

Note that the author cannot use ibid. here. He is referring to two different works by Campbell: one published in 1968, the other in 1966.

included
also ~~includes~~ an excellent coverage of the subject of test evaluation in his work on psychological testing, which has been mentioned earlier in this review. [33]

There are three validities of concern to the test user: content, concurrent, and predictive validities. The validity of the SVIB in each of these traditional areas ~~is~~ was discussed in detail by Strong,[34] by Campbell,[35] and by others.[36] Campbell, in his recent report of factor analysis study found occupational choice determinative.

Now the topic narrows to three validities.

Then we come to Strong and the discussion of these validities as they apply to the Strong approach.

The degree of separation between scales of the SVIB is generally indicated by a determination of the percent of overlapping occasioned

. . . .

The Construction of a Scoring Key

Although Strong has published his procedures for the construction of keys for the SVIB, the literature indicated that refinements in techniques have subsequently occurred. The blanks in scoring and in the weighting system; the format and the items were relatively unchanged.[44] Originally weights of 30 were used. Subsequently, they were reduced to 15; then to 4, and with the current edition, to 1.

If we go back to reread the problem for this research effort we will see how the author has kept his goal constantly in mind while planning his discussion of related literature. In the statement of the problem the author specifically announces that one of his research objectives is to "develop a scale for the revised Strong Vocational Interest Blank to aid recruitment of cartographers." That is precisely what he is discussing here, "the construction of a scoring key—the developing of a scale—to aid in isolating the interests of cartographers from men in general.

Here is a discussion of the evolution of the "revised" SVIB key.

The rationale for adoption of unit weights and reduction in the number of items scored from 400 to 298 ~~is~~ was fully discussed in Strong's last contribution to the literature, published posthumously.[45]

The current procedures, and those to be used in this study, for constructing a scoring key are: first, the SVIB is administered to a criterion group of people in a specified occupation. Length of time employed and the individual's liking of the work are specific requirements for the criteria. Second, the percentage responses for the group are determined for each response and contrasted to men in general. Item choices different for the criterion group and also for the men-in-general group are separated out for use in the scale. Third, all members of the criterion group

The author finally comes to the announcement of the procedures, following those of Strong, that he proposes to use in his study.

[33]Chronbach, op. cit.

[34]E. K. Strong, Jr., Vocational Interests Eighteen Years After College (Minneapolis, MN: University of Minnesota Press, 1955).

[35]Campbell (1966), op. cit.

[36]Buros, op. cit.

[44]E.K. Strong, Jr., et al., "Proposed Scoring Changes for the Strong Vocational Interest Blank," Journal of Applied Psychology, XLVIII (April, 1964), 75-80.

[45]Ibid.

and the men-in-general group are scored on the new scale. Fourth, the norms and standard scores are established if the scale has adequately separated the two groups.

Until the current revision, the weighting system in use employed a mathematical procedure to load the data proportional to

. . . .

In the original document, the discussion of the construction of a scoring key runs on for several pages.

Summary

The extent of research done with the SVIB and its value and reliability as a counseling aid ~~is~~ was well-stated by Cronbach in his summary of the application of interest inventories:

> The Strong blank is undoubtedly the most highly developed and best understood of the inventories; indeed it ranks near the top among psychological tests of all types . . . The great number of keys make interpretation both rich and complex . . . But its length and complexity, together with its research foundation, make the Strong the preferred instrument of most highly trained counselors and psychologists.[56]

[56]Cronbach, op. cit., p. 434.

The heading of this section is somewhat of a misnomer. Actually this is not so much a summary of the discussion of the related literature as it is a justification, by citing an authoritative opinion, for the choice of using the Strong approach over and against any other approach which might have been selected.

Significant and Influential Research

In a recent issue of the *Chronicles of Higher Education,* an article appeared in which 22 leading scholars reported on major trends in research in their respective fields.[3] A brief summary under each of the academic areas covered by these scholars may indicate to you the areas in which the most significant research is now occurring.

Afro-American Studies: Parochialism is vanishing. Black women's studies are increasing. Black hero depicted with both positive and negative qualities. Black history is crossing the color line, becoming more realistic.

Anthropology: Need to close Miocene-Pliocene fossil gap; seeking behavioral and cultural causes of disease in modern world; the patterning of human cognition and memory; nature of economic exchange; learning more about complex societies outside Fertile Crescent; does materialism or idealism explain difference between cultures; positivism or hermaneutics—which is better to study human phenomena?

Art History: Current trend: away from Renaissance study. Interest in decorative or provincial genres, and in media and tradition; interest in eighteenth-century, nine-

[3]"Major Trends in Research: 22 Leading Scholars Report on Their Fields." *Chronicles of Higher Education* 31 (September 4, 1985): 12–14.

teenth-century, and American art and sculpture; interdisciplinary research with historians and literary scholars; art history needs greater critical attention.

Biology: Gene splicing and cloning are active areas; genetic control of enzyme activity and hormone function; defects responsible for genetic diseases; role of cell membranes in metabolism and cell function; discovery of oncogenes and their relation to cancer cells.

Business: Computer processing of large databases will unify scholars in all areas of business research; research needed in operational factors, human-resource management, inventory control, investment, and marketing.

Chemistry: Development of new instruments allowing insight into factors controlling rates of chemical reactions with lasers, molecular beams, computers; transform catalysis from art to science; clarify the molecular basis for the chemistry of life processes.

Cognitive Science: How to learn from experience; artificial intelligence systems, development of intelligent tutor systems (including electronic tutoring); liaison between psychology and computer science.

Economics: Resolution of deep conceptual questions stemming from contemporary reaction to Keynesian model; questions about what makes markets function that general equilibrium theory did not address; application of economic theory to understand how market processes work.

Education: Education lacks a research base. Bring coherence to disparate studies in education; research in curricular alignment: relationship between tests and curriculum.

Engineering: Research opportunities are legion in miniaturization: devices applicable to medicine, for the handicapped (for example, the use of eye motion to direct robots to help patient).

History: History needs cohesion. Recent emphasis on social history has resulted in a fragmentation into highly technical histories; research needed in general developmental patterns and larger integrations of significant events in a multi-integrational interpretation of the historical scene.

Jewish Studies: New emphasis is to treat Judaism as any other religion. Scholars are taking comparative-analytical approach: testing theories and developing hypotheses. Newer studies emphasize the way Jews illustrate broader trends and themes.

Law: New approach is broader and asks questions that penetrate to the root causes of legal problems. Legal empiricism uses social science methodology to look at legal rules and institutions. Much research lies in investigation of the structure and organization of the profession and in the economics and sociology of the law.

Linguistics: More interdisciplinary research on the brain, language, cognition, mental grammar, and human language. Very necessary area: how to put into computer knowledge that a very young child uses in speaking and understanding. Research needed in hard-core linguistics: historical development of languages, their grammars, and the delineation of linguistic universals.

Literature: Present dominant concern: literary theory. New literary insights into blacks and women. Research in reshaping the literary canon as forgotten, neglected, or suppressed texts are rediscovered.

Mathematics: Current research espouses concept that mathematics is one unity. The von Neumann algebras are an open field. Consider Vaughan Jones and relationship between the algebra and analysis of operators. The old classical problems in mathematics still beg for solution and afford research opportunities.

Music: Archival research is growing. Music theory is devoted more to dynamic than static aspects. Research opportunities still exist in preparation of definitive, critical editions of neglected composers.

Nuclear Energy: Survey of consensus in case of a severe nuclear accident. Research in emergency planning in vicinity of nuclear power plants.

Philosophy: Research in applied ethics, especially medical ethics dealing with real moral problems (abortion, euthanasia, human experimentation); in legal practice, relationship between lawyer and client; ethics of agriculture involving environmental issues; the problem of present generation responsibility to future generations.

Political Science: Research in public policy analysis addressing alternatives, costs, and other factors relating to public problems.

Psychology: Contemporary research is focused on behavioral medicine, behavioral toxology, decision theory, and behavioral neuroscience (brain development, memory, relation of brain to immune system); cognitive science and artificial intelligence.

Sociology: Between the macro and the micro perspectives in sociology there is a blank box. Modern research in sociology is beginning to fill that box in establishing the links between the macro processes and individual behavior—between society and the person.

The Computer as a Tool of Research

Word Processing

Ten years ago most students wrote papers, theses, and dissertations on a typewriter. Today, those who have personal computers use word processors. Word processing is a computerized means of composition, whether that composition is a letter or a dissertation.

Many students are just as apprehensive about learning word processing as they are about learning statistics or mathematics. This is an unfounded fear. It is human nature to avoid that which is new, mysterious, and seemingly complicated. But learning word processing is little different than learning to use an electronic typewriter, except that in word processing many more operations are possible and they can be learned in a relatively short time and performed with perfect ease. Correcting spelling errors, moving units of writing from one place to another within the text, automatic numbering of pages, inserting footnotes without apprehension that the space at the bottom of the page will not accommodate the amount of verbiage that the footnote contains, justifying the right margin to avoid "ragged-edge" printing, centering uneven lines of print on the page (as we have done at the beginning of each chapter in this text)—all these and more features are performed with ease in a word processing program. Many people find that word processing is easier and far more efficient and time saving than typewriting and that it increases their speed and accuracy significantly.

Word processing is a software program that is installed in a computer by means of a series of diskettes that give the computer directions as to what to do when the operator wishes to "process" a document. This software usually contains the basic word processing program instructions; a spelling check program, which permits the computer to scan the completed text for misspelled words and word combinations that have been spelled without a space between them; a thesaurus, which permits the operator to call up synonyms for a given word, just as is done in a bound thesaurus; and a printer diskette, which gives instructions to the printer to print out the text with or without headers or footers; to number pages, paragraphs, or lines; to use boldface or regular typeface; to adjust the "pitch" of the type, the spacing, the justification of the text so that even right and left margins are possible; and many other functions.

In word processing, the text as written appears on the computer monitor screen, which gives the writer a chance to correct errors, move words, sentences, or larger blocks of text to different locations within the document or from one document to another, before commanding the computer to print out the text in hard copy. Word processing permits great flexibility in composition. It allows the operator to insert footnotes that will automatically be printed at the foot of the page with the number of the footnote appearing in the text at the proper place. There are many different word processing programs available, and each has its own unique features. You should survey the major ones to determine compatibility with your computer and the range of features that will most nearly suit your requirements.

Most word processing programs are compatible with all IBM and IBM clone computers and have versions for other computer makes (Apple Macintosh, Commodore, etc.). Most current-generation word processing programs produce files that can be read by both Macintosh and IBM systems with equal ease. WordPerfect is probably the most widely used word processing program. Wordstar and Microsoft Word are two other word processors with their own special features and compatibilities.

This is merely a quick and superficial overview. Each program has its own range of functions. Before selecting a word processing system, however, you should discuss the matter with your computer dealer or with a competent software specialist.

For reviews of dozens of word processing programs, see Jim Seymour's articles in *PC Magazine:* "Word Processing: Fast, Flexible, and Forward-looking," *PC Magazine* 7 (Feb. 29, 1988): 92 ff.; and "Having It All: Integrated Word Processing Programs," *PC Magazine* 7 (March 15, 1988): 185 ff. See also current and recent issues of the computer magazines listed in chapter 2. New software is reviewed regularly, and a text such as this cannot hope to list even a portion of the articles.

For Further Reading

Borg, Walter R., and Meredith D. Gall. *Educational Research: An Introduction.* 3d ed. New York: Longmans, 1979. See chapter 4, "Reviewing the Literature."*

Brink, Pamela J., and Marilynn J. Wood. *Basic Steps in Planning Nursing Research.* North Scituate, MA: Duxbury Press, 1978. See chapter 5, "Critical Review of the Literature."

Bryant, David S. *Finding Information the Library Way: A Guide to Reference Sources.* Hamden, CT: Shoe String Press, 1987.

Diers, Donna. *Research in Nursing Practice.* Philadelphia: J.B. Lippincott, 1979. See chapter 3, "Review of the Literature," pp. 66–69.

Galfo, Armand J. *Interpreting Educational Research.* 3d ed. Dubuque, IA: William C. Brown, 1975.

Gephart, William J., and Robert B. Ingle. *Educational Research: Selected Readings.* Columbus, OH: Merrill/Macmillan, 1969. See chapter 3, "The Review of Related Research."

Gilreath, Charles L. *Computerized Literature Searching.* Boulder, CO: Westview Press, 1984.

Good, Carter V. *Essentials of Educational Research Methodology and Design.* 2d ed. New York: Appleton-Century-Crofts, 1972. See chapter 3, "Integration of the Related Literature."

Jackson, C. I., and M. F. Haines. "Look, Before You Research." *Educational Horizons* 63 (Summer 1985): 169.

Lindvall, Carl M. "The Review of Related Literature." *Phi Delta Kappan* 40 (1959): 179–80.

Manheim, Henry L., and Bradley A. Simon. *Sociological Research.* Homewood, IL: Dorsey Press, 1977. See chapter 7, "The Library as a Research Tool."

*As with references on the statement of the problem, very little has been written in the general literature about the review of the related literature. Most of the discussion appears in standard texts on research methodology. This will explain the citations in this reading list.

Moore, Julie. *The Bowker Annual of Library and Book Trade Information.* 30th ed. New York: R. R. Bowker, 1985.

Mouly, George J. *The Science of Educational Research.* New York: Van Nostrand Reinhold, 1970. See chapter 5, "The Library."

Notter, Lucille E. *Essentials of Nursing Research.* 2d ed. New York: Springer, 1978. See chapter 4, "The Literature Search."

Polit, Denise, and Bernadette Hungler. *Nursing Research: Principles and Methods.* Philadelphia: J. B. Lipincott, 1978. See chapter 6, "Locating and Summarizing Existing Information on a Problem."

Shearer, Benjamin F., and Barbara Smith Shearer, compilers. *Finding the Source: A Thesaurus-Index to the Reference Collection.* Westport, CT: Greenwood Press. 1981.

Treece, Eleanor W., and James W. Treece. *Elements of Research in Nursing.* 2d ed. St. Louis, MO: C. V. Mosby, 1977. See chapter 7, "The Library Search."

Verhonick, Phyllis J., and Catherine C. Seaman. *Research Methods for Undergraduate Students in Nursing.* New York: Appleton-Century-Crofts, 1978. See chapter 4, "Review of the Literature."

CHAPTER 5

Planning the Research Project

Architects, before the construction of a building, work out a meticulous and accurate set of plans. This ensures success in the construction of that building. Researchers should be no less precise, detailed, and accurate in the planning of a research project. Plans, specifications, criteria, and design: All of these serve well the architect, the builder, and the researcher alike.

The Scientific Method and Sources of Research Problems

Successful research is planned research. Much research ends in futility because the researcher has plunged into the research activity—going to the library, making notes, gathering data, making observations, computerizing the data—with only a partially thought-out plan and an inconclusive design.

Research planning and architectural planning have much in common. Each requires a conceptualization of the overall organization and a detailed plan before work on the project can begin. For successful completion, a building requires plans that are clearly conceived and accurately drawn. A research project should be no less totally visualized and precisely detailed.

How Is Knowledge Discovered?

But where does planning begin? It begins with an understanding of the manner in which knowledge is discovered. For that is the sole aim of all research: to discover knowledge.

In all of mankind's long history, we have devised only two ways to seek the unknown. One of these is by means of *deductive logic*, the other is by means of *inductive reasoning*, or what is familiarly called *the scientific method*.

Deductive Logic. Up to the time of the Renaissance, insight into most problems was sought by means of deductive logic, a methodology identified with Aristotle. It relied upon logical reasoning and began with a *major premise*. This was a statement, similar to an axiom, that seemed to be a self-evident and universally accepted truth: Man is mortal; God is good; the earth is flat.

The terror that gripped Columbus's sailors was a fear supported by deductive logic. To them, the earth *was* flat. That was their major premise. Then they began reasoning. If the earth were flat, then the flat surfaces would have boundaries. The boundaries of flat surfaces would be the edges of those surfaces. If a ship passed across a flat surface, it would come to the edge of it. There, they reasoned, it would fall off. At this point, they posited a second premise. The earth is afloat on Chaos. Those who travel to the edge of the earth will fall into Chaos and be forever lost! Q.E.D.

The logic was sound; the reasoning, accurate; the conclusion, valid. Where the whole proposition went wrong was that the major premise was incorrect. The reasoning began with a preconceived idea that *seemed* to be true.

But such was Aristotelian logic. It provided answers to problems for which no other answer existed: What is the nature of God? Where are angels found? How many of them can dance upon the point of a needle? It satisfied those who started their quest for knowledge from a dogmatic premise and pursued it to a logical conclusion.

The Origin of the Scientific Method

But with the Renaissance came a new approach to the discovery of knowledge. The method was the result of an interest in humanism. It represented an entirely new way of thinking—an entirely new approach to an unsolved problem, one with a different emphasis. The emphasis was upon *this* world and an intense interest in its phenomena. And it gave rise to a method of thinking known as *the scientific method.*

Its basis was a way of thinking known as *inductive reasoning.* Inductive reasoning begins not with a preconceived conclusion—a major premise—but with an observation. In the Renaissance, people began seeking truth by looking steadfastly at the world around them. They asked questions of Nature. And Nature responded in the form of observable fact.

But fact is fact, and those who seek it must translate it into meaning. During the Renaissance, people soon found that when facts are assembled and studied dispassionately, they frequently suggest hitherto undiscovered truth. Thus was the scientific method born; the words literally mean "the method that searches after knowledge" (*scientia* is the Latin for "knowledge," and derives from *scire,* "to know").

The scientific method gained real impetus during the sixteenth century with such men as Paracelsus, Leonardo, Copernicus, Galileo, Vesalius, Vittorino de Feltre, and others. They introduced scientific methodology to the western world. It is still the most valid method for problem solving and resolving unanswered questions.

What, Then, Is the Scientific Method?

The scientific method is a means whereby insight into an undiscovered truth is sought by (1) identifying the problem that defines the goal of the quest, (2) gathering data with the hope of resolving the problem, (3) positing a hypothesis both as a logical means of locating the data and as an aid to resolving the problem, and (4) empirically testing the hypothesis by processing and interpreting the data to see if the interpretation of them will resolve the question that initiated the research.

Thus, Figure 1.1 in chapter 1, that indicates that research is circular is, in effect, merely a visualization of the scientific method as a basis for research methodology. But, as Figure 1.2 shows, the cycle of research is actually more helical than circular. Each problem begets in the process of inquiry other related problems; and so, the process for solving one problem actually becomes the initiatory process that creates still further problems.

The true researcher looks at the facts *only,* and, as a result of observing *them alone,* draws conclusions as to what they apparently say. For, we can never be *exactly* sure of what the facts do indicate. This statement we shall appreciate more fully when we look more intimately at the nature of data in future chapters. Despite that, the process remains the same. It is a process of *inductive thinking,* and may be best represented by Figure 5.1.

Let's see how this representation applies to an actual research project. A group of neurologists—Silverman, Schwartz, and others—sought the answer to a problem in medicine: How long can a person have a "flat EEG" (an isoelectric brain tracing indicating cerebral death)

Figure 5.1 The Inductive Process.

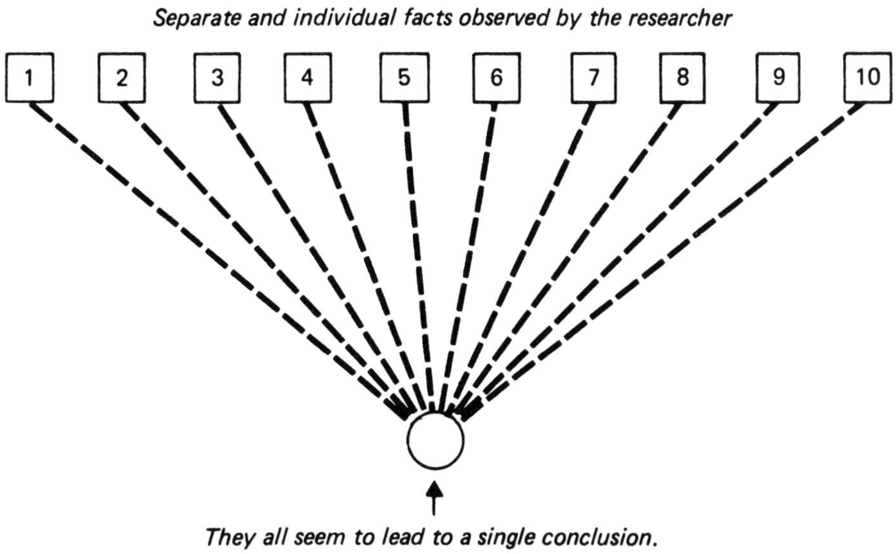

and still recover? Silverman and his colleagues observed actual cases—3,000 of them. They noted that in all cases where the flat EEG persisted for 24 hours or more, *not a single recovery occurred.*[1] All the facts pointed to the same conclusion: *It is tragically unlikely that a recovery might take place with those who exhibit flat EEG tracings of 24 hours or more in duration.* We cannot, of course, rule out the unexplored cases, but *from the data observed* the conclusion reached was that recovery seems impossible. The line from *each* case led to that *one* conclusion.

All Research Has a Basic Format

All research has a basic format. No matter what academic discipline gives rise to the research endeavor, the broad configuration of the research procedure is fundamentally the same. Research is not parochial, and the search for facts to solve a problem seldom fits into the neatly packaged academic disciplines represented by the arrangement of subject areas in a college catalog.

Chapter 6 discusses research methodology as a late arrival, an adjunct area in higher education. Because research was originally introduced by scholars in discrete academic areas—Burford in anthropology, Cattell in psychology, Thorndike in education, among others—this early trend developed into an ongoing attempt to force research methodology into departmental cubicles. We have educational research, nursing research, psychological research, social science research—and on and on, each academic unit attempting to have its own particular brand of research.

In planning a research project, the researcher in quest of the discovery of new knowledge cannot be shackled by curricular restraints. The nature of research is academically global. Research leads the investigator into new and unfamiliar territory that must comprise a part of the journey in pursuit of the resolution of a specific problem and of the advancement of learning. The sociologist in attempting to resolve the unsolved problems in sociology may conceivably come face to face with problems that are psychological or economic; the educational researcher in exploring the causes of learning disability finds that the resolution of the research problem leads through the psychopathology of the central nervous system, endocrin-

[1] *The New England Journal of Medicine* 283 (July 9, 1970): 98,99.

ology, and family counseling. The student in criminal justice may very conceivably be led through the alien territories of abnormal psychology and heredity on the way to finding a solution for a problem in criminology.

Research cannot be monopolized as a departmental mode of investigation. Rather, research methodology must be ancillary to all but free from all. It has its own procedure, unique unto itself, and in its eclecticism draws its data from whatever sources seem to offer productive evidence in resolving the research problem. Figure 5.2 is a general schema for research methodology. We have discussed it in one orientation or another in every chapter of this text. It is the basic format for all research and as such transcends all attempts to compartmentalize it.

We sometimes err in thinking too narrowly, in restricting problems for research to one academic area. Instead of thinking according to departmentalized knowledge, the researcher might do much better to think of problems as arising out of broad generic areas within whose boundaries all research falls: people, things, records, thoughts and ideas, and dynamics or energy.

Briefly, let us consider some problems that may be indigenous to each of these areas.

- *People.* In this category are found research problems relating to individuals, groups, populations, folklore, nationalities, families, sex, community groups and subgroups, employees, management, the disadvantaged, the wealthy, students, ancestors, tribes, mental and physical processes, medical, psychological, educational, social, and sociological problems, learning, motivation, adjustment, crime, criminals, rehabilitation, nutrition, language and linguistics, and religion.
- *Things.* In this category are found research problems relating to biological and vegetable life, viruses, bacteria, inanimate objects (rocks, soil, buildings, furniture, and the phenomenology of nature), matter (molecules, atoms, subatomic matter), chemical and pharmacological problems, space, stars, galaxies, the universe, machines, food, and clothing.

Figure 5.2 The Basic Format For All Research

1
A question strikes!
In the mind of the researcher
a question arises that has no discovered resolution.

2
It's a matter of words.
The researcher converts the question
to a clearly stated research problem.

3
It's worth a guess!
The researcher poses a temporary
hypothesis or series of hypotheses.

4
The search is on!
The literature is searched for
a possible solution to the problem.

5
The search leads nowhere.
Another avenue must be found
to resolve the problem.

6
Fact! Hard Fact! And nothing but the fact!
The researcher looks for facts
that may relate to the problem.

7
What do the facts say?
The facts are subjected to analysis
to reveal their meaning.

8
The facts speak!
The researcher comprehends their
meaning and reaches a conclusion.

9
It's either. . . or—
The facts either seemingly
resolve the research problem,
or they do not resolve it.

10
And, the hypotheses?
Either the facts support the hypotheses
—or they do not.

- *Records.* In this category are found research problems relating to letters, legal documents, lists, journals, memoranda, books, registers, diaries, memoirs, incunabula, interviews, minutes, speeches, monuments, tablets, recordings, census reports, financial and corporate statements, mementos, artifacts, archeological remains, files, newspapers, sketches, drawings, paintings, music, and manuscripts.
- *Thoughts and Ideas.* In this category are found research problems relating to opinions, reactions, concepts, theories, viewpoints, philosophical ideas, political theory, religious beliefs, perceptions, observations, issues, language and semantics, judgments, literature, mathematical concepts and theories, confessions, journalistic columns and commentators' viewpoints, cartoons and caricatures.
- *Dynamics or Energy.* In this category are found research problems relating to human energy and activity, metabolism, bionics, excitation states, radiation, radio and microwave transmission, quantum mechanics, hydrodynamics, hydrologic cycles, atomic and nuclear energy, wave mechanics, thinking, gravity, gravitation, thermodynamics, atmospheric and oceanic energy systems, solar energy, quasars, black holes, and extragalactic radiation.

The above suggestions are not meant to be all-inclusive, but are meant merely to suggest the broad ramifications of categories of research possibilities.

This simplification of the areas from which research problems arise should suggest, however, the folly of attempting to classify research procedures along purely academic and disciplinary lines. The substratum of research principles *is* all-inclusive and, with slight modifications and varying emphases, applies to all disciplines.

The physicist exploring subatomic particles and the sociologist exploring social behavior are both employing the same research principles to their respective problems. Their tools of investigation may differ; and their interpretational techniques may have little in common, but their basic research approach is identical. Both employ the tenets of the scientific method. Both begin with a researchable problem. Both hypothesize concerning it. Both collect data relevant to it. Both interpret the data and draw from that interpretation conclusions that support or nullify the hypotheses they have posited.

In its planning and design, research approaches all problems through certain methodological channels that are particularly appropriate to the nature and type of data that the investigation of the problem requires.

This being so, the researcher must differentiate critically between the terms *research design* or *planning*, and *research methodology*.

Research Planning vs. Research Methodology

Do not confuse research planning with research methodology, to be discussed in chapter 6. One often hears such statements as: Research in physics is *different from* research in philosophy or history. Such statements indicate that the speaker has not made a clear differentiation between *research as a process* and *the methodology employed* by separate academic disciplines in collecting and processing data within the framework of the research process.

Genuine research follows the broad outline of the scientific method. It also exhibits the seven basic characteristics outlined in chapter 1. Not every academic discipline finds it appropriate, however, to employ the same *methodology* in dealing with the data. This is because data vary so widely. You cannot deal with a blood cell in the same way that you deal with a historical fact, and the problem of finding the sources of Coleridge's "Kubla Khan" is entirely different from the problem of finding the sources of radio signals from extragalactic space. The *method* the one researcher employs is entirely different from that which the other researcher uses, because the data in the one situation are entirely different from the data in the other. You cannot investigate chromosomes with a questionnaire (yet).

In planning the research project, therefore, it is extremely important for the researcher not only to choose a viable research problem but also to consider the nature of the data that the investigation of such a problem will demand and the feasible means of collecting and interpreting those data. Many beginning researchers become so entranced with the glamour of the problem that they fail to consider the consequences the pursuit entails as to data availability, collection, and interpretation.

Comparing the brainwave patterns of gifted and normal children may be an engaging project for research, but unless you have subjects who are willing to cooperate in the study, an electroencephalograph at your command, the technical skill to use it, and the ability to interpret the resultant electroencephalographic tracings, and unless you have clearly determined how you will interpret the data and so organize your findings that you can draw conclusions from them, it probably is better that you give up this project in favor of one that you have the knowledge, the resources, and the skill to carry through to completion. Your research should be *practical* research, built upon precise and realistic *planning* and executed within the framework of a clearly conceived and feasible *design*.

Criteria for a Research Project. In planning your research project, certain features common to all true research should serve as guidelines. All research is ultimately tested by certain criteria that must, in fact, be built into the research design in the planning stage. Here, briefly, are those standards.

Universality. The research project should be such that it could be carried out by any competent person other than yourself. The researcher is merely a catalyst, little more than an agent whose function is to collect, organize, and report what the collected data seem to indicate. A surrogate, competent to carry out the research, might take your place and complete the project with essentially the same results without prejudice to the project or the validity of the research.

Replication. The research should be repeatable. Any other competent researcher should be able to take the problem and, collecting data under the same circumstances and within the identical parameters as you have observed, achieve results comparable to those you have secured.

Control. Parameters are important. All research is conducted within an area sealed off by given parametric limitations. By such control, we isolate those factors that are critical to the research. Control is important for replication. An experiment should be repeated under the identical conditions and in the identical way in which it was first carried out. It is also important for consistency within the research design. In certain areas control is more easily achieved than in others. In the physical sciences, for example, control of the experimental factors is possible to a very high degree. Such matters as constancy of temperature, pressure, electrical potential, humidity, and the like, are easily regulated and may be exactly replicated. Control is much less possible in research areas concerned with human data and existential variables.

Measurement. The data should be susceptible to measurement. This, again, is easily accomplished in the physical sciences. In humanistic and social research, it is much more difficult to quantify, measure, or evaluate the critical factors in the research design. The matter of measurement in these latter areas must rely many times upon comparative judgment (arranging factors in a hierarchy of importance), scaling, scoring (correct vs. incorrect responses to a given set of questions), and similar procedures. In the humanities and the social sciences, measurement can never be as precise and as accurate as in the natural and physical sciences.

Research Design. Nothing helps a research effort to be successful so much as planning the overall design carefully. You cannot begin too soon to consider the critical matters that we have been discussing. More research effort is wasted by going off half-prepared, with only a nebulous set of ideas and foggy perceptions, than in any other way. To bring all together, a careful early inventory of your resources, your problem, and the sources of the data may be highly desirable to save you time, money, and effort in getting oriented correctly from the beginning.

The Data: Their Nature and Role in Research

Data: Their Relationship to Both Design and Methodology

The scientific method is a viable approach to any problem only when there are *facts* to support it. Without facts, which within the research community are more properly called *data*, inductive reasoning vanishes and the scientific method collapses. Facts are the lifeblood of research. Let us, therefore, consider the nature of facts—first, from a philosophical standpoint, and then, from a more practical relation of their role in the research process. We begin with the word *data* and its essential meaning.

As stated earlier, the term *data* is plural. We have constantly been referring to data as "they" and "them." In syntactical usage, we employ the word with the plural form of the verb. The word *data* (singular *datum*) derives from the past participle of the Latin verb *dare*, meaning "to give." Data, therefore, are those facts that any particular situation affords or *gives* information, impressions, or other factual data to an observer. Think of data as synonymous with facts. We often refer to data by saying "these are the facts of the situation." In that sense, the plural form of the verb seems perfectly appropriate.

What Are Data? The English word *fact* also comes from the Latin. Its Latin origin is in the word *facere*, meaning "to make"—what the situation "makes" or manifests to the observer.

The etymology provides the first clue as to the nature of data: they are *manifestations* of the truth rather than the truth itself. No one has ever looked upon Truth itself—pure, undisguised, naked Truth. In that sense, data are merely representative, intermediate, elusive surrogates of Truth. Data reflect Truth as a mirror reflects sunlight. We are like those who live in a dungeon, across the floor of which a beam of sunlight passes. That light gives us an idea of what the sun must be like, but if we are never to behold the sun, we shall never know the difference between it and the shaft of light upon the dungeon floor.

The researcher is in a factual dungeon. He will never be able to see the *source* of the data. We glibly talk of populations made up of individuals. But the *individual*—the person "inside"—we shall never know!

Research seeks, through data, to discover what is true absolutely. In a sense, research is a constant pursuit after the complete meaning of the data. Experienced researchers are constantly aware that what they most ardently seek as the ultimate goal of research (Truth) is forever just beyond what is represented by the data and, hence, just beyond human grasp.

The scientist probing the nature of subatomic matter is always conscious of an elusive sub-, sub-, subentity that, like the will-o'-the-wisp, beckons but at the same time evades the researcher. The mind yearns to understand the Ultimate. As a means of access to that goal, we have chosen the pathway of research. But it always ends at the farthest reaches of the data, which are at the brink of the canyon in whose depths lies the inaccessible Ultimate Truth.

What we have been saying about data and their relation to Ultimate Truth may be best represented by Figure 5.3, which depicts the data in their various states.

A careful inspection of the diagram reveals certain important facts concerning the nature of data. Lying farthest away—and, hence, most inaccessible—is the Realm of Ultimate Truth. It can be approached by the researcher only by means of passing through two intermediate areas that we have labeled The Realm of the Data.

Data Are Ephemeral and Ever-changing. Whenever we look at data intently and earnestly, we gain new insight; but at the same time we also discern new problems that demand still further research. Like the asymptotic curve, the researcher approaches but never quite meets the straight line of the Ultimate Quest.

Data are not only elusive, but also ephemeral. Facts that the researcher is permitted to glimpse exist for only a split second. Consider some realistic research situations. A sociologist is interested in studying conditions within a certain city and among a given population. Social workers plan to make a survey. They start at a given point in the hope of eliciting opinions and

Figure 5.3 The Relation between Data and Truth

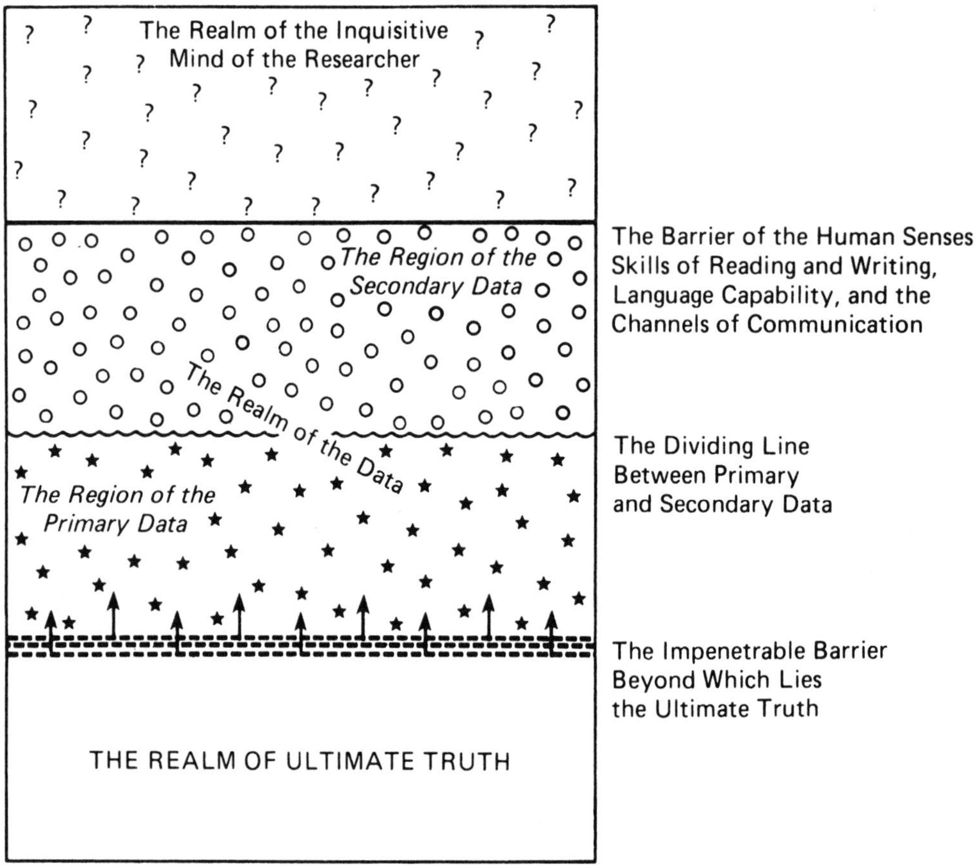

reactions from that population. As they contact family after family, they garner facts and opinions concerning certain matters. Hardly have they surveyed the people of one city block before the data collected are out-of-date. Some people who indicated they held one opinion have now changed their minds and entertain an entirely different opinion. They have seen a television program or heard a discussion that has changed. Some people have moved out; others, moved in; some people have died, others have been born. Tomorrow, next week, next year—what we thought we had "discovered" may have changed completely.

The teacher who presumes to pretest, teach, and posttest the same class may not be testing the same class at all. The individuals in that class may be different at posttest than they were at pretest six weeks earlier. They have been growing, learning, maturing, changing. The pretest-posttest technique seldom takes into account developmental and maturational factors, which bias the data.

We plan an attitude survey. It involves asking people about their interests. It sounds fine, but can we be sure that what they tell us is true? They may answer our questions honestly and represent the truth as they perceive it at that instant. But their interests may be imperceptibly changing because of many factors: age, maturity, a newscast, an item in a newspaper.

Data are, therefore, extremely ephemeral. We catch merely a fleeting glance of what *seems* to be true about the opinions and reactions of people in a city block, about achievement of students after a teaching experiment, about the attitudes of a given population.

Researchers should recognize, therefore, that even the most reliable, most refined, most carefully controlled data may have a very elusive quality about them, and that tomorrow or next week or next year they may, in fact, have no counterpart in reality whatsoever. Data are volatile; they evaporate quickly.

Earlier, we used the simile of the researcher as one who sits in a dungeon and attempts to behold the sun only by means of a shaft of sunlight that falls upon the floor. This represents the *primary data*. We may define primary data as *the data that lie closest to the source of the* Ultimate Truth underlying the *phenomenon*. Primary data reflect Truth more faithfully than any other approach to Truth. Note that in Figure 5.3, an impenetrable barrier exists between the Realm of Ultimate Truth and the region of the primary data. Through a shaft of sunlight, we can tell a great deal about the sun, but it does not compare to seeing the sun itself.

Consider the following incident: I see a car veer off the highway and careen into a ditch. I have witnessed the full occurrence. The driver can afterwards tell me that he had no awareness of the possibility of an accident until the car went out of control. Neither of us will ever be able to fathom the ultimate truth underlying the accident. Did the driver have a momentary seizure of which even he was unaware? Did the mechanism have an imperfection that the accident itself obliterated? Were there other factors that neither of us noticed? The answers lie beyond an impenetrable barrier. The ultimate truth for the cause of the accident may never be known.

The researcher's only perceptions of truth are the layers of various density of truth-revealing fact. The data that lie in juxtaposition to the Truth are most valid, the most illuminating, the most Truth-manifesting. These data are *primary* in the sense that they lie closest to the truth.

Not all data are primary. Beyond the region of the primary data lies the region of the *secondary data*. Think of the two examples we have just used. The researcher in the dungeon sees the sunlight not as a direct beam but as a shimmering light on the wall. It has fallen as primary data upon a mirror and then been reflected—distorted by the imperfections within the mirror—to an image like yet unlike the original shaft of light.

I am a newspaper reporter. I write an account stating precisely what I have observed of the automobile accident. My account is confirmed by the driver of the car. But when my brother reads the account in the paper next morning, he gets, as it were, the sunlight-reflection-upon-the-wall version of the event. The data are of necessity distorted—albeit ever so little—by the channels of communication through which they must pass. My writing skills, my brother's reading skills, and the inability of language to reproduce every nuance of detail that a firsthand observation can provide, all distort, however slightly, what I actually observed.

Another feature of the schematic representation that we have not mentioned is the importance of barriers. In actuality there are, of course, many more of these than we have here represented: the acuity of the human senses, the sensitivity of instrumentation, the failure of language to communicate thought *exactly*, the inability of two human beings to witness the same event and to report it *precisely* as duplicate accounts. The barriers in the research process are legion.

The precise researcher will never forget the overall idea behind Figure 5.3. Recalling it may prevent the researcher from making exaggerated statements or drawing unwarranted conclusions. The remembrance of the philosophical status quo of the several "realms" within the research process reminds the researcher, even in the most exuberant moment of discovery, that no one has ever glimpsed Ultimate Truth, nor can we come to a knowledge of the data that reflect that Truth except through the gross and shadowy channels of our dull and imperfect senses. Such a humiliating awareness helps the researcher to be cautious and adds new respect for such words in the reporting of research findings as *perhaps, it seems, one might conclude,* and *it would appear to be.*

The true researcher is cautious because such a person is wise enough to know that no one can ever be sure that what is beheld is, indeed, even a verisimilitude of what is *actually* the Truth.

Frank Besag, in an article entitled "Striving After the Wind: The Metaphysics and Epistemology of Educational Research," gives an interesting recasting of these thoughts.[2] Here is a brief excerpt.

What Is Perceived and What Is Real?

Educational reality must exist, but where is it and what is it? Certainly, our research attempts to describe an educational reality (our systematic perception of the reality). But just as certainly, our descriptions of the real thing are our perceptions of it and not the same as the thing itself. Therefore, our educational research must be different from educational reality. When we count the number of children in a classroom, we have only the count, not the children, and certainly not the classroom. Even if we exhaustively describe the children and their classroom, we still have only the description of our perceptions and not the children or the classroom. Research is an attempt to describe the reality. It is not reality itself.

What Exists and What Is Real?

The problem of the difference between what we observe is further compounded when we consider the difference between something that is real and something that exists. For example, the color red exists in that we can sense (in this case, see) it. Any object that can be sensed—that is, can be apprehended by our senses—can be said to exist.

Although the color red can be sensed, it cannot be clearly defined. No color can be defined in terms of other colors. A color-blind person will never be able to understand the concept of "red." Describing the wavelength of light occupied by the color red does not improve the situation because the color-blind person still cannot "see" red and therefore is no better able to understand what red is. Philosophers say that for an object to be considered real, it must be amenable to definition.

The color red cannot be defined and therefore is not considered to be real. However, it does certainly exist. Under these circumstances, we can say that red exists, but is not real.

Numbers have the opposite problem. We can describe the number 3 with great detail. We can describe the number 3.00 (a real number) with even greater precision. So long as we use some consistent number system (such as base 10), we can say that the real number 3.00 falls between 2.99 and 3.01. If we wished for greater precision, we could define the number 3.0000 and say that it falls between 2.99999 and 3.00001. We can also say that 3.00 when multiplied by 2.00 (another arbitrary defined number, which falls between 1.99 and 2.01) the product will be 6.00, which in turn falls between 5.99 and 6.01.

The number 3.00 is real in that we can clearly define it. However it does not exist. No one can see or hold on to or in any other way sense the number 3.00. We can sense 3.00 objects, but we cannot see or hold on to the number itself.

Lest this discussion be esoteric, we should remember that many of the objects that we study in educational research are real and do not exist, or exist and are not real. For example, unless we are willing to define intelligence operationally as the score on a test, which is a philosophically inadequate definition, we cannot currently define intelligence. Therefore, intelligence is not real. However, it certainly exists. We can see it in children (like the color red) but we cannot define it. We can also say that we like it and that some children are more intelligent than others, just as we can say that we like some reds better than others and that some reds seem redder than others. Further, just as a color-blind person cannot see red, so a person who is not sufficiently intelligent will not be able to recognize intelligence in others.

This leaves us in a difficult position because there are a whole host of subjects in education that are not clearly definable (are not real) but that do exist and that we feel obliged to study; to name just a few—intelligence, motivation, creativity, spunk, and leadership.

On the other hand, there are a number of subjects that are real (they can be clearly defined), but that do not exist because they cannot be sensed in the usual sense; for example, self-discipline and learning.

[2] Frank Besag, "Striving After the Wind: The Metaphysics and Epistemology of Educational Research," *American Behavioral Scientist* 30 (September–October 1986): 15–22. This is one of a series of papers in this issue of the journal, all of which are provocative commentaries on the material presented in this chapter. Reprinted by permission of Sage Publications.

Practical Application

Thus far we have been discussing the nature and the philosophy of data and the role that they play in the research process. At this juncture, therefore, it is important that you learn to think like a researcher with respect to data and their meaning, for researchers regard data differently than do most people. They look at the facts with which they are confronted more open-mindedly, more comprehensively, and they are more careful in drawing unilateral conclusions from the data that they do consider.

Understanding the Nature of the Data

We have been discussing the care with which a researcher regards data. A study of Figure 5.3 suggests many alternatives to a unilateral interpretation of any quantum of data.

Let us take a specific instance:

A woman screams

Now, with the philosophical structural diagram of the research process, let us fit the happening (the data) into the research structure (Figure 5.4).

Perhaps it should be pointed out that the last column contains only *one* deduction that the observer has made. It could be that this deduction is entirely wrong. The woman may have screamed in surprise; she may have screamed in delight, or in laughter. We cannot be sure merely by *hearing* a woman scream—without other confirmatory data—that she indeed had screamed in fright.

The following is a list of data-bearing situations. Using the skeleton table given in Figure 5.5, try to consider each of these situations in terms of its possible interpretation.

A low moan.
A fireball in the night sky.
The smell of acrid smoke.
A man collapsed on the sidewalk.
The wailing of a siren.

Figure 5.4

Absolute Truth of the Situation	*The Impenetrable Barrier*	Data Reaching the Observer	*First Barrier: Single Sensory Channel (Hearing)*	Channel of Perception	*Second Barrier: Limitations of Human Ear*	Limits (Barrier) of the Channel	*Third Barrier: Data Beyond Reach of the Observer*	Meta-* perceptual Data (Confirm-atory)	*Fourth Barrier: Human Reason and Deductions from Data*	Probable Meaning of the Perceived Data
?		Scream		Human ear (hearing)		Frequency limits of hearing. Human hearing can perceive only within certain limits.		Blood pressure rise. Muscular tension. Adrenalin content.		Fear motivated the scream

* Meta is a combining form from the Greek that means "beyond." Metaperceptual data, therefore, are those available data that are beyond the receptive and sensory channels available to the observer.

Figure 5.5

Data Reaching the Observer	Observer's Channel of Perception	Limits of the Channel	Metaperceptual Data*	Probable Meaning of the Situation	Other Conceivable Meanings

* Metaperceptual data are those data beyond the sensory mode through which the data reach the observer. They are confirmatory data that may assist in substantiating the probable meaning that the researcher deduces from the available data.

A slight tremor of the house.
A distinctly bright spot on the equator of a newly discovered planet.
All of the lights in a room go out.
A sudden flash in a dark area.
An automobile suddenly swerves off the road into a ditch.

Dr. Besag has discussed the metaphysical and philosophical aspects of data. Read again, if necessary, his discussions on "What is perceived and what is real" and "What exists and what is real." Then, copy and fill out the form shown in Figure 5.6.

Criteria for the Admissibility of Data

Not all data that come to the researcher's attention are acceptable for the researcher's use. Data can be defective. If they are, they may affect the validity of the researcher's conclusions.

The imperfections in the data stem from the imperfections and irregularities of nature. If researchers include in the mass of data those that are imperfect or irregular, they corrupt the

Figure 5.6

Type of Data	Does the Data Exist?	Is the Data Real?	Rationale for Your Choice
A rose in your garden			
The odor of a rose			
Chlorophyll in the rose leaves			
Beauty			
A book			
A word			
The meaning of a word			
Conversation			
Body language			
Personality			

entire corpus of the data. We then have no standard against which to measure any performance. For example, a researcher is trying to determine the effect of ultraviolet light on growing plants. But *ultraviolet* is a vague term. It may include any light radiation between 500 and 4,000 angstroms.

One of the axioms of research is that any research effort should be *replicable*; that is, it should be able to be repeated by any other researcher at any other time under *precisely the same conditions*. In order to regulate the precision of the conditions, therefore, certain criteria must be adopted, certain limits established, certain standards set up that all data must meet in order to be admitted for study.

By prescribing such criteria and insisting on standards, we can control the type of data admitted and regulate the conditions under which the research effort proceeds. Those data not meeting the criteria are excluded from the study. It is, of course, much easier to control data in the physical sciences where we can measure the data quantitatively, but such control is also possible in the humanities, the social sciences, and the performing arts. In these latter and "broader" disciplines, these criteria are usually established by definition, and admissible data must meet the definitive parameters.

To return to the agronomist studying the effect of ultraviolet rays on growing plants, we must narrow the parameters of the data so that they will fall within certain specified limits. The agronomist must define precisely what she or he means by ultraviolet light. Within what angstrom range will ultraviolet emission be acceptable? At what intensity? With what time duration? With plants at what distance from the source of emission? What precisely is meant by the phrase "ultraviolet effect on growing plants"? All plants? A certain genus? A specific species?

We hem the data in on all sides, place upon them the restriction of criterion after criterion so that we are able to isolate only those data that are acceptable for our use. The rest of the data are inadmissible. This is what we term the criteria for the admissibility of data.

When we standardize the data, admitting only those that comply with the criteria, we can more nearly control the research effort and conclude with greater certainty what appears to be true. In order, therefore, to ensure the integrity of the research, we must set forth *beforehand* precisely what standards the data must meet. These criteria must be set forth clearly in both the research proposal and the research report. Only in this way can we make the *consumer of the research* a party to the criteria, so that both the researcher and the consumer come to an intelligent understanding of what is being studied.

The Research Methodology

Up to this point in this chapter, we have discussed the *limitations* of the data, data as a communicating linkage between Ultimate Truth and the inquiring mind of the researcher, primary data and secondary data (those that are, respectively, nearer to and farther from the total truth), and data whose value depends on screening them for their admissibility. We are now ready to discuss the ways in which acceptable data may be processed and utilized so that what truth they hold may be extracted from them.

Data are like ore. They contain desirable aspects of the truth, but to extract from the facts their meaning, we employ certain approaches that are broadly termed among professionals *research methodology*. Research methodology is introduced in chapter 6. The following is intended to amplify that discussion.

It is particularly important to recognize the fact that data and methodology are inextricably interdependent. For that reason, the research methodology to be adopted for a particular problem must always recognize the nature of the data that will be amassed in the resolution of that problem. *Methodology is merely an operational framework within which the facts are placed so that their meaning may be seen more clearly.* A review of any standard research textbooks will reveal a broad spectrum of methodological terminology. In practice, however, these many methodologies resolve into only four approaches by which data may be processed.

Let us take one last look at data from a global viewpoint. Actually, data are of two types only: writings and observations. We shall discuss these two main categories under four subcategories:

1. *Observations for whose transmission description is the best vehicle.* These are observations that a researcher makes directly at the scene of occurrence and then relays as facts (commonly called *descriptive survey* or *normative survey* data).
2. *Written records and accounts* of past happenings and events (commonly called *historical* data); literary productions (commonly known as *literary* or *critical* data).
3. *Observations that are quantified and exist in the form of numerical concepts.* These data are expressed in the language of mathematics and must, consequently, be evaluated and interpreted by means of appropriate mathematical or statistical procedures. (Such data are commonly called *analytical survey* or *statistical* data.)
4. *Observations of certain differences and likenesses that arise from comparison or contrast of one set of observations with another set of similar observations.* Generally, these two sets of data have been derived from observations under differing conditions or effected at subsequent time modules. (These data are usually referred to as *experimental* data.)

These four kinds of data demand four discrete and different research approaches, or *methodologies.* It is impossible, for example, to apply a methodology to data that are inappropriate to the demands of that particular method. Historical data, for example, are facts gleaned from written records. There is no possible way that you can take historical writings or literary writings and extract from them any meaning by using experimental methodology. The method is simply not suited to the nature of the data.

The above discussion suggests a basic rule: *The data dictate the research methodology.* Since there are four kinds of data, it is difficult to defend the position that unless research fits an arbitrary prejudice for a given methodology, it fails to be research. Such an attitude denies that we understand Coleridge's poetry better because of the scholarly research of John Livingston Lowes[3] or that we appreciate Western civilization more because of the historiography of Arnold Toynbee[4] because they have not unveiled their findings under the aegis of the experimental method or shown their conclusions by benefit of statistical analysis. No group of scholars has a monopoly upon any one highway that leads toward the enlargement of insight into the unknown. All highways are of equal excellence. Each, however, traverses a different terrain, though they all converge on the same destination: the enlargement of human knowledge, the discovery of new truth.

The four kinds of data demand four principal research approaches (methodologies) to deal with each type of data appropriately. These four research methodologies, in turn, are identified as either qualitative or quantitative, as discussed in chapter 6. For simplicity, we shall keep a one-to-one correspondence between the above categories of data and the methodology appropriate for each. Each methodology is discussed in a separate chapter to come in this text.

1. The *descriptive survey method* (qualitative; chapter 8), or, as it is sometimes called, the *normative survey method,* is appropriate for data derived from simple observational situations, whether these are actually physically observed or observed through benefit of questionnaire or poll techniques.

[3] John L. Lowes, *Road to Xanadu: A Study in the Ways of the Imagination,* rev. ed. (Boston: Houghton Mifflin, 1955).
[4] Arnold Toynbee, *A Study of History,* 12 vols. (London: Oxford University Press, Royal Institute of International Affairs, 1939–1961).

2. The *historical method* (qualitative; chapter 9) is appropriate for those data that are primarily documentary in nature or literary in form.
3. The *analytical survey method* (quantitative; chapter 10) is appropriate for data that are quantitative in nature and that need statistical assistance to extract their meaning.
4. The *experimental method* (quantitative; chapter 11) is appropriate for data derived from an experimental control situation or a pretest-posttest design in which two separate groups, or one group from which data are derived at two separate intervals, is involved. In the instance of two separate groups, one is conditioned by an extraneous variable while the other group is sealed off from the influence that affects the first group. Thus, the *control* or isolated group may be used as a yardstick against which to measure any change that has taken place in the *experimental* group, which has been subjected to the extraneous variable. In the pretest-posttest design, the same group is measured before and after exposure to an extraneous influence.

Each of these several methods has its discrete characteristics. Each, likewise, makes certain demands upon the data, so that the methodology must be able to reveal the meaning of the particular data with which it presumes to deal.

These broad methodological categories generally follow the innate characteristics of the several kinds of data with which the researcher works. Other writers have proposed different categories, the most common of which are given in Table 5.1.

Table 5.1 Methodology and Concomitant Research Goals

Method	Characteristics of the Method and the Research Goals the Method Attempts to Achieve
Action Research	The approach in action research is to do something to see if it works. Will playing videogames improve eye-hand coordination in typing? Method: Get a bank of computers, a group of typists; set up a training session. See if typing skills improve.
Case and Field Study Research	A type of descriptive research in which data are gathered directly from individuals (individual cases) or social or community groups in their natural environment for the purpose of studying interactions, attitudes, or characteristics of individuals or groups. Case study method: AIDS is a good example; case after case has been studied until continually recurring facts have suggested certain conclusions. Field study method: Social workers observe certain recurring features indigenous to given social groups. These observations lead to conclusions.
Correlational Research	A statistical investigation of the relationship between one factor and one or more other factors. Correlational research looks at surface relationships but does not necessarily probe for causal reasons underlying them. Example: An investigation of the degree of relationship between the college grade-point averages of freshmen and selected high school achievement and personality assessment scores.
Descriptive Survey or Normative Survey	This research method is fully discussed in chapter 8 of this text.
Analytical Survey	This quantitative methodology relies largely upon a statistical investigation of the data. Its prime aim is to determine how closely the data of the study approaches ideal data as established by the normal curve and whether the divergence, if any, is "significant" within certain prescribed statistical parameters. See chapter 10 for a full discussion.
Developmental	This is an observational-descriptive type of research that usually stretches over a period of time and is frequently called "the longitudinal study." The classic Gesell-Ilg studies in child development are excellent examples of this type of research. Trend studies and projections of future trends are sometimes considered as developmental research projects.

Table 5.1 continued

Method	Characteristics of the Method and the Research Goals the Method Attempts to Achieve
Ex Post Facto or Casual-Comparative	The ex post facto method is discussed in this text as a subtype of the experimental method (see chapter 11). The method observes existing conditions and searches back through the data for plausible causal factors. It is the "detective method," in which the crime is discovered and then the cause or motivation for the crime is sought.
Historical	The historical research method is fully discussed in chapter 9 of this text. It is the attempt to solve certain problems arising out of a historical context through gathering and examining relevant data.
Quasi-experimental	Quasi-experimental research designs are explained as a subsection of chapter 11 of this text.
True Experimental	This variety of research design is discussed in chapter 11 of this text.

Practical Application

Establishing Research Criteria

In this practical application you will continue writing your research proposal, for which you have developed the review of the related literature (see chapter 4). In writing proposals, we leave nothing unspecified. Here we explore how you will treat each subproblem in terms of its data, the criteria for the admission of those data into your study, and a justification of the methodology you propose to employ. In the form given in Figure 5.7 (a skeleton form and totally inadequate for your purpose; use it as an outline and extend it as needed) we suggest an approach to justify the methodology that you will employ. Do this:

1. Write your principal problem across the page over the two columns.
2. In the left-hand column, write the subproblem.
3. Immediately below the subproblem write a description of the data that you will need to resolve that subproblem.
4. In the right-hand column, write the criteria that you will establish for the admissibility of those data into your research design.
5. Be very specific. Avoid generalized statements.

Justifying the Research Methodology

Refer to the description in this chapter of the four methodologies appropriate to the four types of data. In this part of the project,

1. Describe the characteristics that the data in your research project will exhibit.
2. Indicate with those data that you have just described the methodology that would be most appropriate for the processing of such data. Justify your choice.

Estimating the Feasibility of a Research Project

Many beginning researchers avoid looking the practical problems of research straight in the eye. An exotic investigation, an appealing problem, a consummation-devoutly-to-be-wished-for project sometimes cause the researcher to fail to make an impartial judgment as to the practicability or impracticability of the project. The following Estimation

Figure 5.7

The Problem: (Write it as you stated it in chapter 3.)	
A Statement of each Subproblem together with a Description of those Data needed for its Solution. Subproblem 1: The Data needed for its Solution:	The Criteria which will govern the admissibility of the Data into the Research Design. Criterion 1: Criterion 2: Criterion 3:

Inventory (Figure 5.8) may help you to plan wisely and to accurately evaluate the feasibility of your research project.

To determine the feasibility of the research project you may be considering, study the estimation sheet, and fill it out completely. After you have finished, review it. Then answer this question: Is your study feasible? ( ) Yes ( ) No

If "No," state clearly wherein the unfeasibility of the project lies. Suggest avenues you may explore to resolve your problem or problems.

Research Design and Ethical Standards

Research Design

What is research design? It is planning. It is the visualization of the data and the problems associated with the employment of those data in the entire research project. Research design is the common sense and the clear thinking necessary for the management of the entire research endeavor—the complete strategy of attack upon the central research problem.

The researcher must have some structural concept, some idea of the manner in which the data will be secured and how they will be interpreted so that the principal problem under research will be resolved. All this must be conceived and formulated in the researcher's own mind before he or she begins to write the research proposal.

Research design is a matter of thinking, imagining, and thinking some more. As DeBakey and DeBakey advise, "Thinking through your project clearly and thoroughly before beginning

Figure 5.8 Estimation Sheet to Determine the Feasibility of the Research Project

The Problem

1. With what area(s)* will the problem deal?
   ____ People
   ____ Things
   ____ Records
   ____ Thoughts and Ideas
   ____ Dynamics or Energy

   *Conceivably the problem may involve more than one of these areas. A study of the philosophic viewpoints in the poetry of Robert Frost would deal with the area of people and the concomitant area of thoughts and ideas.

2. State the research problem clearly and in the form of a question:
   ____

3. Are data, which relate directly to the problem, available from one or more of the categories listed in item 1? ____ Yes ____ No

4. What academic discipline is primarily concerned with the problem? ____________________
   ____

5. What academic discipline or disciplines are related to the problem secondarily, or in ancillary relationship? ____________________
   ____

6. What special aptitude have you as a researcher for this problem?
   ____ Interest in the problem
   ____ Experience in the problem area
   ____ Education and/or training
   ____ Other: Specify ____________________

The Data

7. How available to you are the data? ____ Readily available ____ Available, with permission ____ Available with great difficulty or rarely available ____ Unavailable

8. How frequently do you personally contact the source of the data? ____ Once a day ____ Once a week ____ Once a month ____ Once a year ____ Never

9. Will the data arise directly out of the problem situation? ____ Yes ____ No
   If no, where or how will you secure the data? ____________________
   ____

10. How do you plan to gather the data? ____ Observation, ____ Questionnaire, ____ Tests or inventories, ____ Photographic copying of records, ____ Interview and tape recording, ____ Other, Explain: ____________________
    ____

11. Is special equipment or are special conditions necessary to gathering or processing the data? ____ Yes ____ No If "yes" specify: ____________________
    ____

12. If the answer to question 11 was "yes," have you access to such equipment and the skill to use it? ____ Yes ____ No If the answer is "no" how do you intend to overcome this difficulty? Explain: ____________________
    ____

Criterional Evaluation

13. Does your research project meet the criteria proposed in the chapter as applicable to all research?

Universality	____ Yes	____ No
Replication	____ Yes	____ No
Control	____ Yes	____ No
Measurement	____ Yes	____ No

14. As you review this estimation evaluation, are there any of the factors considered, or any other factors, which may hinder a successful completion of your research project? ____ Yes ____ No

to write a proposal is crucial."[5] Or, to take a definition from a research text in political science research methodology, "Research design is the strategy, the plan, and the structure of conducting a research project."[6]

A further definition may make the concept and the purpose of design in research methodology more understandable:

> The design is the plan for the study, providing the overall framework for collecting data. Once the problem has been concretely formulated, a design is developed in order to provide a format for the detailed steps in the study. The design is relatively specific consisting of a series of guidelines for systematic data gathering. The type of design depends upon the statement of the problem.[7]

Some writers seem to consider the design and the proposal synonymous. But they are, in fact, not the same. The design phase *precedes* the proposal phase, as DeBakey suggests:

> A frequent, and grievous, error among novices is to begin writing too soon. The result is a diffuse, rambling, confused proposal that lays bare the incertitude and chaotic thinking of the applicant. An obscurely defined, vaguely described, sloppily developed project is bound to suggest murky thinking and is likely to portend haphazard research. Before you write the first word of the proposal, make sure that the concept you plan to examine has some point of originality, that it is well defined in your own mind, and that it is worthy of support. To satisfy these three criteria, you must have a good grasp of current knowledge of the subject, which means that your preliminary bibliographic research must have been thorough. If you betray an ignorance of certain vital aspects of the subject, you will be judged poorly qualified to perform the study.
>
> First, write down on paper the *precise question* or problem you plan to study. Make sure it is based on a sound premise. Then, write the possible or *expected answer(s)* or solutions. Seeing these two ends of your research project on paper will fix the limits of your study firmly in mind. Next write the *title*. Make it accurate, clear, succinct, and provocative. . . . An informative title is indispensable; select key words carefully to highlight the essence of the subject.[8]

Basic to design, therefore, are four fundamental questions that must be resolved with respect to the data. If the researcher is to avoid serious trouble later on, these questions must be answered specifically, concretely, and without mental evasion or reservation. The forthright answers to these questions will bring any research planning and design into clear focus.

- *What are the data needed?* This question may seem like an oversimplification; but a visualization of the data, an appreciation of their nature, and a clear understanding of their treatment are fundamental to any research effort. Take a sheet of paper. Write down the answers to the following questions and to similar ones that demand resolution before the project can be seen in its global dimensions.

  To resolve the problem, what data are mandatory? What is their nature? Are they documentary? statistical? interview data? questionnaire replies? observations? experimental data, recorded before and after certain processes? Specifically, what data do you need, and what are their characteristics?

- *Where are the data located?* Those of us who have taught research methodology are constantly amazed at students who come up with perfectly fascinating problems for research projects. But then we ask a basic and obvious question, "Where will you get the data to resolve the

[5] Lois DeBakey and Selma DeBakey, "The Art of Persuasion: Logic and Language in Proposal Writing," *Grants Magazine* 1 (1978): 43–60.

[6] M. G. Kweit and R. W. Kweit, *Concepts and Methods for Political Analysis* (Englewood Cliffs, NJ: Prentice-Hall,1981), 357.

[7] Phyllis J. Verhonick and Catherine C. Seaman, *Research Methods for Undergraduate Students in Nursing* (New York: Appleton-Century-Crofts, 1978), 30.

[8] Lois DeBakey, "The Persuasive Proposal," *Journal of Technical Writing and Communication* 6 (1976): 8–9 (slight changes with permission of the author).

problem?" The student either looks bewildered and remains speechless or stutters out a confused remark, such as, "Well, they must be available *somewhere.*" Not *somewhere,* but *precisely where?* If you are doing a documentary study, where are the documents you need? Precisely *what library* and *what collection* do you need to use? What society or what organization has the files that you must see? Where are these organizations located? Specify geographically—by town, street address, and zip code! A nurse or a nutritionist is doing a research report on Walter Olin Atwater, who probably more than any other one individual is responsible for establishing the science of human nutrition in the United States. Where are the data on Atwater located? The researcher can go no further until that basic question is answered.

- *How will the data be secured?* To know where the data are is not enough; you need to know how they may be obtained. With invasion-of-privacy laws, protection of individual integrity, confidentiality agreements, and similar hindrances of access to personal data, securing the information you need may not be as easy as it may first appear. You may indeed know what data you need and where it is located; but an equally important question is, how will you get it? In designing a research project this question cannot be ignored. In the research proposal, the delineation of this matter may spell the difference between a viable research project and a pipe dream.
- *How will the data be interpreted?* This is perhaps the most important question of all. The three former hurdles have been overcome. You have the data in hand. Now, spell out *precisely* what you intend to do with the data to effect the solution of the research problem or subproblem.

At this point, go back and read very carefully the wording of the problem. How must you treat the data to resolve the problem? If you process the data as you propose, what will the result be? How do you propose to measure the data? (Read again "Measurement as a Tool of Research," in chapter 2.)

If you are proposing to test the null hypothesis, are the statistical procedures appropriate for the characteristics of the data? Are you proposing a statistical technique that requires interval or ratio data when the data you have are nominal or ordinal? Are you suggesting a parametric procedure for nonparametric data?

Probably no part of the design requires more detailed thinking and explicit planning than does this section. Analyze your procedure for interpreting the data by using the form shown in Figure 5.9.

Ethical Standards in Research

Within certain disciplines—education, the behavioral sciences, criminology, nursing and the medical sciences, and similar areas of study—the use of human subjects in research is common. This raises the question of ethical standards. The ethics involved in the use of human subjects in research projects should not go without careful scrutiny.

Many disciplines have their own codes of ethical standards with respect to involving human subjects. A listing of some of these codes will be found in the bibliography at the end of this chapter.

The principles of ethical propriety lying at the base of most of these guidelines resolve into simple considerations of fairness, honesty, openness of intent, disclosure of methods, the ends for which the research is executed, a respect for the integrity of the individual, the obligation of the researcher to guarantee unequivocally individual privacy, and an informed willingness on the part of the subject to participate voluntarily in the research activity.

Certainly no individual should be asked to cooperate in any research that may result in a sense of self-denigration, embarrassment, or a violation of ethical or moral standards or principles.

Every researcher should fulfill the commitments made to those who assist in the research endeavor. No research should ever be conducted under circumstances in which total disclosure of the aims and purposes of the research cannot be set forth—preferably in writing.

Figure 5.9 Research Design: Procedure for Interpreting the Data

1. Problem and/or subproblem to be resolved: ______________________________
____
____

2. Data to be employed in resolving the problem: ______________________________
____

3. What kind of data will you employ? ____ Documentary? If documentary, will you use ____ primary data, or ____ secondary data? If secondary data, justify your reason for not using primary sources: ______________________________
____

____ Survey? If survey, which of the following modes of data collection will you employ?
____ Interview ____ Questionnaire ____ Observation ____ Other
If other, explain: ______________________________
____

4. Will the data be processed statistically? ____ Yes ____ No If yes, what type of data, according to measurement, will they be?
____ Nominal ____ Ordinal ____ Interval ____ Ratio

5. What kind of statistical techniques do you plan to employ to interpret the data?*
____ Parametric ____ Nonparametric

6. Is the technique suited to the type of data? ____ Yes ____ No
If no, go back to item 4 to reevaluate your statistical approach.

7. What will you finally have as a result of the statistical technique you plan to use to process the data? ______________________________

8. Will this result resolve the problem? (Compare your answer to item 7 with the statement of the problem, or subproblem, in item 1 and mark the appropriate box.) ____ Yes ____ No
If no, what else needs to be done to resolve the problem? ______________________________
____

9. What criteria have you established to control the quality and limit the admissibility of the data? List the criteria. ______________________________
____
____

10. Does your research project meet all of the ethical standards outlined earlier in this chapter?
____ Yes ____ No

11. Are you still convinced that your research project is feasible and practical?
____ Yes ____ No If "yes," you are, then, ready to consider writing your proposal. If "no," you may then need to reedit the wording of the problem or select another problem entirely.

*The answers to some of these questions may be too advanced for you to respond to at this point in your study of the text. They are, however, pertinent to the research design of your research project.

Nor should any subject be inveigled into cooperating in any research endeavor without knowing fully what participation in the project will involve and what demands may be made upon that subject.

A Résumé of a Professional Code of Ethics. A résumé of the Code of Ethics of the American Sociological Association may be sufficient to indicate the ethical considerations that should govern activity associated with any research project.

1. Researchers must maintain scientific objectivity.
2. Researchers should recognize the limitations of their competence and not attempt to engage in research beyond such competence.

3. Every person is entitled to the right of privacy and dignity of treatment.
4. All research should avoid causing personal harm to subjects used in the research.
5. Confidential information provided by a research subject must be held in strict confidentiality by the researcher.
6. Research findings should be presented honestly, without distortion.
7. The researcher must not use the prerogative of a researcher to obtain information for other than professional purposes.
8. The researcher must acknowledge all assistance, collaboration of others, or sources from which information was borrowed from others.
9. The researcher must acknowledge financial support in the research report or any personal relationship of the researcher with the sponsor that may conceivably affect the research findings.
10. The researcher must not accept any favors, grants, or other means of assistance that would violate any of the ethical principles set forth in the above paragraphs.[9]

Any research endeavor that employs human subjects may raise questions of propriety, create misunderstandings, or ask subjects to go beyond demands consistent with pure research objectivity. A statement signed by the subject, indicating a willingness to cooperate in the research and acknowledging that the purpose and procedure of the research project have been explained, may well be a safeguard for both researcher and subject. Such a statement should contain a clause indicating that if, at any time during the research procedure, the individual should not wish to continue to be associated with the research effort, he or she shall have the right to withdraw. If this situation occurs, the subject should notify the researcher in a written memorandum, in which is set forth the specific reason or reasons for the decision to withdraw.

Ethical practice involves more than the specific area that we have just been discussing. It concerns the personal behavior of the researcher. Researchers are trustees of integrity and truth and, as such, need to be scrupulously aware of the ethics of their own conduct.

In writing a research report, the researcher must be sure that what purports to be the researcher's own work is *indeed* his or her *own* work. Those aspiring to a graduate degree who present a research document in partial fulfillment for the requirements of that degree should at least have fully mastered the common skills and abilities of written communication that are presumed to be part of educational achievement at the public school level. These are, of course, the ability to spell correctly, to write a grammatically correct and effective sentence, and to construct a unified and coherent paragraph. These skills are elemental components of education.

To ask others to check your spelling, correct your grammar, or "ghost" your document is not only unethical but academically dishonest. You are attempting to offer as your own work something that, presumably, you are incompetent to produce. Those who engage in such subterfuge are guilty of fraudulent misrepresentation of their abilities and educational competence.

Any appropriation of writing that belongs to another demands full acknowledgment. Otherwise, it constitutes plagiarism and documentary theft. Full documentation of all material belonging to another person is mandatory. To appropriate the thoughts, the ideas, or the words of another—even though you paraphrase the borrowed ideas in your own words—without acknowledgment is unethical and highly circumspect. Those who are honest will not hesitate to acknowledge their indebtedness to others.

The DeBakeys, writing on "Ethics and Etiquette in Biomedical Communication," summarize the matter succinctly:

> Like other forms of social behavior, ethics and etiquette in . . . communication change with time. Their basis, however, remains the same—honesty, integrity, humanity, courtesy, and consideration. Ethical codes thus depend more on what is morally proper than on what is legally enforceable.

[9] *American Sociological Association Footnotes* 10 (March 1982): 9–10.

The responsible author makes certain that what he publishes has a sound thesis, that his data are ethically obtainable and scientifically valid, that he writes his report himself, that he documents it properly, and that he makes it intelligible and readable. . . . For everyone involved in communication . . . the Golden Rule is a useful guide to [scholarly] ethics and etiquette.[10]

Significant and Influential Research

Astronomers frequently tell us that they have discovered a stellar phenomenon, that they have seen a new solar system being born. The process is dramatic and enlightening. But we need not go to the far reaches of the universe to discover research in progress that is equally exciting, revolutionary, and that, at each new report, debunks our former knowledge or discovers new, engaging fact.

One such area of ongoing activity is research on memory. Exciting developments in memory research promise to affect teaching and learning profoundly. Robert Sywlester, professor of education at the University of Oregon in Eugene, describes contemporary memory research in an article entitled, "Research on Memory: Major Discoveries, Major Educational Challenges."[11] The new research challenges our knowledge of the way the human brain remembers—or forgets—facts and important data. There are, in fact, two kinds of memory: declarative memory and procedural memory. In the first, the brain's hippocampus seems to be particularly influential; in the second, the cerebellum apparently plays a major role.

All of this presents new challenges to curriculum and learning situations. To explore further this aspect of developing research, see Norman Frederiksen, "Implications of Cognitive Theory for Instruction in Problem Solving," *Review of Educational Research* 54 (Fall 1984), pp. 363–407.

Research in memory is an exploding area of knowledge that will revolutionize many of our ideas in psychology, education, and medicine.

The Computer as a Tool of Research

Statistics Software

In chapter 4, we discussed word processing software. The companion area to that discussion is a parallel discussion of statistics software for the microcomputer. This is a developing area and, before this book is in print, other software than that discussed here probably will have been introduced. See reviews in current and recent issues of the computer magazines listed in chapter 2.

Until recently, students who wished to have access to sophisticated statistical procedures done by computers had to rely upon mainframe processing of the data. This was cumbersome, expensive, and time consuming; or, where mainframe access was available to students, required spending many hours in the computer center. Now that bottleneck has been eliminated. More and more statistical software is being introduced for the owner of the personal computer. And these packages are remarkably comprehensive and versatile.

In this section we shall discuss seven packages of statistical software for IBM and other DOS-compatible personal computers. Though statistical packages are becom-

[10] Lois DeBakey and Selma DeBakey, "Ethics and Etiquette in Biomedical Communication," *Perspectives in Biology and Medicine* 18 (Summer 1975): 538–39.
[11] See *Educational Leadership* 42 (April 1985): 69–75.

ing available for Apple Macintosh systems, such as JMP 2.0 from SAS Institute, the majority of educational statistical packages to date are designed to run on DOS-based systems. In discussing some of these programs, we shall lean rather heavily on "Special Report on Statistics Software," by Alan J. Fridlund, which appeared in *InfoWorld,* September 1, 1986, quoting directly as needed.

What, then, does one need to know to deal with a statistical package successfully? What do statistical packages do, and what are the requirements for success in using them?

All statistics packages perform two kinds of statistical analyses: descriptive and inferential. In addition, all statistics packages assume a working knowledge of basic descriptive statistics, the rules of statistical inference (including probability theory) and the major types of statistical procedures.

All the major statistical packages found on mainframe computers now are available in PC versions. These include *SPSS* (Statistical Package for the Social Sciences), *SAS* (Statistical Analysis System), and *BMDP* (Biomedical Data Programs). Several other statistical packages also can be purchased for use on desktop computers. (For a thorough review of the leading statistical packages, see Fridlund's article cited above.)

The available packages all perform the basic range of statistical operations, but they are not all alike. Major differences among these packages include:

Ease of learning and use
Amount of computer memory and disk capacity needed
Number of cases and variables that can be handled
Depiction of results in graphical as well as tabular form
Price

A critical feature that a would-be purchaser of a statistical program must take special care to investigate is *accuracy.* All of the major statistical packages are known to produce accurate results, but some of the lesser-known or newer programs may have "bugs" in them that produce inaccurate results. Anyone contemplating purchasing a statistical package must take care to purchase one that is known to produce accurate results.

The packages of statistics software that we shall inspect follow, with addresses of the companies issuing the software:

1. SYSTAT: Systat, Inc., 1800 Sherman Avenue, Evanston, IL 60201.
   InfoWorld assesses this system as offering "nearly every statistical procedure you'll need, marvelous flexibility, exemplary phone support, and extreme accuracy. For graphics, go elsewhere; but for sheer number-crunching power and analytical breadth, this is the one."
   Systat 3.0 for IBM PC's and compatibles and other MS-DOS machines comes on five double-sided diskettes. It requires only 1.5 megabytes on a hard disk. This leaves ample room for data and other programs. It does not require a numeric coprocessor but analyses are much faster with one. Requirements: PC- or MS-DOS 2.0 or later, 256K of RAM, two floppy disk drives.
2. MYSTAT: Systat, Inc., 1800 Sherman Avenue, Evanston, IL 60201.
   MYSTAT is a condensed version of SYSTAT. It is the personal version of the large package and runs on IBM and MS-DOS personal computers with as little as 256 bytes of memory, and two floppies or a hard disk. MYSTAT can handle up to 32,000 cases and 50 variables. It provides a full screen data editor and full algebraic transformations, as well as sorting and ranking of variables. MYSTAT can handle batch processing with ASCII SUBMIT files. It has a wide range of statistical capabilities.

The entire program functions under a single menu, with online help and an interactive tutorial to demonstrate its use. The user manual is included with the disk.

3. SPSS/PC+: SPSS, Inc., 444 North Michigan Avenue, Chicago, IL 60611.
SPSS/PC+ is an offspring of SPSS mainframe package, which was a statistical package for the social sciences and has been long known to mainframe users. The Special Report calls it "A major contender which provides many features, fast performance, a marvelous editor, a graphics package that works smoothly with Microsoft Chart and a publication-ready output module.

SPSS/PC+ is a large package. It consists of eleven double-sided diskettes. It makes rigorous demands of the hardware: at least a 20 megabyte hard disk. It has five to seven megabytes of programs. It has the best documentation on the market and a capable support staff."

4. Statgraphics: STSC, Inc. 2115 East Jefferson Street, Rockville, MD 20852.
The outstanding feature of Statgraphics is its graphics, which are a dazzling display and are enhanced with graphics hardware. The Special Report rates them as "the best statistical graphics that we have ever seen on a personal computer and they make exploratory data analysis a breeze." The program does have limited capabilities for storing and handling data.

Statgraphics is modest in its demands. It is supplied on four double-sided disks, which provides the researcher with a bewildering variety of statistical procedures. The requirements of the hardware are 384K of memory, (and MS-DOS 2.0 or later) and a graphics display adapter.

5. BMDPC: BMDPC Statistical Software, Inc., 1964 Westwood Boulevard, Suite 220, Los Angeles, CA 90025.

The requirements for BMDPC are intimidating: The complete package takes up about 5 megabytes on the hard disk and requires 640K RAM, plus a math coprocessor. It is not a preferred package for the PC, but it does include these analytical processes not generally found in other packages: bivariate spectral analysis, survival analysis, and nonlinear regression. *InfoWorld* Special Report summarizes the package as follows: "In many ways, BMDPC represents the worst kind of personal computer software. It is minimally interactive, has few user conveniences, does not exploit the computer's features and cannot be used with the common utilities like Sidekick. But for users of the mainframe version, this is as close to an exact copy—warts and all—as possible."

6. PC SAS: SAS Institute, Inc., Box 8000, SAS Circle, Cary, NC 27511.

PC SAS, like mainframe SAS, is complicated. It contains more commands than any other statistics program, and one could make a career out of understanding its capabilities. "It is the most difficult to learn of the five packages that were tested by the *InfoWorld* Report, and the publisher has done little to make the learning easier. We rate the ease of learning as poor."

In summarizing PC SAS the Special Report concludes: "PC SAS brings almost all the tremendous data-handling capacity of mainframe SAS to the IBM PC—but at a cost on performance. It is sluggish even on an AT."

7. PowerStat: Analytical Engineering Corporation, P. O. Box 9, Station P, Toronto, Ontario, Canada M552S6.

A newcomer to the field of statistical packages for the IBM PC is PowerStat. Those who have used it comment upon the ease of using it, the speed of the procedures, and the excellent analysis of variance routines. Among other functions, it is capable of handling basic statistics, regression, analysis of variance, cross tabulation, and multivariate analysis. It consists of four diskettes and an easily understood manual. Its requirements are IBM PC/XT/AT or true compatible, 256 RAM, two DSDD drives or one DSDD drive and a hard disk, and DOS 2.0 or later. The system takes less than two megabytes on the hard drive.

Further details on all of these statistical packages for the microcomputer can be secured by contacting the developers.

For Further Reading

Further Reading in the Scientific Method

Airaksinen, Timo. "Five Types of Knowledge." *American Philosophical Quarterly* 15 (October 1978): 263–74.

Fowler, William S. *The Development of Scientific Method.* New York: Pergamon, 1962.

Giere, Ronald H., and Richard S. Westfall, eds. *Foundations of Scientific Method: The Nineteenth Century.* Bloomington, IN: University of Indiana Press, 1973.

Goldstein, Martin, and Inge F. Goldstein. *How We Know: An Exploration of the Scientific Process.* New York: Plenum, 1978.

Lastrucci, Carlo L. *The Scientific Approach: Basic Principles of the Scientific Method.* Cambridge, MA: Schenkman, 1963.

Ritchie, Arthur D. *Scientific Method: An Inquiry Into the Character and Validity of Natural Laws.* Paterson, NJ: Littlefield, Adams, 1960.

Rougement, D. Translated by R. S. Walker. "Information Is Not Knowledge." *Diogenes* 116 (Winter 1981): 1–17.

Wilson, Edgar B. *An Introduction to Scientific Research.* New York: McGraw-Hill, 1952.

The Design and Planning of Research

Campbell, D. T., and J. C. Stanley. *Experimental and Quasi-Experimental Designs for Research.* Chicago: Rand McNally, 1963.

Davitz, Joel R., and Lois J. Davitz. *A Guide for Evaluating Research Plans in Psychology and Education.* New York: Teachers College Press, Teachers College, Columbia University, 1967.

Ferber, Robert, Sidney Cohen, and David Luck. *The Design of Research Investigations.* Chicago: American Marketing Association, 1958.

Isaac, Stephen, and William B. Michael. *Handbook in Research and Evaluation.* San Diego, CA: Robert R. Knapp, 1971.

Kempthorne, Oscar. *The Design and Analysis of Experiments.* New York: Robert E. Krieger, 1973.

Kirk, R. E. *Experimental Design: Procedures for the Behavioral Sciences.* Belmont, CA: Wadsworth, 1968.

Lakatos, Imre. *The Methodology of Scientific Research Programmes.* Edited by John Worrall and Greg Currie. New York: Cambridge University Press, 1977.

Manten, A. A., and T. Temman, eds. *Information Policy and Scientific Research.* New York: Elsevier, 1983.

Meinbach, Anita M., and Liz C. Rothlein. *Unlocking the Secrets of Research.* Glenview, IL: Scott, Foresman, 1986.

Miller, Delbert C. *Handbook of Research Design and Social Measurement.* 3d ed. New York: David McKay, 1977.

Myers, Lawrence S., and Neal E. Gossen. *Behavioral Research: Theory, Procedure, and Design.* San Francisco: W. H. Freeman, 1974.

Pope, Maureen, and Pam Denicolo. "Intuitive Theories—a Researcher's Dilemma: Some Practical Methodological Implications." *British Educational Research Journal* 12 (1986): 153–56.

"Research Methodology: Behavioral Sciences" in *The International Encyclopedia of Education.* Torsten Husen and T. Neville Postwhaite, eds. Oxford, England: Pergamon, 1985.

Stroud, J. G. "Research Methodology Used in School Library Dissertations." *School Library Media Quarterly* 10 (Winter 1982): 124–34.

The Importance of Ethical Standards in Research

Beauchamp, Tom L., Ruth R. Faden, R. Jay Wallace, Jr., and LeRoy Wallace. *Ethical Issues in Social Science Research.* Baltimore: Johns Hopkins University Press, 1982.

Cassell, Joan, and Murray L. Wax. "Toward a Moral Science of Human Beings." *Social Problems* 27 (February 1980): 259–64.

Davis, A. J. "Ethical Issues in Nursing Research." A series of articles appearing in the *Western Journal of Nursing Research* 7 (February 1985): 125–26; 7 (May 1985): 249–50; 7 (August 1985): 377–79; 8 (February 1986): 100–102.

DeBakey, Lois, and Selma DeBakey. "Ethics and Etiquette in Biomedical Communication." *Perspectives in Biology and Medicine* 18 (Summer 1975): 522–40.

DeBakey, Lois. "Honesty in Authorship." *Surgery* 75 (May 1974): 802–4.

———. "Rewriting and the By Line: Is the Author the Writer?" *Surgery* 74 (January 1974): 38–48.

Freund, Paul A. *Experimentation with Human Subjects.* New York: George Braziller, 1970.

Hoffman, R. "Scientific Research and Moral Rectitude." *Philosophy* 50 (October 1975): 475–77.

Kelman, H. "Human Use of Human Subjects: The Problem of Deception in Social Experiments." *Psychological Bulletin* 67 (January 1967): 1–11.

———. *A Time to Speak Out: On Human Values and Social Research.* San Francisco: Jossey-Bass, 1968.

Schuler, Heinz. *Ethical Problems in Psychological Research.* Translated by Margaret S. Woodruff and Robert P. Wicklund. London: Academic Press, 1982.

Sjoberg, Gideon, ed. *Ethics, Politics and Social Research.* Cambridge, MA: Schenkman, 1967.

Smith, Harmon L. "Ethical Considerations in Research Involving Human Subjects." *Social Science and Medicine* 14 (October 1980): 453–58.

Codes of Ethics of Various Professional Organizations

American Association for Public Opinion Research. *Code of Professional Ethics and Practices of the American Association for Public Opinion Research* (A.A.P.O.R.). 420 Lexington Avenue, Suite 1733, New York, NY 10017.

American Nurses Association. "The Nurse in Research: Guidelines on Ethical Values." *Nursing Research* 17 (1968): 104.

American Psychological Association. "Ethical Principles of Psychologists." *American Psychologist* 36 (June 1981): 633–38.

American Political Science Association. Committee on Professional Standards and Responsibilities. "Ethical Problems of Academic Political Science." *Political Science* 1 (1968): 3–29.

American Sociological Association. *Revised American Sociological Association Code of Ethics.* Washington, DC: American Sociological Association, 1989.

Code of Federal Regulations. Title 45, Public Welfare, Department of Health and Human Services, Part 46: "Protection of Human Subjects." Revised as of January 26, 1981.

Office of Science and Technology, Executive Office of the President of the United States. *Privacy and Behavioral Research.* Washington, DC: U.S. Government Printing Office, 1967.

CHAPTER 6

Research Methodology: Qualitative or Quantitative?

The dogmas of the quiet past sleep quietly beneath the turbulence of the present;
And those who bestir that turbulence: The thinkers of today,
the pioneers of tomorrow create new methodologies that affect us all.

What's In A Name?

A *method* is, very simply, a way of accomplishing an end result. It is how one operates, a way to get the job done. So far, in those two sentences one word has occurred twice. Were you aware of it and, particularly, of its importance? That word is the key to the meaning of method.

Method is a word coined of two Greek elements: *meth-* and *odos*. The *meth-* is an element meaning "after." *Odos* means "way." A method is, therefore, a following *after the way* that someone found to be effective in solving a problem, of reaching an objective, in getting a job done.

Recall a teacher you have known whose inimitable way of presenting subject matter has fixed that educational experience irrevocably in your mind. What you remember is the *way* that teacher taught you: the method and the fact.

Consider Aristotle, his pupils around him, walking with them in the *peripatos* of the Lyceum, imparting his thoughts on physics, on biology, on politics, on ethics, on poetry, and even on the Soul. They took notes on the thoughts of this most unusual teacher who taught them in a most unusual *way*: by the peripatetic method.

So much for method. Now what about the *-ology*? That, too, is Greek. It means "the study of." Hence, *methodology* is merely the study of a particular method, or methods, for reaching a desired end.

Research methodology is a continuing process. It is a continuum that is ever changing, ever developing, and this aspect of research methodology has disturbed some.

To Each One's Own

We should not be disturbed, however, that the methodology of research is in continual ferment. Anyone who follows the literature is aware of this turmoil. It is the restlessness that is characteristic of youth. It is also the restlessness that accompanies the seeking of new worlds of knowledge and more effective ways to deal with the problems of the present, whether of greater (understanding the universe) or lesser magnitude (how do individuals learn?). The academic disciplines whose roots are in the trivium or the quadrivium of medieval education are, perhaps, less vulnerable to methodological turbulence. Compared to these, research, and its methodology, is a relative newcomer to the epistomological hierarchy. Even today it is scarcely beyond its unstable adolescence. In the long history of the human quest for knowledge, the short span from the last quarter of the nineteenth century to the threshold of the twentieth is a miniscule period for the development of any system whose purpose is to solve human problems and enlarge human knowledge.

Modern research probably began as an outgrowth of the empirical methods in psychology promoted by Wilhelm Wundt (1832–1920) in the last quarter of the nineteenth century. Wundt's method of investigation was experimentalism, an early form of research. In 1879, in Leipzig, Wilhelm Wundt instituted the first laboratory for the systematic *experimental* study of experience and the mental processes.

Up to that time knowledge of the human mind and mental behavior was discussed under such labels as mental philosophy, metaphysics, and rational philosophy. The approach was didactic. The concepts were figments of the imagination.

Wundt turned this whole conceptual process around and made the study of psychology an inductive process subject to the scientific method, and in so doing founded the study of mental behavior known as *experimental* psychology. No more was the manic-depressive syndrome attributed to a "disturbance of the soul, a matter of melancholia—black bile," a remnant explanation that invoked the theory of the humors of medieval medicine—or a "fever in the brain." These causes had no foundation in fact and were phantoms of the imagination.

The epistomological revolution spearheaded by Wundt and given momentum by his students was enormous. Such names as Titchner, Cattell, and Thorndike, among others, planted the seeds and nourished the growth of empirical research in American higher education.[1] Hence, the introduction of research as an academic discipline was initially under the aegis of psychologists and educators. But research did not long remain a monopoly of those two areas. Scholars in other disciplines soon adopted the research methodology for the resolution of problems and the enlargement of knowledge in their own areas. Adaptation demanded in many instances a reevaluation of the investigative and methodological goals of the discipline. Seismic tremors soon were felt throughout academia as each discipline began to adapt basic research methodology to its own specific needs.

For example, Lewis Robert Binford jolted archeological research by introducing a new direction to archeological investigation. The older research in archeology was merely concerned with reconstructing the past out of the available clues and artifacts. The "new archeology," introduced by Binford and others, argued that archeological research should be directed not only at reconstructing the past but also at determining the processes responsible for that past thereby injecting a causal factor into the methodology.[2]

In the same decade that Binford was introducing a new research emphasis in archeological research, a major change was taking place in the methodology of geographic research. It was prompted by the desire to make geography more acceptable as an advanced academic discipline and was characterized by an attempt to study the factors, not only with the features of the earth but also with those that control the spacial organization of the human species. This new emphasis in geographic research was known as locational, or spatial, analysis. The new methodology led to the adoption of statistical methods as a major research technique.[3] Statistically constructed models have become the new tools that geographical researchers are adapting to predict future trends, or spatial patterns, in the world of tomorrow.

[1] Edward Bradford Titchener (1867–1927) headed the new psychological laboratory at Cornell University where he was *research* professor, probably the first in the history of American higher education to hold that title. James McKeen Cattell (1860–1944) was among the first American psychologists to introduce the *methods* of psychological experimentation to the American campus. Edward Lee Thorndike (1874–1949), from 1922 served as Director of the Division of Psychology at Columbia University, in the Institute of Educational Research. His principal contributions to research were in the areas of measurement of intelligence and in learning ability.

[2] See Binford, Lewis R., et al., eds., *New Perspectives in Archeology* (1968) and Binford, L. R., *In Pursuit of the Past (1983)*.

[3] This is not to imply that statistics was a new aspect of geographical research. The science of statistics had been used by Torsten Hagerstrand in Sweden and Walter Christaller in Germany as early as the 1930s, but the influence of statistics in affecting research methodology in geography was given a new impetus in the 1960s.

In biological research, a major advancement was introduced with the technique of tissue culture. Tissue culture methodology has let researchers study specific cells and their interactions, which has greatly facilitated the study of cancer cells, the isolation of specific viruses, and the production of viral vaccines and hormones, and has aided in identifying genetic defects, in classifying malignant tumors, and in determining tissue compatibility for organ transplants. Like a mushroom cloud, research has unfolded new methodologies in every academic discipline with startling rapidity.

The Data Controls The Methodology: Qualitative Or Quantitative

All research methodology rests upon a bedrock axiom: *The nature of the data and the problem for research dictate the research methodology.*

All data, all factual information, all human knowledge must ultimately reach the researcher either as words or numbers. This may not sound true, but it is, and it is such a common phenomenon that we seldom notice it. Take this example: I am interested in aerobics, but I do not know how strenuously to exercise. I pick up a medical guide with a chapter on "The Healthy Body" and a subsection of that chapter entitled, "The Essentials of a Good Exercise Program." Here is the first directive I encounter. It tells me exactly what I want to know.

> Have at least 3, and possibly more, exercise sessions every week, preferably at regular intervals and stated times. Make each session 20 minutes or longer, with little or no pause for rest.[4]

I have the *data* I need. But in what form? Binary: 30 *words* and 2 *numerals*: *3* and *20*. It is a tacit acceptance of this fact that forces us, as researchers, to consider for research purposes *basically* a binary methodology.

The nature of the data dictates the methodology. If the data is verbal, the methodology is *qualitative*; if it is numerical, the methodology is *quantitative*. There is, of course, an alternative to this strict dichotomy. It consists of a hybrid variation, discussed in the literature under the designation of *triangulation*.[5] All research methodologies can be classified under one of these categories.

Qualitative Research Methodology

Earlier we commented on the adolescent turbulence characterizing the thought and literature of modern research. Fads, new ideas, contemporary emphases come and go. One decade has its methodological emphasis and that wanes while another arises. To read the literature of qualitative research is to be besieged by conflicting and contrary currents of thought. We must remember that the rise of the qualitative emphasis in research methodology is recent: it did not ascend to prominence in the professional literature until the 1960s. That may account for some of the obfuscation and diversity of interpretation that one meets in the literature.

I did my research and wrote my dissertation in the late 1950s.[6] It was pure qualitative research, but I never referred to it as such. At the time, I never heard the term mentioned from any member of my doctoral committee or in any of my research seminars. In the idiom of that decade it did not exist. So quickly do academic fashions change.

In another sense, nothing is new about qualitative research.[7] Qualitative research has always been a viable mode of investigation, but has not always been welcome in serious graduate

[4] *The American Medical Association Family Medical Guide*, edited by Jeffrey R. M. Kuntz and Asher J. Finkel, New York: Random House, 1987.

[5] See Mary E. Duffy, "Methodological Triangulation: A Vehicle for Merging Quantitative and Qualitative Research Methods," *IMAGE: Journal of Nursing Scholarship* 19 (November 1987): 130–33.

[6] Paul D. Leedy, "A History of the Origin and Development of Instruction in Reading Improvement at the College Level," Ph. D. dissertation, New York University, 1958. Ann Arbor, Michigan: University Microfilms, 1958.

[7] Mary E. Duffy, "Qualitative Research: An Approach Whose Time Has Come," *Nursing and Health Care* 7 (May 1986): 237–39.

research. It was overshadowed by the inordinate recognition given to quantitative research. From this emphasis arose the pronouncement in graduate academia: "If it's not experimental, empirical, or statistical, it's not research!"

Wilhelm Wundt and his emphasis on *experimental* psychology gained dominant influence through his students, who came to Leipzig to study with him and who subsequently taught others. And so, like a virus, the devotion to experimentalism spread throughout graduate academia, biased our thinking about the nature of basic research, and dictated its methodology.

Aftershocks Still Felt

Old ideas die hard. Ideas that have been deeply rooted as accepted *modus operandi* die even harder. Even to this day, some in the academic community look askance at any research that deviates from the experimental or quasi-experimental methodology.

New departures are frequently born among disarray, and need standards and guidelines. Thus has it been with qualitative research: professionals can seldom even agree on what qualitative research really is. One significant and thoughtful statement, by Nancy Burns, appeared in *Nursing Science Quarterly*.[8] In defining the elements of qualitative research, Burns leans heavily upon others who have attempted to formulate the same conditions.[9] Qualitative methodology should

1. be an alternative to the experimental method,
2. consider words as the elements of data,
3. be primarily an inductive approach to data analysis, and
4. result in theory development as an outcome of data analysis.

Another author defines qualitative research in terms of its demands:

> The qualitative research approach is both creative and scholarly. . . . [It] is frequently new to students, and they often become enthusiastic about its use. However, this approach should not be undertaken by students simply because it appears to be interesting, different, and does not require statistical analysis. It is a creative, scientific process that necessitates a great deal of time and critical thinking, as well as emotional and intellectual energy. One must have a true desire to discover meaning[10] develop understanding and explain phenomena in the most thorough way possible. . . . Qualitative research is not slovenly, undisciplined, "soft" research but creative scholarship at its best.[11]

This sets a rigorous agenda for the student who may be considering an alternative to empirical research and statistical analysis; this is perhaps even more true when we consider that quantitative researchers have the computer as a slave to do the statistical computation and to render yeoman's service in many other ways. A glance at the plethora of statistical software will soon change the concept that the modern quantitative researcher is still taking hours to do complicated calculations with pencil and paper.

On the other hand, those of us who write know that dealing with ideas and concepts and converting these to verbal form is quite as exhausting and intellectually demanding as any numerical computation. For this process no computer can achieve or approximate what is

[8] Nancy Burns, "Standards for Qualitative Research," *Nursing Science Quarterly*.

[9] A. K. Cobb and J. N. Hagemaster, "Ten Criteria for Evaluating Qualitative Research Proposals," *Journal of Nursing Education* 26 (1987): 138–43. J. Kirk and M. L. Miller, *Reliability and Validity in Qualitative Research* (Beverly Hills, CA: Sage, 1986); and R. R. Parse, A. B. Coyne, and M. J. Smith, *Nursing Research: Qualitative Methods* (Bowie, MD: Brady, 1985). All are cited in Burns (see note 8).

[10] See the discussion on meaning in chapter 1.

[11] Caria Mariano, "Qualitative Research: Instructional Strategies and Curricular Considerations," *Nursing and Health Care* 11 (September): 354–59.

the sole responsibility of the human brain, although one can certainly alleviate much of the drudgery.

Many students who have never been subjected to the intellectual rigor of thinking in terms of ideas and words, and their representation on paper, fail to comprehend the meaning of the last five words quoted above: "creative scholarship at its best." Creative scholarship at its *very best* is the ultimate criteria for the qualitative researcher, and to achieve it may well require nothing short of "sweat, blood, and tears!"

The task of the qualitative researcher is one of analysis *and* synthesis. Historical data, for example, is almost completely qualitative. History arrives localized, in bits and pieces—isolated events, dates, individuals. Synthesis is indispensable to research history; you must fit the pieces together to form a *meaningful* matrix. Read Toynbee.[12] He gathers analogous situations from many civilizations and national happenings from various periods in time, and from this disparate collection draws from the past the "meaning of history."

Say you are a sociologist or a social worker. The responses of the poor, the homeless, the distressed are telling you something. What is it? It may not be the glib panaceas to "the problems of society" that the "theorists" voice. It may not be as simple as the "specialists" portray it.

It may, in fact, reside in what the homeless tell you, in what the poor in their poverty plead for, what the disenfranchised say. Creative scholarship takes this potpourri of words—*these* are the data—and from them synthesizes the real problems underlying the condition of and causation for poverty. This is the *creative scholarship at its best* to which Mariano refers.

In *The Enlightened Eye,* Elliot Eisner outlines the "six features of a qualitative study."[13] I briefly outline them here.

1. Qualitative studies tend to be field focused. In education, those conducting qualitative research go out to schools, visit classrooms, and observe teachers.
2. Qualitative research [considers] the self as an instrument. The self is an instrument that engages the situation and makes sense of it. This is done most often without the aid of an observation schedule; it is not a matter of checking behaviors, but rather of perceiving their presence and interpreting their significance.
3. A third feature that makes the study qualitative is its interpretive character. Interpretive here has two meanings:
   (a) Inquirers try to account for what they have given an account of.
   (b) Qualitative inquirers aim beneath manifest behavior to the meaning events have for those who experience them.
4. Qualitative studies display the use of expressive language and the presence of voice in the text.
5. A fifth feature of qualitative studies is their attention to particulars.
6. A sixth feature of qualitative studies pertains to the criteria for judging their success. Qualitative research becomes believable because of its coherence, insight, and instrumental utility.

There is a danger that in presenting these three authors' definitions of the nature and character of qualitative research we may be forming a fundamentally erroneous concept of *both* qualitative *and* quantitative methodologies. At this point, you may be thinking in terms of exclusives: that they who practice the qualitative research must eschew quantitative research and vice versa.

Eisner corrects this misconception and sets the record straight:

[12]For example, see Arnold J. Toynbee, *A Study of History,* abridged ed. (New York: Oxford University Press, 1957). See especially vol. 2, pp. 4–10.
[13]Elliot W. Eisner, *The Enlightened Eye: Qualitative Inquiry and the Enhancement of Educational Practice* (New York: Macmillan, 1991) 32–40.

> The term *qualitative* suggests its opposite *quantitative* and implies that qualitative inquiry makes no use of quantification. This is not the case. For some aspects of education, quantification may be the most appropriate means for describing what one needs to say. *Qualitative* also implies that other forms of inquiry—the scientific experiment, for example—have nothing to do with qualities. Nothing could be further from the truth. All empirical phenomena are qualitative. The difference between "qualitative inquiry" and "quantitative research" pertains mainly to the forms of representation that are emphasized when presenting a body of work. The difference is not that one addresses qualities and the other does not.[14]

Qualitative and quantitative data may compatibly live in the same house; the terms refer more to a global atmosphere in which the researcher attempts to solve the basic problem for research, not to any exclusive method of operation.

Let Your Thoughts Be Clear; Your Words, Precise

Mariano has some solid advice for students in terms of writing skills and requirements that pertain especially to verbal presentation in qualitative research.

> Qualitative dissertations and theses are usually book-length narratives.[15] Students desiring to conduct qualitative research should have or develop an articulate and interesting writing style. Timely advisement by the dissertation/thesis committee regarding the need for effective writing skills can often alleviate arduous, frustrating, and nonproductive hours of writing for the student.[16]

In chapter 3, we stated that you must express your thoughts clearly and explicitly. This ability is absolutely required if you are expecting to do qualitative research. The academic areas for which the qualitative approach to the problem is perhaps the most logical methodology are anthropology, business, education, history, home economics, journalism, language and literature, minority studies, nursing, physical education, political science, social work, sociology, urban studies, and women's studies.

That is an impressive list, but not unrealistic. Those who fumble with words will have difficulty in articulating the qualitative research requirements in these subjects using the qualitative methodological approach.

We shall discuss the qualitative approach more fully in chapters 8 and 9, which discuss areas in which problems will likely require qualitative data: "The Historical Study" and "The Descriptive-Survey Study."

Quantitative Research Methodology

The qualitative research methodology might be considered a "warm" approach to the central problem of research. We consider it warm because in great part it is concerned with human beings: interpersonal relationships, personal values, meanings, beliefs, thoughts, and feelings.[17] The qualitative researcher attempts to attain rich, real, deep, and valid data and, from a rational standpoint, the approach is inductive.

As we have called the qualitative approach "warm," we might categorize the quantitative approach as "cold." It is impersonally experimental. The attitude of the quantitative researcher is an either/or attitude. Decisions are made with the coldness of a steel rule.

[14] Eisner, *The Enlightened Eye*, 5.

[15] Earlier, I described my dissertation as "pure qualitative research." The length of that study was 493 pages—7 pages short of one ream of paper!

[16] Mariano, "Qualitative Research," 358.

[17] Leah Ramer, "Quantitative Versus Qualitative Research?" *Journal of Obstetric, Gynecologic, and Neonatal Nursing*, 18 (January-February, 1989): 7–8.

Quantitative methodologies manipulate variables and control natural phenomena. They construct hypotheses and "test" them against the hard facts of reality. Of all quantitative hypotheses, the null hypothesis is perhaps the most often tested: "the researcher decides what factors or variables might cause certain results (cause and effect) and carries out tests to *either* support *or* reject the null hypothesis at some level of statistical probability.[18] The whole process is cold, calculating, deductive logic—from the positing of a hypothesis to the supporting or not supporting it.

We discussed the quantitative approach by inference in the first chapter of this book. Chapters 10 and 11 will be devoted to it as well. Methodologically, therefore, this book is a dichotomy, giving equal emphasis to both qualitative and quantitative methodologies: two chapters devoted to qualitative research methodology and an equal coverage to quantitative methodology.

Triangulation

The basic situation regarding the separateness of qualitative and quantitative methodologies is clearly stated by a quartet of authors in an article entitled, "Blending Qualitative and Quantitative Approaches to Instrument Development and Data Collection."[19] Their opening paragraph states the current attitudes:

> Debate continues over the relative merits and appropriate uses of qualitative and quantitative research. . . . Recently there has been a growing emphasis on combining approaches in single studies. Goodwin and Goodwin[20] concluded that "many studies could be enhanced considerably if a combined approach were taken." In a similar vein, Reichardt and Cook admonished readers that "it was time to stop building walls between methods and starting building bridges."
>
> Despite this recognition of the advantages of combining quantitative and qualitative methods in a single study, few guidelines exist for accomplishing this goal. Texts on research design and methods typically devote separate chapters to quantitative and qualitative methods, with little, if any, discussion of how to combine these approaches. Articles on combining approaches, or triangulation, discuss the potential gains of combining methods without addressing how to implement such an approach.

While the article is valuable in voicing the desirability of triangulation, its authors, too, give no specific guidelines as to implementation. That remains for Duffy to delineate:

1. Theoretical triangulation involves the use of several frames of reference or perspectives in the analysis of the same set of data.
2. Data triangulation attempts to gather observations through the use of a variety of sampling strategies to ensure that a theory is tested in more than one way.
3. Investigator triangulation is the use of multiple observers, coders, interviewers, and/or analysts in a particular study.
4. Methodological triangulation is the use of two or more methods of data collection procedures within a single study.[21]

Further guidance is offered by E. S. Mitchell, who notes that the application of methodological triangulation requires careful application of four principles:

[18] Ramer, "Quantitative Versus Qualitative Research?", 7.
[19] Kathleen A. Knafl, Marian W. Pettengill, Mary E. Bevis, and Karin T. Kirchoff, "Blending Qualitative and Quantitative Approaches to Instrument Development and Data Collection," *Journal of Professional Nursing* 4 (January–February 1988): 30–37.
[20] See "For Further Reading" at the end of this chapter for full reference to the documentation quoted in this paragraph.
[21] Duffy, "Methodological Triangulation," 131.

1. The research question must be clearly focused.
2. The strengths and weaknesses of each chosen method must complement each other.
3. The methods should be selected according to their relevance to the nature of the phenomenon being studied.
4. Continual evaluation of the methodological approach should be done during the course of the study to monitor whether the first three principles are being followed or not.

   It only through such continual vigilance that the researcher can keep track of the playing of each method off against the other so as to maximize the validity of the entire research endeavor.[22]

We close this discussion with a direct contrast between the qualitative and the quantitative methodologies, drawn by Stainback and Stainback (as cited in Duffy).[23]

1. *Outsider/insider perspective.* The quantitative researcher attempts to arrive at an understanding of facts from the outsider's perspective by maintaining a detached, objective view that, hypothetically, is free from all bias. In contrast the qualitative researcher focuses on the perspective of the insider, talking to and/or observing subjects who have experienced firsthand the activities or procedures under scrutiny. The qualitative researcher believes that firsthand experience provides the most meaningful data.
2. *Stable/dynamic reality.* The quantitative researcher focuses on the accumulation of facts and causes of behavior and believes that the facts gathered do not change. The qualitative researcher is concerned with the changing or dynamic nature of reality.
3. *Particularistic/holistic focus.* To gain control of the events under scrutiny, the quantitative researcher structures the situation by identifying and isolating specific variables for study and by employing specific measurement devices to collect information on these variables. In contrast, the qualitative researcher attempts to gain a complete or holistic view of what is being studied. To achieve this end, a wide array of data are needed: documents, records, photographs, observations, interviews, case histories and even quantitative data.
4. *Verification/discovery orientation.* The procedures employed by the quantitative researcher are usually highly structured and designed to verify or disprove predetermined hypotheses. To eliminate as much bias as possible, flexibility is kept to a minimum. In contrast, the research procedures used by the qualitative researcher are flexible, exploratory and discovery oriented. As the study progresses, the researcher can add to or change the types and sources of data gathered. This type of flexibility permits a deeper understanding of what is being investigated than can be achieved through a more rigid approach.
5. *Objective/subjective data.* The quantitative researcher focuses on the objective data that exist apart from the feelings and thoughts of individuals and is typically expressed in numbers. On the other hand, the qualitative researcher focuses on subjective data that exist within the minds of individuals and is typically expressed or reported through language. The qualitative researcher believes that it is essential to understand the meaning that persons attach to events in their environment.
6. *Controlled/naturalistic conditions.* Usually quantitative data are collected under controlled conditions in order to rule out the possibility that variables other than the ones under study could account for the relationships among the variables. In contrast, qualitative data are collected within the context of their natural occurrence. This permits any variables that naturally influence the data to operate without interference.
7. *Reliable/valid results.* Both the quantitative and the qualitative researchers want reliable and valid results. The quantitative researcher focuses heavily on reliability—data that are consistent or stable as indicated by the researcher's ability to replicate the findings. The qualitative researcher tends to concentrate on validity—data that are representative of a true and full picture of what the researcher is attempting to investigate.

[22] E. S. Mitchell, "Multiple Triangulation: A Methodology for Nursing Science," *Advances in Nursing* 8 (1986): 18–26.
[23] S. Stainback and W. Stainback, "Broadening the Research Perspective in Education," *Exceptional Children* 50 (1984): 400–408, as quoted in Duffy, "Methodological Triangulation," 130–31.

Why Research Methodology?

A clear statement of your research methodology, with its rationale, should be an integral part of both your proposal and your research report. Why? It informs your reader exactly how you intend to proceed (proposal) or proceeded (research report) and how you handled the data. It helps to explain what the nature of the data were, and what method you used to process them to arrive at your conclusions. A pragmatic presentation regarding the data may be perhaps most expeditiously handled by spelling out, in concise detail, four principal items with respect to the data:

1. What data do you need?
2. Where are the data located?
3. How do you intend to get the data?
4. Precisely and in detail, what do you intend to do with the data?

This may seem like an elementary exercise, but if you give fully and concisely the information to answer each of the above four questions you will find that you are proceeding with a much clearer awareness, than if you proceed merely by fortuitous hope and relying on a certain amount of luck.

Nothing in the research process should be done secretly or haphazardly. That others may give full credence to your efforts, it is obligatory on your part to lay out to full view every aspect of your research endeavor. Careful researchers, especially in academic research projects, include the data, usually as an appendix to their study (especially if those data are numerical in character). Furthermore, they give any statistical formulae and explain any quantitative approaches or techniques not in common statistical use.

While you are the researcher and have planned and executed the study, you should always be conscious that a host of critical eyes are looking over your shoulder—eyes that are not necessarily unfriendly—but that would like to know exactly what you are planning to do, or have done, and *how* you did what you did, *why* you did what you did, and *what reasoning formed the bedrock upon which the "how" and "why" was justified.* A statement concerning the methodology, whatever that methodology might be, should be clearly expressed and substantiated to validate your study.

Figure 6.1

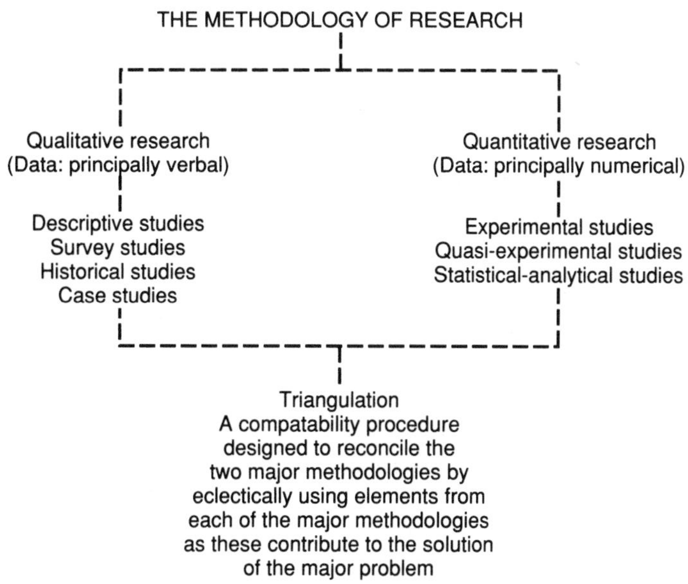

This chapter has discussed the two broad generic types of methodology. Within each of these are submethodologies: the descriptive method, the survey method, the historical method, the case study method, the statistical-analytical method, and the experimental and quasi-experimental methods. Each of these has its own protocol—its paradigm—governing data collection and procedural agenda.

The chapter may be graphically summarized as shown in Figure 6.1.

Significant and Influential Research

In the general population there are unknown numbers of individuals who are suffering from either gross or mild language impairment. Mild cases often go unnoticed except by the skillfully trained specialists in linguistic therapy. Generally, little significant research has been done in the neurological bases for language deficiency.

Innumerable textbooks indicate—as though it were established fact—the cortical areas of the brain that relate to speech, reading, hearing, and allied linguistic manifestations. Most of this insight into the human cortical organization for language has stemmed from the nineteenth century investigations of Broca (1861) or Wernicke (1874). Findings done over the past two decades suggest, however, that revising the earlier models is long overdue. Recent data obtained by various methods of clinical investigation suggest an organization of language in the human brain involving compartmentalization into separate systems subserving different language functions. Instead of a neatly circumscribed area responsible for one aspect of language, as shown in most textbooks, recent research has shown that each neural system subserving a specific language function includes multiple essential areas localized in the frontal and temporoparietal cortex of the dominant hemisphere, as well as widely dispersed neurons.

Studies of many different subject populations have shown a remarkable variance in brain organization for language. Furthermore, different patterns of localization of essential areas for language functions have also gender and verbal differences, as measured by the verbal IQ.

This recent advance in the discovery of knowledge regarding the neurological bases for language proficiency and disability should be particularly interesting to speech and language therapists, teachers, pediatricians, and others who specialize in linguistic phenomena. George A. Ojemann, M. D., of the Department of Neurological Surgery, University of Washington discussed these recent developments in *The Journal of Neuroscience*.[24] The article is accompanied by an extensive list of references.

The Computer as a Tool of Research

Sort and Search Functions

We have said almost nothing so far about the sort and search database functions of the computer. The *sort* function lets you select and sort (alphabetize) words, lines, or rows in a table; it is also possible to sort dates by month, day, and year. This feature should be particularly attractive to those doing historical or archival research.

The *search* capability of the computer is also of great convenience in gathering together all items (words, dates, locations, first names, last names) of the same kind. For those doing questionnaire and mail survey research from a selected population, it is possible to create a sorted list of all who have the same ZIP code.

[24] George A. Ojemann, "Cortical Organization of Language," *The Journal of Neuroscience* 11 (August 1991): 2281–87.

Both search and sort features are especially helpful when compiling an index, a glossary, or a concordance.

Precisely how sorts and searches are performed with each type of software will be outlined in the manual that accompanies the software, but it is well to know that such functions are available and for those who need to amass data of a particular genre, the sort and search capability of the computer is invaluable.

For Further Reading

Bogdan, R., and S. Taylor. *Introduction to Qualitative Research: A Phenomenological Approach to the Social Sciences.* New York: Wiley, 1975.

Das, T. "Qualitative Research in Organizational Behavior." *Journal in Management of Students* 20 (1983): 301–14.

Goodwin, L., and W. Goodwin. "Qualitative vs. Quantitative Research or Qualitative and Quantitative Research." *Nursing Research* 33 (1984): 378–80.

Green, Paul E., Frank J. Camone, and David P. Wachspress. "On the Analysis of Qualitative Data in Marketing Research." *Journal of Marketing Research* 14 (February 1977): 52–59.

Leininger, M., ed. *Qualitative Research Methods in Nursing.* Orlando, FL: Grune & Stratton, 1985.

Mitchell, E. S. "Multiple Triangulation: A Methodology for Nursing Science." *Advances in Nursing Science* 8 (1986): 18–26.

Parse, R. R., A. B. Coyne, and M. J. Smith. *Nursing Research: Qualitative Methods.* Bowie, MD: Brady, 1985.

Pelto, P. and G. Pelto. *Anthropological Research: The Structure of Inquiry.* New York: Cambridge University Press, 1978.

Ramos, Mary C. "Some Ethical Implications of Qualitative Research." *Research in Nursing and Health* 12 (1989): 57–63.

Reichardt, C. and T. Cook. "Beyond Qualitative versus Quantitative Methods." In T. Cook and C. Reichardt eds., *Qualitative and Quantitative Methods in Evaluation Research.* Beverly Hills, CA: Sage, 1979, 7–32.

Sandeldowski, M. "The Problem of Rigor in Qualitative Research." *Advances in Nursing Science* 8 (March 1986): 27–37.

Swanson, J. and W. Chenitz. "Why Qualitative Research in Nursing?" *Nursing Outlook* 30 (1982): 241–45.

Zelditch, M., "Some Methodological Problems of Field Studies." *American Journal of Sociology* 67 (1962): 566–76.

CHAPTER 7

Writing the Research Proposal

Research is never a solo flight—an individual excursion. It begins by researchers communicating their thoughts, their plans, their methods, their objectives for others to read, to discuss, to act upon. The overture opening such a research dialogue is the research proposal. As a point of departure, it must be a precision instrument from the first word to the last.

Research is never a solo flight. It is an activity that involves many people and presumes the accession to and the use of resources far beyond one's personal possessions. For that reason, research is not some "do-it-in-a-corner" activity. It must be aired, laid out, inspected, and, in nearly every instance, approved by others.

The graduate student must get the approval of an academic committee. A researcher seeking a grant must get approval from the university or the organization for which he or she works, and the project must merit the approval of the grant-awarding agency. These approvals are usually secured through the submission to proper authorities of a document known as a *research proposal.* The proposal discusses openly the problem for research, exactly how the research will be executed, and spells out in precise detail the resources—both personal and instrumental—that the researcher has available for producing the proposed results.

Researcher and Architect: Planners in Common

Researcher and architect—two individuals for whom planning is the essence of their art. Essentially, they have the same orientation. The architect plans structural concepts for physical buildings. The researcher plans structural concepts for the solution of problems. With both, structure, conceptualization, practical methodology, and up-front planning are basic requirements.

A proposal is as essential to successful research as an architect's drawing is to the construction of a building. No one would start building a structure by rushing out to dig a hole in the ground for the foundation without knowing in detail how the house will look when finished. Before one turns a shovelful of earth, many questions must be answered, many decisions made. What kind of building do you propose to construct? A dwelling? Will it be a two-story, a split level, or a ranch type? How will the house be placed on the building lot? Where will the openings be located? What kind of roof will it have? What will be its pitch? What kind of heat will it have? Where will the electrical outlets and switches be placed? We could go on and on.

Every one of these questions is extremely important, and each must be answered specifically *before* a pound of dirt can be excavated or a nail driven.

Even then, after you have made all these decisions, do you immediately begin digging? Not at all! Yet another preliminary phase remains. The architect now draws a plan of the entire structure, floor by floor, showing to the fraction of an inch precisely where every detail will be located. Insofar as possible, nothing is left to chance.

Now, you think, everything is ready; you may stake off the position of the building and start to dig for the foundation. Not so fast! Before you do anything, you need *permission*: The contractor must get a building permit, since many communities have building restrictions and building codes. You must observe all of these ordinances—setting the building back the required distance from the street, structure clearances from the property line, and on and on. The point is this: *Permission is indigenous to the plan.* This principle holds in constructing a building and in doing research.

Like the architect, who presents a concept of the building by means of plans and elevations, the researcher presents a concept of the proposed research project, investigating the viability of the undertaking and presenting the plans for it in a written research proposal. In the proposal, the problem and its attendant subproblems are stated clearly, all necessary terms are defined, the delimitations are carefully stated, the hypotheses articulated, and the importance of the study practically and succinctly spelled out. The researcher then gives every anticipated detail of acquiring, arranging, processing, and interpreting the data.

The architect's work is not complete with the executing of the floor plans. The architect then draws a series of elevations of the proposed building, showing each side to scale as it will appear when completed. Finally, the architect will draw up a set of specifications for the building indicating exactly what lumber is to be used, how far apart certain members are to be placed, the sizes and types of windows and doors, and all other details. Nothing is left unspecified.

The researcher does likewise. Parallel to the architect's elevations, the researcher produces an outline of the proposed study. Parallel to the specifications, the researcher sets forth the resources at hand for doing the research: his or her own qualifications (and those of his or her staff, if any); the availability of the data; the means by which they will be secured; computer facilities, if these are needed; and any other aspects of the total research process that merit explanation. Nothing is overlooked: All questions that may arise in the minds of those who review the proposal are anticipated and answered. Any unresolved matter is a weakness in the proposal and may seriously affect its approval. The importance of the proposal *cannot* be overemphasized. It is the magic key that unlocks the door that gives free access to the research endeavor. If it is not clearly and explicitly delineated, it may cause the whole project to be turned down.

Some students—and others seeking research grants—seem to think that the proposal is merely a necessary formality and do not give it the serious consideration it deserves. They try in a few pages to set forth the project. It usually fails. Those sponsoring a project, whether a graduate committee or a funding agency, realize that in doing research there is too much money, time, and effort invested to rush into it without a clearly conceived goal, a practical assessment, and an objective and detached evaluation of all aspects of the research endeavor.

Whether you seek funding of a project from a grant foundation or whether you seek to show your professor or your graduate committee that you have the ability to plan and carry out an investigation independently, a clear, well-written proposal is indispensable. Nothing is a substitute for an explicit setting forth of both problem and procedure. Other names for a proposal are *prospectus, plan, outline, statement,* and *draft.* If you are asked to present any of these, you are asked to present a research proposal.

Characteristics of a Proposal

Research demands that those who undertake it be able to think clearly, without confusion. The proposal will demonstrate, fortunately or unfortunately, whether you possess that quality.

When one reads a proposal that is poorly organized, filled with extraneous details, and foggily focused, one gets the immediate impression that the mind that produced such a mélange of confusion can never be disciplined to regard facts objectively and construe them logically. Unwelcome as the fact may be, your qualification as a researcher more often than not rests squarely upon the quality of the proposal you submit.

Therefore, you should understand and appreciate exactly what characteristics a proposal should have.

A Proposal Is a Straightforward Document

It should not be cluttered with extraneous matter. It begins without introduction, with a straightforward statement of the problem to be researched. It stands upon its own feet; it needs no explanatory props—no introduction, prologue, or statement of reasons why the researcher became interested in the problem or feels a burning need to research it. That may be interesting, but none of it is necessary or appropriate. Those who will review your proposal are not interested in such autobiographical excursions. These, indeed, suggest that you cannot separate essentials from irrelevancies; and *that,* unfortunately, will neither enhance your stature as a researcher nor recommend you as one who can think without irrelevancy and digression.

Whatever does not contribute *directly* to the delineation of the problem and its solution must be eliminated. Anything else only obscures and is diversionary. Remember the architect's drawing: clean, clear, and economical. It contains all that is necessary; not one detail more.

Journalists are taught—or if not taught, soon learn—that the first words they write are the important ones. You capture or lose your reader with the first sentence. It is impossible to overemphasize the importance of the beginning, whether of a speech, a news story, an article, or a proposal.

A proposal begins with these words: "Four decades ago the social and economic status of minority groups in the United States were. . . ." The normal reaction of the reader of such a proposal might readily be: "Who cares, at this moment, what the social and economic status of minorities were forty years ago? What we want to know is not history but prophecy. What does the researcher *propose* to do *now?* C'mon, what's the problem? *State it!*"

You see, your first sentence has irritated your reader, put you immediately at a disadvantage, and perhaps sacrificed your reader's interest; more seriously, it has indicated that you cannot distinguish between history and future planning and so casts umbrage upon your ability as a researcher to think clearly and critically.

In fact, such a beginning might even suggest that the writer does not actually know the meaning of *proposal,* which is a serious indictment, indeed. This is a word that looks *forward,* to what the researcher *plans to do in the future.* It is a document that employs the future tense of the verb. If the writer intended to make an analytical comparison of the social and economic conditions of two groups, he or she should have forthrightly begun: "This study *will* analyze the social and economic status of certain specific minority groups today with their similar status four decades ago for the purpose of. . . ."

This is a no-nonsense beginning, and it indicates that the writer knows what a proposal should be.

A Proposal Is Not a Literary Production

An architect's drawing is not a work of art; a proposal is not a "literary" (in the sense of being consciously a piece of fine writing) production. The mission of neither is to be artistic; the purpose of both is to communicate clearly. As an architect's drawings present an idea of construction with economy of line and precision of measurement, so a proposal indicates how a research project is to be executed to completion, with an economy of words and a precision of expression. It provides no opportunity for fine writing, for literary composition. Stylistically it is generally stark and prosaic. When you have written such a document you may discover, perhaps to your surprise, that direct writing is also elegant writing.

The language must be clear, precise, and sharp. The proposal provides a chance to show with what ultimate clarity and precision the researcher can state a problem, delineate the treatment of the data, and establish the logical validity of a conclusion.

To those who have been nurtured in the idea that writing should be stylistically interesting and artistically creative, the preceding statements may come as a distinct shock. But writing a superb proposal calls for skills of expression quite as demanding as those needed for the forging of an unforgettable sentence.

A Proposal Is Clearly Organized

Proposals are written in conventional prose style, and thoughts are expressed in simple paragraph form. The organization of the thought—the outline, as it were—is indicated by the proper use of heading and subheading. The use of the indented outline is neither conventional nor acceptable in the presentation of formal proposals. Those who employ the indented outline form may lay themselves open to criticism on two counts: They may be suspected of never having learned how to express the outline of their thought by the use of headings and subheadings; but more seriously, outlines hint at brevity, brevity hints at superficiality, superficiality suggests a most undesirable quality on the part of the researcher. Such may, of course, not be so; but no proposal should ever result in its author being represented in an unfavorable light.

Nevertheless, organization and outline are absolutely essential. They hint at an orderly and disciplined mind—one of the highest tributes to a researcher's qualifications. If you are not conversant with the use of headings to indicate thought organization, refer to the section in chapter 12 titled, "Headings Show Organization." There you will find a working knowledge of the basics of this stylistic convention. Efficient readers recognize immediately the outline organization of the thought when expressed with appropriate headings.

There is a rule of thumb that may assist you in reading and writing, headings, and in recognizing their relative importance.

1. The most important headings are in ALL CAPITAL LETTERS and centered on the page. These are headings of the largest units of writing. Chapter headings are thus designated in typescript (corresponding to Roman numerals I, II, III, etc., in an outline).
2. Headings in ALL CAPITAL LETTERS, Capital and lowercase—usually boldface—or other distinctly different typographic presentation flush with the left margin and separated from the text. (These are freestanding sideheads—that is, sideheads separated from the text above by two spaces and from the text following by a single space) are in second order of importance (corresponding to the capital letters A, B, C, etc., in an outline).
3. Headings in capital and lowercase letters, which are also freestanding, are of the next lower order of subheadings (corresponding to the 1, 2, 3, etc., level in an outline). In typescript, underlining means to italicize. This heading is followed by a period. Other headings have no mark of punctuation following them.
4. Paragraph sideheads are headings inserted into the opening of a paragraph. The first word is printed with a capital letter and the rest of the words begin with lowercase letters. All are in italic. These correspond to the a, b, c, etc., level in an outline.
5. Seldom encountered is the least important heading of all. It is a centered heading with the first word capitalized and not underlined. It corresponds to the 1', 2', 3', etc., level in an outline.

Turn back, now, to chapter 4, "The Review of the Related Literature." Notice only the headings in that chapter. They indicate four levels of outline subdivision and the thought organization of the chapter.

Here in structural outline form is the organization of chapter 4 as indicated by the heading and subheadings. The major organizational category is indicated by the wording of the first line: "IV. The Review of the Related Literature." This, then, is marked IV to indicate that it is the fourth major division of the entire book: the chapter. This is part of the organizational plan from the viewpoint of the book as a whole. Now under this main heading the remainder of the chapter is outlined.

IV. The Review of the Related Literature
- **A.** Understanding the role of the review
  - **1.** The purpose of the review
  - **2.** How to begin a search for related literature
    - **a.** Go to the indexes and abstracts
    - **b.** Database access to the literature
    - **c.** The treasury of government publications
    - **d.** Go to the library armed with data-gathering tools
    - **e.** Make as many copies of the bibliographic item as necessary
    - **f.** Computerize as much as possible
    - **g.** Be as fast and as accurate as possible
    - **h.** Be systematic and thorough
    - **i.** Relate your bibliography to your problem
  - **3.** How to write the section on the related literature
    - **a.** Get the proper psychological orientation
    - **b.** Have a plan
    - **c.** Emphasize relatedness
    - **d.** Review the literature; don't reproduce it!
  - **4.** Showing the relatedness of the literature to the research project
  - **5.** Summarize what you have said
- **B.** Points of departure
  - **1.** Abstracts
  - **2.** Indexes
- [Practical application]*
- [A sample research proposal]*
- [Special features of the chapter]*
  - **1.** Significant and influential research
  - **2.** The computer as a tool of research
- **C.** For further reading

Were you aware when you read that chapter that that was the outline of it? You should have been, and you should impart the outline of your thought to your readers in the same way. It is the professional way in which thought organization is expressed. Examine your textbooks—even current magazine articles—and you will find how prevalent the outline structure expressed by headings really is.

Content and Organization of a Proposal

Proposals follow a simple, logical form of presentation. Although there are many ways to arrange the items within the proposal, the following is the outline of the proposal that we will

* These headings are placed in brackets to indicate that they are actually separate sections of each chapter given to continuing topics: (1) Practical Application, and (2) A Sample Research Proposal. Significant and Influential Research and The Computer as a Tool of Research were similarly treated because they do not integrate with the thought organization of the chapter.

follow in this text. A sample proposal for a research project is presented in this chapter and in chapters 3 and 4, and the significant features of the proposal are commented upon in the right-hand column. Refer to it.

I. The problem and its setting
- **A.** The statement of the problem
- **B.** The statement of the subproblems
- **C.** The hypotheses
- **D.** The delimitations
- **E.** The definitions of terms
- **F.** The assumptions
- **G.** The importance of the study

II. The review of the related literature

III. The data, their treatment, and their interpretation
- **A.** The data
  - **1.** The primary data
  - **2.** The secondary data
- **B.** The criteria governing the admissibility of the data
- **C.** The research methodology
- **D.** The specific projected treatment of each subproblem
  - **1.** Subproblem 1 (*The subproblem is here restated*)
    - **a.** Data needed
    - **b.** Where the data are located
    - **c.** How the data will be secured
    - **d.** How the data will be treated and interpreted
  - **2.** Subproblem 2 (*Here, again, the subproblem will be restated and the four steps: a, b, c, and d are detailed. Then each succeeding subproblem will be given similar treatment.*)

IV. The qualifications of the researcher (and the qualifications of each one of the researcher's staff if more than the researcher is involved in the project)

V. The outline of the proposed study

VI. A selected bibliography

One rule governs the writing of proposals and final documents: *The arrangement of the material should be so presented that it forms for the reader of the document a clear, progressive presentation by keeping items together that belong together* (such as the problem and its resultant subproblems; the subproblems and their corresponding hypotheses).

In suggesting ways to write a convincing proposal, Dr. Lois DeBakey gives some valued directives.[1]

> Write the first draft [of the proposal] with attention exclusively to orderly sequence and without consideration for grammatical or rhetorical perfection. Stopping to examine each word phrase or clause will shift your attention from thought to form and will interrupt the rational flow of ideas. You can always refine your compositions later, but if the presentation of your ideas is disorderly, major excision and reconstruction will be required to repair the damage. Use succinct language; and assign to appendices any auxiliary information, to prevent cluttering the text with excessive detail.
>
> *Introduction*
>
> In any unit of exposition, be it a sentence, a paragraph, or a full composition, two of the most important positions are the first and the last. The introduction, therefore, should be prepared

[1]Lois DeBakey, "The Persuasive Proposal," *Journal of Technical Writing and Communication* 6 (1976), 1: 5–25.

with special care, for if you fail to engage the reviewer's interest in the beginning, you may lose it altogether. . . .

State the problem and the aims clearly and promptly, rather than make the reader transverse several pages before he finds out what your central point is. . . . Emphasize what is unique about the project. . . .

Your opening paragraph should inspire confidence and convince the reader that what you wish to do warrants careful consideration. *Remember that cold print alone must sell your idea.*

Materials and Methods

The introduction should lead naturally and smoothly to the section on methods, which is probably the most carefully examined section of the [proposal] and, therefore, one of the most important. . . . Describe clearly the method of selection of subjects or materials and the provision of controls for variables that might later be confused with experimental effect. To defend your choice of procedure, you must obviously be familiar with the capabilities and limitations of all available methods. . . .

Be sure that your experimental design is rational, ethical, and defensible and that it can yield answers to your stated problem. . . .

Never assume that the reader knows anything of vital significance that you have omitted from your presentation. Even if he knows it, he will not know that *you* know it too unless you tell him. Make certain that you have at least described the sample, the experimental design and procedure, the method of collection and analysis of data.

Expected Results

Following the section on methods is that on expected results, which should be written honestly and objectively. Overstated claims . . . should be avoided in favor of sober statements based on logic and reason. Try to estimate the potential generality of the results and the basis for your judgment. When tables and graphs summarize data for this section more efficiently than text, they may be used to advantage. Any tests, instruments, publications, films, or other educational material that may be byproducts of the project should be noted.

Discussion

In the Discussion, you have an opportunity to show your broad familiarity with the various aspects and implications of the problem and to present the potential significance of the prospective results. Be sure to indicate any distinctive qualities of this research as compared with previous studies. Wild speculation is anathema. This is the place to persuade your reader that your proposed study holds real promise. . . . And you may wish to suggest new directions for subsequent or concurrent projects in related research.

Revision

When you have completed the first draft, lay it aside for a couple of weeks or so—long enough to be able to read it with detachment and objectivity. If you re-read it too soon, you may read what you *thought* you wrote, not what you actually put down on paper. Read first for logical order and coherence, accuracy, clarity of purpose, unity of thesis, and consistency; then for grammatical integrity, punctuation, grace of expression, and mellifluence. Note, too, whether the narrative flows smoothly and logically from one statement to the next and from one paragraph to the next. Reading aloud will uncover defective rhythm or cadence, as well as improper balance and emphasis.

If I had to identify the most important literary requisite for [a proposal], I would choose precision—precision in choice of words and their arrangement to convey the intended meaning.

Conclusion

The applicant should remember that the proposal is a kind of promissory note. It is a mistake to promise mountains and deliver molehills, because the day of reckoning will come—when you will have to write a formal report of your research project. It is through writing, therefore, that both the need for the research and the importance of the results are communicated, and the investigator with literary prowess has a distinct advantage in achieving both of these objectives.

Success Begins with the Initial Proposal

It is a frustrating experience for a researcher to have gone through all the activity of gathering data and processing them and then to have a graduate committee turn down the effort because the data have not been interpreted, the hypotheses have not been resolved, or any one of many reasons such committees may give for not approving the student's efforts.

Success begins long before the tumult of activity begins. All research begins with a proposal. The proposal is a clear statement of the problem and subproblems, the data and how these will be processed; and, most important of all, how they will be interpreted. It is at this critical juncture where most students fail to make the nexus that takes the research out of a mere activity and transfers it to a research endeavor.

In planning research, in preparing the proposal, or in writing the research report, researchers come to the point where it is necessary to answer the question, how will the data be interpreted? Here is where the success of the research effort hangs upon a thread.

Let us take a typical situation to see how many students attempt to answer that most important of all questions. We will take a page from one student's proposal. It attempts to spell out how the student will interpret the data for the purpose of resolving a subproblem in a dissertation in economics dealing with labor relations. The general problem was to "analyze the attitudes of professional employees toward certain aspects of management policy and to evaluate the relationship between these attitudes and the responsibility of management to articulate such policy for its employees."

The student is spelling out the manner in which he expects to resolve a particular subproblem. The subproblem is, What does an analysis of the attitudes of employees toward management policy for salary increases and merit pay reveal? A page from the student's proposal, indicating how he intended to resolve this question, is shown in Figure 7.1.

Now, let us look at that page. First, consider the wording of the subproblem:

The first subproblem is to determine *through an analysis of employee responses* the attitudes of employees toward certain aspects of management policy for salary increases and merit pay.

Now read the section "How the Data Will Be Interpreted." What has the researcher really done? Has he *interpreted* (shown what the data mean) any of the data? Has he "determined" anything *through an analysis of employee responses?*

No! He has merely *tabulated* and *graphed* the data. He has rearranged them and presented them in another form. The data remain raw, as they were originally in the questionnaire. Finally, the researcher informs us that he intends to find two points of central tendency for the data—the median and the mean. Why? What do these measures tell us about "attitudes of employees toward certain aspects of management policy"? Median and mean of what? The frequencies or percentages? Which? And for what purpose? What is the rationale for the statistical operation? These are primary questions that should be answered *in the proposal* as well as *in the student's own mind.*

If, at this juncture, the researcher returns to the subproblem and reads it carefully, the fact should be immediately apparent that what has been suggested will never produce an *analysis* of employee responses, but merely an amassing, a tabulating, a conversion, a statistical manipulation of employee responses into another form. Granted, the proposal may be the first step in preparing the data for analysis, but if the researcher does what he intends to do, no analysis will be effected.

If after codifying the data, the researcher had then considered them *analytically,* he would have resolved the responses into various gradational categories, would have classified the

Figure 7.1 Treatment of Each Specific Subproblem

Restatement of Subproblem 1. The first subproblem is to determine through an analysis of employee responses the attitudes of employees toward certain aspects of management policy for salary increases and merit pay.

The Data Needed
The data needed to resolve this subproblem are those employee responses to questions concerning salary increases and merit pay.

Where the Data Are Located
The data are located in the employee responses to questions 3, 7, and 13 of the questionnaire, "Survey of Employee Attitudes Toward Management."

How the Data Will Be Secured
The data will be secured by accurately tabulating all of the responses of employees to the above questions on the questionnaire.

How the Data Will Be Interpreted
From the responses of the questions a table will be constructed similar to the following structural model. It will indicate the employee attitudes, their frequency, and the percentages of these attitudes of the total attitude response to each question.

Attitude	Frequency	Percentage
Totals		

A graph will then be constructed to show which attitudes have received the greatest number of reactions and those which have had the least number of reactions. The median and the mean will also be found for the total group as a basis for comparison.

responses into those supportive of and those opposed to managerial policies. He would have carefully reviewed each of the categories to discern the characteristics of each. Were those who supported management lukewarm in their support? What key words were used in their responses? What did the overall category response indicate about the group psychology behind the *attitudes of the employees* (Read the subproblem!)? What the student intended to do as expressed by the excerpt from the proposal would never have resulted in any indication of employee *attitude.* See chapter 5 for discussion and practical applications of this topic.

Guidelines with Respect to Interpretation of the Data

We have said enough about the example. But from the foregoing discussion, some basic guidelines for handling the data emerge.

Systematically Describe the Treatment of the Data. In the proposal especially, indicate a logical sequence of the steps necessary to solve *each* subproblem *separately.* Refer to the portion of the sample proposal given in this chapter. Note how the author of the proposal has taken each subproblem and clearly presented four steps in the resolution of it: what data were needed, where these data were located, how these data would be secured. Many students know where the data are, but they have no idea how they will gain access to them or, most importantly, how the data will be interpreted. Perhaps you would do well to repeat the subproblem immediately before explaining how the data will be interpreted. This restatement will keep uppermost in the researcher's mind precisely what the subproblem is aiming to achieve. Then read the subproblem carefully. Are there critically important "key" words: "to *determine* through employee responses the *attitudes* of employees"?

State Clearly the Data You Need to Resolve the Subproblem. Under a heading, "The Data Needed," indicate specifically the data you will need for the resolution of the subproblem being investigated. Do not engage in generalities. The sample page just presented was excellent with respect to specifying the precise data needed. It indicated that the researcher needed responses to questions 3, 7, and 13 of the questionnaire.

State Precisely Where the Data Are Located. With respect to the sample page presented, this section was largely a repetition of the preceding statement. Nothing is wrong with this. In research, it is better to repeat than to leave a hiatus that raises unresolved questions in the mind of the consumer of your research.

In some studies, however, where a student may need a certain kind of records—and this is particularly true with respect to historical research—the student should know the exact location of these records. Too many students begin research projects assuming that records are available only to learn too late that either no records exist or that, if they do exist, they are in an inaccessible location or under such heavy restriction that they are not available. Facing the question, "Where are the data located?" frankly, and answering such a question in writing by giving a definite location for such records, may clear the air at the beginning of your research effort.

State without Equivocation How the Data Will Be Secured. Again, with the sample page given above, little difficulty is presented at this point. The student already had the data! But suppose the data are letters of a famous person in possession of that person's family. You may know where the letters are located; the next question is, how do you intend to get them for your research purposes? Perhaps in cases like this—or with any records under the control of others—the name and address should be given of the individual who possesses the data. A statement should be included to the effect that this custodian of the data has consented to your using them for research purposes. This should be clearly stated in the proposal so that your sponsor, your academic committee, the funding agency, or whoever may be interested in reading your proposal before the research is begun can clearly see that you have provided for all contingencies against failure to secure the data, which is common with many students, who dream great dreams and upon the airy substance of them alone undertake research projects without sufficient preliminary groundwork.

State Fully and Unequivocally How You Intend to Interpret the Data. This is often the weakest link in any research endeavor. It is also the most difficult aspect of any research project. Truth, hope, faith are all fine in their place; but they cannot substitute for clear thinking and hardheaded planning.

Some purported researchers skirt this requirement by the subterfuge of employing vague and generalized language—so vague, so generalized that their statements are worthless from a practical research planning and design standpoint. A basic test for the adequacy of your statement of the treatment of the data is the following: *The plan for the treatment of the data should be so unequivocal and so specific that any other qualified person seeing only your proposal could carry out your research project without benefit of your presence, by means of your proposal alone.*

Every contingency should be anticipated; every methodological problem should be resolved. The degree to which you delineate how the data will be interpreted will augur the success or failure of your research endeavor. It is the key to research success, and it should be presented with utmost care and precision.

Spell out Every Step in the Interpretation of the Data. Too many students assume this is unnecessary. They prefer to cut corners. They assume that others know what they mean, and so they avoid taking the trouble to express it. These assumptions are false. Too many students attempt to do in a tenth of a page what they should take ten pages to do. (We may add that those who apply for funding for their projects frequently suffer from the same deficiency.)

Spelling out the treatment and the interpretation of the data is a tedious, time-consuming process. Attempting to relegate it to the broad sweep, the quick and easy statement, the careless approach almost invariably courts disaster. Certain procedural guidelines are therefore given here.

Ask yourself continually just what it is that you are doing. Research is euphoric. Make a clear distinction between *arraying* the data and *interpreting* the data. Tables, charts, graphs, maps—all these contrivances—are merely ways of arraying or repackaging the data. All these intermediate modalities for data may be highly important to the ultimate interpretation of the data, but their *function* is merely to enable you to see clearly without confusion.

Insist that your statistics have a defensible rationale. It is pointless to tell us you will derive the mean and/or standard deviation and stop there. Why do you need these statistical values? How will they help you derive meaning from the data? Is this statistical manipulation of the data indispensable to the understanding of it? What are your formulas? Why did you choose these formulas? Where did you get them? (Footnote your source, and give the symbol equivalents.)

Where does the manipulation of the data cease and your own thinking begin? There is a point in every project where fumbling with the facts ceases and research begins. Unless you can indicate the precise point where you assume control of the data—where the ministrations of computers, graphics, tabulations, and so forth cease—and unless you can describe what role *you* will play in processing the data, you should be very circumspect in calling whatever you have done *interpretation* of the data. Only the genius of human insight can cause dead facts to speak. There is no other way.

The Research Process Is Cyclical. That the entire research process is cyclical was one of the basic propositions with which this book began. Because we have been considering a subunit of the total research design—namely, the treatment of the data with respect to a subproblem—we find that the principle of circularity applies here as well as it does with the overall design. The difference is, however, that here it is only a shrunken orbit of the great circular process.

To test the circularity and, likewise, the validity of your research design use the "If-Test" technique. It goes like this:

The If-Test Technique

1. The point of beginning is the subproblem. State it completely. Then answer the following seven questions.
2. If I have this subproblem, what data do I need to resolve it?
3. If I need these data, where are they located?
4. If they are located there, how can I obtain them?
5. If I can obtain them, what do I intend to do with them?
6. If I do that with the data, will the result of doing it resolve my subproblem?
7. If my subproblem is resolved, then what hypothesis was I testing based on that subproblem?
8. If that was my hypothesis, what do the facts show with respect to the support or rejection of it?
9. If my hypothesis is supported, I hypothesized correctly.
10. If my hypothesis is not supported, then I have discovered something that I did not expect to be so.

Be Sure the Data Support Your Conclusions. Unfounded enthusiasm is one of the hazards you will need to guard against. One mark of immature researchers is that, bewildered by the many data they must handle or dazzled by a newly emerging concept, they make extravagant claims or reach enthusiastic conclusions that are not warranted by the data. Research is indeed an exciting quest, but researchers must learn—particularly those doing a descriptive survey study—that though their data frequently lie close to the vibrant pulse of life, they cannot permit this to influence the objective judgment of their message. Archimedes is perfectly justified running through the streets of Athens screaming, "I have found it" after he is sure that he has found it. Only after the Athenian bathtub ran over did he reach his conclusion. Much research contains unfounded conclusions unsupported by the data and based upon shaky statistical procedures or unwarranted extrapolation of the facts. Research should rest solidly and completely on its own factual foundation.

Look the facts steadfastly in the face. Report honestly what those facts reveal to you. That is good research.

Summary Graphic

The schematic procedural chart shown in Figure 7.2 is from Lawrence Locke, *Proposals That Work*, and will serve as both a guide and a summary of the discussion in this chapter. The boxes represent twenty major procedural steps to a successful proposal. The letters within each circle indicate the sequence in which the questions should be considered. Note that the answers to the questions in the circles are binary in form—they must be answered either "yes" or "no."

The Greatest Weaknesses in Proposals Seeking Funding

The United States government is perhaps the greatest underwriter of research in the country, certainly in funding research projects with grants. Each grant is announced by the division that funds it, that issues invitations for proposals. Specific details may be had by writing to the particular division administering the grant awards and issuing the grant contracts.

Competition is keen. Frequently, thousands of proposals are submitted. These are usually read and evaluated by an award committee. Most of the proposals fail to be funded, usually because of the quality of the proposal itself. Many proposals do not measure up to the excellence that the agency expects and are, thus, eliminated in the winnowing process.

An article in *Science* magazine reported on a study of 605 rejected applications for grants (out of approximately 2,000).[2] In the twelve months that ended June 30, 1959, the National Institutes of Health received and acted upon nearly 6,000 competitive applications for grants to conduct projects in medical and related biological research. Nearly one-third of the proposals submitted were not approved because of obvious research difficulties in the problem, with the research approach, with the researcher, or with other miscellaneous matters.

Table 7.1 sets forth the 26 shortcomings in these proposals. The percentages indicate the frequency of each weakness contributing to disapproval. The percentages corresponding to the four main classes add up to more than 100 percent; also, those within any one of the four groups add up to more than the percentage for that group. In both cases, the excess is due to the fact that a given research proposal may have had more than one adverse characteristic.

Proposals submitted by students for academic research projects share these weaknesses. Study this table carefully, to learn to avoid these problems.

[2]Ernest M. Allen, "Why Are Research Grant Applications Disapproved?" *Science* 132 (November 1960): 1532–34.

Figure 7.2 Twenty Steps to a Proposal

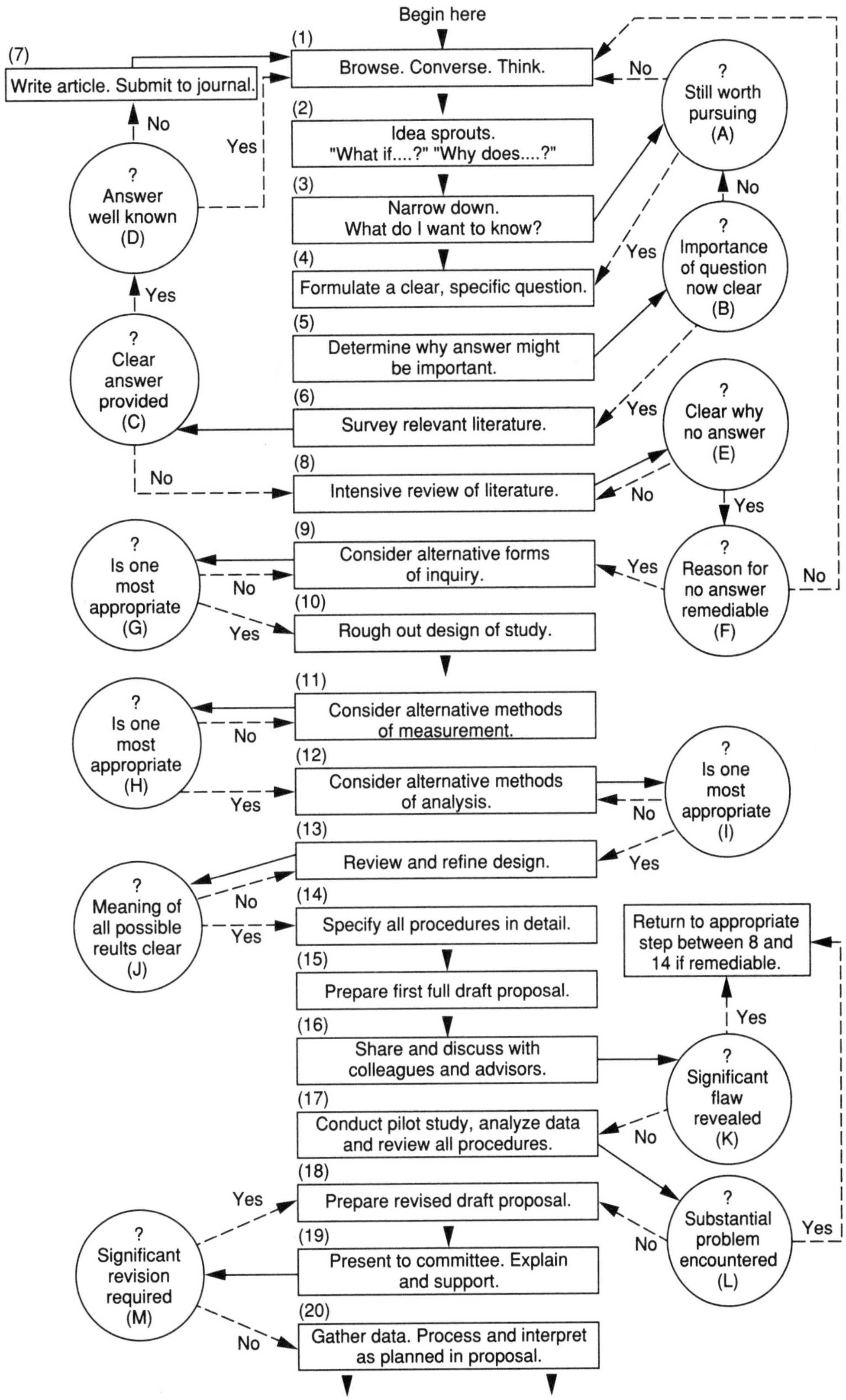

Boxes represent major procedural steps, unbroken lines trace the main sequence of those steps. Circles represent the major questions to be confronted, the broken lines lead to the procedural consequences of the alternative YES or NO answers.

From Lawrence Locke, Waneen W. Spirduso, and Stephen Silverman, *Proposals That Work*, 2d ed. (Newbury Park, CA: Sage, 1987), p. 45. Reprinted by permission of Sage Publications, Inc.

Table 7.1 Weaknesses Found in a Study of 605 Grant Applications Disapproved by National Institutes of Health

No.	Shortcoming	%
	Class I: Problem (58 percent)	
1	The problem is of insufficient importance or is unlikely to produce any new or useful information.	33.1
2	The proposed research is based on a hypothesis that rests on insufficient evidence, is doubtful, or is unsound.	8.9
3	The problem is more complex than the investigator appears to realize.	8.1
4	The problem has only local significance, or is one of production or control, or otherwise fails to fall sufficiently clearly within the general field of health-related research.	4.8
5	The problem is scientifically premature and warrants, at most, only a pilot study.	3.1
6	The research as proposed is overinvolved, with too many elements under simultaneous investigation.	3.0
7	The description of the nature of the research and of its significance leaves the proposal nebulous and diffuse and without clear research aim.	2.6
	Class II: Approach (73 percent)	
8	The proposed tests, methods, or scientific procedures are unsuited to the stated objective.	34.7
9	The description of the approach is too nebulous, diffuse, and lacking in clarity to permit adequate evaluation.	28.8
10	The overall design of the study has not been carefully thought out.	14.7
11	The statistical aspects of the approach have not been given sufficient consideration.	8.1
12	The approach lacks scientific imagination.	7.4
13	Controls are either inadequately conceived or inadequately described.	6.8
14	The material the investigator proposes to use is unsuited to the objectives of the study or is difficult to obtain.	3.8
15	The number of observations is unsuitable.	2.5
16	The equipment contemplated is outmoded or otherwise unsuitable.	1.0
	Class III: Investigator (55 percent)	
17	The investigator does not have adequate experience or training or both, for this research.	32.6
18	The investigator appears to be unfamiliar with recent pertinent literature or methods, or both.	13.7
*19	The investigator's previously published work in this field does not inspire confidence.	12.6
*20	The investigator proposes to rely too heavily on insufficiently experienced associates.	5.0
21	The investigator is spreading himself or herself too thin and will be more productive if he or she concentrates on fewer projects.	3.8
*22	The investigator needs more liaison with colleagues in this field or in collateral fields.	1.7
	Class IV: Other (16 percent)	
23	The requirements for equipment or personnel, or both, are unrealistic.	10.1
24	It appears that other responsibilities would prevent devotion of sufficient time and attention to this research.	3.0
25	The institutional setting is unfavorable.	2.3
*26	Research grants to the investigator, now in force, are adequate in scope and amount to cover the proposed research.	1.5

*The items marked with an asterisk may not be particularly relevant for a student doing academic research.

The above study is reported with considerable fullness, despite the fact that it was done over a quarter of a century ago. It is perhaps the best analysis in the literature specifically outlining the reasons for proposals being disapproved. Basically, most of the causes cited are related to fundamental shortcomings in the individual who wrote the proposal (the inability to think analytically and clearly, insufficient knowledge of the existing research, seeming lack of competence to carry out the proposed study, and the inability to see the global concept of the research in terms of its many ramifications and requirements), and these have apparently not significantly changed since.

The validity of this statement seems to be confirmed by juxtaposing against Table 7.1 a contemporary report from a bulletin of the research branch of the Department of Health and Human Services (Table 7.2). The bulletin, *Preparing a Research Grant Application to the National Institutes of Health: Selected Articles* (May 1987), contains a reprint of an article by Janet M. Cuca and William J. McLoughlin called "Why Clinical Research Grant Applications Fare Poorly in Review and How to Recover." It is interesting to note that from the table, as Cuca and McLoughlin observe, "the most frequent area of shortcoming is that of technical methodology; two thirds of the applications had one or more defects in this area, including all manner of questionable, defective, or unsuitable experimental methods. In about half of the applica-

Table 7.2 Types of Shortcomings in NIH Grant Applications for Clinical Research That Fared Poorly*

		Applications with one or more instances of indicated type of shortcoming	
		Number	**Percent**
Types of Shortcomings			
A. Research Problem:			
Hypothesis: ill-defined, lacking, faulty, diffuse, unwarranted		120	47
Significance: unimportant, unimaginative, unlikely to provide new information		77	30
B. Experimental Design:			
Study group or control: inappropriate composition, number, characteristics		103	40
Technical methodology: questionable, unsuited, defective		168	66
Data collection procedures: confused design, inappropriate instrumentation, timing or conditions		104	41
Data management and analysis: vague, unsophisticated, not likely to provide accurate and clearcut results		80	31
C. Investigator:			
Inadequate expertise or unfamiliarity with literature, poor past performance/productivity on an NIH grant, insufficient time to be given to project		43	17
D. Resources:			
Inadequate institutional setting, support staff, laboratory facilities, equipment; restricted access to patient populations; insufficient involvement of coinvestigators		9	4
Total number of shortcomings:		704	
Number of applications examined:	256		
Mean number of shortcomings:	2.8		

*Disapproved or priority score of 250–500 on scale of 100–500, where 100 = best priority and 500 = worst priority.

Source: Janet M. Cuca and William J. McLoughlin, "Why Clinical Research Grant Applications Fare Poorly in Review and How to Recover," *Clinical Investigation* 5 (1987): 55–58. See also J. M. Cuca, "NIH Grant Applications for Clinical Research: Reasons for Poor Ratings or Disapproval," *Clinical Research* 31 (1983).

tions, the research hypothesis of the study or the problem to be examined was either ill defined, lacking, faulty, diffuse, unwarranted, or all of the foregoing. The third, fourth, and fifth most prevalent shortcomings were data collection procedures (41%); study group or controls (40%); and data management and analysis (31%)."

At this point, a comment by Dr. George N. Eaves in *Grants Magazine* is particularly apropos.

> I have concluded that the single most important qualification for a beginning investigator's successful competition for a grant is a demonstration of outstanding qualifications. These qualifications are not the kind usually presented in a biographical sketch, such as advanced degrees and publications, but the demonstrated ability to think clearly and logically, to express logical thought concisely and cogently, to discriminate between the significant and the inconsequential, to display technical prowess, to handle abstract thought, to analyze data objectively and accurately, and to interpret results confidently and conservatively. These capabilities characterize scholarship, and it is through scholarship that an applicant for a research grant can demonstrate his qualifications.[3]

One might also add that this same constellation of qualities is what graduate professors look for in candidates for the doctorate.

Shortcomings of Many Proposals: View from a Different Perspective

Judith Margolin recently found essentially the same weaknesses in proposals being made today that were indigenous to those of the National Institutes of Health study just cited. Here are Margolin's comments on and her list of shortcomings of many proposals:

> Although I dislike stressing the negative, you should be aware that a large proportion of proposals are turned down. Some say as many as 90 out of every 100 applicants are rejected (depending upon the nature of the grant), though it would be very difficult to verify this statistic. You should not be discouraged by the high rejection rate. If you were to examine the rejected proposals carefully, it probably would become evident that most of the applicants simply had not done their homework properly. All too often their proposals were not worthy, inadequately prepared, or thoughtlessly submitted to inappropriate funders.
>
> My research indicates that, like successful proposals, rejected proposals have much in common. Funding executives report the same reasons for rejection time and time again. Note should be taken of the following shortcomings so that you can avoid these pitfalls yourself.

Ten Reasons Proposals Are Turned Down

1. Inadequately presented statement of need—perceived by funder as either not a significant issue or as one of such magnitude that a few grant dollars would barely make a dent in the problem.
2. Objectives are ill-defined—put forward as vague goals or as personal aims.
3. Procedures are confused with objectives.
4. Lack of integration within the text among components of the proposal.
5. The funder does not accept proposals from unaffiliated individuals.
6. The funder knows that the proposed idea has already been tried and failed.
7. The funder approves of the concept but believes that the applicant is not the proper individual to conduct the project or that the institution with which the applicant is affiliated is not suitable.
8. The individual has adopted a poor approach and appealed on an emotional or a political rather than a factual basis.

[3]George N. Eaves, "Preparation of the Research-Grant Application: Opportunities and Pitfalls" *Grants Magazine* 7 (September 1984): 151.

9. The idea costs too much.
10. The funder does not have enough information.[4]

Figure 7.3 is a checklist covering many of the weaknesses in proposal writing cited above. Check your proposal against each item. This is obviously a checklist for *sponsored* research—for proposals where government, foundation, or other funding is requested. A perfect score results from *no* check mark appearing opposite any item.

This may also be considered an adequate checklist for graduate students preparing a proposal for their academic review committees. The financial factors in such cases do not, of course, apply; otherwise the student will do well to check the proposal to be submitted against the criteria suggested in this checklist.

Figure 7.3 Checklist of Features Detracting from Proposal Effectiveness

Check each item to be sure that your proposal exhibits *none* of the following characteristics

____ 1. The proposal does not follow directions or conform to the guidelines set forth in the informational literature of the funding or approving agency.
___ 2. The statement of the problem is vague or is so obscured by other discussion that it is impossible to find.
___ 3. The problem does not address the research area outlined by the funding agency.
___ 4. The methodology is not clearly stated, and an explanation of exactly how the research will be conducted is not specifically delineated.
___ 5. The proposal is too ambitious for the grant money available.
___ 6. Items included in the budget are disallowed by the terms of the grant.
___ 7. A clear and explicit budget statement outlining program expenditures is either lacking or the summary of estimated costs is ambiguous and indefinite.
___ 8. The deadline for submission has not been met. Late proposals generally do not merit consideration.
___ 9. The section of the proposal explaining the study's importance is not clearly enough set forth for the funding agency to see a relationship of the study to the purpose for which the grant is awarded.
___ 10. The credentials of the chief investigator (the researcher) and others involved in the study are such that they raise questions about the researcher's competence and/or about that of members of the research staff to conduct the study.
___ 11. The application is incomplete; all requested information is either not included or not clearly and explicitly stated in the application.
___ 12. The proposal lacks sharpness. It is not logically organized. Without clear divisions that set forth the several areas of the research project, it rambles. The reader has difficulty in isolating the discussion of the problem, the subproblems, the related studies, the methodology, the interpretation of the data, and other related parts of the proposal.
___ 13. The outline of the proposed study is missing or so indefinite as to fail to communicate a clear concept of the overall structure of the investigation.
___ 14. Criteria for the admissibility of the data are weak or nonexistent.
___ 15. The projected treatment of each subproblem is cursory and is phrased in statements that are too general to convey any clear concept of exactly how each subpart of the entire project will be resolved and the manner in which the data will be interpreted.
___ 16. The whole proposal is phrased in terms that are too general , ambiguous, or inexact to be useful for evaluation. Such phrases as "tests will be given" or "tests will be made" are largely meaningless. The proposal cannot be too specific. Exactly what tests will "be given"? How given? Exactly what "tests" will be made? How made? More proposals are rejected because they are filled with verbal fog that for any other reason.

[4]Judith Margolin, *The Individual's Guide to Grants* (New York: Plenum Press, 1983), pp. 233–34.

A Sample Research Proposal

This will be a somewhat long interlude. It is presented, however, so that you may see how the author of this proposal followed meticulously the directives and suggestions made in this chapter, and elsewhere, for the presentation of a plan for a research project. To review, briefly, you recall that in chapter 3, discussing the problem and its setting, we showed you a facsimile of the first part of an actual submitted research proposal. We presented the proposal in detail, with marginal comment, to illustrate the application of the discussion. In chapter 4, "The Review of the Related Literature," we continued the same practice.

In this chapter we have discussed, meticulously "spelling out," the way you will handle the data. It is in this area that students and professionals alike go wrong. It is also the most tedious part of the proposal to write; most of us are reluctant to spell out every minute detail of procedure and buttress these choices with a rationale that is solidly based on accepted research methodology and analytical thinking. The weakness of many a proposal is the hope that what we find too tedious to state specifically others will *assume* that we will nevertheless do. In a proposal, you cannot ask your reader to make a journey of faith.

Attorneys, in drawing up a contract, meticulously include all of the rights and obligations of the parties to that contract. The proposal writer should prepare a proposal with the same exactitude. For, in a sense, a proposal is, under certain circumstances, a form of contract, or what we might call a *quasi*-contract.

Are you submitting a proposal for a grant to underwrite a research project? If so, you (as the party of the first part) are proposing to undertake a research project in exchange for a monetary consideration from the agency providing the grant (the party of the second part). Looking at this relationship from a legal standpoint, your proposal, upon acceptance by the granting agency, is a formal contractual relationship.

Now, let us look at the situation from an academic standpoint. While considerable difference exists between the proposal presented to a granting agency as an inducement to fund a research venture and that presented by a student to an academic mentor, the basic elements of the research problem, the methodology, and any other factors critical to conducting the research inquiry should be mutually explored and agreed upon before the actual research activity is begun.

Usually mentors will want to see the proposal as it is being developed and, equally, will want to monitor your progress as you proceed with your study. This is a desirable relationship: a process of continual guidance and a process of advice and consent.

Mandatory in many cases, proposals are always advisable irrespective of the magnitude of the research or its academic sophistication. Proposals have two distinct advantages:

1. A proposal helps the student to organize the projected research activity.
2. A proposal provides the student's mentor with a global view of the project and affords an opportunity to counsel and guide the student with respect to areas that may pose exceptional difficulty.

The proposal for an anticipated research endeavor merits words that are carefully chosen, style that is clear and concise, attention to the most minute procedural detail, and a rationale for each procedure that is logically and clearly stated. This is a big order; but it reveals the quality of scholarship of the individual writing the proposal as perhaps no other academic assignment would ever do.

It is an awesome fact to contemplate, but to no small degree, *your proposal is you!* It defines your ability to think critically and to express your thoughts capably. *It is the practical application of one's educational competence laid bare upon a sheet of paper.* It is not a document to be tossed off thoughtlessly an hour before a regulatory deadline or a necessary evil to be dispensed with minimal mental exertion.

Specimen Proposal

THE DATA

AND THE TREATMENT OF THE DATA

The Data

The data of this research are of two kinds: primary data and secondary data. The nature of each of these two types of data will be given briefly below.

The primary data. The responses to the SVIB by cartographers are one type of primary data. The demographic responses to the questionnaire appended to the SVIB comprise another type of primary data.

The secondary data. The normative data and current occupational scales for the SVIB constitute one type of secondary data. The published studies and texts and the unpublished dissertations and theses dealing with interest measurement are another type of secondary data.

The Criteria for the Admissibility of the Data

Only the revised SVIB for men, completed in accordance with the test publisher's instructions, will be used in the study.

Only responses from criterion group cartographers with three or more years of cartographic experience and who indicate on the SVIB that they like their work will be used in this study.

The Research Methodology

Although Hillway pointed out that vague description of the approach to research is indicative of poor understanding of what is to be done and such research potentially will be ineffectual, the classification of educational research method is essentially an arbitrary process[1] Identification

[1]Tyrus Hillway, Introduction to Research (Boston: Houghton Mifflin, 1956), p. 126.

COMMENTS ON THE TEXT OF THE PROPOSAL

We have now come to the very heart of the proposal. This section should, indeed, be the strongest of all the sections of the research proposal in setting forth precisely what it is that the researcher intends to do and precisely how he intends to do it.

The format suggested in this section, if followed scrupulously, will prevent the researcher from becoming nebulous and inexact when faced with difficult problems to solve.

The researcher should begin by describing broadly the types of data she or he plans to use in the study. The statements are direct and informative: "The data of this research are of two kinds...." Each type of data is then clearly described.

The study will utilize two categories of primary data.

The secondary data are described. More detail with respect to both of these types of data will be given later under the heading in each subproblem entitled "The Data Needed."

This is the first page of a new section of the proposal. Note the format, and the very effective way in which "open space" has been used.

First pages of chapters and new sections place the folio (page number) at the bottom, centered.

For the researcher merely to amass data is not sufficient. Data in its raw form is frequently defective or contaminated. The researcher should, therefore, state unequivocally what standards the data must meet or under what conditions she or he will accept the data. Here the researcher has provided a screening process through which the data must pass in order to be acceptable for use in the study.

Immediately after stating what the data are, we state the standards which they must meet to be acceptable.

Having presented the types of data and their refining criteria, the next item to be settled is the methodology to be chosen.

The author has buttressed his comment on method by citing from a standard text on research methods.

of the method or techniques must also include a description of the schema if ambiguity is to be avoided. The classification system suggested by Barr[2] includes the grouping of data-gathering techniques and data-processing methods among others. Within that framework, this research uses the survey method for data gathering and actuarial prediction for data-processing.

Here is the statement of methodology: the survey method will be used. Now we know the methodological framework within which we are operating.

Further description of the data-gathering procedures is suggested by Mouly.[3] His system would classify the data-gathering method proposed for this research as a self-report descriptive survey and the data-processing methods as statistical empiricism.

Now the author goes one step further and suggests that the method will be more closely pinpointed as a descriptive survey—using Mouly's definition—and that the data processing methodology will be "statistical empiricism."

The methods and procedures used in this study are those developed by E. K. Strong, Jr. over a period of forty years and continued by David P. Campbell, Director of the CIMR. Interest measurement research continues to evolve, however; and in spite of the prolific literature centered on the SVIB, the current procedures for scale development are not in print.

Here is an interesting comment. The author indicates that the methods and procedures used in this study are those that the developers of the instrument that he is using have developed "over a period of forty years." He also leaves the door open for new developments.

Now we come to the most critical point in the proposal: the specific treatment of the data for each subproblem. Until now we have been dealing in generalities. No more! Now we cannot be too specific.

Specific Treatment of the Data for Each Subproblem

Subproblem one. The first subproblem is to determine whether male cartographers employed by the Federal Government have a discrete pattern of interests different from men in general as measured by the SVIB.

The author begins by restating the subproblem. Let's get it before our eyes and know precisely what it is we are attempting to resolve.

Each subproblem will be considered under four headings:
The Data Needed
Where the Data Are Located
How the Data Will Be Secured
How the Data Will Be Treated.

The Data Needed

The data needed for the solving of subproblem one are (a) the names of the cartographers within the employ of USATOPOCOM who meet the criteria established earlier in this proposal, (b) the responses of the criterion group to the SVIB, and (c) the responses of the normative men-in-general group to the SVIB.

Here the author states what data he needs to solve the subproblem. Note how specific he is in specifying the data needed.

He is in the same position as a builder who must specify exactly what materials he needs to construct the part of the building he is erecting.

[2]Arvil S. Barr, "Research Methods," Chester W. Harris, (ed.) Encyclopedia of Educational Research (New York: Macmillan, 1960), pp. 1160-1166.

[3]George J. Mouly, The Science of Educational Research (New York: American Book Company, 1963), pp. 300, 301.

A second citation justifies his own choice of method.

The Location of the Data

The identification data are located in the personnel files of the USATOPOCOM, Washington, D. C.

The responses of the criterion group are located within that population.

The responses of the normative men-in-general group are located at the CIMR, University of Minnesota.

While some researchers may feel that the format that we have suggested here is somewhat pedantic, it may be well for you to force yourself to articulate precisely where the data are located that you will need. I have seen entirely too many students who know what data they need but when asked where the data are located, they bewilderingly begin: "Well, I guess it is in...." Let's not guess. There is no guessing in this proposal. We should know with such precision where the data are located that we could send another to get the data for us with specific instructions as to where to get it.

Here we could go to the personnel files of USATOPOCOM (if we had proper credentials) and to the office of CIMR at the University of Minnesota. We know where the data are.

The Means of Obtaining the Data

The identification data will be requested of the Personnel Officer, USATOPOCOM. Prior verbal permission for release of the data has been obtained. Appendix A exhibits the letter requesting these data.

The responses of the criterion group will be obtained by written request from the Commanding General, USATOPOCOM, accompanying the mailed SVIB to the individual members of the criterion group. Appendix B contains a copy of the cover letter. In order to preclude possible compromise and to avoid infringement of copyright, a copy of the SVIB is not included in the appendices to this proposal.

The responses of the normative men-in-general group will be obtained from Dr. David P. Campbell, Director, CIMR, University of Minnesota, 101 Eddy Hall, Minneapolis, Minnesota 55455. Appendix C contains the prior letter offering assistance, and Appendix D displays the letter requesting the data.

All right; you know what data you need and where they are located. The next question is: How will you secure them?

This section spells out the answer to that question without any ambiguity.

Note that for even the criterion group provision is made for obtaining the data. No loose ends remain!

If you are tempted to pass any of these sections off with a generalized comment such as, "The data will be obtained from the sources where they are located," don't. It usually indicates either that you don't know how you will get them, or that you are too careless to bother to spell it out. Either situation will defeat you finally.

The Treatment of the Data

How the Data Will Be Screened. The completed blanks returned by the criterion group will be screened to eliminate those where the respondent fails to meet the criteria for experience and job satisfaction and those forms improperly filled out.

How the Item Analysis Will Be Made. The criterion group response data will be treated by performing an item analysis to determine which of the three responses, i.e., "Like," "Indifferent," or "Dislike," have been made to each of the 298 items on the blanks that are currently used in scoring. The number of persons among the total group selecting each response to each item will be converted to a percent value,

Study the format of the headings in this section of the proposal. Note that the centered heading, unitalicized, follows the paragraph sidehead, and that the next paragraph sidehead has its principal words capitalized to distinguish it from the first paragraph sidehead format. Read the headings consecutively under "The Treatment of the Data" and you will see how logically the author of this proposal proceeds.

The subsection on "The Treatment of the Data" is the vital center of the proposal. Unless this section spells out without any equivocation or ambiguity precisely what the author of the proposal intends to do, the proposal is a failure.

The criterion for this section should be that it ought to explain accurately precisely what is to be done to the data so that, were you inaccessible, anyone competent to do the research could carry out your research project without your assistance.

and this value will be numerically compared with the responses of men in general.

Scoring weights will be assigned for each item where the difference in response between cartographers and men in general is 20 percent or greater. The items will be assigned positive values whenever the difference is in the direction of the cartographers and minus values when the reverse is true.

Table I is hypothetical so far as the data it exhibits, but it is illustrative of the way the data will be treated.

What is the rationale for 20 percent? The researcher should tell us. Why not 10, 15, 25, 30 percent instead of 20?

Note the inclusion of Table I. Many students will say: "A table will be presented," and nothing more. It is not enough to know that a table will be presented but precisely, what the table will indicate, and what will be its data components. To show this treatment of the data, the skeleton "hypothetical" table is presented.

TABLE I

DETERMINATION OF WEIGHTS FOR CARTOGRAPHER SCORING KEY FOR THE SVIB

(Hypothetical Data)

	Percentage of Men in General Tested			**Percentage of Cartographers Tested**			**Differences in Percentages Between Groups**			**Scoring Weights for Cartographers**		
Items on SVIB	L	I	D	L	I	D	L	I	D	L	I	D
Architect	37	41	22	63	31	7	25	−10	−15	1	0	0
. . .	. . .	. . .	. . .	. . .	. . .	. . .	. . .	. . .	. . .	. . .	. . .	. . .
Zoologist	27	41	32	87	11	1	60	−30	−31	1	−1	−1

Note the format of the table. It is entitled TABLE I (all capital letters). Roman numerals are used to number tables. Double lines indicate the boundary top and bottom of the table with the column headings separated from the data arranged under them by a single line.

Perhaps an asterisk after the first "L I D" would explain these cryptic letters for those who do not know the SVIB. These letters are three choices that the respondent has to the item: L= "Like," I= "Indifferent," D= "Dislike."

How The Data Will Be Interpreted. The data will be interpreted by counting the number of weighted items and comparing the resulting total to Strong's criterion.[4] That is, weighted response variance on the last forty items will be construed to mean that cartographers possess a discrete pattern of interests as measured by the SVIB.

Note that we have come full circle. The subproblem sought to determine whether cartographers possessed discrete interest patterns as compared with men in general.

After you have finished with the "Treatment of the Data" section it is always well to go back to read your subproblem again to see if what you have done does indeed provide an answer to the subproblem.

Subproblem two. The second subproblem is to construct a scoring key for the SVIB to differentiate cartographers from men in general and also from other occupational groups.

Now we come to the second subproblem. As before, it is stated (repeated) here so that the reader does not lose sight of what it is we are structuring a solution for.

[4] E. K. Strong, Jr., et al., "Proposed Scoring Changes for the Strong Vocational Interest Blank," Journal of Applied Psychology, XLVIII (April 1964), 75-80.

The Data Needed

The data needed are the scoring weights for the 298 items of the cartographer-criterion group, their original responses to the SVIB, as well as responses from a separate group of male cartographers in the Federal employ, the scoring keys for all other available occupational groups, and their normative data.

Again we go through the same ritual as with subproblem one. The careless researcher will not have the patience and precision to work out each subproblem with meticulous detail. If not, it is an unhappy augury for the remainder of his research effort. All that he does will probably be careless and imprecise. A proposal carefully and meticulously worked out is 50 percent of the research effort completed.

The Location of the Data

Data collection and treatment to be conducted as part of subproblem one will obtain the responses of the cartographer-criterion group and produce, in Table I, the scoring weights. The response data from a separate group of cartographers are located among the male cartographers employed by the U.S. Navy Oceanographic Office, Washington, D.C., and the U.S. Air Force Aeronautical Chart and Information Center, St. Louis, Missouri. The other available occupational scales and their normative data are located at the Center for Interest Measurement Research, the University of Minnesota, Minneapolis, Minnesota.

So accurate are these locations that, again, we could send another with proper credentials to get the material for us.

The Means of Obtaining the Data

The responses of the cartographer-criterion group and the scoring weights will be available at the conclusion of the prior subproblem. The respective commanders of the U.S. Navy Oceanographic Office and the U.S. Air Force Aeronautical Chart and Information Center will each be requested by letter to furnish Strong Vocational Interest Blank responses from a selected sample of sixty cartographers meeting the established experience criterion. A visit will be made to each of these installations to select randomly from the personnel files every fourth name and to facilitate the distribution and return of the blanks. Appendix E contains the letter requesting the data.

Note the way in which the researcher has provided for randomization of his sample: every fourth name in a file.

Letters are important. Note that the researcher exhibits the letters, here in Appendix E, which he will use requesting the data. This gives us an opportunity to see the whole process of selection of the data.

The other available occupational scales and their normative data will be requested from David P. Campbell, Director, Center for Interest Measurement Research, University of Minnesota, 101 Eddy Hall, Minneapolis, Minnesota, 55455. Appendix C contains the letter requesting this data.

The Treatment of the Data

Scale Construction. The new cartographer scale will be construed by selecting those Strong Vocational Interest Blank response items from

The researcher might have strengthened his proposal at this point by giving us the rationale for setting 20 percent as an arbitrary—or seemingly arbitrary—figure.

Table I that discriminate with a 20 percent or greater variance. The scoring key will be comprised of all items having weights of +1 or −1.

Normalizing. Norms for the cartographer scale will be established by:

(1) scoring the criterion group of answer sheets on the new scale,

(2) computing standard scores for the results,

(3) assigning letter ratings to appropriate ranges of standard scores for the criterion group.[5]

Note how clearly the author of this proposal outlines his next three steps. We shall now note each of these steps with specific emphasis.

The criterion-group answer sheets will be scored to obtain the algebraic sum of the previously selected items. Their range and arithmetic mean score will be determined. The standard deviations will be computed by the formula:[6]

← STEP 1

Where statistics are involved it is well to give the formulas that will be used, together with the meaning of each symbol employed in the formula. This was not done here. The authority or origin for the formula should also be given (here Downie and Heath; see footnote).

A slight weakness is discernible at this point in the proposal. The researcher should have told us not only what he was doing statistically, but why he needed to do it. Why does he need the standard deviation?

$$s = \sqrt{\frac{x^2}{N - 1}}$$

The raw scores will be converted to standard scores by the formula:[7]

$$\text{Standard score} = \frac{(x - \bar{X})}{s}(10) + 50$$

← STEP 2

Of course, we see why he needed the "s" in the next formula: to derive the standard score.

Here the researcher does give us the symbols and their meaning. This is always desirable.

Where

x = an individual raw score

$\bar{X}$ = criterion group raw-score mean

s = criterion group raw-score standard deviation

Letter ratings will be assigned to the distribution of standard scores expressed as percentages in the manner developed by Strong.[8,9] The data will appear in Table II and Table III.

← STEP 3

Again, a skeleton table shows exactly how the data assembled from "raw" sources will be displayed.

[5] Campbell (1966), op. cit., p. 9.
[6] N. M. Downie and R. W. Heath, Basic Statistical Methods (New York: Harper and Row, 1959), p. 45.
[7] Ibid., p. 61.
[8] Strong (1943), op. cit., p. 64.
[9] Campbell (1966), op. cit., p. 9.

TABLE II

CARTOGRAPHER-CRITERION-GROUP-LETTER-GRADE DISTRIBUTION

Rating	Standard Score	Percent of Normal Distribution	Value in S. D.	Percent of Cartographers
A	45 & above	69.2	−0.5 and above	- - -
B+	40-44	15.0	−0.5 to −1.0	- - -
B	35-39	9.2	−1.0 to −1.5	- - -
B−	30-34	4.4	−1.5 to −2.0	- - -
C+	25-29	1.6	−2.0 and below	- - -

No researcher should ever be content merely to say: "A table will be presented. . . ." Always that table should be shown in sufficient fullness for the reader to appreciate precisely what the table will show and, thus, be in a position to judge whether, with such data, the subproblem can be solved or the research goal achieved.

To avoid unnecessary repetition, the researcher may refer back to the description of a data treatment delineated in an earlier subproblem. The object of a proposal is not to make it repetitious, but clear.

The criterion group answer sheets will be scored for each available occupational scale, converted to standard scores and percentages as was previously done for the cartographer scale. The results will appear in Table III.

Note the progress through this section of the Treatment of the Data for the second subproblem: The research task as enunciated by the subproblem is to construct a scoring key. The author, therefore, constructs the new cartographer scale, establishes norms for it (presenting the statistics for so doing) and now cross-validates the scale, and—as we shall see next—establishes the validity and, finally, the reliability for the newly developed scale. Read the subheads. That is the complete story. No researcher could do more than that.

Cross Validation. The responses of the cross-validation group will be screened to eliminate those blanks where: (1) the respondent failed to meet the previously established criteria for experience and job satisfaction; and (2) the respondent filled out the forms improperly.

The responses will then be scored with the newly developed (Table I) cartographer scale and all other available occupational scales. The results will be converted to standard scores and percentages. The data will appear in Table III.

The statistical nature of the data will be determined by comparing the difference between the means by using the z test:[10]

Note how carefully the author of the proposal spells out precisely how the statistical matters will be handled.

He also footnotes the authority for each statistical operation. There is, therefore, no question about the appropriateness of the statistic for the research task in which he is applying it.

All of the values that will be later employed in the formulas are presented here for each group.

Scale Group	Cross-validation Group
$\bar{X}_1$ = ________	$\bar{X}_2$ = ________
S_1 = ________	S_2 = ________
N_1 = ________	N_2 = ________

Standard error for $\bar{X}_1$ Standard error for $\bar{X}_2$

$$S_{\bar{X}_1} = \frac{S_1}{\sqrt{N_1}} \qquad S_{\bar{X}_2} = \frac{S_2}{\sqrt{N_2}}$$

Now the computation of the standard error of the mean for each group takes place.

[10]Downie, op. cit., pp. 124-125.

Standard error of the difference between the means:

$$S_{D_{\bar{X}}} = \sqrt{S_{\bar{X}_1}^{\ 2} + S_{\bar{X}_2}^{\ 2}}$$

$$\underset{\sim}{z} = \frac{\bar{X}_1 - \bar{X}_2}{S_{D_{\bar{X}}}}$$

Then the computation of the standard error of the difference between the means.

And now, the computation of the z test.

The resulting data will appear in the $\underline{z}$ column of Table III.

And, finally, an indication of the disposition of the data in Table III.

Validity. The similarities between cartographers and other occupational groups will be determined by the degree and direction of correlation between the standard scores of the criterion group on their own scale and their scores on other scales. The responses, after scoring, will be converted to standard scores by the use of the previously stated formula. The standard scores will then be used to compute the Pearson's product-moment by the formula:[11]

Now, the validity of the new scale will be determined by comparing by means of the Pearson product moment correlation technique the similarities between cartographers and other occupational groups.

Note that the author of this proposal is careful to footnote his source of even so common a technique as the Pearsonian r formula. No opportunity is given for the reader of the proposal to question the integrity of the research approach.

$$\underline{r} = \frac{\Sigma xy}{\sqrt{(\Sigma x^2)(\Sigma y^2)}}$$

The data will be included in Table III.

The amount of overlap between the criterion group and other occupational groups will be determined using the method devised by Tilton:[12]

Here, then, is the statistical procedure to determine the amount of "overlap" between the two groups—again, firmly documented to establish the validity of the statistical tool.

$$Q = \frac{M_1 - M_2}{\frac{SD_1 - SD_2}{2}}$$

Where

M_1 is the mean of group one.

M_2 is the mean of group two.

SD_1 is the standard deviation of group one.

SD_2 is the standard deviation of group two.

The resulting data will appear in Table IV.

Again, the writer indicates the disposition of the statistical data by showing in skeleton form how he will present them in the research report.

[11] Downie, op. cit., p. 127.
[12] Tilton, op. cit.

TABLE III

SIGNIFICANCE OF THE DIFFERENCE BETWEEN THE SVIB MEAN STANDARD SCORE FOR CARTOGRAPHERS AND MEN-IN-GENERAL SCORED WITH THE CARTOGRAPHER SCALE

Group 1 (Criterion)	Group 2 (Cross Validation)	$X_1 - X_2$	$\tilde{z}$	Significance	Pearsonian Correlation Coefficient
Criterion	Men-in-General				
Criterion	Navy Cartographers				
Criterion	Air Force Cartographers				

A $\tilde{z}$ value of 1.96 is significant at the .05 level.

In this table all of the data are gathered together that have been derived during the treatment of the data for subproblem two.

With a design such as this, all the researcher needs to do now is to gather the data, process it statistically as indicated earlier, and fill in the table at the appropriate places with the appropriate data.

With a carefully thought-out proposal design the research is as good as completed!

Recall what we said earlier: A proposal is like the plans for a house. If the plans are carefully worked out, the contractor has no trouble in constructing the building. The simile is equally appropriate for the research effort.

TABLE IV

MEANS AND STANDARD DEVIATIONS OF RAW SCORES OF THE CARTOGRAPHER GROUP ON OTHER CURRENT OCCUPATIONAL SCALES AND THE PERCENTAGE OF OVERLAP

Scale	Mean	Standard Deviation	Percentage Overlap
Actor	–	–	–
Architect	–	–	–
Artist	–	–	–
–			
–			
–			
–			
–			
–			
Zoologist			

The table will present data comparing the cartographer group on other current occupational scales and the percentage of overlap.

Obviously the occupations are to be arranged alphabetically in this table and the respective values for each column will be entered, from Actor to Zoologist.

Reliability. The reliability or internal consistency of the newly developed cartographer scale will be determined by computing a Pearson product-moment correlation between odd-even split halves and correcting the correlation by applying the Spearman-Brown formula:[13]

$$r_{tt} = \frac{2_{r_{oe}}}{1 + r_{oe}}$$

Where many a less experienced researcher would have stopped, the writer of this proposal carries his data one step further: he establishes by statistical means the reliability or internal consistency of his newly developed cartographer scale.

[13]Downie, op. cit., p. 192.

Where

r_{tt} = the reliability of the original test

r_{oe} = the reliability coefficient obtained by correlating the odd items with the even items

Meaning of symbols is again given.

Interpretation of the data. The discreteness of cartographer's interests derived from responses to the SVIB will be interpreted in statistical terms by comparing the resulting numerical values of validity and reliability with standards established through precedence in similar research.

Finally, subproblem two is wrapped up in the final step that describes the manner in which the statistical data will be interpreted. This is the capstone for all that has gone before. Here we see an indication for the use of the "other" data, which the researcher indicated he needed when introducing the subproblem. "The other available scales and their normative data. . . ."

Note also that the researcher has used the data in this subproblem in the order in which he listed having need for it.

We come now to the third and last subproblem.

Subproblem three. The third subproblem is to analyze and to interpret the treated data so as to evaluate the discovered interests in terms of their discreteness in recruiting cartographers.

As with the other two, it is stated at the beginning of the section on the treatment which the researcher will give to the data pertaining to it.

The Data Needed

The data needed are: (1) all treated data developed in previous subproblems, (2) pertinent and selected secondary data gleaned from the literature, and (3) the normative data for the SVIB.

Again he states clearly the data he needs to solve this subproblem.

The Location of the Data

The data will be contained in Tables I, II, III, and IV of the study.

He indicates where the data are found.

The secondary sources—textbooks and journals containing reports and research conducted with the SVIB—are located at the Library of Congress, the Battelle-Tompkins Library on the campus of The American University, and in the microfile publications of University Microfilms, Inc., Ann Arbor, Michigan (which may be secured at the Library of Congress or at the Battelle-Tompkins Library, The American University).

On the first page of this section we indicated the need for secondary data. The reader may have thought that the researcher had forgotten about those data. Not so! Here is the subproblem in which those data will be appropriate. Now we see the comprehensiveness with which he planned. This is the way proposals should be.

The Means of Obtaining the Data

No problems exist with obtaining the primary data for this subproblem. All of the data are those which have previously been secured, and reside in treated form within Tables I, II, III, and IV.

To many readers this section may seem superfluous. Not to this researcher. He is entirely too careful for that. The section takes only a few sentences and he deems these well worth while in order to present the information completely.

The secondary data will be secured at the Library of Congress and from the stacks of the Battelle-Tompkins Library, The American University. The material will be reviewed in place and xerox copies of whatever materials requiring further study will be secured.

A complete statement of how the data will be secured.

Pertinent unpublished dissertations and theses have been obtained through interlibrary loan or purchased from University Microfilms, Inc., Ann Arbor, Michigan.

The section in the Selected Bibliography will indicate the meaning of pertinent. Here those dissertations are fully listed.

The normative data for the SVIB will have been obtained from the CIMR.

The Treatment of the Data

The most as well as the least descriptive discrete interest characteristics of cartographers will be selected from the scoring weight data contained in Table I. Similar and dissimilar occupations will be identified from the data appearing in Tables III and IV. Descriptions of allied and alien occupations will be extracted from the literature.

The researcher will now deal with extremes in terms of cartographer interests.

He will also analyze the data in Tables II and III for similar and dissimilar occupation interest patterns.

The data will be interpreted by consolidating the discrete characteristics into a composite and elucidative description of cartographer interests as compared and contrasted with other occupations.

Now comes a synthesizing of all of the data into "a composite and elucidative description of cartographer interests."

Turn at this point to the sample of the proposal in chapter 3. Read again what the purpose of the research was as stated in the problem. We have indeed come full circle!

THE OUTLINE OF THE PROPOSED STUDY

Many beginning researchers seem to feel that the outline of the proposed study is nothing more than the outline of the proposal. Nothing could be further from the truth.

You do in this section what the architect does when he draws an elevation of the various exposures of the building before a shovel of dirt has been lifted from the site for the foundation. You envision what the completed study will be. What will you have in Chapter I, Chapter II, Chapter III, etc.?

Note how the outline of the study departs from the outline of the proposal.

The first chapter is fairly consistent with the proposal, merely because we need the same information to orient us to the problem and to give us its setting.

PRELIMINARIES

- The Preface and the Acknowledgements
- The Table of Contents
- The List of Tables
- The List of Figures

I. THE PROBLEM AND ITS SETTING

- The Statement of the Problem
- The Statement of the Subproblems
- The Hypotheses
- The Delimitations
- The Definitions of Terms
- Abbreviations Used in This Study
- The Importance of the Study

II. THE REVIEW OF THE RELATED LITERATURE

Interests as Theoretical Concepts

Interests in Counseling and Vocational Choice

The Measurement of Interests

The Strong Approach

The Measurement of Interests among Cartographers

The review of the related literature section is also almost comparable to what we have done in the proposal with the exception of its updating with recent studies.

III. THE POPULATION OF CARTOGRAPHERS

The Population of Cartographers: Distribution and Genesis

The Criterion Group

The Cross-Validation Groups

Now organizationally we depart from the proposal. Chapter III of the proposed study will describe the population of the study and the various subgroups within the population.

IV. GENERAL PROCEDURE

Response Data

Collection Procedures

Treating the Data

Chapter IV will outline the general procedures by which the data will be handled. If the data were to be computerized, here would be a full discussion of the computerization process and the programming of the data.

V. THE RESULTS

The Criterion Group Returns

The Cross-Validation Group Returns

The Cartographer Scale

Other SVIB Scores of Cartographers

In this chapter the results of processing the data are set forth. It will doubtless consist of many tables of summarized data.

The Hypotheses

Hypothesis 1

Hypothesis 2

Hypothesis 3

Now we come to seeing whether the data have supported the hypotheses.

Other Findings

There are always miscellaneous findings. These are presented.

Summary of Results

Finally, the summary.

VI. SUMMARY, CONCLUSIONS, AND RECOMMENDATIONS

Summary

Conclusions

Recommendations

This chapter brings the research to resolution. Here we have summarized for us the findings, the conclusions reached, and the suggestions for further research in the area.

BIBLIOGRAPHY

The bibliography is always an indispensable part of any study. It lists all of the literature referred to in the study.

APPENDIXES

A. Letter of Transmittal

B. Follow-up Letter

The appendixes contain all important matter that has facilitated the research.

C. Item Count and Differences in Group Percentages and Scoring Weights Assigned to the SVIB Key for Army Cartographers

D. Standard Score Means and Standard Deviations of the Cartographer Groups on Other Current Scales of the SVIB

E. Significance of the Differences between Cartographer Group Means on Other Scales of the SVIB

F. Percentage Overlap of Cartographers on Other Current Scales

G. Pearson Product Moment Correlations between Scores of the Cartographer Criterion Group on the Cartographer Scale and Other Occupational Scales Incorporated in the 1971 Revision to the SVIB

H. Significance of the Differences between the Mean SVIB Scores of Cartographers and other SVIB Occupational Groups

The appendixes also contain a set of displays of the "raw" data and the statistical computations that are so necessary if anyone would wish to check your results, redo the study, or compare point for point the results of a later study with your data.

This material, too bulky for inclusion in the main study, is extremely valuable for anyone who might wish to check your statistics or do other computational studies on the basis of your data.

SELECTED BIBLIOGRAPHY

Books

Blum, Milton L., and B. Balinski. Counseling and Psychology. New York: Prentice-Hall, Incorporated, 1951.

Buros, Oscar K. (ed.). The Sixth Mental Measurement Yearbook. Highland Park, New Jersey: The Gryphon Press, 1965.

Campbell, D. P. (revised from E. K. Strong, Jr.). Manual for the Strong Vocational Interest Blank for Men and Women. Stanford, California: Stanford University Press, 1966.

Clark, K. E. Vocational Interests of Non-professional Men. Minneapolis, Minnesota: University of Minnesota Press, 1961.

Clark, K. E., and D. P. Campbell. Minnesota Vocational Inventory. New York: Psychological Corporation, 1965.

. . . .

This is a partial page of the Selected Bibliography section. This section is indicated as dealing with books. Other sections of the bibliography deal with periodical and journal materials; publications of government, learned societies, and other organizations; and unpublished materials (dissertations, theses, etc.).

Note: For personal reasons, the section preceding the Selected Bibliography entitled "The Qualifications of the Researcher" has been omitted. It forms, however, an essential part of every research proposal. Information concerning the competence of the researcher to engage in the research (and in professional research vitas of the participants) is always an expected component of every proposal. This material usually precedes the bibliographical material.

Significant and Influential Research

The research of Professor Vera John-Steiner began with very simple questions:

What are the origins of creativity, and how do creative people think?

Where did Dr. John-Steiner's data come from? What was her research method? This intriguing article may give you some clues.

A psycholinguist, Dr. John-Steiner interviewed more than 100 creative men and women and searched through letters, journals, biographies, and autobiographies of writers, authors, artists, and scientists of the past and present. Was there a single, definitive pattern? Dr. John-Steiner found none. But she did find enough testimony to gain some insight into the origin and nurture of creative minds.

Stephen Spender, the British poet, wrote down many ideas in rough form in notebooks. He has at least 20 of these treasuries of thinking, spanning many years. He reviews them in search of provocative ideas. Mozart delved into his "bag of memories" for his compositions. Einstein could not recall how he acquired his great thoughts. Asked once by an interviewer, he paused awkwardly, then replied, "I don't really know. I've had only one—or maybe two!"

Childhood impressions and experiences—especially involving curiosity and fantasy—seem to have had a strong influence in shaping the creative person, as did the influence of a caring adult, such as a teacher or parent.

What are the characteristics of the creative person? Independence, nonconformity (remember Emerson's remark in his essay on "Self-Reliance": "He who would be a man must be a non-conformist!"), and flexibility.

The report on Dr. John-Steiner's research is contained in a book, *Notebooks of the Mind: Explorations of Thinking,* (University of New Mexico Press, 1986.)[5]

[5] Much of the information in this section was adapted from an article by Fred M. Hechinger, "Origins of Creativity Are Examined," in *The New York Times*, February 25, 1986.

The Computer as a Tool of Research

Backup Files

Whatever is entered into a computer and stored in its disk memory is in danger of being lost. The computer owner who has saved valuable records, important data, and other irreplaceable information in only one disk file should not leave such material to the possibility of chance obliteration. It *can* happen.

For those computers where the files are stored on hard disk, a disk failure, an accidental deletion of an important file, an unexpected power failure—any of these can cause important data to vanish in a flash, forever! If the material has not been duplicated on another disk, it frequently means weeks or months of tedious replacement of what was destroyed.

For this reason, wise computer users "back up" their important files on diskette storage and keep the backup diskettes in a safe place. Nothing is more bloodcurdling than to think that you have your entire dissertation stored in the computer only to realize that by external or human error it might vanish at the speed of light.

Hillel Segal and Jesse Berst, in *How to Manage Your Small Computer . . . Without Frustration,* vol. 2 (Englewood Cliffs, NJ: Prentice Hall, 1983), suggest:

1. Start by making four backup copies of the master program. Refer to these disks as #1, #2, #3, and #4.
2. Begin the first day by using #1 (or the hard disk) as your working copy. After a reasonable time (hour, morning, day), back up the data on disk #2. Note on the diskette envelope the date and brief description of contents, but do NOT write on the envelope with the diskette inside.
3. The second day use #2 as your working disk. Back up the material of the second day on disk #3. Keep rotating the disks.
4. At the end of the week, back up all of the previous week's work on disk #4.

5. Even if you save all your data on diskette, you should have a hard copy (printout) of all the critical matter. In this way, you can be absolutely sure that you will not lose critical data and have to retrace your steps because of an unexpected catastrophe.
6. If you have a hard disk, it is absolutely *essential* that you back up the data on this disk at the end of each installation session. The uncomfortable fact is that these units fail occasionally. When they do, they must be repaired, and *you usually lose all of the material stored on the disk.*

Remember, diskettes should be handled with care. Do not bend, fold, or store them in damp or overheated locations. Keep your fingers away from all the open slots. Oil and perspiration from your fingertips may affect the magnetic surface and cause data dropout in recording. It is always a good idea to view your diskette when placing data on it. In this way you are *sure* that you have saved the data you wish to save.

For Further Reading

Allen, E. M. "Why Are Research Grant Applications Disapproved?" *Science* 132 (1960): 1532–34.

Behling, John H. *Guidelines for Preparing the Research Proposal.* rev. ed. Lanham, MD: University Press of America, 1985.

Berthold, J. S. "Nursing Research Grant Proposals: What Influenced Their Approval or Disapproval in Two National Granting Agencies?" *Nursing Research* 22 (July–August 1973): 292–99.

Brodsky, Jean. *The Proposal Writer's Swipe File II.* Washington, DC: Taft, 1976.

DeBakey, Lois. "The Persuasive Proposal." *Journal of Technical Writing and Communication* 6 (1976): 5–25.

DeBakey, Lois, and Selma DeBakey. "The Art of Persuasion: Logic and Language in Proposal Writing." *Grants Magazine* 1 (1978): 43–60.

Dugdale, Kathleen. *A Manual on Writing Research.* 2d. ed. Bloomington, IN: Indiana University Bookstore, 1967.

Englebret, David. "Storyboarding—a Better Way of Planning and Writing Proposals." *IEEF Transactions on Professional Communication* 15 (December 1972): 115–18.

Gortner, S. R. "Research Grant Applications: What They Are Not, and Should Be." *Nursing Research* 20 (1971): 292–95.

Grant-in-Aid Handbook. Chicago: American Medical Record Association, 1985.

Hall, Mary. *Developing Skills in Proposal Writing.* Corvallis, OR: Office of Federal Relations, Oregon State System of Higher Education, Extension Hall, University Campus, 1971.

Holland, Sherry. "Using Measures of Treatment Strength and Integrity in Planning Research." *New Directions for Testing and Measurement* 27 (September 1985): 49–61.

Jacquette, Lee F., and Barbara L. Jacquette. "What Makes a Good Proposal?" in *The Foundation Directory, Edition Five,* pp. 424–26. New York: Columbia University Press.

———. "What Makes a Good Proposal?" *Foundation News* (January–February 1973): 18–21.

Kiritz, Norton J. "The Proposal Summary." *Grantsmanship Center News* 1 (1974): 7–10.

———. "The Proposal Introduction." *Grantsmanship Center News* 2 (1975): 37–45.

———. "The Problem Statement for Needs Assessment." *Grantsmanship Center News* 2 (1975): 33–40.

Lindvall, Carl M. "The Review of Related Literature." *Phi Delta Kappan* 40 (1959): 180.

Lisk, D. J. "Why Research Grant Applications Are Turned Down." *BioScience* 21 (1971): 1025–26.

Locke, Lawrence F., Waneen W. Spirduso and Stephen Silverman. *Proposals That Work,* Second edition. Newbury Park, CA: Sage, 1987.

Merritt, D. H. "Grantsmanship: An Exercise in Lucid Presentation." *Clinical Research* 11 (1963): 375–77.

National Institutes of Health Staff. *Hints on Preparing a Research Grant Application to the National Institutes of Health.* Bethesda, MD: The National Institutes of Health, August 1987.

Plotkin, Harris M. "Preparing a Proposal Step by Step." *Journal of Systems Management* 23 (1972): 36–38.

Preparing a Research Grant to the National Institutes of Health: Selected Articles. Bethesda, MD: The National Institutes of Health, May, 1987.

Rappaport, Alfred, ed. *Getting a Grant in the Nineteen Eighties.* Englewood Cliffs, NJ: Prentice-Hall, 1982.

Reif-Lehrer, Liane. *Writing a Successful Grant Application.* Boston: Jones & Bartlett, 1982.

Stallones, R. A. "Research Grants: Advice to Applicants." *The Yale Journal of Biology and Medicine* 48 (1975): 451–58.

Stolte, Karen. "A Guide to the Process of Preparing a Research Proposal—Strategies for Teaching Nursing Research." *Western Journal Nursing Research* 3 (Fall 1981): 445–50.

White, Virginia, ed. *Grant Proposals That Succeed.* New York: Plenum, 1983.

Williams, Cortez. *Grantsmanship and Proposal Writing Manual.* Albuquerque, NM: Development of Research and Human Services, 1981.

Wilson, Holly S. "Research Proposal: The Practical Imagination at Work." *Journal of Nursing Administration* 15 (February 1985): 5–7.

Woodford, F. P. "Writing a Research Project Proposal," in F. P. Woodford, ed., *Scientific Writing for Graduate Students.* New York: Rockefeller University Press, 1968.

PART III

QUALITATIVE RESEARCH METHODOLOGIES: DATA PRINCIPALLY VERBAL

CHAPTER 8

The Descriptive Survey Study

To behold is to look beyond the fact; to observe, to go beyond the observation. Look at a world of men and women, and you are overwhelmed by what you see; Select from that mass of humanity a well-chosen few, and these observe with insight, and they will tell you more than all the multitudes together. This is the way we must learn: by sampling judiciously, by looking intently with the inward eye. Then, from these few that you behold, tell us what you see to be the truth. This is the descriptive—the normative—survey method.

The researcher soon learns that the nature of the data dictates the research methodology that must be employed in the processing of those data. For this reason we have several so-called research methods.

The *descriptive survey method,* sometimes called the *normative survey method,* is employed to process the data that come to the researcher through *observation.* These are discrete data, as different from historical data, which come to the researcher through written records, as the subject matter of chemistry is from that of literature.

Survey Research: Observation with Insight

All truth is not apprehended by means of studying past records. We learn some truth by observing the events taking place in the world around us. Historical data is static; records remain records. But events are fleeting. What happens in a public square today may never be exactly repeated in days to come. There is, within limits, conformity and uniformity in life processes, and we are able to judge from what has happened at any fleeting moment what may happen again. The researcher, by drawing conclusions from one transitory collection of data, may extrapolate what is likely to happen again *under similar circumstances.* At best, this is a conjecture and sometimes a hazardous one at that, but it is our only way to generalize from what we see.

The method of research that looks with intense accuracy at the phenomena of the moment and then describes precisely what the researcher sees is called the *descriptive survey,* or the *normative survey.* The name implies the assumption that whatever we observe at any one time is normal and under the same conditions could be observed again in the future. The basic assumption underlying such an approach is that given phenomena usually follow a common pattern, or *norm*.

The beginning of this chapter may provide an opportune moment to turn back to chapter 6 and reread the discussion under the subheading "Data Are Ephemeral and Ever-changing."

So often we read survey studies that seem to suggest that what the researcher found in one sample population at one particular time can be accepted for all time as a constant. What is far more misleading is the strongly implied assumption that these results can be entered into the Book of Eternal Certainties as ever-abiding Truth.

Remember the wisdom of Heraclitus: There is nothing permanent but change.

The Meaning of the Term *Survey*

The word *survey* is composed of two elements that indicate precisely what happens in the survey process. *Sur-* is a derivative of the Latin *super*, meaning "above," "over," or "beyond"; the element *-vey* comes from the Latin verb *videre*, "to look" or "to see." Thus, the word *survey* means "to look or to see over or beyond" the casual glance or the superficial observation.

The word *descriptive*, frequently coupled with *survey* in describing this method, also gives insight into the nature of the method. *Descriptive* comes from *de-*, meaning "from," and *scribere*, "to write." The term, therefore, describes the essential character of the method. In employing this method, researchers do two things: first, they observe with close scrutiny the population bounded by the research parameters; second, they make a careful record of what they observe so that when the aggregate record is made, the researchers can then return to the record to study the observations that have been described there. In this sense, survey research involves, in common with historical research, the study of records.

The point should be clearly emphasized that "looking" or "seeing" is not restricted to perception through the physical eye. In research, we have many ways of seeing that have nothing to do with physical vision. The physician "looks" at the patient's heart through a stethoscope and by means of an electrocardiogram. The educator, the psychologist, the guidance and vocational counselor "look" at achievement, intelligence, attitudes, beliefs, or personality structure through tests, inventories, attitude scales, and other means of evaluation. Hundreds of thousands of survey studies have been conducted in which the "looking" has been done by means of a questionnaire; in interview studies, the "looking" has largely been done by the ear rather than by the eye!

In each instance, observation has been accompanied by the making of a record. The record is always a part of the observation. Look up the word *observe*. Study its etymology. You will discover that it is indissolubly linked with "a record," "a description" of some kind.[1] This preservation of fact—the record—is sometimes narrative, as in the instance of the case study. Glance at any medical journal. What you will find are descriptive survey studies of patients whose symptomatology is discussed at length in the professional article that follows, together with a discussion of treatment and conclusions and recommendations. These latter are the interpretation of the data. A case study lies midway between the descriptive survey method and the experimental method. Other records of facts resulting from observations occur in the form of tables, charts, graphs, and other summary and trend-indicating techniques.

What, then, are the practical considerations in conducting a descriptive survey study? Reduced to its basic elements, the method is essentially simple in design. It is a common approach, used with more or less sophistication in many areas of human activity. From the neighbor who solicits opinions from adjoining property owners or asks them to sign a petition on the granting of a variance that permits a violation of the building code, to the Gallup Poll that aims to determine the attitude of people toward the popularity of a presidential action,

[1] It is from the Latin: *Ob-*, "toward," "before," "completely" + *sevare*, "to save," "preserve," "keep" (in written form). Hence, *observe* suggests a preserving or keeping completely (in the form of a written record).

surveys are commonplace features of contemporary American life. This is not to suggest, however, that because of its frequent use the survey is any less demanding in its design requirements or any easier for the researcher to conduct than any other research method. Quite the contrary, the survey design makes certain specific and critical demands upon the researcher that, if not carefully respected, may place the entire research effort in jeopardy.

Characteristics of the Descriptive Survey

We shall begin by outlining the basic structure of the descriptive survey as a method of research, indicating its salient characteristics.

1. The descriptive survey method deals with a situation that demands the technique of observation as the principal means of collecting the data.
2. The population for the study must be carefully chosen, clearly defined, and specifically delimited in order to set precise parameters for ensuring discreteness to the population.
3. Data in descriptive survey research are particularly susceptible to distortion through the introduction of bias into the research design. Particular attention should be given to safeguarding the data from the influence of bias.
4. Although the descriptive survey method relies upon observation for the acquisition of the data, those data must then be organized and presented systematically so that valid and accurate conclusions can be drawn from them.

Each of the preceding four steps will be discussed at greater length in the pages that follow. Each is important because it deals with a critical area in survey research.

With survey studies, observation in one way or another is absolutely essential. We have already discussed briefly the meaning of observation in its wider connotation. It may be considered to be almost synonymous with *perception* in the broad sense of that term—namely *being aware of data through some means of detecting them.* Many times the researcher may never see, in the conventional sense of perceiving with the eyes, the source of the data.

While researchers in the physical and biological sciences like to think of their research as purely experimental, many aspects of research in these disciplines draw on perspective survey techniques. Therefore, the physicist, the biologist, the psychologist, and others who consider their research to be purely empirical and experimental should recognize that they can and do employ other methodological approaches, among these the descriptive survey.

The Questionnaire

Data sometimes lie buried deep within the minds or within the attitudes, feelings, or reactions of men and women. As with oil beneath the sea, the first problem is to devise a tool to probe below the surface. A commonplace instrument for observing data beyond the physical reach of the observer is the *questionnaire.* The questionnaire may be sent to people thousands of miles away, whom the researcher may never see. In this sense, the social scientist who collects data with a questionnaire and the physicist who determines the presence of radioactivity with a Geiger counter are at just about the same degree of remoteness from their respective sources of data. Neither sees the source from which the data originate. The questionnaire, like the Geiger counter, is a totally impersonal probe. Because of this impersonality associated with the questionnaire, we need to be governed by several practical guidelines when employing it as a tool in survey research.

The Language Must Be Unmistakably Clear. Communication is a deceptive skill. What may be crystal clear to you may be so much meaningless jargon to another person. For example, take a very simple question: "How many cigarettes do you smoke each day?" That seems to be a clear and unambiguous question, especially if we accompany it with certain choices so that all the respondent has to do is to check one of them:

How many cigarettes do you smoke each day?
(Check one of the following.)

__ *more than 25* __ *25–16* __ *15–11* __ *10–6* __ *5–1* __ *none*

The trouble with the question is, of course, the assumption underlying it. The assumption is that people smoke the same number of cigarettes each day. But what happens in an actual situation to an assumption of that kind?

Nervous erratic smokers get that questionnaire. As a group, they do not fit the assumption. At the office or at work, when the pressure is on, and they are working at full speed, they may be chain smokers. When they get home, on holidays and weekends, they may relax and smoke only one or two cigarettes a day—or go without smoking at all. How are the individuals in this group supposed to answer the above question? What box does this type of smoker check?

The first guideline, therefore, for questionnaire construction is: *Inspect the assumptions underlying the question. Do the assumptions fit with the realities of life?*

All questionnaires should be pretested on a small population in what is often referred to as a *pilot study*. Every researcher should give the questionnaire to at least half a dozen friends or neighbors to test whether there are any items that they may have difficulty understanding or that may not ask exactly what the writer of the questionnaire is seeking to determine.

We have hinted at one of the principal causes for ambiguity in the questionnaire and for the inability of recipients to understand the questions that are asked. It is that the researcher has not spent enough time and care in *defining the purpose* for each item in the questionnaire and in *editing* the questions so that each is meticulously and precisely phrased to elicit the answer that the researcher is seeking.

For instance, take the query about smoking. Had the author of that question thought clearly and examined the assumption upon which the question was predicated, he or she would immediately have seen that instead of assuming that all people would conform to the question, a preceding question should have been asked:

Are your daily smoking habits reasonably consistent—i.e., do you smoke about the same number of cigarettes each day?

__ *Yes*
__ *No (If you mark "No," skip the following question.)*

Questionnaires Should Be Designed to Fulfill a Specific Research Objective. Many questionnaires are so inexpertly written that they bear the hallmarks of a quick, effortless attempt "to gather some data" that "may be helpful" in solving the research problem. Aimless, haphazard thinking and careless, imprecise expression are the most commonplace faults in constructing questionnaires. This lack of design and precision of expression may also account for the small return of questionnaires when they are sent to a given population.

Item by item, a questionnaire should be quality-tested again and again for precision of expression, objectivity, relevance, suitability to the problem situation, and probability of favorable reception and return. Have you concentrated on the recipient of the questionnaire, putting yourself in the place of one who is asked to invest time on your behalf? If you received such a questionnaire from a stranger, what would your honest reaction be? These questions are important and should be answered impartially.

We have hinted at a very important matter. The writer of a questionnaire should never forget that he or she is asking of the addressee a gift of time and effort and the favor of a reply. This brings up several important considerations in questionnaire construction.

Be Courteous. A request beginning, "Would you please check . . ." will oil the wheels of cooperation and enhance your chances of having your questionnaire receive more kindly attention than one that continually pushes the questions with only a commanding imperative that exudes an "it-is-your-duty-to-answer-these-questions-for-me" attitude.

Simplify. Make the instrument as simple to read and to respond to as possible. The questionnaire should demand as little effort and time on the part of the respondent as possible. A check-item questionnaire is generally preferable to the completion type or one that asks the respondent to reply with an extended discussion.

Completion questionnaires are time-consuming and mentally debilitating for both respondent and researcher. Don't forget that you are going to have to wrestle with the respondent's words to try to ascertain exactly what the answer is. Those who write in the "Yes-no, and I'll-tell-you-why" style are few and far between. Discussion answers rely entirely upon the skill of the respondent to express accurately in words the thought that he or she wishes to express. With the completion-type questionnaire, the respondent is tempted to ramble, engaging in discussion that does not answer the question or that is beside the point.

Save your respondent from this ordeal. Use your imagination. After answering 15 to 20 completion questions, your respondent will feel that you are demanding the writing of a book! It is a major compositional exercise and unfair to those from whom you request a favor.

Think of the Other Person. Put yourself in the place of the respondent. What would be your reaction if someone you never saw sent you a questionnaire such as you presume to impose upon another? What is the initial impression your questionnaire makes as a stranger draws it from the envelope? Is it inordinately long and time consuming? Is it cleanly and neatly typed? Does it have adequate margins, giving the impression of relaxation and uncluttered ease? Are the areas for response adequate and clearly indicated? Is the tone courteous and are the demands reasonable? Have you provided *return postage* and an *addressed envelope* for the return of the questionnaire?

Concentrate on the Universal. Try to address your questions to universals rather than to specifics, to general problems and ideas rather than to purely personal matters, to local conditions and issues, which fact you have presumably already announced to your addressee.

Make It Brief. The questionnaire should be as brief as possible and should solicit only those data essential to the research project. This need not curtail the adequacy of the instrument, but the researcher should test every item by the following two criteria: (1) What do I intend to do with the information I am soliciting? and (b) Is it absolutely essential to have this information to solve any part of the research endeavor?

Check for Consistency. In questionnaires dealing with debatable or opinion-sensitive issues, or when you suspect that the respondent may give answers that are deemed prudent rather than true, you may wish to incorporate a countercheck question into your list at some distance from the first question. This helps to verify the consistency with which the questionnaire was answered. For example, take the following two questions appearing in a questionnaire as item numbers 2 and 30. This placement causes them to be widely enough separated to test their consistency. Note how they have been answered:

2. Check one of the following choices:
 _x_ *In my thinking I am a liberal.*
 ___ *In my thinking I am a conservative.*

30. Check one of the following choices:
 ___ *I find new ideas stimulating and attractive, and I would find it challenging to be among the first to try them.*
 _x_ *I subscribe to the position of Pope:*
 "Be not the first by whom the new is tried
 Nor yet the last to lay the old aside."

The two responses do not agree with each other. In the first, the respondent claimed to be a liberal thinker, but later, when given the liberal and the conservative positions in another form, indicated a position generally thought to be more conservative than liberal.

Send Return Postage. Accompany your questionnaire with a self-addressed stamped envelope for your respondent's convenience in returning the questionnaire. To impose upon a person's time and spirit of cooperation, and then to expect that person to pay the postage for you to get the data needed to carry out your study is unreasonable.

Offer the Results of Your Study to Your Respondent. In return for the investment of time and the courtesy of replying to your questions, offer to send your respondent a summary of the results of your study, if your respondent wishes it. You might provide a check space, either at the beginning or at the end of your instrument, where your respondent could indicate the desire to have such a summary, together with space for name and address. Ask for a zip code in the address. In questionnaires where anonymity is desirable, a separate postcard may be included to indicate the desire for a summary. It also should request name, address, and zip code and be accompanied by the request that it be mailed separately from the questionnaire.

Think Ahead. The researcher should have clearly in mind, even before constructing the questionnaire, precisely how the data will be processed after the results are received. Data-processing procedures will determine the form the questionnaire should take. If, for example, the data are to be card-punched and computerized, the questionnaire needs to be structured quite differently than if the data are to be handled in more conventional ways.

Questionnaires Succeed as Their Success Is Planned. One researcher who conducted a particularly successful questionnaire study handled it this way: After selecting her population, she sent to each person a letter describing the potential value of the study. The letter emphasized the importance of the study *to the addressee,* and it invited the addressee to cooperate by answering the questionnaire. Here is a copy of the researcher's letter of inquiry with marginal comments on some of its features (Figure 8.1).

Compare the letter in Figure 8.1 with Figure 8.2, a brief note that was sent to the author and that, unfortunately, is all too typical of the hundreds of similar ones that the author has seen proposed by his students in their first attempts at drafting such a letter.

Figure 8.2 represents a flagrant foisting, without benefit of common courtesy, of one's own selfish demands on others. Letters of this sort may be another reason for the poor return of questionnaires when beginning researchers attempt to employ the survey method.

Note the irrelevancies in this letter: "I am a student at XYZ University." That is a bit of autobiography. That's all. It has nothing to do with the purpose of the letter: to solicit my cooperation in replying to a questionnaire. "The enclosed questionnaire is sent to you. . . ." Yes, I know that. My name and address were on the envelope that the mail carrier delivered. You really don't need to tell me that. "I am attempting to get my degree in June." Bully for you, John! That's a laudable endeavor. But, you know, I don't know you and I really don't care whether you get your degree in June. May I put it baldly, young man? Frankly, my reaction is, "So what? Who cares? Why should I do you a favor; your degree means nothing to me! I'm offended by your inability to think clearly, your lack of consideration and absence of courtesy. Get your degree the best way you can!" These reactions are not without justification.

The Initial Letter Is All-Important. It should be carefully and thoughtfully structured, and it should stress the concerns of the person receiving the letter rather than the selfish interests of the sender. Some students forget this and in so doing betray their own self-centeredness without perhaps intending to do so.

Let us return to the letter in Figure 8.1. Mention was made there of an enclosed card that gave the recipient an opportunity to express a willingness to answer the questionnaire. The card was simple and straightforward, containing the following wording. It was addressed and stamped and required only a check mark and a signature on the part of the recipient (Figure 8.3).

Upon receipt of the card indicating a willingness to cooperate, the researcher mailed the questionnaire immediately. A log was kept of questionnaires mailed, the people to whom they were mailed and their addresses, and the date of mailing. In a date book, precisely three weeks after the mailing of each questionnaire, the respondent's name was entered so that if a reply

Figure 8.1 An Annotated Letter of Inquiry

THE AMERICAN UNIVERSITY
Massachusetts and Nebraska Aves., N.W.
Washington, D.C. 20016

The School of Nursing

August 15, 1992

Dear Alumna,

Your School of Nursing is appealing to you for help. We are not asking for funds—all we ask is a few minutes of your time.

It is to your advantage to be recognized as a graduate of a school which has an excellent reputation for the education and training of nurses to meet the realities of nursing practice. You can assist us to maintain—and to improve this reputation—by cooperating in the evaluation of the program of Nursing Education at The American University. What we would like to ask you is to give us your candid, honest opinion of the nursing program in effect when you were a student nurse in training at The American University. We have a questionnaire which we would like to send you, with your permission, and which will take no more than fifteen minutes of your time to answer.

The Lucy Webb Hayes School of Nursing at The American University is growing. With your help it can grow in professional stature and educational excellence. We are sure you will be willing to cooperate with us toward those desired goals.

As an enclosure with this letter, you will find a return post-card on which you may indicate your willingness to cooperate with us by answering the questionnaire. Thank you for the courtesy of your assistance.

Very sincerely yours,

Ruth G. Thomas

Ruth G. Thomas, R. N.

This letter was sent out by a student who was doing an evaluative study entitled: "A Study to Evaluate the Academic Program of the Lucy Webb Hayes School of Nursing at The American University."

The questionnaire was designed to gather information on one of the subproblems of the study: "How adequately do the graduates consider the program to have been in preparing them for a professional nursing career?"

Note the direct "other-fellow" appeal. The author quickly indicates this is not an appeal for money—only a few minutes of time.

The fact is strongly made that it is to the advantage of the addressee to answer the questionnaire.

Note: "with your permission!" Also, an estimate of time required helps to convince.

The positive is emphasized: we are growing; we want to grow in excellence—but we need you!

This is a splendid device for getting a commitment. The card will be reproduced later.

Note the tone. No "yours truly" here. The courteous tone is carried out to the very end of the letter.

was not received by that date, a reminder letter would be sent. The reminder was in the same vein as the initial letter. This second letter, with comments, appears as Figure 8.4.

The letter brought results. In the entire approach of the student, much persuasion was built into the correspondence; but it was done so deftly and tactfully that fine human relations were created and kept throughout the entire procedure. Courtesy, understanding, and respect for others pay large dividends in a situation where a researcher needs the cooperation of others. This is especially necessary in questionnaire survey studies.

Cognitive Approach: A Recent Questionnaire Improvement. Poorly designed questionnaires usually result in poor data quality. A recent study of questionnaire deficiency by Jobe and Mingay has explored analytically what happens cognitively when a subject is faced with a questionnaire.[2] The authors set forth the analytical factors as follows:

[2]Jared B. Jobe and David G. Mingay, "Cognitive Research Improves Questionnaires," *American Journal of Public Health* 79 (August 1988): 1053–55.

Figure 8.2 A Poorly Worded Request for Cooperation

X Y Z UNIVERSITY
Campus Station

April 1, 1992

Dear Sir:

I am a graduate student at X Y Z University, and the enclosed questionnaire is sent to you in the hope that you will assist me in obtaining information for my Master's thesis.

I should appreciate your early reply since I am attempting to get my degree this June.

Yours truly,
John Doe
John Doe

The cognitive approach to questionnaire design conceptualizes the responses to a survey question as involving four distinct stages, each of which can lead to erroneous reporting.[3] The first stage is *comprehension,* in which the respondent interprets the meaning of the question. The second stage is *retrieval* in which the respondent searches long-term memory for relevant information. The third stage is *estimation/judgment* in which the respondent evaluates the information retrieved from memory and its relevance to the question; the respondent may then combine the separate items of information to form, a response or, alternatively, the respondent may decide that the recalled information is inadequate and use that information as a starting point in forming an estimated response. The fourth stage is the *response stage* in which the respondent weighs factors such as sensitivity of the question, social desirability of the answer, probable accuracy of the answer, and so forth, and then decides what answer to provide. . . .

Poorly designed questions are often not revealed even by field questions. That is the bad news. The good news is that this same research has shown that techniques exist to improve questionnaire design. These techniques come from cognitive psychology.

Three [recent] reports from the National Center for Health Statistics demonstrate some of the cognitive methodology which can reduce respondent error in health surveys.[4]

The Interview

Closely allied to the questionnaire is the *structured interview.* The interview, as a data-gathering technique, is frequently misunderstood. Most students think of it as simply asking a person some questions; and, of course, it is that. But it is not asking just *any* questions in *any* way. The questions for the interview should be as carefully planned and as accurately worded as the items in a questionnaire. Interviews should be considered professional situations that demand equally professional planning and conduct on the part of the interviewer. We have seen how the questionnaire demands considerable thought and planning for its effective administration. Equally careful planning is necessary for the interview.

[3] R. Tourangeau, "Cognitive Science and Survey Methods," in T. B. Jabine et al. (eds.), *Cognitive Aspects of Research Methodology: Building a Bridge between Disciplines* (Washington, DC: National Academy Press, 1984): 73–100.

[4] These reports were issued by the National Center for Health and Vital Statistics, Series 6, *Cognitive and Survey Measurement.* For more information on reports from the National Center for Health Statistics, contact the Scientific and Technical Information Branch, 3700 East-West Highway, Hyattsville, MD 20782, telephone (301) 436–8500.

For those interested in this topic, see also P. Royston, D. Bercini, M. Sirken, and D. Mingay, *Questionnaire Design Research Laboratory. Proceedings of the Section on Survey Research Methods* (Washington, DC: American Statistical Association, 1986); 703–7.

Figure 8.3

Dear Mrs. Thomas:

- ❑ Please send the questionnaire; I will be happy to cooperate.
- ❑ I am sorry but I do not wish to answer the questionnaire.

Comments:

Date: ______________ ____________________
Name

Figure 8.4 A Followup Letter

THE AMERICAN UNIVERSITY
Massachusetts and Nebraska Aves., N.W.
Washington, D.C. 20016

The School of Nursing

September 5, 1992

Dear Alumna,

All of us are busier these days than we should be, and most of us have a hard time keeping abreast of those obligations which are essential and required. We know how the little extras sometimes receive our best intentions, but we also know that in reality none of us have the time which we would desire to fulfill those intentions.

From the questionnaire which reached you—we hope—about three weeks ago, we have had no reply. Perhaps you mislaid the questionnaire, or it may have miscarried in the mail—any one of dozens of contingencies could have happened.

In any event, we are enclosing another copy of the questionnaire. We are sure you will try to find fifteen minutes somewhere in your busy schedule to check its several items and drop it in the nearest postal box. Most of them have been returned. We'd like to get them all back. Will you help us?

Thanks. We shall appreciate your kindness.

Very sincerely yours,

Ruth G. Thomas

Ruth G. Thomas, R. N.

This letter applies tactfulness, diplomacy, psychology, and human relations techniques at their very best.

Note the universal and appreciative tone of the letter from the first three words: "All of us...". The first letter began with a "you" approach. This one is much more understanding. It takes any trace of guilt or failure-to-reply out of the situation.

No need for the recipient of this letter to make excuses; the writer has disarmed the situation by offering two and suggesting that there may be dozens more.

By enclosing a second questionnaire, come what may, the recipient has now no excuse for not returning the questionnaire—and she indicated on a card previously that she would carry through.

Note how gently the suggestion is made that she is one of the few delinquent ones.

The faith in this letter is boundless. It would be difficult indeed not to respond in the face of such belief that you will do so.

We have described in detail the approach of a researcher who used the questionnaire in a professional and scholarly way. To illustrate the use of the interview, we will describe how another researcher employed it with equal effectiveness.

The student's problem lay in the field of international relations. He wanted to interview certain United Nations personnel to get their opinions concerning issues within the province of his study. He hoped to gather his data quickly, but systematically, and he planned his approach toward that end. He planned to go to New York City for a series of interviews and wished to schedule them as tightly as possible to conserve both time and expense. His procedure was organized and logical.

How to Arrange an Interview. Approximately six weeks before going for the interviews, the student wrote the United Nations representatives with whom he wished to confer, indicating when he would be in New York and requesting an interview lasting not more than half an hour. He asked each prospective interviewee for an indication of several time slots when the interview might be scheduled. In his letter, he explained clearly what information he was seeking and his reasons for seeking it. (*Not* among his reasons was the fact that he was writing a thesis!) His reasons were mature and meaningful and were so phrased that they held some interest for those he was to interview. If you must reveal that you are collecting the data for a thesis, use the word *study* in lieu of *thesis*. Look at the world realistically. Aside from the student and the graduate adviser, theses hold very little glamour in the everyday world. Studies are much more acceptable.

With the letter, the student enclosed a separate sheet containing the questions that he intended to ask during the interview, arranged in the order that he would ask them. Also, in the letter he suggested that if the interviewee had no objections, taping the conference would facilitate matters considerably, conserving time and lessening the distraction of handwritten notes. He provided a check box on a return postcard for the interviewee to indicate whether there was any objection to recording the interview.

When he received his replies, he set up a master chart of appointments and places and confirmed immediately, by letter, the appointment time, thanking the interviewee for his or her cooperation. Where there was a time conflict, he sought to resolve it by suggesting alternate times that were still open.

Ten days before the interview, he mailed a reminder, together with another copy of the interview questions, just in case the interviewee had misplaced the copy previously sent. He also enclosed his full interview schedule so that his interviewee might appreciate the time exigencies under which he was working.

On the day of the interview, he arrived promptly. When taken in to see the person to be interviewed, he introduced himself, stated briefly that he had come in accordance with previously made arrangements, asked whether his interviewee wished a copy of the questions he had previously sent, and began with the first question. He tried to guide the interview, keeping always to his agenda of questions and seeking to preserve an easy, friendly, yet professional atmosphere.

As the interview drew to a close, he thanked his interviewee for the courtesy of giving his or her time and went off to his next appointment.

In three-and-a-half days, he had interviewed 35 United Nations representatives and had over four-fifths of his data on tape. Subsequently, he transcribed from the tape the substance of the interviews and submitted within ten days following his visit a typed transcript to each interviewee, together with a letter thanking that person for granting the interview. He asked each official interviewed to read the typescript carefully and, if it was correct, to sign at the end of the copy a statement that the typescript was a correct record of the interview. If the official found it inexact or incorrect in any place, the interviewee was requested to correct the script or to edit it as he or she desired. As in all manuscript, the typescript had wide margins and was double-spaced, which permitted ample room for corrections.

In the statement acknowledging the typescript to be correct, the researcher also incorporated a permission clause in which he requested permission to use whatever part of the interview that might provide data for his study, with the full understanding that before the study was released, the interview material would again be submitted to the interviewee for complete approval. This was done, of course, prior to submitting the report as a final document for the degree. In the final document, all acknowledgments were made, and the researcher noted the fact that the authors had inspected and approved all their quoted statements. This is the only way that a researcher or an author can be protected against the accusations of falsification of the facts, libel suits, and other legal entanglements.

Summary. The steps, then, for successfully handling the interview as a technique for gathering data for one's research study are simple, but very important:

1. Set up the interview well in advance.
2. Send the agenda of questions you will ask the interviewee.
3. Ask for permission to tape the conference.
4. Confirm the date immediately in writing.
5. Send a reminder together with another agenda of questions ten days before you expect to arrive.
6. Be prompt; follow the agenda; have a copy of your questions for your interviewee in case he or she has mislaid his or her copy.
7. Following the interview, submit a typescript of the interview and get either a written acknowledgment of its accuracy or a correct copy from the interviewee.
8. After you have incorporated the material into your research report, send that section of the report to the interviewee for final approval and written permission to use the data in your report.

The Checklist and the Sliding Scale Inventory

We shall discuss one further type of observational technique: the *differential sliding scale checklist* or *inventory*.

Researchers need to look purposefully at a situation, in order to have an agenda of objectives or behavioral goals toward which to direct their attention. In its simplest form, such a list of observational goals is the ordinary *checklist*, which is simply a list of items with a check mark after each in one of two columns: in the column "observed" or in the column "not observed."

Often, however, instead of a simple either-or choice, the researcher wishes to record for varying degrees of intensity or a range of frequency for certain events. A scale on which such ranges can be recorded is a checklist, with the checking being done on a variable scale—hence, its name: *a differential sliding scale checklist.* Sometimes this type of observational instrument is known as a *rating scale.*

An example of this type of scale is presented in Figure 8.5. The author constructed it so that readers could evaluate themselves in terms of the development of certain specific habits that are critical to effective reading. Reading is evaluated in terms of effective techniques, visual factors, and emotional factors. The inventory explores exactly 25 items. By so doing, an evaluation system having 5 choices for each item results in a full-scale performance of 100 percent. Similarly, by weighting each of the categories with an assigned value, we can then express any degree of intensity within the entire range of values in terms of percentage strength.

We have discussed at sufficient length the various observational tools and techniques generally employed in the descriptive survey study. In the last analysis, every researcher must devise the particular observational approach most appropriate to the demands of the particular problem and the data that the investigation of the problem will demand.

Figure 8.5 A Reading Habit Inventory

Reading Habit Inventory

For each of the following statements, check under Never, Rarely, Sometimes, Usually, or Always. Do not omit any of the items. Be truthful and utterly realistic. Represent your reading habits as they actually are.

Statement	Never	Rarely	Sometimes	Usually	Always
1. When I pick up a page of print, I notice the paragraphs specifically.					
2. I read as I drive, with varying rates of speed, depending upon varying reading conditions.					
3. While reading, I find it easy to keep my mind on the material before me.					
4. After I have been reading for a while, I stop reading for a few moments and rest my eyes by looking at some distant object.					
5. I am alert to the role which punctuation plays in aiding me to get the meaning.					
6. When I pick up a piece of reading matter for the first time, I look for certain specific items which will aid me in reading the piece more efficiently.					
7. I read groups of words at one glance.					
8. I notice a distinctive style, or flavor, of the author.					
9. I enjoy reading.					
10. I can read for long periods of time without a feeling of eye fatigue or tiredness.					
11. After I read a paragraph, if required to do so, I could sum up the main idea clearly and briefly in my own words.					
12. I make a practice of skimming articles frequently.					
13. In reading a paragraph I usually try to see the organization of its thought content: I look for the main idea, and the details which support it.					
14. I do not lose my place, or skip words or lines, while reading.					
15. I am mildly conscious of grammatical structure while reading.					
16. I feel comfortable and perfectly at ease while reading.					
17. In reading larger units of writing (articles, chapters, etc.) I try to see the outline and total structure of the author's thought.					
18. I have little difficulty in remembering what I read.					
19. When I read, especially for any length of time, I make sure that the page before me is adequately illuminated.					
20. When I read, I am reading for some definite purpose, and I try to keep that purpose clearly in mind as I read.					
21. I read the preface of a book.					
22. In reading more difficult material, after reading a paragraph or a section, I pause to summarize in a momentary flashback the material I have just covered.					
23. While reading, I am aware of questions which arise in my own thinking about the material being read.					
24. While reading, I hold the page 15 to 20 inches from my eyes.					
25. I am aware that with practice a person can improve his reading skills, and I make a conscious effort generally toward that end.					
Count the checks in each column to obtain: (A)					
Multiply by: (B)	0	1	2	3	4
to obtain: (C)		%	%	%	%

Now add the figures in row C for your final score:______%

Analysis of Your Reading Habits

Now, analyze your reading habits. What does the above Inventory mean? If you have marked it carefully and conscientiously, it should prove a helpful guide in aiding you to develop more effective reading habits than those you now have. This means that ultimately you will be a more efficient reader.

To analyze your reading habits, carefully check on the chart below, under the number of the item of the Inventory statement, the category (Always, Usually, Sometimes, Rarely, Never) as you marked it in the Inventory above. Out of the 25 items that you marked, certain of them attempted to appraise your habits associated with certain specific reading techniques. Other items attempted to evaluate the more important matters associated with ocular hygiene and visual efficiency. Finally, a few items sought to probe some of the emotional factors which may aid or hinder your total reading efficiency.

Note the line in the forms below marked, "Danger Line." As you transcribe your check marks from the Inventory above, you will find that you have checked either above or below this danger line. The check marks *below* the danger line indicate that in these matters you need to give attention to your reading habits and practices. Try to put into practice each time you read, the procedures suggested by the Inventory statements of those items which you have checked below the danger line.

1. What does the Inventory indicate as to my reading techniques? To find out, transcribe a check mark from the Inventory to the proper box in the chart following:

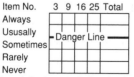

Item No.	1	2	5	6	8	11	12	13	15	17	18	20	21	22	23	Total
Always																
Ususally																
Danger Line																
Sometimes																
Rarely																
Never																

Total number of check marks below the danger line:____

2. What does the Inventory indicate about my visual factors in reading? Check the following chart to find out:

Item No.	4	7	10	14	19	24	Total
Always							
Ususally							
Danger Line							
Sometimes							
Rarely							
Never							

Total number of check marks below the danger line:____

3. What does the Inventory indicate about my emotional factors in reading? Check the following chart to find out:

Item No.	3	9	16	25	Total
Always					
Ususally					
Danger Line					
Sometimes					
Rarely					
Never					

Total number of check marks below the danger line:____

Total number of check marks in all three charts *above* the danger line:__________

Divide 25 into the *total* number of check marks you have *above* the danger line. This will give you your percentage score of *desirable* reading habits:________%

The Mobility Inventory for Agoraphobia. Another type of inventory is given here. This is a type of self-evaluation rating scale, whereby the agoraphobic rates according to a five-item scale his or her feelings in two different situations: when accompanied by another person or when alone. *Agoraphobia* is a morbid fear of open spaces. The word comes from two Greek elements: *agora,* the Greek word for market place, and *-phobia,* meaning "a fear of."

Five investigators in the Department of Psychiatry at the Temple University Medical School in Philadelphia, Pennsylvania, undertook to develop a twenty seven-item inventory to measure the self-reported agoraphobic avoidance behavior and frequency of panic attacks.[5]

The inventory, (Figure 8.6), was their instrument for gathering data for validating the reliability in mirroring the agoraphobic's feelings in a broad spectrum situation-setting.

Selecting the Population

We must now turn to another aspect of the descriptive survey method, namely choosing the population for the study, which we earlier indicated to be the second of the four essential factors of the descriptive survey method.

A basic rule governs the descriptive survey: Nothing comes out at the end of a long and involved study that is any better than the care, the precision, the consideration, and the

Figure 8.6 The Mobility Inventory for Agoraphobia

Name: ____________ Date: ____________

1. Please indicate the degree to which you avoid the following places or situations because of discomfort or anxiety. Rate your amount of avoidance when you are with a trusted companion and when you are alone. Do this by using the following scale.

1. Never avoid
2. Rarely avoid
3. Avoid about half the time
4. Avoid most of the time
5. Always avoid

(You may use numbers half-way between those listed when you think it is appropriate. For example, 3½ or 4½).

Write your score in the blanks for each situation or place under both conditions: when accompanied, and, when alone. Leave blank those situations that do not apply to you.

Places	When accompanied	When alone
Theatres	______	______
Supermarkets	______	______
Classrooms	______	______
Department stores	______	______
Restaurants	______	______
Museums	______	______
Elevators	______	______

[5] Dianne L. Chambless, G. Craig Caputo, Susan E. Jasin, Edward J. Gracely, and Christine Williams, "The Mobility Inventory in Agoraphobia," *Behavior Research and Therapy* 23 (1985): 35–44.

Figure 8.6 *continued*

Auditoriums or stadiums	______	______
Parking garages	______	______
High places	______	______
Tell how high ______	______	______
Enclosed spaces (e.g. tunnels)	______	______
Open spaces	______	______
(A) Outside (e.g. fields, wide streets, courtyards)	______	______
(B) Inside (e.g. large rooms, lobbies)	______	______
Riding In:		
Buses	______	______
Trains	______	______
Subways	______	______
Airplanes	______	______
Boats	______	______
Driving or riding in car		
(A) At any time	______	______
(B) On expressways	______	______
Situations:		
Standing in lines	______	______
Crossing bridges	______	______
Parties or social gatherings	______	______
Walking on the street	______	______
Staying at home alone	NA	______
Being far away from home	______	______
Other (specify)	______	______

We define a *panic attack* as:

1. a high level of anxiety accompanied by
2. strong body reactions (heart palpitations, sweating, muscle tremors, dizziness, nausea) with
3. the temporary loss of the ability to plan, think, or reason and
4. the intense desire to escape or flee the situation. (Note, this is different from high anxiety or fear alone.)

Please indicate the total number of panic attacks you have had in the last 7 days. ______.

thought that went into the basic planning of the research design and the careful selection of the population. *The results of a survey are no more trustworthy than the quality of the population or the representativeness of the sample.* Population parameters and sampling procedures are of paramount importance and become critical factors in the success of the study.

Many students in phrasing their problems forget what we have just been saying. They announce, for example, that their goal is to "survey the legal philosophies of the attorneys of the United States and to analyze the relationship of these several philosophical positions with respect to the recent decisions of the Supreme Court of the United States." A student who words a problem in this way has simply not thought through the meaning of the words themselves. "The attorneys of the United States"! The American Bar Association consists of over 147,000 attorneys, distributed over 3,536,855 square miles in the 50 states. But these are merely first hurdles. As we look at the problem more closely, we begin to discern other, more serious difficulties. What are "philosophical attitudes"? How does one isolate these attitudes in order to study them? How can you show a "relationship of philosophical positions" with "recent decisions of the Supreme Court"? How will this relationship be expressed? Will it be expressed statistically? If so, how will you quantify "philosophical positions" and "decisions"? If not, then what will it be?

Earlier in this book, we discussed the necessity for considering carefully the size, the selection, and the parameters of the survey population. The failure of the researcher to recognize population parameters and their demands upon research procedures and research design, as well as upon the resources available, generally indicates inexperience in the area of practical research planning and design.

But to get back to our more than 147,000 attorneys and their thoughts, it is not necessary, of course, to poll each and every one of them to get some indication of their composite thought. For the purpose of research, the term *universe* means simply "an area surrounding the problem that may contain facts relevant to the problem." Literally, the word suggests the factual area that lies or "turns" around "one"—the central—problem for research. The word comes from the Latin *unus* = one, and *vertere* = to turn. Here we shall define it with particular reference to the data: *A universe of data consists of the totality of those data within certain specified parameters.* Here the "specified parameters" were that those individuals who were to be studied were "the attorneys of the United States." But a universe of data is usually too large to be studied in toto. Where such is the case, we have devised a process that is both logically and statistically sound, namely the *process of sampling.*

Referring back to the attorneys once more, we should point out that the difficulty basically arises out of the statement of the problem. If the researcher has said what he or she means, then he or she proposes to survey "the attorneys"—all of them! If, on the other hand, the student intends to survey only a certain cross section of the attorneys, then the statement of the problem should have said that with such qualifying and accurately descriptive words as *selected, representative, typical, certain, a random sampling of,* and so on. Careful researchers say precisely what they mean. Note the difference in the meaning between "The purpose of this research is to survey the representative legal philosophies of a random sample of attorneys . . ." and the wording as it stands in the student's phrasing: "The purpose of this research is to survey the legal philosophies of the attorneys of the United States. . . ."

How, then, is sampling done? In a number of ways. Perhaps at the outset, the method of sampling is not nearly so important as the purpose of sampling and a careful consideration of the parameters of the population.

Look through the wrong end of a telescope. You will see the world in miniature. This is precisely what the sampling procedure chosen for any particular project should seek to achieve. *The sample should be so carefully chosen that through it the researcher is able to see all the characteristics of the total population in the same relationship that they would be seen were the researcher in fact to inspect the total population.*

That may indeed be a consummation devoutly to be wished, and, ideally, samples are population microcosms. In optics, unless lenses are precision-made and accurately ground, one is likely to get distortion through the spyglass. Similarly, unless the sampling is carefully planned and statistically tested, the conclusions that the researcher draws from the data are likely to be distorted. Such distortion we call *bias.* We will discuss this subject further in the next section. For the moment, however, we will concern ourselves with the types, methods, and procedures of sampling.

Types, Methods, and Procedures of Sampling

One basic rule holds whenever a researcher is considering methodology in relation to data. It matters not whether this methodology concerns sampling, a statistical procedure, or any other type of operation. The general rule is: *Look carefully at the nature of, the characteristics of, and the quality of the data.* After you see this clearly, you can then more intelligently select the proper methodology for the treatment of those data. Not all data lend themselves to sampling. Sampling is appropriate wherever large populations that have an outward semblance of homogeneity are to be investigated.

Nonprobability Sampling

At the outset, let's look at the global view of sampling. Sampling can be divided into two major categories: *nonprobability sampling* and *probability sampling.* In nonprobability sampling, there is no way of forecasting, estimating, or guaranteeing that each element in the population will be represented in the sample. Nonprobability sampling can also be divided into two types: convenience, or accidental, sampling and quota sampling. We shall give a definition and example of each of these.

Convenience or Accidental Sampling. Convenience sampling makes no pretense of being representative of a population. It takes the units as they arrive on the scene or as they are presented to the researcher by mere happenstance. There is also no attempt to control bias. Depending on your purpose and your awareness of the crudity of this type of sampling, convenience sampling may be appropriate to some less demanding kinds of data collection.

For example, I own a diner and want to sample the opinions of my patrons on the quality of food and the quality of service at the diner. I open for breakfast at 6 A.M. Each morning for a week I will sample the first forty patrons to arrive. Customers who have once expressed an opinion will be eliminated upon subsequent arrivals. The opinions that I eventually get are from thirty-eight men and two women. It is a badly skewed poll in favor of men; but I *do* have a sample, one that was derived in the most accidental manner. The individuals who arrive at 6 A.M. are likely to be certain kinds of men who go to work at that time—laborers, construction workers, truck drivers. Women generally do not appear in significant numbers in the diner before 8 A.M.

The data from this accidental sample give me the thoughts of robust, hardy men about my breakfast menu at the diner. That's all. But that may be all I need for the purpose I have. This poll also underscores another fact about the nature of research: All research data do not need to be sterile, highly refined, and controlled by criteria, but without these safeguards, the research may not be trustworthy.

Quota sampling. Quota sampling is a variant of convenience sampling. It selects respondents in the same ratio as they are found in the general population. Let us consider a population in which the number of blacks equals the number of whites. Quota sampling would choose, say, the first twenty blacks and the next twenty whites, regardless of the order in which they arrived.

For example, I am a reporter for a TV station. At noon, I position myself with microphone and television camera at a cross street in the center of a particular city. As people pass I interview them. That whites or blacks may come in clusters of two, three, or four is no problem. All I need are the opinions of twenty from each category of the population.

This is also an unregulated type of sampling. It has no limitations except the size of each category. There is no probability of forecasting how each twenty will arrive. For that reason, we term it nonprobability sampling.

Probability Sampling

In probability sampling, the researcher can specify in advance that each segment of the population will be represented in the sample. This is the distinguishing characteristic that sets it apart from nonprobability sampling.

The composition of the sample is derived by selecting units from those of a much larger population. In survey studies, the *manner* in which the sample units are selected is very important. Generally, the components of the sample are chosen from the larger population by a process known as *randomization.* Such a sample is known as a *random sample.* The two elements that are more important than any others in survey research are *randomization* and *bias.*

Randomization means *selecting a sample from the whole population in such a way that the characteristics of each of the units of the sample approximates the characteristics of the total population.*

Let's explain that. I have a beaker that contains 100 cc. of water. I have another container that has a concentrated solution of 10 cc. of acid. I combine the water and acid in proportions of 10 to 1. After thoroughly mixing the water and acid, I should be able to extract 1 cc. from *any* part of the solution and find that in that 1-cc. sample, a mixture of water and acid is in precisely a 10:1 proportion. In the same way, if we have a conglomerate population with differences of race, status, wealth, education, and other factors, and *if we have a perfectly selected random sample* (a situation usually more theoretical than practical), we will find in the sample those same characteristics that exist in the larger population, and we will find them in the same ratio.

A sample is no more representative of the total population, therefore, than the validity of the method of randomization employed in selecting it. There are, of course, many methods of random selection. We shall look at a few of the more common ones.

The Roulette Wheel Method. If the population is small—seventy-five or fewer individuals—each individual may be assigned a number in some orderly sequence: alphabetically by surname, by birthdate (youngest to oldest or the reverse), by weight, or by any other systematic arrangement. Corresponding numbers are on a roulette wheel. A spin of the wheel and its fortuitous stopping at a particular number selects the individual assigned to that number as a unit within the sample. The process of spinning the wheel and selecting the sample goes on until all the individuals needed to compose the sample have been chosen.

The Lottery Method. In the lottery method, the population again is arranged sequentially and assigned numerical identifications. Corresponding numbers are marked on separate tabs and put into a revolving drum or closed container. The numbers are tossed so that they are thoroughly mixed. Then one tab bearing a number is selected from the container, without the selector seeing the pool. The number selected is recorded, and then *the tab is tossed back into the pool again.* This is an important feature of the lottery method. It ensures that every individual has the same chance of being chosen as every other individual. If, for example, we are selecting 50 people out of a population of 100, and we do not cast each tab back after it has been selected, we will have an ever-diminishing population from which to make choices. Whereas the first choice would have one in 100 chances of being selected, the last would have one in 50 chances of being selected. In other words, the chances of being selected would be twice as great for the last individual as for the first.

If the same number is drawn twice, the second drawing is ignored. The number is returned to the pool, and another drawing is made. Drawing and tumbling go on until 50 tabs have been selected purely by chance.

The Table of Random Numbers Method. The table of random numbers is perhaps the most frequently used method for the random selection of a sample. We can employ this table in any manner. Generally, the researcher enters the table according to some predetermined method.

Entrance into the table may, in fact, be accomplished in many ways. One fundamental principle must be kept in mind, however: *the purpose of randomness is to permit blind chance to determine the outcomes of the selection process to as great a degree as possible.* Hence, in determining a starting point for the selection of random numbers, *pure chance* must always initiate the process.

Consider the table of random numbers presented in Figure 8.7. Ten blocks of random numbers are arranged horizontally, and ten are arranged vertically. Tables of random numbers may be found in most statistics textbooks. In the one presented here, the horizontal and vertical numbering of the columns has been done merely for purposes of convenience in locating a starting point for entering the table. Any block within the table will be at the intersection of two guide numbers. To enter the table you need an entry number of two digits—one will be a guide number designating a location on the horizontal column, and the other a guide number designating a location on the vertical column. But how do we find an entry number?

To find an entry number, pull a dollar bill from your wallet. The one we have just pulled has the serial number C 45 391827A. We choose the first two digits of the serial number, which makes the entry number 45. But which is the vertical and which the horizontal digit? We flip a coin. If it comes down *h*eads, the first digit will be for the *h*orizontal series. The coin comes down heads. This places the 4 in the horizontal series and the 5 in the vertical series. The block where these two digital columns intersect is the location where we begin within the table.

What other ways are there to find an entry number? Let your ingenuity have free rein. Only one rule governs the selection: *pure chance* dictates the choice. We will begin with the technique we have just used.

1. *Look at a dollar bill.* Note the first two digits of the serial number in the lower left- or upper right-hand corner. These will be your entry digits.
2. *Check the stock quotations.* Take any newspaper. Turn to the stock quotation page. Take the first letter of your surname. The first stock listed that begins with that letter will be your predetermined stock. Note its quotation for high and low. Disregard the fractional quotations. Take the two digits in either the high or low quotation column, or, if only one digit appears in each column, take the two digits together.
3. *Ask a friend for his or her social security number.* Select one of your friends at random. Ask for his or her social security number. Take the first two or the last two digits of that number. It will give you an entry number to locate a beginning block within the table of random numbers.
4. *Consult the World Almanac.* Look up any state within the United States. Take the figure representing the area. Select any one of three two-digit numbers: (a) the first two digits of the area, (b) the last two digits of the area, or (c) if it is a six-digit number, the middle two digits of the area. These will be your entry digits to the table.
5. *Use a telephone directory.* Open a telephone directory at random. Take the last two digits of the first number in the first column on either the left-hand or the right-hand page. Toss a coin again to decide. Tails decides the page will be the left-hand one (Tai*l*=*L*eft).
6. *Note a vehicle registration tag.* Step outside. Observe the first vehicle that passes. Note the last (or first) two digits on the registration tag. The digits will serve as an entry number to the table of random numbers.

Having arrived at the digital block location, the next step is to determine the size of the proposed sample. If it is to be fewer than 100 individuals, we will select only two-digit numbers; if it is to be fewer than 1,000, we will need three digits to accommodate the sample size.

Let us go back to the total population for a moment to consider the group from which the sample is to be drawn. It will be necessary to designate individuals in some manner. It is, therefore, advantageous to arrange the individuals within the population in some systematic order (alphabetically, for example, by surname) and to assign each person a serial number for identification purposes.

Now we are ready for the random selection. We start with the upper left-hand digits in the designated block and work first downward in the column; if there are not enough digits for the demand of the total sample in that direction, we will return to the starting digits and proceed upward. Having exhausted all 50 digits in any one column, move to the adjoining columns and proceed as before until the sample requirement is filled. As each digit designa-

Figure 8.7 Random Number Table

	1	2	3	4	5	6	7	8	9	0
1	03 47 43 73 86	36 96 47 36 61	46 98 63 71 62	33 26 16 80 45	60 11 14 10 95	53 74 23 99 67	61 32 28 69 84	94 62 67 86 24	98 33 41 19 95	47 53 53 38 09
	97 74 24 67 62	42 81 14 57 20	42 53 32 37 32	27 07 36 07 51	24 51 79 89 73	63 38 06 86 54	99 00 65 26 94	09 82 90 23 07	79 62 67 80 60	75 91 12 81 19
	16 76 62 27 66	56 50 26 71 07	32 90 79 78 53	13 55 38 58 59	88 97 54 14 10	35 30 58 21 46	06 72 17 10 94	25 21 31 75 96	49 28 24 00 49	55 65 79 78 07
	12 56 85 99 26	96 96 68 27 31	05 03 72 93 15	57 12 10 14 21	88 26 49 81 76	63 43 36 82 69	65 51 18 37 88	61 38 44 12 45	32 92 85 88 65	54 34 81 85 35
	55 59 56 35 64	38 54 82 46 22	31 62 43 09 90	06 18 44 32 53	23 83 01 30 30	98 25 37 55 26	01 91 82 81 46	74 71 12 94 97	24 02 71 37 07	03 92 18 66 75
2	16 22 77 94 39	49 54 43 54 82	17 37 93 23 78	87 35 20 96 43	84 26 34 91 64	02 63 21 17 69	71 50 80 89 56	38 15 70 11 48	43 40 45 86 98	00 83 26 91 03
	84 42 17 53 31	57 24 55 06 88	77 04 74 47 67	21 76 33 50 25	83 92 12 06 76	64 55 22 21 82	48 22 28 06 00	61 54 13 43 91	82 78 12 23 29	06 66 24 12 27
	63 01 63 78 59	16 95 55 67 19	98 10 50 71 75	12 86 73 58 07	44 39 52 38 79	85 07 26 13 89	01 10 07 82 04	59 63 69 36 03	69 11 15 83 80	13 29 54 19 28
	33 21 12 34 29	78 64 56 07 82	52 42 07 44 38	15 51 00 13 42	99 66 02 79 54	58 54 16 24 15	51 54 44 82 00	62 61 65 04 69	38 18 65 18 97	85 72 13 49 21
	57 60 86 32 44	09 47 27 96 54	49 17 46 09 62	90 52 84 77 27	08 02 73 43 28	34 85 27 84 87	61 48 64 56 26	90 18 48 13 26	37 70 15 42 57	65 65 80 39 07
3	18 18 07 92 46	44 17 16 58 09	79 83 86 19 62	06 76 50 03 10	55 23 64 05 05	03 92 18 27 46	57 99 16 96 56	30 33 72 85 22	84 64 38 56 98	99 01 30 98 64
	26 62 38 97 75	84 16 07 44 99	83 11 46 32 24	20 14 85 88 45	10 93 72 88 71	62 95 30 27 59	37 75 41 66 48	86 97 80 61 45	23 53 04 01 63	45 76 08 64 27
	23 42 40 64 74	82 97 77 77 81	07 45 32 14 08	32 98 94 07 72	93 85 79 10 75	08 45 93 15 22	60 21 75 46 91	98 77 27 85 42	28 88 61 08 84	69 62 03 42 73
	62 36 28 19 95	50 92 26 11 97	00 56 76 31 38	80 22 02 53 53	86 60 42 04 53	07 08 55 18 40	45 44 75 13 90	24 94 96 61 02	57 55 66 83 15	73 42 37 11 61
	37 85 94 35 12	83 39 50 08 30	42 34 07 96 88	54 42 06 87 98	35 85 29 48 39	01 85 89 95 66	51 10 19 34 88	15 84 97 19 75	12 76 39 43 78	64 63 91 08 25
4	70 29 17 12 13	40 33 20 38 26	13 89 51 03 74	17 76 37 13 04	07 74 21 19 30	72 84 71 14 35	19 11 58 49 26	50 11 17 17 76	86 31 57 20 18	95 60 78 46 75
	56 62 18 37 35	96 83 50 87 75	97 12 25 93 47	70 33 24 03 54	97 77 46 44 80	88 78 28 16 84	13 52 53 94 53	75 45 69 30 96	73 89 65 70 31	99 17 43 48 76
	99 49 57 22 77	88 42 95 45 72	16 64 36 16 00	04 43 18 66 79	94 77 24 21 90	45 17 75 65 57	28 40 19 72 12	25 12 74 75 67	60 40 60 81 19	24 62 01 61 16
	16 08 15 04 72	33 27 14 34 09	45 59 34 68 49	12 72 07 34 45	99 27 72 95 14	96 76 28 12 54	22 01 11 94 25	71 96 16 16 88	68 64 36 74 45	19 59 50 88 92
	31 16 93 32 43	50 27 89 87 19	20 15 37 00 49	52 85 66 60 44	38 68 88 11 80	43 31 67 72 30	24 02 94 08 63	38 32 36 66 02	69 36 38 25 39	48 03 45 15 22
5	68 34 30 13 70	55 74 30 77 40	44 22 78 84 26	04 33 46 09 52	68 07 97 06 57	50 44 66 44 21	66 06 58 05 62	68 15 54 35 02	42 35 48 96 32	14 52 41 52 48
	74 57 25 65 76	59 29 97 68 60	71 91 38 67 54	13 58 18 24 76	15 54 55 95 52	22 66 22 15 86	26 63 75 41 99	58 42 36 72 24	58 37 52 18 51	03 37 18 39 11
	27 42 37 86 53	48 55 90 65 72	96 57 69 36 10	96 46 92 42 45	97 60 49 04 91	96 24 40 14 51	23 22 30 88 57	95 67 47 29 83	94 69 40 06 07	18 16 36 78 86
	00 39 68 29 61	66 37 32 20 30	77 84 57 03 29	10 45 66 04 26	11 04 96 67 24	31 73 91 61 19	60 20 72 93 48	98 57 07 23 69	65 95 39 69 58	56 80 30 19 44
	29 94 98 94 24	68 49 69 10 82	53 75 91 93 30	34 25 20 57 27	40 48 73 51 92	78 60 73 99 84	43 89 94 36 45	56 69 47 07 41	90 22 91 07 12	78 35 34 08 72
6	16 90 82 66 59	83 62 64 11 12	67 19 00 71 74	60 47 21 29 68	02 02 37 03 31	84 37 90 61 56	70 10 23 98 05	85 11 34 76 60	76 48 45 34 60	01 64 18 39 96
	11 27 94 75 06	06 09 19 74 66	02 94 37 34 02	76 70 90 30 86	38 45 94 30 38	36 67 10 08 23	98 93 35 08 86	99 29 76 29 81	33 34 91 58 93	63 14 52 32 52
	35 24 10 16 20	33 32 51 26 38	79 78 45 04 91	16 92 53 56 16	02 75 50 95 98	07 28 59 07 48	89 64 58 89 75	83 85 62 27 89	30 14 78 56 27	86 63 59 80 02
	38 23 16 86 38	42 38 97 01 50	87 75 66 81 41	40 01 74 91 62	48 51 84 08 32	10 15 83 87 60	79 24 31 66 56	21 48 24 06 93	91 98 94 05 49	01 47 59 38 00
	31 96 25 91 47	96 44 33 49 13	34 86 82 53 91	00 52 43 48 85	27 55 26 89 62	55 19 68 97 65	03 73 52 16 56	00 53 55 90 27	33 42 29 38 87	22 13 88 83 34
7	66 67 40 67 14	64 05 71 95 86	11 05 65 09 68	76 83 20 37 90	57 16 00 11 66	53 81 29 13 39	35 01 20 71 34	62 33 74 82 14	53 73 19 09 03	56 54 29 56 93
	14 90 84 45 11	75 73 88 05 90	52 27 41 14 86	22 98 12 22 08	07 52 74 95 80	51 86 32 68 92	33 98 74 66 99	40 14 71 94 58	45 94 19 38 81	14 44 99 81 07
	68 05 51 18 00	33 96 02 75 19	07 60 62 93 55	59 33 82 43 90	49 37 38 44 59	35 91 70 29 13	80 03 54 07 27	96 94 78 32 66	50 95 52 74 33	13 80 55 62 54
	20 46 78 73 90	97 51 40 14 02	04 02 33 31 08	39 54 16 49 36	47 95 93 13 30	37 71 67 95 13	20 02 44 95 94	64 85 04 05 72	01 32 90 76 14	53 89 74 60 41
	64 19 58 97 79	15 06 15 93 20	01 90 10 75 06	40 78 78 89 62	02 67 74 17 33	93 66 13 83 27	92 79 64 64 72	28 54 96 53 84	48 14 52 98 94	56 07 93 89 30
8	06 26 93 70 60	22 35 85 15 13	92 03 51 59 77	59 56 78 06 83	52 91 05 70 74	02 96 08 45 65	13 05 00 41 84	93 07 54 72 59	21 45 57 09 77	19 48 56 27 44
	07 97 10 88 23	09 98 42 99 64	61 71 62 99 15	06 51 29 16 93	58 05 77 09 51	49 83 43 48 35	82 88 33 69 96	72 36 04 19 96	47 45 15 18 60	82 11 08 95 97
	68 71 86 85 85	54 87 66 47 54	73 32 08 11 12	44 95 92 63 16	29 56 24 29 48	84 60 71 62 46	40 80 81 30 37	34 39 23 05 38	25 15 35 71 30	88 12 57 21 77
	26 99 61 65 53	58 37 78 80 70	42 10 50 67 42	32 17 55 85 74	94 44 67 16 94	18 17 30 88 71	44 91 14 88 47	89 23 30 63 15	56 34 20 47 89	99 82 93 24 98
	14 65 52 68 75	87 59 36 22 41	26 78 63 06 55	13 08 27 01 50	15 29 39 39 43	79 69 10 61 78	71 32 76 95 62	87 00 22 58 62	92 54 01 75 25	43 11 71 99 31
9	17 53 77 58 71	71 41 61 50 72	12 41 94 96 26	44 95 27 36 99	02 96 74 30 83	75 93 36 57 83	56 20 14 82 11	74 21 97 90 65	96 42 68 63 86	74 54 13 26 94
	90 26 59 21 19	23 52 23 33 12	96 93 02 18 39	07 02 18 36 07	25 99 32 70 23	38 30 92 29 03	06 28 81 39 38	62 25 06 84 63	61 29 08 93 67	04 32 92 08 09
	41 23 52 55 99	31 04 49 69 96	10 47 48 45 88	13 41 43 89 20	97 17 14 49 17	51 29 50 10 34	31 57 75 95 80	51 97 02 74 77	76 15 48 49 44	18 55 63 77 09
	60 20 50 81 69	31 99 73 68 68	35 81 33 03 76	24 30 12 48 60	18 99 10 72 34	21 31 38 86 24	37 79 38 86 24	37 79 81 53 74	73 24 16 10 33	70 47 14 54 36
	91 25 38 05 90	94 58 28 41 36	45 37 59 03 09	90 35 57 29 12	82 62 54 65 60	29 01 23 87 88	58 02 39 37 67	42 10 14 20 92	16 55 23 42 45	54 96 09 11 06
0	34 50 57 74 37	98 80 33 00 91	09 77 93 19 82	74 94 80 04 04	45 07 31 66 49	16 90 82 66 59	83 62 64 11 12	67 19 00 71 74	60 47 21 29 68	02 02 37 03 31
	85 22 04 39 43	73 81 53 94 79	33 62 46 86 28	08 31 54 46 31	53 94 13 38 47	11 27 94 75 06	06 09 19 74 66	02 94 37 34 02	76 70 90 30 86	38 45 94 30 38
	09 79 13 77 48	73 82 97 22 21	05 03 27 24 83	72 89 44 06 60	35 80 39 94 88	35 24 10 16 20	33 32 51 26 38	79 78 45 04 91	16 92 53 56 16	02 75 50 95 98
	88 75 80 18 14	22 95 75 42 49	39 32 82 22 49	02 48 07 70 37	16 04 61 67 87	38 23 16 86 38	42 38 97 01 50	87 75 66 81 41	40 01 74 91 62	48 51 84 08 32
	90 96 23 70 00	39 00 03 06 90	55 85 78 38 36	94 37 30 69 32	90 89 00 76 33	31 96 25 91 47	96 44 33 49 13	34 86 82 53 91	00 52 43 48 85	27 55 26 89 62

Figure 8.8 Using a Random Number Table.

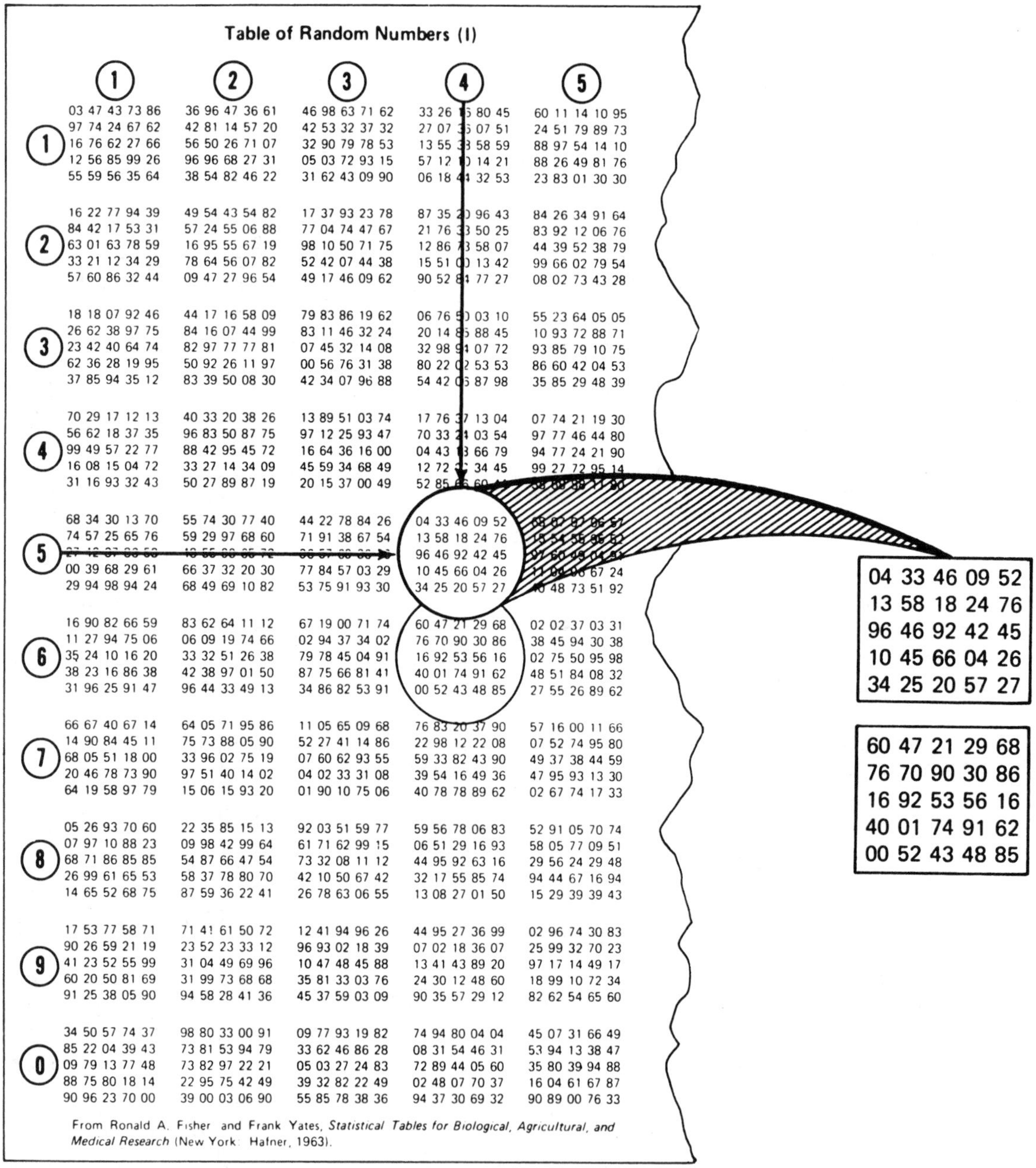

Table of Random Numbers (I)

	1	2	3	4	5
	03 47 43 73 86	36 96 47 36 61	46 98 63 71 62	33 26 [illegible] 80 45	60 11 14 10 95
	97 74 24 67 62	42 81 14 57 20	42 53 32 37 32	27 07 [illegible] 07 51	24 51 79 89 73
1	16 76 62 27 66	56 50 26 71 07	32 90 79 78 53	13 55 [illegible] 58 59	88 97 54 14 10
	12 56 85 99 26	96 96 68 27 31	05 03 72 93 15	57 12 [illegible] 14 21	88 26 49 81 76
	55 59 56 35 64	38 54 82 46 22	31 62 43 09 90	06 18 [illegible] 32 53	23 83 01 30 30
	16 22 77 94 39	49 54 43 54 82	17 37 93 23 78	87 35 [illegible] 96 43	84 26 34 91 64
	84 42 17 53 31	57 24 55 06 88	77 04 74 47 67	21 76 [illegible] 50 25	83 92 12 06 76
2	63 01 63 78 59	16 95 55 67 19	98 10 50 71 75	12 86 [illegible] 58 07	44 39 52 38 79
	33 21 12 34 29	78 64 56 07 82	52 42 07 44 38	15 51 [illegible] 13 42	99 66 02 79 54
	57 60 86 32 44	09 47 27 96 54	49 17 46 09 62	90 52 [illegible] 77 27	08 02 73 43 28
	18 18 07 92 46	44 17 16 58 09	79 83 86 19 62	06 76 [illegible] 03 10	55 23 64 05 05
	26 62 38 97 75	84 16 07 44 99	83 11 46 32 24	20 14 [illegible] 88 45	10 93 72 88 71
3	23 42 40 64 74	82 97 77 77 81	07 45 32 14 08	32 98 [illegible] 07 72	93 85 79 10 75
	62 36 28 19 95	50 92 26 11 97	00 56 76 31 38	80 22 [illegible] 53 53	86 60 42 04 53
	37 85 94 35 12	83 39 50 08 30	42 34 07 96 88	54 42 [illegible] 87 98	35 85 29 48 39
	70 29 17 12 13	40 33 20 38 26	13 89 51 03 74	17 76 [illegible] 13 04	07 74 21 19 30
	56 62 18 37 35	96 83 50 87 75	97 12 25 93 47	70 33 [illegible] 03 54	97 77 46 44 80
4	99 49 57 22 77	88 42 95 45 72	16 64 36 16 00	04 43 [illegible] 66 79	94 77 24 21 90
	16 08 15 04 72	33 27 14 34 09	45 59 34 68 49	12 72 [illegible] 34 45	99 27 72 95 14
	31 16 93 32 43	50 27 89 87 19	20 15 37 00 49	52 85 [illegible]	[illegible]
	68 34 30 13 70	55 74 30 77 40	44 22 78 84 26	04 33 46 09 52	[illegible]
	74 57 25 65 76	59 29 97 68 60	71 91 38 67 54	13 58 18 24 76	[illegible]
5	[illegible]	[illegible]	[illegible]	96 46 92 42 45	[illegible]
	00 39 68 29 61	66 37 32 20 30	77 84 57 03 29	10 45 66 04 26	[illegible] 67 24
	29 94 98 94 24	68 49 69 10 82	53 75 91 93 30	34 25 20 57 27	[illegible] 48 73 51 92
	16 90 82 66 59	83 62 64 11 12	67 19 00 71 74	60 47 21 29 68	02 02 37 03 31
	11 27 94 75 06	06 09 19 74 66	02 94 37 34 02	76 70 90 30 86	38 45 94 30 38
6	35 24 10 16 20	33 32 51 26 38	79 78 45 04 91	16 92 53 56 16	02 75 50 95 98
	38 23 16 86 38	42 38 97 01 50	87 75 66 81 41	40 01 74 91 62	48 51 84 08 32
	31 96 25 91 47	96 44 33 49 13	34 86 82 53 91	00 52 43 48 85	27 55 26 89 62
	66 67 40 67 14	64 05 71 95 86	11 05 65 09 68	76 83 20 37 90	57 16 00 11 66
	14 90 84 45 11	75 73 88 05 90	52 27 41 14 86	22 98 12 22 08	07 52 74 95 80
7	68 05 51 18 00	33 96 02 75 19	07 60 62 93 55	59 33 82 43 90	49 37 38 44 59
	20 46 78 73 90	97 51 40 14 02	04 02 33 31 08	39 54 16 49 36	47 95 93 13 30
	64 19 58 97 79	15 06 15 93 20	01 90 10 75 06	40 78 78 89 62	02 67 74 17 33
	05 26 93 70 60	22 35 85 15 13	92 03 51 59 77	59 56 78 06 83	52 91 05 70 74
	07 97 10 88 23	09 98 42 99 64	61 71 62 99 15	06 51 29 16 93	58 05 77 09 51
8	68 71 86 85 85	54 87 66 47 54	73 32 08 11 12	44 95 92 63 16	29 56 24 29 48
	26 99 61 65 53	58 37 78 80 70	42 10 50 67 42	32 17 55 85 74	94 44 67 16 94
	14 65 52 68 75	87 59 36 22 41	26 78 63 06 55	13 08 27 01 50	15 29 39 39 43
	17 53 77 58 71	71 41 61 50 72	12 41 94 96 26	44 95 27 36 99	02 96 74 30 83
	90 26 59 21 19	23 52 23 33 12	96 93 02 18 39	07 02 18 36 07	25 99 32 70 23
9	41 23 52 55 99	31 04 49 69 96	10 47 48 45 88	13 41 43 89 20	97 17 14 49 17
	60 20 50 81 69	31 99 73 68 68	35 81 33 03 76	24 30 12 48 60	18 99 10 72 34
	91 25 38 05 90	94 58 28 41 36	45 37 59 03 09	90 35 57 29 12	82 62 54 65 60
	34 50 57 74 37	98 80 33 00 91	09 77 93 19 82	74 94 80 04 04	45 07 31 66 49
	85 22 04 39 43	73 81 53 94 79	33 62 46 86 28	08 31 54 46 31	53 94 13 38 47
0	09 79 13 77 48	73 82 97 22 21	05 03 27 24 83	72 89 44 05 60	35 80 39 94 88
	88 75 80 18 14	22 95 75 42 49	39 32 82 22 49	02 48 07 70 37	16 04 61 67 87
	90 96 23 70 00	39 00 03 06 90	55 85 78 38 36	94 37 30 69 32	90 89 00 76 33

From Ronald A. Fisher and Frank Yates, *Statistical Tables for Biological, Agricultural, and Medical Research* (New York: Hafner, 1963).

04 33 46 09 52
13 58 18 24 76
96 46 92 42 45
10 45 66 04 26
34 25 20 57 27

60 47 21 29 68
76 70 90 30 86
16 92 53 56 16
40 01 74 91 62
00 52 43 48 85

tion comes up, select the individual in the population who has been assigned that number. Keep selecting until the entire sample total is reached.

Figure 8.8 recapitulates what we have been describing. You will recall that our random number from the dollar bill was 45. This we selected as the entering number to find the random block within the table. For purposes of illustration, we will assume that the total population consists of 90 individuals from which we will select a sample of 40. We will need random numbers of two digits each.

Beginning in the upper left-hand corner of the designated block, and remembering that there are only 90 individuals in the total population, we see that by going down the leftmost column of numbers, we will begin by choosing from the total population individual number 4 and then individual number 13. The next number does not apply (since we have only 90 persons in the population and this is 96). Our next choices will be 10, 34, 60, 76, 16, 40. We ignore the 00, as well as the next number, 76, which has already been chosen.

We have perhaps said enough with respect to the use of a table of random numbers; for now simply remember that randomization is often affected by the use of just such a table.

What Is a Sufficient Sample?

Two other matters will, however, come to the mind of the practical researcher: How large a sample do I need, and what is the probability of error by taking a sample of the population as opposed to using the entire population?

The Size of the Sample

Let's consider the first question. The basic rule is: *The larger the sample, the better.* But such a generalized rule is not too helpful to a researcher who has a practical decision to make with respect to a specific research situation. Somewhat more definite guidelines should be formulated.

Sample size depends largely on the degree to which the sample population approximates the qualities and characteristics of the general population. Take homogeneity, for instance. How homogeneous or heterogeneous is the general population? Obviously, if the population is markedly heterogeneous, a larger sample will be needed than if the population is more homogeneous. Thus, the researcher should consider three factors in making any decision as to sample size:

1. What is the degree of precision required between the sample population and the general population?
2. What is the variability of the population? (This is commonly expressed as the standard deviation.)
3. What method of sampling should be employed? (We will briefly discuss sampling designs in the pages that follow.)

For those who wish to determine the size of the sample statistically, the following formula estimates the representativeness of the sample on certain critical parameters at an acceptance level of probability:

$$N = \left(\frac{z}{e}\right)^2 (p)\ (1 - p)$$

Where

N = the size of the sample
z = the standard score corresponding to a given confidence level
e = the proportion of sampling error in a given situation
p = the estimated proportion or incidence of cases in the population

In considering the second question, the probability of error by taking a sample of the population as opposed to utilizing the total population, we must consider how far the sample mean deviates from the mean for the total population. This is usually determined statistically through a determination of the *standard error of the mean.* This is determined as follows:

$$SE_{\bar{x}} = \frac{s}{\sqrt{N}}$$

Where

$SE_{\bar{x}}$ = the standard error of the mean
s = the standard deviation of the sample
N = the number of units in the sample

This method of determining the standard error of the mean is true for both large and small samples. The sampling distribution of means is very nearly normal for $N > 30$, even when the population is nonnormal.

Sampling Designs

We should discuss the most common types of sampling designs that are found in normative survey studies. Many times we have commented that all sound research begins with a careful consideration of the data. What is the nature of the data? Methodology depends upon a careful answer to this question. That fact is equally true in sampling. You do not just go out to sample. No researcher is so naive as to think that all you have to do in normative design research is merely pick a sample. Careful consideration of the total population is *most* important. This fact will become ever more important as we review the several types of sampling designs that are available for descriptive survey research.

The descriptive survey method demands that the researcher select from the general population a sample population that will be both logically and statistically defensible. The first step in selecting any sampling design is to analyze carefully the *integral characteristics of the total population.* In view of these, then, the researcher may select the sampling technique most appropriate for the population type.

The following comments have been taken from the Interviewer's Manual of the Survey Research Center of the Institute for Social Research of the University of Michigan.

> Survey sampling is the process of choosing, from a much larger population, a group about which we wish to make generalized statements so that the selected part will represent the total group. Such a sample must be very carefully selected so that it will faithfully represent the particular group being studied. No matter how good the gathering of data is, from such a group, the survey cannot be accurate if the people in the sample are improperly selected.
>
> The sampling procedures the Center uses are based on the same principles that would be used if a choice were made by listing each member of the group to be sampled on identical slips of paper, mixing the slips in a giant hopper, and drawing again and again until a large number of selections had been made. Obviously, it would take an inordinate amount of time and money to list all of the dwellings in the United States on slips of paper and then draw the required number of addresses from some enormous hopper. We can, however, save expense and trouble by *multi-stage sampling of areas.* This is accomplished in various steps:
>
> *Step 1: Primary Sampling Unit Selection.* We divide the entire geographical area of the United States into small areas which we call Primary Sampling Units. These units are usually counties or metropolitan areas because they are convenient units within which the interviewer can operate.
>
> *Step 2: Sample Place Selection.* Each of the Primary Sampling Units is further subdivided into smaller areas. For purposes of illustration, we shall consider the Primary Sampling Unit to be a county. Since there is only one large urban unit within the county no random selection will need to be made. Among the smaller towns selection would be made by randomization.
>
> *Step 3: Chunk Selection.* Each sample place, whether New York City or a rural township in Iowa, is divided into *chunks.* A chunk is an area having identifiable (but not necessarily visible) boundaries: a city block, a rural area bounded by roads, streams, or civil boundaries such as county lines. Chunks usually have an average of 20 to 30 dwelling units, although in large cities a chunk may have many more dwellings.
>
> *Step 4: Dividing Chunks into Segments.* Chunks are subdivided into smaller areas containing about 4 to 12 dwelling units. Always all decisions are made by means of pure random selection.
>
> *Step 5: Dwelling Unit Selection.* About four dwellings are chosen from a given sample segment. If the original address does not produce an interview, the interviewer must not substitute one address for another. An unanswered doorbell does not entitle the interviewer to step next door. Substitutions would quickly destroy the representativeness of the sample.[6]

[6] *Interviewer's Manual,* Survey Research Center, Institute for Social Research (Ann Arbor, MI: University of Michigan, 1969), pp. 8-1–8-3. Some slight liberties have been taken with the wording of the *Interviewer's Manual* to adapt the thought to this textbook.

Reduced to a graphic presentation, the Survey Research Center sampling method can be represented as shown in Figure 8.9.

One further observation should be made concerning the methodology of the Survey Research Center in selecting the Primary Sampling Units. Each of these units is selected by chance. Chance, however, does not mean that they are selected haphazardly. They are chosen by a mathematical procedure so that the selection is random and purely the result of blind chance. The sampling technique employs a process known as *stratification* or *simple stratified sampling.* Stratification helps to select the proper proportion of different types of areas: for example, in selecting Primary Sampling Units, the total population is stratified to select the proper number of urban areas and rural areas, eastern and western areas, and so on. This provides a balanced heterogeneity to the entire sample, and as great a homogeneity within each stratum as possible.

At this point, we may appropriately consider some of the characteristics of populations in general.

1. The population may be generally homogeneous. The separate units may be similar in observable characteristics.
2. The population may contain definite strata of discretely different units.

Figure 8.9 Multi-stage Sampling.

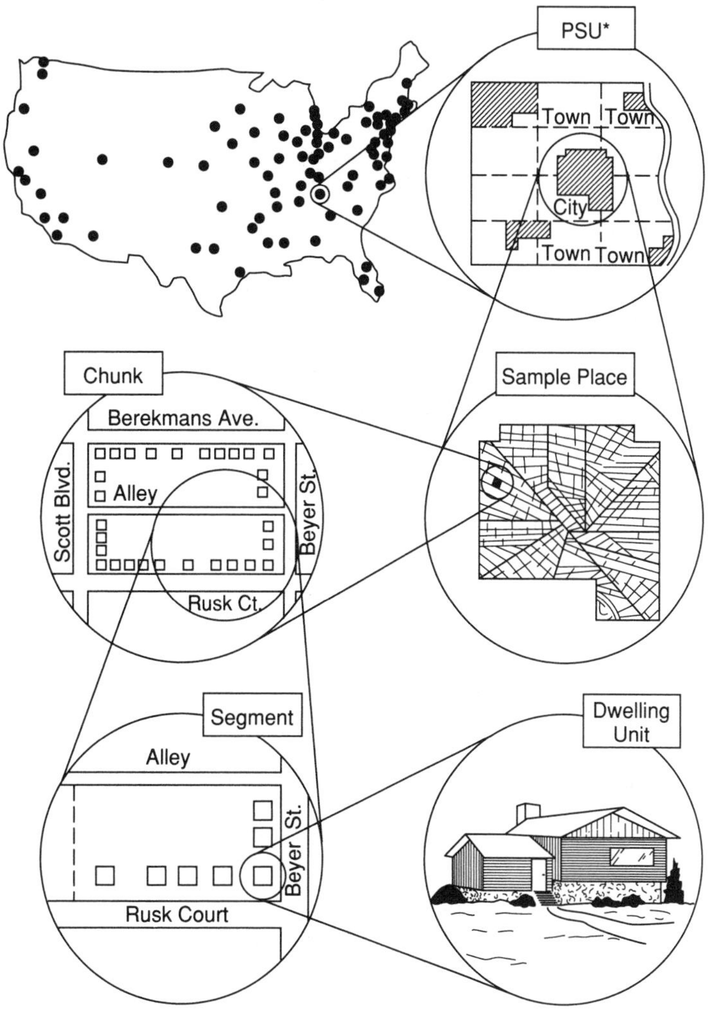

*PSU = Primary Sampling Unit

3. The population may contain definite strata but *each stratum may differ from every other stratum* by a proportionate ratio of its separate stratified units.
4. The population may consist of clusters whose *cluster* characteristics are similar, but whose *unit* characteristics are as heterogeneous as possible.

If this is somewhat confusing to you, Table 8.1 presents the same information in a different format.

All sampling procedures demand processing of the sample. In all sampling, the following three processes are indigenous to the selection of the sample:

1. The population must be identified, an analysis made of its structure, and an assessment made of its characteristics.
2. The process of randomization must be outlined and the selection of the sample from the total population must be made in accordance with a method of the randomization.
3. The data must be extracted from the sample population.

Figures 8.10 through 8.14 show graphically the structure of each of the several methods of sampling.

Table 8.1 Population Characteristics and Sampling Techniques Appropriate for Each Population Type

Population Characteristic	Example of Population Type	Appropriate Sampling Techniques
I Population is generally a homogeneous mass of individual units.	A quantity of flower seeds of a particular variety from which random samples are selected for testing as to their germination quality.	Simple random sampling
II Population consists of definite strata, each of which is distinctly different, but the units within the stratum are as homogeneous as possible.	A particular town whose total population consists of three types (strata) of citizens: white, European-background type; black, African-background type; and Mexican-Indian-background type.	Simple stratified sampling
III Population contains definite strata with differing characteristics and each stratum has a proportionate ratio in terms of numbers of members to every other strata.	A community in which the total population consists of individuals whose religious affiliations are found to be Catholic, 25 percent; Protestant, 50 percent; Jews, 15 percent; nonaffiliated, 10 percent.	Proportional stratified sampling
IV Population consists of clusters whose cluster characteristics are similar yet whose unit characteristics are as heterogeneous as possible.	A survey of the nation's 20 leading air terminals by soliciting reactions from travelers who use them. (All air terminals are similar in atmosphere, purpose, design, etc., yet the passengers who use them differ widely in individual characteristics: age, sex, national origin, philosophies and beliefs, socioeconomic status, and so forth.)	Cluster sampling

Figure 8.10 Simple Random Sampling Design

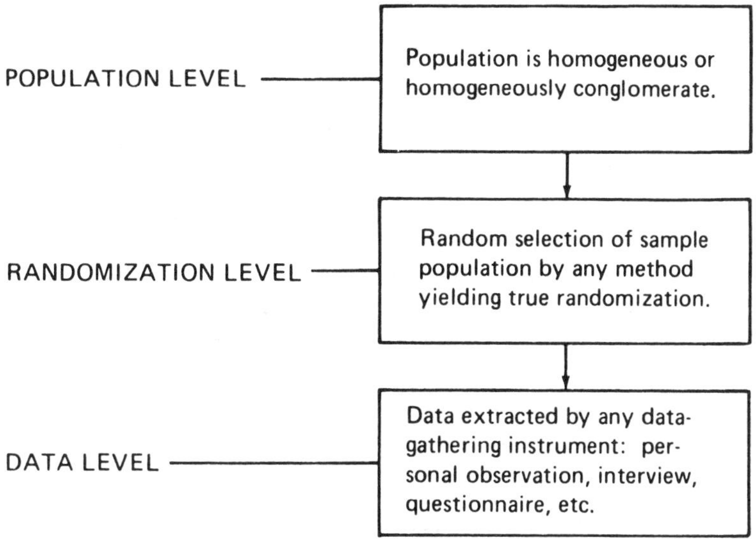

Certain populations, particularly where their compositions consist of disparate elements in proportional ratios, require an equalization process in addition to the three processes indicated above. The equalization process ensures proper balance among all the elements of the population in proportion to their relative strength or significance.

Simple Random Sampling. Simple random sampling is the least sophisticated of all sampling procedures. From a population whose texture is either homogeneous or homogeneously conglomerate, the sample is derived by means of a simple randomization process. Schematically, the process of simple random sampling would resemble Figure 8.10.

Stratified Random Sampling. Certain differences between the stratified random sampling design (Figure 8.11), and the simpler method are at once apparent. Instead of being a homogeneous mass, the population is composed of layers (strata) of discretely different types of individual units.

Think of grades 4, 5, and 6 in a public school. This is a *stratified population.* Generally, the stratification layers are somewhat equal—a schoolroom has just so much seating capacity. If we were to sample a population of fourth-, fifth-, and sixth-grade children in a particular school, we should probably take equal samples from each of the three grades. Our sampling design would look, then, like the figure. Note the addition of one more level, the *equalization level,* at which point we would be careful to see that the sample was indeed representative of the entire population.

In the equalization process, we attempt to get three subpopulations of approximately the same size. To do so preserves equalization in one dimension, and the fact that all students within that particular subpopulation are of the same grade level assures equalization in a second dimension. In this way, we can be reasonably sure that the population is not skewed or biased because of inequality in any of the subpopulations.

Proportional Stratified Sampling. In the simple stratified random sampling design, all the strata of the population were essentially equal in size. But now we come to a population that is markedly different. Consider how different are the strata of religious groups within a community that has, for example, 3,000 Protestants, 2,000 Catholics, and 1,000 Jews. Let us postulate a survey situation. A local newspaper publishes a section dealing with interfaith church news, religious events, and syndicated articles of interest to the religious community in general. The editor wishes to determine certain facts from the paper's readership.

Figure 8.11 Stratified Random Sampling Design

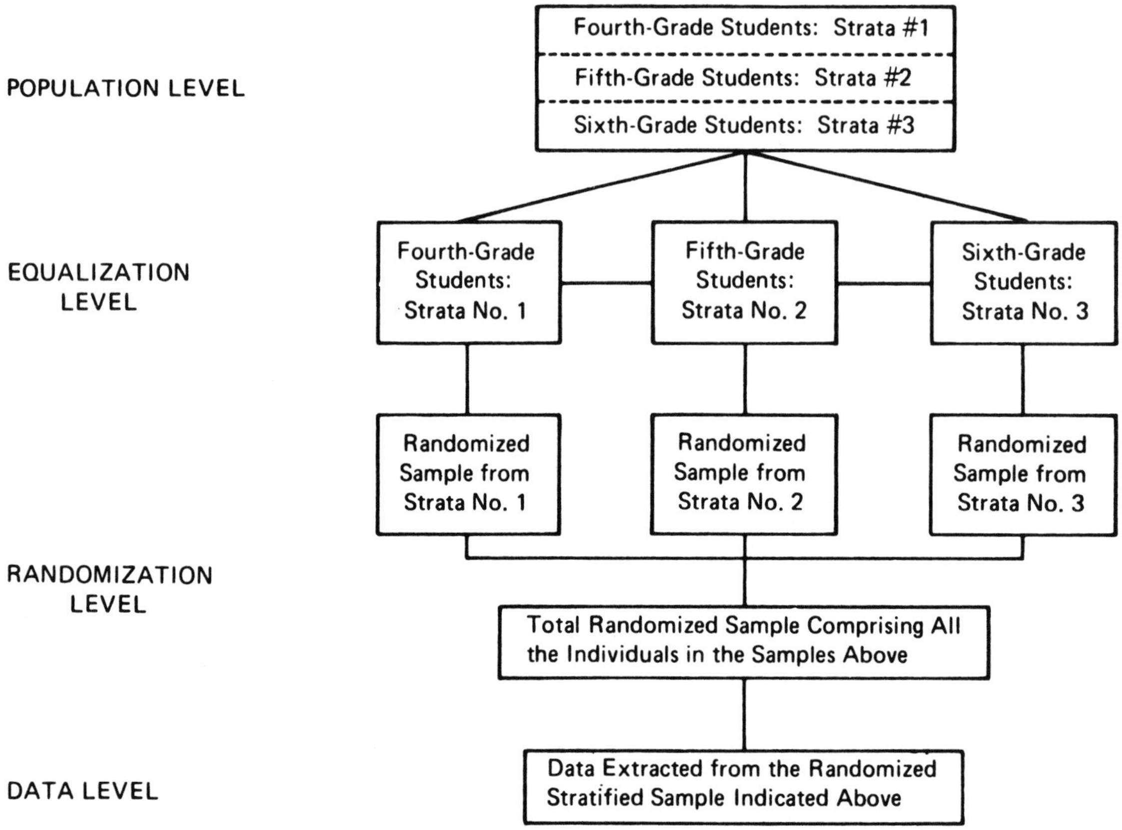

It is now obvious that, instead of an orderly stratification, as in the previous population, the population here is a conglomerate, religiously heterogeneous, proportional mixture in the ratio 3:2:1. Unlike the three public school grades, in which the separate homogeneous strata were arranged one above the other, in this population an *integral mixture of separate disparate units in conglomerate relationship exists.*

The first problem, therefore, is to separate the several discrete elements in the total population and to select from each of the individual groups a random sample proportionately representative of the numerical strength of each of the components within the entire conglomerate.

The proportional stratified design may, therefore, be the answer to the problem. Figure 8.12 schematically represents this type of sampling.

Cluster or Area Sampling. We have not exhausted all of the population variants that exist in real life. Up to this point, the population structure has been homogeneous, composed of layers of different units, or conglomerate; now we come to still another type of population—a large population spread across a large area. Sometimes it is not feasible to make up a list of every person living within a particular area and, from that list, to select a sample for study through normal randomization procedures. In lieu of that, we may secure a map of the area showing political or other types of subdivisions. We can then subdivide an expansive area into smaller units: a city, for example, can be subdivided into precincts, clusters of city blocks, or school boundary areas; a state can be divided into counties or townships. In *cluster sampling,* it is important that each cluster be as similar to the others as possible and that within the clusters the individuals be heterogeneous.

From all the clusters, a random selection of specific clusters is made as the nucleus from which the sample population is ultimately derived, again by random selection. Let us take the example of the religious groups within a community, which we used to illustrate proportional stratified sampling. Let us assume that the community is a large city that we have divided into twelve areas or clusters. The schematic design is shown in Figure 8.13.

Systematic Sampling. Systematic sampling is the final major type of sampling design we will discuss in this chapter. Obviously, there are other ways of sampling, and we have discussed variants of the basic designs. Any good text devoted to survey design or sampling theory will discuss them all. The reason for the elaboration given here is that in a descriptive survey study, the weak links in the chain are usually found in the techniques and procedures of sampling and in the unwitting admission of bias into the study. The subject of bias will be our next consideration; it can be minimized if the researcher has an intelligent and knowledgeable grasp of sampling procedures.

Systematic sampling is precisely what the name implies: the selection of certain items in a series according to a predetermined sequence. The origin of the sequence must be controlled by chance. Let us take the cluster diagram presented in Figure 8.13. Randomization was achieved in the cluster sampling by resorting to the table of random numbers. But there are other approaches that might have been employed.

There are twelve cells, or clusters, of the population as suggested by the schematic. Through the technique of systematic sampling, we might have chosen a group of clusters quite as much by chance as was done by benefit of the table of random numbers.

In a series of twelve numbers a dichotomy exists. Certain numbers within the series are odd, others are even. Using the systematic sampling technique, we would have chosen by *predeter-*

Figure 8.12 Proportional Stratified Sampling Design

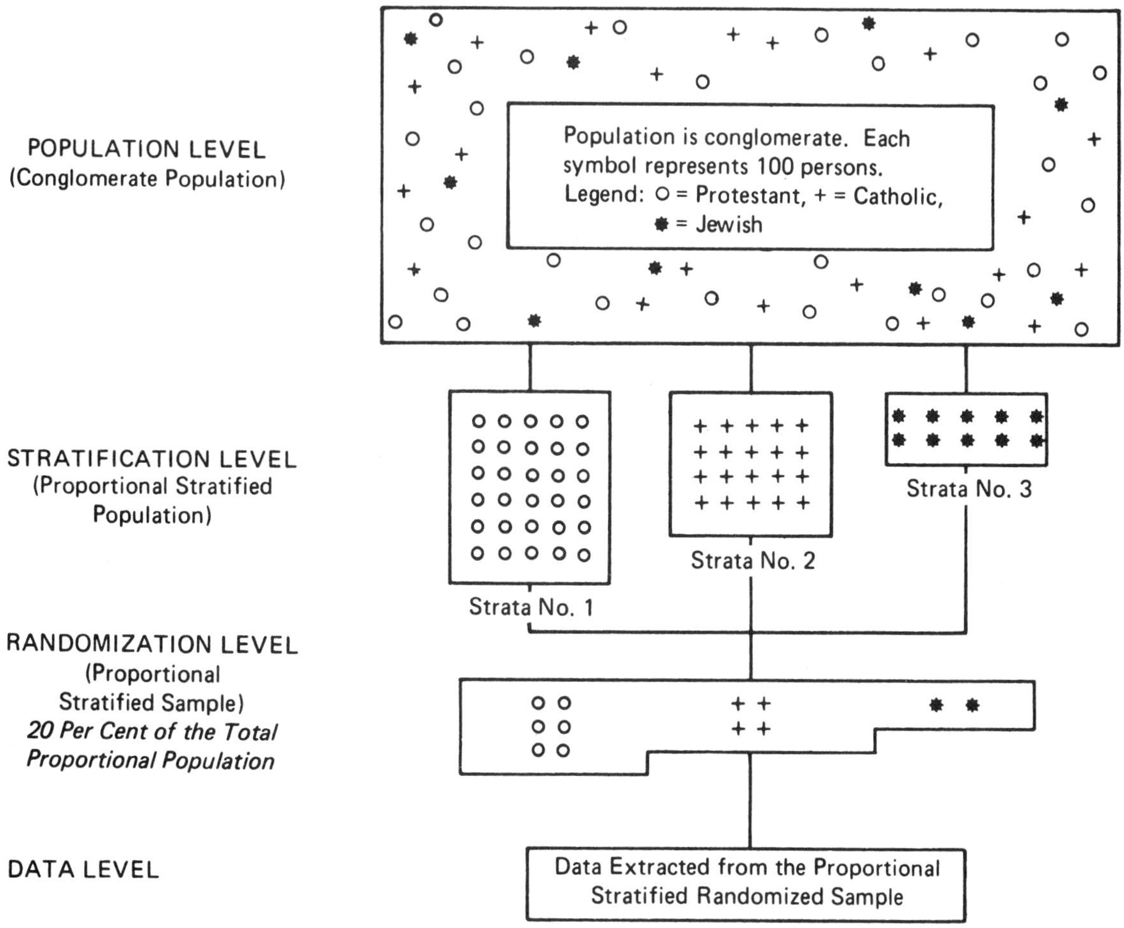

Figure 8.13 Cluster or Areas Sampling Design

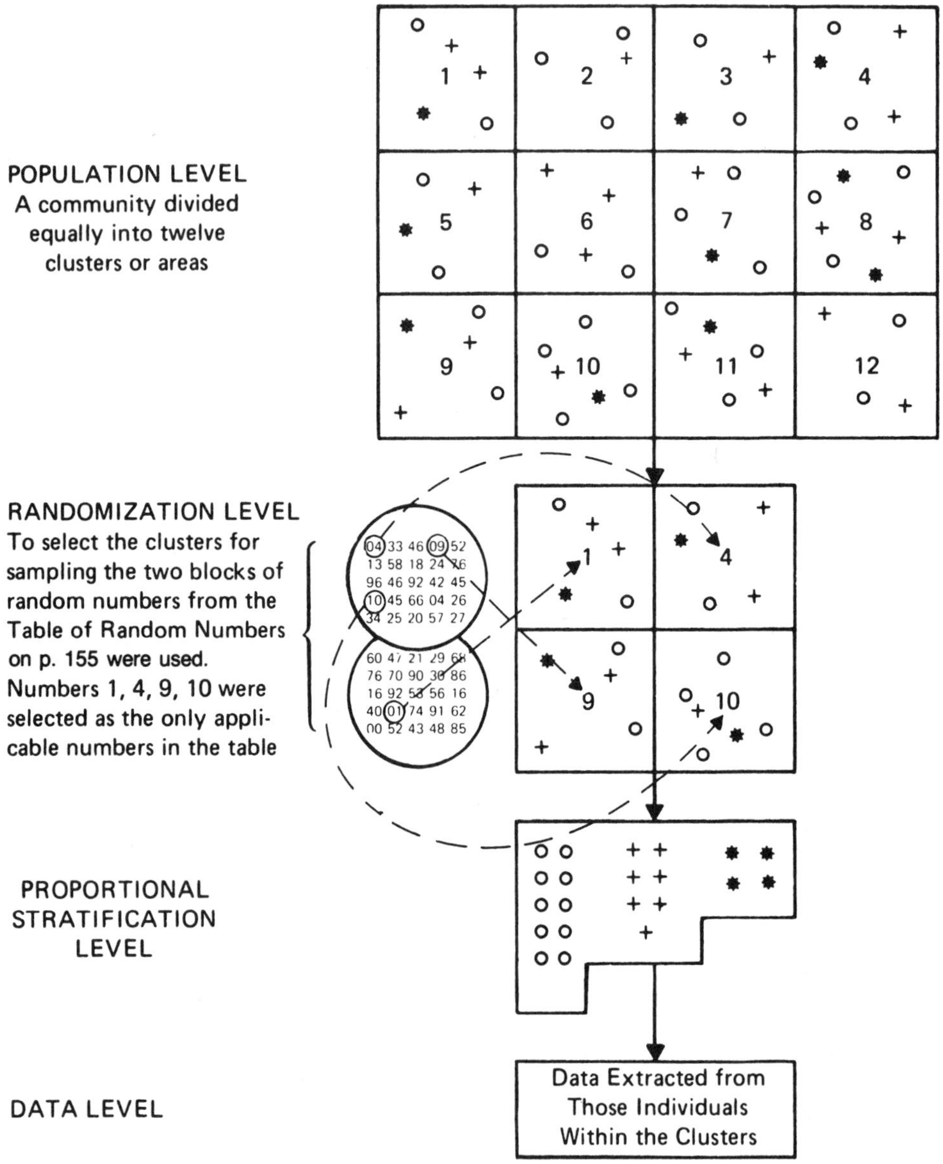

mined sequence the clusters for sampling. Let us toss a coin. Heads dictates that we begin with the first number in the arithmetic progression of odd-numbered clusters. Tails demands that we begin with the even-numbered digit and follow the arithmetic progression in that mode. The coin comes down tails, which means that we start with the first even-numbered digit, which is 2, and select *systematically sequential* clusters 4, 6, 8, 10, 12.

Figure 8.14 shows the systematic sampling design technique.

Before leaving this discussion of sampling design, we should emphasize that the design diagrams presented here emphasize graphically the fact that each design is uniquely suited for the particular characteristics of the various populations. In choosing a sampling design, therefore, you should not choose blindly or willy-nilly. The design should be considered as a tool of research, and this tool should be chosen with a full recognition of the task at hand and its discrete demands on the sampling procedure. A careful study of the diagrams and a consideration of the characteristics of the research population will aid you in selecting the sampling design that is best suited to your population.

Bias in Research Design

We turn now to the matter of bias in the research design. In enumerating the basic characteristics of the descriptive survey method, we indicated that the researcher needed to be particularly alert for the presence of bias in descriptive or normative survey studies. *Data in descriptive survey research are particularly susceptible to distortion through the introduction of bias into the research design. Particular attention should be given, therefore, to safeguarding the data from the influence of bias.*

Bias is, of course, inherent in all research; but because it can infect the descriptive survey more easily than most other methodological procedures and because it is sometimes difficult for the researcher to detect, we have chosen to discuss it here. We may define bias as *any influence, condition, or set of conditions that singly or together distort the data from what may have been obtained under the conditions of pure chance.* Furthermore, bias is *any influence that may have disturbed the randomness by which the choice of a sample population has been selected.*

Data are, in many respects, delicate and sensitive to extraneous influences. We talk about the solid truth, the hard fact, and yet every researcher soon learns that data are neither so hard nor so solid as the hackneyed phrase might suggest. Data are highly susceptible to distortion.

Bias is frequently minute and imperceptible as it infiltrates the research design. It may be easily overlooked by even the most sensitive and careful researcher. Bias attacks the integrity of

Figure 8.14 Systematic Sampling Design

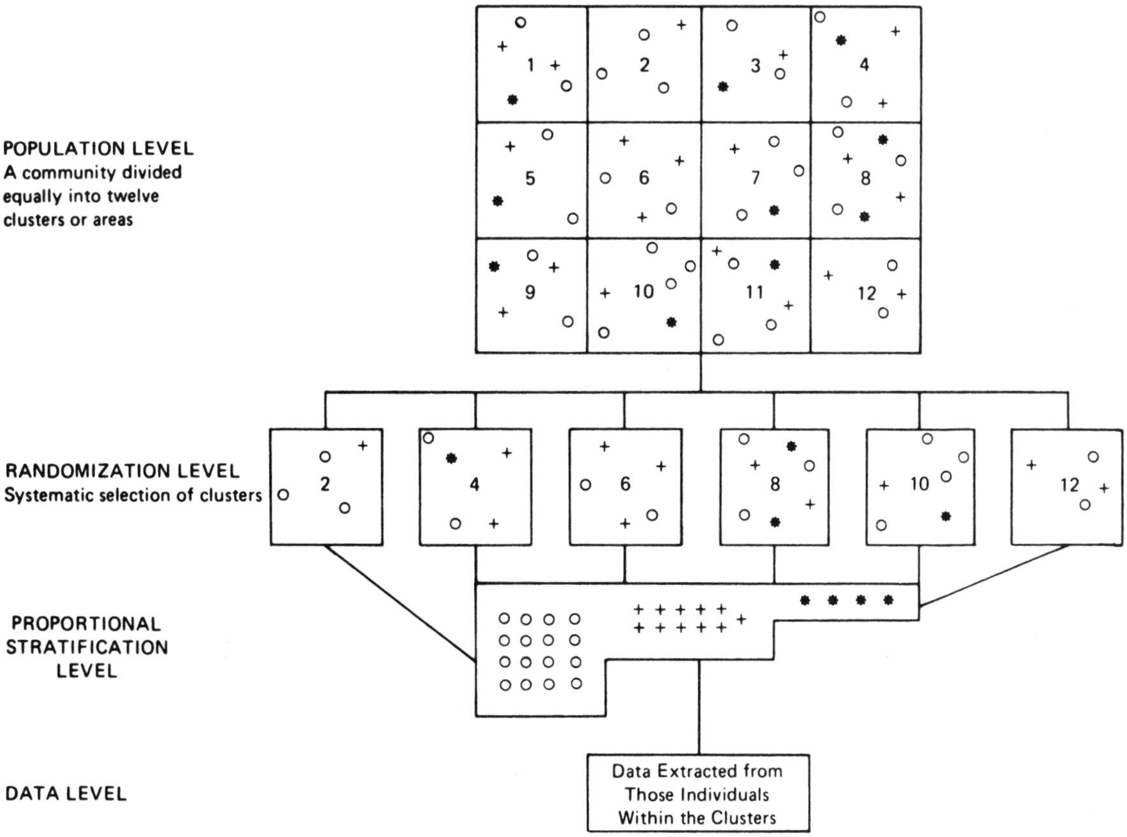

the facts. It is particularly vicious when it enters surreptitiously into the research system and goes undetected. It will render suspect even the most carefully planned research effort.

How Bias Enters the Research Design

The best way to appreciate bias is to see it at work. To understand precisely how bias influences the data, let us take several instances and inspect them carefully. A researcher decides to use a city telephone directory as a source for selecting a random sample. She opens the page at random, closes her eyes, puts the point of her pencil down on the page, and the name that comes closest to the pencil point is selected. You can't get much more random than that, she reasons. But the demon of bias is there. The selection made does not represent the entire spectrum of the general population. The lower economic strata of the population will not be adequately represented because many of them are unable to afford a telephone. The affluent also will not be adequately numbered among the general population because many of them have unlisted phone numbers. Hence, the sample will be biased in the direction of middle-strata population.

Questionnaire studies also frequently fall victim to bias, often without the researcher's awareness. In questionnaire studies, the researcher is frequently more concerned about the percentage of the return of the questionnaire than about the bias that may be exerted by those subjects who do not return the questionnaire.

Let us take a simple situation. A questionnaire is sent to 100 citizens asking, "Have you ever been summoned by the Internal Revenue Service to justify your income tax return?" Of the 70 questionnaires returned, 35 are from people who indicate that they have been summoned, while 35 are from people who have never been summoned. The researcher might conclude, therefore, that 50 percent of the respondents had never been summoned, and that 50 percent had received summonses. On this basis, the researcher may make generalizations concerning the whole population. But the generalizations may be very misleading, since the researcher is basing them on the assumption that a 70 percent return of the questionnaire is a reasonably good return. What the researcher may have overlooked is the inward motivation that may have influenced the 30 percent of the respondents who did not return their questionnaires.

Many people consider being summoned to defend their income tax return to be a reflection of their integrity. For that reason, the nonrespondents may not have wanted to indicate that they had been summoned and may have ignored the whole matter. The bias growing out of an attempt to preserve their integrity may have operated to distort the truth of the situation. Instead of a 50-50 split, a 35 and 65 percent proportion may be more realistic.

Bias may also creep into the research in other undetected ways. In interviewing, one's personality may affect the responses of the interviewee. In asking questions, the tone of one's voice and the inflection or accent within the sentence may influence how a respondent replies. Remember Clever Hans!

Two teachers have been trained exactly alike and teach classes whose compositions are as nearly alike as it is possible to make them. A comparable study of their teaching, in which they apply the same methods, use the same texts, and appear like mirror images of each other, may be grossly influenced by bias, which has seeped into the system from a number of sources:

1. The personality of each teacher is different.
2. Each class, no matter how carefully paired, is composed of different individuals.
3. The inner dynamics of each group are different.
4. Surroundings, modulated by such delicate influences as gradations of light, temperature, noise level, and other imperceptible factors, alter individual reactions to the situation.
5. The home environment of each student may reach into the classroom and affect that student's behavior and reactions.

In each of the preceding situations, which are typical of the normal classroom (we might go on to cite many more), we have influences, conditions, or sets of conditions that may distort the data. When this happens, bias has affected the data arising out of the research situation.

Acknowledging the Probable Presence of Bias

It is almost impossible for people to live in this world without coming into contact with microorganisms. Likewise, in the research environment, the researcher cannot avoid having data contaminated by bias of one sort or another. What is inexcusable, however, is for the researcher to fail to acknowledge the likelihood of biased data or to fail to recognize the possibility of bias in the study. Formulating conclusions about the data without acknowledging the effect that bias may have had in distorting them is naive, and is an immature approach to serious research.

Those with greatest maturity in research skill demonstrate their integrity by admitting without reserve that bias is omnipresent and may very well have influenced their study. The most fearless among them will point out precisely how bias may have infiltrated the research design. With this knowledge, we may then appraise the research realistically and judge its merits honestly. Nothing is gained by ignoring what all of us know exists. Bias for the researchers, like the presence of germs for the surgeon, is next to impossible to avoid. As researchers, we must learn to live with bias, but at the same time to guard against its infective destruction.

Some students, however, strive so hard to make the data support their hypotheses that in so doing they deny the realities inherent in the research situation. Nothing is gained thereby. In research, we cannot force the facts to support anything. The facts should be, as much as possible, immune to influence of any kind and should speak for themselves. If they are tainted with bias, we must accept that as an inevitable condition in most research, particularly in descriptive survey studies, and we should not be unduly upset by its presence.

Presenting and Interpreting Data in the Descriptive Survey Study

Data are of no value merely as data. In this discussion of descriptive research methodology, we have principally discussed the acquisition of fact: how to winnow the data from the general population with appropriate techniques (questionnaires, interviews, sampling); how to protect those data against distortion of bias. We have been thinking of the process of accumulation only; while amassing data is certainly a necessary aspect of research, it is not the end for which the process of research is instituted. The purpose of research is to solve problems. It is to accomplish that purpose that we amass data.

In order to see the descriptive survey method in its proper perspective, let us review some fundamental principles.

Survey Research Is More Than Activity

At this juncture, let us review what has been said in chapters 1 and 7. In these chapters, you were constantly reminded of two basic principles of research:

1. The purpose of research is to seek the answer to a problem in the light of the facts that relate to that problem.
2. Although facts relative to the problem must be assembled for study and inspection, *the extraction of meaning from the accumulated data*—what we have called the *interpretation of the data—is all-important.*

The descriptive survey method is a busy research method from the standpoint of the researcher. Therein lies an element of danger. It perhaps demands more activity than other methodologies. It is also probably the most complex of all the research methodologies. In light of the problem, the researcher must decide upon a population, study it, choose a technique for sampling it, determine how randomness will be guaranteed, minimize the entrance of bias into the study, send questionnaires or conduct interviews (or observe the data directly), record and systematize the facts gleaned through the survey, and perhaps do more that we have failed to mention. All this is enough to keep any researcher busy. The activity connected with descriptive research is complex, time consuming, and distracting. With all this motion going on, it would not seem unreasonable if the researcher lost sight of the nuances of the problem and subproblems. But it is precisely the problem and the subproblems that are the reason for all the rest of the activity.

All the activity is subordinate to the research itself. Sooner or later, all this activity must come to rest in an interpretation of the data and a setting forth of conclusions, drawn from the data, to resolve the problem being investigated.

Inexperienced researchers forget this. Activity for activity's sake is seductive. Amassing great quantities of data gives them a sense of well-being. Like Midas, looking at his hoard of gold, they lose sight of the ultimate demands that the problem itself makes upon those data. They feel that now all they need to do is to present the data in displays and summaries—graphs, charts, tables. Unfortunately, these do nothing more than demonstrate the researcher's acquisitive skills and consummate ability to present the same facts in different settings. Survey research ultimately aims to solve problems.

Practical Application

The Descriptive Survey: Questionnaire Construction

If your research methodology falls within the area of the descriptive survey and you intend to gather some or all of your data by means of a questionnaire, you should duplicate as many copies of the following form for the construction of a questionnaire as you will need to accommodate all your questions. Beginning in the left-hand column with the statement of the question (which you should write out clearly and completely), proceed to analyze that question in terms of the following channels, moving toward the right. With an analysis of each question in this manner, there will be much less chance that you will produce a questionnaire that may be grossly faulty or that may have in it major defects that might impair your study and cast a shadow upon your credibility as a researcher.

The Descriptive Survey: Population Analysis

Take any population and make an analysis of its structure and characteristics. First, identify the population on the following line:

____

Now ask the following questions with respect to the *structure of the population:*

	Yes	No
1. Is the population a conglomerate mixture of homogeneous units?	_____	_____
2. Considered graphically, could the population be considered as consisting generally of equal "layers," each of which is fairly homogeneous in structure?	_____	_____

Guide for the Construction of a Questionnaire

Write the question clearly and completely in the space below	What is the basic assumption underlying the reason for this question? How does the question relate to the research problem?	Type of Question				How do you expect to relate this question to the research effort?
		Multiple Choice	Yes/No Answer	Completion	Countercheck*	

*A "countercheck" question is one included to countercheck the reply given on another question in the questionnaire.

3. Considered graphically, could the population be considered as being composed of separate homogeneous layers differing in size and number of units comprising them? _____ _____
4. Could the population be envisioned as isolated islands or clusters of individual units, with each cluster apparently the same as or similar to every other cluster, but upon close inspection being composed of distinctly heterogeneous units? _____ _____

What is the *randomization process*, i.e., the means of extracting the sample from the total population? Describe on the following lines:

____

____

Refer to Table 8.1. Is the technique of randomization appropriate to the characteristics of the population?

Have you guaranteed that your sample will be chosen by chance and yet will be representative of your population? _____ Yes _____ No

If the preceding answer is yes, indicate *how* this has been done. Explain simply on the following lines:

____

____

____

Indicate what means will be employed to extract the hard facts from the sample:

____

____

____

What are the weaknesses inherent in this method of securing the data?

____

____

____

What safeguards have you established to counteract the weaknesses of the data extraction approach? Be specific.

____

____

____

Significant and Influential Research

"The old order changeth, giving way to new," wrote Tennyson. Research has changed every aspect of our lives: from trashing old and long-reiterated "truths" to bringing to light those never imagined. Those of us who are more than a score of years old may recall reading in our psychology texts that the growth of the human brain was fixed by late childhood and that from then on the organ was merely functional. Its destiny was to think, to reason, to comprehend and associate.

If the foreshadowings of recent studies are substantiated by further research, people are in for a surprise: the growth of the human brain is *not* fixed in late childhood! New evidence points to the growth of the brain even late in life.

In a study discussed earlier, Scheie and Willis suggested that the decline in adult intellectual functioning apparently could be reversed. In a recent report, published in *Experimental Neurology*, Dr. Marian Diamond and her associates found that even in old age the cells of the cerebral cortex respond to an enriched environment by forging new connections to other cells.[7]

Dr. Diamond's study focused on rats 766 days old, the equivalent of 75 years in human terms. These rats were placed in an "enriched" environment and lived there until they reached the age of 904 days. For a rat, an "impoverished" environment means being a solitary occupant in a wire cage a foot square. An "enriched" environment means living with a dozen other rats in a cage a yard square with a variety of toys—mazes, ladders, and wheels.

The elderly rats, after living in such an enriched environment, showed increased thickening of the cerebral cortex. This means that the brain cells increased in dimension and activity and that the glial cells that support the brain cells multiplied accordingly.

If what is good for rats is likewise good for people, we have learned a lesson with tremendous potential for the care, well-being, and happiness of the aging population. This is research that will demand that some of the teachings of our psychology professors and textbooks be completely revised.

[7] Marian C. Diamond, Ruth E. Johnson, Ann Marie Protti, Carol Ott, and Linda Kajisa, "Plasticity in the 904-Day-Old Male Rat Cerebral Cortex," *Experimental Neurology* 87 (1985): 309–17.

The Computer as a Tool of Research

Computer Applications in the Humanities

Over thirty years ago, IBM sponsored a conference at its then-new research facility near Yorktown Heights, New York, to explore the relation of computerization to the humanities.[8] Most of the conferees were employing computers for compiling of concordances and indexes, and similar uses.

Computer-produced concordances and analyses of Shakespeare's works, for example, show a marked difference between the plays published during his lifetime and the "official" editions of those plays published posthumously. What we have considered as the Shakespeare canon might be better considered, through computer-aided study, as a succession of evolutionary stages, or modifications.

In addition to producing concordances, which are valuable in textual analysis and pattern matching, computers have also been employed in creating dictionaries. The *Random House Dictionary* was produced with the aid of computerization. A new edition of the gigantic *Oxford English Dictionary* is available in a machine-readable format under grants from IBM and the British government. The *American Heritage Dictionary* is now available on floppy disk for both IBM-DOS and Apple Macintosh computers, and a host of reference books are now available in CD-ROM format (see chapter 2).

There is also a proliferation of language dictionaries being produced with computer assistance: Old English, Middle English, Old Scots, Old Spanish, Dutch, Indian, and Tibetan.

Machine-readable texts are a recent development. The Kurzwell Data Entry Machine has the amazing ability to learn almost any type of font and to translate printed pages into computer tapes or disks. These machines are now available at a growing number of

[8] This digest was adapted from Joseph Raben, "Computer Applications in the Humanities," *Science* 228 (April 26, 1985): 434-38.

American and British universities, and are beginning to transform many government, business, and academic environments. This development promises to be a boon for research in the humanities for future research scholars. Optical character recognition (OCR) software and hardware is now available in limited form for personal computers. By the time this book is published such systems may be in general use.

One of the most promising developments in the teaching of English composition is a package that has been developed at Bell Laboratories by Nina MacDonald. It is a software package originally developed to eliminate the technical jargon from in-house writing at Bell Laboratories so that its content might be comprehended by the general reader. This package, called the Writer's Workbench, is a computer-assisted program to teach students to write more readable and more literate prose.

The computer promises a bright future for humanists, but one contravening force is the age-old, ingrained idea that humanists are individualists and have a tendency to eschew mechanization as an aid to their studies. New software and computer programs are becoming generally available. This is a promising sign. The Writer's Workbench, Epistle (being developed by IBM), and WANDAH (being marketed by Scribner's) are developments worth watching.

A late bloomer, the humanities is now benefiting from the tremendous assistance that the computer can give to serious scholars and their efforts.

For Further Reading

Further Reading in the Descriptive Survey Method

Babbie, Earl R. *Survey Research Methods.* Belmont, CA: Wadsworth, 1973.

Cartwright, D. P. "Analysis of Qualitative Material." In *Research Methods in the Behavioral Sciences.* Edited by L. Festinger and D. Katz. New York: Holt, Rinehart & Winston, 1953.

Deming, W. E. *Sample Design in Business Research.* New York: Wiley, 1960.

Dillman, Don A. *Mail and Telephone Surveys: The Total Design Method.* New York: Wiley, 1978.

Goldstein, H., and B. H. Kroll. "Methods of Increasing Mail Response." *Journal of Marketing* 22 (1957): 55–57.

Holley, F. S., and L. L. Barker. "Assessing Effect Size in Communication Research: A Case Study." *Communication Quarterly* 56 (September 1979): 269–76.

Miller, Delbert C. *Handbook of Research Design and Social Measurement.* New York: David McKay, 1970.

Namias, Jean. *Handbook of Selected Sample Surveys in the Federal Government.* New York: St. John's University Press, 1969.

Niles, A. G. "Using Survey Research Methodology: An Examination of One Project." *Journal of Continuing Education in Nursing* 12 (November–December 1981): 28–34.

Partan, Mildred. *Surveys, Polls, and Samples.* New York: Harper, 1950.

Selvin, Hanan C. "A Critique of Tests of Significance in Survey Research." *American Sociological Review* 22 (October 1957): 519–27.

Sinquist, John A., and William C. Dunkelberg. *Survey and Opinion Research: Procedures for Processing and Analysis.* Englewood Cliffs, NJ: Prentice-Hall, 1977.

Warwick, Donald P., and Charles A. Lininger. *The Sample Survey: Theory and Practice.* New York: McGraw-Hill, 1975.

Weisberg, Herbert F., and Bruce D. Bowen. *An Introduction to Survey Research and Data Analysis.* San Francisco: W. H. Freeman, 1977.

Williams, Thomas R. "A Critique of the Assumptions of Survey Research." *Public Opinion Quarterly* 23 (Spring 1959): 55–62.

Further Reading in the Use of the Questionnaire

Berdie, Douglas R., and John F. Anderson. *Questionnaires: Design and Use.* Metuchen, NJ: Scarecrow Press, 1974.

Bradburn, Norman M., and Seymour Sudman. *Improving Interview Method and Questionnaire Design.* San Francisco: Jossey-Bass, 1979.

Brandt, K. "The Usefulness of a Postcard Technique in a Mail Questionnaire Study." *Public Opinion Quarterly* 19 (1955): 218–22.

Clausen, J. A., and R. N. Ford. "Controlling Bias in Mail Questionnaires." *Journal of the American Statistical Association* 42 (1947): 497–511.

Colley, R. H. "Don't Look Down Your Nose at Mail Questionnaires." *Printer's Ink* (March 16, 1945): 21–108.

Flitter, H., "How to Develop a Questionnaire." *Nursing Outlook* 8 (October 1960): 566–69.

Frazier, G., and K. Bird. "Increasing the Response to a Mail Questionnaire." *Journal of Marketing* 23 (1958): 186–87.

Futrell, Charles M., and Charles W. Lamb, Jr. "Effect on Mail Survey Return Rates of Including Questionnaires with Follow-up Letters." *Perceptual and Motor Skills* 52 (February 1981): 11–15.

Herzog, A. Regula, and Jerald G. Bachman. "Effects of Questionnaire Length on Response Quality." *Public Opinion Quarterly* 45 (Winter 1981): 549–59.

Kahn, R. L. "A Comparison of Two Methods of Collecting Data for Social Research: The Fixed-alternative Questionnaire Method and the Open-ended Interview." Unpublished Ph.D. Dissertation, Ann Arbor, MI: University of Michigan, 1962.

Kendall, Patricia L. *Conflict and Mood Factors Affecting Stability of Response.* Glencoe, IL: The Free Press, 1954.

Kornhauser, A., and P. B. Sheatsley. "Questionnaire Construction and Interview Procedure." In C. Selltiz, L. S. Wrightman, and S. W. Cook, *Research Methods in Social Relations.* 3d ed. New York: Holt, Rinehart & Winston, 1976, Appendix B.

Oppenheim, Abraham N. *Questionnaire Design and Measurement.* New York: Basic Books, 1966.

Wiasanen, F. B. "A Note on the Response to a Mailed Questionnaire." *Public Opinion Quarterly* 18 (1954): 210–12.

Further Reading in the Use of the Interview

Benney, Mark, David Riesman, and Shirley Star. "Age and Sex in the Interview." *American Journal of Sociology* 62 (1956): 143–52.

Brady, John. *The Craft of Interviewing.* Cincinnati, OH: Writer's Digest, 1976.

Carp, Frances M. "Position Effects on Interview Responses." *Journal of Gerontology* 29 (1974): 581–87.

Dexter, Lewis A. *Elite and Specialized Interviewing.* Evanston, IL: Northwestern University Press, 1970.

Garrett, Annette. *Interviewing: Its Principles and Methods.* 3d rev. ed. Edited by Margaret Mangold and Eleanor Zaki. New York: Family Service Association of America, 1982.

Gordon, R. L. *Interviewing: Strategy, Techniques and Tactics.* rev. ed. Homewood, IL: Dorsey, 1975.

Hyman, Herbert H., and William J. Cobb. *Interviewing in Social Research.* Chicago: University of Chicago Press, 1954.

Katz, Daniel. "Do Interviewers Bias Polls?" *Public Opinion Quarterly* 6 (1942): 248–68.

Maccoby, Eleanor E., and Nathan Maccoby. "The Interview: A Tool of Social Science." In Gardner Lindzey, ed., *Handbook of Social Psychology.* Reading, MA: Addison-Wesley, 1954.

Richetto, Gary M., and Joseph P. Zima. *Interviewing.* Chicago: Science Research Associates, 1981.

Stewart, Charles J., and William B. Cash, Jr. *Interviewing: Principles and Practices.* 3d ed. Dubuque, IA: William C. Brown, 1982.

Survey Research Center Staff, Institute of Social Research. *Interviewer's Manual.* Ann Arbor, MI: Institute of Social Research, University of Michigan, 1976.

Further Reading in the Area of Sampling

Arnold, David O. "Dimensional Sampling: An Approach for Studying a Small Number of Cases." *American Sociologist* 5 (May 1970): 147–50.

Assael, H., and J. Keen. "Nonsampling *vs.* Sampling Errors in Survey Research." *Journal of Marketing* 46 (Spring 1982): 114–23.

Brown, Roscoe C., Jr. "Is There an Optimal Sample Size for Research Involving Human Subjects? Is There a Rule-of-Thumb That Might Be Used in Determining Sample Size?" *Nursing Research* 25 (January–February 1976): 62.

Cochran, William G. *Sampling Techniques.* 3d ed. New York: Wiley, 1977.

Davis, Kingsley, and Wilbert E. Moore. "Some Principles of Stratification." *American Sociological Review* 10 (April 1945): 242–49.

Deming, William E. *Sample Design in Business Research.* New York: Wiley, 1960.

Green, Roger H. *Sampling Design and Statistical Methods for Experimental Biologists.* New York: Wiley, 1979.

Hansen, H. H., William N. Hurwitz, and William G. Meadow. *Sample Survey Methods and Theory.* 2 vols. New York: Wiley, 1953.

Kish, Leslie. *Survey Sampling.* New York: Wiley, 1965.

McCall, Chester H., Jr. *Sampling and Statistics Handbook for Research in Education.* Ames, IA: Iowa State University Press, 1982.

Slonim, Morris J. "Sampling in a Nut Shell." *Journal of the American Statistical Association* 52 (June 1957):143–61. Also issued as a paperback in the Fireside series by Simon and Schuster, New York, 1960.

Som, R. K. *A Manual of Sampling Techniques.* London: Wm. Heinemann, 1973.

Sudman, Seymour. *Applied Sampling.* New York: Academic Press, 1976.

Tumin, Melvin M. "Some Principles of Stratification: A Critical Analysis." *American Sociological Review* 18 (August 1953): 387–94.

Warwick, Donald P., and Chester A. Lininger. *Sample Survey: Theory and Practice.* New York: McGraw-Hill, 1975.

Miscellaneous References

Edwards, Allen L. *Techniques of Attitude Scale Construction.* New York: Appleton-Century-Crofts, 1957.

The RAND Corporation, *A Million Random Digits.* New York: The Free Press, 1955.

Selby, Samuel M. *Standard Mathematical Tables.* 21st ed. Cleveland: Chemical Rubber Co., 1973.

Summers, Gene F., ed. *Attitude Measurement.* Chicago: Rand McNally, 1970.

Tull, Donald S., and Gerald S. Albaum. "Bias in Random Digit Dialed Surveys." *Public Opinion Quarterly* 41 (1977): 389–95.

CHAPTER 9

The Historical Study

Mere happenstance is inimical to the facts of history. Looking behind a random chain of events, historical research descries an underlying matrix of logical cause and effect. And the historical researcher attempts to establish, through the scientific method, a rational explanation for the cause of events and, based upon historical data, a logical interpretation of the effect that such events have upon the lives of individuals and the society in which they live.

Historical Research: The Meaning of Events

Historical research deals with the *meaning* of events. History is merely a transcript of the restless and ever-flowing stream of events and the inexorable changes in human life and its institutions: its language, customs, art, philosophies, and the lives of those who command the attention of their contemporaries—the megafigures, who strut their hour upon the stage and then are heard no more. Historical research deals with this maelstrom. It looks intently at the currents and countercurrents of present and past events and at human thoughts and acts, and seeks to trace them through the tangled web of life, with the hope of unravelling some of its knots, of discerning dynamics that add rationality and meaning to the whole.

Most of us have never been formally introduced to historical *research.* For the most part the academic hierarchy has eschewed any interest in teaching students the specifics of the historical method. Across the board in the curricula of higher education it has been assumed that the ability to do historical research is a genetic trait that anyone who has had a course or two in history is able to perform. This is, of course, false, and the fallacy is that the history course is merely the end product of all the research upon which it is based. Unwittingly and without any guidance, most of us have confused the *study of history* with the *historical method.* They are two entirely different entities and are not to be equated.

Few teachers ever take the time or effort to explain how *history* comes into being. The impression that we have been led to believe is that historical research is merely gathering significant facts about a major event—a war, a depression, the growth of a nation, and similar topics—and organizing these facts in a sequence, usually chronological. This may be a historical narrative. It is not true historical research.

The heart of the historical method is, as with any other type of research, not the *accumulating* of the facts, but the *interpretation* of the facts. Nothing can take the place of that. *The interpretation of the data* is central in all research. Without it, there is no research.

Like so many pieces of a jigsaw puzzle, events seemingly happen without any apparent sequence. But study any chain of events and you will inevitably begin to discern certain "patterns of rationality," of cause and effect that make historical fact appear meaningful. Like the continents, historical events sometimes drift slowly, but to the discerning mind there is, below the mass of data, motion. Historical data is never petrified and static; history is dynamic. Being so, it defines the role of the historical researcher. The task of the historical researcher is not merely to relate *what* events happen but to present a *factually supported* rationale to explain *why* events happen.

The historical researcher digs deep. Historical research makes every effort to go back as nearly as possible to the original event or source—a newspaper clipping, an original memo, a diary entry, a witness to the event—and from such basic sources attempts to establish a rationale and a coherence that will finally culminate in a revelation—an insight into the *meaning* of the event. When this happens, it is truly the historical researcher's "finest hour."

Events do crystallize into meaningful clusters. Just as cause and effect exist in the physical world, so are they equally present in the historical world—in the interaction between humans and their fellows and between humanity and the environment.

In order to appraise accurately the meaning and relationship of events, however, researchers should always seek to get as close to the original events as possible in the hope of thus better reconstructing them. To do this, researchers generally rely on documentary sources, although they occasionally study artifacts, either alone or in conjunction with documentary evidence. In the search for historical truth, therefore, the researcher relies, if at all possible, upon only *primary* data.[1]

Those who made history and influenced human events may indeed be gone forever—they, and their times with them. In attempting to study them, their activities, the events they influenced and that influenced them, we need to reconstruct as nearly as possible the contemporary scene of their day. To try to do this, however, we must discover primary data sources. These consist of portraits, a record of the words they wrote and are reported to have spoken, the testimony of their friends and acquaintances, the personal records that they have left behind, the objects they used, the houses and towns in which they lived, the places where they worked and affected the events important in their times and significant in their lives. Such are the sources of *primary historical data.*

The use of primary data tends to ensure the integrity of the study and to strengthen its reliability. It is, therefore, generally considered to be a sine qua non of historical scholarship.

External Evidence and Internal Evidence

The data of historical research are subject to two types of evaluation. We may judge whether the document is authentic or we may decide, if indeed it is authentic, what the document, or the statement within the document, means. The approaches to data that are concerned with these two problems are known as reviewing the data to determine their *external* or *internal evidence* and subjecting them to *external* or *internal criticism.*[2] The terms *evidence* and *criticism* are interchangeable for all practical purposes. Evidence looks at the problem from the viewpoint of the data; criticism regards the same problem from the psychological attitude of the researcher. Briefly, we shall discuss each of these terms for a fuller appreciation of their use in historical research.

External evidence or external criticism is primarily concerned with the question, is it genuine? External criticism seeks to determine whether the document that has come to the researcher's hands or the artifact that claims attention is genuinely *valid primary data.* Counterfeits are not uncommon. One needs only to recall Thomas Chatterton and the famous "Rowley Manuscripts" to realize how easily a hoax can be perpetrated upon unsuspecting

[1] See the discussion of primary data in chapter 5.

[2] External and internal evidence are sometimes referred to as external and internal *validity.*

scholars. The "Rowley Manuscripts" were famous literary forgeries of the eighteenth century. In the twentieth century, a spurious biography of businessman, motion picture producer, and aviator Howard Hughes appeared, fooled the editors of one of the world's largest publishing houses, and landed the author in jail!

Frauds are not uncommon, nor is their acceptance by the naive scholar and researcher unusual. Remember how thoroughly archaeologists were taken in by the Piltdown Man. Thomas J. Wise for years issued "private editions" of Victorian writings that deceived famous collectors until the fraud was exposed in 1934 by John Carter and Graham Pollard. It is extremely important, therefore, to know whether a document is *genuine.*

External evidence or external criticism of the document is of paramount importance to the credibility of the research. Establishing authenticity of documents is, of course, a study in itself and involves carbon dating, handwriting analysis, identification of ink and paper, vocabulary usage and writing style, and other considerations. This aspect of historical methodology is a study in itself, and we cannot discuss it at length in a text as brief as this one.

Quite apart from the question, "Is it genuine?" is the equally important question having to do with *internal evidence* or *internal criticism.* The question here is not one of authenticity but of *meaning.* In considering a manuscript or a statement, the researcher asks such questions as, "What does it mean?" "What was the author attempting to say?" "What thought was the author trying to convey?" "What inferences or interpretations could be extracted from the words?"

Take a well-known utterance. The time is November 19, 1863. Abraham Lincoln is speaking at the dedication of a national cemetery in Gettysburg, Pennsylvania. In that brief but famous dedicatory address, the president said, "But, in a larger sense, we cannot dedicate—we cannot consecrate—we cannot hallow this ground. The brave men, living and dead, who struggled here, have consecrated it, far above our power to add or detract."

What did Mr. Lincoln *mean* by "the brave men, living and dead"? Did he mean only the brave men of the Union forces? (We must remember that he was dedicating a Union cemetery.) Did he mean the brave Confederate men as well? Or did he mean brave men, indiscriminately, with no thought of North or South but merely of courage and valor? To a researcher studying the life of Abraham Lincoln, it is essential to know precisely what the president did mean by those words.

The matter of internal evidence is not so far from us as we might at first surmise. What does the decision of a court mean? What do the words of the decision convey as to the intent and will of the court? The question comes up all the time in legal interpretation. In such instances, the primary question is *What do the words mean?* This is the sole concern of internal evidence.

The Concept of Historical Time

The student of historical research needs to distinguish very carefully between two concepts that are frequently confused under the general rubric of "the study of history." One of these concepts is genuine historical research—historiography, as it is sometimes called. The historical researcher should be primarily concerned with historiography. The other concept is chronology, the setting down of occurrences and events in the order of their happening. The *Anglo-Saxon Chronicle* is an example of chronology; Toynbee's *A Study of History* is historiography (historical research). Chronology is usually merely a listing of dates and events. It is not research because it does not *interpret the meaning* of those events. It does not point out any significance to the event, as a unit within the larger constellation of events.

The following is chronology:

1492: Columbus discovered America.
1607: First permanent English settlement in America at Jamestown, Virginia.
1620: Pilgrims landed at Plymouth, Massachusetts.

1624: The Dutch settled New Amsterdam.
1630: The Puritans established Massachusetts Bay Colony.
1634: Lord Calvert settled in Maryland.
1682: William Penn founded the colony of Pennsylvania.
1733: Georgia founded by James Oglethorpe.
1754–1763: The French and Indian Wars.
1775–1783: The War of American Independence.
1789: George Washington was inaugurated the first President of the United States of America.
1792: The first political parties appeared in America; the Industrial Revolution began in America with the introduction of Eli Whitney's cotton gin.

In this form, the list is merely a succession of twelve dates marking a series of events in the first three centuries of the history of the original thirteen colonies.

Moreover, format does not change genre. The mere recasting of a chronological list into paragraph form with the amenities of prose composition and appropriate documentary footnotes does not change the nature of the process nor transform pedestrian chronicle into historical research. The paragraph still merely reports happenings and recounts a sequence of events—nothing more.

This is not to imply that chronology does not fill a very important place in historical study. It does. It is the grist of the research mill. It provides the first step in the process of data interpretation, and interpretation is—as we cannot state too often—the indispensable element of all research. You can recognize how essential chronology is in historical research if you attempt to visualize the disadvantage that would result from attempting to reconstruct the history of early England without the *Anglo-Saxon Chronicle.*

In view of what we have just noted, let us now look analytically at the chronology given above. What, in fact, do these events say? What do they mean? Are they merely isolated happenings or do they have a relationship to each other and to the whole 300-year time span? These are questions that the historical researcher is always asking of the data. Such questioning represents a basic attitude in historical research. If we are to do historical research, we must seek not only to identify the chain of events of substantive history but also to understand the meaning of these events, both as to their relationship to each other and to the problem under study.

History is dimensional. It has the *dimension of historical time* and the *dimension of historical space.* Both of these dimensions are extremely important in interpreting historical data. We will discuss, first, the concept of historical time; then, we will explore the idea of historical space. Because history is inseparable from the time in which its events occurred, we should examine the preceding chronology in terms of its time orientation and relationships.

Many beginning researchers fail to become familiar with the time dimension; hence, they do not appreciate the significance that the temporal relationship gives to the data. The more angles from which data are regarded, the more meaningful those data become. Historical data are no exception.

In the chronology that we gave you above, the time span was 300 years: 1492 to 1792. Draw a line 150 millimeters long. For a 300-year span, a line of such length makes each millimeter equal 2 years. So divided, the period 1492 to 1792 will look as shown in Figure 9.1.

Now, within the preceding time frame, let us insert at the proper points the events listed in the chronological sequence. The linear chronology now appears as shown in Figure 9.2.

How different the chronology now appears. It is no longer merely a list of items. It has become, rather, a series of events placed along a time continuum at the precise points of their relative occurrence. The dynamics of history are now becoming apparent. Note also the *rhythms* along the time line. An event happens—the discovery of America. Then, an apparently sterile 115 years (1492–1607) elapse between that event and the first permanent English set-

Figure 9.1

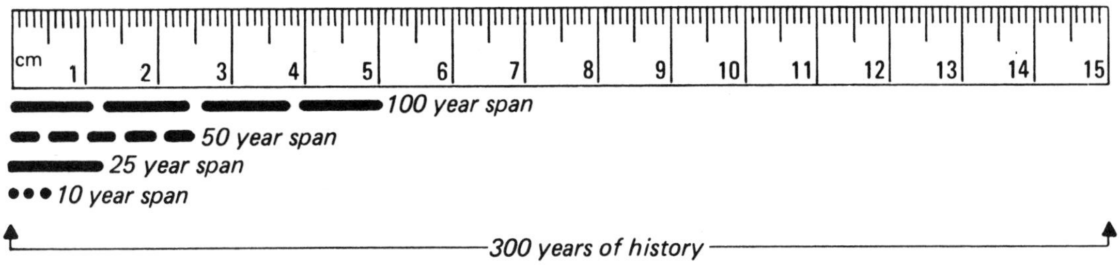

tlement at Jamestown, Virginia. But such, of course, was not the case. The *total* stage of history was, of course, crowded with events during that 115-year hiatus. In what is now the United States of America, Spanish conquistadors and missionaries were busy in the Southwest and Florida. The French were in the Mississippi Valley. But if we look at the activity in the original 13 colonies, the historical record offers only silence during that span of years.

Then, beginning with 1607, for slightly more than a quarter of a century, events occur in rapid succession: the English settle in Virginia and Massachusetts, the Dutch settle in New Amsterdam, and the Calvertists settle in Maryland. Other events, unmentioned, of course, were taking place: Roger Williams and the Antinomians settled in Rhode Island; the Swedes, in Delaware; John Mason and David Thomson, in New Hampshire. This quarter-century of American colonial history teemed with activity! But for our purposes within the particular chronology we have cited, we have not mentioned these other events.

The timeline proceeds. Another century is unbroken except for the one event—the founding of Pennsylvania. Then, the final half of the third century is again a time of renewed activity, of turbulent events: the birth of a nation and the beginning of an industrial revolution.

We need only a little imagination to realize that the device that we have been discussing briefly—and merely for the purpose of presenting a historiographical method—has great potential. It is also capable of numerous variations. The historical researcher who is studying more than one set of chronological data within the same time frame may gain increased

Figure 9.2

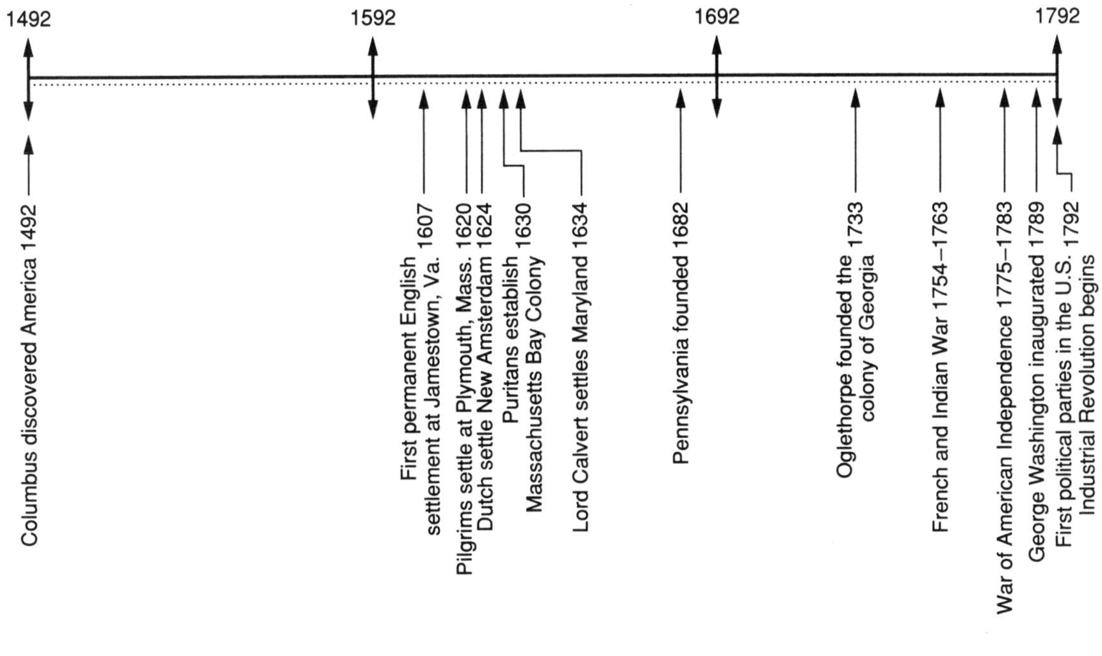

insight by arranging multiple timeline scales in slide-rule fashion. We might superimpose above the events we have plotted on one timeline another series of events—for example, the principal events in the history of England that determined the discoveries and settlements in the New World. Similarly, we could plot on a third scale the meaningful events from European history over the same 300-year period. We would then read the chart as we read a slide rule: one scale against the other.

Sometimes, a realistic way to regard the time-distance dimension in historical perspective is to see it in reverse. As historical data stand in perspective at a distance of centuries from the researcher, they have a tendency to telescope and to become unrealistically crowded upon each other. Historical time has a subtle way of becoming deceptive unless we are very alert to its realities. A pencil and some simple subtraction will reveal a great deal that may otherwise escape our awareness. If we lay a particular historical period backward from the present, we dramatically focus the slowness or the rapidity with which events moved in times past. Into the block of time that elapsed between the discovery of America and the establishment of the first permanent English settlement at Jamestown, you could pack all of American history from the invention of the telephone in 1876 to the present moment!

The Concept of Historical Space (Historical Geography)

We have been discussing history as a time phenomenon, and we have demonstrated the role of time in seeking the interpretation of historical fact. But events also happen in a particular *place.* They have a *space dimension.*

In trying to understand the significance of historical fact, the *where,* or spatial dimension, is frequently as important as the *when.* Let us now consider the same events that we have plotted above in relation to the geographical location where the action took place. Study the map shown in Figure 9.3 carefully. Note how English colonization began at the extremes (Virginia and Massachusetts), with the Dutch settling at New Amsterdam approximately 275 miles north of Jamestown and 225 miles south of the Massachusetts Bay Colony. Calvert founded Maryland. Half a century later, Penn settled Pennsylvania. In the interim, the Swedes had come to Delaware, and New Jersey was being negotiated between Dutch and English with the whole situation complicated by conflicting deeds and permissions granted by authorities ignorant of each other's acts. The colonization that began at the fringes was now closing in toward the center. Only a map can reveal this phenomenon.

Now, see what we have done with one set of facts. We have arranged the same historical data in three separate ways: first, as a simple chronological listing; next, along a timeline continuum; and, finally, in geographical relationship. Each arrangement provides a different insight into the meaning of the data. In each instance, we more fully answered the basic question every researcher asks of any data, what do these facts *mean?* The geographical placement of the information reveals a number of new insights aside from those apparent through the chronological and timeline presentation. These may be tabulated as follows:

1. Colonization, as represented by the timeline chronology, was not equally spread along the Atlantic coast. It clustered north of the 36th parallel of latitude.
2. The first English colony, at Jamestown, Virginia (represented on the map by a star), was pivotally located. It was just about equidistant from the northernmost and southernmost points of colonization activity.
3. Inscribe an arc on the map using Jamestown as the pivotal point and include the area in which almost all of the events of the first 300 years of colonial American history took place. Compare the radius of the arc to the scale of miles and you will see that it inscribes an area of just about 500 miles equidistant from Jamestown.
4. By referring to the limits of such an arc, we see that the French and Indian War took place in the hatched area lying across the outer and northern limits of such an arc. With imagination, we must also realize that such a war must probably have seemed as remote

Figure 9.3 The Spatial Dimension of History

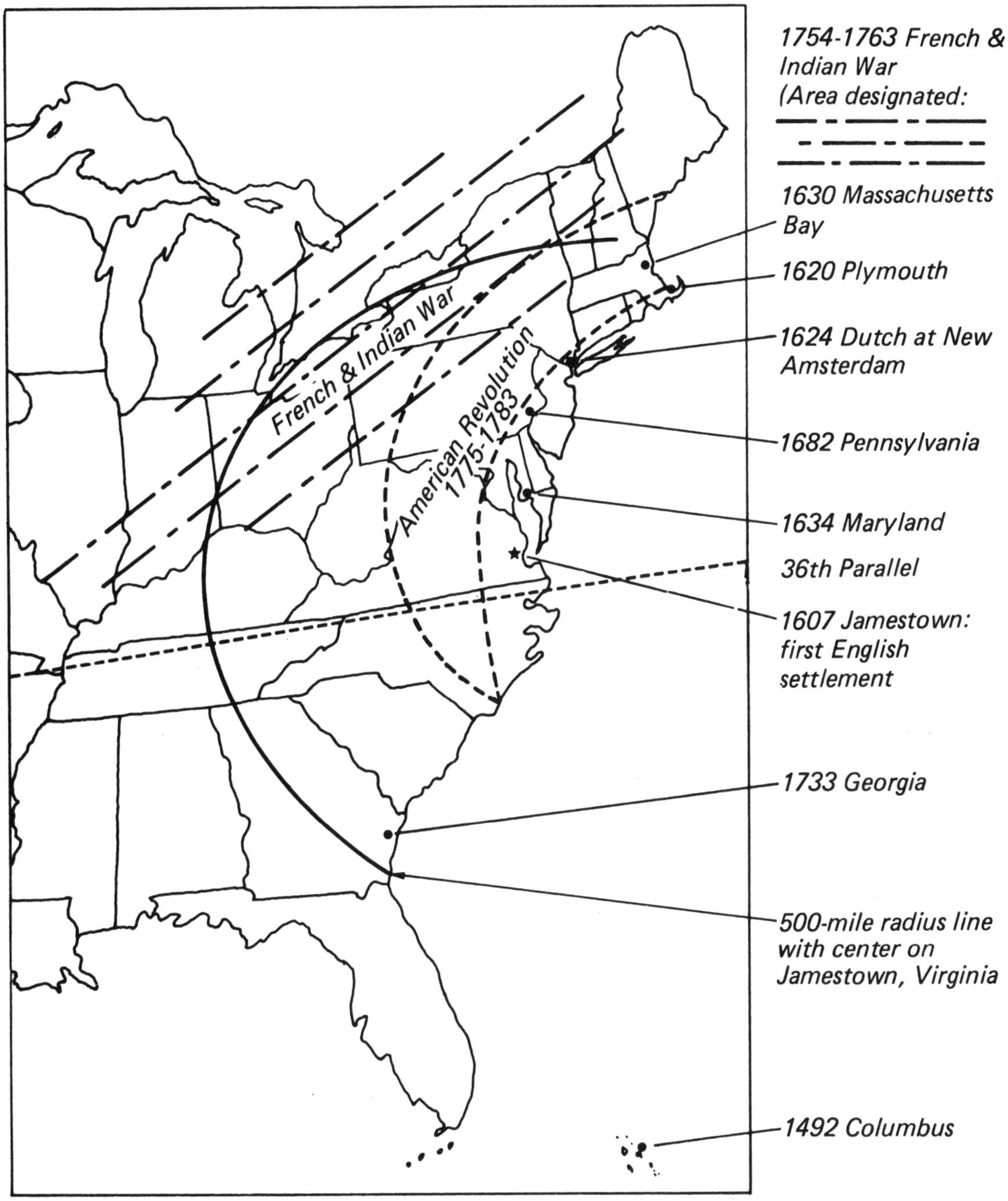

to the colonists of Jamestown, Philadelphia, New York, and Boston as Vietnam and the Middle East seem to people of today.

5. The war for American Independence, on the other hand, was a very intimate struggle. It swept through the colonies in a north-to-south direction. The only variation to this pattern was the Vincennes exploit of George Rogers Clark (1779). The broad arrows on the map indicate the general direction of events from 1775 to 1781.
6. The landing of Columbus on San Salvador is perhaps the only event lying outside the area of principal activity as bounded by the 500-mile radial line. Not only is it some 950 miles south of Jamestown but it is also removed from the settlement at Jamestown by 115

years of history. Probably this one event does indeed lie outside the corpus of historical fact that we are studying and is convenient only as a point of chronological reference.

Systematic Handling of Historical Data

We have perhaps said quite enough about the several ways in which historical data may be studied. Because, however, most of the data of the historical researcher will be gathered from documents and will finally be studied in terms of hundreds or even thousands of note cards, it is imperative for the researcher to have some means of gathering and controlling the data so that he or she reaps the greatest return from the innumerable hours spent in archives, document rooms, and libraries. In historical investigations, perhaps more than in any other type of research, the investigator can soon become lost in a morass of notes, note cards, bibliography cards, and memoranda. It is easy to read and to take notes, but it is difficult for many students to organize those notes into useful and meaningful facts for interpretation. Historical data collecting demands a systematic plan, not only for the collection of the data, but also for retrieving and analyzing them. Before beginning historical research, therefore, you should have a specific plan for the acquisition, organization, storage, and retrieval of the data. Some of the following suggestions may assist you in developing that systematic approach.

Note Cards and Bibliography Cards

The planning for the organization of note cards and bibliography cards should be done with a thorough understanding of the importance of such foresight. Despite the widespread use of filing cards for note and bibliographical purposes, they have their disadvantages. Quantities of them take up an inordinate amount of file space. In chapter 4, we discussed your system of bibliographic reference cards. Here we discuss a note card system designed to coordinate with your bibliography. We suggested that you consider using 20-pound paper for notes and bibliographical information. Cut the sheets to 3 × 5-inch size for bibliographical notes. Cut other sheets to 4 × 6 or 5 × 7-inch sheets for substantive notes. For your own convenience, you may well wish to have certain items duplicated on these sheets. Such prepared sheets will save you time and ensure that you do not overlook important information that may be essential at a later date. By photocopying forms and sizes on regular 8½ × 11-inch or 8½ × 14-inch sheets, these can then, before use, be cut to smaller size with an ordinary hand paper cutter. From a regular typewriter-size sheet, four 3 × 5-inch bibliography cards or two 4 × 6-inch and two 3 × 5-inch cards can be cut. A sample 4 × 6-inch note card for notes of a substantive nature is given in Figure 9.4.

The importance of the box in the upper right-hand corner of the card is apparent when making an extended note. For example, you know precisely where the particular card belongs if it reads, "Card 2. One of 3 cards." At the bottom of the note card is a brief but exact short form for bibliographical reference. To find the complete bibliographic reference, all you have to do is refer to your bibliographical file, which should be alphabetically arranged by the author's last names (see chapter 4).

Multiple Files and Color Coding

All notes should be kept in multiple copies—probably in triplicate or quadruplicate, depending upon your ultimate analysis of the data. Behind the suggestion of substituting 20-pound paper for filing cards was the thought of making multiple copies. (Most photocopying paper is of similar weight.) Earlier we discussed the multidimensional nature of historical data. A fact may lie simultaneously in the province of time, of space, of personality, and perhaps of subject matter. Take, for example, a note that a researcher might make in studying Edgar Allan Poe's poem "Annabel Lee." Poe wrote that poem in 1849 while living in a small cottage in the

Figure 9.4 A Sample Note Card

Main Heading Classification	Subheading	Card No.____ One of ____cards
		Check here if note is continued on reverse side ☐
Source Information: Author's last name ______________	Date of book _____ pp. _____	
First significant word of title ________________	Bibliog. card No. ______________	

Fordham section of the Bronx (now part of New York City). A student studying this poem may wish to see it from various angles, and a note on the poem may have various facets. The student may be interested in studying all of Poe's poems written in 1849, in studying Poe's life in Fordham, in studying the poems Poe wrote about his wife, Virginia Clemm, or in having a quick reference to all the information collected on the poem "Annabel Lee." Thus, one item of information might conceivably be studied from four separate angles.

Leaving the heading blank, make four copies of the note. Add the headings to each card as appropriate. The headings of these four identical notes might appear as shown in Figure 9.5.

If you continue to produce cards in quadruplicate, then these notes will result in four separate but parallel files of the same data. Through this method all chronological data can be gathered together into a progressive file, day by day, month by month, year by year. The geographical place data (in this case, for Fordham) can be assembled as one body of information. By arranging the geographical data alphabetically according to place locations, quick reference may be had to Poe's activities in every location where he lived: Baltimore, Fordham, Richmond, and so forth. Another file will hold all the information about separate poems. A final file may be devoted to people important to the life of the subject being studied. These may also be filed alphabetically for rapid reference.

For each of these areas of study, the researcher may wish to use color coding for ready identification. Select a different colored note card for each category of information. If dates, for example, are all on white cards, and blue cards are used for cross-referencing information, not only do the blue cards stand out among the other cards of the category, but they afford an efficient and rapid means of relating the data of one category to that of another. When seen thus in a three-, four-, or five-dimensional matrix, interpretation of historical data is greatly facilitated. By such a system, one can readily see meanings and interpretations that might have been missed in a one-card system.

Figure 9.5 Filing Multiple Note Copies

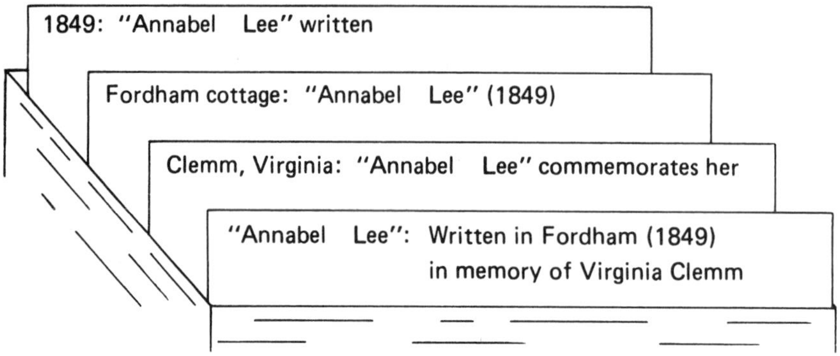

Use the Computer to Manage the Data

We have just described the conventional note-taking and filing system. For those who own computers, an even more effective and less laborious method of data management is available. Let's simplify and increase efficiency as much as possible. We begin with the note-taking process.

Instead of using the note card and manual copying of the data, go to the library, or archives, or wherever the data may be available with a micro- or minicassette recorder. Dictate the data (notes) instead of transcribing them. Returning, enter your notes into a document file in your computer.

From here on the management of your data is only limited by the capacities of your software. Most word processing programs will permit you to search through your data for recurring words or phrases and to collect these in a separate file. Much database software will also sort, alphabetize, create tables, summaries and abstracts, permit you to enter comments into the text that are not printed when the document is printed, and arrange your data in an ascending or descending order of date and event. Other special features, such as Hypertext, which make data management feasible and flexible are becoming common components. Computerizing the data offers a broad spectrum of techniques for data management. Your best guide for availability of data management features is the manual to your software package. Scan the index; it will outline the features available.

Psychological or Conceptual Historical Research

Thus far we have discussed historical research with respect to happenings, events, and personalities. This is conventional historical research. But this chapter would not be complete without a brief discussion of another quite valid type of historical research—namely, research concerned not only with events and personalities but also with tracing the origin, development, and influence of ideas and concepts.

Ideas and concepts have origins, growth, and development, and exert an influence upon their age as strong as the influence of the growth and development of a civilization, a nation, or a local area. The *idea* of democracy was born in Greece; its development has run parallel to the events of the Greco-Roman world, the Middle Ages, and modern times. Perhaps the fragile remains of the monumental concept that began in ancient Athens is found in its purest form today in the New England town meeting.

One might also say the same of any of the principal ideas of civilization—capitalism, socialism, rationalism, individualism, communism, utopianism. Each of them, and other ideas akin to them, has its own developmental history, which is the history of the creative human mind. Each history is as valid as the history of western civilization, the United States, or your hometown.

There are spinoffs from any human idea that are minuscule and discrete enough for any individual researcher to examine. In some cases the researcher may find a new area of investigation that will prove both exciting and challenging.

Turn to the sample proposal section entitled "The Review of the Related Literature" given in chapter 4. Note that the author of the proposal gives a very sketchy history of the role of interests within the behavioral sciences. It is certainly not his purpose to present anything remotely resembling a history of interests. But there is a broad hint in this sketchy presentation that a most fertile field may lie fallow, one in which no scholar has hitherto set an investigative spade.

As a very simple point of departure, open the *Encyclopedia Britannica* to any of the principal ideas of civilization cited above. You may be surprised at the extent of the treatment in every encyclopedia article, yet it still hints at the historical research possibilities of the idea *qua* idea.

Look into Arnold Toynbee's monumental *A Study of History.* Here, you will find not the traditional approach to history—the relating and interpreting of events—so much as the dynamic *ideas* that have powered the histories of nations and civilizations and that have been instrumental in bringing about cataclysmic changes in those histories.

For the researcher who wants to get away from the surface facts of the day, regardless of the century in which that day exists, probing the growth of the thoughts and ideas of that day may prove refreshing and exciting.

The Fascination of Searching for Roots

We mentioned earlier in this text the fascinating research of John Livingston Lowes, presented in *The Road to Xanadu.* Lowes's book is remarkable because it is in a sense research in reverse. In it, Lowes searches for "the genesis of two of the most remarkable poems in English, 'The Rime of the Ancient Mariner' and 'Kubla Khan.'"[3]

This type of research, which is the counterpart of a genealogical search of one's family origins, begins with such questions as, where did it come from? how did it all begin? The search is antecedent to the fact. This is precisely the type of research astronomers and astrophysicists are doing to try to account for the creation of the universe.

One does not have to design a research project on such an astronomically cosmic scale to engage in the same kind of detective work that reels backward in search of answers instead of forward, as is usually done.

The process of beginning with a phenomenon and regressing to locate the causal factors is generally known as ex post facto research. You will find a more extensive discussion of this research paradigm in chapter 11.

Practical Application

Practicum in Historical Research Writing

Historical research evidences broad variations, depending upon the historian and that individual's style of writing. We make the point in chapter 13 that research writing need not be dull. This statement is certainly obvious when reading some historians. Their pages are as varied and as interesting as life itself.

To appreciate how various scholars have handled the same subject matter, take one significant event in history—the Peloponnesian War, the Sacking of Rome by Alaric in 410 A.D., the Battle of Tours, or the march of Hannibal across the Alps—and compare the treatment of the event by various historical writers. In view of the matters discussed

[3] John Livingston Lowes, *The Road to Xanadu* (Boston: Houghton Mifflin, 1927), 3.

Figure 9.6

Criterion or Evaluative Standard	Yes	No	Your Comment Based on Your Observations
Are the accounts essentially the same? If not, what is the difference between them?	___	___	
The accounts reveal some attempt at textual criticism of sources.	___	___	
The accounts show an awareness of "historical time."	___	___	
The accounts show some awareness of "historical space."	___	___	
The account is a prose form of chronology.	___	___	
The account is interspersed with interpretations of the historical data presented.	___	___	

General critical reactions:	
Author: ____________________	Author: ____________________
Title: ____________________	Title: ____________________
Source 1	Source 2

in chapter 9, compare the historical accounts on the basis of the criteria in Figure 9.6.

For a variation on the preceding project, look up some event in the *Cambridge Ancient* (or *Medieval*, or *Modern*) *History* and choose the identical event in, for example, Will Durant's *The Story of Civilization.* The purpose of this project is to give you an opportunity to develop skill at critically evaluating historiography and historical research.

Significant and Influential Research

Hernando DeSoto. His name is familiar to all of us. In grade school we learned that he was the Spanish explorer who discovered the Mississippi River and who was buried in it so that hostile Indians would not find his body and mutilate it. We also learned that he was ruthless and cruel. Beyond that, we learned very little about this Spanish adventurer, who passed across the pages of history like an insubstantial wraith, leaving only a shadowy impression behind.

Now all that is changed. Researchers—archaeologists and historians—are on the trail of the first large party of Spanish conquistadors as they plunged into the aboriginal wilderness and traveled across much of what is now the southern United States. They ranged far and covered thousands of miles; theirs was no inconsequential expedition.

How do we know all this? In this chapter we discussed the importance of documentary evidence and the desirability of going to the primary sources of the evidence. This record of the DeSoto expedition is an excellent example of this methodology.

Following this discussion is a map (Figure 9.7). It appeared in the *New York Times* on May 19, 1987. The news story that accompanied it described the finding, in Tallahassee, Florida, of an Indian-Spanish site. It was a major discovery in the DeSoto story. The map delineates the wanderings of DeSoto through the southern states.

How do we know this? Primary documentary evidence! There are at least five on-the-spot records, written by actual members of the expedition, of what happened in that expedition, including the record left by Rodrego Ranjel, DeSoto's private secretary. But this is not all. In Spanish archives there are additional documents and letters relating to the DeSoto travels through the southern United States.

The story of the DeSoto expedition is a fascinating one. A record of the piecing together of this chapter in our early history is available through the Department of Anthropology, The Florida State Museum, Gainesville, FL 32611. It is entitled, "Hernando DeSoto and the Expedition in *La Florida*" and is by Jerald T. Milanish (Miscellaneous Project Report No. 32).

Ongoing research at a second site in Florida has yielded important artifact evidence on DeSoto and the Spaniards' contacts with the American aborigines. It is described in a

Figure 9.7

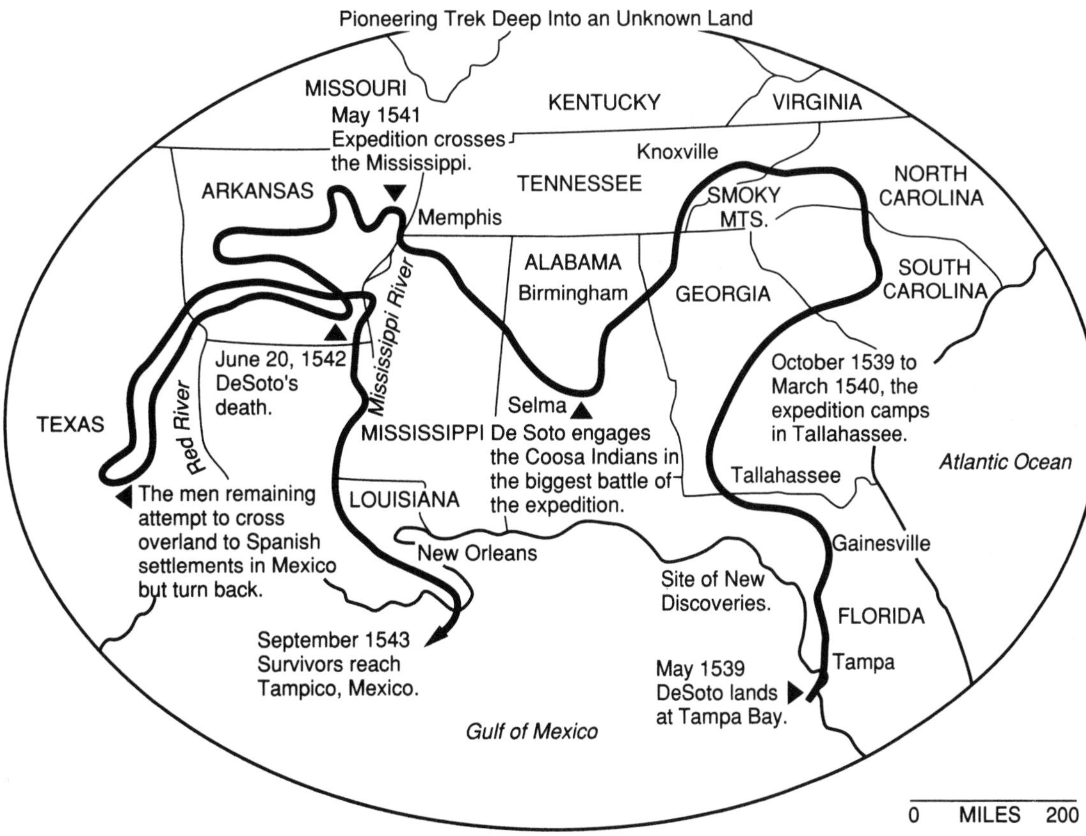

series of interim reports on excavations at the Tatham burial mound in Citrus County. These reports, entitled, "Interim Report on Archaeological Research at the Tatum Mound, Citrus County, Florida," are available from the Florida State Museum (Miscellaneous Project Report Series No. 30, Florida State Museum, 1987). There are, to date, three interim reports on this project.

For those interested in historical research, with archeological and documentary evidence, the work going on in Florida is contemporary and exciting. This significant and influential research will rewrite a chapter in our history that has been shadowy and indistinct and will change many of our previous concepts with respect to DeSoto and the exploration of the South.

As an adjunct to this discussion of historical research, mention of significant, contemporary doctoral research that employs the methodology of historical research may be appropriate. The following recent dissertations were noted in the 1989–1990 volume of *American Doctoral Dissertations,* a publication of University Microfilms International compiled for the Association of Research Libraries:

"Rebels Against the Cold War: Four Intellectuals Who Campaigned to Recast World Politics 1945–1985," by Michael D. Bess (University of California: Berkeley, 1989).

"British Observers of America 1890–1950," by Robert P. Frankel (Harvard University, 1990).

"The Idea of Sociability in Pre-Revolutionary France," by Daniel L. Gordon (University of Chicago, 1990).

"Music, Race, and Culture in Urban America: The Creators of Jazz," by Burton W. Peretti (University of California: Berkeley, 1989).

"Bourgeois Women, Local Politics and Social Change: The Women's Movement in Hanover, 1880–1933," by Nancy R. Reagin (Johns Hopkins University, 1990).

"Charged with Sexuality: Feminism, Liberalism, and Pornography, 1970–1982," by Elizabeth A. Smith (University of Pennsylvania, 1990).

The Computer as a Tool of Research

Computer Applications in Historical Research

There was a time when the primary function of computers was to crunch numbers. But times have changed. No longer is the computer merely a giant calculator; it fills many other roles. Can computers deal with language, or the academic disciplines to which language is the principal vehicle of communication? The answer is, emphatically, yes!

With the advent of word processing, the computer became literate. Some of us still have trouble envisioning the computer having a central place in research in the fields of history, literature, philosophy, and religion. But in these areas the computer can be a most helpful research tool.

As long ago as 1970, two professors, one at Oklahoma State University and the other at the University of Illinois, had a dream and a vision. It was a vision of the computerization of research in history. They wrote a book: *Historian's Guide to Statistics.*[4] In this volume they devoted nearly a hundred pages to data processing fundamentals and computer applications in historical research. Their approach was to analyze certain tables of statistical data.

Over the years word processing has won a leading role in handling verbal data. It has opened up such possibilities as searching a body of text to compile lists, to determine the frequency of use of some material, to study context, and for similar procedures.

[4]Charles M. Dollar and Richard A. Jensen, *Historian's Guide to Statistics* (New York: Holt, Rinehart and Winston, 1979). The chapters referred to are chapters 5 and 6: "Fundamentals of Data Processing," (pp. 139–86) and "Computer Applications of Historical Research" (pp. 187–235).

Probably the most spectacular use of computers in historical research occurred in two studies undertaken at Hull University in Great Britain. In one study, researchers used census schedules and poll books from the elections held before the introduction of the secret ballot in 1872 to examine electoral behavior in the eighteenth and nineteenth centuries. In the second study, researchers examined the Domesday Book to explore the social and economic structure of England in 1066.

We have said enough about the historical method for the purposes of the beginning researcher. We now turn to another of the research methodologies, as another avenue to the discovery of truth. Chapters 8 and 9 have dealt with qualitative methodologies; chapters 10 and 11 will explore quantitative research.

For Further Reading

Austin, Anne L. "The Historical Method in Nursing." *Nursing Research* 7 (February 1958): 4–10.

Aydelotte, William O. "Quantification in History." *American Historical Review* 71 (1966): 803–25.

Barnard, K. "Research Designs: The Historical Method." *American Journal of Maternal Child Nursing* 6 (November–December 1981): 391.

Barzun, Jacques, and Henry F. Graff. *The Modern Researcher.* New York: Harcourt, Brace, 1957.

Bauer, Richard H. *The Study of History with Helpful Suggestions for the Beginner.* Philadelphia: McKinley, 1948.

Berkhofer, Robert F. *A Behavioral Approach to Historical Analysis.* New York: Macmillan, 1969.

Bloch, Marc. *The Historian's Craft.* New York: McGraw-Hill, 1964.

Boehm, Eric, and Adolphus Lalit. *Historical Periodicals: An Annotated World List of Historical and Related Serial Publications.* Santa Barbara, CA: Clio Press, 1961.

Bybee, R. W. "Historical Research in Science Education." *Journal of Research in Science Teaching* 19 (January 1982): 1–13.

Caron, Pierre, and Marc Jaryc. *World List of Historical Periodicals.* New York: H. W. Wilson, 1939.

Christy, Teresa E. "The Methodology of Historical Research: A Brief Introduction." *Nursing Research* 24 (May–June, 1975): 189–92.

Clive, John. *Not by Fact Alone: Essays on the Writing and Reading of History.* New York: Knopf, 1989.

Clubb, Jerome M., and Howard Allen. "Computers and Historical Studies." *Journal of American History* 54 (1967): 599–607.

de Certeau, Michel. *The Writing of History.* New York: Columbia, 1988.

Dollar, Charles M., and Robert J. Jensen. *Historian's Guide to Statistics: Quantitative Analysis and Historical Research.* New York: Holt, Rinehart & Winston, 1971.

Felt, Thomas E. *Researching, Writing, and Publishing Local History.* Nashville, TN: American Association for State and Local History, 1981.

Floud, Roderick. *An Introduction to Quantitative Methods for Historians.* Princeton, NJ: Princeton University Press, 1973.

Freudlich, Y. "Methodology of Science as Tools for Historical Research." *Studies in the History and Philosophy of Science* 11 (December 1980): 257–66.

Gawronski, Donald V. *History: Meaning and Method.* 3d ed. Glenview, IL: Scott, Foresman, 1975.

Gottschalk, Louis R. *Understanding History.* New York: Alfred A. Knopf, 1950.

Gray, Wood, et al. *Historian's Handbook: A Key to the Study and Writing of History.* 2d ed. Boston: Houghton Mifflin, 1964.

Greenwood, Val D. *The Researcher's Guide to American Genealogy.* Baltimore: Genealogical Publishing, 1973.

Hale, Richard W. *Methods of Research for the Amateur Historian.* Technical Leaflet No. 21. Nashville, TN: American Association for State and Local History, 1969.

Heller, G. N., and B. D. Wilson. "Historical Research in Music Education." *Bulletin of the Council on Research in Music Education* 69 (Winter 1982): 1–20.

Hockett, Homer C. *The Critical Method in Historical Research and Writing.* New York: Macmillan, 1955.

Hoover, Dwight W., ed. *Understanding Negro History.* New York: Quadrangle, 1968.

Humphries, R. Steven. "The Historian: His Documents and the Elementary Modes of Historical Thought." *History and Theory* 19 (February 1980): 1–20.

Kaplan, Abraham. *The Conduct of Inquiry: Methodology for Behavioral Science.* Scranton, PA: Chandler, 1964.

Kent, Sherman. *Writing History.* New York: F. S. Crofts, 1941.

Lichtman, Allan J., and Valerie French. *Historians and the Living Past: The Theory and Practice of Historical Study.* Arlington Heights, IL: AHM, 1978.

Marston, Doris R. *A Guide to Writing History.* Cincinnati, OH: Writer's Digest, 1976.

Maynes, M. J. "Theory and Method in Recent German Historical Studies." *Journal of Interdisciplinary History* 10 (Autumn 1979): 311–17.

McCoy, F. N. *Researching and Writing in History.* Berkeley, CA: University of California Press, 1974.

McMurtie, Donald. "Locating the Printed Source Materials for United States History, with a Bibliography of Lists of Regional Imprints." *Mississippi Valley Historical Review* 31 (1944): 369–78.

Milligan, J. D. "Treatment of an Historical Source." *History and Theory* 18 (No. 2, 1979): 177–96.

Mommsen, W. J. "Social Conditioning and Social Relevance of Historical Judgements." *History and Theory* 17 (No. 4, 1978): 19–35.

Morison, Samuel Eliot. "Faith of a Historian." *The American Historical Review* 56 (January 1951): 261–75.

Murphy, George G. S. "Historical Investigation and Automatic Data Processing Equipment." *Computers and the Humanities* 3 (1968): 1–13.

Platt, Jennifer. "Evidence and Proof in Documentary Research, I and II (I. Some Specific Problems of Documentary Research; II. Some Shared Problems of Documentary Research)." *The Sociological Review* 29 (February 1981): 31–52, 53–66.

Poulton, Helen J. *The Historian's Handbook: A Descriptive Guide to Reference Works.* Norman, OK: University of Oklahoma Press, 1972.

Rowney, D. K., and J. Q. Graham, Jr. *Quantitative History: Selected Readings in the Quantitative Analysis of Historical Data.* Homewood, IL: Dorsey, 1969.

Rubicam, Milton, ed. *Genealogical Research Methods and Sources.* Belcherville, MA: American Society of Genealogists, 1966.

Sabin, Joseph, and continued by Wilberforce Eames and R. W. G. Vail. *Dictionary of Books Relating to America from the Discovery to the Present Time.* 29 vol. New York: J. Sabin, 1868–1936.

Shafer, R. I. *A Guide to Historical Method.* rev. ed. Homewood, IL: Dorsey, 1974.

Shorter, Edward. *The Historian and the Computer: A Practical Guide.* Englewood Cliffs, NJ: Prentice-Hall, 1971.

Siegel, S. *Nonparametric Statistics for the Behavioral Sciences.* New York: McGraw-Hill, 1956.

Stevenson, Noel C. *Search and Research: Addresses of Libraries Having Genealogical Collections.* Salt Lake City, UT: Deseret, 1959.

Swierenga, Robert P. "Computer and American History: The Impact of the 'New Generation.'" *The Journal of American History* 60 (March 1974): 1045–70.

Thernstrom, Stephan. "Quantitative Methods in History: Some Notes." In S. M. Lipset and Richard Hofstadter, eds., *Sociology and History: Methods*. New York: Basic Books, 1968.

Veyne, Paul. *Writing History*. Reading, MA: n. p., 1984.

Weitzman, David. *Underfoot: An Everyday Guide to Exploring the American Past*. New York: Scribner's, 1976.

Westmoreland, Guy T. *An Annotated Guide to Basic Reference Books on the Black American Experience*. Washington, DC: Scholarly Resources, Inc., 1974.

Wheeler, Helen. *Womanhood Media: Current Resources about Women*. Metuchen, NJ: Scarecrow Press, 1972.

Yeomans, K. A. *Statistics for the Social Scientist*. Volume 1: *Introductory Statistics*; Volume 2: *Applied Statistics*. Baltimore: Penguin, 1968.

PART IV

QUANTITATIVE RESEARCH METHODOLOGIES: DATA PRINCIPALLY NUMERICAL

CHAPTER **10**

The Quantitative Study

By the mystery and expressiveness of numbers we can express what is inexpressible, describe what is indescribable, predict what is reasonable to expect, or infer a logical conclusion to a series of events. Statistics is a language that can speak where other tongues are mute. Words cannot express the concepts that have been reserved for the eloquence and expressiveness of statistics alone.

In this chapter, we will discuss a form of quantitative study called the analytical survey. We begin on a note of contrast. We can understand the analytical survey best by comparing the difference between it and the descriptive survey. The descriptive survey method concerns itself largely with what the researcher *sees, observes,* with what can be *described in words* and can be concluded from those words. It is one way of arriving at truth. It is the method that in modified form is used in every judicial proceeding in the country. The vital questions are: What did you actually see? What do you know on the basis of your observations only? From the answers to these two questions, judge or jury arrives at conclusions which, hopefully, represent the truth of the situation.

Now, we come to an entirely different road that leads toward the discovery of truth. It uses a totally different language—the language not of words but of numerals. The grammar of that language is the syntax of mathematical operations. Its purpose is not to report data verbally, but to represent those data in numerical values. We can express with numbers what is impossible to state in words. You cannot pile up words and deduce an average from them. You cannot take the square root of a sentence. It is impossible to square a word, a phrase, or a paragraph.

The analytical survey method exists, therefore, in an entirely different milieu than either of the two preceding methods of research. The analytical survey method, which in this chapter we will call simply the quantitative study, is different because its data are different. In historical and descriptive studies, the data are verbal because the means to elicit the data are verbally oriented: questionnaires, interviews, written records, descriptive observational reports. This is not to imply that calculations are not used in these methodologies. They are. But they are not the *major* form in which the data exist. We think of the data of historical and descriptive studies as *qualitative data,* and the data of analytical survey studies as *quantitative* data. We measure each kind of data with a different research yardstick.

Statistics: The Language of Facts

Statistics is merely a way of thinking about the facts of the real world. In a sense, statistics is measurement by means of numbers. Statistics measures the data of the real world on a "how much," "how many" scale.

Facts reach us in various ways: the size of human communities, the intensity of heat, of pressure, of the pull of gravity on physical mass. We also represent and attempt to comprehend the facts of the not-so-real world: intelligence level, the strength of one's preferences and beliefs, academic achievement, the worth of an employee to an organization, and so forth. These facts we usually express in the form of a *numerical* symbol—a *statistical value:* the *number* of people in a group, the *number* of degrees of heat, the *number* of pounds of pressure, the intelligence *quotient*, the *numerical* grade a student earns, and so on. Thus, many aspects of life are represented statistically.

It is unfortunate, therefore, that so many students regard statistics as a necessary evil—an ogre lying astride their path of progress in research. Thousands of students may "love to do research" but shudder at the thought of having to encounter statistics. The strange mathematical symbols, the multistoried and complex equations, and the unfamiliar terminology frighten them unnecessarily.

Statistics is really a very simple matter, and a powerful tool in the hands of the researcher. It is merely a type of language into which facts are constantly translated. When we translate facts into numerical values, the facts speak more clearly, and the researcher is able to see their nature and interrelationships more understandably. Through statistics, therefore, the researcher is able to conceptualize what otherwise might be incomprehensible.

Put very simply, *statistics is a language that, through its own special symbols and grammar* (the symbols are the numbers; the grammar is what you *do* with the numbers, e.g., +, −, ×, etc.) *takes everyday facts and translates them into a numerical form of expression and, by so doing, makes those facts more meaningful than they would otherwise be.*

The question that any researcher must ask of statistics is: How does the use of statistics assist in understanding the facts more completely?

The answer to that question should be concrete and unequivocal. Statistics uses numbers to reveal hidden truth. When the Arabs invented the numbers system, they gave to civilization one of its greatest miracles. Numbers allow us to do what we cannot do with words alone. For example, take this paragraph and the one directly above it. Now, express how, by using words only, these two paragraphs compare in size. Here is what you get:

The second paragraph is *larger* than the first.
The second paragraph is *longer* than the first.

But what does that *mean?* What does "larger" mean? "Longer"? Remember, in research we are dealing with data and, especially, the *meaning* of those data. Suppose you had only words to express the idea. You would be stuck! It's impossible (without numbers) to say anything *meaningful* about those two paragraphs with respect to their size—to go beyond the words themselves to express the fact precisely.

Now, let us translate a description of the size of those two paragraphs into another "language"—the language of numbers, of statistics—and compare this with what words alone could do.

The first paragraph contains 23 words.
The second paragraph contains 69 words.

Now, we can say something *meaningful* about those two paragraphs. We can say, for instance, that

1. paragraph 1 has only one-third the number of words as paragraph 2;
2. paragraph 2 has exactly three times as many words as paragraph 1;

3. paragraph 1 has 14 one-syllable words out of a total of 23 words;
4. paragraph 1 has about 61 percent of its total verbiage as one-syllable words;
5. paragraph 2 has 40 one-syllable words out of a total of 69 words;
6. paragraph 2 has about 58 percent of its total verbiage as one-syllable words.

Now, aside from showing how precisely we can differentiate the two paragraphs using numbers, we might actually employ the above data to analyze the two paragraphs to determine the author's writing style, to estimate the reading ease of the text, and to compare the paragraphs for various other reasons. We could, for instance, compare the number of Anglo-Saxon word derivatives with the total verbiage of each paragraph to get an estimation of the linguistic characteristics of the writing. All this would help us understand the difference between paragraph 1 and paragraph 2.

The advent of numbers, and statistical ways of using them, opened up a whole new horizon of meanings that we never dreamed existed when we were trying to describe the difference between those two paragraphs through the medium of words only.

Statistics is a very simple and elemental tool of research. It demands, procedurally, little more than a knowledge of basic arithmetic. It involves the basic procedures of addition, subtraction, multiplication, and division. Its formulas, while they sometimes appear threatening and complex, are merely shorthand recipes to indicate what one does to get the result on the left-hand side of the equal sign.

For example:

$$\overline{X} = \frac{\Sigma x}{N}$$

Now, to some, that mixture of Greek and Arabic nomenclature may be meaningless. But remember that we have said that statistics is a language. Like any language, it has its own vocabulary, its own symbols, its own way of expressing its thoughts and writing its sentences.

Here is a translation of that statistical formula:

To find the arithmetic average,
add up all of the values and
divide by the total number of values.

Look:

Where $\overline{X}$ always means the arithmetic average
(the common average)
Σ always means "the sum of"
x always means "the individual values,
the separate scores"
N always means "the total number of
values, counted individually"

These are standard symbols with constant meanings. Whenever you see them in any formula, they will always have the same meaning.

Conventions in Symbol Usage

Greek letters generally are used to denote the characteristics of *population parameters.* Roman letters generally express the characteristics associated with samples. For example, we may have the mean of the population or the mean of a sample drawn from the population. If the *population mean* is meant, it is represented by the Greek μ, whereas the *sample mean* is indicated by M. Frequently in statistics, the italic form of the alphabet is used where the Roman letter is appropriate. Likewise, σ denotes the standard deviation of the *population*, whereas s would indicate the standard deviation of the *sample*.

A bar above a symbol, $\overline{X}$, $\overline{Y}$, indicates the *arithmetic mean* of the several items. Generally, the letters x, y, z denote *variables* and observations on individual cases. Constants are represented by letters at the beginning of the alphabet. Small letters from the middle of the alphabet, particularly i and j, used as subscripts, indicate reference to specific individuals or groups.

A few other symbols that you should know are the following:

$>$: $a > b$ means "*a* is greater than *b*"
$<$: $a < b$ means "*a* is less than *b*"
$\gg$: $a \gg b$ means "*a* is very much larger than *b*"
$\ll$: $a \ll b$ means "*a* is very much less than *b*"
$\geqslant$: $a \geqslant b$ means "*a* is greater than or equal to *b*"
$\leqslant$: $a \leqslant b$ means "*a* is less than or equal to *b*"
$=$ means "equal to"
$\neq$ means "not equal to"
$|a|$ means "the absolute value of *a* without + or − designation"
∞ means "infinity"
$\sqrt{a}$ means "the square root of *a*"
H_0 means "the null hypothesis"
! means "factorial, or multiply the number by each succeeding number below it to 1"; thus, 4! means $4 \times 3 \times 2 \times 1 = 24$

It's All Greek to Me! In addition to the above symbols, you will need to learn the meaning of certain Greek letters that have specific meanings to researchers. Here is a list of those letters with their meanings:

Σ = sum of, or the summation of (upper case sigma)
ϵ = base of natural logarithms (epsilon)
π = product of (pi)
Δ = increment of (delta)
ϕ = the phi coefficient (phi)
τ = Kendall's tau (tau)
r = correlation coefficient, especially the Pearson coefficient of correlation (italic *r*: English)
χ^2 = chi square test (chi—squared)
σ = standard deviation of a population (lower case sigma)
μ = the mean of a population (mu)
η = correlational ratio (eta)
ρ = Spearman rank order correlation (rho)

These are standard symbols with *constant* meanings. Wherever you see them, in any formula, they will always mean the same. The first thing to do, therefore, is to learn the vocabulary of statistics—those symbols that you will meet again and again in statistical expressions. But this is nothing new; learning the vocabulary is the first requirement to learning any language. Statistics is no different, except that the vocabulary of statistics is delightfully brief, and its meanings are usually given following each statistical expression.

There are other conventions used in statistical communication that every student should know. These are the meanings of subscripts and exponents, summation, and multiplication and division.

Subscripts and Exponents. Common to statistical expressions are small letters or figures written slightly below a quantity. These are called *subscripts*. They function as adjective or qualitative descriptors whose function is to tell *what kind* of quantity is indicated. For example, in the expression M_g, the subscript g tells the kind of M, where M stands for the mean. The symbol stands for "mean geometric," or the geometric mean.

Where a small symbol is written slightly above the quantity, it is called an *exponent.* An exponent is a quantitative descriptor, telling not what kind but *how much.* M^2, for example, is read "*M* squared," meaning, of course, that *M* is multiplied by itself, thus increasing the value of *M.*

Summation. Another symbol frequently seen in equations is the summation symbol. It is an overgrown Greek uppercase sigma, Σ, and it simply means "add." Sometimes it, too, has smaller symbols below and above it to indicate the limits of the additive process. For instance,

$$\sum_{i=1}^{N}$$

simply means "add all the items from 1 (i=1) to N (the last item)." Thus, if you had the series 1, 2, 3, 4, 5, and it was expressed as

$$\sum_{i=1}^{5}$$

it would mean: 1 + 2 + 3 + 4 + 5 = 15.

Multiplication and Division. Multiplication is indicated in one of two ways: either by two quantities standing in juxtaposition to each other, as XY, or by a quantity in parentheses juxtaposed to another quantity in parentheses, or a symbol juxtaposed to a quantity in parentheses, for example, $(a + b)(a + b)$ or $N(N + 1)$.

A horizontal line always means *divide.* Furthermore, the quantity below the line is always divided into the quantity above the line. Thus,

$$\frac{1}{3}$$

means divide 1 by 3, or divide 3 into 1. Likewise,

$$\frac{\Sigma X}{N}$$

means divide N into the sum (Σ) of all the Xs.

Another skill that you should develop is the way to read a statistical formula. Most books do not tell you how; most instructors take for granted that you know how. This is not always the case.

How to Read and Execute a Statistical Formula

Take, for example, the following formula for finding the standard deviation:

$$s = \sqrt{\frac{\sum_{i-1}^{N}\left(X_i - \overline{X}\right)^2}{N}}$$

Where $\overline{X}$ = the arithmetic mean
X_i = each individual observation
N = the number of cases
s = the standard deviation of the sample

This is merely a directive in statistical shorthand for finding the standard deviation. It is to a researcher what a recipe is to a cook: It tells the researcher what steps to execute to produce the final product. All recipes are presented in standard format: first the ingredients, usually in the order in which they are added, then the specific directions for mixing the ingredients. Statistical formulas are like that. A statistical formula always has two principal parts. The first part is the symbol to the *left* of the equal sign. This is the final product. It is what you will get after you have followed the procedural directions. The second part of a statistical formula is to the *right* of the equal sign. This is the procedural part—the directions to be followed so that you get the result indicated.

Here are some basic guidelines that may help you to read any statistical formula:

1. Be sure you know what result you will obtain after doing all of the statistical operations. It may be well to check whether this is an *appropriate* statistical technique to use in terms of the data that you are processing. How have the data been measured? The statistical technique is indicated by the symbol to the left of the equal sign.
2. Now, go to the right of the equal sign. Begin to read from the *extreme right* reading always toward the left. This is the *reverse* of the normal reading procedure.
3. Where there are quantities in parentheses, read (and calculate) *inside* the parentheses *first,* doing all the operations there indicated. Work from *right* to *left.* For example, take this expression: $5(6 + 2)(3 + 4)$. Start from the right, inside the parentheses, add the 4 to the 3, then, working right to left and always *inside* the parentheses *first,* add the 2 to the 6. You then have $(7)(8) = 56$. Now going farther to the left, we next encounter a 5, which is the multiplier of the product of the parentheses: 5×56.
4. Where there is an exponent, do as it directs—before going any further.
5. Perform all the operations *above* the line *first.*
6. Then perform the operations *below* the line. A horizontal line always means *divide:* Divide what is below the line into what is above the line.
7. Perform the division.
8. Finally, if there is an all-encompassing symbol—a radical (which we have in the above formula), a parentheses, a bracket—perform the operation indicated by the symbol.

The following jingle may help you remember the above procedure:

Right, left! right, left!
Inside, outside;
Upside, downside;
Do as you are told.

If you read statistical expressions intelligently and knowledgeably, you will dispel most of the foreboding you may feel in the presence of unfamiliar nomenclature. By following the above directions stepwise, you can solve any statistical formula and find any statistical product.

Look again at the statistical expression that we presented above. Figure 10.1 shows that statistical formula with the above eight steps applied to it.

This discussion has been merely a general orientation to statistics *as a tool of research.* Later we will discuss some basic statistical approaches to the treatment and interpretation of the data.

The Nature of the Data in Quantitative Studies

In the quantitative study, we analyze data statistically so that we may infer meanings that lie hidden within the data, or discern certain potentials and dynamic forces that may be clues to areas that warrant further investigation. We are concerned primarily with *problems of estimation* and with *testing statistically based hypotheses.* The methods we employ are those of *inferential statistics.*

Figure 10.1 Reading and Executing the Formula for Standard Deviation

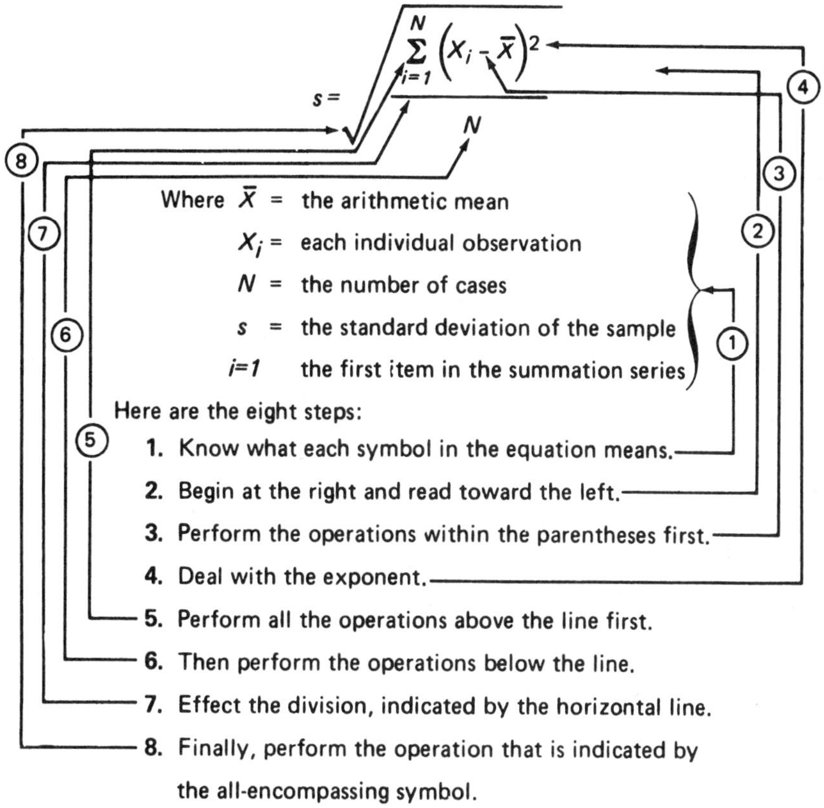

We stressed earlier the necessity of considering the data in terms of their basic qualities and essential nature, of seeing their distinguishing characteristics before adopting a particular methodological approach. Here, as elsewhere, the general rule is that *the data determine the research method.*

Data and Their Characteristics

Not only do all data have certain clearly recognized characteristics, which we shall discuss in a moment, but every statistical approach has its own specific requirements in terms of the type of data appropriate to the demands of that particular statistical procedure. A glance at the classification of statistical techniques in Figure 10.6, which charts the domain of statistical methodology, will show the necessity of knowing something about the nature of the data before one considers statistical treatment of it.

Data may be characterized and classified in four separate ways:

1. THE KIND OF DATA:
   Discrete data exist independently of each other; examples include individuals, bacteria, apples, nationalities.
   Continuous data together form a continuum; examples include millibars, degrees of temperature, chronological age.
2. THE SCALE OF MEASUREMENT OF DATA:
   Nominal data are distinguished from other data by assigning them a name; examples include pine tree, Sirius, inner-city children, farmers.
   Ordinal data are assigned an order of sequence; examples include days of the week, faculty rank in a university, rank of a percentile scale.

Interval data are those data that are measured in terms of difference in standard units; examples include a board three feet longer than another, an IQ thirty points higher than another, Nicky is five pounds heavier than Ginger; Tom is three inches taller than Kathy.
Ratio data indicate that one item is so many times as large as, as bright as, or as powerful as another (some statisticians contend that the ratio scale must originate at zero); examples include degrees of a circular compass, a percentage scale, or amperage of electrical current.

3. THE NUMBER OF GROUPS FROM WHICH DATA ARISE:
   One-group data arise from a single group of subjects. This type of data is often encountered in pretest or posttest investigations of variables in one group of individuals.
   Two-group data arise from a study of two groups such as is typical in experimental studies involving a control group and an experimental group.
   Many-groups data arise from multigroup populations in which contrasting variables are studied against several varying group contexts.
4. VARIABLES:
   Univariate data involve one variable within a population. Such studies are of the simplest type and belong to the older order of research. All variables are held constant except the one being studied.
   Bivariate data, as the name suggests, contain two variables. Studies that measure relative achievement in two areas for each individual within a certain population are of this type.
   Multivariate data contain a number of variables that are usually isolated and then studied by the multivariate analysis technique.

Look Closely at the Data

Nothing takes the place of looking carefully, inquiringly, critically, even naively at the data. Data are the raw materials of your research. Inspect them carefully. Do not ignore any data configuration, no matter how elusive or remote it may be from the central axis of your research. Think of data as you might think of chess pieces: how many positions can they occupy; what difference does any shifting of position, rearrangement of sequence, or change of observational orientation make? Are the data nominal, ordinal, interval, or ratio? From how many viewpoints can you contemplate them?

Before considering any further statistical treatment, every researcher needs to develop the skill of looking closely at the data only. All too few researchers do so. It is more exciting to run off into a statistical treatment of the data, to possess raw fact before we know what we are dealing with. Eyes, sometimes, are much better interpreters of the data than statistics. Look! Think! Look again!

You need to doodle with data. Try them out in every conceivable arrangement. See what various patterns the data will fit before beginning to think in terms of means, deviations, correlations, and tests of hypotheses.

Data in a table look different from data in a graph. Arrange them both ways. Data assume an added dimension when arranged in some configurational order: ascending, descending, categorical, alphabetical, and so on.

Nowhere in the whole research process is inexperience so evident as when researchers are so impatient to get involved in the treatment of the data that they rush into statistical sophistication before they have played with the data long enough to get acquainted with them. The complexity of the Law of Universal Gravitation began in a very simple way: An apple hit Isaac Newton on the head!

Primitive simplicity, an open mind, the ingenuity of imagination to see as much as can be seen without benefit of computational complexity—this is the genesis of true research.

Now, with all this exhortation, let's take a very simple example to illustrate the point. Here are the reading achievement scores of 11 children: Ruth, 96; Robert, 60; Chuck, 68; Margaret, 88; Tom, 56; Mary, 92; Ralph, 64; Bill, 72; Alice, 80; Adam, 76; Kathy, 84.

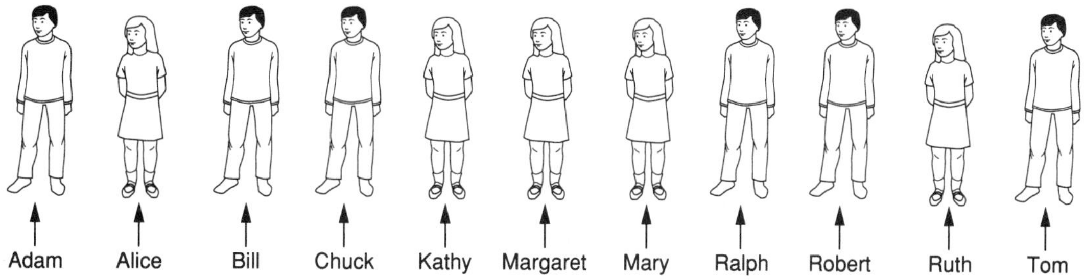

What do you see? Stop at this point to jot down as many observations as possible. Then read further.

First, let's try as many arrangements of those scores as possible to see just how much information we can extract from them before subjecting them to statistical treatment. Some of the information may not be of any use to us in terms of our research problem. No matter. What we are after is what we can see by the process of looking. Careful researchers discover everything possible about the data, whether it is immediately useful or not. They leave no stone unturned. They overlook no lurking significances because their investigations do not seem to be uncovering golden revelations or big yields of meaningful information.

We shall start simply. What will an alphabetical arrangement of those students' names reveal? Let's see. Remember, we are merely on the lookout for *any* meaning of whatever kind or type, no matter how seemingly trivial, no matter how artificial the method of extracting it may appear. This is merely an illustration.

Adam	76	Mary	92
Alice	80	Ralph	64
Bill	72	Robert	60
Chuck	68	Ruth	96
Kathy	84	Tom	56
Margaret	88		

In columnar form and alphabetical arrangements, the array may not be much more meaningful, but we have isolated individuals and grades more clearly. If nothing else, it is somewhat easier to inspect them in this form. We have, of course, listed the data *nominally*. But does it show anything? Yes. It shows that the highest grade was earned by a girl and the lowest grade belongs to a boy. Silly, you say, and meaningless. Perhaps. But it's an observable fact, and that *is* important. It is the whole point of this exercise.

Let's keep the nominal arrangement, now, but view it in another way. We see these 11 boys and girls lined up in a straight row, still arranged in alphabetical order according to their given names.

Look! Now we can discern a *ratio* pattern in these children that was not apparent before. We have a *symmetrical pattern*. Starting from either end the ratios are as follows:

Expressed Verbally	*Expressed Mathematically*
one boy-one girl	1:1
one girl-two boys	1:2
two boys-three girls	2:3
three girls-two boys	3:2
two boys-one girl	2:1
one girl-one boy	1:1

Now, let's do another very simple arrangement. We will separate girls from boys, arranging the group according to sex. The data will then appear as follows:

Girls		*Boys*	
Alice	80	Adam	76
Kathy	84	Bill	72
Margaret	88	Chuck	68
Mary	92	Ralph	64
Ruth	96	Robert	60
		Tom	56

Represented graphically in Figure 10.2, this diverse trend is even more dramatic:

What have we seen? Whatever we have seen may have no importance whatsoever for any project, but because it represents *dynamics within the data,* it is important that we see it. That is the point we are making: that the researcher should be aware of the dynamics, the phenomena, that are active within the data, whether those phenomena are important to the purpose of the research or not. The astute researcher overlooks *nothing.*

As we originally presented the data, we should never have guessed that when the names were arranged in an alphabetical order and the group divided by sex the scores of the girls formed an *ascending* series of values, with the first girl on the list getting the lowest score among the girls, the last girl, the highest score. With the boys, the situation is reversed. When they are arranged alphabetically, their scores form a *descending* series of values.

Not only is there a divergence of trends, but now we are aware of a very obvious fact that may, up to this point, have escaped our attention: The intervals between the scores are *equidistant in scalar value.* Each score is four points either above or below the preceding one.

We have spent enough time manipulating the data. There is perhaps much more to discover. With children and reading scores this may have been an exercise in futility, but for the researcher working in an area of science, observations of a similar kind may reveal very important new knowledge. Take the case of a paleontologist and an astronomer who noticed data

Figure 10.2

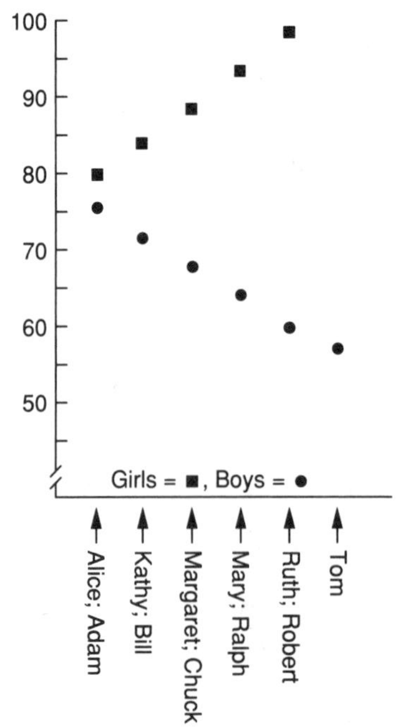

recorded in the form of growth marks on the shells of the chambered nautilus.[1] They noticed that each chamber had an average of 30 growth lines and deduced that the growth lines had appeared at the rate of one a day and that one chamber was laid down every lunar month—every 29.53 days. They also concluded that, if their interpretation of the data was correct, then it might be possible to determine from fossil shells the length of the ancient lunar months. Since the distance of the moon from the earth can be calculated from the length of the lunar month, the scientists examined nautilus fossils—some of them 420 million years old—and noticed a gradual decrease in the number of growth lines in each chamber as the fossils receded farther and farther into prehistoric time, indicating that formerly the moon was closer to the earth and revolved around it more rapidly than it does now—an observation consistent with generally accepted scientific theory.

The fact that the data that we examined above and the various constellations of that data were spurious is beside the point. Certain basic principles regarding the observation of data begin to emerge. These we note at this point.

For example, where two facts are concerned (grades and names; growth rings and lunar month cycles), *one of them becomes dominant* and governs the meaning that emerges from the other. In the data that we have been inspecting about the children, meaning emerged from the last arrangement of data primarily because we used an alphabetized list of the students' names. By arranging the data in other ways, different meanings would probably have been obvious. This suggests a fundamental guideline for looking at the data: *Whatever the researcher does with the data to prepare it for inspection or interpretation will affect the meaning that those data will reveal, so that every researcher should be able to defend the procedure underlying the interpretation of the data with a clear and logical rationale.*

We had no rationale whatever for arranging the data according to the given names of the children. Had we used their last names, which would have been equally illogical, the entire boy–girl ratio would have gone to the wind. Had we done that, we would have had a simple one-to-one ratio; alphabetized, the surnames of the children arranged in a boy–girl sequence would have looked like this:

Angel, Ralph	Murray, Bill	Street, Robert
Brown, Kathy	Nichols, Mary	Thomas, Margaret
Daniels, Tom	Oglethorpe, Chuck	Vaughn, Adam
George, Ruth	Smith, Alice	

As we have remarked, from a research standpoint there is no defensible rationale for using the given name over the surname or the reverse. The *nominal data,* therefore, were not critical to the research purpose. The *ordinal data* may have been. So, also (and probably with more likelihood), may have been the *interval* and the *ratio data.*

With so-called scientific data, the problem is less complex. Data come to the scientist generally prepackaged and prearranged. The growth rings on the nautilus shell are there. They cannot be altered. What such data need for interpretation is a pair of keen eyes and a curious and inquiring mind. From the standpoint of dealing with the data, therefore, the researcher working in the physical or biological sciences may not have the problems of arranging data prior to interpretation that a colleague working in the social sciences, education, or the humanities may face.

But irrespective of arrangement, there is enough in both situations above to pique our curiosity. For example:

1. Why were all the scores of the girls higher than those of the boys?
2. Why were all the scores of the boys lower than the lowest score for the girls?

[1] Peter G. K. Kahn and Stephen Pompea, "Nautiloid Growth Rhythms and Dynamical Evolution of the Earth-Moon System," *Nature* 275 (October 19, 1978): 606–11.

3. Why were the intervals between each of the scores for both boys and girls equidistant?
4. What caused the nautilus to record a growth mark each day of the lunar month?
5. Is the relationship between the forming of the partitions and the lunar month cycle singular to the nautilus or are there other like occurrences in nature?

Beware of Snap Judgments

Research springs from questions like these. Looking at these situations, we may be inclined to draw hasty and unwarranted conclusions, such as *girls read better than boys.* Again, we are not looking at the data; we are not thinking accurately.

Much research goes wrong at this juncture. Reading is a complex skill. The data do not say that girls read better than boys. What the data do say is that *on a particular test* given *on a particular day* to 11 children—5 girls and 6 boys—the scores of the girls were *for this particular situation* higher than those of the boys and that each score was precisely equidistant from every other score *for both boys and girls.* Furthermore, the apparent excellence of the girls over the boys was limited to test performance in those reading skills and aptitudes measured specifically by this test.

Honesty and precision dictate that all the conditions in the situation be considered and that we may make generalizations only in strict accordance with the facts. The time-operant-condition relationship is a very unstable one. The same test given to another 11 children, as similar to the first group as we can possibly pair them, on the next day (or the next four, for that matter) may produce vastly different data.

The chart shown in Figure 10.3 may suggest some ways in which the various categories of data may be studied. This chart is, in a sense, a transition between the observation of pure data, categorized by type of measurement, and the processing of that data by means of appropriate statistical techniques.

The Role of Statistics in Making Data Meaningful

In statistics, we attempt to comprehend the facts of the real world with the aid of numbers. The real world is filled with abstractions and intangibles: the *size* of human aggregations, the *intensity* of heat, the *pounds* of pressure, the *volts* of electromotive force. We are also aware of concepts of the not-so-real world: the *level* of intelligence, the *strength* of one's preferences or beliefs, one's academic *achievement* or *skill* in sports, or the *worth* of an employee to an organization. All of the italicized words are abstractions. Add to these *points of central tendency,* extent of *dispersion,* degree of *relationship* of one *factor* to another, and the testing of *hypotheses* and you have a world of abstract concepts that defy words to capture adequately. Only numerals can suggest a means by which our minds can comprehend these intangibles.

In a real sense statistics is a never-never land where seemingly substantial concepts are merely elusive ghosts conjured up by the mathematical imagination. But elusive and insubstantial as these concepts may be, the only way in which we may capture them with any degree of comprehension is with statistical procedures.

The concepts above we usually express in terms of the *number* of individuals in a group, the *number* of degrees of temperature, the *number* of pounds of pressure, the *numerical* grade of the student, the intelligence *quotient,* and so on. Thus, many aspects of everyday life are statistical.

Statistics is really a very simple and helpful aid to the researcher. It is a language into which facts are constantly translated. When this happens, facts speak more clearly and forcefully, and consequently the researcher may see their nature and interrelationships more clearly.

Figure 10.3 Methods of Studying Categories of Data

Scale	Question
	1. What general picture do the data convey? Answer: Frequency Distributions.
Nominal	*Bar graphs:* only the relative heights of the bars have mathematical significance.
Ordinal	Discrete data: *Bar graphs:* order and heights of bars have mathematical significance. Continuous data: *Histograms:* order and heights of bars have mathematical significance, and adjacent bars must be contiguous. *Frequency polygons:* horizontal distances between points are arbitrary. *Cumulative frequency and cumulative percentage graphs:* horizontal distances between points are arbitrary.
Interval	Discrete data: *Bar graphs:* heights, order, widths, and spacing of bars have mathematical significance. Area inside bars is proportional to number of cases. Continuous data: *Histograms:* as for bar graphs; adjacent bars must be contiguous. *Frequency polygons:* horizontal spacing of points has mathematical significance, and area under curve is proportional to number of cases. *Cumulative frequency and cumulative percentage graphs:* horizontal spacing of points has mathematical significance. The shape of the distribution is meaningful. *Skewness* and *kurtosis* can be described. Theoretical distributions (e.g., normal) can be approximated by obtained data.
Ratio	*Bar graphs* *Histograms* *Frequency polygons* *Cum. freq. and cum. percentage graphs* *Skewness and kurtosis* *Theoretical distributions* } *as for interval scale.* *Transformed measurements* can be used to approximate a theoretical distribution from obtained data.

From *Measurement and Statistics: A Basic Text Emphasizing Behavioral Science*, by Virginia L. Senders.

Put very simply, for those who may feel uncomfortable with statistics, a simple definition might be: *Statistics is a language that, through its own special symbols and grammar, takes the intangible facts of life and translates them into comprehensible meaning.* The first and last question of statistics is precisely the same question that every researcher always asks of the facts themselves: What do they *mean*? What *message* are they attempting to communicate?

We saw earlier, through an intense scrutiny of 11 children and their reading grades, how facts may be forced to give up their meaning without benefit of statistics. Let us now repeat that process, this time relying only upon the lowest level of statistical processing.

Take an everyday example. Joe is in high school. During February, he gets the following grades: 92, 69, 91, 70, 90, 89, 72, 87, 73, 86, 85, 75, 84, 76, 83, 83, 77, 81, 78, 79.

These are the raw numerical facts—the data—directly from a life situation. As they stand in the above array, they do not say very much; other than the fact that Joe's performance seems to be inconsistent.

Now, suppose that we treat these data statistically, employing at first only the very simplest of statistical (or quasi-statistical) processes. We begin by arranging Joe's grades in a table, under the respective day of the week, Monday through Friday, on which the grade was earned.

February

	Monday	Tuesday	Wednesday	Thursday	Friday
First week	92	69	91	70	90
Second week	89	72	87	73	86
Third week	85	75	84	76	83
Fourth week	83	77	81	78	79

We now have the scores within a *time sequence.* Formerly we presented the data in *simple linear sequence.* (Is this getting to sound like the language of statistics? If so, do not be concerned. The terms merely describe the status or nature of the data; that is all that statistical terminology ever does.)

Now, we may inspect Joe's grades in a two-dimensional relationship. We may read them horizontally as well as vertically within the time frame of a month. Reading them horizontally, we note that the grades on Monday, Wednesday, and Friday are considerably higher than those on Tuesday and Thursday.

As we read the columns vertically, we note another striking phenomenon. Whereas Joe's grades seemingly deteriorate during each successive week on Monday, Wednesday, and Friday, they steadily improve during successive weeks on Tuesdays and Thursdays. Such behavior of the data should alert the researcher; for such an effect, there must be a cause. Discovering the probable cause is the function of research; in this process, which involves an analysis of the data, the role of statistics is frequently indispensable.

Remember the definition? *Statistics takes the numerical facts of life and translates them meaningfully.* Let's pursue this thought a little further.

We have already read some meaning into Joe's grades. With a little further statistical treatment, subjecting these grades to one or two additional (although extremely elemental) statistical processes, we shall force the data to tell us still more than they have already done. Let us represent Joe's grades in the form of a simple line graph (Figure 10.4).[2]

Note the difference between the three presentations of the same set of facts. Each has its own unique characteristic. Each shows certain emphases that no other form of presentation sets forth nearly so well. First, we merely *listed* Joe's grades in the order in which they were earned. The result was a *straight linear sequence.* Of all arrays, this was the simplest and least

Figure 10.4 Line Graph of Daily Grades

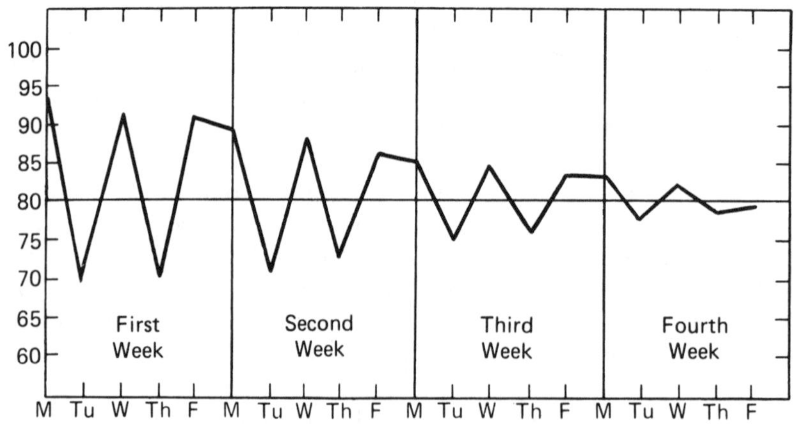

[2] For a discussion of reading graphic material, see chapter IV in my *Read with Speed and Precision* (New York: McGraw-Hill, 1963) entitled "Reading Graphic Presentations—the Ability to See Facts in Action," pp. 76–87.

meaningful. Then, we added the day-month dimension. It placed the data for the first time in a two-dimensional grid setting. The data became more meaningful. Finally, we arranged that same array of data in the form of a line graph. It presented the most dramatic view of all.

In the line graph, we see some phenomena dramatically set forth that were not apparent in the two previous arrays of the data. No one can miss the wide disparity in grades during the first and second weeks of the period. Also, just as apparent is the leveling-out process emphasized in the second half of the third week and in the fourth week. A profile of this sort should raise questions and suggest to an alert researcher the possibility that underlying causal factors and undiscovered data may explain the eccentricity and erratic behavior of the graph.

Thus far, we have discovered an important fact. *Looking at data in only one way yields but a fractional view of those data and, hence, provides only a small segment of the full meaning that those data contain.* For that reason, we have many statistical techniques. Each technique extracts but *one* segment of meaning from the same set of facts. Each time you rephrase the data into different statistical language (i.e., apply a new statistical treatment to the data), you derive new insight and see more clearly the meaning of those data.

We have already looked at Joe's academic performance in three different ways, but all of them have been on a day-to-day basis. Let us now broaden our viewpoint. In contrast to the nervous fluctuations in the graph presented above, let us by means of statistics take out the jagged irregularities of daily performance by leveling them into a smooth total weekly average. The result will be represented by a broken line extending from week's end to week's end (Figure 10.5). By so doing we get a whole new view of Joe's achievement. Whereas the graph originally showed only an erratic zigzagging between daily extremes, whose amplitude lessened as the weeks went by, the dotted line shows that, week by week, very little change actually occurred in Joe's average level of achievement.

One point should be clearly emphasized: *All presentations of the data are equally important.* Inspecting data is like turning a diamond. With a diamond, each new facet gives forth a different hue. The light from one facet is not *more* beautiful than that of any other; each is, rather, *unique* in its separate glory. So is the inspection of data. Each statistical manipulation of the data gives forth a new illumination of the facts. One is not *more* significant than another.

By means of statistics, we have already seen Joe's achievement in four different ways: (1) as a linear set of grades, (2) as a day and weekly set of grades, (3) as a graphic line showing the amplitude of Joe's grades, and (4) as a weekly average of Joe's grades. We have not exhausted the means by which we might view these same data. We could go on and on, subjecting these data to additional statistical analyses. By so doing, we would learn more and more about Joe's

Figure 10.5 Line Graph of Weekly Average Grades

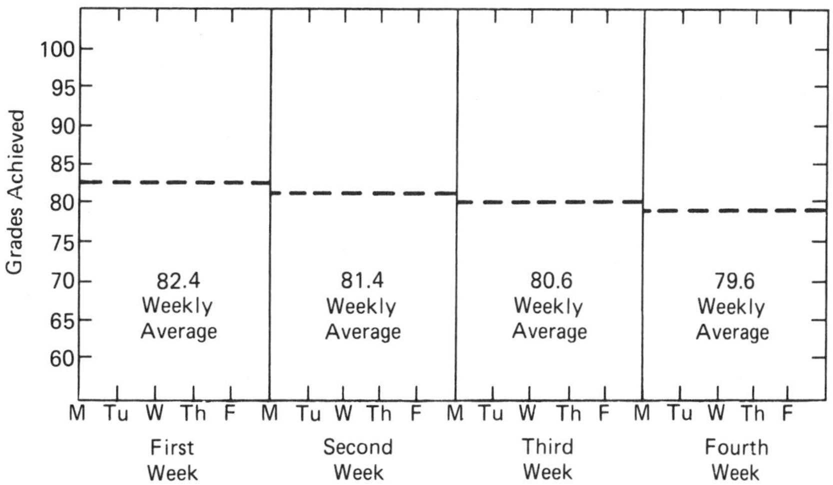

academic performance. But that is not the purpose of this discussion. We have merely cited this situation to illustrate that statistics *as a tool of research* may assist us in seeing what otherwise we may never have known.

Looking Backward

Perhaps at this point we should pause to see precisely what we have been doing. The chapter began on a basis premise: *The quality and type of the data determine the research method.* We distinguished between qualitative data and quantitative data. We used the example of the 11 children and their reading scores to show that by viewing the data from every possible angle—merely *looking at them*—without benefit of any other tool except one's eyes and mind, we were able to derive many meanings from the 11 scores. This was a purely qualitative examination made by shifting the data into different configurations and studying them to determine what they revealed. "Look Closely at the Data" was the advice in the subhead preceding the section.

But we also learned that researchers have a tool for further assisting them in looking at the data. That tool is statistics. To illustrate the window that this tool gives us on the landscape of the data, we took 20 grades that Joe received during the month of February. Beginning, again, with a simple linear recording of these grades, we subjected them to some very elementary statistical techniques: We arranged them in a day/week table; we converted the data within the table into a line graph showing a differential magnitude of the data on a weekly basis; we finally telescoped the individual scores for the week and represented them as a single line—the weekly average score. In the closing statement, we suggested that there might be dynamic forces lying below the surface that could explain the behavior of the data.

Now we will look at statistics in historical perspective and structurally. We shall learn the meaning of the term, see a brief history of the subject, comprehend the fact that statistics is organized into two main divisions, and we will discuss each of these divisions as they assist in interpreting the data in the quantitative study.

A Brief History of Statistics

Statistics as a part of the science of mathematics goes back to earlier times. The word comes from the word *state,* and it was as a function of the business of the state that statistics first arose. Originally, statistics was used by early states and kingdoms to count their resources, and their people. Moses was commanded to count the children of Israel and the Book of Numbers in the Bible is precisely that, a census of the Israelites. Ancient Egypt (as early as 3050 B.C.), as well as Babylonia and Rome all used statistical data for levying taxes and assessing their military strength. Perhaps the earliest and most famous statistical compilation among English-speaking peoples is the famous Domesday Book, dating from A.D. 1086, in which William the Conqueror directed that a complete record be made of the lands, resources, and population of early England.

The Oxford Universal Dictionary indicates the old as well as the more recent meaning of the word *statistics:*

> In early use, that branch of political science dealing with the collection, classification, and discussion of facts bearing on the condition of the state or the community.
>
> In recent use, the department of study that has for its object the collection or arrangement of numerical facts or data, whether relating to human affairs or to natural phenomena.[3]

[3] *The Oxford Universal Dictionary on Historical Principles,* 3d edition, edited by C. T. Onions (Oxford: The Clarendon Press, 1955), 2007.

The Organization of Statistics

Statistics as an academic discipline has made great advances in recent years. At this point, we should indicate the broad divisions of statistics and the purpose and function of each division, particularly the role of inferential statistics in dealing with the problems inherent in quantitative studies.

The following organizational chart of the realm of statistics (Figure 10.6) should be viewed with some tolerance. The more one knows about research (which is another way of saying that the more one knows about life and the nature of its factual matrix), the less one is sure that anything as closely associated with life processes—such as statistics is—can be neatly isolated into discrete cubicles. Although determining the mean is generally thought of as lying in the domain of descriptive statistics, testing an assumption about a population mean (as postulated from the sample) is conceded to be a problem in the area of statistical inference.

Researchers, especially those whose mathematical backgrounds are somewhat weak, regard statisticians in much the same way as the general public once regarded medieval alchemists: as wizards wielding unnatural powers, all enshrouded in statistical jargon and expressed as a bizarre statistical formula. The researcher who neither understands the logic nor appreciates the expressive power of statistics is awed by it.

Statistics is a language that expresses concepts and relationships that cannot be communicated in any other way. In its proper perspective, statistics is a language, eloquent and adequate, that is capable of expressing facts—frequently hidden from the mind as well as from the eye—that can be articulated or made manifest to our understanding through no other channel of communication.

As we have said in an earlier chapter, we do not presume in this text to make any attempt at teaching statistics. Any library will furnish adequate volumes to this end. What we will attempt to do here is to clear away some of the underbrush that so often confuses and impedes the

Figure 10.6 The Realm of Statistics

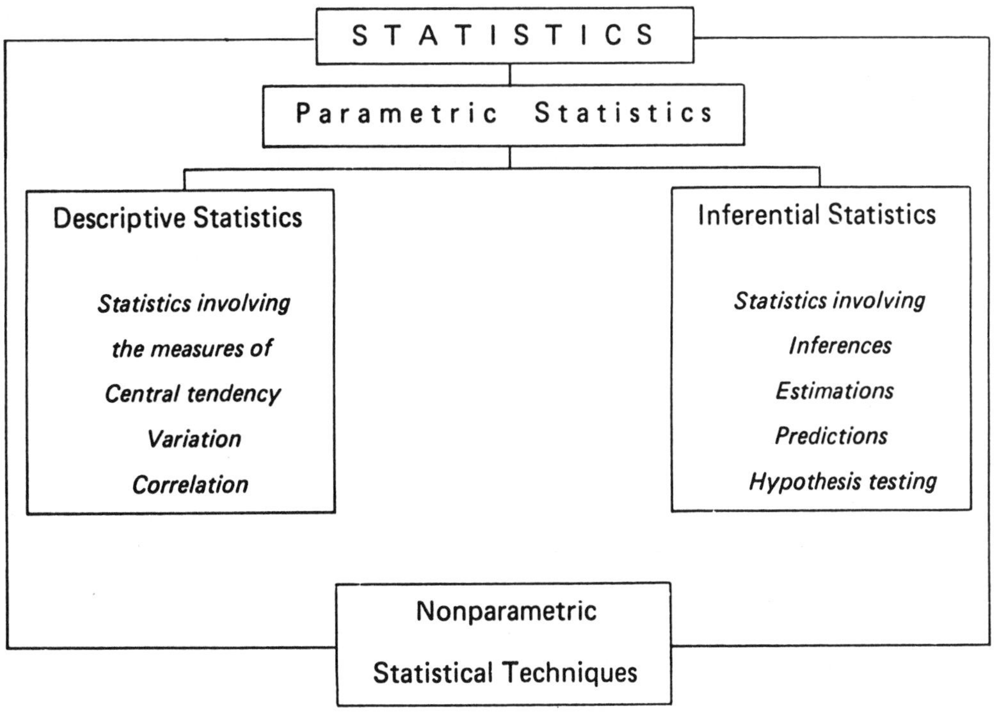

progress of students because they become bewildered in an area whose overall plan they do not comprehend and whose potential for solving their research problems they do not appreciate. We will try, therefore, to clarify only a few basic concepts and principles with respect to the application of statistics to the demands of the quantitative study. We will attempt to make you aware of the role of statistics in terms of function, possibilities, and limitations in dealing with those problems that rely upon analytic survey research methodology to resolve them.

The Division of Statistics

Statistics divides in two ways: first in terms of its *functional* aspects—namely, statistics whose function is to *describe the data.* This branch of statistics describes what the data look like: where their center is, how broadly they spread, and how they are related in terms of one aspect to another aspect of the same data. Hence, we call the statistics performing such functions *descriptive statistics.*

Another function of statistics is to *infer.* Suppose you had never been to Australia, but you were an immigration officer and had seen small groups of Australians debark from incoming planes and ships. Suppose that you had learned to know small groups of Australians intimately. From this minute sample of the Australian population, you could probably *infer* what Australians in general would be like.

Statistics takes small samples of a population and from those samples makes inferences as to the *statistical* characteristics of the population in general. Slightly different types of inference are *estimation* and *prediction.* These statistics do not describe what is here and now, but look into the distance and postulate what is beyond the horizon by examining the small sample that they are permitted to explore.

In an age in which we have brought back rocks from the moon, we can infer what the total surface of the moon is like from the samples we have seen. That is the function of *inferential statistics:* to extrapolate beyond the known into the realms of the unknown.

Statistics also divides qualitatively into *parametric* and *nonparametric statistics.* Before we discuss either of these areas, however, it is necessary for us to clarify what a *parameter* (of which *parametric* is the adjective) is.

A *parameter* is a function, a characteristic, a quality of the population that in *concept* is a constant but whose *value* is variable. Does that confuse you? Let's make it simple. Consider a circle. One of the parameters, or characteristics, of a circle is its radius, which has a functional relationship to the circle. In *concept* it is a constant: It is always the same for every circle—the distance from the center of the circle to the perimeter. In *value,* it constantly varies, depending on the size of the circle. Large circles have long radii, small circles, short radii. The *value*—that is, the length of the radius as expressed in so many linear units (centimeters, inches, feet)—is variable.

Thinking of a parameter in this way, we see that each circle has a number of parameters: circumference, area, diameter. We define these parameters in terms of concepts that are *constants:* The diameter is always twice the radius, the circumference is always $2r\pi$, the area always $\pi r.^2$

Parameters are always characteristics of a population (or a *universe,* as it is sometimes called). When we have a similar characteristic of a sample, we call the sample parameter a *statistic.* A statistic is not to be confused with *statistics,* which is the science that deals with the collection, classification, description, mathematical analysis, and testing of facts, usually for research purposes. In fact, there is a difference in the symbol representing the same characteristic common to both the population and the sample or samples drawn from it.

And so, it is important for us to distinguish between *statistics* and *a statistic.* It is, likewise, important to distinguish between *parametric* and *nonparametric* statistics. *Parametric statistics* assumes that most populations have at least *one* parameter. The parameter that is perhaps the most persuasive and generally encountered is the great *Gaussian curve of normal frequency distribution,* which seems to be as universal as any phenomenon that man has observed. The *normal*

Table 10.1 Conventional Statistical Notation for Various Parameters

The Factor Being Designated	The Symbol Employed for Designating the Factor: In the Case of a Population	The Symbol Employed for Designating the Factor: In the Case of a Statistic †
The mean	μ	$\overline{X}$ $M_g M_h$*
The standard deviation	σ	s
Proportion or probability	P	p
Uncertainty in	H	H
Number or total	N	n

*M_g = geometric mean, M_h = harmonic mean
†Notice the wording: *a* statistic

curve is a humpbacked curve. In reality, however, each "normal" curve describes an actual life situation and so departs in varying degrees from the *ideal* Gaussian curve.

Table 10.1 shows the conventional parameter symbols employed in statistical notation.

The Role of Statistics

Statistics is merely a tool. It is not a be-all and end-all for the researcher. Those who insist that research is not research unless it is statistical display a myopic view of the research process. There are others who are equally adamant that unless research is "experimental research," *it* is not research. Again, the cardinal rule applies: *The nature of the data governs the method that is appropriate to interpret the data and the tool of research that is required to process those data.* A historian seeking answers to problems associated with the assassination of President John F. Kennedy or Martin Luther King, Jr., would be hard put to produce either a statistical or an experimental study, and yet the research of the historian can be quite as scholarly and scientifically respectable as that of any statistical or experimental study.

The purpose of this chapter is to discuss statistics merely as one of the tools of research. It does not try to summarize the principles of basic statistics or to teach the student the statistical procedures necessary for most research projects. It assumes that the student already has this background. For those who wish to learn the fundamentals of statistics or who desire to refresh their minds with references to statistical principles, a selected bibliography is given at the conclusion of the chapter.

At this point, a further observation should be made with respect to the nature of a statistic. You should always be aware that what statistically seems very plausible may in the *real* world have no counterpart whatsoever.

Statistics many times describe a *quasi world* rather than the real world. For example, if you add up a series of grades and divide by the number of students in the class, you may get an average grade of 82. Having done this, you may feel that you have discovered a substantial fact. If you look down over the class list of individual grades, however, you may be astonished to find that *not one student in the entire class actually received a grade of 82!* What you accepted statistically as solid fact became empirically an illusion in the actual grades earned by the individuals.

Consider the man who read in the paper that the Bureau of Census had just announced that there were 1.75 children in the average American family. With heartfelt gratitude, he exclaimed, "Thank God, I was the *first*born!" What is accepted statistically is sometimes meaningless empirically. All this, however, does not disparage the importance of statistics as *a tool of research.*

Some statistical concepts, even though they have no counterparts in the real world, may assist us in understanding the phenomena of the real world. Many ideas we accept as being substantial have no real substance. Take the North Pole, for example. The North Pole provides a prime reference point for many types of human activity; it is essential in determining linear units of the metric system and as a basis of commerce between nations. It provides a basic reference point for navigation, for terrestrial latitude, for geodetic measurements, and for many other activities. Yet if you travel to the Arctic wastes, you will have to imagine that one particular spot on the ice—which looks precisely like every other spot on the ice, which stretches from horizon to horizon—is the North Pole. In the same way a statistic is a valuable benchmark, a reference point, even though in the hard world of reality no such point actually exists. The same is true of many statistical concepts.

If you know what statistics can and cannot do, you may appreciate more fully the role of statistics as a tool of research. If the data are expressed as numerical values, then statistics may assist you in four ways:

1. It may indicate the central point around which the data revolve.
2. It may indicate how broadly the data are spread.
3. It may show the relationship of one kind of data to another kind of data.
4. It may provide certain techniques to test the degree to which the data conform to or depart from the expected operations of the law of chance or approximate an anticipated standard.[4]

We will discuss each of these functional roles briefly so that you may see the landscape of statistics at a glance.

Points of Central Tendency

Statistics may indicate the central point around which the data revolve. To understand this concept, it may help you to think of data as being comparable to a physical mass. The central axis for any mass of data is called the *point of central tendency.* One large segment of statistics is devoted to ways of determining how to locate the midpoint around which the mass of data is equally distributed. In statistical language, we call the techniques for finding such a point the *measures of central tendency.* Of these, the most commonly employed are the *mode,* the *median,* and any of the several *means:* the *arithmetic mean,* the *geometric mean,* and the *harmonic mean.* Each of these measures has its own applications and characteristics. As a careful researcher, you will choose the particular indicator of central tendency with full knowledge of its unique capability for indicating accurately the point of central tendency for any particular type of data. Statisticians always look at the data first, then choose the statistical technique that is most appropriate to explore those data.

To see more clearly the concept of central tendency, think of the median and the mean as the fulcrum points for a mass of data. Both median and mean are points of exact balance, but it is important to understand what each balances. The median is the *numerical center* of the array, with exactly as many grades *by number* above the median point as below it. The word *median* comes from the Latin word meaning "middle," and so the median grade is the one precisely in the middle of the series. Joe's record has a total of 20 grades. Ten grades will be above the median, ten will be below it. The fulcrum point will be, therefore, midway in the series between the 10th and the 11th grade, or 10.5

The mean is also a fulcrum point. It is the precise center of all the amalgamated *values* in the array. The mean balances the *weight* of each grade. Think of 69 as the lightest of all the grades and 92 as the heaviest. The mean indicates the point where the weight of the entire statistical mass is in delicate equilibrium around the center of its own gravity. The median indicates the *distance,* the mid*point,* from one end to the other of an array of figures; the mean indicates the mid*point* where the *weight* of the scores on one side of the mean exactly balance

[4] The considerations subsumed under items 1, 2, and 3 belong to *descriptive statistics,* because the principal function of the statistical process is to *describe* the data. Item 4 deals with *inferential statistics,* because the principal function of the statistical process is to *infer* how closely the data conform to or depart from a hypothetical norm. Hence, we sometimes refer to this statistical area as being concerned with testing the *null hypothesis.*

the *weight* of the scores on the other side of the mean. The median is a tape measure; the mean, a set of scales.

While we are clarifying the concepts underlying the central tendency, let us explain the terminology of dispersion. We may say that the *range* is simply the full extent of the data from the lowest value to the highest. Joe's grades, from 69 to 92, have a range of 23 points.

The Normal Curve

Take any fortuitous happening and analyze its distribution pattern—the corn production of the state of Iowa in any given year, for example. If we could survey the per acre yield of every single farmer in Iowa (literally, the total population, the universe of the cornfields and corn farmers in Iowa), we would find that probably a few farmers had a remarkably poor yield of corn per acre, for no discernible reason except that "that's the way it happened." A few other farmers, for an equally unaccountable reason, had excessively heavy yields from their fields. Generally, however, most farmers will have had a middle-of-the-road yield, sloping gradually in either direction of the greater or the lesser yield categories. The normal curve will describe the Iowa corn production. No one planned it that way; it is simply the way Nature behaves.

Walk into any clothing store. Take an inventory of men's suit sizes or women's dress sizes. Again, the normal curve will be confirmed. Test all the children in a given school system. Their IQ scores will describe a Gaussian curve, as will their heights, their weights, and their various abilities to spell correctly.

Look at blind, impersonal Nature. Watch an approaching thunderstorm. An occasional flash of lightning will herald the coming of the storm. Soon the flashes will occur more frequently. At the height of the storm, the number of flashes per minute will reach a peak. Gradually, with the passing of the storm, it will subside. The normal curve is again confirmed. Dip again into Nature and you will find the parameter of the Gaussian curve occurring repeatedly.

We could think of thousands of situations, only to find that Nature behaves generally according to the normal frequency curve. The curve is a *constant.* It is always bell-shaped. In any one situation, the *values* within it vary. The mean is not always at the same place; the shape is overall more broadly spread or more compressed depending upon the situation being represented.

Because the curve is a universal representation of the distributional pattern of populations generally, statisticians consider it a *basic parameter* that fits *most* life situations and that therefore may be used as a norm against which to measure population data generally (Figure 10.7).

Curves Determine Means

We emphasize *most* life situations to call attention to the fact that the normal frequency curve is not the *universal* curve of life. Some phenomena do not fit its curvaceous contour. Growth is one. It follows an ogive curve and flattens into a plateau. Speed, is another. Driving to work, I accelerate, decelerate, cruise along for a few moments at maximum speed, then stop for a traffic signal, my speed dropping to zero. No normal curve here. For this reason we have various *means.* Each type of mean is statistically designed to measure the particular phenomena peculiar to it.

If I am recording the growth of bean stalks in an agronomy laboratory, I do not find the average growth by means of the normal curve, or *arithmetic mean.* The statistical technique does not fit the natural fact. For growth phenomena, we use the *geometric mean* for a very simple reason: *that* is the way things grow, that is the way cells divide—*geometrically.*

In every statistical situation, one basic rule applies: *The configurational characteristics of the data dictate the statistical treatment that is most appropriate for that particular situation.* If the data assume the distribution approximating the normal curve—as most data do—they call for one type of central tendency determination. If they assume an ogive-curve configuration, characteristic of a growth or developmental situation, they demand another method of statistical management. A polymodal distribution, such as one might find in the fluctuation of the stock market, may call for still a third type of statistical approach to locate the point of central tendency. Only

Figure 10.7 Normal Curve Distributions For Selected Standard Scores

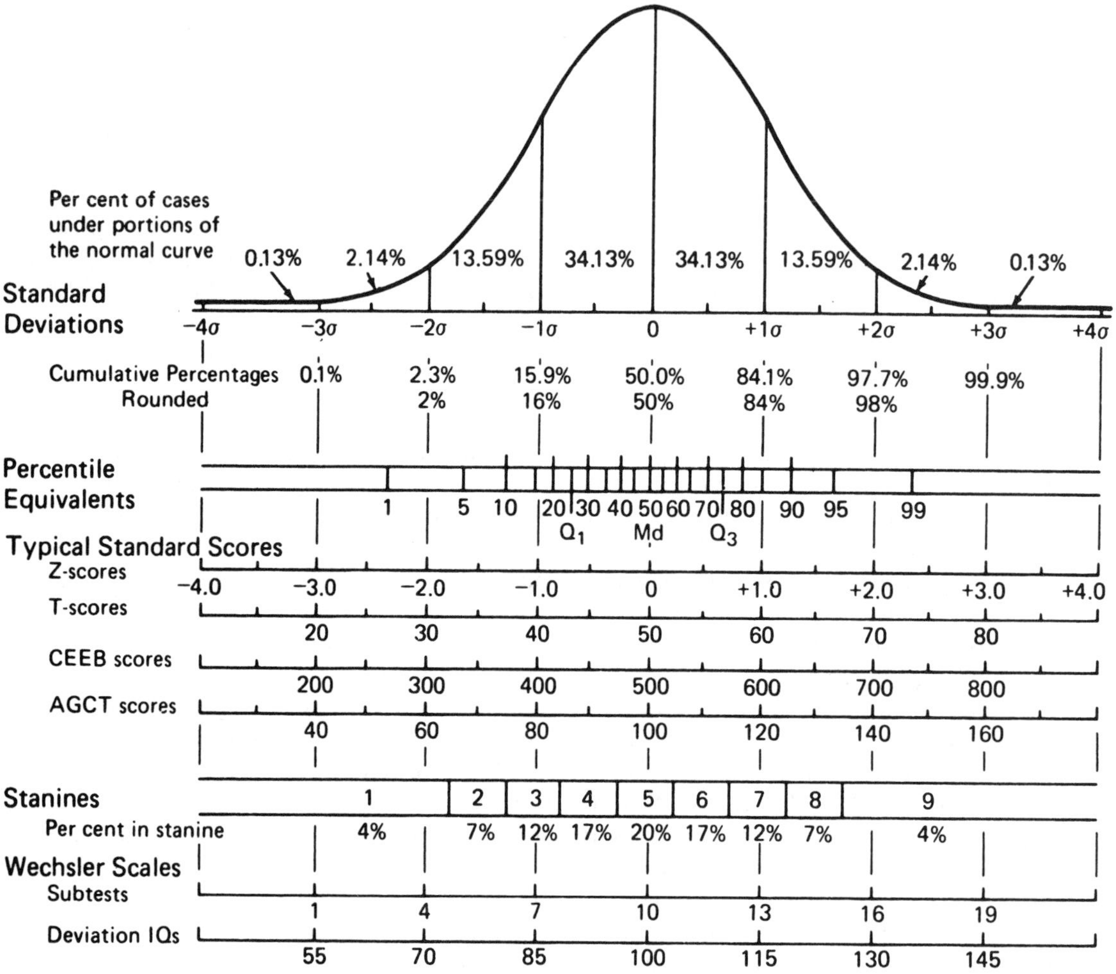

NOTE: This chart cannot be used to equate scores on one test with scores on another test. For example, both 600 on the CEEB and 120 on the AGCT are one standard deviation above their respective means, but they do not represent "equal" standings because the scores were obtained from different groups.

Source: *Test Service Bulletin,* No. 48 (January 1955), The Psychological Corporation.

after careful and informed consideration of the characteristics of the data and the configurational patterns that those data assume, when plotted as a frequency curve, can the researcher select the most appropriate statistical procedure.

Too many students try it the other way around: They attempt to select the statistical technique before they have adequately considered whether that particular treatment is appropriate to the data at hand. They have been conditioned by statistics textbooks and courses in basic statistics to think always in terms of the *arithmetic* mean, when the nature of the data may dictate that the geometric mean, or the harmonic mean, or perhaps the contraharmonic mean may be *statistically* a much better choice. The arithmetic mean may, indeed, be perhaps the *least* desirable. Such sensitive discrimination in the choice of a statistical tool is a distinguishing mark of the skilled researcher.

A Matter of Means

Some researchers, however, regard the matter of central tendency from a somewhat different standpoint. They consider it from the angle of optimal chance: What is the best prediction?

In the normal curve, the greatest mound of data always occurs at the point of central tendency. Take an example. You are driving down the street. Suddenly you come upon a crowd of people forming in contour a human normal-curve configuration. Where is the best prediction that you will find the cause for the crowd forming? The answer is simple. Where the crowd is deepest, where the crest of the curve and the greatest mass of people are, there probably is the cause for the gathering of the crowd. It may be a street fight, an accident, a man giving away wooden nickels. But whatever the occasion, your best guess lies at the point where the human mass—the statistical median, the mean, or the mode of the crowd—is at its peak.

Similarly, wherever the point of convergence of data is located, that is the most likely point to find the best prediction of the meaning of those data. We speak of "the average American" "the average student," "the average wage earner" when we refer to those Americans, those students, those wage earners that we are most likely to find huddled around the point of central tendency in any random sampling of Americans, or students, or workers that we may take. In the broad spectrum of possibilities, we are betting on the average as being the best guess as to what is most characteristic of the total population.

Aside from the points of central tendency—the mean, the median, and the mode—that we have mentioned, there are others that are seldom mentioned in textbooks but that competent researchers should know about if they are to fit the statistical tool to the contour and characteristics of the data. These are the *geometric mean,* the *harmonic mean,* and the *contraharmonic mean.* We shall discuss each of these briefly.

The *geometric mean,* as we have suggested earlier, is employed when the researcher wishes to find the point of central tendency of a growth phenomenon. We must again look at the data configuration. When the data are in the configurational pattern of a normal or humped curve, then the *arithmetic mean* is appropriate. The growth curve is quite different, however. If growth were represented by the normal curve, individuals who begin from two cells might grow to a point of maximum development and then wither away until they return to a two-celled state again. But, as we all know, growth does not occur like that—not in individuals, or towns, or cities. The growth curve for these things is the normal ogive, or "S," or its variants: the Gompertz curve, the modified exponential curve, or the logistic curve.

Growth is a function of geometric progression. Recall Thomas Robert Malthus, an English clergyman and economist, who was the first to warn the human race about the population explosion and the possibility of worldwide famine. Malthus's *An Essay on the Principle of Population as It Affects the Future Improvement of Society* was the first serious discussion of the effects of growth mathematics. He contended that population, when unchecked, increases in a *geometric ratio:* 2, 4, 8, 16, 32, 64, 128 . . ., whereas subsistence increases only in *arithmetic ratio:* 2, 4, 6, 8, 10, 12, 14 . . . . Malthus also saw that the eventual flattening of the growth curve was determined by the arithmetic progression factor, subsistence.

Hence, the growth curve appears as follows:

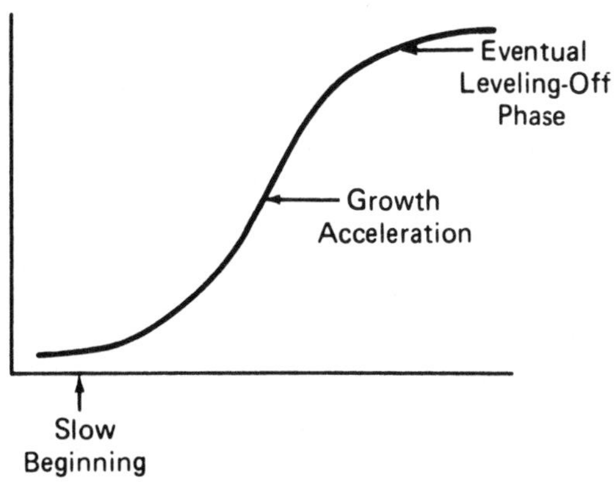

Typical Growth Curve

Biologists, physicists, ecologists, economists all encounter the growth and decay phenomena in one form or another. They all witness the same typical aspects of growth: a slow beginning—a few settlers in an uninhabited region, a few bacteria on a culture; then, after a period of time, rapid expansion—the boom period of city growth, the rapid multiplication of microorganisms; the leveling-off period—the land becomes scarce, and the city sprawl is contained by geographic and economic factors, the bacteria have populated the entire culture.

Examples of situations where the application of the geometric mean is appropriate are the following:

1. biological growth situations
2. population growth situations
3. increments of money at compound interest
4. in averaging ratios or percentages
5. decay or simple decelerative situations

We usually calculate the geometric mean in practice by the use of logarithms.

$$\text{G. M.} = \sqrt[n]{X_1 \cdot X_2 \cdot X_3 \cdot X_4 \cdot \cdot X_5 \ldots X_n} =$$

$$\log \text{G. M.} = \frac{\log X_1 + \log X_2 + \log X_3 + \log X_4 \ldots \log X_n}{N} =$$

$$\text{G. M.} = \frac{\Sigma \log X}{N}$$

The *harmonic mean* is employed for data derived from fluctuating situations. You drive a car from one point to another. If you had a graphical record of your speed, it would resemble the profile of a series of major and minor peaks in a mountain range. Leaving the point of origin, you accelerate to a speed of 20 miles per hour for a given time; then you climb to 35 miles per hour; then, being impeded by a truck in a no-passing zone, you drop to 10 miles per hour and follow the truck. With a chance to pass it, you accelerate to 50 miles per hour. And so, fluctuating in speed, you finally reach your destination. You want to find your *average* speed. The harmonic mean will help you. Any fluctuating phenomenon may call for the employment of the harmonic mean. A good elementary discussion of both the geometric mean and the harmonic mean can be found in Wert.[5] An article by Ferger gives advice about conditions that may call for the use of the harmonic mean.[6]

The harmonic mean is computed as follows:

$$\text{H. M.} = \frac{1}{\frac{1}{N}\left(\frac{1}{X_1} + \frac{1}{X_2} + \frac{1}{X_3} + \frac{1}{X_4} \cdots \frac{1}{X_n}\right)} = \frac{1}{\frac{1}{N}\Sigma\frac{1}{X}} = \frac{N}{\Sigma\frac{1}{X}}$$

One further statistic of the mean, very useful in certain instances, is the *contraharmonic mean.* It is a statistic that approximates a more realistic mean in situations where a few individuals contribute disproportionately to the total number of contributions. Take the instance of a college that attempts to show that the average income of its graduates, 20 years after graduation, is about $50,000 per year per graduate. It cites the average income (the *arithmetic average* income!) of the graduates in its twentieth-anniversary class. The figures look fine. They do not reveal, however, that one of the members of the class is an oil tycoon with an income of $1.75

[5] J. E. Wert, *Educational Statistics* (New York: McGraw-Hill, 1938), 63–80.
[6] Wirth F. Ferger, *Journal of the American Statistical Association* 26 (March 1931): 36–40.

million a year. Another graduate is a corporation president whose income from salary, stocks, and other sources totals $875,000 per year; another is president of a land speculation and realty firm with an income upward of $500,000 per year. A fourth is a corporation lawyer with earnings of $375,000 per year. The rest of the graduates are professionals whose incomes range between $20,000 and $40,000 per year. There are 478 of these out of a class of 493. A few graduates earn between $40,000 and $100,000 a year. If plotted, badly skewed curves should alert us to consider in such instances the possibility that the contraharmonic mean may be more appropriate in determining the point of central tendency.

We can employ the contraharmonic mean in only those instances where each X in the following formula is itself expressed in terms of a *number* of this or that: the *number* of dollars, the *number* of arrests, the *number* of accidents, and so forth.

The formula for deriving the contraharmonic mean is as follows:

$$\text{C.M.} = \frac{\Sigma f X^2}{\Sigma f X}$$

If, in driving my car, I could see my acceleration and deceleration curves as they might appear on a cathode tube in an oscilloscope, I would find not one bell-shaped curve but a series of oscillations and harmonics such as the tone from an organ pipe produces. To find my average speed, I must employ a mean that measures such a situation—in this case the *harmonic mean.* Thus, we come to the first rule for researchers who anticipate employing statistics in their research: *The data—the facts of life—govern the statistical technique, not the other way around.* Statistics is the maidservant of reality, and statisticians labor to produce a statistical tool for every life contingency. As the physician must know what drugs are available for specific diseases, so the researcher must know what statistical techniques are suited to specific research demands.

The Standard Error of the Mean

Let us pick up the matter of means, curves, and population samples. We will think of total populations and the samples drawn from them for a moment to discover a very important fact, what statisticians call *the standard error of the mean.*

Random samples from populations display in general the same characteristics as the parent population from which they were selected. There are, of course, slight deviations in every sample: Samples are not *facsimiles* of the parent population. But the deviations, if the sample has been selected randomly, so that it is truly representative, are presumably not of such magnitude as to be *significantly* different from the population from which the sample was drawn. The several means of the various samples, however, do form a normal frequency distribution of their own, and that frequency distribution has its own mean. In other words, the mean of each sample varies slightly from the mean of the general population from which the sample was drawn. It is axiomatic, however, that the larger the sample, the more the sample mean approximates the population mean. But the distribution of the several sample means gives us a variance phenomenon known as the *standard error of the mean,* which statistically is represented as

$$SE_{\bar{x}} = \frac{\sigma}{\sqrt{N}}$$

Here we are faced at once with a difficulty. This formula involves using the *population* standard deviation (σ), and the purpose of using the sample was that, since we cannot use the population as a whole because of its size, we must then work *backward* through an *estimation* technique that statisticians have devised to estimate the standard deviation of the total population with reasonable accuracy. This formula is as follows:[7]

$$\tilde{\sigma} = \frac{s}{\sqrt{N-1}}$$

Although statistics may indeed assist in estimating parameters when the size of the population prohibits complete surveying of every individual, two important considerations must be recognized:

1. Statistical predictions and estimates are no more accurate than the fidelity with which the parameters of the sample mirror those of the total population.
2. Statistical procedures must be appropriate to the character of the data being analyzed. *Nothing* substitutes for a careful and intelligent appraisal of the characteristics of the data and matching statistical procedures to those characteristics.

Figure 10.8 summarizes the measures of central tendency and their several uses, together with the various categories of data with which each measure is appropriate.

Figure 10.8 Uses of Measures of Central Tendency with Categories of Data

	Question
Scale	What is the best prediction? Answer: Measures of central tendency.
Nominal	*Mode:* The mode is the numeral representing the category with the highest frequency of occurrence. It is the prediction most likely to be right.
Ordinal	*Mode:* The same as for nominal scale. Appropriate for discrete data only. *Median:* The point above and below which lie 50 per cent of the cases. It is the prediction that is just as likely to be too high as too low. It is more stable than the mode.
Interval	*Mode:* } as for ordinal scale. *Median:* } as for ordinal scale. The prediction that minimizes average error. Mean: $\bar{X} = \frac{\Sigma X}{N}$: The prediction that makes the sum of the errors zero, and makes the sum of the squares of the errors a minimum. More stable than the median.
Ratio	*Mode:* *Median:* as for interval scale. *Mean:* *Geometric mean:* $GM = \sqrt[N]{X_1 \cdot X_2 \cdot \ldots \cdot X_n}$ *Harmonic mean:* $HM = \frac{N}{\Sigma \frac{1}{X}}$ *Contraharmonic mean:* $CM = \frac{\Sigma fX^2}{\Sigma fX}$ } Statistics for special situations.

From *Measurement and Statistics: A Basic Text Emphasizing Behavioral Science*, by Virginia L. Senders. Copyright © 1958 by Oxford University Press, Inc. Reprinted by permission.

[7] Virginia L. Senders, *Measurement and Statistics* (New York: Oxford University Press, 1958), 467.

Dispersion or Deviation

The Message of Curves and Deviations

We have been discussing basically the question, what is the best guess? Now we turn to the opposite question, what are the worst odds? Both questions are important. Some of us would like to look at the first question and forget the second. Such a reaction means merely that we need to cultivate a more objective and unemotional response to cold fact.

If, as we have been discussing, the probability index of the correct guess rises with the tendency of the data to cluster about the point of central tendency, then it is also true that the farther the data are dispersed from the central pivotal axis, the greater the margin of predictive error becomes. Consider, for example, the two curves shown in Figure 10.9.

The data are more uniform when they cluster about the mean. Scatter them, and they lose some of their uniformity. They become more diverse, more heterogeneous. As they recede from the mean, they lose more and more of the quality that makes them "average." It is easy for us to talk about one, two, three standard deviations from the mean. That type of language keeps everything impersonal, faceless. But just as there is a difference in living, in culture, in life as one goes farther and farther from a metropolitan center, so data change in character as they recede into the second and third standard deviations from the mean.

Also, a high, peaked curve—*leptokurtic,* as it is called—indicates a data accumulation more homogeneous. A low, flat, spreading curve—*platykurtic,* as this type is called—hints at greater heterogeneity within the data.

Statistics and surveying are somewhat similar. Each needs a point of origin from which to make further measurements. With surveying, the origin of measurement is a triangulation point; with statistics, it is one of the parameters of the data, usually the mean, which establishes a measurement point for the mass of data. If we can establish a mean, then from it we can initiate further measurements. In this way, we can learn more about the data, discern their characteristics, and identify their quality.

It is important to see two parameters of the data to make a sound judgment. We need to discern not only their centrality but also their spread. And we need to see these characteristics in terms of quantitative values. Only by seeing the data quantitatively, in terms of *number values,* can researchers know anything about those data. Researchers are like cartographers charting an unknown land; they must "chart" the data, appreciate the meaning of the "peaks and valleys," and evaluate the effect of the expansiveness or narrowness of the spread. Such information aids greatly in interpreting the data later.

How Great Is the Spread?

We have several statistical measures that assist us in describing the dispersion of the data from the mean or from the median.

Figure 10.9

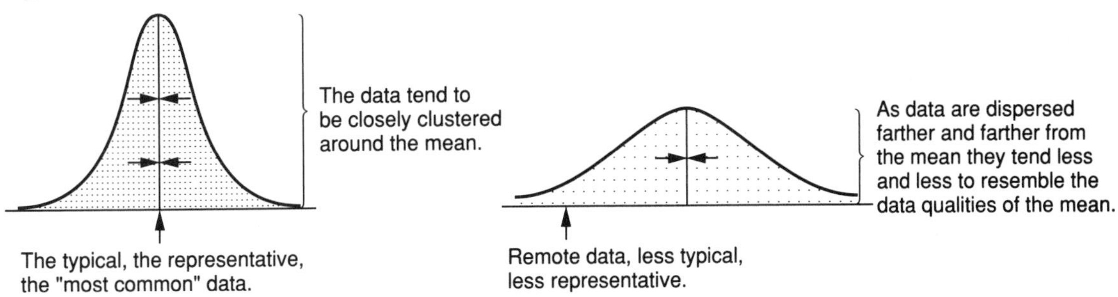
The data tend to be closely clustered around the mean.
The typical, the representative, the "most common" data.
As data are dispersed farther and farther from the mean they tend less and less to resemble the data qualities of the mean.
Remote data, less typical, less representative.

Perhaps the most unrefined of the measures of dispersion is the *range.* The range merely measures the spread of the data from their lowest to their highest value. The range has, however, limited usefulness as a measure of dispersion and may even be misleading if the extreme upper or lower limits are inordinately atypical of the other values in the series. Take an example. The following is the range of the number of children in six families: 15, 6, 5, 4, 3, 0. Now we might say that the families range from a childless couple to a family of 15 children. But drop off the extremes and the situation is much more realistic when we say that two-thirds of the families surveyed had from three to six children.

The next measure of dispersion is the *quartile deviation.* The quartile deviation divides the data into four equal parts. Quartile 1 will lie at a point where 25 percent of the items are below it. Quartile 2 will divide the items into two equal parts and will be identical to the median. Quartile 3 will lie at a point where 75 percent of the values are below it.

If, instead of dividing the data into four equal parts, we divide it into ten equal parts, then each part will be a *decile;* if into 100 equal parts, each part will be a *percentile.*

The *quartile range* is important in several ways, one of which is to provide a means of measuring *skewness.* Because quartiles are associated with the median, any statistical approach employing the median as a measure of central tendency should also consider the quartile deviation as an appropriate statistical measure for variability. Furthermore, the interquartile range includes within its limits the middle 50 percent of the cases in the distribution. The *interquartile range* is a combination of quartile measurement and range measurement and includes those data that lie from the first to the third quartile.

A test for the symmetry of the distribution is, therefore, the equidistance of Quartile 1 and Quartile 3 from the median. A *skewed distribution* will not present such symmetry. A *measure of skewness* takes advantage of asymmetry. The measure gives a value of 0 when Quartile 1 and Quartile 3 are equidistant from the median. The equation, with a lower limit of 0 and an upper limit of 1, may be stated as follows:[8]

$$SK_q = \frac{Q_3 + Q_1 - 2Md}{Q_3 - Q_1}$$

We will have more to say about measures of skewness when we discuss standard deviation. For all practical purposes, one may consider this index of skewness as comparable to a percentage index.

If we measure the dispersion of the data to the right and to the left of the mean, sum the deviations (disregarding the algebraic signs), and divide the summed differences by the number of cases, we get the *average deviation.* The equation for the average deviation is

$$AD = \frac{\Sigma|x|}{N}$$

where $|x| = X - \overline{X}$, disregarding algebraic signs.

We can, of course, take the average deviation around any point of central tendency. When calculated from the median, the average deviation is *less* than when taken from any other point of central tendency. The equation is

$$AD_{mdn} = \frac{\Sigma(x - M_{dn})}{N}$$

[8] William A. Neiswanger, *Elementary Statistical Methods,* rev. ed. (New York: Macmillan, 1956).

The average deviation is very readily understood and, for that reason, has some merit. It is acceptable when no further statistical procedure is contemplated. It is a little-used value, however, and the measures of standard deviation and variance have largely supplanted it in practical research projects.

The *standard deviation* is the standard measure of variability in most statistical operations. It is an expression of variability from the arithmetic mean, and it is the accepted measure of dispersion in modern statistical practice. To understand the reason for using the standard deviation, we must recall what happens numerically when we find the average deviation, which we have just discussed. In finding the average deviation, as we subtract all the deviations lesser than the median (which lie on the normal curve distribution to the left of the median), all of them become *negative* values. Thus, the values to the left of the median (which are all negative) and those to the right of the median (which are all positive) tend in summation to cancel out one another. This is because these values are linear. In practice, we can change this situation by ignoring the algebraic signs, which we suggest that you do in finding the average deviation. But this is a rather dubious procedure. It is neither sound mathematics nor sound statistics to ignore what you do not like. We can, however, change negatives to positives in a perfectly acceptable mathematical manner. In algebra, if we multiply a negative value by itself, it becomes positive. Thus, by squaring all negative derivations, they become positive:

$$-2^2 = (-2)(-2) = +4$$

Then:

$$\sqrt{+4} = +2$$

Thus, we change linear numbers to square numbers and then take the square root of the square number. By changing all the linear numbers to square numbers, then summing the squared values and dividing by the *number of deviation values,* and, finally, taking the square root of the quotient, we have gone full-circle mathematically and are back again to an average of the deviations from the mean in which all the values, regardless of what sign they bore originally, have been transformed to positive integers. It is important to note that we divide the *summed squared deviations* (not the summed deviations, squared!) by the total number of deviations from the mean. Finally, we take the square root of the resultant quotient, which, in turn, will give us the standard deviation. In terms of an equation, the standard deviation is

$$s = \sqrt{\frac{\Sigma x^2}{N}}$$

A careful distinction should be made at this point. For the average deviation we measure the deviations from the *median;* for the standard deviation we measure the deviations from the *mean.*

For analyzing data, we need another measure of dispersion based upon the standard deviation. This statistic is known as the *variance,* which is merely the standard deviation squared.

$$s^2 = \frac{\Sigma x^2}{N}$$

In discussing the quartile deviation, we presented a method of determining skewness in the normal distribution and suggested that another method of determining it would be presented after we had discussed the standard deviation. In this latter method, devised by Karl Pearson, we make use of the major parameters of the normal distribution: the mean, the median, and the standard deviation. It is sometimes referred to as the *Pearsonian measure of skewness.*

The formula for the Pearsonian coefficient is

$$Sk = \frac{3(\overline{X} - Md)}{s}$$

where

$\overline{X}$ = the arithmetic mean
Md = the median
s = the standard deviation

For normal distributions the coefficient value is 0. It varies ±3, but a coefficient in excess of ±1 is unusual.

These measures—central tendency, dispersion, and skewness—should provide us with sufficient means of analyzing the data. Because we call on the aid of statistics to this end, this quantitative methodology has also been termed *the analytical survey method.* A composite approach to the data, it consists of first surveying the data to note their configuration and fundamental characteristics, then through statistical means analyzing those data—seeing, through the eyes of statistical procedures, what the mass of data appears to be.

Up to this point, we have been considering data en masse by looking at the parameters inherent to that mass. We have attempted to analyze the mass by determining where the center of it lies, how far it spreads, and whether the spread shows distortion or skewness. We have piled up, as it were, all the data and attempted to find the exact point where they are exactly balanced. We have also viewed the spread on either side of this delicate equilibratory point to see how the data were distributed. We come now to a closer look at those data and their innate characteristics. But, before proceeding, let us summarize in Figures 10.10 and 10.11 what we have been discussing with respect to the measures of dispersion. We are using Joe's grades that, earlier in this chapter, we used to show how we can view data from several different per-

Figure 10.10 Measures of Central Tendency and Dispersion

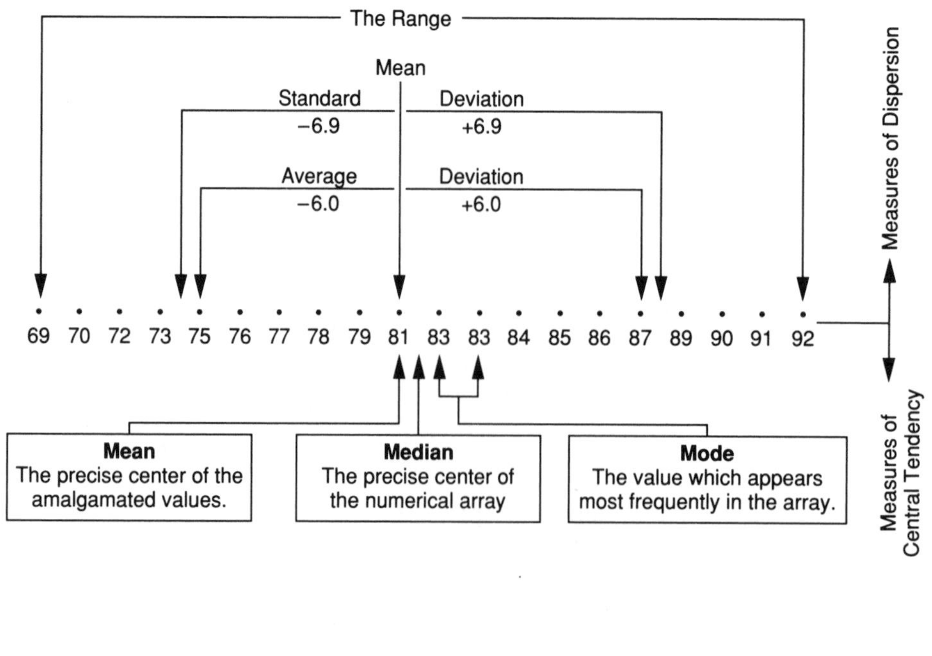

Figure 10.11 Uses of Measures of Dispersion with Categories of Data

	Question
Scale	What are the worst odds? Answer: Measures of dispersion.
Nominal	Except for verbal descriptions ("longer than") this category is inappropriate for indicating measures of dispersion.
Ordinal	Range: $X_{max} - X_{min} + 1$. Unstable. Interquartile range: 75th percentile–25th percentile. Semi-quartile range, Q. Half of interquartile range. Other interpercentile ranges.
Interval	Range, quartile ranges, as for ordinal scale *Average deviation: AD*: $AD = \frac{\Sigma\|x\|}{N}$ *Standard deviation,* s, *and variance,* s^2: $s = \sqrt{\frac{\Sigma x^2}{N}}$ $s^2 = \frac{\Sigma x^2}{N}$ More useful in later computations than *AD*.
Ratio	Various ranges, *AD*, s and s^2 } as for interval scale. *Coefficient of variation, V*: $V = \frac{100s}{\overline{X}}$ Expresses variability in terms of absolute size of measured objects.

From *Measurement and Statistics: A Basic Text Emphasizing Behavioral Science*, by Virginia L. Senders.

spectives. Here are those same grades to show the measures of central tendency and the simple measures of dispersion.

In the early pages of this chapter, we used only the simple statistical average to inspect the array of Joe's grades. Now, with this display, we see how statistics is giving us greater insight into Joe's academic performance. We are also able to see how the topics that we have been discussing—points of central tendency and measures of dispersion—appear when applied to these data.

So that we do not lose perspective, we should remind ourselves that this is all merely statistical manipulation of the data. It is not research, for research goes one step further and demands *interpretation* of the data. In finding means, medians, quartiles, and standard deviations, we have not interpreted the data; we have not extracted any *meaning* from the data. We have merely *described* the center of the data mass and its spread. We have attempted only to see what the data looked like. After we know what the data are and what their basic nature is, we can then attempt to say what those data mean. Then we can descry whether there are forces, which are the real culprits in forcing the data to behave as they do, acting upon those data. For example, apropos of skewness, if we toss a die 100 times and it comes up "5" 53 times out of the 100, we will have a skewed distribution. It may suggest to us that a reason lurks *behind the skewness*. We may hypothesize that we are playing with a loaded die!

But, let us consider other ways of analyzing the data.

Correlation

Measuring Relationships

Statistics Can Show You the Existence of Relationships. Up to this point, we have been discussing statistics from the viewpoint of only the central tendency and dispersion. These are phenomena that happen with relation to only one parameter of the data: the pivotal axis that we have called the *mean.*

But the facts of life are not always so simple. Nor can life be adequately described by a static system where only the central balance point and the amplitude of dispersion account for the world around us. The *raison d'être* of statistics is that it takes the disparate facts of life and translates these into quantitative concepts and formulations that are manageable and meaningful.

In the real world, facts exist not only in a static linear arrangement but also in dynamic interrelationships with each other. There is a relationship, for example, between age and mental maturity, emotional state and physical health, the incidence of rainfall and the price of food in the marketplace. Relationships and interrelationships are all around us. Consider the relationship between temperature and pressure, between the wavelength and intensity of light and the growth of plants, between the administration of a certain drug and the resultant platelet agglutination in the blood. We could go on and on. Relationships between one kind of data and another are everywhere. Because life is filled with these interrelationships, one of the functions of statistics is to *describe* or *indicate the intensity and magnitude* of such related factors.

To many students, the mere discovery of a relationship between one type of data and another is the prime goal of research. It is nothing of the kind. Those students think they have discovered something. Not so. They have not so much discovered something as described something that already existed, that a statistical technique caused to float to the surface. What they have done with a statistical formula, a computer can do better. But computers cannot do research. There is no *interpretation of fact* in what either such students or the computer does. What we are saying does not disparage either the function of statistics or the function of the computer. It merely aims to put both tools into proper perspective with respect to the purposes of research.

The statistical process by which we discover the relationship between different types of data is called *correlation.* It is always a decimal fraction, indicating the degree of relatedness between the factors being correlated. Such a fraction is called a *coefficient of correlation.* Finding a coefficient of correlation is not doing research; it is merely discovering a signpost. That signpost points unerringly to a fact that two things are indeed related. It also reveals the *nature of the relationship:* whether the facts are closely or distantly related.

So you come up with a coefficient of correlation. This should spark a barrage of questions in your mind: what is the nature of the relationship; what is the underlying cause of the relationship; if two things are related, how are they related? Answer these questions and you are *interpreting* what the correlation *means.* You are doing research.

Mention coefficient of correlation and most students immediately think of only the Pearsonian product moment correlation, commonly called the *Pearsonian r.* Although this probably is the commonest of all correlational techniques, there are perhaps a dozen more. As in the case of the mean, the nature of the data must always determine the correlational technique that is most appropriate.

Correlations are merely statistical descriptions. They describe the strength of the relationship between one variable and the other. At best, correlations are statistical conclusions of what happens within a correlational matrix, and a correlational matrix is nothing more than a convention for representing graphically facts that, presumably, have some connection with each other.

Data should be thought of as having within them a certain energy potential that reacts within a framework of vertical and horizontal dynamics. Gas, for example, has under normal conditions certain dynamics of pressure and temperature. A child has the dynamics of age and reading achievement. These dynamic dimensions are interactive and changeable. We call such dimensions *variables,* because their nature is to vary. We call other data that do not exhibit such variable characteristics *constants.*

In the case of the gas, the pressure varies with the temperature. Similarly, in the case of the child, the data vary continually. The child is constantly changing with respect to age, growth, achievement, reading proficiency, and other academic skills.

To represent these variables statistically to show a relationship between one group of data and another, we use a grid—a two-dimensional statistical representation called a *correlational matrix. A correlational matrix is a dynamic area within which the forces of the variables interact.*

Presented in Figure 10.12 is a correlational matrix on which data variables are represented as interacting: They form a statistically dynamic field of "forces." Thus, any fact expressed in terms of *one data factor* is also expressed in relation to the *other factor* and is, therefore, located on the grid at some point where the lines extending from the point of magnitude for each variable intersect.

Also presented, in Figure 10.13, is a grid representing the other situation that we mentioned above. On the *ordinate* (the vertical axis), we have represented chronological age. On the *abscissa* (the horizontal axis) is the reading grade expectancy. We identify the child mentioned above with the symbol Δ on the grid. She has made normal progress in reading: at age six, she was reading at the first-grade level; at seven, at the second-grade level; at eight, at the third-grade level; and so on. The relationship of age to reading grade expectancy is a perfect one-to-one correspondence: one year of age, one grade of reading achievement. The straight-line vector that connects these points is an equilibrium between grade achievement in reading and chronological age. In statistics, such a line is called the *line of regression,* which in this instance represents a perfect, positive correlation of the one factor (age) to the other (reading achievement) in progressive equilibrium. In practice, we represent a coefficient of correlation with the symbol r; in this instance we would describe the correlation as $r = 1.0$.

Figure 10.12 A Correlational Matrix

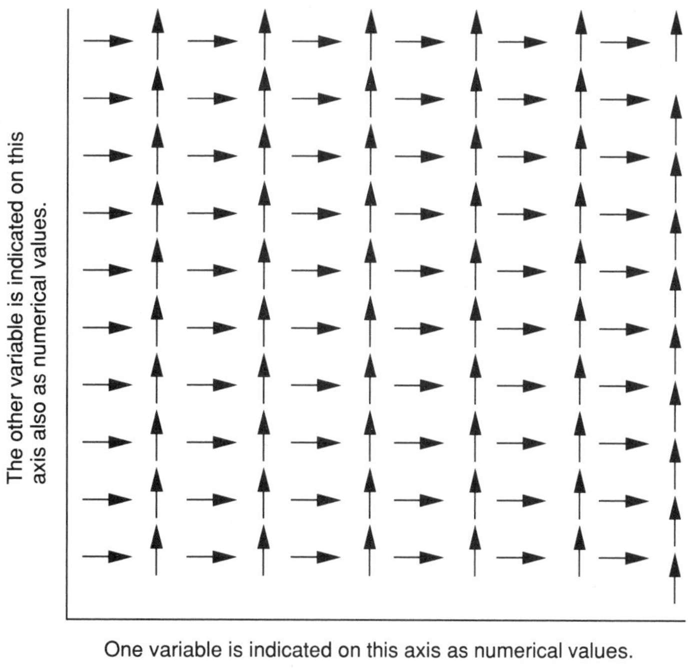
The other variable is indicated on this axis also as numerical values.
One variable is indicated on this axis as numerical values.

Figure 10.13 Dynamic Relationship between Age and Achievement

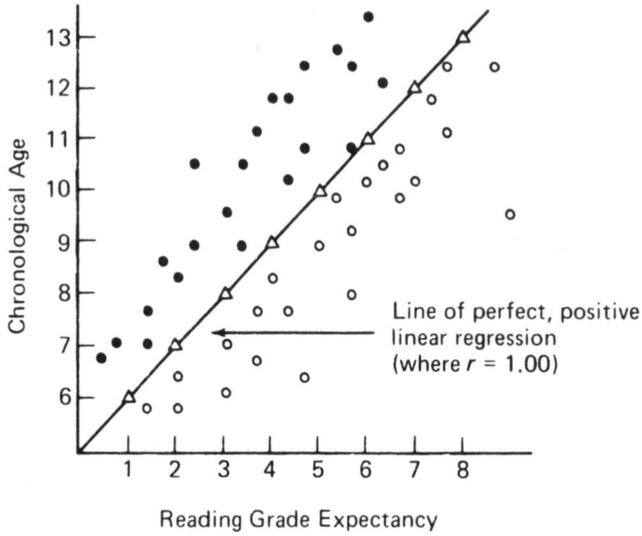

In contrast to this perfectly linear correlation, we can plot the ages and reading levels of classmates of the child we have just been discussing. Some—represented by the symbol ○—are advanced for their age. Others—represented by the symbol ●—are lagging with respect to their reading grade expectancy. The following graph plots the reading grade placement for each child.

As we inspect this matrix, what can we say about it? We can make two statements. We can merely *describe* the homogeneity or heterogeneity of the data in terms of the statistical dynamics. This description we express in the form of an r, a coefficient of correlation represented by a decimal fraction: the larger the decimal value, the greater the homogeneity of the data.

On the other hand, we can *interpret* the meaning of these data within the matrix by investigating the juxtapositions or remotenesses and by considering the data configuration as a whole, which considerations seem to hint at further and more significant meanings than that of a mere decimal fraction.

Research, by its very nature, goes beyond simple statistical description to probe the meaning within the data. Its goal is to discover a rationale for the appearance of such data within the matrix itself. We might, for example, analyze the placement of the data that represent achievement below the level of reading grade expectancy. Let us look at each ● in relation to all other ●s; in relation to factors that have conditioned the placement; in relation to the overall configuration of the ●s; and corresponding cases of the ●s and the ○s with respect to their proximity or remoteness from the norm of expected behavior—the line of perfect, positive, linear regression. When we regard the data in this way, we get insight that is not apparent from a correlation coefficient. The matrix has dramatized certain of the events within the data that can now claim our attention.

What we have done with the underachievers, we might also do with the overachievers. Then, by combining, contrasting, and permuting these two subpopulations, we can probe for further facts. Thus, we are attempting to dig underneath the correlational coefficient to see the reason for it! We seek a knowledge of the internal structure of the entire matrix, which may give us further insight into the causes for its being the way it is.

Statistical techniques are thus helpful in providing us with overall views and conclusions about data masses that we could not achieve in any other way. What is important, however, is that the researcher know the limitations of each correlational technique employed and the specific way in which it may allow a fuller understanding of the data.

In all relationship studies, however, you should be alert for faulty logic. A tacit assumption is sometimes made that if one factor can be shown to have a statistical relationship to another, then these two factors must necessarily have an influence on each other. In some instances, the influence may indeed be intimate and direct, as in the case where chronological age seems to have a direct bearing upon physical and mental development. But to infer that merely because a correlation exists, it therefore implies an interaction between the correlational variables is very questionable reasoning.

Take a logically absurd yet statistically demonstrable instance. We could conceivably establish a statistically correct correlation between the number of elephants in Thailand and the size of the Florida orange crop. The facts may be very clear: As the size of the elephant population increases, the Florida orange crop increases! To reason, however, that because we can show a positive correlation there must therefore be a causal bond at the root of that relationship is erroneous. There is no connection whatsoever between the elephant population in Thailand and the production of oranges in Florida. *One variable correlates meaningfully with another only when there is a common causal bond that links the phenomena of both variables in a logical and causal relationship.* This causal bond always lies below the mere statistical operation.

But where in an extreme situation we recognize the absurdity of the reasoning (as in the elephant–orange crop correlation), in research studies we occasionally find this same kind of questionable reasoning proposed quite seriously. We assume, for instance, that a correlation between low socioeconomic level and poor academic performance implies that one *causes* the other: *Because* the family paycheck, the family living conditions, and so forth are inadequate, the achievement of the boys and girls of such families is also deficient. Improve the family economic status and you will improve the learning quality of the children of that family. Does not the coefficient of correlation indicate that's what happens?

We assume on the basis of the correlation coefficient that one situation determines the other. There may be some connection between paycheck size and children's grades; but such an inference may also be utter nonsense. Unless we inspect the causal premise very carefully, we may be misled by a statistical statement that, in fact, may have no validity whatever. If we reason this way about socioeconomic status and academic performance, we may find it difficult to account for the world's geniuses and intellectual giants, many of whom have been born of indigent parents and have lived in constant poverty. For example, Robert Burns, the greatest of Scottish poets, did not have even a common school education because of the poverty of his family. Enrico Caruso was born in Naples of a poor family; George Washington Carver was born of slaves; Franz Schubert's father was a peasant and his mother was a cook. He himself lived in poverty most of his life. The case of Abraham Lincoln, born in a log cabin, walking miles to borrow a book belies the impoverished environment–deprived child theory modern thinking so glibly accepts.

If you begin to correlate low socioeconomic status with failure and draw conclusions as to causal relationships, read the biographies of the world's great and forthrightly face the fact that the correlational approach is highly questionable. If you are going to draw one conclusion to suit your premise, you must account as well for those exceptions to the rule that belie your conclusion. You cannot glibly get rid of an uncomfortable fact by apotheosis. Correlations are correlations, and those who employ them must be ready for absolute intellectual honesty.

Figures may not lie, but the causal assumptions that we make with respect to some of our figuring may at times be extremely circumspect. The genuine researcher is never content to stop at merely finding a correlation. Such a researcher is always aware that *below the correlation* lies a universe of fact whose interpretation may conceivably lead to the discovery of new and exciting truth. The coefficient of correlation is, therefore, merely a signpost pointing to further discovery. The forces within the data that are correlated determine the validity of the correlation. As shown in Figure 10.12, *a correlation is not a static entity; it is a field of dynamic forces that must always be recognized, especially when using the correlation as the main support in drawing a conclusion.*

Think of a datum as you think of an atom. Within the atom lies a whole organization of forces: the central proton, the kinetic electrons, the mesons, the neutrons, the neutrinos. These forces, each dynamic within itself, each interacting within the structure, cause each atom to be a structure of complex forces. The same is true of data. Within the data are forces, dynamics, and measurable trends that when discovered and expressed as one data "force" in relation to another data "force" make the entire data mass more meaningful and significant.

We should remember, however, that correlational data are generally plotted on a grid. Convention suggests that the independent variable be plotted along the horizontal axis, the dependent variable along the vertical axis. When neither factor can be said to be the cause of or dependent upon the other, then the *variable to be predicted* should be plotted along the vertical axis.

Always keep in mind that *the nature of the data governs the correlational procedure that is appropriate to those data.* All too many would-be researchers begin by deciding, for instance, that they will use a Pearsonian coefficient of correlation for showing a relationship between two factors when, in fact, that technique may be entirely inappropriate to the data being correlated. Don't forget the cardinal rule: *Look at the data! Determine their nature; scrutinize their quality; then select the appropriate correlational technique suited to the type of data with which you are working.*

In Table 10.2 we have characterized the several techniques by the type of data required for each variable. Having taken you thus far, the rest is merely a matter of some further searching among the broad range of statistical texts for appropriate formulas and relevant discussions as to the specific application and the discrete characteristics of each statistical approach. We will not attempt to go any further into the statistical realm of correlational concerns.

Inferential Statistics

Refer to Figure 10.6—the map of the statistical landscape. We are still in the realm of parametric statistics, but we now leave descriptive statistics to discuss inferential statistics.

Inferential statistics has two principal functions:

1. to predict or estimate a population parameter from a random sample; and
2. to test *statistically based* hypotheses.

Prediction: One of the Roles of Inferential Statistics

Prediction is a division of statistics that has many ramifications. In this text, we cannot venture too far into this area. Again, statistical texts will provide you with this information. We will, however, comment briefly concerning some general underlying concepts and principles.

Earlier, we discussed prediction or estimation of values in terms of measures of central tendency. We then balanced our estimate of "goodness of guess" with "badness of guess" as indicated by the degree of dispersion or variation. We also considered the predictive implications of the line of regression. These estimating techniques are not, however, the ones that we usually consider within the realm of inferential statistics.

Inferential statistics is more concerned with estimating *population parameters from sample statistics.* The population estimates that we commonly attempt to make are estimates of *parameters* with respect to frequency distributions or parts thereof, estimates with respect to the population μ (central tendency of the population), the σ (variability of the population), or the proportion or probability, the P. These values in the population compare with the $\overline{X}$, the s, and the p of the sample.

To understand exactly what we mean by estimation, let us take a simple illustration. Jan is a production manager of a manufacturing corporation. She has a sample lot of connecting-rod pins. These pins fit snugly into assembly units, permitting the units to swivel within a

Table 10.2 Digest of Correlational Techniques

Correlational Technique	Symbol	Variable Characteristic X	Y	Comment
		Parametric Correlational Techniques		
Pearson product moment correlation	r	Continuous	Continuous	The most commonly used coefficient.
Biserial correlation	r_b	Continuous	Continuous, but forced into an artificial dichotomy	Much used in item analysis. An array of grades in which some are "pass," others "fail" is an artificial dichotomy.
Point biserial correlation	r_{pb}	Continuous	True dichotomy	Example: heights and weights of boys and girls.
Tetrachoric correlation	r_t	Artificial dichotomy	Artificial dichotomy	Less reliable than Pearson *r*. Do not use with nominal or ordinal data.
The phi coefficient (fourfold coefficient)	ϕ	True dichotomy	True dichotomy	Statistic is related to χ^2. Assumes variable can have values of only +1 or −1.
Widespread biserial correlation	r_{wblc}	Widespread artificial dichotomy	Continuous	Used when interested in cases at extremes of dichotomized variable.
The triserial correlation	r_{tri}	Continuous	Trichotomy	Developed by N. Jaspen. See *Psychometrika,* 1946, 11, 23–30.
Correlational ratio	η	Continuous	Continuous	Nonlinear relationship between variables. Scattergram necessary to determine linearity.
		Nonparametric Correlational Techniques		
Spearman rank-order correlation (rank difference correlation)	ρ	Ranks	Ranks	Similar to the Pearson *r*. Particularly well suited to situations of 25–30 cases.
Kendall's coefficient of concordance	W	Used with three or more sets of ranks		Value of *W* varies between 0 = no agreement to 1 = perfect agreement.
Kendall's tau correlation between ranks	τ	Ranks	Ranks	Can be used wherever ρ is appropriate but preferable to ρ when number is less than 10.
Contingency coefficient	C	Two or more categories	Two or more categories	Similar to r_t. Closely related to χ^2. Correlations similar to Pearson *r* with large sample and at least five categories for each variable.
Partial correlation	$r_{12\cdot3}$	Correlational method involving more than two variables		The partial *r* is used when the relationship between two variables is influenced by a third variable.
Multiple correlation	$R_{1\cdot234}$	One variable (criterion) vs. many variables		Employed where two or more variables are used to predict a single variable. In the symbol subscript $R_{1\cdot234}$, the subscript 1 stands for the criterion variable; the 234 for the predictor variables.

From *Educational Research: An Introduction*, 3d ed., by Walter R. Borg and Meredith D. Gall.

given arc. The diameter of the pins is critical. If the diameter is too small, the assembly will wobble in turning; if too large, the assembly will stick and refuse to move. Jan has received a number of complaints from customers that the pins are faulty. She wishes to estimate, on the basis of a sample, how many of the units may have to be recalled for replacement. The sample is presumably random and representative. From this sample, Jan wants to know three facts relative to the hundreds of thousands of pins that have been manufactured and sold on the market.

1. How many of them are within acceptable tolerance limits?
2. How widely do they vary in diameter measurement—what is the deviation, the variance?
3. What proportion of the pins produced will be acceptable in the assemblies already marketed?

The problem is to judge population parameters on the basis of the sample statistics. From the sample, she can estimate the mean, the variation, and the probability of acceptable pins within the population universe. There are the values represented by the μ, σ, and the P.

Certain basic assumptions underlie all prediction procedures: (1) Estimates of whatever kind assume that the sample is random and representative of the total population. Only by its being so can we have any congruity between the sample and the population universe from which the sample was chosen and toward which the prediction will be made; and (2) the sample should ideally be a microcosm of the greater universe of the population. The closer this correspondence, the greater is the predictive accuracy of the sample. When such a situation exists, we then have statistical techniques to project from the statistic of the sample to the corresponding parameter of the population. Whatever we can determine with respect to a *statistic* of the sample, we can estimate with respect to a *parameter* of the population.

Point vs. Interval Estimates

In making estimates of population parameters from sample statistics, we can make estimates of two types: *point estimates* and *interval estimates.*

A *point estimate* is a single statistic that is taken as the best indication of the corresponding population parameter. We have discussed the variability within samples—the error of the means of random samples from the true mean of the total population. We must recognize and take into account this variability when making any kind of estimate, particularly point estimates, where we are shooting for a statistical bull's eye.

Point estimates afford us very little freedom. We seek the parallel population parameter value with the sample statistic value. Although point estimates have the virtue of being precise, precision has its own price; the price for precision is that the point estimate will generally not exactly correspond with the true population equivalent.

An estimate is a statistical flight into the unknown. The prediction of population parameters is at best a matter of dead reckoning. It takes its sightings from a randomly selected sample and, taking into account the other conditioning factors, makes its predictions on the basis of these contingencies. We have seen earlier that the accuracy in estimating the population mean depends upon (1) the size of the sample, and (2) the degree of its variability.

In the example of the connecting-rod pins, if we had been told that the company had produced 500,000 pins, of which Jan had a sample of 1,000 with a given mean diameter and a standard deviation of .005 inch, we then would have been able to make a parametric estimate. Although the values we had predicted may not have been accurate for the total production of connecting pins, they would certainly have been better than nothing.

So much for point estimation. A much more comfortable procedure is the *interval estimate* of parameters. In this type of prediction, we specify a band within whose limits we estimate that practically all the values will lie. Such a band is commonly called the *confidence interval* because we have confidence that between the values we have set, 95 percent of all the data values will be found. At times, depending upon the research refinement that we seek, we may set the limit at 99 percent confidence. Statisticians usually consider these two values as standard for confidence levels. Sometimes, however, we phrase the same concept in terms of *level of significance.* This is looking at the concept of the confidence interval in reverse.

Any factor that causes more than a 1 percent variability in 99 percent of the data or (in the case of a 95 percent confidence limit) a 5 percent variability in the data values is considered to be the result of some influence other than mere chance. We speak, thus, of a factor as being *statistically significant* at the 5 percent level or at the 1 percent level of significance. In brief, what this means is that we permit a certain narrow margin of variance, which we deem to be natural and the result of pure chance. Any variation *within* this statistically permissible band is not considered to be important enough to claim our attention. Whatever *exceeds these limits,* however, is considered to be the result of some determinative factor other than chance, and so the influence is considered to be a significant one. The term *significant,* in the statistical sense in which we have been using it, is very close to its etymological meaning, namely, "giving a signal" that something is operating below the surface of the statistic that merits further attention and investigation. Thus, is new research born. In investigating one problem, we discover a force, a dynamic that we had not anticipated—and a new investigation faces us. This is only one of the places in the research structure that we may come upon such unexpected events. Wherever they appear, there is the opening of a new avenue leading toward Truth.

We have said enough about estimation for you to appreciate its importance. To venture further would get us involved in a statistical methodology and specific operational procedures that are not the province of this text. For those who wish a guide to such procedures, see Table 10.3 for a Summary of Point and Interval Estimates of Parameters. The student must consult the textbooks in statistics for these matters.

There still remains the last of the functions of inferential statistics in the analytical survey method, namely, the *testing of hypotheses,* to which we now turn.

The Testing of Hypotheses

At the very outset, we should clarify the matter of terminology. The term *hypothesis* can bewilder you hopelessly unless you understand that it has two entirely different meanings in the literature of research. The first of these two meanings restricts the word *hypothesis* to a *research problem-oriented hypothesis.* The second usage of the term is limited to *a statistically-oriented hypothesis.* In the first meaning of the word, a hypothesis exists because the research problem, or the subproblems issuing from it, arouses a curiosity in the researcher's mind, which, in turn, results in the positing of a *tentative guess* relative to the resolution of the problematic situation. This type of hypothesis we discussed earlier in connection with the discussion of the nature of research. It concerned the perplexed home owner whose living room failed to light. The hypothesis is in one sense, therefore, a reasonable and logical conjecture, an educated guess. Its purpose is a practical one: It provides a tentative objective, an operational bull's-eye, a logical construct that helps researchers look for the data.

Based on conclusions to which the data force them, researchers must either confirm or deny the hypothesis they have posited. In a sense, a problem-oriented hypothesis in research is comparable to a scaffold in construction engineering. Each has its purpose as a function of an ongoing operation. In the case of the hypothesis, it is the pursuit of the data that, when inspected and interpreted, will help solve the problem being researched; in the case of the scaffold, it is the erection of an architectural structure. The completion of the project makes both the hypothesis and the scaffold of no further use. Both are vitally necessary, though intermediary functionaries. Their sole purpose is to facilitate the achievement of the ultimate goal.

However, when one comes across the phrase *tests of hypotheses,* the matter is entirely different. Here the word *hypothesis* refers to a *statistically-based hypothesis,* commonly known as a *null hypothesis.* The null hypothesis postulates that there is no statistically significant difference between phenomena that occur by pure chance and the statistically evaluated behavior of the data as they have been observed by the researcher. If a difference does occur, and the magnitude of that difference is such as to exceed the possibility of its having been caused by random error or pure chance, then we conclude that some intervening variable aside from the fortuitousness of nature is energizing the data. In consequence, we reject the null hypothesis. It is this comparison of observed data with expected results of normative values that we call testing the hypothesis or, perhaps more accurately, *testing the null hypothesis.*

Table 10.3 A Summary Table of Point and Interval Estimates of Parameters

Scale	Kind of Measure: Frequency distributions or parts thereof	Central Tendency	Variability	Correlation
Nominal	$\tilde{P} = p \quad \sigma_p = \sqrt{PQ/N}$ $\frac{p-P}{\sigma_p}$ is normally distributed when $NP \geq 5$. Confidence bands for estimating *P* from *p*. Chi-square test for correspondence of obtained and espected frequency distributions.		$\tilde{H} = \hat{H} + 1.3863N$	$\tilde{T} = \hat{T} - \frac{(r-1)(k-1)}{1.3863N}$
Ordinal	Confidence interval for any population percentile made in terms of sample percentiles. Kolmogorov-Smirnov confidence band for entire cumulative percentage histogram.	$\tilde{\text{Mdn}}_{\text{pop}} = \text{Mdn}$ Confidence intervals in terms of sample percentiles.	Confidence intervals for Q_1 and Q_3 in terms of sample percentiles.	
Interval and Ratio	Chi-square and Kolmogorov-Smirnov tests can be used to determine goodness of fit of any theoretical distribution —e.g., normal.	$\tilde{\mu} = \overline{X}, \ \tilde{\sigma}_{\overline{x}} = s/\sqrt{N-1}$ $\frac{\overline{X}-\mu}{\tilde{\sigma}_{\overline{x}}}$ has *t*-distribution for samples from normal populations. For small samples from nonnormal populations, use Tchebychev's Inequality. Same principles for Mdn., but $\tilde{\sigma}_{\text{Mdn}} = 1.253\tilde{\sigma}_{\overline{x}}$.	$\tilde{\sigma}^2 = s^2\left(\frac{N}{N-1}\right)$ For samples from normal populations, Ns^2 has chi-square distribution with N-1 degrees of freedom.	Confidence bands for estimating ρ from *r*. $Z_r = 1.1513 \log_{10} \frac{1+r}{1-r}$ $(z_r - z_\rho)(\sqrt{N-3})$ has unit normal distribution if population is normal bivariate.

From *Measurement and Statistics: A Basic Text Emphasizing Behavioral Science*, by Virginia L. Senders. Copyright © 1958 by Oxford University Press, Inc. Reprinted by permission. (Modified at the direction of the author.)

What is frequently confusing to the uninitiated researcher is that testing the null hypothesis involves nothing more than a statistical comparison of the data from two situations. One of these we consider mathematically ideal because it conforms to the parameters of the normal distribution; the other we derive from life. To these latter data, we apply certain statistical processes to determine whether their calculated values diverge from the statistical ideal sufficiently to reject the postulation that there is no difference (*null* difference) between the two sets of data. It is important to keep clearly in mind, therefore, the difference between the two kinds of hypotheses. You cannot test the first type statistically as you can the second type. In the literature, the null hypothesis is generally represented by the symbol H_0.

We should also look at hypothesis testing from another point of view. Testing the null hypothesis does not contribute much to the fulfillment of the basic aim of pure research, which we defined early in this book as "a systematic quest for undiscovered truth" under the aegis of the techniques of the scientific method. Also, we have indicated that statistics is merely a "tool of research," whose function is to take the data, quantify them, and inspect them in their quantified form so that, having been converted into the language of mathematics, they may reply to the researcher in terms of quantitative values and, by so doing, give some indication of the characteristics of the data and the dynamics that affect them.

Statistics has its function, but that function is ancillary: to inspect the data so that aspects of them, of which we might not otherwise be aware, are revealed. Testing the null hypothesis frequently leaves us with merely an indication that factors or forces that may influence the data either are or are not present.

In the last analysis, testing the null hypothesis merely confirms or denies the deeper presence of something that is working within the data. It is this all-important *something* that the researcher seeks to identify and evaluate. To stop with a mere indication that something is there that accounts for a significant difference between one set of data and another is to settle for a ghost, and research is not a systematic quest for ghosts. It is a systematic search for Truth.

Statistical hypothesis testing is an important component in decision theory. As such, it has value for those who must make decisions on the basis of statistical characteristics of samples. All researchers must ultimately develop an intellectual acuity that looks with unprejudiced candor at their procedures and results. If those results reveal facts newly discovered and those facts result in new insight, then the data have been interpreted. That is quite a different matter from running those data through a statistical formula and coming out with a numerical value. The one process ends in a decimal fraction; the other, in a deeper understanding of the meaning of the data. The latter includes the former, but they should never be confused.

What Is Statistical Hypothesis Testing? We can only offer a sketch here. The domain of statistical hypothesis testing is extensive, and we leave detailed discussion to statistics texts. Briefly, it involves testing, or rather, comparing the distribution of data that *you have,* when these data are plotted over, or *compared with an ideal,* or *hypothetical distribution,* as measured by the normal, or Gaussian, curve.

Nothing is perfect. Your data always will show divergence when superimposed upon the distribution of the normal curve. We expect some variance between the two configurations. But we set limits as to how far those variations may vary. These limits we call *confidence limits*; and, depending upon how rigorously we wish to approach the perfection of the normal curve, we allow a 1 percent or a 5 percent variance between the two sets of data.

The larger the population from which *your data* were obtained the less the variance between *your* data and those of the normal curve will be. To interview 1,000 people on a particular viewpoint will give you less variance than to interview 100. As the size of the population decreases the higher the variance becomes until it reaches 100 percent with a population of two individuals. You ask them, "Do you like orange juice for breakfast?" From one person you get a categorical "yes." From the other, an equally vehement, "no." The scale swings from a total positive to a total negative. But what does this prove for the manufacturer of orange juice? Nothing. Ask 1,000 persons and you begin to get a trend.

But we cannot always have large sample populations. We have only twenty-nine students in a class. We want to measure them statistically against the normal distribution. How do we do this without small-population distortion? In 1907, William S. Gosset, statistician for the Guinness Brewing Co., published, under the pseudonym, "Student," the *Student's t distribution,* a statistical technique for measuring populations of fewer than thirty individuals known, somewhat erroneously, as the *t* test, for it is not a *test* at all, but merely a way of statistically obtaining a distribution of the data in small samples that can be measured against a parameter known as *the number of degrees of freedom.* Having determined the degrees of freedom, you head off for a table, usually in the back of your text, to find a value for *t*.

But here the water may be getting somewhat deep; for wading further into this statistical sea you are referred to any comprehensive statistical text and to its index, where you will undoubtedly find further information under the listing "Student's *t* distribution" or "*t* distribution," or "*t* test."

Nonparametric Statistics

Before we leave the discussion of the quantitative study, we should present briefly the nonparametric methods of dealing statistically with certain types of data. Thus far, we have assumed *that all populations and the samples drawn from them demonstrate certain parameters.* We have assumed that the mean and the standard deviation are common attributes of all data. This is not universally so. Not all data are parametric. Nature does not invariably behave as a Gaussian curve. Consider a page of print. It presents a binary world. No normal distribution there. Any given point on the page is either black or white. Human beings are either male or female, alive or dead. Just as we have a world of the bell-shaped curve, so also do we have the world of the sharp dichotomy: the world of either/or.

Sometimes the data world looks more like a stairway than a bell-shaped curve: the data occur at graduated elevations—data ranked above or below data in a well-escalated arrangement. Take a graduating class. When each student is ranked in academic subjects, Luis ranks first in English, fifteenth in mathematics. Other students have individual rankings up and down the academic staircase. A statistical system based upon the assumption of normal distributions, means, and standard deviations is simply not applicable to a ranked situation of this kind.

Data with the characteristics such as we have just been describing demand a statistical methodology that will recognize the particular characteristics of non-normal curve data and provide specialized approaches that will take the singular characteristics of such data into account. Such a methodology is found in *nonparametric statistics.*

The system of nonparametric statistics is less powerful than parametric techniques. By less powerful we mean that, in general, they require larger samples in order to yield the same level of significance. They also are less likely to reject the null hypothesis when it should be rejected or to differentiate between groups as sensitively as the parametric methods do.

The Principal Nonparametric Techniques

- *The Chi Square Test.* Perhaps the most commonly used nonparametric test, the *chi square (χ^2) test* is generally used in causal comparative studies. We also employ χ^2 in instances where we have a comparison between observed and theoretical frequencies or in testing the mathematical fit of a frequency curve to an observed frequency distribution. Chi square is applicable when we have two variables from independent samples, each of which is categorized in two ways. It is likewise valuable in analyzing data that are expressed as frequencies rather than as measurements. In electronics, for example, a sine wave has a certain wavelength amplitude. This can be measured in standard lengths. It also has a certain number of frequencies per second. For frequency evaluation in certain research instances, χ^2 is probably the most appropriate statistical technique.

There are, however, other nonparametric approaches that have specialized application. Although we cannot go into a discussion of these in detail, we here list the principal ones with brief comments as to their significances and usual applications. Any text dealing with nonparametric statistics will discuss these in full and indicate their application to the data.

- *The Mann-Whitney U-test* is the counterpart of the *t*-test in parametric measurements. It may be used in determining whether the medians of two independent samples differ from each other to a significant degree.

• *The Wilcoxon Matched Pairs, Signed-Rank Test* is employed to determine whether two samples differ from each other to a significant degree when there is a relationship between the samples.

• *The Wilcoxon Rank Sum Test* may be used in situations where measures are expressed as ranked data in order to test the hypothesis that the samples are from a common population whose distribution of the measures is the same as that of the samples.

• *The Kolmogorov-Smirnov Test* fulfills the function of χ^2 in testing goodness of fit and the Wilcoxon rank sum test in determining whether random samples are from the same population.

• *The Sign Test* is important in determining the significance of the differences between two correlated samples. The "signs" of the sign test are the algebraic plus and minus values of the difference of the paired scores. Where the difference between the paired scores favors the *X* variable a plus sign is given; those favoring the *Y* variable are assigned the minus designation. The null hypothesis postulates a 0 value with the pluses equaling the minuses. To test for significance between the plus and minus signs, χ^2 can be used.

• *The Median Test* is a sign test for two independent samples in contradistinction to two correlated samples, as is the case with the sign test.

• *The Spearman Rank Order Correlation,* sometimes called Spearman's rho (ρ) or Spearman's rank difference correlation, is a nonparametric statistic that has its counterpart in parametric calculations in the Pearson product moment correlation.

• *The Kruskal-Wallis Test* is sometimes known as the Kruskal-Wallace *H* test of ranks for *k* independent samples. The *H* in the title of the test stands for null hypothesis; and the *k* (from the German *klasse,* "class") for the classes or samples. The test looks for the significance of differences among three or more groups, and it has been developed along the same general lines as the Mann-Whitney *U*-test. The Kruskal-Wallis test is a one-way analysis of variance and is the nonparametric correspondent to the analysis of variance in parametric statistics. Its purpose is to determine whether *k* independent samples have been drawn from the same population.

• *The Kendall Coefficient of Concordance* is also variously known as Kendall's concordance coefficient *W* or the concordance coefficient *W*. It is a technique that can be used with advantage in studies involving rankings made by independent judges. To analyze the rankings, the Kendall coefficient will indicate the degree to which such judges agree in their assignment of ranks. The Kendall coefficient *W* is based on the deviation of the total of each ranking. To test the significance of *W*, we simply employ the null hypothesis and test it by employing the χ^2 technique.

• *The Corner Test.* A little-known test is the corner test, whose function is to test the hypothesis that two continuous variables are independent. The test is a graphical one. The data are plotted as for a conventional correlation study. Medians are drawn. The *X* median will be parallel to the *X* axis. A *Y* median is also drawn through the plotted data to divide them equally in a horizontal direction. The four quadrants are then assigned the conventional plus and minus signs. The plotted data falling within each quadrant thus become either positive or negative. Now, inspect the data in the four quadrants. Draw a line to the left and a line to the right, also similar lines above and below the median lines at the extremity of the lesser of each of the respective groups of data. The test of significance will be based upon the count of the number of points lying outside the lines marking the boundaries of the lesser groups of data. If a point lies beyond one of the demarcation lines, it is given a value of 1; if it lies beyond two of these lines, it rates a value of 2. The algebraic sum of all the outlying points is the test statistic. From it is computed the degree of association and the nature of that association.[9]

[9]A full explanation of the corner test is given in Albert Rickmers and Hollis N. Todd, *Statistics: An Introduction* (New York: McGraw-Hill, 1967), 403–05.

Tables 10.4 and 10.5, are summary tables of both parametric and nonparametric techniques applicable to testing *statistical* hypotheses. You may find them helpful in selecting the proper tool for the specific situation.

Looking Backward

At this juncture, after what has been a somewhat long and at times involved discussion, turn to the opening pages of this chapter and review there the purpose of this discussion: to probe data by means of statistics so that we may infer certain meanings that lie hidden within the data or discern the presence of certain potentials and dynamic forces that may be clues to areas that warrant further investigation.

It may also be helpful to review Figure 10.6, the map of the statistical landscape—the flowchart showing the organization of statistics; and the tables throughout the chapter. All of these may help you to see what this chapter has been about.

Practical Application

We derive a clear understanding of statistics and statistical procedures by seeing these in actual practice and by encountering them in the literature. To give you an opportunity to see more clearly some of the matters the following Practical Application will serve in two ways: (1) to apply some of the items covered in the chapter, and (2) to help you in clarifying some statistical aspects of your own proposal—if your research project is quantitative in its methodology.

Guide to the Management of Data for the Quantitative Study

If your research methodology falls within the area of procedure normally considered to belong to the analytical survey methodology, the following guide to the consideration and management of the data will help you with the necessary groundwork for such a study.

The Characteristics of the Data

1. Are the data ___ discrete or ___ continuous?

2. What are the characteristics of the data? Are they
- ___ nominal
- ___ ordinal
- ___ interval
- ___ ratio

3. What do you want to do with the data?
- ___ *Find a measure of central tendency? If so, which?* ______________
- ___ *Find a measure of dispersion? If so, which?* ______________
- ___ *Find a coefficient of correlation? If so, which?* ______________
- ___ *Estimate parameters? If so, which?* ______________
- ___ *Test the null hypothesis? If so, at what confidence level?* ______________
- ___ *Test the significance? If so, which?* ______________
- ___ *Other (specify)* ______________

4. With respect to correlational techniques, what are the characteristics of the variables?
Independent variable: (identify) ______________
Nature of the data? ______________
Dependent variable: (identify) ______________
Nature of the data? ______________
Correlational technique for dealing with these types of data: ______________

Table 10.4 Tests of Hypotheses

Scale	Hypothesis							
	Two independent samples have:		Two correlated samples have:	*k* independent samples have:		*k* correlated samples have:	Two variables are:	
	Equal variability	Same central tendency or proportion	Same central tendency	Equal variabilities	Same central tendency	Same central tendency	Uncorrelated or independent	Linerally related
Nominal		$P_1 - P_2$ is normally distributed with $\sigma_{D_p} = \sqrt{p_a q_a\left(\frac{1}{N_1} + \frac{1}{N_2}\right)}$			Chi-square test for equality of several sample proportions.		Chi-square test of independence. Likelihood-ratio chi-square. If $T = 0$, $1.3863NT$ has chi-square distribution with $(r - 1)(k - 1)$ degrees of freedom.	
Ordinal	Run test (also sensitive to differences in central tendency).	Run test (also sensitive to differences in variability). Median test. Rank-sums test.	Sign test.		Median test Kruskal-Wallis test.	Friedman test (sometimes called 'analysis of variance by ranks').	Contingency test of association. Test of hypothesis that $p_o = 0$.	
Internal and Ratio	F test. Assumes normality of populations.	$\tilde{\sigma}_{\bar{x}_1 - \bar{x}_2} = \tilde{\sigma}\sqrt{\frac{1}{N_1} + \frac{1}{N_2}}$ $\frac{\bar{x}_1 - \bar{x}_2}{\tilde{\sigma}_{\bar{x}_1 - \bar{x}_2}}$ has t-distribution with $N_1 + N_2 - 2$ degrees of freedom when samples are from normal populations with equal variances.	Wilcoxon Test for Paired Replicates. For large samples, or small samples from normal populations $\frac{\bar{D}}{sD/\sqrt{N-1}}$ has a t-distribution with $N - 1$ degrees of freedom.	Bartlett's Test for Homogeneity of Variance.	Analysis of variance. $\frac{\tilde{\sigma}^2_B}{\tilde{\sigma}^2_W}$ has F distribution if samples are from normal populations with equal variances.	Analysis of variance (two dimensional). Assumes normality and homogeneity of variance.	Test hypothesis that $\eta = 0$ by use of F ratio. Test hypothesis that $p = 0$ by use of F ratio or t-test.	Test hypothesis that $p = \eta$ by use of F ratio.

From *Measurement and Statistics: A Basic Test Emphasizing Behavioral Science*, by Virginia L. Senders. Copyright © 1958 by Oxford University Press, Inc. Reprinted by permission. (Modified at the direction of the author.)

Table 10.5 Classification of Statistical Techniques and Guide to Their Use

Number of Groups	Type of Analysis	Purpose	Type of Data: Categorical*	Rank-order†	Measured††
One	Univariate	Description	(1) One-way tables; bar, pie diagrams; modal class; conversion to proportions	(7) Array; ranking; cumulative frequencies and proportions	(13) Frequency distribution; histogram; frequency polygon; ogive; percentiles; averages; measures of variability, skewness, and kurtosis
		Inference	(2) Binomial test; chi-square goodness-of-fit test	(8) Kolmogorov-Smirnov goodness-of-fit test	(14) Normal curve theory; *z* and *t* tests; chi-square variance test
	Bivariate	Description	(3) Two-way tables; comparative diagrams; conditional and marginal proportions	(9) Bivariate arrays; rank-order correlation coefficient	(15) Scatter diagrams; prediction equations; Pearson correlation coefficient; standard error of estimate
		Inference	(4) Chi-square tests of independence and experimental homogeneity	(10) Testing significance of rank-order correlation coefficient	(16) Bivariate normal distribuiton; testing significance of Pearson coefficient
Two or *More*	Univariate	Description	(5) See cell 3	(11) Comparative tables and cumulative proportions	(17) See cell 13
		Inference	(6) See cell 4	(12) Kolmogorov-Smirnov two-sample test; Mann-Whitney U test	(18) *F* test of homogeneity of variance; analysis of variance

*Data that result from the application of a *nominal* scale of measurement.
†Data that result from the application of an *ordinal* scale of measurement.
††Data deriving from either an *interval or ratio* scale of measurement.

Reprinted by permission from C.M. Dayton and C.L. Stunkard, *Statistics for Problem Solving* (New York: McGraw-Hill, 1971), p. 10.

5. State clearly your rationale for planning to process the data as you have indicated you intend to do in sections 3 and 4.

The Interpretation of the Data

6. After you have treated the data statistically to analyze their characteristics, what will you then have? (Explain clearly and succinctly.)

7. Of what will your interpretation of the data from a research standpoint consist? What has the statistical analysis done to help solve any part of your research problem? (Explain precisely.)

8. What yet remains to be done before your problem (or any one of its subproblems) can be resolved?

9. What is your plan for carrying out this further interpretation of the data? (Explain clearly.)

Significant and Influential Research

"We were all kids of one big family!"

How often have you heard that expression? There are implications behind those words: that we all experienced the same things; that we all grew up under the same influences; that generally, under the skin, we were all pretty much alike. Don't you believe it! According to recent research—by Dr. Robert Plomin, a behavioral geneticist at Pennsylvania State University, and Dr. Denise Daniels, a psychologist at Stanford University, School of Medicine—environmental influences affecting the psychological development of the individual operate in a way quite different from the way most psychologists thought they worked.

It is probably a case of taking too much for granted, of drawing superficial conclusions from what seemed too obvious to be questioned. There's a lesson here for all researchers, the best of whom always question what seems too obvious to be questioned.

Dr. Daniels said, "All psychological theories point to the family as the basic unit of socialization. If so, you would expect children from the same family to be largely similar. But it is really quite the opposite. The assumption that the family environment operates the same for all children in it does not hold up."

To find similarities, we must delve deeper than the outward environmental influences. What similarities there are seem to come largely from shared genes rather than from shared environment. Dr. Daniels's research methodology centered around a comparison scale on which siblings compare themselves with one another on such factors as parental love, control, attention, favoritism, sibling jealousy, and popularity with peers. Several facts began to surface. The key differences in the family may be more obvious to the children themselves than to their parents. The differences, or the different perceptions of them by each individual, may be the source of friction within the family. When parents treat children differently, the children in turn will be more hostile to each other when they are alone.

The study seems to point to one overriding conclusion: Each sibling experiences a *different* family. Researchers are working on the problem, each from a different angle and emphasis: Drs. Daniels and Plomin; Dr. Gene Brody, a psychologist at the University of Georgia; Dr. Stella Chess, a psychiatrist at New York University Medical Center; and Dr. John Loehlin, at the University of Texas, whose studies have been on identical and fraternal twins. The research is broad and significant. The bibliography is too extensive to give in this chapter, but it appears in *The Journal of Personality and Social Psychology, Child Development,* and *Behavioral and Brain Sciences.* A look into the periodical indexes under any of the names mentioned will lead you to the research.

The Computer as a Tool of Research

Spreadsheets

We should talk of spreadsheets in a chapter dealing largely with statistics. Statistical research frequently demands an array of figures arranged in columns. This is a perfect situation for the spreadsheet.

A spreadsheet is an electronic worksheet with rows and columns. The typical electronic spreadsheet is large: 63 columns across, 254 rows down. Obviously, such a mammoth array cannot be displayed on a monitor screen, so only a part of the sheet, called a *window*, will be displayed at any one time. A window usually displays 12 columns and 20 rows. But you can move the window around to view data residing in any part of the spreadsheet.

The spreadsheet is a versatile tool. Any numbers displayed on the sheet can be added, subtracted, multiplied, or divided. Any value can be raised to any power, averages can be obtained, percentages taken, and frequently, according to the software package used, other functions can be added, such as trigonometric or statistical functions.

The way to determine if a spreadsheet will profit you in your calculations is to determine if you will be working with a table that has a vertical column of separate items, and if you will have a series of values for each item in the vertical column that will be appropriate for columnar display in succeeding columns (such as values for each month of the year or other stated designations). If so, a spreadsheet may solve some of your analysis problems. You should know, however, that spreadsheeting is not for all hardware. How much random-access memory (RAM) does your computer have?

This is not a tool that all researchers need, but we mention it here because for certain operations spreadsheeting is a versatile tool and fills a specific requirement.

Certain types of researchers will welcome the spreadsheet; others will find it superfluous. Business administration students, for instance, may find it most helpful, since it is a business-oriented tool. For mathematical relationships and calculations, for financial analyses, for cash-flow forecasting, investment analysis, budgeting, planning, engineering analysis, and similar applications the spreadsheet program may be a real boon. All leading microcomputer manufacturers sell either Lotus, Excel, or Multiplex, or lookalikes—and they all do the same job.

For Further Reading

(See also the Further Readings in the Statistics section at the end of chapter 2.)

Further Reading in General Statistics

Baum, P., and E. M. Scheuer. *Statistics Made Relevant: A Casebook of Real Life Examples.* New York: Wiley, 1981.

Box, George E. P., William G. Hunter, and J. Stuart Hunter. *Statistics for Experimenters: An Introduction to Design, Data Analysis, and Model Building.* New York: Wiley, 1978.

Brieman, Leo. *Statistics with a View toward Applications.* Boston: Houghton Mifflin, 1973.

Castle, Winifred M. *Statistics in Small Doses.* New York: Churchill Livingston, 1977.

Christensen, Howard B. *Statistics: Step-by-Step.* Boston: Houghton Mifflin, 1977.

Cole, F. L. O. "Content Analysis: Process and Application." *Clinical Nurse Specialist* 2(Spring, 1988): 53–7.

Dapkus, F. *Statistics One: A Text for Beginners.* Elmsford, NY: Collegium, 1979.

Fogiel, Max. *Statistics Problem Solver: A Supplement to Any Class Text.* New York: Research and Education Association, 1978.

Froelicher, E. S. S. "Understanding and Reducing Measurement Error." *Cardiovascular Nursing* 24 (November–December, 1988): 48.

Holm, K. "The Interface of Physiological and Psychological Variables. Editorial. *Cardiovascular Nursing* 25 (November–December, 1989): 35.

Klugh, Henry E. *Statistics: The Essentials for Research.* 2d ed. New York: Wiley, 1974.

Laczun, M. E. "Introduction to Quantitative Research and Analysis." *Journal of Post Anesthesia Nursing* 4 (February, 1989): 46–8.

Larsen, Richard J. and Donna F. Stroup. *Statistics in the Real World: A Book of Examples.* New York: Macmillan, 1976.

Mattson, Dale E. *Statistics: Difficult Concepts, Understandable Explanations.* St. Louis: C. V. Mosby, 1981.

Neave, H. R. *Statistics Tables.* Winchester, MA: Allen Unwin, 1977.

Ostle, Bernard, and Richard Mensing. *Statistics in Research.* Ames, IA: Iowa State University Press, 1975.

Rowntree, Derek. *Statistics Without Tears: A Primer for Non-Mathematicians.* New York: Scribner's, 1982.

Taylor, D. "Time Series Analysis: Use of Autocorrelation as an Analytic Strategy for Describing Pattern and Change." *Western Journal of Nursing Research* 12 (April 1990): 254–61.

Ukens, Ann S. *Statistics Today.* New York: Harper & Row, 1978.

Wonnacott, Thomas J., and Ronald J. Wonnacott. *Statistics: Discovering Its Power.* New York: Wiley, 1981.

Further Reading in the Behavioral Sciences

Johnson, M., and R. Liebert. *Statistics: Tool of the Behavioral Sciences.* Englewood Cliffs, NJ: Prentice-Hall, 1977.

Lindner, William A., and Rhoda Lindner. *Statistics for Students in the Behavioral Sciences.* Menlo Park, CA: Benjamin-Cummings, 1979.

Mendenhall, William, and Madeline Ramey. *Statistics for Psychology.* North Scituate, MA: Duxbury Press, 1977.

Palumbo, Dennis J. *Statistics in Political and Behavioral Science.* New York: Columbia University Press, 1977.

Further Reading in Biology and the Health Sciences

Bishop, O. N. *Statistics for Biology.* 2d ed. New York: Longman, 1981.

Bliss, Chester I. *Statistics in Biology.* 2 vols. New York: McGraw-Hill, 1967.

Broyles, Robert, and Colin Lay. *Statistics in Health Administration.* 2 vols. Rockville, MD: Aspen Systems Corporation, 1980.

Buncher, C. Ralph, and Jai Yeong Tsay. *Statistics in the Pharmaceutical Industry.* New York: Marcel Dekker, 1981.

Campbell, R. C. *Statistics for Biologists.* New York: Cambridge University Press, 1974.

Colton, Theodore. *Statistics in Medicine.* Boston: Little, Brown, 1975.

Finny, D. J. *Statistics for Biologists.* London: Methuen, 1980.

Goldstone, Leonard A. *Statistics in the Management of Nursing Services.* London: Pitman Books, Ltd., 1980.

Hammerton, Max. *Statistics for the Human Sciences.* New York: Longman, 1975.

Kviz, Frederick J., and Kathleen A. Knafl. *Statistics for Nurses: An Introductory Text.* Boston: Little, Brown, 1980.

Larsen, Richard J. *Statistics for the Allied Health Sciences.* New York: Merrill/Macmillan, 1975.

Mike, Valerie, and Kenneth E. Stanley. *Statistics in Medical Research: Methods and Issues with Applications in Cancer Research.* New York: Wiley, 1982.

Remington, R., and M. A. Schork. *Statistics with Applications to the Biological and Health Sciences.* Englewood Cliffs, NJ: Prentice-Hall, 1970.

Schefler, William C. *Statistics for the Biological Sciences.* Reading, MA: Addison-Wesley, 1979.

Von Fraunhofer, J. A., and J. J. Murray. *Statistics in Medical, Dental, and Biological Studies.* Montclair, NJ: Tri-Med Books (England), 1981.

Further Reading in Business, Economics, and Management

Ashford, John. *Statistics for Management.* Brookfield, VT: Renouf USA, 1977.

Ben Horim, Mosche, and Haim Levy. *Statistics: Decisions and Applications in Business and Economics.* New York: Random House, 1981.

Chao, Lincoln L. *Statistics for Management.* Monterey, CA: Brooks-Cole, 1980.

Clark, John J., and Margaret T. Clark. *Statistics Primer for Managers: How to Ask the Right Questions about Forecasting, Control, and Investment.* New York: Macmillan, 1982.

Davies, Brinley, and John Foad. *Statistics for Economics.* Exeter, NH: Heinemann Educational Books, 1977.

Fisher, Walter D. *Statistics Economized: Basic Statistics for Economics and Business.* Lanham, MD: University Press of America, 1981.

Haack, Dennis G. *Statistics Literacy: A Guide to Interpretation.* Boston: PWS, 1978.

Heitzman, William R., and Frederick W. Mueller. *Statistics for Business and Economics.* Boston: Allyn & Bacon, 1980.

Lapin, Lawrence L. *Statistics for Modern Business Decisions.* 3d ed. New York: Harcourt Brace Jovanovich, 1982.

Levin, Richard I. *Statistics for Management.* 2d ed. Englewood Cliffs, NJ: Prentice-Hall, 1981.

Mandel, B. J. *Statistics for Management: A Simplified Introduction to Statistics.* 4th ed. Baltimore: Dangary, 1977.

Mansfield, Edwin. *Statistics for Business and Economics.* New York: Norton, 1980.

Matlack, W. F. *Statistics for Public Policy and Management.* North Scituate, MA: Duxbury Press, 1980.

McClave, James T., and George Benson. *Statistics for Business and Economics.* 2d ed. Santa Clara, CA: Dellen, 1982.

Mendenhall, William, and James E. Reinmuth. *Statistics for Management and Economics.* 4th ed. North Scituate, MA: Duxbury Press, 1982.

Mills, Richard L. *Statistics for Applied Economics and Business.* New York: McGraw-Hill, 1977.

Plane, Donald R., and Edwin B. Oppermann. *Statistics for Management Decisions.* rev. ed. Plano, TX: Business Publications, 1981.

Sobol, Marion G., and Martin K. Starr. *Statistics for Business and Economics: An Action Learning Approach.* New York: McGraw-Hill, 1983.

Further Reading in Criminal Justice

Griffin, John I. *Statistics Essential for Police Efficiency.* Springfield, IL: Charles C. Thomas, 1972.

Further Reading in Education

Cohen, Louis, and Michael Holliday. *Statistics for Education.* New York: Harper & Row, 1979.

Crocker, A. C. *Statistics for the Teacher.* Atlantic Highlands, NJ: Humanities Press, 1974.

McIntosh, D. M. *Statistics for the Teacher.* 2d ed. Elmsford, NY: Pergamon Press, 1967.

Talmage, Harriet. *Statistics as a Tool for Educational Practitioners.* Berkeley, CA: McCutchan, 1976.

Townsend, Edward A., and Paul J. Burke. *Statistics for the Classroom Teacher.* New York: Macmillan, 1963.

White, David. *Statistics for Education with Data Processing.* New York: Harper & Row, 1973.

Further Reading in Geography

Ebdon, David. *Statistics in Geography: A Practical Approach.* Oxford, England: Blackwell, 1977.

Mandal, R. B. *Statistics for Geographers and Social Scientists.* Atlantic Highlands, NJ: Humanities Press, 1981.

Further Reading in Language and Linguistics

Anshen, Frank. *Statistics for Linguists.* Rowley, MA: Newbury House, 1978.

Further Reading in the Physical Sciences

Chatfield, Christopher. *Statistics for Technology: A Course in Applied Statistics.* 2d ed. New York: Methuen, 1978.

Martin, B. R. *Statistics for Physicists.* New York: Academic Press, 1971.

Schaeffer, Richard, and James McClave. *Statistics for Engineers.* North Scituate, MA: Duxbury Press, 1982.

Wine, Russell L. *Statistics for Scientists and Engineers.* Englewood Cliffs, NJ: Prentice-Hall, 1964.

Youmans, Hubert L. *Statistics for Chemistry.* New York:. Merrill/Macmillan, 1973.

Further Reading in the Social Sciences

Bohrnstedt, George W., and David Knoke. *Statistics for Social Data Analysis.* New York: Bantam, 1982.

Cohen, Louis, and Michael Holliday, *Statistics for the Social Sciences.* New York: Harper & Row, 1982.

Hagood, Margaret J., and Daniel O. Price. *Statistics for Sociologists.* New York: Holt, Rinehart & Winston, 1952.

Horwitz, Lucy, and Lou Ferleger. *Statistics for Social Change.* Boston: South End Press, 1980.

Iversen, Gudmund R. *Statistics for Sociology.* Dubuque, IA: William C. Brown, 1979.

Sharp, Vicki F. *Statistics for the Social Sciences.* Boston: Little, Brown, 1979.

Yeomans, Keith A. *Statistics for the Social Scientist.* Baltimore: Penguin, 1968.

CHAPTER 11

The Experimental Study

Progress is relative. We measure progress by noting the degree of change between what was and what is. And we attempt to account for the change by identifying the dynamics that have caused it. This concept is the experimental approach whose purpose is to keep "what was" unchanged, and to see how much "what is" has changed because of an extraneous influence to which we attribute whatever change there is. In brief, this is the research approach that we call the Experimental Method.

General Considerations

The experimental study is the last major methodological approach in research that we will consider. This methodology goes by various names: the experimental method, the cause and effect method, the pretest-posttest control group design, the laboratory method. By whatever name, the basic idea behind the experimental study is to attempt to account for the influence of a factor or factors conditioning a given situation. In its simplest form, the experimental study attempts to control the entire research situation, except for certain input variables that then become suspect as the cause of whatever change has taken place within the investigative design.

Underlying Concepts

The matter of *control* is so basic to the experimental study that we frequently refer to this means of searching for truth as the *control group-experimental group design.* At the outset, we assume that the forces and dynamics within both groups are equistatic. We begin, as far as possible, with *matched groups.* These groups are randomly selected and paired so that, insofar as possible within the limits of the crude evaluative instruments we have available (especially in the social and humanistic areas of study), each group will resemble the other in as many characteristics as possible, especially those that are critical to the experiment. Mathematically, we can represent the equivalent status of these groups at the beginning of the experiment as

$$\text{Experimental group} = \text{Control group}$$

Although we assume that both groups at the beginning of the experiment have identical characteristics, values, and status, perfect identity is more theoretical than real. In recognition of this fact, therefore, we employ the phrase *matched groups,* or we say that they are "groups matched on the basis of *x, y,* and *z.*" The *x, y,* and *z* are the qualitative parameters that provide the basis for matching.

A glance backward will bring into contrast the distinctive nature of the experimental study. Reviewing the various research methodologies, we see that each provides a unique way to handle the data that fall within its methodological boundaries: The historical study deals with the study of documents; the descriptive survey, with the study of observations; the quantitative study, with the investigation of data dynamics and interrelationships of these dynamics through appropriate statistical techniques. We will now look at the experimental study to see its characteristics.

The Characteristics of the Experimental Method

The experimental method deals with the phenomenon of *cause and effect.* We assess the cause and effect dynamics within a closed system of controlled conditions. The basic structure of this methodology is simple. We have two situations. We assess each to establish comparability. Then, we attempt to alter one of these by introducing into it an extraneous dynamic. We reevaluate each situation after the intervening attempt at alteration. Whatever change is noticed is presumed to have been caused by the extraneous variable. Basically, the experimental method is the method practiced in research laboratories.

We must clarify the difference between an *experiment* and the *experimental method.* They are not the same. An illustration will establish the distinction. Consider a problem that arose in the laboratory of Thomas Edison in the early days of the incandescent electric light. Edison had given his engineers the well-known tapering and rounded bulb for them to calculate its volume. They brought all their mathematical knowledge to play on the problem. When they reported to Edison, each of them had a different answer. Edison then went into his laboratory, drew a container of water, measured its volume, immersed the incandescent bulb in it, and snipped off the pointed glass tip. Water rushed into the bulb (because it was a vacuum), filling it completely. Edison then measured the difference between the water in the container after filling the bulb and subtracted that volume from the water in the container originally. The difference between the two was the cubic capacity of the bulb.

That was an experiment. It was not research, nor was Edison's method the experimental method of research. Had there been any factual meaning behind the experiment and had this meaning been discovered, the experiment would then have become a research experiment. As it was, the experiment merely determined a fact, and for that particular fact there was no further meaning.

Experimental research needs to be planned. We call this planning the *design of the experiment.* In experimental research, however, the word *design* has two distinct meanings. Because of this, the inexperienced researcher may frequently be confused. In one sense, the word *design* refers to *the propriety of the statistical analysis necessary to prepare the data for interpretation.*

Frequently students come to a professor, who advises them that they need the assistance of a statistician to help them with the "design" of their research. Pick up many texts in psychological, physical, or biological scientific research methodology and what you will find is essentially a statistics text. Hence, what *experimental design* means here is that the statistical techniques for analyzing the quantitative data must be properly selected and utilized in accordance with their nature. The meaning of the term in this sense is beyond the province of this text. This is not a text in statistical design. We have made reference to proper statistical approaches in the tables of the last chapter and elsewhere. Many statistical textbooks on experimental design are available, and you should refer to them as needed.

The word *design,* as it is employed in a purely research connotation, refers, of course, to *the total architectural plan, the tectonic structure of the research framework.* This goes far beyond the mere selection of statistical tools to process data, test hypotheses, or effect prediction.

We shall explore design in this sense further in this chapter. Where the term *experimental design* is used, it will mean, of course, the planning of the entire experimental approach to a research problem. The statistical aspects are only one phase in that total approach and merely prepare the data so that the researcher can better assess their meaning and interpret their significance.

Classification of Experimental Designs

Experimental designs have been variously categorized by different writers in the field of research. Perhaps the simplest of these is the dichotomized classification of Wise, Nordberg, and Reitz. They classify all experimental designs into two types: (1) *functional designs* and (2) *factorial designs.*[1] The difference between the two design types is whether the researcher is able to control the independent variable at will (the functional design) or whether, during the course of the experiment, the researcher *cannot* control the independent variable (the factorial design). Earlier, we indicated that the matter of control was fundamental to the experimental method. So basic is it, indeed, that its presence determines the nature of the variable. If the investigator has control over the variable and is able to manipulate it or change it at will, then we say that the variable is an *independent variable.* If, on the other hand, the investigator has no control over the variable and it occurs as the result of the influence of the independent variable, then that variable is known as the *dependent variable.*

To illustrate these two kinds of variables, we take a very simple situation. The investigator has a potentiometer connected to a voltage source and, by means of it and by turning a knob, is able to control the voltage that passes through it. The voltage is the *independent variable.* The potentiometer is in turn connected to a voltmeter. The deflection of the indicator hand on the face of the voltmeter *depends* upon the voltage potential, which is controlled by the investigator and is, thus, the *dependent* variable.

We do, however, experiment with factors and forces over which we have no control whatsoever. A person's reaction time, intelligence quotient, age—no investigator can control these.

A more conventional categorization of experimental designs has been made by others. Perhaps the most complete categorization has been made by Campbell and Stanley.[2] They divide experimental studies into four general types: (1) *pre-experimental designs,* (2) *true experimental designs,* (3) *quasi-experimental designs,* and (4) *correlational and ex post facto designs.*

So that we may see the experimental design configurations and the function of each within the context of the experimental method, we present in Table 11.1 a summary table of the experimental method, according to the schema outlined by Campbell and Stanley. We will now discuss each of the designs of the experimental method.

Pre-Experimental Designs

The One-Shot Case Study. The one-shot case study is probably the most primitive type of observational activity that might conceivably be termed research. For the studies that we will outline, we will employ a conventional symbolism: When a group, an individual, or an object is exposed to an experimental variable, the letter X will be used. The letter O will indicate an observation or measurement of the data.

The one-shot case study may, therefore, be represented by the following symbolic formula.

$$\text{Paradigm of Design I:} \qquad X \rightarrow O$$

This is the simplest and most naive experimental procedure. This is the method behind many superstitious folk beliefs. We see a child sitting on the damp earth in mid-April. The

[1]John E. Wise, Robert B. Nordberg, and Donald J. Reitz, *Methods of Research in Education* (Boston: D. C. Heath, 1967), 133–37.

[2]Donald T. Campbell and Julian C. Stanley, "Experimental and Quasi-Experimental Designs for Research on Teaching," in N. L. Gage, ed., *Handbook of Research on Teaching* (Chicago: Rand McNally, 1963), 171–246. Also published separately by Rand McNally, 1966.

Table 11.1 Summary of Experimental Methodology

Aim of the Research	Name of the Design	Paradigm*	Comments on the Research Design
		Pre-Experimental Designs	
To attempt to explain a consequent by an antecedent.	One-shot case study	$X \rightarrow O$	An approach that has spawned many superstitions and that is the least reliable of all experimental approaches.
To evaluate the influence of a variable.	One group pretest-posttest design	$O_1 \rightarrow X \rightarrow O_2$	A naive approach that relies upon supposition and coincidence in validating the conclusion.
To determine the influence of a variable on one group and not on another.	Static group comparison	Group I $X \rightarrow O_1$ Group II $- \rightarrow O_2$	Weakness lies in no examination of pre-experimental equivalence of groups. Conclusion is reached by naively comparing the performance of each group to determine the effect of a variable on one of them.
		True Experimental Designs	
To study the effect of an influence on a carefully controlled sample.	Pretest-posttest control group design	R -- [$O_1 \rightarrow X \rightarrow O_2$ $O_3 \rightarrow - \rightarrow O_4$	This design has been called by Mouly "the old workhorse of traditional experimentation." Borg and Gall suggest analysis of covariance as best statistical tool for analyzing the data.
To minimize the Hawthorne effect.	Solomon four-group design	R -- [$O_1 \rightarrow X \rightarrow O_2$ $O_3 \rightarrow - \rightarrow O_4$ $- \; X \rightarrow O_5$ $-- \rightarrow O_6$	This is an extension of the pretest-posttest control group design and probably the most powerful experimental approach. Data are analyzed by doing analysis of variance on posttest scores.
To evaluate a situation that cannot be pretested.	Posttest only control group design	R -- [$X \rightarrow O_1$ $- \rightarrow O_2$	To be used in situations that cannot be pretested. An adaptation of the last two groups in the Solomon four-group design. Randomness is critical. Probably simplest and best test for significance in this design is the t test.
		Quasi-Experimental Designs	
To investigate a situation where random selection and assignment are not possible.	Nonrandomized control group pretest-posttest design	$O_1 \rightarrow X \rightarrow O_2$ $O_3 \rightarrow - \rightarrow O_4$	One of the strongest and most widely used quasi-experimental designs. Differs from experimental designs because test and control groups are not equivalent. Comparing O_1 with O_3 pretest results will indicate degree of equivalency between experimental and control groups.

Table 11.1 *continued*

Aim of the Research	Name of the Design	Paradigm*	Comments on the Research Design
To determine the influence of a variable introduced only after a series of initial observations and only where one group is available.	Time series experimental design	$O_1 \rightarrow O_2 \rightarrow O_3 \rightarrow O_4 \rightarrow X \rightarrow O_5 \rightarrow O_6 \rightarrow O_7 \rightarrow O_8$	If substantial change follows introduction of variable then variable can be suspect as to the cause of the change. To secure more external validity, repeat the experiment in different places under different conditions.
To bolster the validity of the above design with the addition of a control group.	Control group time series design	$O_1 \rightarrow O_2 \rightarrow O_3 \rightarrow O_4 \rightarrow X \rightarrow O_5 \rightarrow O_6 \rightarrow O_7 \rightarrow O_8$ $O_1 \rightarrow O_2 \rightarrow O_3 \rightarrow O_4 \rightarrow - - \rightarrow O_5 \rightarrow O_6 \rightarrow O_7 \rightarrow O_8$	A variant of the above design by accompanying it with a parallel set of observations without the introduction of the variable—the experimental factor.
A variant of the above design with the purpose of controlling history in time designs.	Equivalent time-samples design	$[X_1 \rightarrow O_1] \rightarrow [X_0 \rightarrow O_2] \rightarrow [X_1 \rightarrow O_3] \rightarrow [X_0 \rightarrow O_4]$	This is an on-again, off-again design in which the experimental variable is sometimes present, sometimes absent. Gilbert Sax has extrapolated the design with two extensions (explained in the text).
	Correlational and Ex Post Facto Designs		
To seek for cause-effect relationships between two sets of data.	Causal-comparative correlational studies	$\overset{\longrightarrow}{\underset{\longleftarrow}{O_a = O_b}}$	A very deceptive procedure that requires much insight for its use. Causality cannot be inferred to be a *quid pro quo* merely because a positive and close correlation ratio exists.
To search backward from consequent data for antecedent causes.	Ex post facto studies 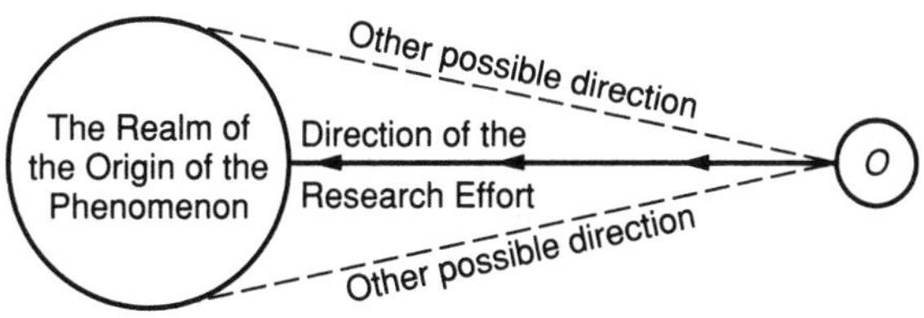		This approach is experimentation in reverse. Seldom is proof through data substantiation possible. Logic and inference are the principal tools of this design.

*The symbols in each paradigm will be explained fully in the discussion of each design type in the pages following.

next day he has a sore throat and a cold. We conclude that sitting on the damp earth causes one to catch cold. According to the above paradigm, the design of our "research" thinking is something like this:

X = exposure of child to cold, damp earth (*variable*) $\rightarrow$ O = observation that the child has a cold

This type of "research" is represented in such beliefs as: If you walk under a ladder, you will have bad luck; Friday the 13th is calamity day; 13 is a number to be avoided; a horseshoe above the doorway brings good fortune to the house. Someone observed a fact, then observed a following fact, and the two were linked together as cause and effect.

The One-Group Pretest-Posttest Design. The one-group pretest-posttest design is a type of experiment where a single group (1) has a pre-experimental evaluation, then (2) is influenced by the variable, and, finally, (3) is evaluated after the experiment. The paradigm for this type of research is represented as follows:

Paradigm for Design II: $O_1 \rightarrow X \rightarrow O_2$

A teacher wants to know how effective hearing a story read masterfully on a tape-recorder would be in improving the reading skills of her class. She selects a group of students, gives them a standardized reading pretest, exposes them to daily taped readings, and tests them with a variant form of the same standardized test to determine how much progress they have made because of (so she supposes) the tape-recorder technique.

An agronomist hybridizes two strains of corn. He finds that the hybrid strain is more disease-resistant and has a better yield than either of the two parent types. He concludes that the hybridization process has made the difference.

The Static Group Comparison. The static group comparison is a familiar control group–experimental group procedure. It is represented by a paradigm as follows:

Paradigm for Design III: Random Group Selection

Group I	$X \rightarrow O_1$
Group II	$— \rightarrow O_2$

Here is a design in which two randomly selected groups are designated by the dictates of chance, one to be a control group, the other to be the experimental group. The experimental group is exposed to variable *X*; the control group is not. Control groups isolated from the experimental factor are represented in the paradigms as with Group II above. At the close of the experiment, both groups are evaluated, and a comparison is made between the evaluation values of each group to determine what has been the effect of factor *X*. In this design, no attempt is made to obtain or examine the pre-experimental equivalence of the comparison groups.

These three designs, although commonly employed in many research projects reported in scholarly journals, are loose in structure and leave much to be desired in terms of factors that, not being controlled, could inject bias into the total research design.

True Experimental Designs

In contrast to the somewhat crude designs that we have been discussing to this point, the *true experimental designs* offer a greater degree of control and refinement and a greater insurance of both *internal* and *external validity*. These are new terms. They have nothing to do with the internal and external evidence with respect to historical research, which we discussed in Chapter 9.

With experimental designs, *internal validity* is the basic minimum without which any experiment is uninterpretable.[3] The question that the researcher must answer is whether the experimental treatment did, indeed, make a difference in the experiment.

External validity asks the question, how generalizable is the experiment? To what populations, settings, treatment variables, and measurement variables can the effect, as observed in the experiment, be generalized?[4]

Of the two types of validity, internal validity is certainly the more important insofar as the integrity of the study is concerned. The following suggested designs are those that are more likely to be strong in both types of validity, which is certainly the aim of every experimental researcher.

[3]Campbell and Stanley, "Experimental and Quasi-Experimental Designs," p. 175.
[4]Campbell and Stanley, "Experimental and Quasi-Experimental Designs," p. 175.

As we emphasized so strongly in the discussion of the descriptive survey method, randomization is one of the greatest guarantees of validity. In each of the three designs that follow, randomization is a necessary and constant factor in the selection of all groups, both experimental and control. In the paradigms, randomization will be indicated by the letter *R.*

The Pretest-Posttest Control Group Design. The pretest-posttest control group design is, as Mouly remarks, the "old workhorse of traditional experimentation."[5] In it, we have the experimental group and the control group carefully chosen through appropriate randomization procedures. The experimental group is evaluated, subjected to the experimental variable, and reevaluated. The control goup is isolated from all experimental variable influences and is merely evaluated at the beginning and at the end of the experiment. A more optimal situation can be achieved if the researcher is careful to match the experimental against the control group and vice versa for identical correspondences. Certainly, where matching is effected for the factor being studied, the design is thereby greatly strengthened. For example, if we are studying the effect of reading instruction on student IQ levels, wisdom would dictate that the members of both the control and experimental groups should be selected, as nearly as possible, so that a one-to-one correspondence with IQ scores be achieved.

The paradigm for the pretest-posttest control group design is as follows:

$$\text{Paradigm for Design IV:}\quad R\text{——}\left[\begin{array}{l} O_1 \rightarrow X \rightarrow O_2 \\ \\ O_3 \rightarrow \text{—} \rightarrow O_4 \end{array}\right.$$

The bracketing of both groups shows that *R*, the randomization process, is common to both groups. The *R*—— shows that before separation these two randomized samples were kept isolated from the influence of the experimental variable *X*. O_1 and O_2 are the two evaluations of the experimental group, before and after its exposure to the experimental variable *X*. O_3 and O_4 are the evaluations of the control group.

Campbell and Stanley indicate that good experimental design is separable from the use of statistical tests of significance; but because this is such a common design in the experimental methodology, researchers often use incorrect statistical procedures in an effort to analyze such data. Borg and Gall caution against this and recommend that the best statistical method to use is analysis of covariance, in which the posttest means are compared using the pretest means as the covariate.[6]

The Solomon Four-Group Design. In 1949, R. L. Solomon proposed an "extension" of the control group design, a refinement on the previous design discussed.[7] For the first time, consideration was given to a design that emphasized factors of external validity.

The design is obviously an "extension" of Design IV, as is seen from analyzing the following paradigm:

$$\text{Paradigm for Design V:}\quad R\text{——}\left[\begin{array}{l} O_1 \rightarrow X \rightarrow O_2 \\ O_3 \text{ —} \rightarrow \text{— } O_4 \\ \text{— } X \rightarrow O_5 \\ \text{— —} \rightarrow O_6 \end{array}\right. \quad \text{"extension"}$$

The fact that the pretest disappears in groups 3 and 4 constitutes a distinct advantage. It enables researchers to generalize to groups that have not received the pretest in cases where they may suspect that the pretest has had no adverse effect on the experimental treatment. It removes a kind of Hawthorne effect from the experiment. A group of subjects is pretested.

[5]George J. Mouly, *The Science of Educational Research,* 2d ed. (New York: Van Nostrand Reinhold, 1970), 336.
[6]Walter R. Borg and Meredith D. Gall, *Educational Research: An Introduction,* 2d ed. (New York: David McKay, 1971), 383.
[7]R. L. Solomon, "An Extension of Control Group Design," *Psychological Bulletin* 46 (1949): 137–50.

The question now is, "What effect does the pretesting have?" It may provide them with additional motivation to do well under experimental conditions. It may contaminate the effect of the experimental variable. The "extension" takes care of these contingencies.

The Hawthorne effect is named for a series of research studies conducted during the 1920s and 1930s at the Western Electric Company's Hawthorne plant near Chicago. It is an important series because many textbooks cite them as central in the historical development of industrial or organizational psychology. In its simplest form, the Hawthorne effect states that any workplace change, such as a research study of all or some employees, makes people feel a heightened degree of importance and thereby improves their efficiency and productivity. In other words, people alter their behavior when they know they're being observed. There were five phases to the Hawthorne studies. The Hawthorne effect is reported at length in the *Encyclopedia of Psychology*, Raymond J. Corsini, editor, NY: Wiley, 1984, pp. 95–96.

In terms of experimental designs, the Solomon four-group design is probably our most powerful experimental approach. The data are analyzed by doing an analysis of variance of the posttest scores. This rigorous bivariate structure does require, however, considerably larger samples and demands much more energy on the part of the researcher to pursue it. Its principal value is in eliminating pretest influence, and where such elimination is desirable, the design is unsurpassed.

The Posttest-Only Control Group Design. We come now to the last of the generally employed true experimental designs. Some researchers, especially those in education, psychology, and the social sciences, think that the phrase *pretest-posttest* is used so habitually that they cannot imagine sloughing off the first half of the phrase and having anything left in terms of scientific research.

Some life situations, however, defy pretesting. You cannot pretest the forces in a thunderstorm or a hurricane; you cannot pretest growing crops or growing children. These phenomena happen only once. The design here proposed may be considered as the last two groups of the Solomon four-group design—the "extension" part. The paradigm for the posttest-only approach is:

$$\text{Paradigm for Design VI:}\quad R \text{——} \left[\begin{array}{l} X \rightarrow O_1 \\ \\ \text{—} \rightarrow O_2 \end{array}\right.$$

To test for significance in this design, the t test would probably be the simplest and best. Randomness is critical in the posttest-only design and should be carefully considered as an important element in the success of employing such an approach.

Quasi-Experimental Designs

Thus far in the experimental designs, we have been emphasizing the importance of randomness of group composition. Life occasionally presents situations where random selection and assignment are not possible. Experiments carried on under such conditions must rely upon designs called *quasi-experimental designs*. In such designs, it is imperative that the researcher be thoroughly aware of the specific variables the design fails to control and take these into account in the interpretation of the data.

The Nonrandomized Control Group Pretest-Posttest Design. The nonrandomized control group pretest-posttest design configuration is similar to the first of the true experimental designs that we discussed, except for the lack of randomization:

$$\text{Paradigm for Design VII:}\quad \left[\begin{array}{l} O_1 \rightarrow X \rightarrow O_2 \\ \\ O_3 \rightarrow \text{—} \rightarrow O_4 \end{array}\right.$$

This design is not to be confused with the pretest-posttest control group design (Design IV), in which the composition of the groups is randomly chosen. The researcher might well consider using Design VII in situations where the true experimental designs (Designs IV, V, and VI) are not feasible.

To minimize the differences that might exist between the experimental and the control groups, the researcher might attempt to match the two groups as closely as possible (and on as many variables as possible) in a kind of quasi-randomization before beginning the experiment.

Again, the researcher might consider, if feasible, consolidating the so-called control group and the so-called experimental group into one amalgamated group and from this supergroup randomly dividing the total number of students into two groups. One of these may then be designated as the control group, and the other as the experimental group. Still another way to compensate for initial differences, as suggested by Borg and Gall, is by the analysis of covariance technique. Analysis of covariance reduces the effects of initial group differences statistically by making compensating adjustments of final means on the dependent variable.

The Time-Series Experiment. The time-series experiment consists of taking a series of evaluations and then introducing a variable or a new dynamic into the system, after which another series of evaluations is made. If a substantial change results in the second series of evaluations, we may reasonably assume that the cause of the difference in results was the factor introduced into the system. This design has the configuration shown in the following paradigm:

Paradigm for Design VIII: $O_1 \rightarrow O_2 \rightarrow O_3 \rightarrow O_4 \rightarrow X \rightarrow O_5^* \rightarrow O_6^* \rightarrow O_7^* \rightarrow O_8^*$

In this paradigm, the O^* indicates that these observations are different in character from those in the series before the introduction of the variable.

This is the design that was formerly widely used in the physical and the biological sciences. The classic discovery of Sir Alexander Fleming that *Penicillium notatum* could inhibit staphylococci is an example of this type of design. Dr. Fleming observed the growth of staphylococci on a culture plate *n* number of times. Then, unexpectedly, a culture plate containing well-developed colonies of staphylococci was contaminated with the spores of *Penicillium notatum.* Dr. Fleming observed that the colonies in the vicinity of the mold seemed to undergo dissolution. The experiment was repeated with the bacillus and the mold in company with each other. Each time the observation was the same: no staph germs near the mold. These were the O_5, O_6, O_7, O_8 of the paradigm.

The weakness of this design is in the probability that a major event may enter the system unrecognized along with, before, or after the introduction of the experimental variable. The effects of this extraneous factor are likely to be confounded with those of the experimental factor, and the wrong attribution of the cause for the effect observed may be made.

Control Group, Time Series. A variant of the time-series design is one that accompanies it with a parallel set of observations, but without the introduction of the experimental factor. This design would, then, take on a configuration like the following:

Paradigm for Design IX:

$$O_1 \rightarrow O_2 \rightarrow O_3 \rightarrow O_4 \rightarrow X \rightarrow O_5 \rightarrow O_6 \rightarrow O_7 \rightarrow O_8$$

$$O_1 \rightarrow O_2 \rightarrow O_3 \rightarrow O_4 \rightarrow - \rightarrow O_5 \rightarrow O_6 \rightarrow O_7 \rightarrow O_8$$

Such a design tends to assure greater control for internal validity. The advantage of a design of this construction is that it adds one further guarantee toward internal validity in drawing conclusions with respect to the effect of the experimental factor.

Equivalent Time-Samples Design. A variant of the previous design is the equivalent time-samples design. The object of its construction is to control history in time designs. The intervening experimental variable is sometimes present, sometimes absent. Suppose we have a class in astronomy. One approach is to teach astronomy through audiovisual materials; another is to teach the subject by means of a textbook. An equivalent time-samples design of the teaching method for this class might look like the following:

Paradigm for Design X: $[X_1 \rightarrow O_1] \rightarrow [X_0 \rightarrow O_2] \rightarrow [X_1 \rightarrow O_3] \rightarrow [X_0 \rightarrow O_4]$

In this paradigm, X_1 indicates the time when the audiovisual approach was used, and X_0 the time when the textbook approach was used. We see also that the instructional cells are such that we can compare observations such as O_1 with O_3, and O_2 with O_4.

Gilbert Sax has suggested two variants of this basic design.[8] One utilizes two variables in the study, so that the schematic of the design looks like this:

Paradigm for Design X_a:
$[X_1 \rightarrow O_1] \rightarrow X_0 \rightarrow O_2 \rightarrow (X_2 \rightarrow O_3) \rightarrow X_0 \rightarrow O_4 \rightarrow [X_1 \rightarrow O_5] \rightarrow X_0 \rightarrow O_6 \rightarrow (X_2 \rightarrow O_7)$

If pursued over a long enough time span, some multivariate comparisons might be made. For example, in the preceding sequence, we could

Compare	*With*	*To Explore Variable*
O_1	O_5	X_1
O_2	O_6	X_0
O_3	O_7	X_2

Whereas in the preceding design, Sax introduces a second variable in the time-samples design, he goes even further to suggest an equivalent *materials* design:

Paradigm for Design X_b:
$[M_a \rightarrow X_1 \rightarrow O] \rightarrow [M_b \rightarrow X_0 \rightarrow O] \rightarrow [M_c \rightarrow X_0 \rightarrow O] \rightarrow [M_c \rightarrow X_1 \rightarrow O] \ldots$

Sax comments on this design: "This design is exactly the same as the equivalent time-sampling design except that the different materials are introduced throughout the course of the experiment. Assuming that these materials are equivalent, experimental controls would seem to be adequate."[9]

Correlational and Ex Post Facto Designs

Correlational designs are usually attempts to establish cause-effect relationships between two sets of data. We might represent the situation by the following diagram:

$$O_a \underset{\leftarrow}{\overset{\rightarrow}{\neq}} O_b$$

Correlational studies are always particularly hazardous. So often researchers think that if they can show a positive correlation between two factors that *they deem to be related,* then they can *assume* causality (i.e., that one factor is the cause of the other). This is erroneous reasoning. The fact that one can demonstrate a statistically positive correlation between two sets of data in no way implies any causality between them. Remember the Florida orange crop and the elephant population of Thailand in chapter 10!

[8]Gilbert Sax, *Empirical Foundations of Educational Research* (Englewood Cliffs, NJ: Prentice-Hall, 1968), 363.
[9]Sax, *Empirical Foundations,* 363.

The preceding diagram indicates the possibilities within any correlational situation. We have indicated the observed data with respect to each factor as O_a and O_b. Now, given two variables of this type, with O_a as the independent variable, three conclusions might be drawn with respect to these data:

1. O_a has caused O_b: $O_a \rightarrow O_b$
2. O_b has caused O_a: $O_a \leftarrow O_b$
3. Some third variable is responsible for both O_a and O_b: $O_a \neq O_b$

Perhaps some of the difficulty with the causal-comparative correlational studies has been the fact that we have failed to recognize the structure of the correlational factors with which we work. We have a tendency to simplify. Especially in a research endeavor, we think of a certain effect as having *a* cause when, in fact, because of the complexity of many situations, we are not dealing with *a* cause for a particular phenomenon but with *a constellation of causes,* all of which may contribute to a greater or lesser degree to causing the phenomenon. Arbitrarily selecting any two (or even several) factors for a given phenomenon and then attempting to ascribe the cause of the phenomenon to the limitation of *our selection of causative factors* may be both irrational and foolhardy, especially in the face of extremely complex problems, whose tributaries of causality may spread far beyond anything that we have conceived as being remotely relevant to the problem and its co-related data.

Correlation is too simple an answer for most of the complex realities of life, and its simplistic approach disarms the researcher. It is an extremely deceptive tool, and one that the researcher needs to employ with the utmost caution.

Ex Post Facto Studies. The ex post facto study belongs to a no man's land in the discipline of research. Although it is usually considered under the heading of experimentation, it has little that is experimental about it. We indicated in the early pages of this chapter that control was the one condition that was characteristic of the experimental method. But after an event has happened, how can it be controlled? Mouly asserts that

> A relatively questionable quasi-experimental design is the *ex post facto* experiment, in which a particular characteristic of a given group is investigated with a view to identifying its antecedents. This is experimentation in reverse: instead of taking groups that are equivalent and exposing them to different treatment with a view to promoting differences to be measured, the *ex post facto* experiment begins with a given effect and seeks the experimental factor that brought it about. The obvious weakness of such an "experiment" is that we have no control over the situations that have already occurred and we can never be sure of how many other circumstances might have been involved.[10]

Strictly because of the lack of the control element, the methodology may be somewhat difficult to classify. Yet it is a method that pursues truth and seeks the solution of a problem through the analysis of data. Science has no difficulty with such a methodology. Medicine uses it widely in its research activities. Physicians discover a pathological situation, then inaugurate their search "after the fact." They sleuth into antecedent events and conditions in order to discover the cause for the illness.

The research that has gone on in laboratories with respect to the moon rocks is purely ex post facto research—so much "post" indeed that the research is separated from the causal fact by millions and even billions of years. Research that inquires into the origin of the universe is this type of methodology. Yet no one will deny that this is research, that it is oriented to specific problems, supported by specific data, and given direction by underlying hypotheses.

[10]George J. Mouly, *The Science of Educational Research,* 2d ed. (New York: Van Nostrand Reinhold, 1970), 340.

Figure 11.1 The Ex Post Facto Paradigm

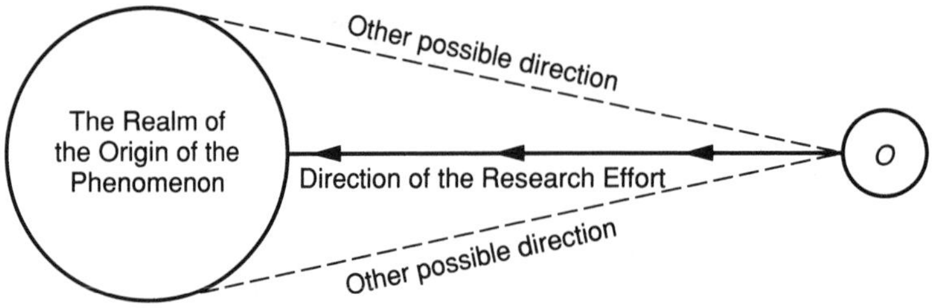

Ex post facto research might be adequately represented by the diagram shown in Figure 11.1.

The entry to the diagram is at the right-hand side. Here is where the researcher encounters the observed fact (O). That observed fact originated in a much larger area of events, which is represented by the larger circle at the left: the Realm of the Origin of the Phenomenon, of which the observed fact is but a small part. It is from the area of the observed fact that researchers must formulate all their hypotheses and aim their research effort. Because of the disparity between the size of the observed instance and the expanse of the possibility out of which the observed fact may have arisen, it is always possible that the direction of the research effort in ex post facto studies may lead nowhere.

We seek the cause of a disease, for instance. Our efforts may come to naught. So vast is the realm of the origin of the phenomenon and so miniscule the single observed fact that to attempt to construct a nexus of cause and effect and to extract meaning from the situation may be very difficult indeed. A cell begins to multiply spontaneously, a neoplasm results, the neoplasm metastasizes. The problem facing the cancer research team is an ex post facto one. What caused the cell to grow inordinately at first? The cytological complexity of the cell is such that careful as the aim of our research effort may be, we are like hunters drawing the bead of a rifle on a little bird, flitting in a thicket a mile away. We are indeed doing, as Mouly has suggested, "experimentation in reverse."

Conclusion

Let us conclude this broad section of the book, which has dealt generally with methodology, with a word about methodologies other than those we have been discussing here. In any new area—and research is a relatively new academic discipline—there is always confusion of terminology and many names for the same process.

The methodologies that we have suggested in this chapter have been generic ones within which other approaches can be accommodated. These are sometimes discussed separately as discrete methodologies in themselves. Inspected closely, you will usually find that these minor methodologies take on definite characteristics of the broader forms discussed here.

One author, for example, indicates that predictive methods are a separate type of methodology.[11] But we have chosen to discuss prediction as an aspect of analytical statistics and to consider it under the quantitative study. Others have decided to include the case study method as a discrete methodology, but because it is an approach that keeps observational details of the behavior of one or more individuals, we have deemed it appropriate to include the discussion of this research approach under the heading of the descriptive survey study. Still other writers have chosen to indicate other methodologies: the cross-cultural method, the developmental method, the causal-comparative method, the correlational method, the statistical method, and even the so-called philosophic method.

[11] Mouly, *The Science of Educational Research*, 357–76.

You should not be disturbed, therefore, if you find some disagreement and some discrepancy in the terminology and organization of the discipline of research. Some academic areas, notably the physical and natural sciences, and English and the languages, do not have a discrete and identifiable methodology associated with their research efforts; other areas such as education, psychology, nursing and the social sciences have a well-defined and recognized academic discipline of research that is found in the curriculum as educational research, psychological research, nursing research, or social research.

Research, in a very real sense, is a new discipline. It is also a chaotic discipline. We pointed out in the first chapter the multiple meanings that the word *research* has. It is used to mean all things to all people. Little wonder then that the divisions, the discussions within the larger framework, the terminology, the basic viewpoints, and individual opinions should differ so widely. Unsettledness is characteristic of youth; this is true of both young people and young disciplines. Some writers on research do not mention any discrete methodologies. Many think of statistics as being synonymous with research. Some will quarrel violently with some positions that are taken and some of the concepts that are articulated in this book. This may not be too serious. It is but an indication of the growing pangs of a discipline that is as yet very young and of indecisive mind. So long as we are fair in our judgments and respect the honest convictions of others and are willing to consider *both* sides of any question, little harm can come from sincere differences of viewpoint.

Practical Application

1. You have a pretest-posttest control group design. When you have the statistical data collected, what statistical treatment of the data would be the recommended procedure to use?

2. Researchers talk so much about the importance of the pretest in the pretest-posttest design experiment. Name ten instances where life phenomena do not lend themselves to pretesting techniques.

3. In such instances as those cited above, indicate how you would employ the experimental method of research to resolve problems associated with them.

4. We have cited the instance of Fleming and experimentation with penicillin as an example of the

$$O_1 \rightarrow O_2 \rightarrow O_3 \rightarrow O_4 \rightarrow X \rightarrow O_5 \rightarrow O_6 \rightarrow O_7 \rightarrow O_8$$

design. Name some other experimental situations that would be appropriate for testing by the same design structure.

5. You have two types of material (conventional textbook and programmed textbook). You wish to test experimentally the effectiveness of the use of the one type of material as against that of the other type. Indicate what experimental research design you would employ and give the procedure in paradigm form.

Significant and Influential Research

Research that cost $4.4 million, covered a six-year period, and involved 22,071 male physicians aged 40 to 84, promises to be a most significant and influential project for a great segment of the American population in danger of heart attack. This was a double-blind, randomly selected population assigned to receive one of four types of treatment. Two research studies were being run with the same population of volunteers: one investigated the effect of taking a five-grain aspirin tablet every other day for the prevention of a heart attack, and the other investigated the effect of taking beta carotene for the prevention of cancer.

In the aspirin study, half of the physicians took a 325 mg aspirin tablet every other day, and the other half received a placebo. The results seemed to indicate that the "study provides the first conclusive evidence that aspirin will reduce the risk of fatal and nonfatal heart attacks in otherwise healthy men. After an average of 4.8 years of follow-up, the total number of myocardial infarctions among physicians who had been taking aspirin had been reduced by nearly half." With data like these, the monitoring board of the study decided that the results were sufficiently compelling to terminate the study and issue a preliminary report. That report appeared in the January 28, 1988, *New England Journal of Medicine* (vol. 318, no. 4, pages 245–46). The report is short. We will reprint it here in its entirety, with footnotes. The concluding remarks of the preliminary study justify its inclusion here as "significant and influential research": "If the highly promising preliminary results withstand the test of subsequent full reporting and further peer review, the Physicians' Health Study will be regarded as a milestone in the continuing struggle against myocardial infarction."

*ASPIRIN FOR THE PRIMARY PREVENTION OF MYOCARDIAL INFARCTION**

Under the somewhat ill-defined rubric "Special Report," we publish in this week's issue a preliminary report from the Physicians' Health Study, a double-blinded, controlled trial of aspirin in the prevention of cardiovascular disease and of beta carotene in the prevention of cancer.[1]

After more than 59,000 volunteers were screened, 22,000 male U.S. physicians 40 to 84 years of age were entered in the trial and randomly assigned to receive one of four treatments: (1) buffered aspirin (325 mg) and beta carotene (50 mg), (2) buffered aspirin and beta carotene placebo, (3) aspirin placebo and beta carotene, and (4) aspirin placebo and beta carotene placebo. Each type of pill, active or placebo, was given on alternate days, so that all participants received a single dose of either an active agent or a placebo each day. After an average of 4.8 years of follow-up, the total number of myocardial infarctions among the physicians taking aspirin had been reduced by nearly half. Strokes, on the other hand, were slightly, although not significantly, more numerous among the aspirin takers. Aspirin had no effect on the total number of vascular deaths or deaths from all causes. When the numbers of important vascular events were combined (nonfatal myocardial infarctions plus nonfatal strokes plus vascular deaths from all causes), those receiving aspirin still had a significant 23 percent reduction in risk.

Given these findings, an independent board that had been monitoring the data recommended last month that the aspirin component of the trial be halted (but not the beta carotene component) and all participants be promptly notified by mail of the results. The board also recommended that a preliminary summary of the essential aspirin data be published immediately (preferably when the participants were notified), to be followed as soon as possible by a detailed report. The article in this issue represents the first of these reports. Results have also been mailed this week to all physicians participating in the trial. The final

*Arnold S. Relman, M.D., *The New England Journal of Medicine* 318 (January 28, 1988).

[1]The Steering Committee of the Physicians' Health Study Research Group. Preliminary report: findings from the aspirin component of the ongoing Physicians' Health Study. N Engl J Med 1988: 318:262–4.

report on the aspirin part of the trial will be prepared for publication within the next few months, but the authors hope to continue their study of beta carotene until the originally scheduled end of the trial in 1990.

Has the Physicians' Health Study been properly designed, conducted, and analzyed, and can the results be taken at face value? The preliminary report suggests that this is a meticulous trial, but we shall have to wait for the full report to be sure. However unlikely it appears to be in this case, a clinical trial of such magnitude and complexity, particularly one that depends so heavily on reporting by participants, could be flawed in ways not immediately apparent in a preliminary report. Yet, so clear an effect of aspirin on the incidence of myocardial infarction is unlikely to be explained by methodological error.

These considerations raise other questions: Were the investigators right to terminate the aspirin part of the study, and was it necessary to publish a preliminary report? The cardiovascular mortality in this population of physicians was much lower than would be expected in the general U.S. male population, and critics may argue that there was no urgent need to terminate the study or notify participants, since the risks were so small. I believe the investigators' decision was correct; the results to date appear to show decisively that aspirin greatly reduced the incidence of myocardial infarction in their subjects and delay in notifying them could hardly have been justified. Furthermore, the unexpectedly low cardiovascular mortality rate among the participants in the study made it highly improbable that a significant effect of aspirin on this end point could have been detected by the end of the trial, so no definitive answer to this question would have been gained by waiting. And if the 22,000 participants were to be notified, why not make the information available simultaneously to all physicians through publication in a journal? Without formal publication, the news would still have circulated widely, but probably not without inaccuracies and misinterpretation. Far better to have the data on the record, available to all.

Assuming that the major findings of this study are basically correct, what therapeutic conclusions can be drawn? Do the results now justify the widespread use of aspirin for the primary prevention of myocardial infarction? Any answer at this time must be tentative and carefully qualified. The results of this study were obtained in a highly selected population: male physicians with no history of myocardial infarction, stroke, or transient ischemic attacks and with no contraindications to the use of aspirin. Those with liver or renal disease, gout, or peptic ulcer were also excluded. Furthermore, all those who could not tolerate aspirin or comply with the study protocol during a four-month preliminary period were eliminated from the study before randomization. The trial results provide good reason to consider using aspirin in patients meeting those criteria, but they do not demonstrate the value and safety of aspirin in the general population—particularly in those at risk for hemorrhagic strokes or other hemorrhagic complications of aspirin therapy.

A recent randomized trial of aspirin (500 mg daily) in some 5000 British physicians[2] showed no significant effect on the incidence of first myocardial infarction. However, the 95 percent confidence limits were wide, and the smaller number of subjects as well as the larger dosage in the British trial may well account for the difference between its results and those reported in this issue.

A recent meta-analysis of all published trials of aspirin (and other anti-platelet agents) in the secondary prevention of vascular events among patients with a history of vascular disease[3] seems to confirm the value of this intervention in such patients. But secondary and primary prevention are not necessarily equivalent, and a final judgment on the general prophylactic use of aspirin in apparently healthy subjects cannot yet be made with any confidence.

If its highly promising preliminary results withstand the test of subsequent full reporting and further peer reviews, the Physicians' Health Study will be regarded as a milestone in the continuing struggle against myocardial infarction. That it may still leave many important questions unresolved should not diminish the importance of its achievement.

[2]Peto R, Gray R, Collins R, et al. A randomized trial of the effects of prophylactic daily aspirin among male British doctors. Br Med J (in press).

[3]Anti-Platelet Trialists Collaboration. Secondary prevention of vascular disease by prolonged anti-platelet therapy. Br Med J (in press).

The Computer as a Tool of Research

Its Use in Various Disciplines

We have already explored the use of the computer as a tool of research in historical research and in the humanities. But there are many disciplines that are experimenting with ways to use the computer for their own purposes. Below is a brief bibliography of the use of the computer in various other academic disciplines.

Nelson, Allen H. "Computer Use and Nursing Research: Application of Micro-Computers in Nursing Research." *Western Journal of Nursing Research* 8 (February 1986): 117–21.

Moore, Richard. *Introduction to the Use of Computer Packages for Statistical Analysis.* Englewood Cliffs, NJ: Prentice-Hall, 1978.

OSIRIS III: An Integrated Collection of Computer Programs for the Management and Analysis of Social Science Data. Ann Arbor, MI: Institute for Social Research, 1973.

Patton, Peter C., and Renee A. Holoien, eds. *Computing in the Humanities.* Lexington, MA: D. C. Heath, 1981.

Rossman, Parker. "Computers and Religious Research." *National Forum* 63 (Spring 1983): 24–26.

Shorter, Edward. *The Historian and the Computer: A Practical Guide.* Englewood Cliffs, NJ: Prentice-Hall, 1971.

Singer, B. "Exploratory Strategies and Graphical Displays." *Journal of Interdisciplinary History* 7 (Summer 1976): 57–70.

For Further Reading

Anderson, Virgil L., and Robert A. McLean. *Design of Experiments: A Realistic Approach.* New York: Marcel Dekker, 1974.

Beck, S. L. "The Crossover Design in Clinical Nursing Research." *Nursing Research* 38 (September–October, 1989): 291–93.

Campbell, Donald T. "Factors Relevant to the Validity of Experiments in Social Settings." *Psychological Bulletin* 54 (1957): 297–312.

Campbell, Donald T., and Julian C. Stanley. *Experimental and Quasi-Experimental Designs for Research.* Boston: Houghton Mifflin, 1966.

Campbell, P. H. "Using a Single-subject Research Design to Evaluate the Effectiveness of Treatment." *American Journal of Occupational Therapy* 42 (November 1988): 732–38.

Christensen, Larry B. *Experimental Methodology*. 2d ed. Boston: Allyn & Bacon, 1980.

Coombs, Clyde H. *A Theory of Data.* New York: Wiley, 1967.

Edwards, A. L. "Experiments: Their Planning and Execution." In G. Lindzey, ed., *Handbook of Social Psychology*. Vol 1. Cambridge, MA: Addison-Wesley, 1954, 259–88.

———. *Experimental Designs in Psychological Research.* New York: Holt, Rinehart & Winston, 1972.

Fairweather, George W., and Louis G. Tornatsky. *Experimental Methods for Social Policy Research.* Elmsford, NY: Pergamon Press, 1977.

Holtgrave, D. R. "A General Strategy for Single-subject Research." *Psychological Reporter* 65 (October, 1989): 687–90.

Hulica, Irene H., and Karel Hulica. "To Design Experimental Research." *Americal Journal of Nursing* 62 (February 1962): 100–103.

John, J. A., and M. H. Quenouille. *Experiments: Design and Analysis.* 2d ed. New York: Macmillan, 1977.

Myers, J. L. *Fundamentals of Experimental Design.* Boston: Allyn & Bacon, 1966.

Natrella, Mary G. *Experimental Statistics.* Washington, DC: U.S. Goverment Printing Office, 1963.

Peng, K. C. *The Design and Analysis of Scientific Experiments.* Reading, MA: Addison-Wesley, 1967.

Ridgman, W. J. *Experimentation in Biology: An Introduction to Design and Analysis.* New York: Wiley, 1975.

Robinson, Paul W. *Fundamentals of Experimental Psychology.* Englewood Cliffs, NJ: Prentice-Hall, 1976.

Rosenthal, Robert. *Experimenter Effects in Behavioral Research.* New York: Halstead Press, 1976.

Rubin, Z. "Designing Honest Experiments." *American Psychologist* 28 (1973): 445–48.

Sidman, Murray. *Tactics of Scientific Research.* New York: Basic Books, 1960.

Sidowski, Joseph B., ed. *Experimental Methods and Instrumentation in Psychology.* New York: McGraw-Hill, 1966.

Winer, B. J. *Statistical Principles in Experimental Design.* New York: McGraw-Hill, 1971.

PART V

PRESENTING THE RESULTS OF RESEARCH

CHAPTER **12**

Writing the Research Report

To write a report of one's research that shows fidelity to the facts, the ability to organize them logically, to present them clearly, and to remember there will be a reader who will ultimately read your report—this is to bring one's research effort to its destined conclusion and to share with others your findings and whatever nuggets of truth they may contain.

The Report as a Communicative Document

The research report is a straightforward document that sets forth clearly and precisely what the researcher has done to resolve the research problem. In structure, it is factual and logical. It makes no pretense at being a literary production. It must, however, be readable, which is another way of saying that the writer of the research report must know how to communicate clearly.

Many reports suffer because those who attempt to write them need greater skill in English expression. The basics of sentence and paragraph structure must be thoroughly mastered. Unity, coherence, and emphasis are rhetorical principles with which every writer needs a functional acquaintance. Punctuation also facilitates the expression of thought. All nine marks of punctuation should be ready expressional tools of those who would write communicative and easily read reports. But we will say more on matters of style and readability in the next chapter.

The Parts of a Research Report

The research report has a relatively simple format. In general, it should achieve three objectives:

1. It should acquaint the reader with the problem that has been researched and explain its implications adequately enough so that all who read the report have a clear orientation to the problem.
2. It should present the data fully and adequately. The data within the report should substantiate all the interpretations and conclusions that the report contains.
3. It should interpret the data *for* the reader and demonstrate exactly how the data resolve the problem that has been researched. A report that merely *presents* raw data and uninterpreted fact (in the form of tables, graphs, histograms, and other data–summary devices) is of little help to the reader in deriving *meaning* from those data.

Briefly, we will discuss each of these matters and amplify their significance insofar as they relate to the writing of the research report.

Acquainting the Reader with the Research Problem

The first section of the research report should have but one purpose: to create between the writer and the reader of the report a meeting of minds. The reader should be able to comprehend from the report alone what the problem is and what its ramifications are. The reader should appreciate the setting in which the problem was conceived. Much report writing is of poor quality because the writer has not approached the task of writing the report from the standpoint of reconstructing the problem for the reader, setting it forth clearly and adequately. Often the reader may not grasp the precise concept that was in the writer's mind. We cannot assume that the reader will be aware of important facts that the writer has never set forth.

After a few paragraphs of introductory remarks (if the writer chooses to make them) stating the rationale and the background or the relevance of the study, the document should set forth clearly and unmistakably the problem that has been researched. This might be further emphasized for the reader if it is announced with a proper subheading, which has presumably been done already in the proposal. The statement of the problem, as well as other information needed to understand it comprehensively, should comprise the first chapter of the final report.

At this juncture, turn again to the sample proposal in chapter 3 to review there the section entitled "The Problem and Its Setting." The final report will in a sense merely amplify what is set forth here, and its contents will be identical.

If the problem has been divided into subproblems, these should be stated following the statement of the problem (and, likewise, announced with a proper subhead). The object of the first section of the research document is to present the reader with as clear an understanding of the *principal* thrust of the research effort as possible. The reader will then be in a better position later on to understand the interpretation of the data and to judge the merits of the research. The research methodology is also stated and justified in the opening pages of the report.

Terms that may be ambiguous, or that may be used in a specialized sense, must be defined. For a meeting of minds, it is imperative that the reader and the researcher be concerned with precisely the same orientations to the problem, the same concepts, the same ideas. This is accomplished by a careful definition of any terms in either the problem or the subproblems that may be open to varied interpretation. In case you have forgotten what we said earlier about these matters, you might want to review chapter 3.

Any delimitations should also be clearly set forth. All who read the research report should know precisely how far the research effort extended and where the limits were set. Into what relevant areas did the research effort not intrude? What aspects of the problem have not been studied? Readers want answers to these questions, and they should be provided with them in the opening pages of the study report.

The research report provides no opportunity for imprecise thought or inexact expression. We should see explicitly what hypotheses have been tested; we should know exactly what the assumptions were upon which the researcher relied.

In addition, the first chapter of the research report should indicate the importance of the study both to the academic audience and to the practical reader. It should perhaps end with a section bearing a heading such as "The Organization of the Remainder of the Study" in which, chapter by chapter, the writer of the report delineates said organization. This prepares the reader with an advance summary.

These matters might well comprise the first chapter of the research report, the thesis, or the dissertation. We assume, of course, that the organization will be indicated by the use of appropriate headings, and subheadings. Because some students may never have acquired the habit of using headings and subheadings in an outline, we take a brief detour at this point to discuss the proper use of such format devices.

Headings Show Organization

The outline is indicated by the headings in the document. The most important of all headings is, of course,

THE CENTERED HEADING

which appears in the manuscript exactly as we have represented it here, centered on the type page and typed entirely *in capitals.* In manuscript writing, it is always reserved for announcing the major divisions of thought. The printer, because of the wide variety of type weights and faces to choose from, can be much more versatile in heading style and placement than the manuscript writer, who should rely on the limitations of type alone to express the thought and its relative degrees of importance. Although word processors offer type flexibility approaching that available to a printer, the various head levels will bear the same relationship as discussed here. By and large, we urge you to stay simple—dissertation committees tend to prefer a uniform style, and may even suspect you of trying to disguise inadequate research with a fancy presentation! If you simply *must* play with your computer, maintain the format shown here, and use a single type family; use boldface and italics judiciously, and do not vary the point size by more than four points.

In printed material, centered headings are usually set in the largest type size and, although the printer may not always center them, they are always the main divisions of the textual matter (such as chapter headings and other divisions of prime importance in the document). Such headings would ordinarily correspond to the parts of the outline that would be assigned the importance of Roman numerals: I, II, III, and so forth.

The Free–Standing Sidehead

Here the head is printed to show exactly how it would appear in typescript. This heading is written in capitals and lowercase letters with each word of the heading underscored. No punctuation follows the free–standing sidehead. The initial letters of the principal words of the heading are capitalized, the rest of the word and the prepositions and articles (except, of course, unless these are the first words of the heading) are typed in lowercase.

In print, free–standing sideheads are commonly italicized; they are *always* italicized in typescript. Italicization in typescript is indicated by underlining the words to be italicized. Note that the spaces are *not* underlined. The reason is obvious: you cannot italicize a blank space!

In importance, the free–standing sidehead is next below the centered heading. In an outline, this level would ordinarily be represented by the capital letters A, B, C, of the first indentation under the Roman numerals. Usually free-standing sideheads are set four single spaces below the preceding text and three single spaces above the text that follows. They are placed flush with the left-hand margin of the textual material—exactly as we have done here.

The paragraph sidehead. The paragraph sidehead, as the term indicates, is a heading set into the paragraph, as we have done here. It is always indented to line up with the other paragraph indentations of the page, and it always has a period as a terminal point of punctuation. Only the *first word* of the paragraph sidehead is capitalized; the rest of the words are in lowercase. The heading indicates the next lesser degree of thought under the free–standing sidehead and would normally correspond to the 1,2, 3 level in the conventional outline. The paragraph sidehead is *always* italicized (underlined), as we have done here. For ease of reading, three spaces usually follow the period of the paragraph sidehead before the paragraph proper begins.

The use of these three types of heading is illustrated throughout the sample proposal in chapters 3, 4, and 7.

Should you desire a fourth-level heading, such further diminution of thought importance is indicated by a centered heading, but this time by one quite different from the heading-of-first-importance discussed above. We have shown this type of heading in the sample proposal. It is typed in capitals and lowercase and centered on the text page as follows:

The Fourth-Level Heading

Note that it is not italicized. When placed in the text, the head is set four single spaces below the preceding text and three single spaces above the text that follows. Such a heading would indicate an importance of thought corresponding to the a, b, c level in the conventional outline.

The treatment of the fourth-level heading will be fully appreciated by referring to the sample proposal in chapter 7, where it is used along with the free-standing sidehead and the paragraph sidehead. This, incidentally, is the professional manner in which fourth-level headings are indicated. It differs somewhat from some academic style book recommendations.

Headings are used to show the outline of thought and, at the same time, to keep the left-hand margin of the type page straight. Outlining has its place, but with headings of the type described above, there is no need to accompany them with the conventional outline symbols I, A, 1, a, and so forth.

Study the use of headings in this text. They illustrate the style suggested in the above discussion.

We are back from our detour and will discuss one further matter under the general heading of acquainting the reader with the research problem.

In the document or dissertation, the review of the related literature should probably be given the status of a major division and be dignified with a centered first-importance heading. Such divisions always begin on a new page and a more-than-usual amount of space is generally left before the heading to mark it as a new major division of the document.

The review of the related literature section is designed to acquaint the reader with the corollary research literature. We need, at times, to see a particular research endeavor against the broad background of the efforts of others. This gives us a better understanding of the orientation of the problem to the larger research environment. Review chapter 4, where we have discussed the function of the review of the related literature. What has been said there is highly appropriate to the writing of the report document.

The Presentation of the Data

After we appreciate fully just what the problem is and the research setting in which it has been investigated, the next question is, "What are the facts?"

The research document is not a unique production that only you can write. It is, instead, a report that, being given your problem and your data, *anyone* should be able to write. This is one of the criteria by which to judge the adequacy of the research proposal: The proposal should be so self–contained that, should you be unable to complete the research, anyone with the requisite skill and ability could, by virtue of your proposal and the facts you have amassed, carry the research to its completion.

The data are presented *in terms of the problem.* You have gathered a mass of data. You then codified, arranged, and separated them into segments, each of which corresponded to a particular section of the problem being studied. The problem has presumably been expressed in subproblems in order to facilitate the management of the problem as a whole. There is, then, a one-to-one correspondence: certain data relate to each subproblem. You then exhibit these in logical sequence within the report. As each subproblem and its attendant data are discussed, it is helpful to restate, at the beginning of such discussion, the subproblem in the exact wording in which it appears both in the proposal and in the first chapter of the study. To do so will keep your reader oriented to the progress of the research as it is being reported; it will, likewise, focus the reader's attention on the specific subtopic of the research problem under discussion.

Generally, the report is divided into chapters. A logical division is to devote one chapter to each subproblem and its pertinent data. Present the subproblem, present the data germane to it, analyze and interpret those data, and present conclusions warranted by the data. Each chapter normally ends with a summary section in which the findings of that particular chapter are shown in relationship to the general problem and the previous subproblems. In this way, a tightly woven web of communication is established throughout the report.

The data should be presented *completely*. They may, of course, be organized into charts, tables, graphs, statistical summaries, lists of responses to questionnaire inquiries, and so on. But it is imperative that the data be exhibited as evidence for the conclusions that you draw from them. Where the data are extensive and you choose to present them in summary form in the body of the study, give them in full array in an appendix. In this way, anyone wishing to take the same data should be able to replicate the results of the research effort and should be able to reach substantially the same conclusions.

Let us not forget that we are also testing a hypothesis. Somewhere, therefore—probably in the closing paragraphs of the chapter—you should give some indication as to whether the data did or did not support the hypothesis being tested. Restate the hypothesis, and state clearly the fact of its support or nonsupport by the data.

Where the data were subjected to statistical analysis, present your rationale for employing the particular statistical approach. It is important to know, for example, not *that* one employs a particular correlational technique but *why* that particular correlational technique was used. In fact, throughout the entire research process, it is well for you to keep in mind that generally the answer to the question "What?" is not nearly so important as the answer to the question "Why?" One of the weakest links in research is frequently the failure to substantiate *what* one has done with a solid rationale as to *why* one has done it. We shall have more to say about this in the next section.

The Interpretation of the Data

All too frequently, researchers feel that having once presented the facts and figures, they have done all that needs to be done. This is self-delusion, and a misunderstanding of the research process. That is doing nothing more than a grand exercise in compiling minutiae. To display the data is certainly important, but it is the *interpretation of the data* that is the sine qua non of research.

In *Teaching for Thinking*, the following passage epitomizes the point: "The teacher who asks what the data are (the *who, what, when, where* questions) is concerned with a lower mental process, albeit he elicits the responses with pedagogical flourish. The teacher who gives the student some data and then asks what they *mean* is concerned with a higher mental process."[1] Without inquiring into the intrinsic meaning of the data, no resolution of the research problem or its subproblems is possible.

Many researchers, however, fail to exploit the data fully. One cannot turn over the facts too often, look at them from too many angles, or chart, graph, and arrange them in too many ways. Don't be satisfied. Ask simple questions of those facts. Doodle with them. This is not to suggest that you take a superficial or trifling approach. But sometimes very simple questions, very naive approaches will afford you startling insights. Have you thought of plotting the

[1]Louis E. Raths, Selma Wasserman, Arthur Jones, and Arnold Rothstein, *Teaching for Thinking* (Columbus, OH: Merrill/Macmillan, 1967), 117.

data? What has caused the plotted data to peak? To reach a plateau? To dip or plummet? Does the behavior of the data have any relationship to events that lie outside them?—a question the historical researcher should ask as a standard procedure, and all researchers might seriously consider.

Questions like these may sometimes crack the shell of the data and reveal the meaning within. Every data configuration may not be meaningful, but that is beside the point. What is important is that you leave no stone unturned, no data unnoticed, no arrangement untried. As a general rule, data have many more meanings than most researchers discover. This is because having processed the data by one means only, many researchers are unaware that other processes applied to the same data may reveal additional meanings in those same facts.

This discussion also suggests another matter. Researchers are sometimes so intent on proving their point that their enthusiasm takes control of their judgment. In the last analysis, *the facts must speak for themselves.* The researcher is only the mouthpiece. You may not like what the facts say. They may not confirm your fondest hopes or support your preconceived opinions, but the researcher is the servant of the scientific method. That method looks at facts squarely and without prejudice; it reports candidly and precisely what the impersonal fact affirms.

There is danger here. Beginning researchers need to ferret out every generalization, underscore it in red, and then be sure that the facts in the tables, graphs, and other exhibits will solidly support what those words, underlined in red, declare.

Defending one's research effort is an academic tradition. *Defend* in this sense means "to justify one's conclusions, to support one's statements with the backing of solid fact that has been presented in the document." Nothing short of this will suffice.

As a final section to the interpretation of the data, the report should close with a chapter entitled "Summary, Conclusions, and Recommendations." In this chapter, all loose threads should be gathered together. Here is the place for looking backward, for distilling into a few paragraphs precisely what has been accomplished in each phase of the research activity. One should be able to see the research endeavor as through the wrong end of a telescope: clearly, minutely, and at some distance, with all significant aspects brought together in proper perspective. On the basis of this summary, the researcher should state clearly the findings and conclusions reached with respect to the problem and the subproblems. The conclusions should be entirely supported by the facts presented. Then, the researcher is ready for two final steps: (1) to state whether the hypotheses have been supported or not, and (2) to make recommendations for further study, perhaps in those areas related to the problem that, during the research, the researcher has recognized as worthy of further investigation.

A word should be said about summaries. One of the weakest aspects of all research report writing is the failure of writers to summarize adequately. They forget human psychology. They overlook the psychological necessity of the reader who comes to the report. The whole research project—the problem, the organization of the data, the facts, the figures, the relationships and interrelationships—these are all so clear in the minds of those who have been involved with the research that they sometimes give little thought to the fact that the reader is not so intimately acquainted with the project. Researchers should always be mindful of the fact that through their long acquaintance with their study they have an awareness of the master plan, the relation of each component to the total study, the parts as they fit into the whole.

Readers, however, are not so fortunate. They need to stop occasionally as they proceed through the report, to orient themselves with respect to the totality of the investigation. To this end, use guideposts in the form of headings, transitional words and paragraphs, and other means of directing your reader. Instead of a long rambling discussion of related literature, help the reader to keep oriented by employing any of the several means that we have mentioned. One of the best directive devices is a summary at the close of each extended discussion. By pausing long enough to summarize what has been happening and what relevance such discussion has to the larger considerations within the report, you give a higher desirable unity to the whole, which is tantamount to keeping one's eye on the goalpost when, in the frenzy of the game, we need orientation and reference points. Pure frenzy can leave us greatly bewildered. Discussions that ramble on and on tend to produce psychological numbness, bewilderment, and confusion. Summaries avoid such reader disorientation.

A Schematic Model of the Research Report

The writer of a research report needs to visualize clearly the total schema of the report. What is central needs to be distinguished from what is peripheral; what is basic, from what is ancillary. The writer should understand the dynamics of the report and, seeing these matters, should never leave the reader in doubt for a moment as to what is happening during the entire discussion.

At the close of chapter 1, we presented figures showing the cyclical and helical nature of research. At this point, we present the same schema, only in a slightly different form (Figure 12.1).

Let us conceive of the research problem as metaphorically covering a certain "area" of investigation. The subproblems, then—we will assume that we have three—will each cover one-third of the area occupied by the problem. The main dynamics of the research effort will take place in a more or less vertical system of activity localized under the area indicating the

Figure 12.1 The Schema of a Research Report

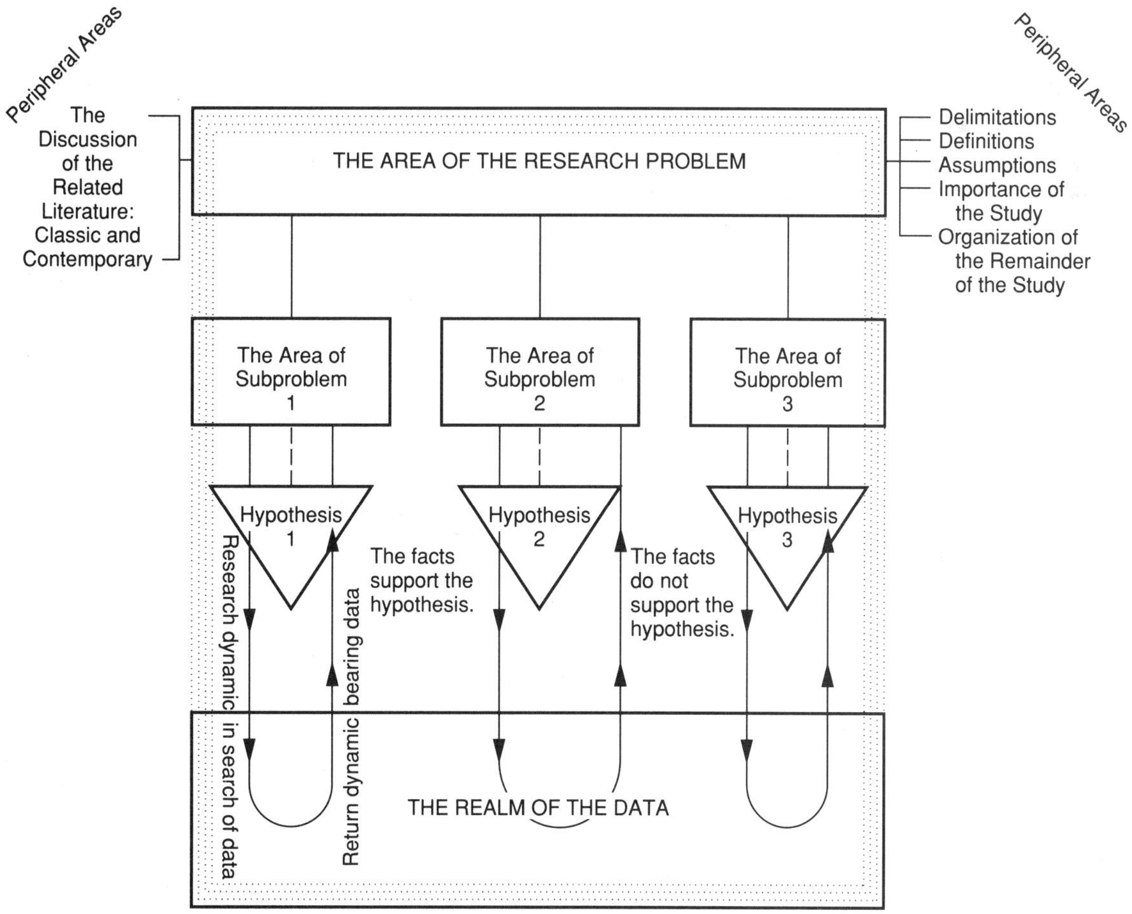

"spread" of the problem. Peripheral to the problem will lie those other items whose principal function is to throw light on the problem by explaining the meaning of its terms, delimiting the extent of its boundaries, presenting the assumptions that the researcher has made, delineating the importance and the relevance of the study, and outlining the remainder of the report organization. These matters help us to understand the problem, but they are not an integral part of it.

The review of the related literature is in the same peripheral relationship. This discussion, although helpful in allowing us to see the problem under study in relation to other studies, classical and contemporary, merely orients us within the total research environment. It does for us what a map does for the traveler. The schema of a research report presented here indicates within the dotted boundary lines what is essential to any research activity. It places outside those boundaries what is necessary for an intelligent reading of the research report but is not a part of the activity itself. At the top of the diagram is the area of the unsolved research problem; at the bottom is the realm of the data where the potential for solving the problem lies. In vertical paths that originate in the problem, but principally in the subproblem areas, is the research activity itself. This activity passes through and is focused in the direction of the facts by the hypotheses. The hypotheses point in the direction of the data. The activity loop contains two types of energy: *efferent,* the activity that originates in the researcher and in the problem area and flows out toward the realm of the data in search of the facts; and *afferent,* the return flow on the opposite side of the loop that is the data-bearing dynamic in the system. This returns to the area of the subproblem. If the data have supported the hypothesis, they pass through the hypothesis itself. If they have not supported the hypothesis, they miss it entirely in returning to the subproblem. In the schema, the facts do not support the hypothesis of subproblem 2.

The Outline of the Research Report

The following is the outline of the final document written as a development of the sample proposal used throughout this text. It is presented here in conventional outline form. It is presumed, however, that when you write your report, you will not employ the indented form given here (which is entirely inappropriate for formal written documents) but will indicate the organization of your report in the usual professional manner by the use of conventional headings and subheadings as we discussed these earlier in this chapter and as they appear in the proposal.

The purpose of an outline, in its initial stage and in the form in which we have presented it here, is obvious: The overall consideration in the writing of any report is to present to the reader a document that is both logical in structure and organized in thought. It is the spinal column of the discussion. You should not be disturbed if you see variant organizational patterns for research documents. There are many equally acceptable ways of arranging the report.

Compare the outline with the proposal itself. The outline shows the skeleton—the barebones organization. The proposal adds some substance to the skeletal structure; the complete report will present the body of research, fully developed, muscular with facts, and dynamic because of the mental processes of the researcher, who has taken those facts and *interpreted* them so that they manifest their meaning to the readers.

Of particular interest is the material that the researcher of the sample proposal presents in the eight appendices, A through H. By including these data, the researcher invites those who read the study to check the validity of the conclusions against the facts. This augurs well for the integrity of the research and the honesty of the researcher. It is a forthright presentation of the raw data, insofar as this is feasible, so that those who read the research may follow the footsteps of the researcher conducting the research.

Preliminaries

Title Page	Table of Contents
(Copyright Notice)	List of Tables
Acknowledgments	List of Figures

Text

Chapter

I. THE PROBLEM AND ITS SETTING
- The Problem
- The Subproblems
- The Hypotheses
- The Delimitations
- The Definitions of Terms
- Abbreviations Employed in the Dissertation
- The Assumptions
- The Need for the Study
- The Organization of the Remainder of the Study

II. THE REVIEW OF THE RELATED LITERATURE
- Interests as Theoretical Concepts
- Interests in Counseling and Vocational Choice
- The Measurement of Interests
- The Strong Approach
- The Measurement of Interests among Cartographers

III. THE POPULATION OF CARTOGRAPHERS
- The Population of Cartographers; Distribution and Genesis
- The Criterion Group
- The Cross-Validation Groups

IV. GENERAL PROCEDURES
- Response Data
- Collection Procedures
- Treating the Data

V. THE RESULTS
- The Criterion Group Returns
- The Cross-Validation Group Returns
- The Cartographer Scale
- Other *SVIB* Scores of Cartographers
- The Test of the Hypotheses
  - Hypothesis 1
  - Hypothesis 2
  - Hypothesis 3
  - Reliability and Validity
- Other Findings
- Summary of Results

VI. SUMMARY, CONCLUSIONS, AND RECOMMENDATIONS
- Summary
- Conclusions
- Recommendations

BIBLIOGRAPHY

APPENDIXES
- Appendix A: Letter of Transmittal
- Appendix B: Follow-up Letter

The Preliminary Matter and Appendix Content

The preliminary matter is all of the material of an introductory nature that precedes the actual text of the study. This includes the title page and, on the page following, the copyright notice. Following this is a page for the dedication (if any), a section of prefatory remarks and acknowledgment of indebtedness to those who have assisted in the research, the table of contents, the list of tables, and the part-title page (if any), in that order.

Perhaps a word should be said about copyright. Copyright is the protection given by law (U.S. Code, Title 17) to the authors of literary, dramatic, musical, artistic, and other intellectual works. Because of the great expenditure of time, effort, monetary resources, and other investment in a scholarly work such as a thesis or dissertation, it would seem only prudent to protect that investment by copyright. Formerly, the first term of statutory copyright ran for 28 years and could be renewed for a second term of 28 years. Under the current law, which took effect in 1978, copyright protection lasts for 50 years following the author's death, and is not renewable. For full information, write to the Copyright Office, Library of Congress, Washington, DC 20540.

Some theses and dissertations have later been turned into very remunerative and well-known books. Consider John Livingston Lowes's *The Road to Xanadu* (which we have discussed) or Rudolf Flesch's many books on readability. Sometimes, under pressure of writing a dissertation, a student may not realize how important or publishable one's efforts may be. For the low cost of protective literary insurance, it is a good idea to have the dissertation or the thesis copyrighted—just in case.

The acknowledgments page usually graciously acknowledges the assistance of those through whose kindness the research effort has been made possible. This assistance may include those responsible for providing the researcher with an entree to data sources that aided in completing the research or those who have guided the study and have given counsel—an academic dissertation committee, a faithful typist and proofreader, and those in one's family who have encouraged and assisted in the research effort. The guild mark of education is to say thank you to those who have given their time and their assistance to forward your efforts and aspirations. The acknowledgments page is the proper place for the gracious expression of such indebtedness.

The rest of the front matter is largely material intended to indicate the content and organization of the text. The most important of this material is the table of contents. The table of contents is a bird's-eye view of what the document contains and its organizational structure. The illustrative material appearing in the manuscript is indicated by two types of lists: a list of tables and a list of figures. A *table* is usually an arrangement of words, numbers, signs, or combinations of them in parallel columns for the purpose of exhibiting certain information in compact and comprehensive form. A *figure*, on the other hand, indicates any kind of graphic illustration other than a table: a chart, photograph, schematic, drawing, sketch, or other device to convey an idea by other than verbal means.

The back matter usually contains supplementary aids or addenda that may be valuable in understanding the text more completely but that are not absolutely essential to the comprehension of the body of the report. A rule of thumb is that the material appearing in the appendix enables one to go further with the document, if that is so desired. In our sample proposal, the appended data are largely numerical scores, statistical computations, mean values, and other similar data, so that if readers wish to do so, they can check the researcher's statistics to confirm their accuracy or the statistical procedures to determine their appropriateness. In reporting research, nothing is hidden. All the data are laid before the reader. The researcher's integrity is, thus, preserved, and the results and conclusions of the study can be readily verified.

The bibliography is also a part of the back matter and is in the nature of reference material. Should one wish to read further in the problem area or in corollary areas, the bibliography provides directions and suggestions. The bibliography likewise speaks pertinently of the researcher's awareness of the literature in the field of investigation and his or her own critical evaluation of that literature. A glance at the bibliography is usually enough to convince us that the researcher knows the principal scholarly works underlying the entire area of the study. Bibliographic materials are often categorized into two principal types: the classic studies that one might find almost invariably appearing with respect to any particular area and the items that are especially appropriate to the specific problem under investigation.

Learn by Looking

Perhaps the best way to appreciate the nature and the various forms of research reports is to inspect a number of them. Any university library will have a collection of theses and dissertations. State and federal agencies issue research reports in many areas. Notable available reports include the Surgeon General's report on smoking, and the numerous research reports issued by the National Institutes of Health, the American Medical Association, the many learned societies, professional associations, and occupational and trade groups.

You need only to let your imagination roam, to inquire, and to request; soon a research report will reach you in the mail. Not all reports will follow the somewhat formal and academic format and style we have outlined here. All of them, however, should exhibit the basic characteristics of a research report. Perhaps the best way, therefore, to become acquainted with what a research report is—and, conversely, to become aware of what a research report is not—is to learn by looking, keeping in mind the guidelines presented in this chapter. In your looking, you might profit a great deal by spending several hours perusing the research as reported in *Dissertation Abstracts International* (bear in mind that they are nothing more than *abstracts*, not full–blown reports.

Also, the United States Government Printing Office, Public Documents Department, Washington, DC 20402, issues a free periodical listing of published governmental research in a leaflet entitled *Selected U.S. Government Publications.* You should request it from the Superintendent of Documents.

Be Sure You're Right, Then Go Ahead—and Publish

Nothing is more embarrassing and more damaging to a researcher's reputation than to have words irrevocably fixed in type and have a glaring example of failure to check and recheck every detail of the research procedure and the precision with which your report is presented. Dr. Cheryl Beck, a professor at Florida Atlantic University, a registered nurse, and a member of the American Nurses' Association, in "The Research Critique: General Criteria for

Evaluating a Research Report," an article for nursing students and professional colleagues engaging in research, presents a set of penetrating questions that every researcher should answer satisfactorily *before publishing*.[2] Here is the list. Where the author has addressed the questions specifically to nursing personnel, I have generalized the statement and enclosed the altered wording in brackets.

Criteria for Critiquing a Research Report

Step 1. The Problem

1. Is the problem clearly and concisely stated?
2. Is the problem adequately narrowed down into a researchable problem?
3. Is the problem significant [enough to warrant a formal research effort]?
4. Is the relationship of the identified problem to previous research clear?

Step 2. Literature Review

1. Is the literature review logically organized?
2. Does the review provide a critique of the relevant studies?
3. Are gaps in knowledge about the research problem identified?
4. Are important relevant references omitted?

Step 3. Theoretical or Conceptual Framework

1. Is the theoretical framework easily linked with the problem, or does it seem forced?
2. If a conceptual framework is used, are the concepts adequately defined and are the relationships among these concepts clearly identified?

Step 4. Research Variables

1. Are the independent and dependent variables operationally defined?
2. Are any extraneous or intervening variables identified?

Step 5. Hypotheses

1. Is a predicted relationship between two or more variables included in each hypothesis?
2. Are the hypotheses clear, testable, and specific?
3. Do the hypotheses logically flow from the theoretical or conceptual framework?

Step 6. Sampling

1. Is the sample size adequate?
2. Is the sample representative of the defined population?
3. Is the method for selection of the sample appropriate?
4. Are the sample criteria for inclusion into the study identified?
5. Is there any sampling bias in the chosen method?

Step 7. Research Design

1. Is the research design adequately described?
2. Is the design appropriate for the research problem?
3. Does the research design control for threats in internal and external validity of the study?
4. Are the data collection instruments described adequately?
5. Are the reliability and validity of the measurement tools adequate?

Step 8. Data Collection Methods

1. Are the data collection methods appropriate for study?
2. Are the data collection instruments described adequately?
3. Are the reliability and validity of the measurement tools adequate?

Step 9. Data Analysis

1. Is the results section clearly and logically organized?
2. Is the type of analysis appropriate for the level of measurement for each variable?
3. Are the tables and figures clear and understandable?
4. Is the statistical test the correct one for answering the research question?

[2]Cheryl T. Beck, "The Research Critique: General Criteria for Evaluating a Research Report," *Journal of Gynecology and Neonatal Nursing* 19 (January–February 1990): 18–22.

Step 10. Interpretation and Discussion of the Findings

1. Are the interpretations based on the data obtained?
2. Does the investigator clearly distinguish between actual findings and interpretations?
3. Are the findings discussed in relation to previous research and to the conceptual/theoretical framework?
4. Are unwarranted generalizations made beyond the study sample?
5. Are the limitations of the results identified?
6. Are implications of the results for clinical nursing practice discussed?
7. Are recommendations for future research identified?
8. Are the conclusions justified?

Significant and Influential Research

We have alluded throughout this text to a monumental piece of research in English literature—John Livingston Lowes's *The Road to Xanadu.* We give special place to it here because it is a colossal effort to trace the influences on the writing of two of Samuel Taylor Coleridge's principal poems, "The Rime of the Ancient Mariner" and "Kubla Khan." As a research endeavor it is unique. The subtitle of the book is "A Study in the Ways of the Imagination."

For many researchers, that quest would seem too ephemeral—too diaphanous—to pursue and substantiate with hard, objective data. For that reason alone, it should command the attention of all researchers.

In a thinly veiled disguise of language that is both graceful and precise, Lowes sets forth his research goal—not in stark and angular language, but clearly and definitively. Note the statement of the research problem: "There are two matters about which I want to be quite clear. In the first place this is not a study of Coleridge's theory of the imagination. *It is an attempt to get at the workings of the faculty* (i.e., the imagination) *itself . . . our interest is in a study of the imaginative processes themselves*" (italics added). The words define the goal of the study. Notice that he repeats it *twice.* There is no possibility of mistaking where this research is headed.

For those who read perceptively, the delimitations are clearly stated: ". . . This is not a study of Coleridge's theory of the imagination." "Coleridge wrote a great deal about the imagination; he evolved the nebulous theory propounded in the twelfth and thirteenth chapter of the *Biographia Literaria. With that I have just now nothing to do.*" What could rule out closely adjunct areas with clearer delimitation? He also eschews "considerations of obvious importance" to the study that do not bear directly upon his problem: "to study the ways of the imagination." No forays here into irrelevant territory simply because they are interesting! This is straight-line research: "This one thing I do!"

The book is eminently readable. But in reading it you never forget that Lowes is in quest of the roots of the imagination and is seeking them through objective and verifiable fact. This is research, stripped of its formalism yet not pandering to popularism. You are always aware that this is a serious quest by an eminently respected scholar. W. A. Neilson wrote of the book: "It transformed source hunting into something new—a sort of sublimated detective process." Douglas Bush, who wrote the biographical sketch of Lowes in the *Dictionary of American Biography,* notes, "The minute and precise documentation . . . might in other hands have been merely mechanical, but Lowes vitalized it by the imaginative insight of a critic working, as it were, within the poet's mind." In the book, the documentation is amply given following the discussion of the data.

The book is just short of 575 pages in length, 58 percent of which is *discussion* of the data; 42 percent is *presentation* of the data or references to their sources. *The Road to Xanadu,* while a classic of literary research, has all the benchmarks of a dissertation. In chapter 13 we make the point that research need not be dreary reading. *The Road to Xanadu* is an inspired example of that assertion.

You will find it in most libraries. Come, see what research outside of the professional journals can be.

The Computer as a Tool of Research

Database Management

A database management program is a tool for organizing information. It is particularly helpful in organizing information from several files and getting it all together into one massive electronic filing system. In chapter 9, we suggested filing data under several headings so that the same fact might be available in various data orientations. The birthdate of a historical figure may be filed under the date, the place, the name of the person, the month of birth, and even the astrological sign under which the person was born. Each of these categories would be a separate file, and manually we might manipulate them and study them for various reasons, depending upon the purpose of the study or the desire of the researcher. It can be done, but it is an awkward and cumbersome operation.

With a computer all of this information can be assembled and interrelated by means of database software. Data is most useful when seen in association with other data. Such association can reveal dynamic relationships not otherwise apparent.

What are the advantages? With a manual filing system you must create multiple files and place the same data in each in a given order of sequence. With an electronic filing system (database), you file the data *once*. The computer does the rest—sorting and resorting the data as the researcher wants them.

Database programs come in two basic forms—simple and complex. Simple databases usually are easy to learn to use and hence are attractive. Simple databases produce what are called "flat" files, which means simply that all the data elements for a case are stored in a single file.

Complex database programs (such as FileMaker Pro and 4th Dimension) differ from the simple ones in significant ways. Chiefly, instead of producing a single file of data for each case, a user can construct several different files, each of which may contain some information about a particular case. The files are *related* by the common data elements in each, and hence are called *relational* databases. While much more versatile than simple database programs, relational programs are usually much more expensive and take considerably more effort to learn to use.*

To illustrate the differences, consider the example discussed above, about storing historical personages' birthdates. In a *flat file* database, one might store such information as date of birth, location, and any other information desired as separate variables or data elements in a file organized by names. In a *relational* database, in contrast, one could create separate files for birthdates, locations, etc. in which varieties of information could be stored, among which might be included the names and birthdates of historical persons.

We cannot go into this topic in depth in this text. The purpose of these sections throughout the book is merely to alert you to the fact that certain possibilities exist that facilitate the handling of data, the writing of a document, or the presentation of the data in various constellations so that their interpretation is more obvious to the researcher. To every one of these sections, much more might be added. They merely aim to show you some light at the end of the tunnel. If they pique your interest, follow toward the light.

*For good reviews of database programs, see Jim Seymour, "Flat-File Databases: Easy to Use Sophisticates," *PC Magazine*, Vol 7, No. 7, April 12, 1988: 155–ff; and Jim Seymour, "Project Databases: Relational Databases Taking the Middle Ground," *PC Magazine*, Vol 7, No. 8, April 26, 1988: 53–ff. See also various reviews of database software in current and recent issues of the computer magazines listed in chapter 2.

For Further Reading

Allen, Eliot D. *A Short Guide to Writing a Research Paper, Manuscript Form and Documentation.* Deland, FL: Everett Edwards, 1976.

Barzun, Jacques, and Henry Graff. *The Modern Researcher.* 3d ed. New York: Harcourt Brace Jovanovich, 1977.

Cooper, Bruce M. *Writing Technical Reports.* Baltimore: Penguin, 1964.

Cummins, Martha H., and Carole Slade. *Writing the Research Paper: A Guide and Sourcebook.* Boston: Houghton Mifflin, 1979.

Davis, Gordon B., and Clyde A. Parker. *Writing the Doctoral Dissertation.* Woodbury, NY: Barrons Educational Series, 1979.

Doubleday, Neal F. *Writing the Research Paper.* rev. ed. New York: D.C. Heath, 1971.

Gallagher, William J. *Writing the Business and Technical Report.* Boston: CBI, 1981.

Harris, M. B. "Accelerating Dissertation Writing: Case Study." *Psychological Reports* 34 (1974): 984–86.

Hauser, Travis, and Lee L. Gray. *Writing the Research Term Paper.* New York: Dell, 1965.

Hubbell, George S. *Writing Term Papers and Reports.* 4th ed. New York: Barnes & Noble, 1969.

Jones, Paul W., and Michael L. Keen. *Writing Scientific Papers—Reports.* 8th ed. Dubuque, IA: William C. Brown, 1981.

Koefod, Paul E. *The Writing Requirements for Graduate Degrees.* Englewood Cliffs, NJ: Prentice-Hall, 1964.

Lester, James D. *Writing Research Papers: A Complete Guide.* 3d ed. Glenview, IL: Scott, Foresman, 1980.

Martin, Roy. *Writing and Defending a Thesis or Dissertation in Psychology and Education.* Springfield, IL: Charles C. Thomas, 1980.

Moore, G. E. "Approved Practices in Reporting Quantitative Research." *Journal of Vocational Education Research* 11 (Fall, 1986): 1–24.

Morse, Lawrence. *Writing the Economics Paper.* Woodbury, NY: Barrons Educational Series, 1981.

Nelson, Joseph R. *Writing the Technical Report.* 3d ed. New York: McGraw-Hill, 1952.

O'Connor, Maeve, and F. Peter Woodford. *Writing Scientific Papers in English.* Amsterdam: Elsevier, 1976.

Passmore, D. L. "There Is Nothing So Practical as Good Research." *Journal of the Industrial Teacher Education* 24 (Winter, 1987): 7–14.

Samuels, Marilyn S. *Writing the Research Paper.* New York: AMSCO School Publications, 1978.

Scientific Writing for Graduate Students. Rockville, MD: Council of Biology Editors, 1968.

Sternberg, Robert J. *Writing the Psychology Paper.* Woodbury, NY: Barrons Educational Series, 1977.

Stromberg, M., and Jo Ann Wegmann. "The Fine Art of Writing Research Abstracts." *Oncology Nursing Forum* 8 (Fall 1981): 67–71.

Weidenborner, Stephen, and Domenick Caruso. *Writing Research Papers: A Guide to the Process.* New York: St. Martin's Press, 1982.

Willis, Hulon. *Writing Term Papers: The Research Paper—the Critical Paper.* New York: Harcourt Brace Jovanovich, 1977.

Winkler, Anthony C., and Jo Ray McCuen. *Writing the Research Paper: A Handbook.* New York: Harcourt Brace Jovanovich, 1979.

Woodford, F. P., ed. *Scientific Writing for Graduate Students.* New York: Rockefeller University Press, 1968.

"Writing a Market Research Report." *International Trade Forum* 16 (October–December 1980): 22–27.

CHAPTER 13

The Style, the Format, the Readability of the Report

Dr. Samuel Johnson once said to a young man who was seeking employment with the lexicographer, "Boy, open thy mouth, that I may see thee!" With equal poignance, one might say to every researcher, "Hand me thy written page—thy research report—that I may see thee." For what you put on paper, and how you put it there, reveals your standards of excellence, your knowledge, and the quality of your thinking more eloquently than anything else about you!

Technical Details and Stylistic Matters

We have discussed in the previous chapter and at various other places throughout the book matters of style and format as these have seemed appropriate to the discussion at hand. This chapter will be devoted to methods of presenting the thought upon the page and to some suggestions of practical importance that will facilitate the production of the document.

Write on the Right Side of the Paper

Few students know that there is a right and a wrong side of a sheet of paper. Every piece of paper has one side that has a smooth, feltlike appearance. This is called the *felt side* and is the side on which the typing is done. Typing or printing on the felt side of the paper gives the manuscript a soft, clean appearance and the letters a sharp, clear configuration. The reason for this will be seen by taking any sheet of paper and looking carefully at one side and then at the other with a high-powered magnifying glass. One side will be, as we have said, soft and felty in appearance. The other side will look like a window screen or will have a rough, fibrous appearance. In fact, this side is called the *screen side.*

In the papermaking process, the pulp and rag issue from the Jordan macerating machine and flow onto the first stage of the papermaking machine as a thin milklike fluid. An oscillating trough drains away the water carrying the fibers, the shaking orients the fibers, and the soft pulp comes to rest upon a very fine screen bed. The impression made by the webbing of the screening is never entirely eradicated from the surface of the paper in the processes that follow. Because of its pitted texture, the screen side of the paper does not register the full force of the typed character as well as the felt side, and although the difference is miniscule, to those who observe closely there *is* a difference. Papers printed or typed on the screen side do not have the snap, the vitality, or the finesse of appearance that those typed on the felt side do.

With watermarked paper, it is a very simple matter to identify the felt side. Hold up the paper to the light, looking at the watermark. When the watermark is oriented in the proper right-side up reading position, you are facing the felt side of the paper on which you should type. For papers without a watermark, the outside wrapper of the package will usually bear the words "felt side" to identify it, but inspection under magnification will always reveal one side as more granular than the other. The granular side, the dead–looking side, is *not* for typing.

A further word about paper. In making paper, both wood pulp and rags are used. Wood pulp paper, sometimes merely called pulp paper, is cheaper, less durable, and after a time has a tendency to turn yellow or brown and become brittle. Other types of paper are composed of various proportions of rag content, which gives the paper durability and a flexibility that pulp paper lacks. The proportion of rag content is usually indicated as 25, 50, 75, or 100 percent rag. Many universities specify a particular make and proportion of rag content for their dissertations. You should check with your university librarian, registrar's office, or the office of the graduate dean to ascertain whether, indeed, a special paper requirement is designated for your thesis or dissertation. If it is, it will doubtless be watermarked. Check the orientation of the watermark before you begin printing or typing.

Follow Accepted Guidelines

If you are writing a thesis or a dissertation, be sure to check with the office of the graduate dean to ascertain whether the university has a prescribed set of guidelines for writing theses. Check such matters as paper size, width of margins, and size and style of typeface. (Some universities specify 12–point pica, others will accept either pica or elite face.) Double-spacing the manuscript is a universal requirement. Stylistic customs differ. What is permitted in one institution may be entirely unacceptable in another. You should make sure, then, whether your university has a style manual for writing research documents or whether it recommends that you follow a particular style manual and, if so, which one. Some of the principal manuals of style are the following:

The Chicago Manual of Style. 13th ed. Chicago: University of Chicago Press, 1982.

Manual for Authors of Mathematical Papers. 8th ed. Providence, RI: American Mathematical Society, 1980.

Campbell, William G., Stephen V. Ballou, and Carole Slade. *Form and Style: Theses, Reports, Term Papers.* 6th ed. Boston: Houghton Mifflin, 1982.

CBE Style Manual. 5th ed. CBE Style Manual Committee. Bethesda, MD: Council of Biology Editors, 1983.

MLA Handbook for Writers of Research Papers, Theses, and Dissertations. 2d ed. Edited by Joseph Gibaldi and Walter S. Achtert. New York: Modern Language Association, 1984.

Parker, William Riley, compiler. *MLA Style Sheet.* rev. ed. New York: Modern Language Association, 1954.

Publication Manual of the American Psychological Association. 3d ed. Washington, DC: American Psychological Association, 1983.

Trelease, Sam F. *How to Write Scientific and Technical Papers.* Cambridge, MA: MIT Press, 1969.

Turabian, Kate L. *A Manual for Writers of Term Papers, Theses, and Dissertations.* 5th ed. Chicago: University of Chicago Press, Phoenix Books, 1987.

United States Government Printing Office. *Style Manual.* 28th ed. Washington DC: U. S. Government Printing Office, 1984.

Words into Type. 3d ed. Englewood Cliffs, NJ: Prentice-Hall, 1974.

Barclay, William R., ed. *Manual for Authors and Editors: Editorial Style and Manuscript Preparation.* East Norwalk, CT: Appleton and Lange, 1981.

Footnotes and Documentation

We will not prescribe any footnote form here. There are too many styles. Almost every academic discipline has its own preference for footnote and bibliographic documentation. But beneath all of them lie some basic principles of reference notation. What you need is to grasp the *purpose* of the footnote that lies behind the variant forms.

First, we will discuss the general idea of documentation. The documentary footnote has two principal functions. One of these is to invest the footnoted statement with an aura of authority. You buttress your statements with an authoritarian source to establish their validity. Again, the footnote acknowledges your indebtedness for quoted material or data appropriated. Ethics among writers requires that if material is borrowed from any source, whether it is a direct quotation or not, and if those who know the source would recognize the appropriated material, then both author and source should be acknowledged by a footnote citation. Where the quotation is extensive and the writer is contemplating having his or her document published in any form or copyrighted, he or she should secure *in writing* from the publisher or the author of the material—whoever holds the copyright to the material—permission to reprint the material. In addition to the footnote citing the source, the words *Reprinted by permission of the publisher* (or author) should be added to the footnote.

The purpose of the footnote is to convey information. That information may generally be categorized as follows:

1. the authorship data
2. the source data
3. the publication data
4. the chronological data
5. the locational data

We shall discuss each of these items briefly.

The Authorship Data. Generally in footnotes the author's name is listed in the natural order: given name and surname. In bibliographic entries, the author's name is usually reversed: surname, given name, and middle initial or middle name. Where multiple authors are involved, the names are separated by commas with *and* joining the name of the last author to the series. Except for the first author's name, the others in the series are usually presented in given name-surname sequence. Academic degrees or titles of respect are always deleted in listing authors' names.

The Source Data. The source data tell the source of the information. Did you get the information from a book? a journal? an interview? an address? Acknowledge it. Generally, the complete title of the source is listed as it appears on the title page of the book or in the masthead of a journal. The rule is, put the title in *italics* when the source document is a separate publication. In typing, italics are indicated by underscoring the words with a straight line. When the reference is only a part of a larger published whole (such as the title of an essay within a book of essays, the title of a poem in a volume of poetry, the title of a chapter within a book, or an article within a journal), then put the title in quotation marks. Titles of books and journals are *never* enclosed in quotation marks.

The misuse of quotation marks is a common fault among writers who do not know how this punctuation is used. Quotation marks have five specific uses. Any dictionary with a section on punctuation will give you these uses. Quotation marks are not to be inserted at the whim of the author, nor are they to be scattered willy-nilly. Learn to employ them properly.

The Publication Data. With books, the publication data usually consist of the city and state in which the publisher is located and the full corporate name of the publisher. The place of publication is available from the title page of the book or the masthead of the periodical. In the case of books, the title page may carry a list of cities; for example, Van Nostrand Reinhold Company, New York, Cincinnati, Toronto, London, Melbourne. The place of publication is always the first city mentioned in such an array—in this case, New York.

The publication information for a periodical, in addition to the title, is the title of the article being cited, the volume—usually with the month and date in parentheses, following the volume—and the page or pages on which the citation appears. With periodicals issued quarterly the quarter of publication is also included among the publication information: e.g., winter, spring, summer, fall.

The Chronological Data. With books, chronological information is the year of publication as indicated on the title page. If it does not appear there, the date of copyright is used as indicated on the copyright page. The chronological information usually follows immediately after the name of the publisher and is separated by a comma. With periodicals, the chronological data are usually the year, the month, and in the case of daily or weekly periodicals, the day of the month. Newspaper citations usually also include section, page, and, at times, column location.

The purpose of all documentation is to permit the reader to go with the least difficulty to the source cited. To that end, the documentary data should assist the reader.

The Locational Data. The locational data identify the reference by its page location within the book or the periodical. Usually this information is the last item cited in the footnote. A widely used convention is to include the abbreviation p. or pp. for page references with book citations and to *omit* the page abbreviations for periodical citations—for example: *Research/Development* 24:33 (1973). In this citation, 24 is the volume and 33 is the page. Many journals number their pages consecutively throughout all the issues in a year. Styles vary widely, depending on the manual used. The basic rule is, *be consistent.* Once you have adopted a style, do not vary it throughout your document. This, too, is to assist the reader. Be precise: sloppy documentation form implies sloppy research!.

Think of each issue of a periodical as one section of a bound volume. A journal issued monthly will have 12 sections that are often compiled into a single volume. These volumes will be found on the bound periodicals shelves or the reference shelves of the library. The spine of the volume will show the title of the periodical and the volume number.

Bibliographies are usually appended to extended discussions either as a recapitulation of the works cited in the document or as an additional reading list of related literature for the reader who wishes to pursue the subject at greater length.

Two other types of footnotes that we have not mentioned are the *informational footnote,* in which supplementary information (considered by the author as not particularly appropriate for inclusion in the text proper) is placed in footnote position, and the *internal reference footnote,* in which the reader is referred to a page earlier or later in the same work in which a particular topic is discussed.

The Prose Style of the Report

The research report is precisely that—*a report.* It is the researcher reporting upon what he or she has done in the progress of the research effort. As we have said earlier, the researcher is acquainting the reader with the problem, with the data brought to bear upon the resolution of that problem, the means employed in gathering those data, the processes of analysis to which they were submitted, and the conclusions reached. All of this, from the actual research effort standpoint, is history.

Because the researcher is reporting upon what has already happened, *the manuscript should be written in the past tense.* The document will also be restricted by another convention of document writing; namely, that—except for the title page or the by-line—*the researcher, qua researcher, should be anonymous.* The use of the first-person pronoun or reference to the researcher in any other way is particularly taboo. Research permits only one "character" upon the stage: *the facts!* All of the action within the drama of research revolves around *the data*; they, and they only, speak.

This, however, creates a concomitant problem: It forces the writer to employ the less forceful, more impersonal *passive voice.* In case you are uncertain on matters of grammar, do not confuse the *past tense* with the *passive voice.* They have nothing in common. Past tense relates events as happening in time past: "The Treaty of Paris *brought* the Revolutionary War to an end." This is a simple statement of an event that happened in the past. The passive voice, on the other hand, is used to indicate that no identifiable subject is performing the act. It is a kind of ghostly form of the verb that causes events to happen without any visible cause being present. We assume that someone or something caused the events to occur, but on the face of the record no evidence of it appears. Note the passive voice construction in this sentence: "A survey *was made* of the owners of the Rollaway automobiles." We have no indication of *who* made the survey, only of *the fact* that the survey "was made." The passive voice plays down the person; it emphasizes the fact. We might indeed have said, "A survey was made *by the researcher* of the owners of the Rollaway automobiles" or "*The researcher made* [here we have the active voice] a survey of the owners of Rollaway automobiles." But both of these versions are unacceptable. Here we have a quasi-first-person intrusion of the researcher, and some readers may frown upon it. The best research reporting does not use it.

The passive voice is always identifiable by two features: It always contains some form of the verb *to be*, and it always contains a past participle of a verb. It need not suggest events happening in the past at all. We can suggest events that will happen in the future without any indication of who will do them by using the *future* passive form of the verb. Take, for example, this statement: "The test *will have been given* before the students are permitted to read the novel." The italicized words indicate the essential verbal components of the passive voice construction: a part of the verb *to be (been) + a past* participle *(given).*

The general rule for the style of the research report is, therefore:

1. Write it in the past tense as a report of events that have already happened.
2. In the interest of keeping the person of the researcher subdued upon the face of the report, employ the passive voice in writing the report.

Preparing the Report

The report should be a clean, neat, attractive document. City planners are conscious of open spaces in the design of urban communities. Research report writers should be no less aware of their importance. Between text and free-standing sideheads, ample space should be allowed. Four single spaces between the end of the text material and the sidehead, then three single spaces between the sidehead and the continuing text, give an openness to the discussion that suggests a definite break in the pursuit of one topic and a turning to another. Margins are probably the most important factor in creating the impression of uncrowded open space. Leave two inches at the top of the paper, one inch at the bottom, 1.75 inches on the left, and one inch on the right. This will give your page a spaciousness and will conform to the best typographical quality standards.

Such a page fulfills the specifications laid down by typographers and printers of quality books. The following sets forth the principle clearly:

> Enough of the paper is exposed to make its contribution of a surface sympathetic to the type, texture, and pliability pleasant to the touch, and color pleasing to the eye. The classic page relationships are in the neighborhood of 50 percent for type page and paper respectively. The Gutenberg 42-line Bible has 45 percent for type, 55 percent for paper page area.

> The distribution of margins from the esthetic viewpoint is governed by the principles of design relating to spatial areas. This means simply that there should be a pleasing difference between front and back and top and bottom margins.[1]

In preparing your report there are three cardinal principles that are requisite: (1) neatness and clarity, (2) precision, and (3) clarity of outline and logical structure.

You must remember that your report *is* you. Your report is a powerful psychological weapon. Without your meaning to do so, a report can say more about you to your reader than you can possibly imagine. It reveals the inner you, and from that standpoint sends an indelible message as to what is vitally important to the acceptance of your research.

Neatness and Clarity

Your report should show signs of a clean, clear mind that presents the evidence in the form of facts that resolve your problem. Each subproblem should be a clear stepping stone to the resolution of the main problem. Little things leave lasting impressions. Your page should be easy to read: double-spaced lines, sharp-impression type, placed attractively upon the page.

Let's look at the last two of those three requirements. The computer is becoming the substitute for the outmoded manual typewriter. Even the so-called typewriters of today hold little resemblance to their ancestor. Many typewriters are word processing machines, and fill an economical gap for those who cannot afford computers. But whatever the input mechanism, the output must be clear, crisp letters whose intensity of blackness is the antithesis of the pure whiteness of the page on which they rest.

Whether you have a word processor or a computer, your typeface will be created with a printer. There are a wide range of printers, from dot–matrix machines to laser jet printers. The results from dot–matrix printers vary widely, depending on how many pins produce the printed character, from a printing head with nine pins to a maximum of 24 pins. The more pins, the better the impression. Even with letter-quality printing, however, most dot-matrix printing is "grainy" in appearance, approximating but not equalling the quality of printing produced by a laser jet machine. Consult your local source for thesis and dissertation manuscript requirements to learn whether a dot-matrix document will satisfy typography guidelines.

Placing the block of print on the paper is also important. You should strive for the block of print to occupy no more than fifty to fifty–five percent of the total page space. If you plan to have running heads at the top of each page, measure from the top of any capital letter to the farthest extension of the lowest descender in the last printed line on the page. (Descenders are those letters that extend below the baseline: g, j, p, q, y.) Measure also the width of the type line. Multiply the one dimension by the other.

You will probably be using 8.5-inch by 11-inch paper. Multiplying these gives you a paper page of 93.5 square inches. The print that you place on that page should not exceed 51.5 square inches. All white space should be deducted from the "print page," but not, of course, the space between the lines in double-spaced typing.

Think of your reader. Nothing is more depressing than page upon page of solid-block text. Guide the reader through your text with free-standing sideheads and paragraph sideheads. Put the organization of your proposal on the face of the research report. Where you have a list of items, set each item off serially with a number to distinguish each item from all the others. Try to mimic the organization of an easily read text in organizing and presenting your report. No one will object. Many will bless you for making what could otherwise be dreary fact after fact without relief a stimulating reading experience.

While I have never seen it done, with computerization and the capacity of most word processing software, you might consider adding an index to your research report (with the

[1] *Typography and Design: United States Government Printing Office Training Series* (Washington, DC: U.S. Government Printing Office, revised 1963), 66.

approval of your research advisor, of course, and providing that the report's complexity and length warrant such an effort) to guide your reader to specific topics or areas that would otherwise be difficult to find.

With a computer or word processor, you can format an attractive page by setting the margins to control the line and type page length. You can also insert footnotes, either as footers or as end notes to the chapter, and produce professional-looking tables, presenting numerical facts neatly in perfect columns.

Precision

A research report must be crisp with precision. There is no place in it for "I-guess-so's." This is not the time for guessing, or ambiguous or foggy terms. Your document should be clean-cut and should present its facts plainly.

An example will contrast foggy writing with precise writing. A student, writing an historical account of Napoleon's preparations to march against Russia described the situation in these words:

> Napoleon, having grandiose dreams, was not one to attack without adequate preparations. He amassed a vast army, not only from France, but from various other countries, and stationed detachments along the route to Russia.

Note the fog. Nothing is precise. What are "grandiose dreams"? What are "adequate preparations"? What is a "vast" army? Which countries were "various other" countries?

Now see how Will and Ariel Durant in *The Story of Civilization*, volume 11, "The Age of Napoleon" describe the same situation:

> Napoleon explained that his dream was only to found a United States of Europe, to give the Continent one modern legal code, one coinage, one system of weights and measures, one court of appeals—all under one three-cornered hat. And this immense, unprecedented army, which he had so toiled to assemble and equip—how could he send it home now, and walk through the rest of his life with his tail between his legs?
>
> It was verily an immense army, 680,000 men including 100,000 cavalry, not counting political officials, servants, and attendant women. Of the total, less than half were French; the rest were contingents requisitioned from Italy, Illyria, Austria, Germany, and Poland. There were half a hundred generals—Lefevbre, Davout, Oudinot, Ney, Murat, Victor, Augereau, Eugène de Beauharnais, and Prince Jósef Antoni Poniatowski, nephew of Poland's last and knightly King. All these forces were gathered into separate armies, at various points, en route to Russia, each general with specific instructions when and where to lead his host.[2]

Note how these historical researchers have illuminated with precise fact every one of the student's foggy, questionable phrases. Is it any wonder that one reviewer of this volume called it "a masterpiece and an enduring classic, as breathlessly readable in narrative as it is informative in fact"?[3]

Get the facts. Some call them the *dusty* facts. Blow off the dust, more imaginary than real, and you will find that they will sparkle like jewels when viewed by a precise and imaginative mind. James H. Breasted blew the centuries-thick dust off of the ancient facts and artifacts of Egypt, and his *History of Egypt* (New York, 1912) brings ancient Egypt to life with precision of fact and the scintillating insight of an intellect that perceived the beauty and potential in bare fact alone.

Precision is beautiful in its own right. Look at a finely jeweled watch or read a research classic and you will be viewing basically the same beauty: the precise working of a human mind.

[2]Durant, Will and Ariel, *The Age of Napoleon,* 698–99. New York: Simon and Schuster, 1975.

[3]Quoted from the jacket of the book.

Clarity of Outline and Logical Structure

Here the basic structure of your proposal will be made manifest. You may have wondered why we were so fastidious and particular in drafting a research proposal. The purpose was to discipline your thinking, and to construct a logical plan upon which you could later build a clear, logical research report.

Every fact has its precise place within the research report structure. You may remember the weeks, the months, perhaps the years ago when you garnered a particular fact or constellation of facts. You did not gather these as a child gathers wildflowers in a field—willy nilly, without a guiding purpose. You gathered each fact because you envisioned it as a single building block that would support and advance the basic raison d'être of all research: to enlighten a corner of the darkness of a specific problem. We have come almost full circle, very close to the place this book began. Everything that you have done, all of the procedures that you have understood, have been for one purpose: to take one problem, one atom of darkness in human experience and cause it to glow with the light of fact and interpretation.

This cannot be done haphazardly. The steps you take toward resolving a problem must be as ordered as the steps you would take emerging from a cave toward a blaze of clear sky and sunny landscape. Every step must progress logically toward cracking open the shell of the enigma that you chose at the very beginning as the goal of your quest. You may understand better now why we entitled the third chapter, "The Problem—the *Heart* of the Research Process."

After you have written several pages of your research report, go back and read your headings and subheadings. Do they form a logical whole, are they as progressive as the steps of one emerging from a cave? They should be. Recall the inverted pyramid in chapter 4, "The Review of the Related Literature." There we counselled you to "begin your discussion . . . from a comprehensive perspective, like an inverted pyramid: broad end first. Then you can deal with more and more specific or more localized [data] that focus more and more on your [central research] problem."

That's logic in practice. Logic comes from the Greek word *logos,* which means reason, order, speech, word. That's the idea precisely in your research report. Think of your research proposal as an x-ray of the human body. You see the skeleton; the bones that hold the whole together; the framework upon which everything else depends. That is your proposal: the skeleton of your final research report. Now adorn that skeleton with fact: clear, convincing, relative fact. March through each of your subproblems, laying fact upon fact, with as deliberate a precision as a mason cements masonry blocks in a skyscraper's wall. Reason, order, and fact, carefully placed and cemented by the precise word, are the logic of the research report. Nothing will substitute.

Setting your words on paper is much more than rattling your fingers over the typewriter, the word processor, or the computer keyboard. That's an utterly superficial act and has nothing to do with the *real* business of getting your thought so clearly displayed that it becomes indisputable, progressive evidence. And perhaps what we have said here has hinted at the message of the next subsection, giving your work a polish that makes us enjoy the beauty that was sleeping within the once dull, dusty facts.

And, Finally, the Research Report Need Not Be Dull Reading!

There is no reason why a report should be dull—anymore than there is a reason why a textbook should be dull. Both of them deal with the excitement of human thinking prompted by the fascination of facts in the world around us. It is unfortunate that the research report, the academic thesis, and the dissertation have been considered an almost certain cure for insomnia. The only reason research reports are dull is because they are the products of dull writers. Phlegmatic attitudes and unimaginative minds will never set ablaze dry, lifeless fact.

Discovery is one of the most exciting of human activities. And research is discovery! It is sailing upon seas where no one has ever been before. It is looking across vast wastelands of mere data and seeing in them features previously missed by other observing eyes. Imagine the thoughts of those who have walked upon the moon. To them it was a thrilling adventure, not just because it was the moon, but because in that dull and lifeless world lay the facts that might provide evidence for the birth and age of the earth, the origin of the solar system, and the birth of the moon itself. It offered a means of testing our theories. It was the end of an observation that began in Padua in the seventeenth century when Galileo first discovered the mountains of the moon! In the gray and lifeless dust, more completely dead than anything that we had ever looked upon in all our long history, lay exciting facts, pregnant with the possibilities of extending human knowledge.

There is no such thing as a dull and lifeless fact. When facts die, something more important than the fact has first succumbed: the imagination, the insight, the excitement of discovery, the creative thought within the mind of the researcher. When this goes, all goes, and research dies. The writing of the report then becomes a dull exercise that produces an uninspired account of the researcher's efforts. Passive voice does not mean passive mind.

We have come full circle. Now we understand why the selection of a problem that fascinates researchers is so important. Only by being engrossed with a problem will researchers be able to keep their enthusiasm until the last word of the report is typed. That enthusiasm is infectious; it will spread to the words of the report itself.

Many years ago, I started to investigate the origins and influences that have contributed to the history and development of reading improvement as a subject at the college level. I expected that my quest would take me back perhaps a quarter of a century and that the causes would have shallow roots. Instead, this study became a quicksand, taking me down, down, down into a historical abyss I had not bargained for and of whose cavernous reaches I had little dreamed.

Coming back from the historical depths, I brought with me data. In writing the research report, I was faced with essentially the task of uncovering a hitherto undiscovered chapter in American higher education. A few paragraphs indicate what I did with what was otherwise pedestrian and uninspiring fact. These paragraphs probably illustrate that the difference between the soporific narrative and one alive with the dynamic force of imagination is in the *way in which* you present the facts. Unless you are alive with enthusiasm for the newly discovered fact, the thought will be delivered to the page stillborn: dull, uninteresting, and prosaic.

Here are some of the dullest data with which I had to deal.

> Many reasons contributed to the discouragement of reading in the mid–nineteenth century college. The libraries grew slowly, and even the oldest—and, presumably, the best—fell far short of what a college library might have been. Harvard and Yale, had, doubtless, the acme of collegiate libraries in America; but even they left much devoutly to be wished by men of vision who saw what books and reading could mean in the educational program of the American college. . . .
>
> While no particular data can dichotomize the moment when the old order ceased, giving way to the new, 1876 seemed an especially noteworthy year. Influences which accumulated strength for years seemed suddenly of a moment to materialize into concrete fact. When this happens, certain historical moments become pivotal. In retrospect, 1876 seemed to be such a moment. . . . In 1876, the American Library Association was formed. Perhaps in the light of this fact, Shores says that modern librarianship generally dates from 1876. In this year also R. R. Bowker became the first editor of the newly founded *Library Journal,* a publication that was to voice again and again in its columns the pertinency of reading to higher education. On the first of January of this year, Daniel C. Gillman, the new president of The Johns Hopkins University, issued his first annual report.[4] In this initial report to the trustees of the new university, President Gilman said,
>
> > The idea is not lost sight of that the power of the university will depend upon the character of its resident staff of prominent professors. It is their researches in the library and the labora-

[4]Refer to chapter 9, where we discuss keeping a multiple file of the same data. Without a chronological file of data, I would probably not have noticed these facts and their apparent relationship.

> tory . . . which will make the University in Baltimore an attraction to the best students and serviceable to the intellectual growth of the land.

And the University in Baltimore did, indeed, have a far-reaching effect upon the "intellectual growth of the land."[5]

The Elements of Style

The elements of style are there in the extract above—readability, topic sentences. These are developed and the facts are documented. See what variety of structure the author has used. The first three sentences have a normal subject-predicate order. The fourth sentence begins with a dependent clause. Then sentence five assumes the subject-predicate form again. In succeeding order sentences begin with a phrase, an adverb, another phrase. Variety is the spice of life; it is also the life of a readable style. Short sentences alternate with longer ones. These are all features that make for easy interesting reading.

You might do well, if you are not sure what makes writing readable, to study two books: *The Elements of Style* and *The Art of Readable Writing*.[6] Eschew the exaggerated expression; look sharply at your ill-advised and thoughtlessly chosen adjectives. Stick to the facts. Report them accurately, but, in so doing, enliven your prose with a variety of sentence structure, sentence length, and precision of verb and noun. You may have to write your report in the unappealing passive voice, but there is much compensation in the skill and art of readable writing.

More do's and don'ts are probably to no avail. Distilled into a brief stanza by an anonymous hand is a broad guideline for all your writing. Follow it.

The written word
Should be clean as bone:
Clear as light,
Firm as stone;
Two words are not
As good as one.

Significant and Influential Research

Occasionally a graduate student's doctoral dissertation becomes more than a dissertation. It becomes a bestseller, a helpful text, a well-known book published by a well-known publishing house. This is a consummation devoutly to be wished. This is the situation behind the example of significant and influential research with which we choose to close this text.

Dr. Rudolf Flesch wrote a 68-page dissertation for his doctorate at Teachers College, Columbia University. His problem was simple: What makes English prose easy to read and comprehend?

One needs only to look at the serpentine sentences, the involuted prose of the late nineteenth century to appreciate the poignancy of the problem. Dr. Flesch decided to analyze English prose to see what elements made writing either difficult or easy to read. The result was a dissertation, "Marks of a Readable Style," which reduced readability to a statistical formula.

In attempting to make the dissertation more readable, Dr. Flesch found that he had written an entirely new book. That book was *The Art of Plain Talk*, which was published in

[5]Paul D. Leedy, "A History of the Origin and Development of Instruction in Reading Improvement at the College Level," (Ph.D. dissertation, New York University, 1958; Ann Arbor, MI: University Microfilms, 1958), 94, 97–98.

[6]K. W. Strunk, Jr., and E. B. White, *The Elements of Style*, 3d ed. (New York: Macmillan, 1979); Rudolf Flesch, *The Art of Readable Writing* (New York: Harper & Row, 1949).

1946 by Harper and Row and has had tremendous success throughout the years. Here is graduate research in casual dress. It is available in most public libraries. This simple beginning has spawned a whole series of books by Dr. Flesch dealing with simplicity and clarity in reading, writing, and speaking.

Go into any library, and look under the author cards for Flesch, Rudolf. You will doubtless come up with one or more of this scholar's many titles. When you do, remember that this long chain reaction of writing was sparked by—of all things—a graduate student's doctoral dissertation!

The Computer as a Tool of Research

Last Words

To many people computers are mysterious and incomprehensible. Therein lies a danger. We are likely to feel either that these modern electronic creations are capable of doing almost anything or that they are totally beyond our amateur grasp. Do you face a problem? Feed it into the computer and let the computer solve it. But the danger is overestimating the machine.

Never forget that computers are inanimate and faithful slaves of the master who sits before the keyboard. They have no will of their own, no initiative, no ingenuity. They are what we have been calling them throughout this text—merely a *tool* for the researcher. They can crunch figures with the speed of light and perform all of the arithmetic and algebraic operations long before you can wink an eyelid. They are faithful servants. If you ask them, as the author has done many times in revising this text, to pick up a sentence or a paragraph or a whole section of prose and deliver it to another location, the computer will do it easily.

We should be profoundly thankful for this help. But we must know where to stop in our expectations.

Computers are not human. They cannot think, they cannot originate new ideas, they cannot be creative. They solve no design difficulties; they *interpret* no data. Only a human being can perform these functions.

There is an old anagram used to describe the function of computers: GIGO—meaning Garbage In, Garbage Out! You cannot expect an electronic network to take the place of the neural network. Always behind the computer is the human brain: The port of last call is the human intellect and the critical thinking and judgment of the human being.

Computers are helpful, obedient, faithful servants. They are merely tools to assist the researcher in doing what is either tedious routine or tiresome repetition. They will do menial tasks. But that is the end of their genius. Use them, let them save you hours of slow plodding with pen and pencil. But do not be disappointed or dismayed if you realize that the work of thinking, planning, and critically creating is still a domain where you must work alone to gather flashes of insight.

For Further Reading

Barzun, Jacques. *Simple and Direct: A Rhetoric for Writers.* New York: Harper & Row, 1975.

Barzun, Jacques, and Henry E. Graff. *The Modern Researcher: A Manual on All Aspects of Research and Writing.* 3d ed. New York: Harcourt Brace Jovanovich, 1977.

Baker, Sheridan. *The Practical Stylist.* 3d ed. New York: Thomas Y. Crowell, 1973.

Cather, Willa. *On Writing.* New York: Alfred A. Knopf, 1949.

DeBakey Lois. "Literacy: Mirror of Society." *Journal of Technical Writing and Communication* 8 (1978): 279–319.

———. "Medical Writing: Let Thy Words Be Few." *International Journal of Cardiology* 2 (1982): 127–32.

———. "Medical Writing: Grammar. Word Order: The Misplaced Modifier." *International Journal of Cardiology* 1 (1982): 447–48.

DeBakey, Lois, and Selma DeBakey. "Syntactic Orphans and Adoptees: Unattached Participles I. Mischievous Intruders." *International Journal of Cardiology* 3 (1981): 67–70.

———. "Syntactic Orphans and Adoptees: Unattached Participles II. Medical Misconstructions." *International Journal of Cardiology* 3 (1983): 231–36.

Koefod, Paul E. *The Writing Requirements for Graduate Degrees.* Englewood Cliffs, NJ: Prentice-Hall, 1964.

Mandel, Siegfried. *Writing for Science and Technology: A Practical Guide.* New York: Dell, 1970.

Words into Type. 3d ed. Englewood Cliffs, NJ: Prentice-Hall, 1974.

Index

ISBN 0-02-369242-1

90000>

9 780023 692420